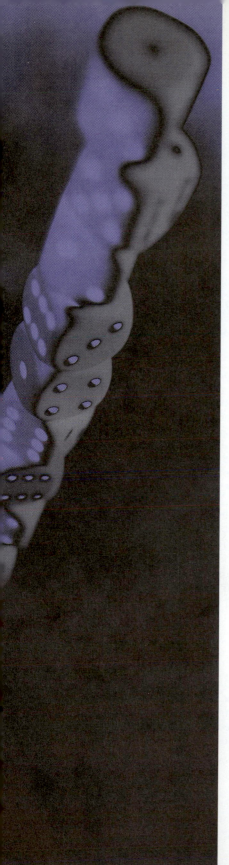

THE OBJECT OF JAVA™

Introduction to Programming Using Software Engineering Principles

David D. Riley

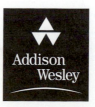

Addison Wesley

Boston San Francisco New York
London Toronto Sydney Tokyo Singapore Madrid
Mexico City Munich Paris Cape Town Hong Kong Montreal

Executive Editor: *Susan Hartman Sullivan*
Associate Editor: *Elinor Actipis*
Executive Marketing Manager: *Michael Hirsch*
Managing Editor: *Pat Mahtani*
Production Supervisor: *Diane Freed*
Cover Design: *Susan Carsten Raymond*
Cover Image: *©2002 PhotoDisc, Inc.*
Text Design: *Susan Carsten Raymond*
Design Manager: *Regina Hagen*
Composition: *Gillian Hall, The Aardvark Group*
Copyeditor: *Roberta Lewis*
Proofreader: *Brooke Albright*
Prepress and Manufacturing Coordinator: *Caroline Fell*

Access the latest information about Addison-Wesley titles from our World Wide Web Site: *http://www.aw.com/cs*

Many of the designations used by manufacturers and sellers to distinguish their products are claimed as trademarks. Where those designations appear in this book, and Addison-Wesley was aware of a trademark claim, the designations have been printed in initial caps or all caps.

The programs and the applications presented in this book have been included for their instructional value. They have been tested with care but are not guaranteed for any particular purpose. The publisher does not offer any warranties or representations, nor does it accept any liabilities with respect to the programs or applications.

Library of Congress Cataloging-in-Publication Data
Riley, David D., 1951–
 The object of Java: introduction to programming using software engineering
 principles / David Riley.
   p. cm.
 Includes bibliographical references and index.
 ISBN 0-201-71585-6 (pbk.)
  1. Java (Computer program language) 2. Computer software--Development. I Title.

QA76.73.J38 R54 2002
005.13'3--dc21   2001033535

ISBN 0-201-71585-6

2 3 4 5 6 7 8 9 10—DOC—040302

This book is dedicated to my wife, Sandra, and children, Kasandra and Derek. These three remarkable individuals provided endless assistance, encouragement, and inspiration.

TABLE OF CONTENTS

CHAPTER 4 Methods   87

CHAPTER 5 Numeric Processing   129

CHAPTER 6   Supplier Classes   **159**

CHAPTER 7   Logic and Selection   **211**

CHAPTER 8   Inheritance   **257**

PREFACE

The Object of Java—This title directly parallels the objectives of this textbook. Java was designed as a vehicle for modern software development. Similarly, this text was designed as a vehicle for instruction in modern software development. Both are powered by the object-oriented paradigm and properly driven with sound software engineering practices. The goal of this presentation is to convey programming skills, object-oriented skills, software engineering skills, and Java skills—and through these skills to provide a firm foundation for future study in computer science.

By ACM/IEEE conventions the target audience for this text is categorized as students in the CS1 course. Readers need not have ever written computer programs before, but having a reasonable level of analytic sophistication is important. A background of three years of high school mathematics is all that is required to understand any notation in this book.

P.1 OBJECT ORIENTATION AND JAVA

In the words of James Gosling and Henry McGilton, "To function within increasingly complex network-based environments, programming systems must adopt object-oriented concepts." Such emphasis on object orientation requires more than an "objects first" curriculum; it requires an *objects-centric* approach. Software classes, methods, inheritance, and event-driven code should be just as much in today's programmer repertoire as are variables, loops, and arrays. The goal of the objects centric approach goes well beyond a presentation of object terminology. The objects-centric approach seeks to educate software developers who are able to reason with object orientation.

Part of the beauty of the objects-centric approach is that it subsumes the older imperative and functional paradigms. In order to use object-oriented programming (OOP) you must still write assignment instructions, pass parameters, return values from functions (nonvoid methods), and become proficient with all of the basic control structures. This means that when students are transitioning from OOP to other programming paradigms, they encounter few of the obstacles that are often experienced when transitioning in the opposite direction.

This book is based upon six years of experience using the object-oriented (O-O) approach in our CS1 classes. For the past three years we have used the Java programming language. Java works well in this course because it incorporates a reasonable implementation of the object model, and it is ubiquitous in both academic and professional circles. Java has the added benefit of a C-like notation. This is helpful for students who might have completed an Advanced Placement course in C++, as well as individuals who may need to use C or C++ in the future. As Gosling and McGilton put it, "The Java programming language is designed to be object oriented from the ground up."

P.2 SOFTWARE ENGINEERING EMPHASIS

Like good writing, good programming requires skill and discipline. The guidelines and techniques of software engineering are critical for developing such skill and discipline. A software engineering emphasis is evident throughout this book. The following textbook features are specifically included to convey proper software engineering:

Software Engineering Tips

You will find Software Engineering Tip boxes sprinkled throughout the chapters. These offer a collection of software-developer "best practices." A Software Engineering Tip might suggest how to format a language construct for good programming style or it might explain how experienced programmers approach a common design problem.

Programming by Contract

The importance of specifications is amplified by OOP. Method preconditions and postconditions, as well as class invariants, are especially critical for conveying code behavior. Such assertions are used consistently to document examples and to define example classes. Programming by contract is introduced in Chapter 2 and used regularly thereafter. Additional discussions about logical expressions, loop invariants, and special assertion notations are included.

Patterns

The software engineering principle of design patterns reminds us that our software development skills are often based upon our memory for commonly used structures. This book extends the notion to include patterns for frequently encountered code expressions, instructions, algorithms, and design patterns that serve as programming templates. These patterns are highlighted so that the reader may become familiar with a commonly required solution and learn how and when it is applicable.

Software Testing

Testing is a part of any good software engineering model. Special sections are included to ensure that the reader will develop basic debugging skills, as well as knowledge of simple path testing and black-box testing.

The Java Inspector

Software engineering studies confirm that the most useful of all testing comes in the form of informal desk checks, code reviews, and walkthroughs. Such practices require fundamental knowledge of what to "check," "review," or how to "walk through." Every chapter provides this information in the form of The Java Inspector. These end-of-chapter sections not only provide a useful review of salient points from the chapter, but they do so in the form of practical "how to" ideas.

UML

Pictures play a key role in object-orient design and programming. Numerous object diagrams are interspersed in many places to illustrate the run-time nature of computation. Class diagrams are also included frequently to depict the visible interface of a class and to picture relationships among various classes. In addition, activity diagrams are included to show control flow.

To remain true to the software engineering theme, this book restricts diagramming notations to those from the Unified Modeling Language (UML). Using UML diagrams exposes students to the same notations that have now become standard in the software development industry. The subset of UML used in this book is summarized in Appendix E.

P.3 ORDER OF TOPICS

Our experiences of teaching OOP in the CS1 course have taught us several lessons. Arguably the most important discovery has been how sensitive this material is to proper ordering. Instructional time is the scarcest of resources in today's CS1; there is no time to waste. After experimenting with various alternatives, we've found that the order of topics in this text works well for our students.

You may notice that the table of contents of this book looks somewhat unique. The objects-centric approach demands that key object-oriented material be presented as early as possible so that it can be properly applied throughout the text.

The first chapter begins with a brief overview of objects and classes, almost like a "preview of coming attractions." An example object-oriented program is used to illustrate some basic notations, the software development tools (editors, compilers, and virtual machines), and to provide a glimpse of the overall process of software development. This chapter is expected to require no more than a class period of coverage.

Objects-centric

The second chapter begins with the basic object-oriented construct, namely the method call. After demonstrating how to perform methods upon objects, the chapter continues to examine simple sequences of these instructions. The chapter also explores declaring, instantiating, and assigning objects. Including the swap algorithm as a code pattern helps to illustrate object bindings. Chapter 2 also includes all of the Java facilities needed to write initial programs.

Early O-O Strategies

The third chapter is a somewhat unique blend of basic software design skills and some additional language facilities. In this chapter the reader is shown two strategies for attacking programming problems in an OOP context: top-down design and design by prototyping. Under the assumption that every CS1 student will be expected to write several programs, these strategies help to minimize the "Where do I begin?" questions. Chapter 3 also discusses other fundamental software development skills, such selecting good identifier names and using output instructions (System.out.println) to assist in debugging.

Methods

The primary instruction of OOP, the method call, introduced in Chapters 1 and 2, is explored more fully in Chapter 4. This presentation also examines how to create methods, including such issues as parameter passage, local variables, and nonvoid methods.

Primitive Types

Only after the reader has had four chapters to explore objects, classes, and methods does the presentation turn to primitive data types in Chapter 5. We have found that delaying a discussion of primitive types, such as numeric expressions, eliminates many early distractions. This approach allows the reader to become relatively comfortable with manipulating reference data before confronting the issue that Java treats numbers in a non–object-oriented way. This later presentation of primitive types also tends to expose primitive variables as anomalies, although sensible anomalies, in an object-oriented environment. It seems to take no more time to present primitive expressions at this later time, and it definitely improves the students' comfort level with reference data/objects.

Writing Supplier Classes

There appears to be a significant cognitive difference between writing client code that utilizes other classes and writing the supplier side code of those external classes. Chapter 6 is included to assist readers in making the leap. This chapter confronts not only design decisions of which class is the best site for a particular method, but also explores the importance of proper information hiding and encapsulation.

Control Structures

Why not present selection and loops before Chapters 7 and 10? The answer is that delaying the discussion of these control structures allows object-oriented topics to be explored earlier, and therefore used throughout more of the remainder of the course. When presented at these later times, the utility of *if* instructions and *while* loops is pretty obvious, and students eagerly assimilate such useful material. In the object-oriented model, control structures are no longer the centerpiece of programming skills. Nonetheless, selection and repetition are still important programming tools, and we have found this placement to provide students with sufficient exposure to master these constructs.

Delaying the presentation of selection and repetition is possible, in part, because of event-driven code. A quick glance at the programming assignments and examples in this book should provide convincing evidence that interesting and challenging programming is quite possible without selection instructions or loops.

Using extensive event-driven programming has other benefits. Event-driven code is a natural companion of OOP. We are all accustomed to the behavior of buttons, menus, and scrollbars that rely upon event-driven control. Indeed, it is the program-control model that tends to be awkward for anyone who has grown up with graphical user interfaces.

Inheritance

The core of the object-oriented tools and techniques is covered in three phases:

1. Utilizing objects, classes, and methods (Chapters 1–4)
2. Writing supplier-side code (Chapter 6)
3. Using inheritance (Chapters 8–9)

It would be wonderful to introduce inheritance earlier, but we have had the best success with presenting inheritance beginning at roughly the middle of the course. This timing still permits sufficient opportunity to use inheritance in many course projects.

Containers, including Arrays

Chapter 11 is included to separate the issues of container classes from the specific concepts of arrays (Chapter 12). The inherently sequential nature of a list makes it a bit easier to use than a direct access container such as an array. More importantly, a list is a better example of the object-oriented approach for implementing a container (data structure). Since Java integrates array notation into the language, an array gives the initial appearance of being unlike other objects. Chapter 11 also takes the opportunity to include useful discussions of the Object class, wrapper classes, and a sorting algorithm that is naturally suited to lists—insertion sort.

P.4 ORDER DEPENDENCIES

Although the order of presentation in this text works well at our institution, there are many factors that can dictate the need for variations. Therefore, every reasonable effort was made to minimize dependencies of topics. Figure P.1 diagrams significant chapter dependencies. An arrow in this diagram is drawn from A to B to indicate that Chapter B relies substantially upon the material presented in Chapter A.

Figure P.1 Chapter dependencies

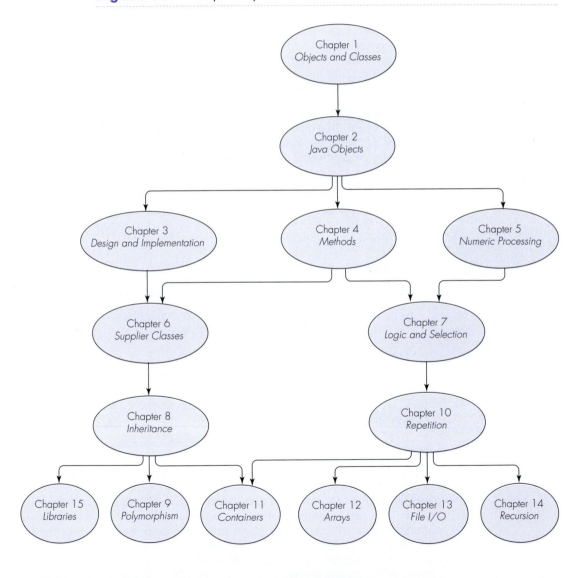

This book should be viewed as an attempt to be as inclusive of CS1 topics as was deemed reasonable. In an ideal world it would be nice to cover all 15 chapters in a course. This is a considerable undertaking, and I suspect that most CS1 courses will sacrifice coverage of part or all of some of the later chapters.

Appendix A is also included for those courses that prefer to begin with an introduction to computer hardware. This material can be used as an introductory chapter, or as outside reading material for students. The choice to place this material in an appendix was made because it lies outside the object model focus.

P.5   APPLICATIONS OR APPLETS—YOU CHOOSE

The programs in this book are all written in such a way that they can be executed as either Java applications or as Java applets. Each program incorporates a class called Director that defines a controller object for the program.

Two separate classes are included with each program—one for executing the program as an application and the other to run it as an applet. The *go.java* class, illustrated below, is included to use the program as an application.

```
public class go  {
    public static void main(String args[])  {
        Director   director = new Director();
    }
}
```

The *appletStarter.java* can be used if you would prefer to run a program as an applet.

```
import java.applet.*;
public class AppletStarter extends Applet  {
    private Director  director;
    public AppletStarter()  {
        director = new Director();
    }
}
```

The details of the distinction between applications and applets, along with *go.java* and *AppletStarter.java*, are thought to be Java-isms that detract from the early presentation. Therefore, a complete discussion of these issues is delayed until Chapter 15.

P.6 ALIBRARY (AVAILABLE WITH SOURCE)

Objects are built from classes, and classes come from libraries. Therefore, an objects-centric approach would be incomplete without the inclusion of software libraries. However, detailed knowledge of any repertoire is far less important to a programmer than the ability to quickly adapt to different library codes. Such abilities are best acquired through experiences reading and using library classes beginning from class diagrams and class specifications.

A separate library of Java classes, known as *aLibrary*, accompanies this text. With *aLibrary* it is easily possible to develop Java programs that display animations, utilize simple list data structures, or access real calendar and clock information. However, the bulk of classes in *aLibrary* are included to provide a graphical user interface (GUI) for student-written Java code.

Why use graphical libraries?

In our experience there seems to be no collection of classes that motivate beginning programmers better than GUI libraries. This motivation is sufficiently strong that we have found that the *aLibrary* classes require very little of our precious lecture time. After we have demonstrated the basics of one or two initial *aLibrary* lectures, our students are quite capable of teaching themselves about *aLibrary* classes by reading their specifications. A complete set of *aLibrary* class diagrams and class specifications, in the form of class invariants with method preconditions and postconditions, is included in HTML form so that students can learn to teach themselves.

Graphical classes also have the pedagogical advantage of visibility. The GUI objects provide a fertile field for examples of objects and object relationships that are easily visualized.

The final reason for using GUI classes is that the alternative seems to be the same tired interactive terminal stream type I/O that CS1 courses have used for thirty years. A generation that was raised with compact disks and electronic games will find terminal I/O to be pretty artificial and unappealing.

Why not use the *jdk* libraries?

The Java *jdk* libraries, such as *swing* and *awt*, were designed for use by production programmers, not first-time programmers. The *aLibrary* classes are designed as a pedagogical tool. For the accomplished programmer, it is acceptable to master the intricacies of the `paint` method, `repaint` method, `update` method, and `Graphics` class that are required to draw even a rectangle with *swing/awt*. However, for the individual writing his/her first program, it is more sensible to instantiate the `ARectangle` class from *aLibrary*. For the experienced programmer, event delegation via Java `interfaces` is a powerful and flexible tool, but *aLibrary* classes that already incorporate event handlers are better for learning about inheritance and method overriding.

Even though *aLibrary* is a separate library, it is not intended to depart from *jdk*. Every graphical *aLibrary* class inherits from some *swing/awt* class, and *aLibrary* preserves naming consistency with *swing/awt*. This means that someone familiar with *aLibrary* should find it relatively simple to transition to the use of the *swing/awt* libraries. To further facilitate such a transition, Appendix D is included.

P.7   OPENING BLACK BOXES

Bertrand Meyer has defined the concept of "successive opening of black boxes" as a pedagogical approach that begins with the use of predefined components (i.e., the black boxes) that little by little reveals the tools and techniques that were used to compose the black boxes. As an example black box, this text avoids the distraction of static methods early in the presentation by using the aforementioned *go.java* static class to instantiate an initial Director object. The reader is initially asked to ignore the *go.java* class until later in the text when static methods are explained and the code for the *go.java* class is shown as an illustration. Similarly, an *aLibrary* class called A3ButtonWindow provides for convenient access to a window with integrated buttons. A3ButtonWindow is used for program examples long before its implementation is revealed as an example of inheritance.

CLOSED Black Box

When a black box is employed and the reader is expected to assume something "on faith," a special Closed Black-Box section, accompanied by the appropriate icon, appears in the text. Correspondingly, Opening the Black-Box sections indicate locations in the book where these black-box concepts are revealed.

OPENING the Black Box

P.8   CLASS TESTED

I have used much of this approach while teaching CS1 for several years, and various versions of this book in manuscript form have been class-tested for the past three semesters. More importantly, three of my colleagues have used a near-final version for the past semester, and all have reported success. Our classes are composed of a mixture of students from first-semester freshman to nontraditional students with degrees in other disciplines. The largest two population groups in our CS1 course are those students who plan to major in Computer Science and those who plan to major in Information Systems, but there are also significant numbers of students planning to major in other disciplines.

P.9   SUPPLEMENTS

Below is a list of supplementary materials associated with this textbook. These supplements are made available online for adopting instructors:

- A complete set of answers to all exercises
- The source code for sample solutions to programming exercises
- The source code for the example programs used in the book (over 70 programs), included in both application and applet form
- All *aLibrary* classes, including source code
- Class diagrams and class specifications for all *aLibrary* classes (in HTML form)

- Abridged class diagrams and class specifications for selected Java *jdk* classes, including `Byte`, `Character`, `Color`, `Double`, `Float`, `Integer`, `Long`, `Math`, `Object`, `Short`, `String`, and `Timer`.
- A set of PowerPoint lectures that parallel the chapter presentations

P.10 ACKNOWLEDGMENTS

I am indebted to Barbara Barkauskas, Keith Burand, and Kasilingam Periyasamy for their trust, their helpful comments, and their friendship. These three fine colleagues had sufficient faith in this project (or perhaps it was disappointment with other CS1 textbooks) that they were willing to teach for a full year from a manuscript of this book. Barb deserves a special commendation, because she also consented to act as a reviewer. She provided the unique perspective of one who teaches the material in precisely this way.

I am also grateful for the remarkable collection of talented reviewers from widely varying programs that the folks at Addison-Wesley contracted. Good reviewers probe, question, suggest, and criticize, and these knowledgeable computer scientists did all of that.

Thomas W. Bennet, Mississippi College
Robert Burton, Brigham Young University
W. Sam Chung, Pacific Lutheran University
Eck Doerry, Northern Arizona University
Aaron J. Gordon, Metropolitan State College of Denver
Le Gruenwald, University of Oklahoma
Mark S. Hutchenreuther, California Polytechnic State University
Cerian Jones, University of Alberta
Blayne E. Mayfield, Oklahoma State University
Bina Ramamurthy, State University of New York at Buffalo
John M. Samaras, Valdosta State University
Carolyn J. C. Schauble, Colorado State University
John A. Trono, Saint Michael's College
Phil Ventura, State University of New York at Buffalo

Robert Burton is one of those outstanding individuals who is both a fine researcher and a consummate teacher. I am especially indebted to Robert for the extra time he spent working with me on this project—an effort that was above and beyond the normal role of textbook reviewer.

Dave Riley

PREFACE FOR THE STUDENT

So why are have you decided to take this course? Are you committed to a career as a computer scientist? Are you seeking to sharpen your analytic problem-solving skills? Are you testing the waters to see whether or not computer programming might be in your future?

Whatever your reasons, it is important to realize that the lifeblood of computer science is software development. This is why a large part of the computer science curriculum is devoted to the study of how to develop software. This book is an introduction to computer science in the form of an introduction to software development.

Learning to develop software is a participatory sport. You didn't learn to write a theme or a poem by merely reading them, and you won't learn to create software by just reading this text or listening to your instructor. You need to do it. You'll find several programming assignments suggested at the end of each chapter. Plan on writing at least one program per chapter using these or other assignments.

At the heart of software development is problem-solving. Your problem-solving skills will grow as you develop software. Sometimes this is frustrating, and sometimes it is energizing. Computer scientists find excitement in tackling problems. The more difficult the path that leads to the solution, the greater the feeling of accomplishment when the program is written.

S.1   SOFTWARE ENGINEERING TIPS

The world's understanding of software development has matured through the years to the point that we now refer to the best practices as "software engineering." Software engineering principles and processes can be complicated, especially in an introduction to software development. However, software engineering is really just a collection of procedures that we know to be effective, and it is always wise to learn from the experience of others.

Like any craftsman, the software engineer must learn how to best use the tools of the craft. Sprinkled throughout this text you will find highlighted Software Engineering Tips. These Tips offer "how to" suggestions. Often they discuss how software engineers choose from alternative approaches or solutions. It is a good idea to read each Software Engineering Tip when you read the associated section.

> **SOFTWARE ENGINEERING TIP**
>
> It is wise to go back and review the Software Enineering Tips after you have had the opportunity to try out the technique in a software project or two.

A secondary reason for including the Software Engineer Tips is to help you gain some appreciation for future software engineering issues that you may encounter. Software development, like other problem solving, tends to follow a three-step sequence:

1. Analyze the problem.
2. Design a solution.
3. Implement the solution.

Unfortunately, the first two steps are difficult, if not impossible, to fully appreciate prior to a thorough understanding of the last step. Therefore, software development is generally taught in the opposite order. In other words, we begin by studying how to implement a solution. The Software Engineering Tips often provide a glimpse at the problem analysis and design steps as a means to see important connections in software development.

S.2   THE JAVA INSPECTOR

One of the practices that has proven itself to be invaluable in software engineering is the **inspection**. The names "design review," "code inspection," "structured walkthrough," and "desk check" all refer to different kinds of inspections. Inspections are really just what their name implies, an informal inspection or a perusal of some aspect of the software. Just like a painter must step back from the painting to discover imperfections, so too must a software engineer step back from the software to look for problems or potential improvements. The Java Inspector sections are included to provide guidance on how to inspect software. Just like Software Engineering Tips, it is best to examine The Java Inspector both before and after you have had the opportunity to utilize the chapter's material.

S.3 SUCCESSIVELY OPENING BLACK BOXES

Imagine that you are asked to learn to speak a new language and that you are told you must speak only in complete sentences. This analogy is remarkably close to what it is like to begin developing software (computer programs) using any modern programming language. The difficulty is that you will be expected to create complete programs almost from the very start. However, it is impossible to learn all of the rules for punctuation and grammar of any useful language without taking your time.

CLOSED
Black Box

In order to assist you, this book includes Black Box sections, like this. Such Closed Black Box sections indicate a black box in the sense that you are being asked to use some language feature or technique without questioning how or why. You should view the language feature as a black box that performs as explained, but you should not worry about what makes the black box work. If you simply can't wait for the solution, Closed Black Box sections also contains the section number from this text where the black box is opened and its secrets are revealed. Usually, it is best to ignore these references unless you return to this page for reference and you have already studied the section that opens the box.

OPENING
the Black Box

One of the simple pleasures in life can be a moment when we discover a secret. When a black box is opened, we discover why and how things work that had previously been a mystery. These times when black boxes are opened are indicated by Opening the Black Box sections like this, and they refer back to the previous Closed Black Box sections to which they correspond. If you are willing to accept a few of these black box concepts on faith, you should find that it is easier to learn to program

S.4 TERMINOLOGY

The computing industry has spawned a rather rich vocabulary all its own. Just a few years ago, if you mentioned "the Web" most people would assume you were talking about spiders. Today, we tell friends to "e-mail me" as frequently as we ask them to "give me a call."

Software development also has its own terminology. Some of these terms may be familiar to you, but most are likely to be new. Throughout this text we have tried to identify the most important vocabulary and boldface these terms when they first occur. You will also find a summary of these keys terms at the end of each chapter.

S.5 A FINAL COMMENT

If you are reading this book as an assigned text for a course, then I am honored that your instructor has chosen this book. However, I didn't write this text for instructors; I wrote it for you, the student. With the assistance of the good folk at Addison

Wesley Longman, some fine colleagues in my Department, and some excellent reviewers, I've tried to make the organization logical, the presentation clear, and the writing readable. The first semester that I used an early draft of this material I did so in parallel with another well-known textbook, and my students told me that they greatly preferred my manuscript. (Of course, I was the one who assigned their grades at the end of the semester, not the author of the other textbook. ;-) So you are the true judge of the quality of this book. If you find that it helps you to begin your journey into computer science, then my efforts will have been a success.

Dave Riley

CHAPTER 1

OBJECTS AND CLASSES

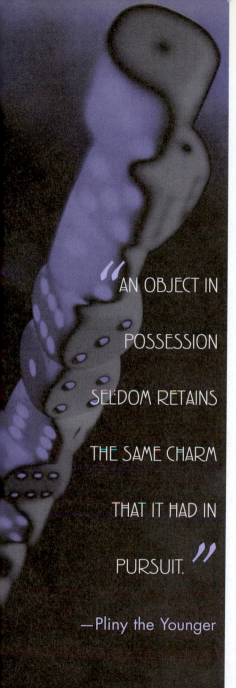

"AN OBJECT IN

POSSESSION

SELDOM RETAINS

THE SAME CHARM

THAT IT HAD IN

PURSUIT."

—Pliny the Younger

OBJECTIVES

- To provide a basic definition of an object as an entity with state and behavior

- To present the fundamental similarities and differences between objects and their classes

- To provide an initial example of how objects and classes can be used to construct a simple program

- To introduce the notation of class diagrams

- To explain the edit-compile-run process and its realization for the Java programming language

- To introduce the terminology of the waterfall software development model and use it to illustrate the role of various key processes in software development.

The world is a collection of **objects**. When you (an object) got up this morning you might have retrieved a box of cereal (another object) from the cupboard (still another object) and poured cereal into the bowl (a fourth object). Then you turned to the refrigerator (an object) to remove the gallon of milk (an object) to cover your cereal. Just as objects play a central role in "real life," they can also play a central role in computer programming.

1.1 OBJECTS EVERYWHERE

Examining objects with a bit more care leads to the conclusion that every object has two facets, namely:

- its state
- its behavior

The particular characteristics of an object constitute its **state**. The amount of milk within the container, the location of the milk container, and whether or not the container is open, are all characteristics that contribute to the state of the milk container. Of course, an object's state changes as time passes. When milk is poured out of the container, the amount of milk that remains has been altered. The changable nature of state means that state is related to time.

The refrigerator also exhibits state. For example, the temperature inside the refrigerator is a significant part of its state. Also, when the refrigerator's door is closed, the state of the refrigerator includes the fact that the light within is off. As the door is opened and the light turns on, the state of the refrigerator has changed.

Behavior refers to the tasks that an object is capable of performing. Typically, behavior takes the form of operations that can be performed upon the object. For example, the act of pouring milk from a container is an operation that is part of the normal behavior for a milk container. Other common operations for the milk container include placing the container in the refrigerator and removing the container's lid. Operations such as sitting on a milk container or using it to paint a picture would not be considered typical behavior for such an object.

Objects are routinely categorized into groups, also known as **classes**. The milk container in your hand is a particular object, but it belongs to a class called "milk container." Similarly, the refrigerator in your home belongs to the class of all refrigerators.

Classes define the state and behavior that is shared by all of the class members. An operation, like pouring, is part of the milk container class because it is common to all milk container objects.

1.2 OBJECTS IN SOFTWARE

A **program** is a collection of instructions that, when performed, cause a particular task to be performed on a computer. Individuals who write programs are, therefore, called **programmers**. The terms **software** and **code** refer to a collection of one or more programs, so programmers are also referred to as **software developers**.

Today, the strategy most often employed by knowledgeable software developers is called **object-oriented programming (OOP)**. A programmer using an object-oriented (O-O) strategy begins by selecting objects that can collectively solve the given problem.

Example 1 illustrates how a particular program might be developed in an OOP fashion. The software developer begins with a set of **program requirements** that specifies the desired task for the program.

EXAMPLE 1: PROGRAM REQUIREMENTS

Write a program to display a gray circle in a window.

SOFTWARE ENGINEERING TIP

Object-oriented design begins by selecting the objects. A good O-O designer looks for nouns in the program requirements, because these often indicate the key objects needed for a solution.

The program requirements document for Example 1 suggests that there are two significant objects, namely a circle and a window. One way to discover objects in requirements is to search for nouns. The circle and window are examples of such nouns.

Once a programmer identifies the objects in the program, the next step is to find or create a class corresponding to each object. Classes are essential because they serve as the places where the code of an object-oriented program resides. In fact, it is correct to say that an object-oriented program consists of a collection of classes.

SOFTWARE ENGINEERING TIP

Programmers should always seek to reuse existing software, rather than waste time creating something that already exists.

Ideally, a programmer **reuses** an existing class, as opposed to writing the code for a new class. Such software reuse by a programmer makes sense in the same way that an architect designs new structures from commonly available lumber with standard dimensions or an engineer designs new automobile engines using spark plugs that are available at most hardware stores.

For the purpose of a first example, Example 1, assume that two classes already exist: SimpleWindow for the window object and GrayCircle for the circle object. Given the appropriate supporting classes, the code from Figure 1.1 provides the rest of the program to accomplish the Example 1 task.

CLOSED
Black Box

Programming languages are like other foreign languages—the first exposure to a written sample is bound to seem pretty mysterious. The program code in Figure 1.1 is included to illustrate a few key points about software and its connection to the process of programming. However, you are not expected to read this code just yet. It is best to think of the notational details of this example as a black box to be opened (explained) in Chapters 2 and 3.

Figure 1.1 Driver class for Example 1

```
// Example 1
import  aLibrary.*;
public class Director  {
    private SimpleWindow  window;          ⎫ object declarations
    private GrayCircle  circle;            ⎭

    public Director()  {                   ⎫
        window = new SimpleWindow();       ⎪
        circle = new GrayCircle();         ⎬ instructions
        circle.place(window);              ⎪
        window.repaint();                  ⎭
    }
}
```

The execution of an object-oriented program begins with an initial object. This initial object plays a special role because it serves as the starting point for the entire program and often coordinates much of the program's activity. For Example 1, the initial object belongs to the Director class. The name Director is chosen because the object is responsible for *directing* the execution of the program and its other objects.

The state of an object depends upon its components (other objects). This particular Director object includes two component objects, declared in the two lines that begin with the word private.

1. The window object is declared to belong to a class called SimpleWindow. This object serves as a window (a rectangular display region) on the computer screen.

2. The circle object is declared to belong to a class called GrayCircle. This object draws the gray circle upon window.

An object's behavior is determined by **instructions**. When a program executes, the program's instructions are performed. There are four instructions for the Director object. These instructions are found in the four lines following the "public Director() {" line.

- The first instruction will cause a new SimpleWindow object, named window, to be constructed.
- The second will cause a new GrayCircle object, named circle, to be constructed.
- The third will cause the circle object to be placed upon the window object.
- The fourth will cause the window object with the circle upon it to be displayed.

Example 1 illustrates the tools that a software developer must use to write a program. A program is built from classes that the programmer writes or reuses. Classes are composed from instructions, and these instructions are used in such a way that they manipulate objects to perform the desired task.

The work of a programmer is something like that of a songwriter. The songwriter composes songs, while the programmer writes classes. A song is composed from notes and words, while a class is composed from declarations and instructions. A performer takes the notes and lyrics of a song and performs the music. A computer takes the declarations and instructions of a program and executes the program. Sometimes the results of a program execution are images drawn on a computer screen, sometimes they are complex calculations, and sometimes they retrieve and update important information.

1.3　ANATOMY OF A SOFTWARE CLASS

Since all of the code in object-oriented programs resides within classes, the skilled programmer needs to become familiar with writing and using classes. Indeed, most of this textbook is devoted to learning how best to compose classes. This section introduces the basics.

A **software class** consists of two groups of members:

- attributes
- methods

An **attribute**, often represented by an **instance variable**, is an entity that names a single characteristic of an object's state. A **method** is an operation that can be performed upon an object. It is useful to picture the attributes and methods as a **class diagram** with the following general form.

The class diagram is a rectangle with three compartments separated by two horizontal lines. The top compartment contains the name of the class. The middle compartment lists the attributes of the class, and the bottom compartment shows the class methods.

This class diagram notation is part of the **Unified Modeling Language (UML)**. UML is the most widely used set of notations in today's software engineering industry.

The `Director` class of Example 1 is diagrammed as shown in Figure 1.2. The class diagram for `Director` specifies that this class contains two attributes: `window` and `circle`. Notice that each attribute is preceded by the name of the class to which it belongs.

Figure 1.2   Class diagram for `Director` class of Example 1

The methods of the class are listed in the bottom compartment of the class diagram. The only method in the `Director` class has the same name as the class (`Director`). It may seem strange for a method to have the same name as its class, but this is a common occurrence in some programming languages.

Example 1 also makes use of two other classes: `SimpleWindow` (the class of the `window` object) and `GrayCircle` (the class of the `circle` object). The class diagrams for these two classes are shown in Figure 1.3. This figure illustrates a couple of new notations that are typical of class diagrams.

Figure 1.3 Class diagrams for `SimpleWindow` and `GrayCircle`

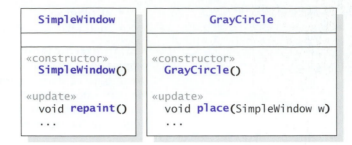

Neither the `SimpleWindow` class nor the `GrayCircle` class have any interesting attributes. Therefore, the attribute region of each class diagram in Figure 1.3 is left blank. When attributes are omitted in this way, it means that either the class has no attributes or (more often) that the attributes of the class aren't relevant to the discussion at hand.

The list of methods shown within a class diagram can also be incomplete. The "..." notation in the `SimpleWindow` and `GrayCircle` diagrams indicates that there are more methods in these classes than are shown. These additional methods are not shown, because they are not relevant to Example 1.

You may also notice that the `repaint` and `place` methods are preceded by the word `void`. The inclusion of `void` is used commonly in Java to denote a method that is designed for updating.

UML class diagrams frequently include labels to categorize the class methods. Such labels are bracketed within « » symbols. In Figure 1.3, the `SimpleWindow` and `GrayCircle` methods are both categorized as *constructor* methods, while `repaint` and `place` are *update* methods. The distinction between constructor and update categories will be explained in Chapter 2.

1.4 THE DIFFERENCE BETWEEN OBJECTS AND CLASSES

An object is very closely associated with the class to which it belongs. An object has attributes as defined by its class. An object's behavior is restricted by the methods that are included in its class. The instructions that are executed by an object are the instructions that are written in the class. However, there are significant differences between objects and class.

A class

- is a template that defines attributes and methods.
- is written by a programmer as a part of a program.
- does not exist when programs execute, except in the form of one or more member objects.
- is static in the sense that its code cannot be altered during program execution.
- is named by a class name.

An object

- must belong to some class.
- exists during the time that a program executes.
- must be explicitly declared *and* constructed by the executing program.
- has attributes that can change in value and methods that can execute during program execution. (The class to which the object belongs defines these attributes and methods.)
- is often referenced using a variable name.

Classes can be compared to automobile assembly lines. The purpose of an assembly line is to produce automobiles, just as the purpose of a class is to produce objects. A single assembly line is designed to produce a single basic type of auto. Similarly, the objects from the same class all share common characteristics.

Each object must **belong** to one particular class, and the object is said to be a **member** of the class to which it belongs. The `window` object from Example 1 belongs to the `SimpleWindow` class. This means that the program is permitted to perform `SimpleWindow` methods (operations) upon `window`. This also means that performing `Director` methods or `GrayCircle` methods upon `window` is *not* permitted; these methods are designed for a different kind (class) of objects.

Despite the fact that every object belongs to a single class, it is possible for a class to have multiple member objects. The `Director` class could be revised to create not one, but two `SimpleWindow` objects. Each of these two objects would have its own unique attribute values, just as two cars from the same assembly line might be painted different colors. However, both `window` objects are the product of the same assembly line called `SimpleWindow`, and this class membership defines the methods that can be performed upon them.

1.5 EDIT, COMPILE, AND RUN

This discussion of classes and objects raises a fundamental distinction between actions that occur during the time a program executes and actions that occur prior to program execution. In order to explore such issues, it is useful to examine the process that is used to bring a program into production.

Computers are **hardware**; that is to say they are made of electrical circuits, perhaps with a few mechanical devices. A key part of that hardware is a unit called **main memory**. The main memory stores each object, including all of its attributes.

The **processor** is a second key device within every modern computer. It is the processor that is responsible for executing the program. Unfortunately, processors are restricted to executing only a primitive type of instructions, known as **machine instructions**. Machine instructions are extremely difficult for humans to read and to write, because they are designed for the convenience of the computer hardware and not for programmers. Therefore, modern software development relies upon **high-level programming languages**. The term "high-level" implies that these languages are closer to a notation that is comfortable for programmers.

The use of a high-level language dictates the need for a three-step process to bring a program from the programmer's mind into production. Figure 1.4 illustrates this process. Step 1 occurs when the programmer enters the program into the computer. A programmer uses a software tool, called an **editor**, to perform this task. Each software class is typed into the editor, and the editor is used to save each class in a separate **file** (generally on the computer's disk storage). Such files are often called **source code** because they are the original (source) program components as created by the programmer.

Figure 1.4 The edit-compile-run process

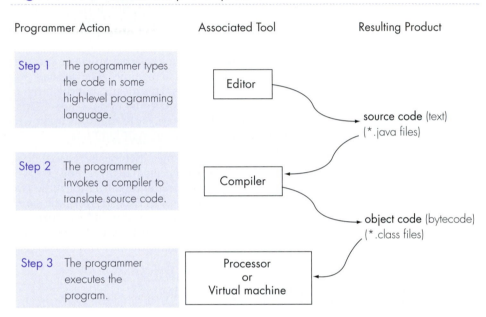

In order to type the source code, a programmer must first choose a particular **programming language**. Each programming language has its own unique notations and conventions, just as each different natural language has its distinctive conventions.

In this text all programs are written in a programming language called **Java**. Java is the result of a research project, directed by James Gosling and funded by Sun Microsystems. In May of 1995 Sun formally announced the new language. Java shares many of its notations with the earlier C and C++ programming languages. However, being designed later, Java incorporates several different language features, including many features specifically to support object-oriented programming and World Wide Web applications.

When programming in Java, the programmer usually stores each class in a separate file and the name of each file should be the same as the class with ".java" appended. For example, the Director class would be stored in a file named *Director.java*. Note that Java is a **case-sensitive language**, which means that capitalization patterns must be identical if they are to refer to the same thing. Case sensitivity dictates that "director" or "DIRECTOR" or "DiReCtOr" are all different names. Some file systems are also case sensitive.

Once the classes have been stored in source files, the second step of the process is to **compile** the source code. A **compiler** is a program that translates source code into an executable form. Not all computing systems use the same Java compiler or the same technique for invoking the compiler. One common procedure for compiling code is to place the source code files into a single folder, making certain that this folder is the working folder (current directory), then to enter the following command:

```
javac *.java
```

This command invokes the standard Sun Microsystems Java compiler and compiles all files whose names end with a ".java" suffix. Assuming the compiler detects no errors in the source code, it will store the translated form of each class in its own file. Each of these translated **object code** files will be named the same as the original class with ".class" appended. In other words, the Java compiler will read the *Director.java* file and store the translated form of this class in a second file called *Director.class*. (The source file remains unaltered by the compilation process.)

> ### SOFTWARE ENGINEERING TIP
> Compilers are extremely unforgiving. In English, a missing comma or semicolon is often unimportant, but not so for a compiler. The wise programmer reviews source code for typographical errors and avoids using conventions that encourage such errors.

In the event that the programmer has mistyped the program, the compiler will detect an error. Such errors are called **compile-time errors** or **syntax errors**; they are errors in the allowable **syntax** or form of the code. When a syntax error is detected, it is reported by the compiler and no object code is produced. Such an error is a signal to the programmer to return to the editor and alter the file(s), then compile again. It may take several repetitions of edits and compiles before the programmer gets the code corrected.

Once all syntax errors have been fixed and the classes compiled, the third step of the process is to **execute** (or **run**) the program. Many compilers produce object code that is in machine code format, so the computer's processor can execute such object code directly. Most Java compilers do not translate into machine code, but instead their object code is stored in a format known as **bytecode**. Like machine code, bytecode is in a form that is of little value to humans but unlike machine code, bytecode cannot be directly executed by a processor.

One solution to the problem of how to execute bytecode is to use a **Java Virtual Machine** (or **Java VM**) to execute the code. The Java VM is another program that knows how to execute the ".class" files. A Java VM is typically invoked by typing "java" followed by a blank and the name of the class where execution is to begin. In the case of Example 1, the folder contains a class called "go.class" that is an appropriate starting class for this code. (The go class is used by early examples in this text in order to create an object of type Director, thereby invoking the Director constructor method.) A typical command to execute the Example 1 program is as follows:

```
java go
```

The program expressed in the Director class from Example 1 together with the go class is called an **application**, which means that it is designed to be executed by a Java VM. In Chapter 15 a different type of Java program that does not require the same sort of Java VM will be presented.

When the Example 1 application is executed, the result is that a window containing a gray circle is displayed on the computer monitor. Figure 1.5 contains a picture of such a window. This window may look slightly different on computers with different operating systems. However, the window will always consist of a bar across the top that names it as "AWindow" and a white rectangular region that serves as the drawing canvas of the window. In this case, a gray circle is displayed within the white region.

Figure 1.5 Window displayed when Example 1 executes

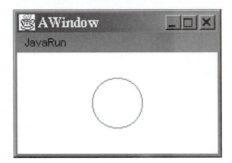

Program execution must end at some time. The Java applications in this book provide the user with two ways to exit the entire program: (1) close every window that the program creates, or (2) select the Quit command from the application's menu. The user closes a window by clicking the close button (usually marked "X" in the upper-right corner of the window.

The second option for terminating program execution uses the *JavaRun* menu, illustrated in Figure 1.6. This action consists of selecting the *JavaRun* pull-down menu and then the Quit entry of this menu. On some operating systems the *JavaRun* menu is located within the window(s) created by the application (as shown), while other operating systems have their own separate place for the menu for the executing application.

Figure 1.6 *JavaRun* menu for quitting a Java application

The Java bytecode that is created by a compiler on one computer can generally be executed on any Java VM running on any computer. This ability to easily transport executable code from one computer to another is called **portability**; it is the primary reason for using a compiler that produces bytecode rather than machine code. Machine code is not portable because each different family of computer processors has its own machine code.

> **SOFTWARE ENGINEERING TIP**
>
> Beginning programmers sometimes make the mistake of believing a program to be correct if the compiler fails to find syntax errors. The wise programmer knows that logical errors can occur independent of syntax errors and are frequently more difficult to find and correct.

Just as there are compile-time errors, there are also **logical errors**. A logical error results in a program that doesn't perform the intended task. Sometimes logical errors are so grievous that they can be detected by the Java VM, in which case an error is reported to the programmer. Such reported errors are known as **run-time errors**. However, many times the program with a logical error appears to run normally but simply produces incorrect results. For example, the programmer may have written a program to display a blue square in a window, when the program requirements stated that a gray circle was to be displayed.

> **SOFTWARE ENGINEERING TIP**
>
> Programs are neither correct nor incorrect by themselves. It makes sense to talk about program correctness only with respect to the specified purpose for the program. Programmers must scrutinize and rescrutinize the specifications (requirements) documents throughout the processing of writing and testing their code.

Programming errors, whether they be compile-time errors or logical errors, are also called **faults**. More informally, faults are called **bugs**. The process of identifying faults is referred to as **testing**, and the act of testing together with correcting faults is known as **debugging**.

1.6   INTRODUCTION TO SOFTWARE ENGINEERING

In the 1970s it became apparent that much of the world's software was being created by haphazard methods. Unlike other engineering disciplines that had strict rules for how to approach a new design and how to measure the quality of a product, computer programming was a kind of "grab bag" of programming strategies often learned through on-the-job experiences. The term **software crisis** was frequently used to describe a software industry in which programming projects rarely met schedules and the resulting software typically contained many faults. The phrase "computer error," which almost always means "software error," became a common excuse for many everyday problems.

The result of this bit of history was a new emphasis on **software engineering** as a disciplined approach to software development. Today's software developers practice their craft on sizable programs consisting of thousands, or even millions, of instructions. Teams of cooperating software developers, devoting hundreds of man-years of time, are required for this so-called **programming in the large**. This textbook explores the fundamental tools of the software development trade. The examples and exercises are necessarily smaller than large-scale programming, but it is essential to keep in mind that the ultimate goal is to develop the habits and skills needed for programming in the large.

Large programming projects tend to follow a pattern known as a **software lifecycle**. An early form for a software lifecycle, called the **waterfall model**, is illustrated in Figure 1.7.

Figure 1.7 The waterfall model of software development

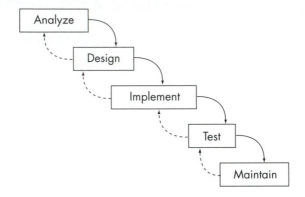

The waterfall model describes the process of creating a program as a five-step procedure. The process begins with the **analysis phase** in which the software developer must analyze the problem that is to be solved. The purpose of analysis is to discover what the customer wants and to formulate a detailed set of software requirements.

The **design phase** of software development is the time at which the basic structure of the program is chosen. Object-oriented design includes tasks such as identifying the objects needed in the program, as well as outlining the classes and their relationships. Documents such as class diagrams are produced during the design phase.

The actual code for each class is created during the **implementation phase**. The difference between the design phase and the implementation phase is analogous to the difference between the work of an architect and a contractor. Design work produces the architectural blueprint whereas implementation turns the blueprint into bricks and mortar. Any software implementation must be expressed using the notation of some programming language, but designs are often language independent.

> **SOFTWARE ENGINEERING TIP**
>
> Introductory computer science texts, like this one, tend to concentrate on issues relating to the implementation phase of the software lifecycle. However, history has shown that implementation is easier (and faster) when more effort has been invested in analysis and design.

The waterfall model suggests that the implementation phase is followed by a **testing phase** in which the code is tested for correctness with respect to its requirements. Software rarely ends its lifecycle with testing. Most significant programs live through many revisions (also called "versions" or "releases"). Each subsequent revision purports to improve the software by correcting earlier deficiencies and/or adding new and improved features. This process of modifying the code to produce later revisions is known as the **maintenance phase**.

Few, if any, software development projects follow the exact five-step sequence of the waterfall model. For most projects testing is an ongoing process, not just a single step between implementation and maintenance. It is also commonplace to discover a deficiency during the implementation that requires revisiting the basic design or even the requirements documents. Despite the imperfections in the waterfall model, all programmers can benefit by understanding the five phases of the model because they represent five fundamental activities of software engineering.

1.7   A SAMPLE OF OBJECT-ORIENTED SOFTWARE DEVELOPMENT

To glimpse the way that a large object-oriented programming project might proceed, consider the task of automating a grocery store. This software development project begins by analyzing the entire grocery operation to discover the requirements for the software. Senior software developers then talk with the store owners to understand their needs and wishes for the software. The developers also study the store's equipment, including the computer upon which the software executes along with customer check-out devices and systems for recording new inventory arrivals. Store policies and personnel responsibilities are also investigated during this phase of the project.

Once the store owners and the senior programmers have agreed upon a set of system requirements, software design begins. The initial stages of software design, sometimes called **high-level design**, are likely to rely heavily upon information gathered during analysis. As the design begins, objects are identified and classes emerge. Suppose the grocery store has 14 check-out lanes, each equipped with bar-code scanners, credit-card readers, and manually operated cash drawers. Additionally, the store receives weekly printed price lists from suppliers. Objects that begin to emerge from analyzing this system include the following:

- a bar-coded can of beans
- the cash drawer in Register 3
- the order form to be submitted to a supplier
- the cash stored in the store's safe
- a single sale by credit card

The objects must be grouped into classes, such as BarCodedProduct that can include objects like corn chips and bars of soap. Similarly, a CashDrawer class has member objects that include those cash drawers in use at check-out lanes, as well as any cash drawer that is being counted down by the store bookkeeper.

The design process proceeds to identify the attributes and methods of each individual class. For example, the attributes of BarCodedProduct include items like the product's name, the supplier, the cost, the selling price, the quantity on hand, and the bar-code number. The operations that are performed upon bar-coded objects, such as *change the price* and *sell one item* become methods of the class. Figure 1.8 contains a sample class diagram that might result from designing the BarCodedProduct class.

It is common for programmers to discover unexpected objects during the design process. For example, consideration of the BarCodedProduct class and its quantityOnHand attribute might lead to the need for an out-of-stock-alert object. There are likely to be hundreds of classes needed for the grocery store system.

An architect creates house plans by performing a kind of high-level design to draw graphical blueprints. But the architect must also supply more detailed descriptions of things such as wall thickness, materials, and insulation requirements. Similarly, software designers must perform both high-level design and **detail design**. Writing a class diagram is usually viewed as high-level design, but supplying precise specifications for the behavior of each of the class's methods can be considered to be detail design. An example of a detail design decision is whether or not to design the sellOneItem method so that it triggers immediate product orders when inventory is low.

Figure 1.8 Class diagram for BarCodedProduct

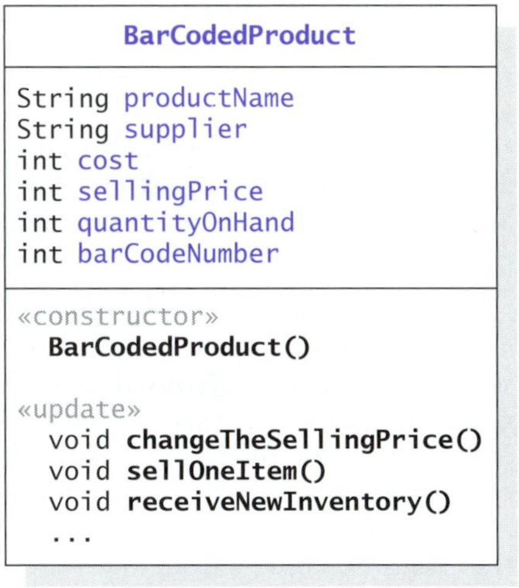

```
                    BarCodedProduct

        String productName
        String supplier
        int cost
        int sellingPrice
        int quantityOnHand
        int barCodeNumber

        «constructor»
          BarCodedProduct()

        «update»
          void changeTheSellingPrice()
          void sellOneItem()
          void receiveNewInventory()
          . . .
```

After the detail design has specified the desired behavior for a method, the method can be implemented. During the implementation process, a software developer writes the actual Java instructions (the code) that execute when the method is invoked. This developer, and others, are likely to examine and test the code under various conditions to gain confidence that it performs the intended task.

The execution of the complete program consists of a collection of objects that perform methods upon one another. When an item is scanned for sale by the checkout scanner object, a method must be called to update the quantity on hand from the product object and another method might add the item's cost to the customer's bill object. It is the combined execution of numerous methods upon many objects that belong to various classes that characterize a typical running object-oriented program.

JAVA INSPECTOR

Software engineering teaches that the most productive way to improve code quality is to perform frequent and thorough **desk checks**. A desk check consists of scrutinizing the code manually. Compilers can discover syntax errors and executing a program can uncover certain logical errors. However, many of these errors can be avoided if the programmer simply spends a little time examining the code.

Below is a collection of hints on what to check when examining code that involves the concepts of this chapter.

✓ Compilers are uncompromising. As a programmer you must learn to spell and punctuate precisely. The Java syntax rules presented throughout this book are a guide.

✓ Java is case sensitive. It is always worth checking for proper use of capitalization.

✓ Every class should be checked to be certain that it is stored in a file, named with the class name and a suffix of .java.

✓ Before a program can be executed, it must have compiled properly. Always check for the presence of syntax errors prior to executing your program.

TERMINOLOGY

analysis phase (of software development)

application (as used in Java)

attribute

behavior

belong (as an object "belongs" to a class)

bug

bytecode

case-sensitive language

class (in software)

class diagram

code

compile/ compiler

compile-time error

debug

design phase (of software development)

desk check

detail design

editor

edit-compile-run process

execute

fault

file

hardware (of a computer)

high-level design

high-level programming language

implementation phase (of software development)

instance variable

instruction

Java (the programming language)

Java Virtual Machine (Java VM)

logical error

machine instruction

main memory (computer memory)

maintenance phase

member (of a class)

method

object

object code

object-oriented programming (OOP)

portability

processor
program
program correctness
program requirements
programmer
programming in the large
programming language
reuse (of software)
run

run-time error
software
software class
software crisis
software developer
software engineering
software lifecycle
source code
state
syntax

syntax error
testing
testing phase (of software development)
Unified Modeling Language (UML)
waterfall model (of software development)

EXERCISES

1. Consider an object called cruise ship. Which of the following would you classify as contributing to the state of the cruise ship, and which is better associated with its behavior?

   a. the ship's color
   b. the act of slowing the ship down to 5 knots per hour
   c. the length of the ship's deck
   d. turning the ship back toward its home port

2. For each of the following objects, select a class to which this, and other objects, belongs.

   a. your mother
   b. Sun Microsystems
   c. your favorite item of clothing
   d. the writing utensil you use most often
   e. your favorite pet

3. Identify as many objects as you can within each of the following requirements statements.

   a. Write a program to draw a clown with a red nose and green hair.
   b. Write a program to simulate a farm tractor pulling a plow through a field.
   c. Write a program to show three dogs leaping through three hoops.

4. For each class diagram below, identify the name of the class, the name of every attribute and the class to which the attribute belongs, and the name of every method.

a.

Director
SimpleWindow window rectangle blueSquare rectangle greenSquare
Director()

b.

PhoneAnsweringMachine
Button playButton Button eraseButton Counter messageCount
PhoneAnsweringMachine() void playNextMessage(); void rewind() void eraseAll()

5. Each statement below lists an activity that might take place within the development of a particular piece of software. As best fits, label each of these activities as

> analysis phase
> design phase
> implementation phase
> testing phase
> maintenance phase

a. Sending an early version of the software to a group of prospective buyers to get their reaction

b. Formulating a collection of classes from the program requirements

c. Writing the code for a particular method

d. Correcting syntax errors

e. Discussing a typical scenario for how the software should function

f. Announcing version 1.2 of the program

PROGRAMMING EXERCISES

1. Compile and run the program called Example 1 (Figure 1.1). This may require assistance to learn how to use the Java compiler and run-time environment on your system. Don't forget to include the go class.

2. Use your editor to remove the third instruction from Example 1 (Figure 1.1). (The third instruction consists of the following line.)

```
circle.place(window);
```

When you compile and run this new version of the program, you should see a window with no gray circle.

3. Use your editor to remove a semicolon anywhere from Example 1 (Figure 1.1). Recompile the program to see how the Java compiler reports compile-time errors.

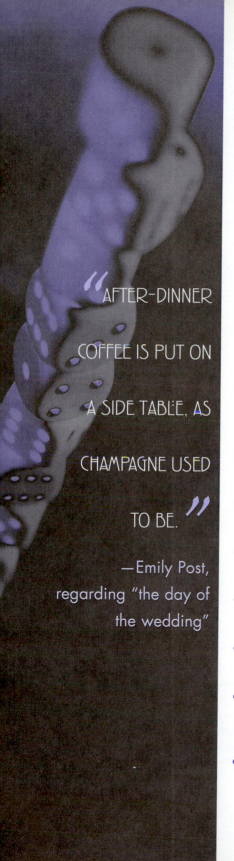

INTRODUCTION TO JAVA OBJECTS

OBJECTIVES

- To introduce the basic Java language concepts necessary to write an initial program in the form of a class, called `Director`

- To present the concept of syntax diagrams as a notation to be used in defining Java syntax throughout this text

- To describe the syntax and semantics of a sequence of statements

- To describe the syntax and semantics of a parameterless method call instruction

- To describe the syntax of an assignment instruction used to construct new objects

- To describe the syntax and usage of instance variable declarations

- To examine the need for class specifications and present a means for expressing them in the form of class invariants, as well as method preconditions and postconditions

- To describe the syntax of Java comments and suggest how best to use comments to express software specifications

How does a programmer "speak" Java? Much of this textbook is devoted to explaining the Java programming language and how to express programs in Java. This chapter focuses on the basics of how to write simple Java classes to construct and manipulate objects.

2.1 SYNTAX DIAGRAMS

Every programming language has two defining characteristics:

- its **syntax**
- its **semantics**

Syntax refers to form and semantics refers to meaning. Spelling and punctuation within a program are syntax issues, whereas the program's behavior at run time depends upon its semantics.

To maintain the necessary precision for illustrating syntax, this text will use a common notation known as **syntax diagrams**. Each syntax diagram is a picture containing text and arrows that define a single portion of the language's notation. This section contains three syntax diagrams to illustrate how to read and write such pictures. Figures 2.1, 2.2, and 2.3 do not, however, define any part of the Java programming language.

Figure 2.1 An example syntax diagram

FourSentences

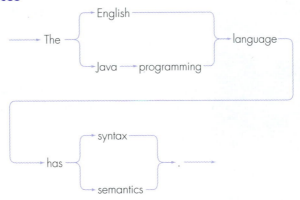

Each syntax diagram has a name that identifies the portion of syntax that it represents. Figure 2.1 names its syntax diagram *FourSentences*. Correct syntax is defined by any path that proceeds all the way from the arrow entering the diagram on the left through the arrow leaving the diagram on the right. Any such path through defines a syntactically valid sequence of symbols based upon the order that symbols are encountered along the path. The *FourSentences* diagram defines four possible paths and, therefore, four sequences of symbols. These four alternatives are as follows.

The English language has syntax.
The English language has semantics.
The Java programming language has syntax.
The Java programming language has semantics.

Any one of these four alternatives is said to be valid syntax for *FourSentences*. Furthermore, there are no other syntactically valid *FourSentences* alternatives.

Sometimes syntax diagrams contain arrows that loop backward. Figure 2.2 illustrates this type of syntax diagram.

Figure 2.2 A second syntax diagram

WhyProgram

The *WhyProgram* syntax diagram from Figure 2.2 matches each of the following sentences.

Programming is subtle.
Programming is very subtle.
Programming is very, very subtle.
Programming is very, very, very subtle.

It also matches an infinite number of other sentences resulting from repeating the backward loop more times.

Syntax diagrams are given names so that they can be used in other syntax diagrams. Figure 2.3 contains a reference to the *FourSentences* diagram. (Note that such references to other diagrams should be denoted differently to avoid confusion. In this text a rectangle encloses such a reference to another syntax diagram.)

Figure 2.3 A third syntax diagram

ManySentences

Valid syntax for the *ManySentences* diagram of Figure 2.3 would include any one of the following lines, along with an infinite number of others.

(The English language has syntax.)
(The English language has semantics.)
(The Java programming language has syntax.)

(The Java programming language has semantics.)
(The English language has syntax.) (The English language has syntax.)
(The English language has syntax.) (The English language has semantics.)
(The English language has syntax.) (The Java programming language has syntax.)

Most programming languages contain a certain amount of flexibility that is ignored by syntax diagrams. The issue of **separators** is one particular topic ignored by syntax diagrams. The sentences described as valid for the preceding syntax diagrams all contain blanks between consecutive words, despite the fact that the syntax diagrams do not contain these blanks. Blanks are used as separators between consecutive symbols of English sentences. Java allows various kinds of white space (one or more blanks, tabs, or the end of a line) to serve as a separator. Unless otherwise stated, white space is permitted, but not required, wherever an arrow is placed in a syntax diagram.

Sometimes a version of a syntax diagram is labeled abridged in an early presentation because it is incomplete. An unabridged collection of syntax diagrams for Java is included in Appendix B.

2.2 THE METHOD CALL

The **method call** is the fundamental instruction in any object-oriented program. A method call (see Figure 2.4) involves two things: an object and a method. Executing a method call causes the method to be performed, or executed, upon the object.

Figure 2.4 ParameterlessMethodCall description

ParameterlessMethodCall (abridged version of *MethodCall*)

Syntax

Notes

- *ObjectRef* is the name (or valid reference) to an object and *MethodName* is the name of a nonconstructor method from the class to which the *ObjectRef* object belongs.

- No separators are permitted before or after the period.

Semantics

Executing ParameterlessMethodCall causes the method to be performed upon the object.

To see how method calls are used, suppose that the task is to draw lines on a computer window. Further assume the use of a DrawingTool class. The following class diagram describes DrawingTool to have at least four nonconstructor methods named moveForward, turnClockwise, dontDraw, and draw.

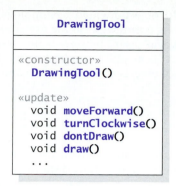

If `pencil` is the name of an object belonging to the `DrawingTool` class, then according to the rules of `ParameterlessMethodCall`, each of the following are valid Java instructions.

```
pencil.moveForward();
pencil.turnClockwise();
pencil.dontDraw();
pencil.draw();
```

The following illustrate some *invalid* attempts at method call instructions. (The reason that each is invalid is explained in the text to the right)

`pencil.moveForward;`	(missing parentheses)
`pencil.moveforward();`	(misnamed method—moveforward should be moveForward)
`chalk.moveRight();`	(incorrect object name—chalk)
`pencilmoveForward();`	(missing period)
`pencil .moveForward();`	(blanks not permitted prior to the period)
`pencil.DrawingTool();`	(constructor methods cannot be called with this syntax)

The last invalid instruction points out that Java divides methods into two categories: those methods that are **constructors** and those that are not. Constructor methods are easily identified because they always have the same name as their class. As will be seen later, constructor methods are called somewhat differently.

When a method call is executed, that method is performed upon the indicated object. Therefore, executing the instruction

```
pencil.moveForward();
```

causes the `pencil` object to move forward. If there is a second object, named `pen`, the following Java instruction is appropriate to move the `pen` object.

```
pen.moveForward();
```

In object-oriented terminology, executing a method is often referred to as sending a **message**. So the execution of the previous instruction can be explained as a moveForward message being sent to the pen object. This way of thinking about objects is helpful in understanding that a program is nothing more than a collection of objects that are sending and responding to messages.

2.3   INSTRUCTION SEQUENCES

Executing a single instruction performs one task, such as moving a DrawingTool object forward a short distance or causing it to turn. However, a more complete task generally requires multiple instructions. To allow for such tasks, Java supports a StatementSequence, as described by Figure 2.5. (Note that Java instructions are often referred to as "statements.")

Figure 2.5   StatementSequence description

StatementSequence

Syntax

Note

Statements in a sequence are best placed one per line and each line justified to the same left position (i.e., tabbed the same distance from the left margin).

Semantics

Executing StatementSequence causes the *OneStatements* to execute in order.

When a **sequence of statements** executes, each of the statements is executed in turn. That is to say, the first statement executes, and when it completes, the second executed; when the second statement completes executing, the third is executed; etc. As an example, executing the following sequence of Java statements/instructions causes the pencil object to begin drawing, move forward twice, turn clockwise, and then move forward three more times.

```
pencil.draw();
pencil.moveForward();
pencil.moveForward();
pencil.turnClockwise();
pencil.moveForward();
pencil.moveForward();
pencil.moveForward();
```

2.4   CONSTRUCTING AND ASSIGNING OBJECTS

Before an executing program can call a method (send a message) it must first construct the object that is to receive that message.

Figure 2.6 ParameterlessConstruction description

ParameterlessConstruction (a version of *Expression*)

Syntax

Note

ConstructorName is the name of a constructor method.

Semantics

Evaluating `ParameterlessConstruction` causes a new object to be constructed and the constructor method named *ConstructorName* to be performed upon the object.

According to this description of `ParameterlessConstruction` from Figure 2.6, the notation for constructing an object consists of the keyword new followed by a constructor method call. For example, evaluating the following expression constructs a DrawingTool object.

```
new DrawingTool()
```

Such a construction is called an **instantiation**, because it creates an *instance* (an object) of type DrawingTool. This instantiation is not a complete instruction. Furthermore, an object instantiation by itself does *not* associate the newly constructed object with a name. An **assignment instruction** (see Figure 2.7) is frequently used in conjunction with an object instantiation in order to make a complete instruction, as well as give the object a name.

Figure 2.7 AssignmentInstruction description

AssigmentInstruction (a version of *OneStatement*)

Syntax

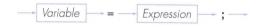

Note

The type of *Expression* must conform to the declared type of *Variable*.

Semantics

Executing `AssignmentInstruction` causes *Expression* to be evaluated. *Variable* is assigned the result of the *Expression* evaluation.

Executing an assignment instruction assigns (or binds) a variable name to the result of an expression evaluation. If the expression in the assignment instruction is an object instantiation, then the result of executing an assignment instruction is to construct a new object and to bind the **variable** to that object. The instruction below is an example.

```
pencil = new DrawingTool();
```

Following the execution of the above instruction, a new `DrawingTool` object has been constructed. This new object is bound to the name `pencil` so the variable refers to the object.

Assume that a program has two `DrawingTool` variables, namely pen and pencil. Prior to executing any instructions, these variables are considered to be unbound. In Java an unbound variable is said to be `null`. This means that the state of pen and pencil prior to any bindings can be pictured as follows. The downward lines in this picture don't connect to anything because the variables are unbound.

pen   pencil

(null)   (null)

Programmers must be cautious about variables that are `null`. Attempting to execute a method call upon a variable that is `null` results in a run-time error something like the following.

```
Exception Occurred:
java.lang.NullPointerException
...
```

This error is avoided by binding variables to objects. For example, executing the following instructions would cause two separate `DrawingTool` objects to be created, each bound to one of the variables. This binding is pictured in the form of object diagrams to the right of the instructions. The shaded rectangles represent objects, showing both the name of the object (before the colon) and the class to which the object belongs (after the colon).

```
pen = new DrawingTool();
pencil = new DrawingTool();
```

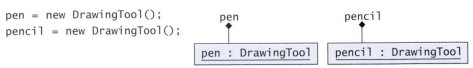

Assignment instructions can also be used to assign one variable to another. (Any variable name by itself is considered to be a valid *Expression*.) When one variable is assigned to another, the result is for the left variable to take on the value/binding of the one on the right. The second instruction in the example below illustrates this concept.

```
pen = new DrawingTool();
pencil = pen;
```

As can be seen in the picture above, pencil becomes bound to the same object as pen. In a sense, the two variables are both **aliases** for each other. (Since there are two names for the same object, the object name has been omitted within the object rectangle.) Failure to recognize aliases can lead to programmer confusion. For example, normally a method performed upon pencil would have no effect upon the pen object. However, if the two variables are aliases, then any change in one is a change to both.

Sometimes assigning one variable to another produces objects known as **orphans**. An orphan is an object that is no longer bound to anything. The example below shows how the object previously bound to pencil becomes orphaned when the third assignment instruction executes.

```
pen = new DrawingTool();
pencil = new DrawingTool();
pencil = pen;
```

pen   pencil

: DrawingTool   : DrawingTool

Creating such orphans is not necessarily a bad thing, so long as this is the programmer's intent. However, it is important to remember that an orphaned object becomes inaccessible to program instructions. The Java VM automatically recovers any computer memory space that might otherwise have been lost to orphan objects.

It is also possible to create orphans by constructing another object. Each of the two instructions below constructs a new object and binds that object to pencil. Since a variable can be bound to only one object at a time, the object bound by the first instruction becomes an orphan when the second instruction executes.

```
pencil = new DrawingTool();
pencil = new DrawingTool();
```

pencil

: DrawingTool   pencil : DrawingTool

Assigning null to a variable is yet another way to create an orphan. The first instruction below instantiates a DrawingTool object, and the second causes the object to become orphaned by assigning to pencil the value null.

```
pencil = new DrawingTool();
pencil = null;
```

pencil

(null)

: DrawingTool

Programmers must be careful not to create unnecessary objects, nor to orphan objects that are needed.

2.5 SWAPPING

Some programming ideas occur with enough frequency to be called **patterns**. A pattern is a general programming template that is used in many programs. Coding patterns are programming expressions or instruction sequences that are useful for solving many problems.

One such coding pattern is known as a **swap**. The swap pattern is applicable any time that two variables must interchange their objects (values). Such an interchange provides insight into the behavior of assignment instructions.

Suppose that it is necessary to swap pencil and pen. A typical mistake made by novice programmers is to attempt to perform the interchange with the following code.

```
pencil = pen;
pen = pencil;
```

A logic error can be discovered by tracing the execution of these instructions. Prior to the execution of this code it is presumed that each variable is bound to some object as shown in the object diagram below.

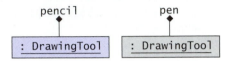

Executing the first instruction (pencil = pen;) results in the following.

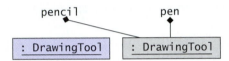

Executing the second instruction changes nothing, because both variables are already bound to the right object.

The key shortcoming of the previous attempted swap is that the first instruction causes one of the objects to be orphaned. This shortcoming can be resolved by using a third DrawingTool variable, call it tempTool. The resulting swap code is shown below.

```
tempTool = pen;
pen = pencil;
pencil = tempTool;
```

Suppose that prior to this code the three variables are bound as follows:

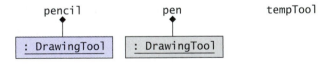

Below is the state following the execution of the first instruction: tempTool = pen;

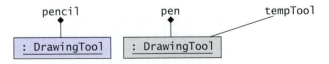

Next is the state following the execution of the second instruction: pen = pencil;

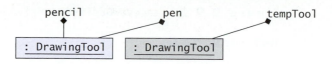

Below is the state following the execution of third instruction: `pencil = tempTool;`

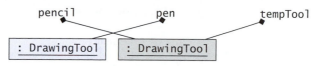

SOFTWARE ENGINEERING TIP

Just as basketball players recognize certain typical defenses, programmers learn to recognize software patterns. Knowing commonly used patterns like swapping is essential in software engineering.

This three-instruction sequence can be extended to a coding pattern by considering any two variables, call them *varA* and *varB*. Figure 2.8 contains this pattern.

Figure 2.8 Swap pattern for interchanging *varA* and *varB*

> *aThirdVar = varA;*
>
> *varA = varB;*
>
> *varB = aThirdVar;*

2.6 PUTTING IT TOGETHER IN A JAVA CLASS

Every Java variable must be declared before it can be used. Figure 2.9 describes a common way to accomplish such a declaration. Variables declared as decribed in this figure are known as **instance variables**.

Below are two example declarations that appropriately declare the instance variables discussed earlier, namely `pencil` and `pen`.

```
private DrawingTool pencil;
private DrawingTool pen;
```

Since both variables are declared with the same class, the two lines can be combined into the following equivalent one-line declaration:

```
private DrawingTool pencil, pen;
```

The declarations of instance variables and the code that manipulates the objects bound to those variables is typically placed within the same class. Figure 2.10 describes a `DirectorClass` for the purpose of writing programs that combines variable declarations and executable instructions. `DirectorClass` contains

Figure 2.9 InstanceVarDecls and PrivateVarDecl description

InstanceVarDecls

Syntax

Notes

- Each variable declaration should be on a single line and justified one tab setting (three or four spaces) from the left.
- Variable names should be meaningful.
- Variable names should be nouns or noun phrases.

PrivateVarDecl (abridged version of *OneVarDecl*)

Syntax

Note

Each *ClassName* and *VarName* must be named by an *Identifier*.

Usage

Each *VarName* is declared to have a type of *ClassName*, and the scope of this declaration is the class in which it is included.

many of the aspects of the complete Java class syntax, and will be expanded in future chapters.

The Director Java class described in Figure 2.10 is designed to allow flexibility in writing initial programs with minimal programming language distractions. To produce a working program, the programmer need only supply the desired code in place of StatementSequence and any necessary variable declarations in place of InstanceVarDecls. Director works well in conjunction with a class called *go.class* (supplied with many of the examples of this text). Compiling *Director.java*, followed by executing the *go.class* file, causes the StatementSequence code from Director to execute.

CLOSED
Black Box

Most of the programming examples in this book begin with a class called Director. When you execute the *go.class* file, an object of type Director is constructed and the Director method is called. Chapter 15 describes how these actions are accomplished.

Figure 2.10 DirectorClass description

DirectorClass (abridged version of *Class*)

Syntax

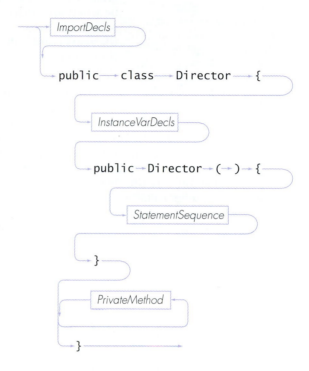

Semantics

Director is a specific type of class that is used in conjunction with *go.class* and the example programs of early chapters of this book. When the Director method is called (and the *go.class* performs such a call) the *StatementSequence* code is executed.

Notes
- *PrivateMethod* is described in Chapter 4.
- *ImportDecls* is described in Chapter 3.

Style notes (for enhancing code readability)
- The line beginning public class and ending with { should be on a single line and left justified. The final } symbol should also be left aligned.
- All *InstanceVarDecls* should be indented by one tab (three or four spaces) from the left.
- The line beginning public Director should be indented by one tab, as well as the matching (second from the last) } symbol. *StatementSequence* code should be indented two or more tabs.

Figure 2.11 contains a complete class containing the Java code explained thus far. This particular program declares a single variable named pencil. This program will begin execution by constructing a new DrawingTool object, binding the pencil name to this object. The remainder of the Director method starts the pencil object drawing, moves it forward twice; then three times in a row, pencil is turned clockwise and moved forward.

There are two file constraints that must be observed when compiling and running the Figure 2.11 code. The go class is a convenient way to execute Director. To use this technique, the *go.class* file must also be included in the folder containing *Director.java*. The second constraint is that the DrawingTool class must be available to Director. The easiest way to do this for now is to include a *DrawingTool.class* file in the same folder as the *Director.java* file. (Chapter 3 introduces the import declaration as another solution.)

Figure 2.11 Example Director class to manipulate pencil

```java
public class Director   {
    private DrawingTool  pencil;

    public Director()    {
        pencil = new DrawingTool();
        pencil.draw();
        pencil.moveForward();
        pencil.moveForward();
        pencil.turnClockwise();
        pencil.moveForward();
        pencil.turnClockwise();
        pencil.moveForward();
        pencil.turnClockwise();
        pencil.moveForward();
    }
}
```

CLOSED
Black Box

The syntax of Java, like any new language, may raise questions for the first-time reader. Why is the word "public" placed at the front of the class line and also the beginning of the Director constructor method? What is the meaning of the "private" prefix in front of the pencil declaration? Why all of the parentheses and braces?

For now, these things must be taken "on faith." The meaning of private and public declarations, as well as Java punctuation, are topics that will be discussed later; it is premature to worry about these details at this stage.

Figure 2.11 illustrates a second coding pattern. This pattern is the most fundamental of all object-oriented coding patterns because it describes the preliminary steps that are necessary in order to call a method. Figure 2.12 contains this so-called declare-instantiate-bind pattern.

Figure 2.12 Declare-instantiate-bind coding pattern

Three steps are essential prior to calling a method upon any variable.

Step 1   *Declare* the variable, specifying the class to which it belongs.

Step 2   *Instantiate* an object with a class conforming to the variable.

Step 3   *Bind* the variable (declared in Step 1) to the object instantiated in Step 2.

After these three steps, methods can be called freely upon the variable.

The three-step pattern from Figure 2.12 is perhaps the most fundamental of all coding patterns in object-oriented programming. This pattern outlines the three requirements that need to be observed in order to call a method upon a variable without error.

The first step of the declare-instantiate-bind pattern is to declare the variable. Java, like most modern programming languages, does not permit any variable to be used without declaration. The program in Figure 2.11 carries out this first step with the following instance variable declaration:

```
private DrawingTool pencil;
```

After this declaration, both the name of the variable, `pencil`, and its class association, `DrawingTool`, are known.

As described in Section 2.4, a newly declared variable, such as `pencil`, is initialized to `null`; and calling a method upon a `null` variable results in a run-time error. Therefore, the variable must be assigned an object prior to calling a method. Steps 2 and 3 explain that this requires both *instantiating* and *binding* the object— in that order. Often instantiating and binding occurs in the same instruction, as in the following example from the Figure 2.11 program.

```
pencil = new DrawingTool();
```

Once an object is instantiated (`new DrawingTool()`) and bound (`=`) to `pencil`; then, and only then, the code is free to call methods upon that variable.

2.7   PROGRAMMING BY CONTRACT

An accomplished software engineer would find prior descriptions of the `DrawingTool` class to be excessively vague. Where and how is the tool's movement displayed? How far does the tool move in a single `moveForward` call? What is the initial position of a newly constructed `DrawingTool`? These and other similar questions cannot go unanswered if the programmer is expected to compose programs that correctly satisfy their requirements.

The imprecise nature of code, like that in Figure 2.11, stems from a vague understanding of the behavior of DrawingTool. The DrawingTool class diagram (shown in Section 2.2) and the names of the DrawingTool methods provide clues regarding the behavior of DrawingTool objects, but they lack precision and completeness.

One widely accepted solution to the problem of ill-defined class behavior is to provide **class specifications**. A class specification for DrawingTool contains sufficient explanation about the state and behavior of DrawingTool objects so that a programmer can confidently use such objects.

The notation used for expressing class specifications in this text consists of two elements:

- a **class invariant**
- **precondition/postcondition** specifications for each method

A class invariant defines a collection of facts that are true about class objects. The name "invariant" comes from the understanding that these facts must be true throughout the object's execution lifetime. A suitable invariant for the DrawingTool class is given in Figure 2.13. From this invariant it is discovered that DrawingTool objects appear as an arrow within a *DrawingCanvas* window. The invariant specifies two additional constraints on DrawingTool objects: (1) they must be pointing in one of only four directions and (2) they are either in a *drawing* mode or a *moving* mode.

> **SOFTWARE ENGINEERING TIP**
>
> A complete class specification must include the information from the class diagram plus
>
> - a class invariant
> - a specification for the behavior of each method
>
> Method behavior specifications consist of
>
> - an optional precondition
> - a postcondition
> - an optional *modifies* clause.

Figure 2.13 DrawingTool class invariant

DrawingTool Class Specifications

Invariant

A DrawingTool object

- appears as an arrow within the *DrawingCanvas* window. (This window is 200 pixels wide and 150 pixels high.)
- is directed either up, down, left, or right.
- is either in drawing mode or in moving mode.

The class invariant doesn't tell the whole story because it fails to explain anything about the behavior of the various class methods. Therefore, a complete class specification must also include specifications for each method. Such a method specification includes two parts:

1. The changes that result from executing the method (known as the method's postcondition)

2. Any preliminary conditions that are required for the method to execute properly (known as the method's precondition).

In the next chapter a third clause, called *modifies*, will be examined as an optional part of method specifications. Taken together, the precondition and postcondition form a **software contract**. This contract states the following:

The Precondition/Postcondition Contract

If

the calling code ensures the precondition is true at the time it calls the method,

then

the postcondition is guaranteed to be true at the time the method completes execution.

This Precondition/Postcondition Contract places a burden upon the code that calls any method. This so-called "caller" is responsible for ensuring that the state of execution satisfies the precondition portion of the contract. The role of the precondition is to identify requirements for using the method. Violating a precondition should be considered to be a logic error.

So long as the precondition is true when the method is called, the contract states that the method is obligated to ensure the postcondition is true when the method finishes. In other words, the postcondition is the portion of the specification that defines the actions that are performed when the method executes.

Figure 2.14 illustrates by providing specifications for the five methods from the `DrawingTool` class. This notation uses a bulleted list format for preconditions and postconditions. *All* of the bulleted assertions must be true to satisfy the specification. For example, the specifications make it clear that immediately after executing a `DrawingTool` constructor, the associated object will be positioned in the center of the window *and* it is in drawing mode *and* its arrow is pointed up *and* this arrow is colored green.

Figure 2.14 DrawingTool class specifications

DrawingTool Class Specifications

Constructor Methods
public `DrawingTool`()

postcondition

- A new `DrawingTool` object is created and placed in the center of the *DrawingCanvas* window. (Note that if two tools occupy the same location, only one will be visible.)

- This object is set to drawing mode.

- The arrow for this object is pointing up.

- This `DrawingTool` arrow is colored green.   Continued on next page.

Update Methods

`public void` **`draw`**`()`

postcondition

- This object is set to drawing mode.

- This `DrawingTool` arrow is colored green.

- A 0.5 second delay occurs following this method's execution

`public void` **`dontDraw`**`()`

postcondition

- This object is set to moving mode.

- This `DrawingTool` arrow is colored red.

- A 0.5 second delay occurs following this method's execution.

`public void` **`turnClockwise`**`()`

postcondition

- This object is rotated by 90 degrees clockwise from its old (previous) direction.

- A 0.5 second delay occurs following this method's execution.

`public void` **`moveForward`**`()`

precondition

- A minimum of 20 pixels remain in front of this `DrawingTool` arrow before an edge of the *DrawingCanvas* window.

postcondition

- This `DrawingTool` object is moved in the arrow's direction by 20 pixels from its old (previous) location.

- If this object is in drawing mode, a line segment is drawn across the 20 pixel path just traversed.

- A 0.5 second delay occurs following this method's execution.

The precondition for `moveForward` specifies that the programmer using a `DrawingTool` must take care not to let it get too close to the edge of the window before calling `moveForward`. Notice that the Precondition/Postcondition Contract explains the situation when the precondition is true, but makes no promises for the outcome when the precondition is false. Therefore, if `moveForward` is called when the `DrawingTool` is 20 or less pixels (roughly 100 pixels equal one inch) from the window edge ahead of it, then the behavior of the `moveForward` method is unpredictable. (Obviously, programmers must avoid such situations where preconditions are not true.)

Sometimes there are no constraints on calling a method. In these situations it is common to omit the precondition. This means that it is possible to execute the DrawingTool constructor method at any time, regardless of any particular state of execution. Similarly, there is no precondition for calling the draw, dontDraw, or turnClockwise methods.

Even without the presence of a precondition there is one precondition that is understood for every method excepting constructors. As explained previously, a run-time error will occur whenever a method is called upon a variable name that is null. Therefore, with or without a precondition, all nonconstructor methods have an implicit precondition that the object be nonnull. Constructor methods are an exception to this rule, because their purpose is to create a new object.

Writing class specifications takes some practice. Effective specifications communicate accurately and succinctly. The items in postconditions should not explain unnecessary detail, but they must include enough information for the programmer to understand behavior precisely. The DrawingTool specifications are given in English, which is informal. Such informality tends to improve readability, but can result in ambiguities. Later in this text slightly more formal notations will be introduced for expressing specifications.

Armed with the DrawingTool specifications from Figure 2.14, we can now analyze the behavior of the Figure 2.11 Director method. The first instruction from this method is repeated below:

```
pencil = new DrawingTool();
```

This causes the DrawingTool constructor method to construct a new object and assign the object to the pencil variable. The postcondition for the DrawingTool method specifies that the new tool will be centered in the *DrawingCanvas* window as a green arrow pointed up.

The next three instructions in this program are as follows:

```
pencil.draw();
pencil.moveForward();
pencil.moveForward();
```

When the first of these three instructions executes, the `pencil` object is set to the drawing mode and the arrow is turned green. This instruction is unnecessary for a newly constructed `DrawingTool` object, but isn't harmful. Executing the next two methods moves the arrow forward (upward) by a total of 40 pixels, drawing a line across this path. Notice that the preconditions to both of these method calls are met, since `pencil` is near the center of the window and the window is 150 pixels high. (The window height is given in the class invariant.)

The next two instructions are as follows:

```
pencil.turnClockwise();
pencil.moveForward();
```

The postcondition for the `turnClockwise` method states that the object should be turned "90 degrees in the clockwise direction." This means that executing the first line above will cause `pencil` to rotate to point to the right; then the second instruction draws another 20-pixel line segment.

The final four instructions are shown below:

```
pencil.turnClockwise();
pencil.moveForward();
pencil.turnClockwise();
pencil.moveForward();
```

Executing these instructions rotates pencil to point down, draws a 20-pixel line, then rotates pencil to point left and draws a final 20-pixel segment. The resulting window shows the end result of this program.

2.8 COMMENTS

Class specifications can be made available in a number of different formats. The specifications used within this book are included in HTML (Web page) format to make them most accessible when programming. It is also important to embed class specifications within the source code. This makes the specifications readily accessible to future maintenance programmers, as well as keeping them handy for the initial implementation.

The device used by programmers to place specifications within a program is called a **comment**. Figure 2.15 describes the Java comment. Comments allow any text to be placed at almost any location within a program without altering the program's run-time behavior.

Syntactically, there are two possible types of comments:

1. single-line comments

2. multiline comments

The single line comment begins with "//" and continues through the end of the same text line. A multiline comment can spread across several lines of text. Multiline comments begin with "/*" and extend until the first subsequent instance of "*/". This means that a two-line comment such as

```
/*       Author: David D. Riley
         Date: May 9, 2000 */
```

can also be written as two consecutive single-line comments.

```
//       Author: David D. Riley
//       Date: May 9, 2000
```

Figure 2.15 Comment description

Comment

Syntax

Notes

- A comment is permitted anywhere that a separator, such as a blank, is allowed.
- *AllCharactersUntilEndOfLine* denotes any sequence of characters as terminated by the first end of a line encountered.
- *AnythingButCommentEnd* denotes any sequence of characters and/or ends of lines as terminated by the first occurrence of */.

Semantics

Comments do nothing at run time.

Figure 2.16 shows an improved version of the Director class from Figure 2.11. This improved code is the same except for the inclusion of initial comments to identify the author and date and appropriate specifications.

Figure 2.16 Improved version of an earlier Director class

```java
// Author: David D. Riley
// Date: May 9, 2000

/* This class draws a block letter "P" that is
   40 pixels high and 20 pixels wide upon
   a window named Drawing Canvas. */
public class Director  {
    private DrawingTool pencil;
    public Director()    {
        pencil = new DrawingTool();
        pencil.draw();
        pencil.moveForward();
        pencil.moveForward();
        pencil.turnClockwise();
        pencil.moveForward();
        pencil.turnClockwise();
        pencil.moveForward();
        pencil.turnClockwise();
        pencil.moveForward();
    }
}
```

JAVA INSPECTOR

Below is a collection of hints on what to check when examining code that involves the concepts of this chapter.

✓ Syntax diagrams are like a dictionary to a programmer. Just as you look up words in a dictionary when writing prose, it is equally important to refer to syntax diagrams when writing programs. Appendix B contains a syntax diagram collection for Java.

✓ Checking a program's style can easily improve readability and may also uncover well-hidden problems. A key style issue raised in this chapter is proper indentation. See Figure 2.10 for proper class indentation. All statements in the same sequence should be indented by the same amount.

✓ Objects must be instantiated before calling a method upon them. Check to ensure that constructor method calls precede the use of variables to avoid run-time errors.

✓ Every assignment instruction should be checked to see if it will create an orphan object at run time.

✓ Any variable used within a section of code must be declared in some way. Checking for variable declarations is a good idea.

✓ When performing a desk check, keep class diagrams and class specifications handy. If the program being checked uses another class, then it is always helpful to consult the specifications of the class's behavior.

✓ If a precondition is violated, then the program's behavior is unpredictable. Therefore, it is wise to review each method call to ensure that the precondition will be satisfied.

✓ Classes that make use of other classes require extra attention. The Java compiler and Java VM can locate outside classes so long as they are in the same folder as the class using them. This is why any class that uses DrawingTool must have the *DrawingTool.class* file in its folder. Chapter 3 shows how to compile classes from different folders.

✓ It is easy to forget either the "/*" (at the beginning) or the "*/" (at the end) of a multiline comment. By checking to see that these symbols occur in matched pairs you will avoid potentially confusing compile-time errors. Also, remember that one multiline comment cannot be nested inside another.

TERMINOLOGY

alias (via variable names)

assignment instruction

bind (a variable name to an object)

class invariant

class specification

comment (within a program)

constructor (method)

design by contract

instance variable

instantiation

message (as used to call a method)

method call

new (the Java reserved word)

null

orphan

pattern

postcondition

precondition

semantics

send (a message)

separator (in Java syntax)

sequence of statements

software contract

swap

syntax

syntax diagram

variable

EXERCISES

1. Suppose that you are writing a class that has declared three objects named `redWagon`, `blueWagon`, and `greenWagon`. All three of these variables belong to a class called `Wagon`, and the `Wagon` class contains two methods, as shown in the following class diagram:

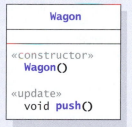

Each part below is an attempted instruction that is either a method call (see Figure 2.4) or an assignment instruction (see Figures 2.6 and 2.7). Identify whether or not each instruction has correct Java syntax.

a. `redWagon.push();`

b. `redWagon.push;`

c. `greenWagon.Wagon();`

d. `blueWagon.pull();`

e. `redWagon = new push();`

f. `redWagon = new Push();`

g. `blueWagon = new Wagon();`

h. `redWagon = new blueWagon;`

i. `redWagon = new redWagon.push();`

2. Figure 2.9 shows how to declare instance variables.

    a. Show the complete declaration of the instance variable redWagon from Exercise 1.

    b. Give a single declaration that declares *all* three Wagon variables: redWagon, blueWagon. and greenWagon. (See Exercise 1 for a description of these two variables.)

3. Trace the execution of each of the following statement sequences by drawing an object diagram after each instruction. Identify every orphan that is created, and every alias that occurs by this execution.

    a. ```
        greenWagon = new Wagon();
        blueWagon = new Wagon();
        redWagon = new Wagon();
        greenWagon = blueWagon;
        redWagon = blueWagon;
        ```

    b.  ```
        greenWagon = new Wagon();
        blueWagon = greenWagon;
        redWagon = blueWagon;
        ```

    c. ```
        greenWagon = new Wagon();
        blueWagon = null;
        greenWagon = blueWagon;
        redWagon = greenWagon;
        ```

    d.  ```
        greenWagon = new Wagon();
        blueWagon = greenWagon;
        greenWagon = new Wagon();
        redWagon = greenWagon;
        greenWagon = new Wagon();
        blueWagon = greenWagon;
        greenWagon = new Wagon();
        redWagon = greenWagon;
        greenWagon = new Wagon();
        ```

4. Write a segment of Java code that swaps the object bound to blueWagon with the object bound to redWagon. (You may use greenWagon any way you wish.)

5. Even if the following push method has no precondition, there is still an implicit precondition for the following instruction. What is it?

    ```
    greenWagon.push();
    ```

6. Each part below makes a statement regarding one or more of the following assertions.

    class invariant
    method precondition
    method postcondition

Select all of the previous assertions that function as described.

a. If the method is to function properly, this condition must be true at the time the method is called.

b. If the method is functioning properly, this condition must be true at the time the method completes.

c. Ensuring this condition is the responsibility of the programmer writing the code for the method.

d. Ensuring this condition is the responsibility of the programmer writing the code that calls the method.

7. Show the lines that are drawn in the *DrawingCanvas* window as a result of executing each of the following Java Director constructors.

a.
```java
public class Director {
    private DrawingTool pencil;
    public Director() {
        pencil = new DrawingTool();
        pencil.draw();
        pencil.moveForward();
        pencil.dontDraw();
        pencil.moveForward();
    }
}
```

b.
```java
public class Director {
    private DrawingTool pencil;
    public Director() {
        pencil = new DrawingTool();
        pencil.moveForward();
        pencil.moveForward();
        pencil.dontDraw();
        pencil.turnClockwise();
        pencil.moveForward();
        pencil.draw();
        pencil.draw();
        pencil.turnClockwise();
        pencil.turnClockwise();
        pencil.turnClockwise();
        pencil.moveForward();
        pencil.turnClockwise();
        pencil.moveForward();
    }
}
```

c. ```java
public class Director {
    private DrawingTool pencil, pen;
    public Director() {
        pencil = new DrawingTool();
        pen = new DrawingTool();
        pen.dontDraw();
        pen.turnClockwise();
        pen.moveForward();
        pen.turnClockwise();
        pen.draw();
        pencil.moveForward();
        pen.moveForward();
    }
}
```

## PROGRAMMING EXERCISES

1. Compile and run the program called *Director* (Figure 2.11).

2. Write a program that uses a `DrawingTool` object to create a square that has sides 40 pixels long.

3. Write a program to display the "HI" message shown below. These letters should be 40 pixels tall.

```

4. Write a program that draws two side-by-side rectangles that are 40 pixels high and 20 pixels wide. Use two different `DrawingTool` objects to draw them in parallel. In other words, one object should draw the left rectangle and one draw the right, and immediately after each action of the left `DrawingTool` object, the right object should take the corresponding action. (The final image is shown below.)

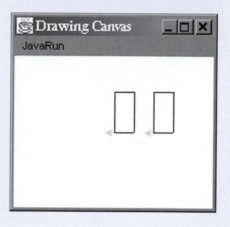

INTRODUCTION TO DESIGN AND IMPLEMENTATION

OBJECTIVES

- To investigate the process of designing an implementation

- To present the concept of top-down design with stepwise refinement as one strategy for developing software

- To present prototyping as a strategy for developing software

- To describe the syntax of Java identifiers and discuss the importance of careful identifier selection

- To introduce parameter passage as a means of passing an argument to a method

- To introduce a class library, called *aLibrary*, especially the `AWindow`, `ARectangle`, `AOval`, and `ARoundRectangle` classes

- To describe the Java `import` declaration and its role for accessing external software classes

- To introduce the use of output instructions, such as `System.out.println`, for use in debugging

Reading a program is a task that all programmers must master. Chapter 2 presented enough of the Java basics to explain how to read many programs. However, the task of programming is really about *writing* (designing) code. This chapter introduces some of the fundamental techniques used by programmers to design programs. A couple of additional Java language constructs are included in this presentation.

3.1   TOP-DOWN DESIGN—REFINING ALGORITHMS

The carpenter assembles furniture from raw materials such as lumber, glue, and paint. In a similar way software developers assemble programs from classes and their component declarations and instructions. This software assembly phase is often called **implementation**.

Implementation isn't possible without a strategy. The carpenter relies upon a strategy to assembly all of the parts in the proper manner. Similarly, good programming requires design strategies to compose each program.

Perhaps the most useful of all design strategies is called **divide and conquer**. As its name implies, a divide-and-conquer strategy consists of two parts:

1. *divide* a larger component into its constituent subcomponents

2. *conquer* each of the subcomponents

Dividing and conquering is fundamental to object-oriented software development. O-O design first divides a problem into its constituent objects, then conquers the objects by identifying or creating a software class for each object. Next, O-O design proceeds to divide each class into its attributes and methods, then conquers each attribute and method by supplying its code. Both of these uses of divide and conquer will be revisited again and again throughout this book.

This chapter focuses in part on designing individual methods where **top-down design**, a type of divide-and-conquer strategy, is employed. As an example of top-down design, consider the need to write a method that uses `DrawingTool` to create two squares. One square is required to be 20 pixels on each side, and it must be centered inside an outer square that is 60 pixels on each side. The picture in Figure 3.1 illustrates the arrangement.

Rather than the programmer attempting to write the entire method, it is advisable to divide and conquer the problem. Figure 3.1 illustrates a four-stage procedure for drawing the two squares. This shows that a single task can be divided into separate subtasks. This is called the top level of design in a top-down design.

The four-stage task from Figure 3.1 uses another design technique typically employed by good software developers. These subtasks are expressed in English, instead of Java or any other programming language. Programmers frequently use such informal notations during a design process. These four subtasks do not constitute a syntactically valid Java program, but they do form an **algorithm** that can eventually be transformed into a Java program.

The term "algorithm" refers to any collection of instructions (or subtasks) that define a procedure for performing some task. Humans frequently think algorithmically. There is an algorithm for creating your favorite chocolate cake. There is an algorithm for driving from home to the nearest department store. There is an algorithm for getting prepared to go to work each day. None of these example algorithms are likely to be coded in Java, but all consist of a specific sequence of subtasks that, when performed in order, produce a desired result. Java software also contains algorithms. In a Java program, the algorithms take the form of a method.

Figure 3.1 A four-step algorithm to draw nested squares

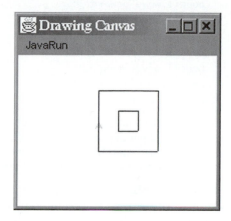

Subtasks
1. Create a `DrawingTool` object.
2. Use object from Step 1 to draw an inner square that is 20 pixels on each side.
3. Stop drawing, move the `DrawingTool` object outward by 20 pixels, and restart drawing.
4. Use the `DrawingTool` object to draw an outer square that is 60 pixels on each side.

The particular four-stage algorithm in Figure 3.1 is not the only solution for drawing these particular nested squares. As with most programming problems there are many alternative solutions. For example, drawing the outer square before the inner square would use a different algorithm, but the end result might be the same.

The top level of design in the Figure 3.1 algorithm results from the divide phase of the divide-and-conquer strategy. In order to implement this algorithm the programmer must proceed to conquer each subtask. In top-down design, each level of design is conquered by applying the divide-and-conquer strategy several times—once for each subtask. The technique of dividing a single stage/subtask into its own algorithm is commonly called **refinement**, and the repeated application of divide and conquer to refine one task into subtasks, then subtasks into subsubtasks, and so on, is known as **stepwise refinement**.

The first subtask from Figure 3.1 is conveniently refined from

1. *Create a* `DrawingTool` *object.*

into the following single Java instruction.

```
pencil = new DrawingTool();
```

The second subtask from the Figure 3.1 algorithm requires a bit more thought.

This refinement proceeds from

2. *Use object from Step 1 to draw an inner square that is 20 pixels on each side.*

to the following Java instruction sequence.

```
pencil.moveForward();
pencil.turnClockwise();
pencil.moveForward();
pencil.turnClockwise();
pencil.moveForward();
pencil.turnClockwise();
pencil.moveForward();
```

These seven Java instructions rely on Subtask 1 instantiating a `DrawingTool` object, named `pencil`, and `pencil` being in drawing mode. This code also depends upon knowing that a single `moveForward` method call advances the `DrawingTool` by 20 pixels and that a `turnClockwise` method performs a 90-degree rotation.

Refining Subtask 3 relies upon an understanding of the location of `pencil` following the inner square drawing. A review of the instructions from Subtask 2 leads to the conclusion that `pencil`'s last location is at the lower-left corner of the inner square, and that it is directed to the left. Armed with this knowledge of the location and direction of pencil, Subtask 3:

3. *Stop drawing, move the* `DrawingTool` *object outward by 20 pixels, and restart drawing.*

can be refined as follows.

```
pencil.dontDraw();
pencil.moveForward();
pencil.draw();
```

Immediately after the three instructions are executed, `pencil` will be directed to the left and its vertical height will be the same as the bottom of the inner square. This position and direction, together with the additional complexity of the larger square, mean that this fourth subtask is more complicated than the other three. Therefore, it is wise to refine Subtask 4 into other subsubtasks as shown below.

4. *Use the* `DrawingTool` *object to draw an outer square that is 60 pixels on each side.*

is refined into these eight stages:

```
pencil.turnClockwise();
pencil.moveForward();
pencil.moveForward();
```

4.4. Turn right 90 degrees and draw forward 60 pixels.

4.5. Turn right 90 degrees and draw forward 60 pixels.

4.6. Turn right 90 degrees and draw forward 60 pixels.

```
pencil.turnClockwise();
pencil.moveForward();
```

The final step in the stepwise refinement is to recognize that

> *Turn right 90 degrees and draw forward 60 pixels.*

can be refined into the following:

```
pencil.turnClockwise();
pencil.moveForward();
pencil.moveForward();
pencil.moveForward();
```

All of this refinement is summarized in Figure 3.2. The non-Java parts of the algorithm are shaded in blue with their refinement to their right. The original four-stage algorithm is shown in the left column.

Figure 3.2 Refinement of the square within a square algorithm

Step 1 Create a DrawingTool object.

```
pencil = new DrawingTool();
```

Step 2 Use object from Step 1 to draw an inner square that is 20 pixels on each side.

```
pencil.moveForward();
pencil.turnClockwise();
pencil.moveForward();
pencil.turnClockwise();
pencil.moveForward();
pencil.turnClockwise();
pencil.moveForward();
```

Step 3 Stop drawing, move the DrawingTool object outward by 20 pixels, and restart drawing.

```
pencil.dontDraw();
pencil.moveForward();
pencil.draw();
```

```
pencil.turnClockwise();
pencil.moveForward();
pencil.moveForward();
```

Step 4.4 Turn right 90 degrees and draw forward 60 pixels.

```
pencil.turnClockwise();
pencil.moveForward();
pencil.moveForward();
pencil.moveForward();
```

Step 4 Use the DrawingTool object to draw an outer square that is 60 pixels on each side.

Step 4.5 Turn right 90 degrees and draw forward 60 pixels.

```
pencil.turnClockwise();
pencil.moveForward();
pencil.moveForward();
pencil.moveForward();
```

Step 4.6 Turn right 90 degrees and draw forward 60 pixels.

```
pencil.turnClockwise();
pencil.moveForward();
pencil.moveForward();
pencil.moveForward();
```

```
pencil.turnClockwise();
pencil.moveForward();
```

Following all of this refinement, the original algorithm has been transformed into the sequence of Java instructions. These instructions are gathered with the appropriate instance variable declaration and class syntax in Figure 3.3. Blank lines are included in this program to separate the code into the portions corresponding to the four stages of the original algorithm.

Figure 3.3 Director class to draw a square within a square

```java
public class Director {
        private DrawingTool pencil;

        /* postcondition
                This class draws a 20-pixel square within
                a 60-pixel square. */
        public Director()    {
                pencil = new DrawingTool();

                pencil.moveForward();
                pencil.turnClockwise();
                pencil.moveForward();
                pencil.turnClockwise();
                pencil.moveForward();
                pencil.turnClockwise();
                pencil.moveForward();

                pencil.dontDraw();
                pencil.moveForward();
                pencil.draw();

                pencil.turnClockwise();
                pencil.moveForward();
                pencil.moveForward();
                pencil.turnClockwise();
                pencil.moveForward();
                pencil.moveForward();
                pencil.moveForward();
                pencil.turnClockwise();
                pencil.moveForward();
                pencil.moveForward();
                pencil.moveForward();
                pencil.turnClockwise();
                pencil.moveForward();
                pencil.moveForward();
                pencil.moveForward();
                pencil.turnClockwise();
                pencil.moveForward();
        }
}
```

SOFTWARE ENGINEERING TIP
When the desired task for any method becomes complicated (more than six or seven instructions), programmers are well advised to use a design strategy such as top-down design.

Stepwise refinement is the technique employed in order to achieve top-down design. In fact, the name "top-down" results from the fact that each step in the design refines a more abstract (**higher-level algorithm**) into an algorithm that is closer to code.

3.2   SELECTING IDENTIFIERS

During the process of program design, the programmer must frequently choose names for various program entities. For example, the designer of the previous program (see Figure 3.3) chose to name the drawing object `pencil`.

Names for program entities are called **identifiers**. In addition to naming instance variables with identifiers, like `pencil`, programs also name classes with identifiers, like `Director` and `DrawingTool`, and methods, like `moveForward`, `turnClockwise`, `draw`, and `dontDraw`. Figure 3.4 explains the Java rules for identifiers.

Figure 3.4 Identify description

Identifier

Syntax

An *Identifier* begins with either an alphabetic letter ("a" through "z" or "A" through "Z") or an underscore ("_") and is followed by zero or more consecutive alphabetic letters, digits ("0" through "9") and/or underscores. Dollar signs ($) are also permitted within identifiers but generally reserved for system use.

Notes

- Java is case sensitive, so two identifiers that have the same sequence of letters with different capitalization are considered to be different identifiers.
- Some identifiers are reserved words (see Figure 3.5) and may not be used for other purposes.
- A separator *must* be used immediately after an identifier when the symbol just after the identifier is an alphabetic character, an underscore, or a digit.

Style note

When selecting an identifier the programmer should generally capitalize the first letter of any English word embedded within.

Certain identifiers, like `class` have special meaning in Java. These identifiers are called **reserved words**. Figure 3.5 enumerates all Java reserved words. Programs are not permitted to use reserved words to name other program entities.

Figure 3.5 Java reserved words

abstract	double	instanceof	static
boolean	else	int	super
break	extends	interface	switch
byte	false	long	synchronized
case	final	native	this
cast	finally	new	throw
catch	float	null	throws
char	for	package	transient
class	generic	private	true
const	goto	protected	try
continue	if	public	void
default	implements	return	volatile
do	import	short	while

In the interest of making Java programs easier to read, software developers follow two important conventions:

1. Every identifier should be descriptive of the entity it names.

2. If the identifier contains multiple English words, then each word (except possibly the first) should begin with a capital (uppercase) letter.

A descriptive name, such as `DrawingTool`, assists any programmer who reads the code. Similarly, capitalizing individual words in an identifier makes it easier to read the name. For example, the identifiers

`turnClockwise` and `moveForward`

are easier to read than

`turnclockwise` and `moveforward`.

Another convention that is generally followed in Java programs is to capitalize the first letter of an identifier that names a class name and use a lowercase letter to begin other identifiers. This first-letter convention allows the class identifiers to be distinguished at a glance.

It is also best to select an identifier based upon its usage. Identifiers that are nouns or noun clauses are preferable for variables, classes, and nonvoid methods. (Nonvoid methods are discussed later.) Void methods, like the ones shown thus far, are better named with identifiers that are action verbs or verb phrases.

3.3 A SECOND DESIGN EXAMPLE

As a second example of top-down design, consider the task of making a cheese pizza. In particular, the pizza should be made according to the following recipe.

> Using a premixed ball of crust dough, flatten the dough to the desired thickness. Next, pour two cups of pizza sauce onto the crust. Spread the sauce evenly across the crust. Spread three cups of mozzarella cheese on top. Cook the pizza for 15 minutes at 400 degrees Fahrenheit.

Cooking recipes are algorithms because they explain a procedure for preparing food. The cheese pizza recipe is no exception. This recipe can be recast as a five-stage algorithm as shown in Figure 3.6.

Figure 3.6 Top-level algorithm for making a cheese pizza

Subtask

1. Using a premixed ball of crust dough, flatten the dough to the desired thickness.
2. Pour two cups of pizza sauce onto the crust.
3. Spread the sauce evenly across the crust.
4. Spread three cups of mozzarella cheese on top.
5. Set pizza oven to 400 degrees Fahrenheit and cook pizza for 15 minutes.

As explained earlier, the first step in any object-oriented design is to identify the objects. In the case of the pizza recipe, the objects seem to be

dough (crust)

sauce

cheese

oven

Often a software developer can find existing software classes from which to construct the necessary objects. It is important to discover such classes early, because they impact the way the design needs to proceed toward implementation. In this case, assume that the five classes diagrammed in Figure 3.7 have been discovered for use in implementing the cheese pizza recipe.

The plus sign (+) shown in Figure 3.7 is a notation commonly used within class diagrams. A plus sign prefix on a method of a class diagram indicates that this method is available for use outside of the class. (Alternatives to the plus sign will be explained in subsequent sections.)

A second important difference between Figure 3.7 and earlier presentations of methods is the inclusion of **parameters**. Parameters are indicated in a class diagram by the name of a type (class) inside the parentheses following a method. Figure 3.7 shows that the following methods have parameters: `placeInOven`, `pourInto` (from both the Sauce and Cheese classes), and `pourOnto`.

Figure 3.7 Class diagrams for pizza-related classes

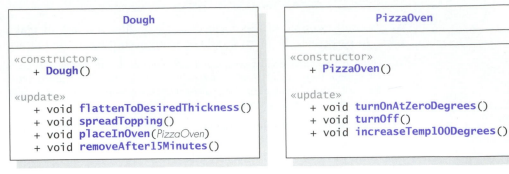

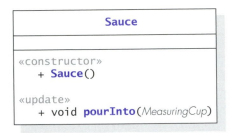

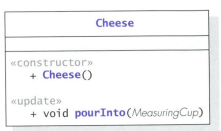

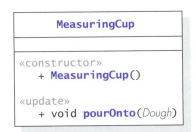

The use of parameters often stems from the need to involve multiple objects in a single method. For example, the act of pouring pizza sauce into a measuring cup involves two objects—the sauce and the cup. Using a parameter permits one object to be **passed** to a method performed upon a second object. As a second example, the following instruction is used to cause a Dough object, called crust, to be placed into the PizzaOven named oven.

```
crust.placeInOven( oven );
```

The five classes from Figure 3.7 introduce a new object into the algorithm that wasn't obvious by reading the original pizza recipe. In particular, it will be necessary to use measuring cups to transfer sauce and cheese to the dough. This additional class will impact the subsequent refinement of the algorithm.

The next stage of the top-down design is to refine each of subtasks from the top-level design. Figure 3.8 shows an algorithm that results from refining each of the individual five subtasks.

Figure 3.8 The second-level algorithm for making a cheese pizza

```
// 1.  Using a premixed ball of crust dough, flatten the dough to the
desired thickness.
        crust = new Dough();
        crust.flattenToDesiredThickness();

// 2.  Pour two cups of pizza sauce onto the crust.
        sauceCup = new MeasuringCup();
        mySauce = new Sauce();
        mySauce.pourInto( sauceCup );
        sauceCup.pourOnto( crust );
        mySauce.pourInto( sauceCup );
        sauceCup.pourOnto( crust );

// 3.  Spread the sauce evenly across the crust.
        crust.spreadTopping();

// 4.  Spread three cups of mozzarella cheese on top.
        cheeseCup = new MeasuringCup();
        // 4.2. Use cheeseCup to spread three cups of mozzarella on the
        pizza.

// 5.  Set pizza oven to 400 degrees Fahrenheit and cook pizza for 15
minutes.
        oven = new PizzaOven();
        oven.turnOnAtZeroDegrees();
        // 5.3. Set the temperature to 400 degrees.
        crust.placeInOven( oven );
        crust.removeAfter15Minutes();
        oven.turnOff();
```

The second-level refinement from Figure 3.8 names several objects. These objects are listed below, along with the classes to which each belongs.

crust—of type Dough

sauceCup—of type MeasuringCup

mySauce—of type Sauce

cheeseCup—of type MeasuringCup

oven—of type PizzaOven

The designer has been careful to select proper Java identifiers for these object names. In writing the program for this algorithm the programmer must provide declarations for these five instance variables.

When the six instructions from Stage 2 execute, sauceCup and mySauce are instantiated. The mySauce.pourInto(sauceCup); instruction causes the measuring cup to be filled with sauce, then sauceCup.pourOnto(crust); empties the cup onto the pizza crust. These two instructions are repeated to pour a second cup of sauce on the crust. The decision to use a separate MeasuringCup variable, called cheeseCup, in Stage 4 was made in order to use a clean cup for the cheese. (The sauceCup might be messy.)

It is evident that another level of refinement is needed, because there are two instructions (Stage 4.2 and Stage 5.3) in the Figure 3.8 algorithm that are not yet expressed in Java. The complete program in Figure 3.9 results from refining these two comments and including the necessary instance variable declarations.

Figure 3.9 Program to make a cheese pizza

```java
public class Director  {
    private Dough  crust;
    private MeasuringCup  sauceCup, cheeseCup;
    private Cheese  mozzarella;
    private PizzaOven oven;
    /* postcondition
        A cheese pizza is ready to eat. */
    public Director()   {
        crust = new Dough();
        crust. flattenToDesiredThickness();
        sauceCup = new MeasuringCup();
        mySauce = new Sauce();
        mySauce.pourInto( sauceCup );
        sauceCup.pourOnto( crust );
        mySauce.pourInto( sauceCup );
        sauceCup.pourOnto( crust );
        crust.spreadTopping();
        cheeseCup = new MeasuringCup;
        mozzarella = new Cheese();
        mozzarella.pourInto( cheeseCup );
        cheeseCup.pourOnto( crust );
        mozzarella.pourInto( cheeseCup );
        cheeseCup.pourOnto( crust );
        mozzarella.pourInto( cheeseCup );
        cheeseCup.pourOnto( crust );
        crust.spreadTopping();
        oven = new PizzaOven();
        oven.turnOnAtZeroDegrees();
        oven.increaseTempBy100Degrees();
        oven.increaseTempBy100Degrees();
        oven.increaseTempBy100Degrees();
        oven.increaseTempBy100Degrees();
        crust.placeInOven( oven );
        crust.removeAfter15Minutes();
        oven.turnOff();
    }
}
```

3.4   A GUI SOFTWARE LIBRARY

Earlier in this chapter software development was compared to carpentry. Yet another key similarity between these two professions is the need for proper tools. The carpenter relies upon saws, hammers, sanders, and drills. The software developer relies upon editors, compilers, and other types of software.

Among the key tools of the software developer are software classes, such as `DrawingTool` and `MeasuringCup`, to supply types for objects. Sometimes these classes are so important that they are gathered into libraries to be shared by many programmers. Such libraries behave like extensions of the programming language. If the programming language doesn't contain instructions to control the color of display images, then perhaps there is a library class for declaring `Color` objects. If the programming language doesn't incorporate facilities for creating objects to store checking account information, perhaps there is a `CheckingAccount` class in some library.

Among the most frequently used of all software libraries are those that supply classes to build a **graphical user interface** or **GUI** (commonly pronounced "goo - ee"). The term "GUI" refers to the interaction between a computer and its **user**, where any person who executes the program is thought of as a user. Typically, the interaction between user and program takes the form of GUI elements, such as windows, buttons, menus, and images. Several example programs in this book use a supplied library of classes for constructing GUIs. The name of this library is *aLibrary*.

The GUI classes within *aLibrary* are an extension of two standard Java libraries called **swing** and **awt**. The classes provided by *aLibrary* assist with conveying important concepts in object-oriented software engineering, while retaining most *swing/awt* conventions. Chapter 14 reveals many of the techniques used to create *aLibrary*, and Appendix D shows how to use *swing/awt* without using *aLibrary*.

GUIs rely upon graphical drawings that appear on some **computer display** (**screen**). The **window** is the primary object that GUIs use to support such drawing. Each window is a rectangular region of the screen that is devoted to containing the graphical elements created by the associated program. The region in which the `pencil` object from previous examples drew its image was a window. Some types of windows permit the user to provide control, such as dragging the window to a different location, resizing the window, and closing the window. The primary class included in *aLibrary* to support window objects is called `AWindow`. A class diagram including many `AWindow` methods is shown in Figure 3.10.

This class diagram introduces a new notation that is common for class diagrams. A minus sign (–) has been inserted in front of all class attributes. A minus sign prefix signifies that a feature is *not* available for use outside the class. In other words, the five `AWindow` attributes cannot be used by other programs. The reason that these five attributes are included in the class diagram is that they are essential for describing the class behavior. Methods also share this notation. Prefixing with a plus sign (+) signifies that the attribute or method is available for public use, and prefixing with a minus sign (–) means that the attribute or method is private to the class and not available elsewhere.

Figure 3.10 AWindow class diagram

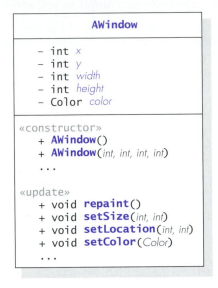

The class specification in Figure 3.11 includes more detailed information about AWindow.

Figure 3.11 AWindow class specifications

AWindow Class Specifications

Invariant

An AWindow object

- is a rectangular window.
- is placed on a computer screen with its upper-left corner x pixels from the left and y pixels from the top. (The upper-left corner of the screen is (0, 0).)
- has a visible region that is *width* pixels from side to side and *height* pixels from top to bottom; the region has a background color of *color*.

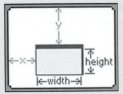

At left is an AWindow with a gray *color* on a white screen.

Continued on next page.

Constructor Methods

```
public AWindow ( )
```

postcondition

A new AWindow object is created with attributes as follows: $x == 0$ AND $y == 0$ AND width $== 10$ AND height $== 10$ AND color $==$ Color.white

```
public AWindow ( int newX, int newY, int w, int h )
```

postcondition
A new AWindow object is created with attributes as follows: $x == newX$ AND $y == newY$ AND width $== w$ AND height $== h$ AND color $==$ Color.white

Update Methods

```
public void repaint ( )
```

postcondition
This AWindow will be redrawn as soon as possible.

```
public void setSize ( int w, int h )
```

precondition
$w >= 0$ AND $h >= 0$

modifies
width, height

postcondition
width $== w$ AND height $== h$

```
public void setLocation ( int newX, int newY )
```

modifies
x, y

postcondition
$x == newX$ AND $y == newY$

```
public void setColor ( Color c )
```

precondition
c is a valid Color

modifies
color

postcondition
color $== c$

aLibrary uses the same two-dimensional coordinate scheme as many standard Java graphical classes. In such a scheme x represents the horizontal coordinate of any screen position and y represents the vertical coordinate. The class invariant for AWindow indicates that the upper-left corner of an AWindow has x and y values that measure the distance to the upper-left corner of the computer screen. (When x = 0 and y = 0, the AWindow is located in the screen's upper-left corner.) The value of x increases from left to right and the value of y increases from top to bottom.

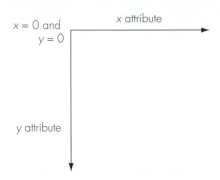

It is also typical in Java to measure screen distances in terms of **pixels** (an abbreviation for picture elements). Computer displays range from about 1024 to 1600 pixels horizontally and 768 to 1200 pixels vertically. The x and y values for an AWindow object measure its distance (in pixels) from the left and top edge, respectively, of the computer display. The class specification of AWindow also illustrates the Java standard of using width, and height attributes to represent size (in pixels) of the displayable region of an Awindow.

The methods of Figure 3.11 include **modifies clauses** in addition to preconditions and postconditions. Including a *modifies* clause helps to clarify which aspects of the object's state can be changed by a given method. An attribute should be included in the *modifies* clause whenever that attribute might be altered by some execution of the method.

The class specifications in this text often make use of special Java notations. Two consecutive equal signs (i.e., "==") is one such notation that appears frequently. (See Figure 3.11.) Java uses two consecutive equal signs as the notation for "equals," whereas a single equal sign denotes assignment. Therefore, the specification for the AWindow constructor method states that following this method's execution, the AWindow is located newX pixels from the left edge of the screen (*x* == newX) and newY pixels down from the top of the screen (*y* == newY).

3.5 CALLING METHODS WITH PARAMETERS

The concept of parameters was first encountered in the cheese pizza example from Section 3.3. The AWindow class demonstrates more extensive use of parameters, and introduces some new options related to parameter passage.

Like instance variables, every parameter has both a name and a type. As shown in the AWindow class specification, the setColor method has a single parameter, named c, that is of type Color (i.e., c belongs to the Color class).

Parameter names are useful for expressing a method's preconditions and post-conditions. For example, consider the setColor postcondition.

postcondition
    color == c

This postcondition asserts that the AWindow attribute called *color* has a value of c (the parameter) following a call to the setColor method. As a result, the execution of the following instruction sets the *color* attribute of the myWindow object to be green (Color.green).

```
myWindow.setColor( Color.green );
```

Whenever a method containing parameters is called, the method call must specify an **argument** for each parameter. The description of MethodCallWithParameters in Figure 3.12 explains that each argument must also conform to the class of its corresponding parameter. For now, conformance should be interpreted to mean that both must belong to the same class.

Figure 3.12 MethodCallWithParameters description

MethodCallWithParameters (abridged version of *MethodCall*)

Syntax

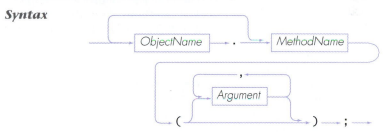

Notes

- *ObjectName* is the name of an object, and *MethodName* is the name of a nonconstructor method from the class to which the *ObjectName* object belongs.
- No separators are permitted before or after the period.
- The number and class type of each *Argument* must conform to the class of the corresponding parameter.

Semantics

- Executing MethodCallWithParameters causes each argument to be assigned to its corresponding parameter, followed by an execution of the method body.
- If *ObjectName* is omitted, the call is assumed to be to a local method.

Since the setcolor class has a parameter that belongs to the Colorclass, any argument must come from the same class. Figure 3.13 contains a list of such valid Color arguments.

While the setColor method has a single parameter, two of the other AWindow methods, namely setSize and setLocation, have two parameters, and one AWindow constructor has four parameters. When multiple parameters are used, Java uses a common technique, known as **positional parameters**, to keep track of the correspondence between argument and parameter. Each argument is passed to the parameter in the same position. For example, the first parameter of setLocation always refers to horizontal placement and the second parameter to vertical placement. When arguments are supplied in a call to setLocation, the programmer must know the meaning of each position in order to place the arguments in their proper order.

Figure 3.13 Color constant values

```
Color.black          Color.green          Color.pink
Color.blue           Color.lightGray      Color.red
Color.cyan           Color.magenta        Color.white
Color.darkGray       Color.orange         Color.yellow
Color.gray
```

(Note that the use of these constants requires an import of Java.awt.Color. See Section 3.7.)

All parameters from the setLocation and setSize methods are specified to be *int*. This allows the user to utilize an integer constant (i.e., a consecutive sequence of decimal digits) as an argument. The following section of code illustrates use of the setLocation and setSize methods. Executing this code constructs and displays a window object that is 400 pixels wide, 500 pixels tall, located with upper-left corner at coordinate (10, 20), with a yellow background color.

```
bigWindow = new AWindow();
bigWindow.setSize( 400, 500 );
bigWindow.setLocation( 10, 20 );
bigWindow.setColor( Color.yellow );
bigWndow.repaint();
```

Figures 3.10 and 3.11 also point out that AWindow has two constructor methods. Java rules require that all constructor methods have identical names (the same name as their class). However, it is possible for a single class to have multiple constructor methods so long as they have different numbers and/or types of parameters. In the case of AWindow, the first constructor method has no parameters and the second has four. Using this second constructor, the function of the code above can be expressed more succinctly as shown below.

```
bigWindow = new AWindow( 10, 20, 400, 500 );
bigWindow.setColor( Color.yellow );
bigWndow.repaint();
```

An AWindow object isn't very interesting unless there are other objects that can be displayed upon it. One of the *aLibrary* classes that is included to draw images upon a window is ARectangle. Figure 3.14 gives a class diagram for ARectangle, and Figure 3.15 contains a class specification for the same class.

The ARectangle class contains many of the same methods as AWindow. The repaint, setLocation, setSize, and setColor methods have identical syntax and perform analogous functions. Even the constructor method has the same parameter list (although the name of the constructor must necessarily change to match the class).

Figure 3.14 ARectangle class diagram

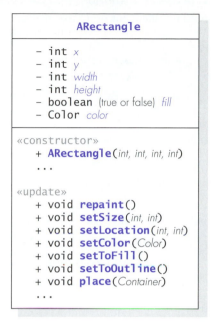

Figure 3.15 ARectangle class specifications

ARectangle Class Specifications

Invariant

An ARectangle object

- is a rectangular region that is displayed when placed upon a Container object.

- has an upper-left corner x pixels from the left and y pixels from the top of the Container on which it is placed. (The upper-left corner of an ARectangle is (0, 0).)

- is displayed either as an outline (when fill == false) or a filled figure (when fill == true). The width, height, and color of the image are given, respectively, by width, height, and color. (Note that any portion of the ARectangle that lies outside the Container on which it is placed will not be visible.)

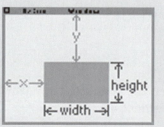

At left is a darker ARectangle inside an AWindow on which it is placed.

Continued on next page.

Constructor Method

```
public ARectangle ( int newX,int newY, int w, int h )
```

postcondition

A new ARectangle object is created with attributes as follows:
x == *newX* AND y == *newY* AND width == *w* AND height == h AND
fill == *false* AND color == Color.black

Update Methods

```
public void repaint ( )
```

postcondition

If this ARectangle is placed, then its image is updated (redrawn) as soon
as possible.

```
public void setSize ( int w, int h )
```

precondition

w >= 0 AND *h* >= 0 ("*>=*" denotes *greater than or equal to*)

modifies

width, height

postcondition

width == *w* AND height == *h*

```
public void setLocation ( int newX, int newY )
```

modifies

x, y

postcondition

x == *newX* AND y == *newY*

```
public void setColor ( Color c )
```

precondition

c is a valid Color

modifies

color

postcondition

color == *c*

```
public void setToFill ( )
```

modifies

fill

postcondition

fill == true

```
public void setToOutline ( )
```

   modifies

   fill

   postcondition

   fill == false

```
public void place ( Container c )
```

   precondition

   c != null (i.e., the *c* argument must be validly constructed)

   postcondition

   This ARectangle is placed upon *c* and removed from any prior placement.
   Any portion of the ARectangle that lies outside the object upon which it
   is placed will not be visible. (Call repaint to ensure image update.)

Only the setToFill, setToOutline, and place methods are new. A call to setToFill is used to create a solid rectangle figure, and a call to setToOutline creates a rectangular figure border.

An ARectangle object is visible only when it has first been placed on some other visible Container object. The place[1] method is included for this purpose. Every AWindow object is a valid Container. Therefore, executing the following code causes mySquare to display as a 50 by 50, black, filled square to be placed upon bigWindow.

```
bigWindow = new AWindow( 120, 90, 400, 300 );
mySquare = new ARectangle( 200, 150, 50, 50 );
mySquare.setToFill();
mySquare.place( bigWindow );
mySquare.repaint();
```

The place method positions the ARectangle object relative to the background object upon which it is placed. This means that the above code positions mySquare so that it is 200 pixels from the left side of bigWindow. Figure 3.16 shows a picture to illustrate the result of executing this code segment.

ARectangle objects are also valid Containers. This means that one ARectangle object can be placed upon another.

```
outerRect = new ARectangle(100, 150, 200, 200);
innerRect = new ARectangle(10, 20, 30, 30);
innerRect.place(outerRect);
```

Execution of the code above places innerRect on top of outerRect so that the upper-left corner of innerRect is 10 pixels right and 20 pixels down from outerRect's corner.

---

[1]The *swing* and *awt* classes use a method called add that performs a similar function to place.

Figure 3.16 A square placed on an AWindow

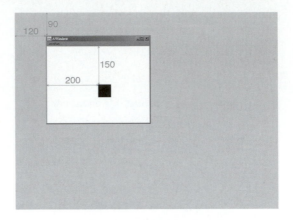

Overlapping ARectangle objects are explained by three rules:

1. Any portion of a graphical *aLibrary* object that lies outside the boundary of the object on which it is placed is invisible.

2. When two objects are placed on the same underlying object, the one placed last will appear to be on top of the one placed first (i.e., the last placed object may cover part or all of an earlier placement).

3. Any object placed upon another an underlying object will appear to be on top (i.e., the placed object may cover part or all of the underlying object).

These three rules are intended to make a place behave just as though one graphical object were physically placed upon another. The object on top may cover all, or part, of the object underneath. Redrawing an *aLibrary* object (resulting from calling repaint) causes the object receiving the message to be redrawn *followed* by all objects placed upon it. Redrawing the placed objects repeats the same procedure. To illustrate these placement and drawing rules, Figure 3.17 shows a sequence of instructions and the corresponding ARectangles that are displayed. This code assumes four ARectangle variables that are called darkOutlined, lightFilled, whiteFilled, and blackOutlined.

CLOSED Black Box

The place method has another unusual characteristic in that it results in a hidden binding. It happens that every object is bound to the object upon which it is placed. Consider the execution of the following:

```
blackOutlined = new ARectangle(30, 30, 30, 30);
blackOutlined.place(theWindow);
blackOutlined = null;
```

When this instruction sequence completes execution, blackOutlined is bound to a 30 by 30 ARectangle by virtue of the first instruction. After this object is placed, blackOutlined is assigned null. The 30 by 30 rectangle does *not* disappear, however. The place method has bound this rectangle to theWindow, so it will continue to be visible even when it has no variable name.

Figure 3.17 Example place calls and their result

```
theWindow = new AWindow( 10, 10, 300, 220);
lightFilled = new ARectangle(10, 10, 200, 200);
lightFilled.setToFill();
lightFilled.setColor(Color.lightGray);
lightFilled.place(theWindow);
darkOutlined = new ARectangle(50, 50, 40, 200);
darkOutlined.setColor(Color.darkGray);
darkOutlined.place(lightFilled);
whiteFilled = new ARectangle(80, 80, 50, 50);
whiteFilled.setToFill();
whiteFilled.setColor(Color.white);
whiteFilled.place(lightFilled);
blackOutlined = new ARectangle(30, 30, 30, 30);
blackOutlined.setColor(Color.black);
blackOutlined.place(whiteFilled);
theWindow.repaint();
```

Two other *aLibrary* classes that are very similar to ARectangle are ARoundRectangle and AOval. All three classes have the same methods, excepting for constructor methods, and even the constructor methods have the same parameters. The ARoundRectangle image differs from ARectangle because its corners are rounded, as shown below.

An AOval object is an elliptical image that is inscribed in a rectangle. The width attribute is the horizontal distance across the center, and the height attribute is the vertical distance from top to bottom through the AOval's center. Below is a diagram of an AOval.

CLOSED
Black Box

Note that consecutive changes to *aLibrary* objects without the time to repaint do not appear; only the final appearance is displayed. For example, if an AOval object is created and then resized via setSize or relocated via setLocation, only the final size or position is displayed on the computer screen. (The key for revealing this black box is given in Section 10.7.)

3.6 IMPORT DECLARATIONS

The ultimate goal of a software design is to produce a working program, and the program can only work if each class includes the proper references to the other classes it utilizes. In particular, the Java compiler needs some help finding external classes. For example if the *Director.java* file makes use of `DrawingTool` or `ARectangle`, then the compiler must know where to find vital information (i.e., the *DrawingTool.class* or *ARectangle.class* file). One way to be certain that the compiler can locate such external files is to include a copy of the ".class" files in the same folder as the *Director.java* file. This was the approach suggested in Chapter 2.

For libraries, such as *aLibrary*, *swing*, or *awt*, it isn't practical (nor is it always possible) to copy all the necessary ".class" files into other folders. For this reason the Java language includes **import declarations**. An `import` declaration is a line placed before the `public class` line. Each import declaration specifies one or more files that the compiler can search to locate external classes. Figure 3.18 provides more detail.

Figure 3.18 `ImportDecls` description

ImportDecls

Syntax

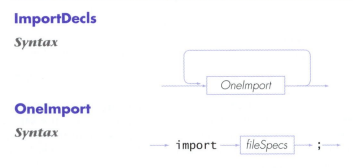

OneImport

Syntax

Note

fileSpecs denotes the pathname of a file relative to the system classpath variable. The notation uses a period as a separator between consecutive folder/file names.

Usage

The class in which the *ImportDecls* is included can access the imported classes.

Java programming environments use a **CLASSPATH** system variable to maintain the addresses of major library folders[2]. The *fileSpecs* folder (named in Figure 3.18) specification must specify a file pathname that is relative to *CLASSPATH*. For example, any class that uses one of the `Color` constants, such as `Color.green`, must include an import declaration such as the following:

```
import java.awt.Color;
```

This import informs the compiler that it can locate the *Color.class* file within the *awt* library of the *java* folder. An alternative import that allows access to all classes in the *awt* folder uses an asterisk (*) in place of `Color` as shown below.

```
import java.awt.*;
```

---

[2] The CLASSPATH system variable is usually predefined to identify the standard Java library folders. When a new library is added, the classpath system variable must be updated to include the library. Many of the examples in this text assume that *aLibrary* has been loaded and the classpath appropriately updated.

Similarly, if *aLibrary* is properly loaded and CLASSPATH set, the following import declaration permits access to all of the classes in *aLibrary*.

```
import aLibrary.*;
```

Figure 3.19 illustrates the use of import declarations to complete a working Director class. (The program is included in electronic form in the folder for the bullseye program.) Executing the program in Figure 3.19 creates a bull's eye by overlaying one circle upon another. Since the Director class uses both *aLibrary* classes and Color constants, both import declarations are needed.

Figure 3.19 A Director class to draw a bullseye

```
// Author: David Riley
//           (January, 2000)
/* invariant
        A bullseye is drawn in a window.  This bullseye consists of
        three concentric circles, getting progressively lighter
        from outside in.   */
import aLibrary.*;
import java.awt.*;

public class Director {
    private AWindow   theWindow;
    private AOval outerCircle, midCircle, innerCircle;

    /* postcondition
            a window is constructed and bullseye displayed. */
    public Director()    {
        theWindow = new AWindow( 10, 10, 500, 400);
        outerCircle = new AOval(100, 100, 90, 90);
        outerCircle.setToFill();
        outerCircle.setColor(Color.darkGray);
        outerCircle.place(theWindow);

        midCircle = new AOval(15, 15, 60, 60);
        midCircle.setToFill();
        midCircle.setColor(Color.lightGray);
        midCircle.place(outerCircle);

        innerCircle = new AOval(15, 15, 30, 30);
        innerCircle.setToFill();
        innerCircle.setColor(Color.white);
        innerCircle.place(midCircle);

        theWindow.repaint();
    }
}
```

3.7   PROTOTYPING

Section 3.1 examined the top-down design strategy for writing software. In this section a different strategy, called **prototyping**, is introduced. The process of prototyping consists of developing a sequence of programs, known as **prototypes**. The early prototypes provide only partial functionality, but are sufficient to exhibit key aspects of the desired program behavior. Each succeeding prototype adds functionality.

Software that produces graphical images is often well suited to the use of prototyping. A customer may not know, or care to specify, details of color or of placement. Prototypes can be used to assist the customer in making these software requirements decisions. For example, consider the problem of drawing a caricature of a caterpillar. An initial prototype of code and the associated picture are shown in Figure 3.20.

Figure 3.20 A first prototype for the caterpillar program

```java
import aLibrary.*;
import java.awt.Color;
public class Director   {
    private  AWindow   theWindow;
    private  AOval  head, frontSegment, midSegment, rearSegment;

    public Director()    {
        theWindow = new AWindow( 10, 10, 500, 220);
        head = new  AOval( 110, 70, 80, 80 );
        head.place( theWindow );
        frontSegment = new AOval( 180, 100, 50, 50 );
        frontSegment.place( theWindow );
        midSegment = new AOval( 230, 100, 50, 50 );
        midSegment.place( theWindow );
        rearSegment = new AOval( 280, 100, 50, 50 );
        rearSegment.place( theWindow );
        theWindow.repaint();
    }
}
```

This prototype makes use of an AWindow object, named theWindow, and four AOval objects. Following the instantiation of theWindow, each of the four AOvals is instantiated and placed upon theWindow. The final instruction ensures the display of all objects.

The customer can execute this first prototype and observe the drawing produced. This allows the customer to make key decisions. It is also important to note that the programmer has not invested much time in the prototype, so the cost of changing the requirements are minimal. Suppose that the customer decides that this three-segment body and enlarged head are good, but legs and a face are needed. A second prototype might take the form shown in Figure 3.21. The newly inserted code is boldfaced.

Figure 3.21 A second prototype for the caterpillar program

```java
import aLibrary.*;
import java.awt.Color;
public class Director  {
    private  AWindow  theWindow;
    private  AOval  head, frontSegment, midSegment, rearSegment;
    private  AOval leftEye, rightEye, mouth;
    private  ARectangle  frontLeg;

    public Director()  {
        theWindow = new AWindow( 10, 10, 500, 220);
        head = new  AOval( 110, 70, 80, 80 );
        head.place( theWindow );
        leftEye = new AOval( 15, 30, 15, 10 );
        leftEye.setColor( Color.blue );
        leftEye.place( head );
        rightEye = new AOval( 50, 30, 15, 10 );
        rightEye.setColor( Color.blue );
        rightEye.place( head );
        mouth = new AOval( 25, 50, 30, 10 );
        mouth.setColor( Color.red );
        mouth.place( head );
        frontSegment = new AOval( 180, 100, 50, 50 );
        frontSegment.place( theWindow );
        frontLeg = new ARectangle( 200, 150, 10, 20 );
        frontLeg.place( theWindow );
        midSegment = new AOval( 230, 100, 50, 50 );
        midSegment.place( theWindow );
        rearSegment = new AOval( 280, 100, 50, 50 );
        rearSegment.place( theWindow );
        theWindow.repaint();
    }
}
```

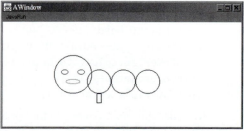

The second prototype includes two eyes and a mouth. These are drawn as AOval outlines and are placed upon the head. The second prototype also includes just one leg, hoping to get the customer's reaction. The additional legs are easier to include once the desired leg form has been determined. For the final program, assume that the customer wants the following changes:

- All of the following should be filled: three body segments, two blue eyes, and all legs.
- Each leg needs a "foot" pointing forward.
- The mouth should be filled, red, and turned up in a smile.
- The white face must move backward to partially cover the front body segment.

Figure 3.22 contains the desired drawing.

Figure 3.22 The final caterpillar drawing

The two most difficult tasks in reaching this final program are

- making the mouth smile
- causing the face to partially cover the front body segment

Turning the mouth into a smile is accomplished by creating two filled AOvals. The initial AOval is a red mouth. A smile results from placing a white filled AOval on top of the red one. The following instruction sequence draws such a mouth:

```
mouth = new AOval( 25, 50, 30, 10 );
mouth.setColor( Color.red );
mouth.setToFill();
mouth.place( head );
mouthCover = new AOval( 0, 0, 30, 5 );
mouthCover.setColor( Color.white );
mouthCover.setToFill();
mouthCover.place( mouth );
```

To make the head cover the first body segment suggests that the head should be constructed from two AOval objects. The underlying object, headBackground, is a filled white AOval. A black outlined AOval is placed on top. This code is shown below. The final completed program is available electronically:

```
headBackground = new AOval( 110, 70, 80, 80 );
headBackground.setColor( Color.white );
headBackground.setToFill();
head = new AOval( 0, 0, 80, 80 );
head.place( headBackground );
```

The caterpillar example illustrates that prototyping is useful for discovering requirements, but there are many other reasons for using prototyping. One such reason is that prototyping assists with debugging. Since each prototype alters only a portion of the code, the most likely location to begin searching for the cause of any error is in one of these alterations.

3.8 DEBUGGING—SYSTEM.OUT.PRINTLN

Design by prototyping highlights the closely interconnected nature of the design, implementation, and testing activities. By definition, a prototyping strategy requires repeated design of implementation prototypes, each of which should be tested prior to proceeding to the next prototype.

Even the most careful programmers make errors. If those errors are syntactic, such as a misspelled variable identifier or a misplaced comma, then the compiler reports the error, and the programmer makes the necessary correction.

Logic errors do not generally involve bad syntax. Instead a logic error is an incorrect algorithm that results from faulty thinking. Logic errors can be more difficult for a programmer to locate and correct because

- They aren't manifest until run time.
- They may or may not result in a reported error.
- They may not cause trouble for every program execution.

For example, suppose that the caterpillar program (discussed in the previous section) was rewritten so that leftEye is placed upon rearSegment, rather than head. This is not a syntax error, because it is valid Java code to place one AOval (leftEye) upon another AOval (rearSegment). Therefore, the Java compiler will not report any errors for this new program.

Logic errors, like the misplaced leftEye, are sometimes discovered when the program executes. There are two possible run-time manifestations of this particular error:

1. If the place method is called prior to constructing either leftEye or rearSegment, then a null pointer exception occurs.

2. If the place method is called after both leftEye and rearSegment are constructed, then the left eye image is drawn in the wrong location.

Debugging can be difficult, because logic errors can take so many different forms. In addition, it is often difficult to associate the visible behavior of a logic error with its cause.

The first step in debugging logic errors is to **trace** the program to identify its cause. In program trace, the programmer pretends to be the Java VM and executes the program. Each instruction is considered in the order that it would be executed by the VM, and as each is considered, the programmer records the result. (This record is typically a picture of the state of each program object.) Throughout this book there are examples of program traces, sometimes using pictures of the resulting graphical output (like the examples in this chapter), and sometimes using object diagrams (like Section 2.4).

Occasionally a logic error is so ornery that tracing doesn't help. In such cases a useful debugging aid is to let the program assist by periodically reporting its run-time state. There are software development tools, called **debuggers**, that are sometimes used.

An even simpler approach is to "let the program trace itself" by inserting output instructions within the program to observe the run-time state of a program. Each output instruction is designed to report the content of a selected variable at some key location within the program. The programmer inserts the desired output instructions, recompiles the program, and observes the output that results from program execution.

Many Java objects, including those from *aLibrary* classes, support a method called `System.out.println`, designed specifically for such debugging. `System.out.println` has a single parameter, and when it is called, the state of its argument is output to the **standard output stream**. Note that the standard output stream is different for different systems. Sometimes it is displayed in a separate run-time window. Sometimes the standard output stream is the *shell* in which you type the "javac" and "java" commands. Sometimes a designated file is used for the standard output stream.

A typical call to `System.out.println` is shown below:

```
System.out.println( leftEye );
```

When this instruction executes, it will display information about the state of the `leftEye` variable at that particular point in execution. A sample of such output is shown below.

```
AOval object .... (#03)
      x: 15, y: 30 width: 15, height: 10
      is placed, is filled, color: blue
```

This display shows the type of the object (`AOval`) and several of its attributes. The output for other types of objects may differ. Variable names are *not* output by `System.out.println` because there could be several such bindings. However, each object does display a number that is unique to the object. The output above identifies this object as the "03" object. (The "3" indicates that this is the third `AOval` object created by the program.)

When `System.out.println` calls are "sprinkled" among program instructions, it is possible to observe changes in state that occur during program execution. For example, consider the following code segment:

```
leftEye = new AOval( 15, 30, 15, 10 );
    System.out.println( leftEye );
leftEye.setColor( Color.blue );
    System.out.println( leftEye );
leftEye.setToFill();
leftEye.place( head );
    System.out.println( leftEye );
```

The output resulting from executing this segment of code is shown below.

```
AOval object .... (#03)
    x: 15, y: 30 width: 15, height: 10
    not placed, is outlined, color: black
AOval object .... (#03)
    x: 15, y: 30 width: 15, height: 10
    not placed, is outlined, color: blue
AOval object .... (#03)
    x: 15, y: 30 width: 15, height: 10
    is placed, is filled, color: blue
```

This kind of output provides valuable trace information for debugging. These instructions should be either removed or turned into comments for the production program.

CLOSED Black Box

There are a couple of things that may seem odd about System.out.println. Its name is long and unusual. Furthermore, it is strange to have a method that accepts arguments of virtually any type. The reasons behind these features are discussed later in Chapters 9 and 15.

3.9 RECAP

This chapter has explored several of the fundamental techniques that are required to transform a set of software requirements into a working program. The process begins by designing one or more algorithms, and culminates with a working program. Along the way, the software developer must select proper identifiers and use preexisting software wisely.

Psychological studies have shown that the human mind can only retain roughly seven thoughts simultaneously. Programmers need to remember the limitations of their own memory as they design software solutions. Programming design strategies like top-down design and prototyping are powerful techniques for addressing human limitations.

Software implementation also relies upon designing correct algorithms. Sometimes a top-down design is the best approach to finding this algorithm, and sometimes prototyping is more useful. Furthermore, top-down design and prototyping are not independent, but complementary, design strategies. Skilled programmers tend to borrow techniques from both top-down design and prototyping as they perform the task of software design and implementation.

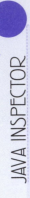

Below is a collection of hints on what to check when examining code that involves the concepts of this chapter.

✓ Retain higher (earlier) levels of a top-down design. These earlier steps can be compared to the resulting code to check for omissions.

✓ Checking identifiers can greatly improve readability. Are instance variables named with nouns? Are methods named with verbs? Is the first letter of each class name uppercase and the first letter of every variable and method lowercase? Most importantly, are the names meaningful?

✓ There are only two ways for your class to have access to other classes: (1) these other classes are located within the same file folder as yours or (2) an import declaration is included at the top of your class. If *aLibrary* facilities are used, then check for

```
import aLibrary.*;
```

If Color constants are used, then check for

```
import java.awt.*;
```

✓ For every method call, check to see that the number and type of the arguments in the call are the same as the number and type of the parameters expected by the method.

✓ When using the place command from the *aLibrary* classes, do not forget that the placement is relative to the upper-left corner of the background object, and not relative to the window or the computer display.

✓ A frequent problem when using *aLibrary* graphics is that some graphical object doesn't appear at run time. Below is a checklist of probable reasons for nonappearance. These should be checked in the order they are listed.

1. The program terminated with a run-time error prior to ever placing the object.
2. The object was never placed.
3. The object was placed, but not repainted. (Calling repaint isn't always needed, but it isn't harmful.)
4. The object is located outside the boundaries of its underlying background.
5. The object is covered up by another object.
6. The Java VM is having difficulty updating the window. (This is a remote possibility, but it happens with certain operating systems, complicated graphics, and/or graphics that overlap boundaries.) Sometimes resizing a Java window will cause it to redraw properly.

EXERCISES

1. Imagine that `pencil` is an instance variable of type `DrawingTool` that is located near the left edge of its window and directed to the right. Refine each of the following algorithms into a short piece of Java code using `pencil`. These algorithms are simple enough that this refinement can occur in a single step.

   a. Rotate `pencil` 90 degrees in the counterclockwise direction.
   b. `pencil` draws two 20-unit horizontal line segments separated by 20 units.
   c. `pencil` draws three stair steps heading downward from its initial position.

2. Imagine that `pencil` is an instance variable of type `DrawingTool` that is located near the left edge of its window and directed to the right. Perform top-down design on each of the following algorithms, converting them into a piece of Java code using `pencil`. Do not attempt to translate each of these directly into code. Instead, you should refine each algorithm gradually into subalgorithms.

   a. Use `pencil` to draw the number 950 on the window.
   b. Use `pencil` to draw the word "STEP" in uppercase letters on the window.
   c. Use `pencil` to draw a house that contains two windows and a door.

3. Top-down design and prototyping both provide techniques for progressing gradually toward a final program. However, they do so in different ways. Identify each of the following statements as describing either a top-down concept or a prototyping concept.

a. Writing a research paper beginning with an outline is similar to this design technique.

b. This technique can be described as somewhat like "trial and error."

c. This technique is better suited to an ongoing involvement from customers.

d. The very first version of the code might be the last using this technique.

4. A class diagram (shown below) and class specifications (on the next page) are given for a class called AlarmClock. Using this class, show how to perform a top-down design of a program to set two alarm clocks. One alarm should be set for 5 o'clock and the other for 4:32.

```
┌─────────────────────────────────────┐
│            AlarmClock               │
├─────────────────────────────────────┤
│   – int  hour                       │
│   – int  minute                     │
├─────────────────────────────────────┤
│ «constructor»                       │
│   + AlarmClock()                    │
│                                     │
│ «update»                            │
│   + void  advanceOneHour()          │
│   + void  advanceOneMinute()        │
│   + void  advanceTenMinutes()       │
└─────────────────────────────────────┘
```

AlarmClock Class Specifications

Invariant

An AlarmClock object

- keeps track of a single alarm time in terms of *hour* and *minute*.

- cannot distiguish between A.M. and P.M. times

- has attribute values restricted to the following ranges:

    $1 \le$ hour ≤ 12 and $0 \le$ minute ≤ 59

Constructor Method

public **AlarmClock** ( )

> *postcondition*
> A new AlarmClock object is created with attributes as follows:
> *hour*== 1 AND *minute* == 0

Update Methods

public void **advanceOneHour**( )

> *precondition*
> *hour* < 12

> *modifies*
> hour

> *postcondition*
> The value of *hour* is one unit greater than before this method was called.

public void **advanceOneMinute**( )

> *precondition*
> *minute* < 59

> *modifies*
> minute

> *postcondition*
> The value of *minute* is one unit greater than before this method was called.

public void **advanceTenMinutes**( )

> *precondition*
> *minute* < 50

> *modifies*
> minute

> *postcondition*
> The value of *minute* is 10 units greater than before this method was called.

5.
```
private AWindow window;
private ARectangle rectA, rectB;
private AOval oval, circle;
```

Using the instance variable declarations above, sketch the images or output that result from executing each of the following segments of code.

a.
```
window = new AWindow(10, 10, 200, 100);
rectA = new ARectangle(50, 20, 100, 30);
rectA.setColor( Color.black );
rectA.place(window);
rectB = new ARectangle(50, 60, 5, 30);
rectB.setColor( Color.gray );
rectB.setToFill();
rectB.place(window);
window.repaint();
```

b.
```
window = new AWindow(10, 10, 200, 100);
rectA = new ARectangle(20, 10, 100, 30);
rectA.setColor( Color.black );
rectA.setToFill();
rectA.place(window);
rectB = new ARectangle(50, 60, 5, 10);
rectB.setColor( Color.white );
rectB.place(rectA);
window.repaint();
```

c.
```
window = new AWindow(10, 10, 200, 100);
rectA = new ARectangle(50, 20, 200, 30);
rectA.setColor( Color.green );
rectA.setToFill();
rectA.place(window);
rectB = new ARectangle(50, 60, 10, 100);
rectB.setColor( Color.blue );
rectB.place(rectA);
circle = new AOval(0, 0, 20, 20);
circle.setColor( Color.red );
circle.place(rectB);
oval = new AOval( 160, 50, 100, 40 );
oval.setToFill();
oval.setColor( Color.yellow );
oval.place( window );
window.repaint();
```

d. ```
window = new AWindow(10, 10, 200, 100);
oval = new AOval(10, 10, 50, 50);
oval.place(window);
oval = new AOval(20, 20, 50, 50);
oval.place(window);
oval = new AOval(30, 30, 50, 50);
oval.place(window);
window.repaint();
```

e. ```
window = new AWindow(10, 10, 200, 100);
oval = new AOval(10, 10, 50, 50);
window.repaint();
```

f. ```
window = new AWindow(10, 10, 200, 100);
oval = new AOval(10, 10, 50, 50);
oval.place(window);
oval.place(window);
window.repaint();
```

g. ```
window = new AWindow(10, 10, 200, 100);
oval = new AOval(10, 10, 50, 50);
oval.place(window);
oval.setSize( 100, 25 );
oval.setLocation( 50, 20 );
window.repaint();
```

h. ```
window = new AWindow(10, 10, 200, 100);
oval = new AOval(10, 10, 50, 50);
oval.place(window);
System.out.println(window);
System.out.println(oval);
```

## PROGRAMMING EXERCISES

1.  Write a program that produces a window with the following image. The face must be yellow on a black background. The mouth is red. The eyes are black.

```

2. Write a program that produces a window with the following image. The pattern is blue on a white background.

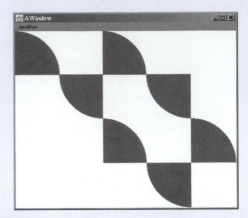

3. Write a program that produces a window with the following image. The snake eye must have a blue pointed iris and a small black slit for a pupil. The background of the window is gray.

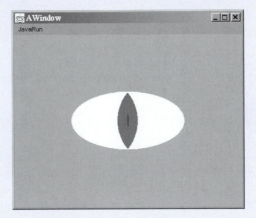

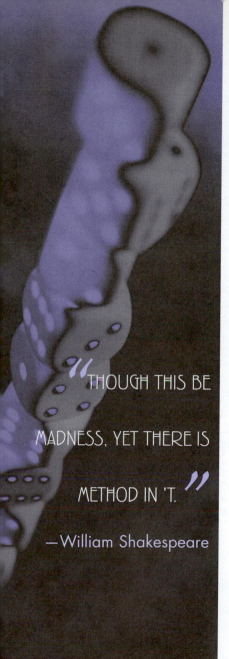

CHAPTER 4

METHODS

OBJECTIVES

- To examine the need to partition large algorithms into subprograms

- To explore the syntax and semantics of private methods

- To examine the concept of parameter passage

- To introduce nonvoid methods

- To present local variables in support of objects needed only within one method

- To show the utility of this as a means for referring to an object from inside the class to which that object belongs

- To introduce event handling and an A3ButtonWindow class that uses events

- To introduce result and previous value notations for expressing postconditions

Methods are the code repositories of an object-oriented program. Prior chapters have shown how programmers use external classes with precoded methods. This chapter explores how methods are written and used within the Director class.

"THOUGH THIS BE

MADNESS, YET THERE IS

METHOD IN 'T."

—William Shakespeare

4.1   THE NEED FOR A SUBPROGRAM

Novels are written in chapters. Manuals are divided into sections. Television mini-series are shown in episodes. Whether in a chapter, a section, or an episode, humans seem to prefer to have their information partitioned into segments. Therefore, it isn't surprising that good computer programs are subdivided into smaller portions.

Historically, computer programs have been constructed from **subprograms**. Each subprogram performs some portion of the complete task of the program. More importantly, each subprogram can be designed, implemented, and tested as a separate entity. The use of subprograms is, therefore, an effective way to partition a lengthy algorithm into smaller units.

SOFTWARE ENGINEERING TIP

Programmers decompose their code into subprograms because shorter segments of code are easier to implement, to debug, and to read. A good rule of thumb is to divide code into pieces that fit on one computer screen or less.

A method is a subprogram. When code becomes long or repetitive, it is often helpful to be able to decompose the task into separate methods. Such decomposition has the effect of making each piece (method) smaller and therefore easier to write and to read. As an example, consider writing a program to make a backup copy of an audio compact disk. Figure 4.1 explains background information on compact disks.

For this program it is necessary to assume that the computer running the program will have two CD drives, at least one of which is capable of burning CDs. Figure 4.2 contains an algorithm designed to copy one audio CD that contains eight tracks (songs) onto another.

SOFTWARE ENGINEERING TIP

If the same task is repeated several times, it is a likely candidate to become a subprogram. One such example is found in Steps 3 through 9 of Figure 4.2.

Even though there are nine steps in the algorithm for copying the 8-track CD, there appear to be just three different tasks. The first step of the algorithm is unique and represents one task. The second step copies the first track of the source CD onto the destination. The last seven steps are all identical, so they represent the same task being performed seven times. These three different tasks are potential candidates for individual subprograms (methods).

Figure 4.3 contains a partial program for this algorithm. The Figure 4.3 program is missing the subprograms indicated by the nine numbered comments within the code.

The Director class in Figure 4.3 includes the declarations for two instance variables, sourceCD and destinationCD. The designer of this program decided to refine the first step of the algorithm into two Java instructions that instantiate sourceCD and destinationCD. Such instructions rely upon a class called CDdrive,[1] described by the following class diagram.

---

[1]CDdrive is a class invented for this example and not a part of the software supplied with this text.

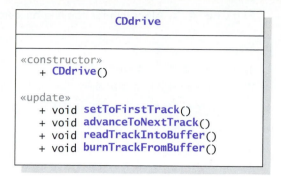

Figure 4.1 Information about compact disks

Compact disks, also known as CDs, are flat plates of plastic that can store various types of data. An audio CD is a CD that stores data representing sound (usually music). A CD player spins the CD under a beam of light and a sensor detects the associated reflections. Sensing the reflected light beam is called reading the disk's data.

The audio data on the disk is stored in groups, known as tracks. One track generally corresponds to a separate song. The tracks are arranged in concentric circles from the inside of the CD outward, as shown in the picture below.

There are three kinds of devices (drives) capable of reading CDs; they are called CD-ROM, CD-R, and CD-RW. Two of these devices (CD-R and CD-RW drives) can also write new data onto the proper types of compact disks. The process of writing to a CD is often called burning.

Figure 4.2 Algorithm for copying an 8-track CD

Step
1. Initialize both the source CD drive and the destination CD drive.
2. Read first track from the source CD and burn a copy onto the destination CD.
3. Read the next track from the source CD and burn a copy onto the destination CD.
4. Read the next track from the source CD and burn a copy onto the destination CD.
5. Read the next track from the source CD and burn a copy onto the destination CD.
6. Read the next track from the source CD and burn a copy onto the destination CD.
7. Read the next track from the source CD and burn a copy onto the destination CD.
8. Read the next track from the source CD and burn a copy onto the destination CD.
9. Read the next track from the source CD and burn a copy onto the destination CD.

Figure 4.3 Partial Director to copy an 8-track CD

```java
public class Director {
        private CDdrive sourceCD;
        private CDdrive destinationCD;

        /* modifies
              destinationCD
           postcondition
              destinationCD has the same first 8 tracks as sourceCD */
        public Director() {
              sourceCD = new CDdrive();
              destinationCD = new CDdrive();
              // 2) Copy first track from sourceCD to destinationCD
              // 3) Copy the next track from sourceCD to destinationCD
              // 4) Copy the next track from sourceCD to destinationCD
              // 5) Copy the next track from sourceCD to destinationCD
              // 6) Copy the next track from sourceCD to destinationCD
              // 7) Copy the next track from sourceCD to destinationCD
              // 8) Copy the next track from sourceCD to destinationCD
              // 9) Copy the next track from sourceCD to destinationCD
        }
}
```

The CDdrive class contains a method to instantiate an object (CDdrive), a method to position the read/burn mechanism at the first track (setToFirstTrack), and a method to advance the read/burn mechanism from one track to the next (advanceToNextTrack).

The readTrackIntoBuffer method is designed to read data from the current track, and the burnTrackFromBuffer is designed to burn data to the current track.

Both readTrackIntoBuffer and burnTrackFromBuffer make use of a reserved segment of computer memory called a **buffer**. Executing readTrackIntoBuffer causes this buffer to receive a copy of the current track from the CD drive. Executing burnTrackFromBuffer causes whatever track was last placed into the buffer to be burned onto the current track of the CD.

4.2   PRIVATE PARAMETERLESS METHODS

Java subprograms take the form of methods. Figure 4.4 describes the kind of method that can be used to accomplish the necessary subprogram tasks needed for the CD copying program. This particular version of method is called **private**, because it is called only within its class.

From Figure 4.4 it is evident that private methods have a syntax that is similar to the Director method. The differences are the following:

- the private prefix
- the void qualifier before the class name
- a method name other than Director

Figure 4.4 PrivateVoidParameterlessMethod description

PrivateVoidParameterlessMethod (abridged version of *PrivateMethod*)

Syntax

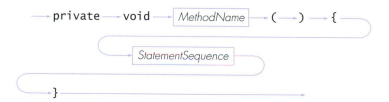

Semantics

When this method is called, the *StatementSequence* code is executed.

Note

MethodName is an identifier. Each parameterless method within the same class must have a unique name.

Style notes

- The line beginning private and ending with "{" should be on a single line and one tab setting inside the containing class. The final "}" symbol should also be aligned directly under private.
- All *StatementSequence* instructions should be indented at least one tab inside private.
- *MethodName* should be an action verb or a verb phrase.
- *precondition*, *modifies*, and *postcondition* clauses are a good inclusion in each method.

CLOSED
Black Box

In Java the private and public prefixes are important, but they may seem annoying to a novice programmer. The following rules are sufficient for now.

1. The Director class is public.
2. The Director constructor method is public.
3. leftAction, midAction, and rightAction (see Section 4.8) are public.
4. Everything else is private. This includes all nonconstructor methods and all instance variables within the Director class.

Chapter 6 will clarify the meaning of these declarations, and explain in general how to select between public and private.

Below is an example private method that can be used in the CD copy program as the subprogram to advance both drives by one track, then copy the new track from sourceCD to destinationCD.

```java
private void copyNextTrack() {
    sourceCD.advanceToNextTrack();
    destinationCD.advanceToNextTrack();
    sourceCD.readTrackIntoBuffer();
    destinationCD.burnTrackFromBuffer();
}
```

SOFTWARE ENGINEERING TIP

The selection of the name of a method deserves care. The name should reflect the task that the method performs. It helps to use action verbs or verb phrases for void methods.

The code between the initial "{" and last "}" symbols of a method is often called the method **body**. Every method body consists of a sequence of statements (instructions). The body of copyNextTrack contains four instructions.

A private method executes in response to a **method call**, or **method invocation**, instruction. When a method is called, its body executes. Following the method body execution, the method is said to **return** to the location of the call. Figure 4.5 shows the syntax for calling a private parameterless method.

Figure 4.5 PrivateVoidParameterlessMethodCall description

PrivateVoidParameterlessMethodCall (abridged version of *MethodCall* and a possible *OneStatement*)

Syntax

Notes
- *MethodName* is the name of a nonconstructor method from the same class as this call.
- No separators are permitted before or after the period.

Semantics
Executing *PrivateVoidParameterlessMethodCall* causes the method to be executed.

All methods that are members of the same class are accessible throughout that class. As Figure 4.5 indicates, the syntax for calling a method within the same class is different from calling external methods; there is no object prefix required within the same class. For example, the `Director` class simply includes the following instruction in order to call the `copyNextTrack` method:

```
copyNextTrack();
```

The execution of the call instruction above behaves as if the body of the `copyNextTrack` method were substituted in its place.

This run-time behavior of a method call can be pictured in the form of an activity diagram (another Unified Modeling Language diagram form). Activity diagrams show the sequence of activities or actions that occur at run time.

Figure 4.6 contains an excerpt of code that calls `copyNextTrack`, along with an **activity diagram** to illustrate how this code executes. The action boxes (rectangles with rounded sides) on the left represent the execution of instructions from the `Director` method, and the actions on the right represent the body of `copyNextTrack`. This figure demonstrates that executing the call instruction causes the body of the method to execute followed by a return to the code following the call.

Figure 4.6 Activity diagram for calling copyNextTrack

Code Excerpt (from the `Director` class)

```
. . .
    // Instruction before the call
    copyNextTrack();
    // Instruction after the call
. . .
```

Activity Diagram

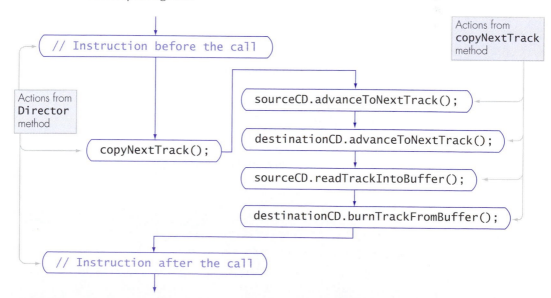

The complete program for copying an 8-track CD is shown in Figure 4.7. This class contains three methods—the Director constructor and two private methods. When Director executes, it instantiates both CDdrive variables, then calls the copyFirstTrack method. Following the return from this first call, the Director method proceeds to call the copyNextTrack method seven times in succession, thereby copying the remaining seven tracks.

Figure 4.7 Program to copy an 8-track CD

```
public class Director {
    private CDdrive sourceCD;
    private CDdrive destinationCD;

    /* modifies
            destinationCD
       postcondition
            destinationCD has the same first 8 tracks as sourceCD */
    public Director() {
        sourceCD = new CDdrive();
        destinationCD = new CDdrive();
        copyFirstTrack();
        copyNextTrack();
        copyNextTrack();
        copyNextTrack();
        copyNextTrack();
        copyNextTrack();
        copyNextTrack();
        copyNextTrack();
    }

    /* precondition
            sourceCD instantiated AND destinationCD instantiated
       modifies
            first track of destinationCD
       postcondition
            sourceCD positioned at first track
            AND destinationCD positioned at first track
            AND 1st track of destinationCD == 1st track of sourceCD */
    private void copyFirstTrack() {
        sourceCD.setToFirstTrack();
        destinationCD.setToFirstTrack();
        sourceCD.readTrackIntoBuffer();
        destinationCD.burnTrackFromBuffer();
    }

    /* precondition
            sourceCD instantiated AND destinationCD instantiated
       modifies
            one track of destinationCD
```

```
            postcondition
                sourceCD positioned at next track (from time of call)
                AND destinationCD positioned at next track
                AND current track of destinationCD == current track of
                sourceCD */
        private void copyNextTrack() {
            sourceCD.advanceToNextTrack();
            destinationCD.advanceToNextTrack();
            sourceCD.readTrackIntoBuffer();
            destinationCD.burnTrackFromBuffer();
        }
}
```

Figure 4.7 also illustrates the use of specifications (in comment form) for *pri-vate* methods. Each of the three methods includes an appropriate set of *precondition*, *postcondition*, and *modifies* clauses. The use of these specifications demonstrates how each method can be thought of as a self-contained algorithm (a subprogram) that is part of the complete solution.

It should be noted that the 8-track CD copy problem can be solved by other programs that do *not* contain private methods. The most obvious such program results from replacing each call of a private method with the body of that method. The resulting Director method is over 30 instructions long, which is probably acceptable. However, the private methods, as shown in Figure 4.7, do a better job of clearly delineating and explaining the subalgorithms; they are easier to read and easier to modify. For larger methods, the advantage of using private methods becomes even more obvious.

4.3 USING PARAMETERS

Parameter passage was used in examples from Chapter 3 to communicate the dimensions, location, and color of various graphical objects. Now it is time to examine how to include parameters when writing methods. Figure 4.8 shows the Java requirements for private methods with parameters.

Figure 4.8 PrivateMethod and ParamDecls description

PrivateMethod

Syntax

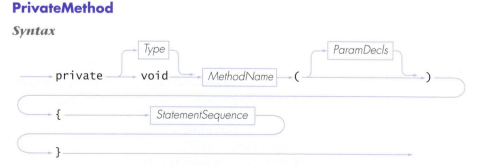

Continued on next page.

ParamDecls

Syntax

Semantics

When this method is called, each *ParameterName* is assigned its corresponding argument. Then the *StatementSequence* code is executed.

Notes

- *MethodName* is an identifier. Each method within the same class must either have a unique name or a different number and/or types of parameters.
- *ParameterName* is an identifier that identifies the formal parameter.
- *Type* can be any accessible class name or Java primitive type.
- The use of *Type*, rather than void, in a private method is described in Section 4.5.

Style notes

- The line beginning with private should be one tab setting inside the containing class. The final "}" symbol should also be aligned directly under private.
- The initial "{" should be on the end of the first line of the method, or directly underneath private (in the event that there is no room on the first line).
- All *StatementSequence* instructions should be indented at least one tab inside private.
- If void is used, then *MethodName* should be a verb or a verb phrase. Otherwise, it should be a noun or noun phrase.
- *precondition*, *modifies*, and *postcondition* clauses are good inclusions in each method.

> **SOFTWARE ENGINEERING TIP**
> Methods are subprograms within classes, so their formatting style parallels that of a class. Their bodies should be indented from the surrounding curly braces.

Declaring parameters (see ParamDecls in Figure 4.8) is similar to declaring variables. Each parameter must be named by an identifier. This parameter name is known as a **formal parameter**, or simply **parameter**. The formal parameter identifies the particular parameter within the body of the method (but nowhere else). The following copySecondTrack method illustrates.

```
/* precondition
        s instantiated AND d instantiated
    modifies
        first track of d
    postcondition
        first track of d == second track of s */
private void copySecondTrack( CDdrive s, CDdrive d ) {
    s.setToFirstTrack();
    s.advanceToNextTrack();
    s.readTrackIntoBuffer();
    d.setToFirstTrack();
    d.writeTrackFromBuffer();
}
```

The `copySecondTrack` method has two formal parameters, named s and d. Both parameters belong to the `CDdrive` class. When this method executes, s and d are assigned their corresponding arguments. Consider the execution of the following method call:

```
copySecondTrack( sourceCD, destinationCD );
```

At the time this method is called, the parameter passage behavior is equivalent to executing these two instructions.

```
s = sourceCD;
d = destinationCD;
```

The resulting execution of the `copySecondTrack` body burns a copy of the second track from s, which is an alias for `sourceCD`, onto the first track of d, an alias for `destinationCD`. If a different call, like the following, is used, then the association of formal parameter to argument is different:

```
copySecondTrack( sourceCD, blankCD );
```

During the execution of this new call instruction, s is assigned `sourceCD` as before, but d is assigned `blankCD`. This has the effect of copying from `sourceCD` onto `blankCD`.

Formal parameters are destroyed following each method execution. Therefore, calling the same method multiple times results in new argument assignments every time with no lingering formal parameter values from previous calls.

As a second example of parameter passage, consider the following `placeFillAndColor` method. This method uses the `AWindow`, `ARectangle`, and `Color` classes described in the previous chapter.

```
/* precondition
        window has been constructed AND
        r has been constructed AND
        c is a valid Color
    modifies
        window, r
    postcondition
        r is set to color c AND r is filled AND r is placed on
        window */
private void placeFillAndColor( ARectangle r, Color c ) {
    r.setToFill();
    r.setColor( c );
    r.place( window );
}
```

The `placeFillAndColor` method has two formal parameters with differing types. The first parameter is an `ARectangle` named r, and the second parameter is a `Color` named c. Figure 4.9 shows the execution of the following method call with three object diagrams. This figure contains an activity diagram followed by three snapshots of the state of computation. These snapshots take place just before, during, and just after the execution of the method that is initiated by the following call:

```
placeFillAndColor( rectangle, Color.green );
```

SOFTWARE ENGINEERING TIP
The code example pictured in Figure 4.9 includes variables called **rectangle** and **window**. It is a common practice to use variable names that are similar to the name of the class to which they belong. The convention of using a lowercase letter at the beginning of a variable and an uppercase letter at the beginning of a class avoids conflicts, even when the same name is used for a variable and its class.

Prior to executing `placeFillAndColor` there are three relevant objects: an `ARectangle` object named `rectangle`, an `AWindow` object named `window`, and a `Color.green` object. When `placeFillAndColor` is called, the two arguments from the call instruction are assigned to the corresponding formal parameters as if the following instructions were executed:

```
r = rectangle;
c = Color.green;
```

Figure 4.9 illustrates the resulting situation by showing that the first parameter (r) is bound to the `rectangle` object, and the second parameter (c) is bound to the `Color.green` object. The resulting execution of the method's second instruction

```
r.setColor( c );
```

causes `rectangle` to be colored green, because both `r` and `rectangle` are bound to the same object. The formal parameters are destroyed when the method returns, so they have been removed from the final snapshot in Figure 4.9.

Figure 4.10 contains a program that uses the `placeFillAndColor` method to draw a window containing three blue squares as shown in the window at the top of the figure. This program includes three call instructions like the one just explained.

Parameter passage adds utility to a method because the same method can be applied to different arguments. The `placeFillAndColor` method is applied to three different `ARectangle` objects in the three squares program.

4.4 LOCAL VARIABLES

Methods are truly subprograms in the sense that each method has its own environment. Each method has its own

- name
- executable body of instructions
- formal parameters

and so on.

SOFTWARE ENGINEERING TIP
Local variables are best suited to situations in which the need for an object is restricted to the execution of a method. Local variables are the preferred alternative to instance variables, whenever either one would work.

Each method can also have its own variables, called **local variables**. Local variables belong to a single method execution, unlike instance variables that belong to the entire object and can be shared by several methods. The syntax of a local variable declaration (described in Figure 4.11) is similar to the syntax for declaring a formal parameter, together with the optional assignment portion.

Figure 4.9 Objects before, during, and after calling `placeFillAndColor`

Activity Diagram (annotated to match object diagrams that follow)

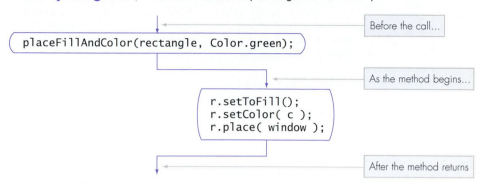

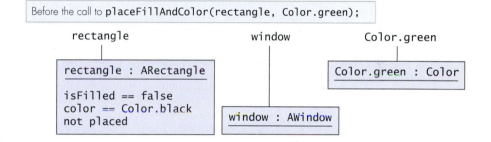

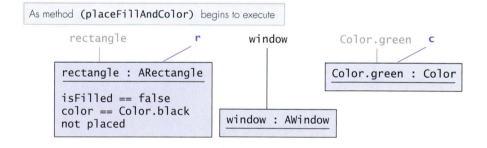

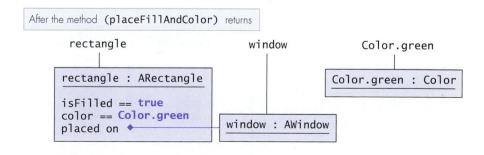

Figure 4.10 Three squares program

```
// Three Squares Program
// Author: David Riley
// Date: May, 2000
import aLibrary.*;
import java.awt.*;

public class Director {
    private AWindow window;
    private ARectangle leftSquare, midSquare, rightSquare;

    /* postcondition
           a window with three blue filled squares is drawn */
    public Director() {
        window = new AWindow(10, 10, 450, 250);
        leftSquare = new ARectangle(100, 100, 50, 50);
        placeFillAndColor(leftSquare, Color.blue);
        midSquare = new ARectangle(200, 100, 50, 50);
        placeFillAndColor(midSquare, Color.blue);
        rightSquare = new ARectangle(300, 100, 50, 50);
        placeFillAndColor(rightSquare, Color.blue);
        window.repaint();
    }


    /* precondition
           window has been constructed AND
           r has been constructed AND
           c is a valid Color
       modifies
           window, r
       postcondition
           r is set to color c AND r is filled AND r is placed on
           window */
    private void placeFillAndColor( ARectangle r, Color c ) {
        r.setToFill();
        r.setColor( c );
        r.place( window );
    }
}
```

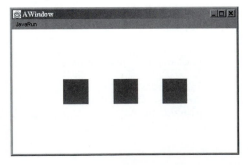

Figure 4.11 LocalVariableDecl description

LocalVariableDecl (a possible *OneStatement*)

Syntax

Semantics

- Executing *LocalVariableDecl* causes each *VariableName* to begin its lifetime. (The lifetime ends when the method returns.)
- If the optional = *Expression* syntax is used, then *Expression* is evaluated and the result is assigned to *VariableName*. If = *Expression* is not included, then *VariableName* is assigned a default value (null for objects).
- The lifetime of *VariableName* ends with the completion of execution of its method.

Notes

- The type of *Expression* must conform to *Type*.
- *Type* can be any accessible class name.

Style notes

- Local variable declarations are best placed immediately after "{".
- Local variable naming conventions should follow the same style as instance variable naming.

If a variable is needed only for the duration of a method's execution, then that variable is an obvious candidate for local declaration. For example, consider the problem of writing a `private` method to draw a happy face, like the one shown in Figure 4.12.

Figure 4.12 A happy face image

Figure 4.13 contains a `private` method to draw such a happy face. This `makeHappyFace` method requires a single parameter that is an `AOval` with a width and height of 100. `makeHappyFace` has four local variables, all belonging to the

AOval class. These local variables are declared in the first statement of the method body. Thereafter, local variables can be used within the method's body in the same way as instance variables. The lifetime of the four local variables comes to an end when makeHappyFace completes its execution. Fortunately, the images that are produced by the variables remain, because they have been placed. (Recall that the place command binds an *aLibrary* object to the object upon which it is placed.)

Figure 4.13 makeHappyFace method

```
/* precondition
        v has been constructed with a radius of 100
    modifies
        window, v
    postcondition
        v is colored yellow AND v is filled
        AND two black eyes are placed on v
        AND a black smile is placed on v */
private void makeHappyFace( AOval v ) {
    AOval leftEye, rightEye, mouth, mouthCover;
    v.setColor( Color.yellow );
    v.setToFill();
    mouth = new AOval( 20, 20, 60, 60 );
    mouth.setToFill();
    mouth.place( v );
    mouthCover = new AOval( -10, -30, 80, 80 );
    mouthCover.setColor(Color.yellow);
    mouthCover.setToFill();
    mouthCover.place(mouth);
    leftEye = new AOval( 20, 30, 15, 15 );
    leftEye.setToFill();
    leftEye.place( v );
    rightEye = new AOval( 65, 30, 15, 15);
    rightEye.setToFill();
    rightEye.place( v );
}
```

Private methods are particularly helpful for applying the same operation to different objects by passing each object as an argument in a separate method call. Figure 4.14 illustrates with a method to create a window with four happy faces. Each of the four calls to the makeHappyFace method passes a different AOval object.

SOFTWARE ENGINEERING TIP

Methods are an effective means for shortening the overall program when repetitive tasks are involved. For example, the program in Figure 4.13 draws four happy faces by calling **makeHappyFace** four times, as opposed to having four similar copies of the code.

Figure 4.14 Director to make four happy faces

```
/* postcondition
        a window with four happy faces is drawn */
public Director() {
    window = new AWindow(10, 10, 230, 230);
    topLeftFace = new AOval(10, 10, 100, 100);
    topLeftFace.place(window);
    makeHappyFace( topLeftFace );
    topRightFace = new AOval(120, 10, 100, 100);
    topRightFace.place(window);
    makeHappyFace( topRightFace );
    botLeftFace = new AOval(10, 120, 100, 100);
    botLeftFace.place(window);
    makeHappyFace( botLeftFace );
    botRightFace = new AOval(120, 120, 100, 100);
    botRightFace.place(window);
    makeHappyFace( botRightFace );
    window.repaint();
}
```

One difference between local variables and instance variables is that each method call creates a *new* set of the method's local variables. These local variables are available to the method throughout the remainder of its execution, and they cease to exist once the method returns. As a result, the execution of the Director method in Figure 4.14 is four separate happy faces with four separate left eyes, four separate right eyes, and four separate mouths.

4.5 NONVOID METHODS

Earlier in this book, calling a method was described as sending a message. One object (sometimes referred to as the "caller object") sends a message to another object (the "called object"). The called object executes its method body and then returns to the caller. Parameter passage provides a mechanism for the caller to share objects (arguments) with the called method.

Java's style of parameter passage is a one-way form of communication in the sense that the caller's actual arguments are assigned to the called object's formal parameters, but the called object cannot alter the binding of any argument. The called method can alter the object that is passed as a parameter, it just cannot pass back a different object. For example, consider the erroneous program in Figure 4.15. When testReturn is called, it is passed an argument (oneOval) that is null. The execution of the testReturn method constructs a new object and binds the formal parameter a to the newly constructed object. However, this new binding has no effect upon oneOval, which is still null. Executing this program results in a run-time error, because oneOval is still null when the place instruction executes.

Figure 4.15 Erroneous attempt to return an object via a parameter

```
/* This program is a vain attempt to return
   a new object via parameter passage. */

import aLibrary.*;
public class Director {
    AWindow window;
    AOval oneOval;

    public Director() {
        AWindow window = new AWindow(10, 10, 400, 500);
        testReturn( oneOval );
        oneOval.place(window); // This line fails.
        win.repaint();
    }

    private void testReturn(AOval a) {
        a = new AOval(10, 10, 20, 20); //This line is useless.
    }
}
```

Fortunately, Java includes a different mechanism that permits methods to return data. Such a method is called a **nonvoid** method. The name nonvoid method stems from a syntax that replaces the "void" with the method's return type (i.e., the name of the class to which the object to be returned by the method belongs). A nonvoid method returns a single object for each call.

Below is an example nonvoid method. The placement of the AOval identifier just after private signifies that aFilledRedCircle is a nonvoid method to return an object of type AOval. Executing aFilledRedCircle causes a new AOval object, called circle, to be instantiated. The method causes circle to be colored red and filled.

SOFTWARE ENGINEERING TIP

Identifiers that represent nouns or noun phrases are best for naming nonvoid methods.

```
private AOval aFilledRedCircle() {
    AOval circle;
    circle = new AOval(0, 0, 20, 20);
    circle.setColor( Color.red );
    circle.setToFill();
    return circle;
}
```

The aFilledRedCircle method above also illustrates the use of a new instruction, namely the **return instruction**. A return instruction is required for every nonvoid method, and the preferred location for a return is the last instruction of the method. Figure 4.16 describes this instruction.

Figure 4.16 NonvoidReturnInstruction description

NonvoidReturnInstruction (a possible *OneStatement*)

Syntax

$$\longrightarrow \text{return} \longrightarrow \boxed{Expression} \longrightarrow ;$$

Notes

- The type of *Expression* must conform to the declared type of the surrounding method.
- Nonvoid methods require a return instruction.

Semantics

Executing *NonvoidReturnInstruction* causes *Expression* to be evaluated and its value returned to the place of the call.

Style Note

It is best to locate a return instruction at the bottom of the method body.

Executing a return instruction results in two actions:

1. *Expression* is evaluated.

2. The method's execution is terminated and the value of *Expression* is returned to the point of the call.

Nonvoid methods are sometimes called **functions**. Just like a mathematical function, a nonvoid method yields a value. Also like a function, nonvoid methods are invoked as expressions. In other words, a nonvoid method is called a bit differently than void methods. The call to a nonvoid method is properly located anywhere in the code where an *Expression* of the method's type is permitted. One good location for such a call is at the right side of an assignment instruction. For example, consider the following instruction:

```
theOval = aFilledRedCircle();
```

When this instruction executes, the `aFilledRed-Circle` method is called. The value of the expression in the subsequent `return` instruction (i.e., a newly instantiated `circle` object) is returned and assigned to `theOval`.

4.6   THIS

The distinction between class and object is subtle. Classes contain methods and their associated code. However, at run time it is *objects* that exist, not classes. So whenever a method is called, the code for that method is applied to an object, even though the instructions are written within the object's class. For example, consider that a `Director` class includes the following instruction.

```
window.repaint();
```

Figure 4.17 contains an object diagram to illustrate this run-time action.

Figure 4.17 `Director` object calling `repaint` on `window` object

The `window` object can be thought of as a run-time *proxy* for the `AWindow` class. A programmer wrote the instructions for the `repaint` method within the `AWindow` class. These instructions are applied to the class's proxy, namely `window`, when the program executes. But how does an instruction refer to the proxy (object) of its own class?

Java includes a special notation to name this otherwise anonymous object. The reserved identifier

```
this
```

always denotes the run-time proxy for the object from the class in which it occurs. So within the code of the `AWindow` class, the `window` object can be referred to as `this` for the duration of the `window.repaint()` instruction call.

Within the `Director` class, the name `this` will always refer to the `Director` object (pictured as an anonymous object in Figure 4.17). One use for such notation is in calling a private method. If the `Director` class contains a private method such as `makeHappyFace` (from Figure 4.13), then it can call this method with the following instruction:

```
this.makeHappyFace(topLeftFace);
```

The previous instruction demonstrates that calling a method within the same class is like sending a message to one's self or applying a method to one's self, because the code for the method is within the same class as the calling object. As shown earlier, Java provides an abbreviated notation for calling private methods without **this**. Using the abbreviated syntax, the previous instruction is written as follows:

```
makeHappyFace(topLeftFace);
```

4.7 INTRODUCTION TO EVENT HANDLING

All of the programs examined thus far can be described as **program-driven code**. As the name implies, program-driven code executes under the control of the program. The execution of each instruction is triggered by the completion of the program's previous instruction.

Program-driven code is not well suited to user interactions. When users strike keys or move the mouse, they expect that these actions will affect the program. However, program-driven code is incapable of the necessary immediate reactions.

A different style of program execution, known as **event-driven code**, is more appropriate for interacting with the user. Event-driven code is essentially reactive, remaining dormant until some action (an **event**) occurs. Typically, an event is the result of some activity on the part of the program's user. Moving a mouse, clicking a mouse button, and striking a key on the keyboard are all examples of events.

In response to an event, the program executes an **event handler**. In Java, event handlers are methods. However, unlike other methods, event handlers do not need to be called from an instruction, because they respond automatically to events.

Object-oriented programming is a natural companion for event handling. Buttons, scrollbars, and even rectangles are objects that support event-driven control. Such objects are largely inactive until the user manipulates them. Events occur in situations such as the following:

- When the mouse is moved from a location outside a rectangle to inside, a mouseEntered event occurs upon the rectangle and a mouseEntered event handler is called.
- When the mouse is positioned over a button and the mouse button is pressed, an actionPerformed event occurs upon the button object, causing actionPerformed to be called.
- When the user drags the scrollbar slider, an adjustmentValueChanged event occurs upon the scrollbar object and the associated adjustmentValueChanged method executes.

aLibrary includes a special class, called A3ButtonWindow, that utilizes event-handling to provide more user control over program execution. This class is very similar to AWindow, except that it has three buttons horizontally arrayed across the bottom. Below is a picture of an A3ButtonWindow object, and Figure 4.18 describes the syntax that is necessary for a Director to make use of A3ButtonWindow.

An A3ButtonWindow object supports three different kinds of events, one event for clicking each of its three buttons. When the LEFT button is clicked, a leftAction event occurs; when the MID button is clicked, a midAction event occurs; and when the RIGHT button is clicked, a rightAction event occurs. To make event handling more convenient, every one of these events is handled by a method with the same name as the associated event. These three methods (event handlers) should be located within a Director class, using the syntax of Figure 4.18.

There are three new requirements for a Director class that wishes to use an A3ButtonWindow object.

1. The public class line of Director must include the following syntax following the class name:

   extends A3ButtonHandler

2. Director must construct an A3ButtonWindow object upon which the user can generate events. The A3ButtonWindow constructor method has a single parameter that must be passed the Director object (this).

3. The Director class must include void parameterless methods for any of three desired event handlers. These methods must be named leftAction, midAction, and rightAction, and each must be specified as public rather than private.

Figure 4.19 contains the class diagram for this kind of Director class. The three event handler methods are illustrated in this diagram. Figure 4.20 contains a sample Director class.

Figure 4.18 DirectorForA3ButtonWindow description

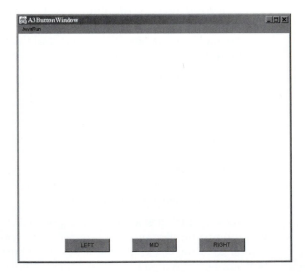

Continued on next page.

DirectorForA3ButtonWindow (abridged version of *Class*)

Syntax

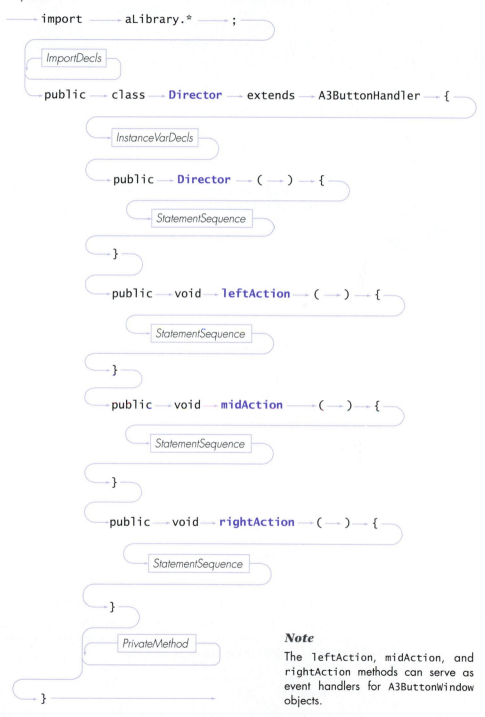

Note

The leftAction, midAction, and rightAction methods can serve as event handlers for A3ButtonWindow objects.

Figure 4.19 Class diagram for Director used with A3ButtonWindow

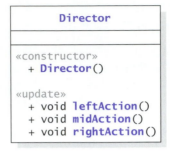

Director
«constructor»   + Director()

«update»
    + void leftAction()
    + void midAction()
    + void rightAction()

CLOSED
Black Box

Event handling via A3ButtonWindow can look like magic at first. As you run the program, every click to one of the three window buttons "magically" calls the corresponding event-handler method. Of course, this isn't really magic; instead, this event handling requires careful coordination by the Java VM and several library classes.

Chapters 8 and 15 explain several of the details that make it possible for A3ButtonWindow to provide for event handling in this way.

It is typical for event-driven programs to begin with a segment of program-driven code to initialize the objects needed to accomplish event handling. In the Figure 4.20 program, the Director method serves to perform this needed initialization. When Director completes, an A3ButtonWindow has been created and an ARectangle object (bound to square) has been placed upon the window.

The instruction that instantiates the object named window deserves extra attention. A3ButtonWindow uses a different constructor method than AWindow. This new constructor has just one parameter; this parameter is required to pass the identity of the object that will handle events for the A3ButtonWindow. Since it is the Director object that contains the event handlers, the A3ButtonWindow constructor call passes this as its argument.

Following the initialization of the Director method, the program execution becomes truly event driven. At this time the program becomes inactive until the user chooses to click on one of the three buttons. If the user clicks on the LEFT button, then an event occurs, and the leftAction method executes as event handler. Similarly, a user click to the MID button generates an automatic call to midAction, and a click on the RIGHT button invokes rightAction. Following the execution of any event handler, the program again becomes inactive, awaiting the next event.

Each event handler from the program in Figure 4.20 is designed to recolor the square object. A leftAction event colors square green, a midAction colors square red, and a rightAction colors square blue.

Figure 4.20 Program to recolor a square

```
// Three Squares Program
// Author: David Riley
// Date: June, 2000
import aLibrary.*;
import java.awt.*;
public class Director extends A3ButtonHandler{
    private A3ButtonWindow window;
    private ARectangle square;

    /* postcondition
            a window with a 100 by 100 filled black square is drawn
            AND button actions control recoloring of the square */
    public Director() {
        window = new A3ButtonWindow(this);
        square = new ARectangle(200, 150, 100, 100);
        square.setToFill();
        square.place(window);
        window.repaint();
    }

    /* precondition
            square is constructed
        modifies
            square
        postcondition
            square is colored green AND square is repainted */
    public void leftAction() {
        square.setColor( Color.green );
        square.repaint();
    }

    /* precondition
            square is constructed
        modifies
            square
        postcondition
            square is colored red AND square is repainted */
    public void midAction() {
        square.setColor( Color.red );
        square.repaint();
    }

    /* precondition
            square is constructed
        modifies
            square
        postcondition
            square is colored blue AND square is repainted */
```

Continued on next page.

```
public void rightAction() {
    square.setColor( Color.blue );
    square.repaint();
}
}
```

The period of program inactivity between consecutive events is actually quite important to the Java Virtual Machine. This apparent "down time" from program execution is used by the Java VM to do such things as update the computer display. The instruction

```
square.repaint();
```

included within each event handler informs the Java VM that the square object needs to be redrawn. Calls to repaint don't ensure immediate screen updates, but they should be included in order to assist the Java VM to properly update the display when it has the opportunity.

4.8   POSTCONDITION NOTATION

A method's postcondition must always reflect the task performed when the method executes. Each postcondition is expressed in the form of an assertion regarding the state of computation at the time that the method returns. Sometimes this state involves instance variables from the class, and sometimes it involves parameters that were passed to the method. For example, the following method is passed an ARectangle; and the method colors its parameter blue, assigns it new dimensions, and places it upon an instance variable, called window. The postcondition reflects all of these changes using the names window and r to refer to the objects that are altered.

```
/* precondition
        r is instantiated
   modifies
        r
   postcondition
        r.color == Color.blue
        AND r.width == 100 AND r.height == 50
        AND r placed upon window */
public void positionColorAndPlace( ARectangle r ) {
    r.setColor( Color.blue );
    r.setSize(100, 50);
    r.place( window );
}
```

It *is* proper for a postcondition to refer to
- formal parameters from its class
- instance variables from its class

However, it *is not* proper for a postcondition to refer to
- arguments passed to the method
- local variables of the method
- local variables of other methods
- inaccessible instance variables of other classes

Parameters are known by their formal parameter names within a method. Therefore, they should also be known by their formal parameter names within the *precondition*, *modifies* clause, and *postcondition*. The arguments that are passed to these parameters are determined by the calling code and should not appear anywhere in the postcondition or precondition.

When a method returns, all of its local variables are eliminated and are no longer available at the time the postcondition applies. Similarly, local variables from other procedures and inaccessible instance variables are not available for use within a method, so they also shouldn't be used within the method's postcondition (or precondition).

Nonvoid methods have another object that must play a role in their postcondition, namely the object returned by the method. This book uses the convention of calling this object `result`. For example, a method that returns an `int` value that is double its parameter can be expressed with the following postcondition.

```
/* postcondition
        result == k * 2 */
public int parameterDoubled( int k ) { ... }
```

Since `result` is a name for the object returned, it is proper to use `result.` as a prefix to attributes of the return object. For example, consider the following method:

```
/* postcondition
        result.x == 100 AND result.y == 20
        AND result.width == 5 AND result.height == 5
        AND result.color == Color.black */
public ARectangle newBlackSquare() { ... }
```

The notation `result.x` refers to the x coordinate of the `result` object. So the above postcondition describes that the `ARectangle` returned by the method has an upper-left corner at (100, 20), is a square with 5 pixels on each side, and is colored black.

When a method must instantiate a new object to be returned, some programmers find it convenient to name this object as a local variable called `result`. This is the one time when a local variable makes sense in a postcondition. Following is a `newBlackSquare` method that illustrates using `result` for a local variable.

SOFTWARE ENGINEERING TIP

The name **result** should be avoided as a variable name. One acceptable exception is for a nonvoid method that instantiates the object it returns. In such cases the name **result** may be used for a local variable bound to the return object.

```
/* postcondition
        result.x == 100 AND result.y == 20
        AND result.width == 5 AND result.height == 5
        AND result.Color == Color.black */
public ARectangle newBlackSquare() {
    ARectangle result;
    result = new ARectangle(100, 20, 5, 5);
    result.setColor( Color.black );
    return result;
}
```

Sometimes postconditions must refer to previous values of a parameter of an instance variable. For example, imagine a program to maintain the credit-card balance and a method called chargeIt to post a new charge to your account. The primary impact of posting a new charge is to add this new charge to your account, thereby increasing the amount due. One way to denote a postcondition for such alterations is illustrated as follows:

```
/* modifies
        amountDue
    postcondition
        amountDue == old amountDue + newCharge */
public void chargeIt( int newCharge ) { ... }
```

> ## SOFTWARE ENGINEERING TIP
> Previous value notations are necessary for expressing many specifications. In this text the notation
>
>   old *expression*
>
> denotes the value of *expression* at the time the method is *called*. The old notation is only needed within postconditions, and should be used only when required.

The postcondition for chargeIt uses **old** as an expression prefix. This use of old is called a **previous value** notation, because the old expression denotes the value of the prefixed expression from the time the method *begins* to execute. Any postcondition expression without an old is referring to the expression's state at the *end* of the method execution. Therefore, chargeIt's postcondition describes that the resultant amount due consists of the amount due prior to executing the method plus the value of the newCharge parameter.

4.9   A DESIGN EXAMPLE USING AVIEW

This section explores the design of a particular program to draw and manipulate coffee cups. Several of the concepts of this chapter are revisited along the way. The particular software requirements for this program are explained in Figure 4.21.

From these requirements three objects are evident:

1. a window of type A3ButtonWindow

2. a red coffee cup

3. a blue coffee cup

Furthermore, the use of A3ButtonWindow dictates syntax for Director that follows the form shown in Figure 4.18.

Figure 4.21 Requirements for the coffee cup program

Initial State

The program displays an A3ButtonWindow object containing two coffee cups. Both cups are roughly 40 pixels wide and 20 pixels high. One coffee cup is centered near the top of the window and colored red. The second coffee cup is centered just above the MID button and is colored blue.

LEFT

Every time the LEFT button is clicked, the red coffee cup moves downward by five pixels and the blue coffee cup moves upward by five pixels.

MID

Every time the MID button is clicked, the two coffee cups are relocated to their positions from the initial state.

RIGHT

Every time the RIGHT button is clicked, the red coffee cup moves to its left by 10 pixels and the blue coffee cup moves to its right by 10 pixels.

One of the key parts of the design for this program will be the code to draw a coffee cup of the shape shown in the picture above. Because this task is nontrivial, it is reasonable to design a separate method to construct a cup object. It is also wise to use a nonvoid method to return the cup as a single graphical unit.

The coffee cup picture seems to be a composition of three ovals: a black filled oval for the top of the cup, a colored oval for the handle, and a portion of a filled colored oval for the cup body. There are two difficulties in drawing this image:

1. Grouping the three ovals into a single graphical unit

2. Clipping off the top and bottom of the oval that forms the body of the cup

Both of these difficulties can be solved with a new *aLibrary* class, called AView.[2]

---

[2]The standard *awt* and *swing* libraries contain classes with similar purpose to AView. The corresponding *awt* class is called Container and the corresponding *swing* class is called JComponent.

Figure 4.22 is a class diagram for `AView`.

An `AView` object is very much like an `ARectangle`. The major difference is that an `AView` object is completely transparent. The `AView` methods duplicate `ARectangle` methods with the same behavior. Since an `AView` is invisible, there is no need to include methods such as `setColor`, `setToFill`, or `setToOutline`.

Figure 4.22 AView class diagram

```
AView
------------------------------
  - int x
  - int y
  - int width
  - int height
------------------------------
«constructor»
  + AView()
  + AView(int, int, int, int)
  ...

«update»
  + void repaint()
  + void setSize(int, int)
  + void setLocation(int, int)
  + void place(Container)
  + void translate(double, double)
  ...
```

`AView` objects are intended for use as backgrounds upon which to place other *aLibrary* objects. An `AView` is also like an `ARectangle` in the sense that any objects placed upon an `AView` are clipped to the `AView` boundaries. This clipping is helpful for drawing the body of the coffee cup. Executing the code segment below places an `AOval` on an `AView` so that it overlaps the top and bottom.

```
cupBackground = new AView(0, 5, 30, 15);
cup = new AOval(0, -18, 30, 35);
cup.setToFill();
cup.place(cupBackground);
```

The result of executing this code is pictured in Figure 4.23. Only the portion of the `cup` object that is shown in blue is actually visible, since the gray portions lie outside of the `AView` named `cupBackground`.

`AView` objects are also a good way to group other *aLibrary* objects into a single graphical object. The complete coffee cup image consists of the `AView` shown in Figure 4.23 along with an `AOval` cup handle and an `AOval` for the top of the cup. If all three of these parts of the coffee cup are placed upon the same underlying `AView`, they behave as a group.

Figure 4.23 A cupAOval placed upon cupBackground (an AView)

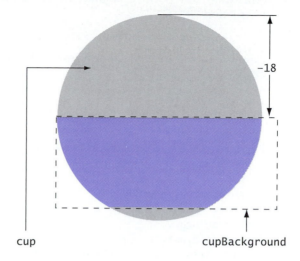

cup   cupBackground

A complete Director class for this program is shown in Figure 4.24. The work of constructing a coffee cup is performed by a method called newCup. This method instantiates and returns an AView object upon which all of the parts of the coffee cup have been placed. The parameter of the newCup method determines the color of the cup, so that the same method can be used to create different colored cups. In this program newCup is called once to create the red cup and once for the blue cup.

There are five local variables declared in newCup. The background variable represents the AView upon which the coffee cup is constructed. Additional local variables are used for the individual parts of the cup. These variables are properly declared to be local to newCup because they are not used elsewhere in the program.

One of the advantages of placing *aLibrary* objects upon an underlying object is that they can be moved around as a unit. In the Figure 4.24 program, the red coffee cup is placed upon an AWindow and then moved into place with the following two instructions.

```
redCup.place(window);
redCup.setLocation(280, 10);
```

The second instruction repositions the AView object named redCup. The cup body, handle, and top are moved along with their underlying AView. The blueCup is positioned in the same way.

Moving the cups, as required for clicks of the LEFT and RIGHT buttons, is accomplished using an AView method called translate. The translate method is available in many of the *aLibrary* classes, but was not discussed previously because it wasn't needed. This method has two numeric parameters. (double is a type permitting arguments with decimal points in addition to integers.) When translate is called, the graphical object changes its position by distances determined by its parameters. The first parameter determines horizontal movement (positive arguments produce right movement and negative produce left movement). The second parameter determines vertical movement upward (for negative arguments) or downward (for positive arguments). As shown in the program, the following instruction

```
redCup.translate(0, 5);
```

causes the red cup to move downward by five pixels. Likewise, the instruction below

```
blueCup.translate(10, 0);
```

causes the blue cup to move to its right by 10 pixels.

Figure 4.24 A program to draw two coffee cups

```
// Coffee Cups Program
// Author: David Riley
// Date: August, 2000
import aLibrary.*;
import java.awt.*;
public class Director extends A3ButtonHandler {
    private A3ButtonWindow window;
    private AView redCup, blueCup;

    /* postcondition
            a window is created with two cups
            (a red one above a blue one) */
    public Director() {
        window = new A3ButtonWindow(this);
        redCup = newCup(Color.red);
        redCup.place(window);
        redCup.setLocation(280, 10);
        blueCup = newCup(Color.blue);
        blueCup.place(window);
        blueCup.setLocation(280, 420);
        window.repaint();
    }

    /* postcondition
            result is a new AView with a coffee cup
                colored c placed on top
            AND result.width == 40 AND result.height == 20 */
    public AView newCup(Color c) {
        AView background, cupBackground;
        AOval cup, handle, top;
        background = new AView(0, 0, 40, 20);
        handle = new AOval(28, 1, 8, 12);
        handle.setColor(c);
        handle.place(background);
        cupBackground = new AView(0, 5, 30, 15);
        cup = new AOval(0, -18, 30, 35);
        cup.setColor(c);
        cup.setToFill();
        cup.place(cupBackground);
```

```
            cupBackground.place(background);
            top = new AOval(0, 1, 30, 6);
            top.setToFill();
            top.place(background);
            return background;
        }


    /* precondition
            redCup instantiated AND blueCup instantiated
       modifies
            redCup, blueCup
       postcondition
            redCup.y == old redCup.y + 5
            AND blueCup.y == old blueCup.y - 5 */
    public void leftAction() {
        redCup.translate(0, 5);
        redCup.repaint();
        blueCup.translate(0, -5);
        blueCup.repaint();
    }


    /* precondition
            redCup instantiated AND blueCup instantiated
       modifies
            redCup, blueCup
       postcondition
            a new redCup is repositioned at the top center of
                window
            AND a new blueCup is repositioned at the bottom center
                of window */
    public void midAction() {
        redCup.setLocation(280, 10);
        redCup.repaint();
        blueCup.setLocation(280, 420);
        blueCup.repaint();
    }


    /* precondition
            redCup instantiated AND blueCup instantiated
       modifies
            redCup, blueCup
       postcondition
            redCup.x == old redCup.x - 10
            AND blueCup.x == old blueCup.x + 10 */
    public void rightAction() {
        redCup.translate(-10, 0);
        redCup.repaint();
        blueCup.translate(10, 0);
        blueCup.repaint();
    }
}
```

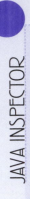

JAVA INSPECTOR

Below is a collection of hints on what to check when examining code that involves the concepts of this chapter.

✓ Methods that are too long become difficult to read. Check for methods that are longer than one computer screen. Find a way to break up long methods into logical pieces.

✓ The `public` and `private` prefixes should be checked so that most things are `private`. The exceptions for now are the `Director` class, the `Director` constructor method, and the `leftAction`, `midAction`, and `rightAction` event handlers.

✓ Remember to include the `void` type when declaring methods that aren't functions. A quick scan can detect missing the missing `void`. Don't forget that constructor methods, like `Director`, must *not* include void.

✓ Always check method call instructions to be certain that their argument lists match the parameter list in number, type, and order.

✓ Nonvoid methods should be called by an expression within an instruction, unlike void methods, where the call is a complete instruction.

✓ Remember to include a `return` instruction in the body of all nonvoid methods.

✓ When using `A3ButtonWindow` objects, ask three questions:

1. Is extends `A3ButtonHandler` included as a suffix on the `public class` line of `Director`?
2. Are the `leftAction`, `midAction`, and `rightAction` parameterless void methods included in `Director`?
3. Does the `Director` code construct an `A3ButtonWindow` object passing `this` as an argument?

✓ When using graphical images, each event handler method should be reviewed to ensure that `repaint` is called for any displayed object whose appearance has changed.

A3ButtonWindow

activity diagram

AView

body (of a method)

buffer

divide and conquer

event

event-driven code

event handler

formal parameter

function

local variable

old (postcondition
   clause notation)

method call

method invocation

nonvoid method

parameter

parameter passage

previous value
   (postcondition clause
   notation)

private (method)

program-driven code

public (method)

return

return instruction

result (postcondition
   clause notation)

subprogram

this (reserved word)

1. Which of the following should be declared using `public` and which declared using `private`?

   a. the `Director` class

   b. the `Director` constructor method

   c. the `leftAction` method

   d. any instance variable of the `Director` class

   e. private methods of the `Director` class that aren't event handlers

2. Below are three parameterless methods that are included within your `Director` class.

```
private void makeRedDot() {
    circle.setColor( Color.red );
    circle.setToFill();
}
private void drawGraySquare() {
    ARectangle graySquare;
    graySquare = new ARectangle( 20, 20, 50, 50 );
    graySquare.setColor( Color.gray );
    graySquare.place( window );
}
private void makeSpottedView() {
    AOval spot;
    spottedView = new AView(0, 0, 100, 100);
    spot = new AOval( 30, 30, 20, 20 );
    spot.setToFill();
    spot.setColor( Color.red );
    spot.place( spottedView );
}
```

a. Each of these methods makes use of an instance variable that *must* be declared in Director. Name each instance variable.

b. Draw a picture of the window that results from executing the following code. (Assume that window is declared to be an instance variable of type AWindow.)

```java
public Director() {
    window = new AWindow( 10, 10, 500, 500 );
    drawGraySquare();
    makeSpottedView();
    spottedView.place( window );
    window.repaint();
}
```

c. Draw a picture of the window that results from executing the following code. (Assume that window is an AWindow instance variable and that circle is an AOval instance variable.)

```java
public Director() {
    window = new AWindow( 10, 10, 500, 500 );
    makeSpottedView();
    drawGraySquare();
    spottedView.place( window );
    circle = new AOval( 20, 20, 50, 50 );
    circle.place( window );
    makeRedDot();
    window.repaint();
}
```

d. What happens at run time when the program from part (c) is modified to remove the two instructions involving circle?

3. Use the following private method to complete parts (a) through (d).

```java
private void makeGreenBorderedDot( int x, int y, AWindow w ) {
    AOval dot, border;
    dot = new AOval(x, y, 100, 100);
    dot.setColor( Color.green );
    dot.setToFill();
    dot.place( w );
    border = new AOval( 0, 0, 100, 100 );
    border.place( dot );
}
```

a. Assuming that window is an AWindow instance variable, explain why the Java compiler detects a syntax error in each of the following instructions.

```java
makeGreenBorderedDot();
makeGreenBorderedDot( 20, 20 );
makeGreenBorderedDot( 20, window, 20 );
```

b. Show the results of executing the following code. (Assume that window is an AWindow instance variable.)

```
public Director() {
    window = new AWindow( 10, 10, 300, 300 );
    makeGreenBorderedDot( 20, 20, window );
    makeGreenBorderedDot( 150, 0, window );
    makeGreenBorderedDot( 80, 80, window );
    window.repaint();
}
```

c. Explain the run-time error that results from executing the following code. (Assume that window is an AWindow instance variable.)

```
public Director() {
    makeGreenBorderedDot( 20, 20, window );
}
```

d. Rewrite the following code to produce an equivalent method without using this. (Assume that window is an AWindow instance variable.)

```
public Director() {
    window = new AWindow( 10, 10, 300, 300 );
    this.makeGreenBorderedDot( 50, 50, window );
    this.makeGreenBorderedDot( 100, 100, window );
    window.repaint();
}
```

4. Use the following private method to complete parts (a) through (c). (Recall that s*2 denotes s multiplied by 2 and s*3 means s times 3.)

```
private AView makeChex( int s ) {
    ARectangle leftSquare, rightSquare, topSquare, bottomSquare;
    AView result;
    leftSquare = new ARectangle( 0, s, s, s );
    leftSquare.setToFill();
    rightSquare = new ARectangle( s*2, s, s, s );
    rightSquare.setToFill();
    topSquare = new ARectangle( s, 0, s, s );
    topSquare.setToFill();
    bottomSquare = new ARectangle( s, s*2, s, s );
    bottomSquare.setToFill();
    result = new AView( 0, 0, s*3, s*3 );
    leftSquare.place(result);
    rightSquare.place(result);
    topSquare.place(result);
    bottomSquare.place(result);
    return result;
}
```

a. Assuming that the only two instance variables are `window` (belonging to `AWindow`) and `view` (belonging to `AView`), explain why the Java compiler detects a syntax error in each of the following instructions:

```
window = makeChex( 100 );
view = makeChex( 100, view );
view = makeChex( s );
```

b. Assuming that the only two instance variables are `window` (belonging to `AWindow`) and `view` (belonging to `AView`), explain why the following instruction is wrong. (Incidentally, the Java compiler will *not* detect this as an error.)

```
makeChex( 100 );
```

c. Show the results of executing the following code. (Assume that `window` is an `AWindow` instance variable and `smallView` and `largeView` are `AView` instance variables.)

```
public Director() {
    window = new AWindow( 10, 10, 270, 270 );
    largeView = makeChex( 90 );
    largeView.place( window );
    smallView = makeChex( 30 );
    smallView.place( window );
    window.repaint();
}
```

5. Consider the following program in which `myVar` is declared as both an instance variable and a local variable of the `Director` method.

```
// Example of the meaning of this
public class Director {
    private int myVar = 1;
    public Director() {
        int myVar = 2;
        System.out.println( myVar );
        System.out.println( this.myVar );
    }
}
```

a. What do you expect this program to output when it executes?

b. Test your answer to part (a) by running the program.

c. Explain the behavior of this program by discussing the difference between `myVar` and `this.myVar`.

6. Explain each of the following postconditions in a few English sentences:

a.
```
/* postcondition
       result == a + b */
public int mysteryMethod1(int a, int b) { ... }
```

b. ```
    /* precondition
             spot1 and spot2 are both instantiated
        modifies
            spot1, spot2
        postcondition
            spot1 == old spot2
            AND spot2 == old spot1 */
    public void mysteryMethod2(AOval spot1, AOval spot2) { ... }
    ```

c.  ```
    /* precondition
             spot1 and spot2 are both instantiated
        modifies
            spot1, spot2
        postcondition
            spot1.width == old spot1.width - 1
            AND spot2.Color == Color.green */
    public void mysteryMethod3(AOval spot1, AOval spot2) { ... }
    ```

7. Below is a Director class that is suppose to create a circle on an
    A3ButtonWindow and allow the user to halve the size of the circle by clicking
    the left button and double the size of the circle by clicking the right button.
    (Note that the two scale method calls correctly accomplish these respective
    tasks.) This code contains several errors. Fix them.

    ```
    import aLibrary.*;
    import java.awt.*;
    public class Director extends A3ButtonHandler{
        private A3ButtonWindow window;
        private AOval circle;
        /* postcondition
                 a window with a 100 by 100 black circle is drawn */
        public Director() {
            window = new AWindow();
            circle.place(window);
            window.repaint();
        }
        /* precondition
                 circle is instantiated
            modifies
                 circle
            postcondition
                 circle is half the size of old circle */
        public void leftAction() {
            circle.scale( 0.5, 0.5 );
            circle.repaint();
        }
    ```

```
/* precondition
      circle is instantiated
   modifies
         circle
   postcondition
         circle is double the size of old circle */
public void rightEventHandler() {
    circle.scale( 2, 2 );
    circle.repaint();
}
}
```

PROGRAMMING EXERCISES

1. A seven-segment display is sometimes used in devices such as calculators to display decimal digits (0-9). The concept of a seven-segment display is to use seven bars arranged as shown in the window below. By lighting some of the seven bars, and not others, any digit can be displayed in a legible form. (The window below displays the digit 8 by lighting all seven bars.)

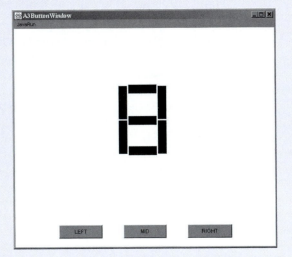

Write a program that uses this concept together with A3ButtonWindow so that initially the program displays the "8" digit with black bars as shown above. Thereafter, the buttons behave as follows:

LEFT   Causes the digit to become a "2" with all bars colored red.

MID   Causes the digit to become a "7" with all bars colored orange.

RIGHT   Causes the entire digit to move to the right by two pixels. (*Hint*: Using an AView background and the `translate` method makes this easier.)

Include the use of the following private methods in your program:

`removeAllBars()`   To remove all seven bars from their placement.

`colorBars( Color )`   To recolor all seven bars to the color of the method's argument.

2. Write a method that returns a symbol that looks like a U.S. Interstate sign, similar to the one shown in the upper-left corner of the window below. (This sign has a blue bottom and a red border across the top.) This method needs two parameters to pass the coordinates of the upper-left corner of the road sign. Call your method appropriately to fill the window with the eight signs as arranged below.

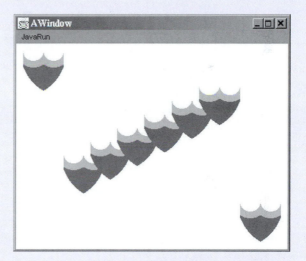

3. Write a program to utilize an `A3ButtonWindow`, and use other private methods efficiently. Initially your program should draw four log cabin quilt blocks all centered in the middle of the window. A log cabin block consists of nine rectangles arranged and sized as shown below. Each of your blocks should consist of eight `ARectangle` objects with a center that is blank (contains nothing). You may color all of the blocks as you choose with three restrictions: (1) all blocks must be filled; (2) no two blocks that touch on their sides may have the same color; and (3) the leftmost block is red for one block, black for another block, dark gray for one block, and light gray for the

remaining block. When all blocks are placed initially, only one block is visible, because they are all placed on top of each other. The button clicks should behave as follows:

LEFT   Each of the four quilt blocks must move two pixels closer to their respective corners. Note that if the center of each quilt block is empty, the blocks underneath should show through as they move.

MID   This button does nothing.

RIGHT   This button should cause each quilt block to move in the opposite direction as the LEFT button.

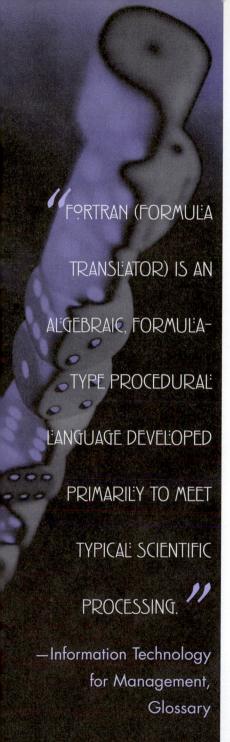

CHAPTER 5

NUMERIC PROCESSING

"FORTRAN (FORMULA TRANSLATOR) IS AN ALGEBRAIC, FORMULA-TYPE PROCEDURAL LANGUAGE DEVELOPED PRIMARILY TO MEET TYPICAL SCIENTIFIC PROCESSING."

—Information Technology for Management, Glossary

OBJECTIVES

- To explore the similarities among and differences between primitive types and reference types

- To examine integer data types, including `int`, `short`, `byte`, and `long`

- To examine real data types, including `double` and `float`

- To examine the order in which numeric expressions are evaluated at execution time

- To explore mixed-type numeric expressions and the use of casting

- To introduce the `Math` library class and some of its more useful methods and constants

- To demonstrate how to create numeric constants and nonvoid primitive methods in Java

- To examine a few common numeric expression/instruction patterns

Numbers have always played a key role in computer programming. In the earliest programming languages, the instructions themselves were numbers. Today, computers frequently manipulate numeric data, whether that data represents scientific formulas, accounting ledger information, or engineering calculations.

5.1   PRIMITIVE TYPES

Object-oriented programming makes use of data in many forms. All instance variables and local variables presented thus far in this text have been of **reference type**. Reference type variables belong to classes. The name "reference" derives from the fact that a variable of this type *refers* (is bound) to its object.

There are eight Java data types that are too simple to require the overhead of a class. These "simpler" data types are called **primitive types**. Primitive types have three characteristics that distinguish them from reference types.

1. Primitive types are *atomic* in the sense that they contain no attributes (instance variables).
2. Primitive types are *built into* the Java language, requiring no external class.
3. A primitive variable represents a *value*, rather than an object binding.

The complete list of primitive types is given in Figure 5.1. As the names in this figure imply, the majority of the primitive types are devoted to storing numbers.

Figure 5.1 The primitive data types

```
boolean                          float
byte                             int
char                             long
double                           short
```

Primitive types are similar to classes, since programs can use them to specify the types of instance variables, local variables, parameters, and methods. However, primitive type data have key differences, mostly related to efficiencies that can result from the simpler, built-in types. These differences will become clearer as the types are examined.

5.2   PRIMITIVE INTEGER DATA TYPES

The int **data type** is arguably the most commonly used Java data type for integer data. (This data type was encountered previously as a parameter type for such methods as setLocation and setSize.) A variable of type int can store any non-negative or negative integer with nine or fewer digits. Figure 5.2 contains a summary of int and describes the key characteristics of the int data type. The name of the type, int, can be used to declare the type of an instance variable, a local variable, a parameter, or the return type of a method.

Figure 5.2 Summary of the int data type (operators abridged)

Name of the type: int

Usage:

An int is an integer within the range from –2,147,483,648 through 2,147,483,647

Constants:

Any consecutive sequence of nine or fewer decimal digits (0–9) optionally preceded by a "+" or "–" symbol.

Prefix Operator (int → int)

[++ and –– cannot be applied to constants or constant expressions.]

syntax	*semantics*
–	negation
++	autoincrement
––	autodecrement

Infix Arithmetic Operators (int × int → int)

syntax	*semantics*
+	addition
–	subtraction
*	multiplication
/	division (quotient)
%	remainder after integer division (modulo)

Infix Relational Operators (int × int → boolean)

syntax	*semantics*
==	equal to
!=	not equal to
<	less than
<=	less than or equal to
>	greater than
>=	greater than or equal to

Postfix Operator (int → int)

[++ and –– cannot be applied to constants or constant expressions.]

syntax	*semantics*
++	autoincrement
––	autodecrement

A **constant**, also called a **literal**, is a single value of the primitive type that is acceptable Java notation. For example, Java permits all of the following as int constants.

```
      73
+64710
       0
      -3
```

The Java syntax for constants is generally similar, but not identical, to common mathematical notations. In the case of int constants, blanks and/or commas are *not* permitted within a constant, even though such notations are frequently used for everyday communication among people.

The following are illegal constant attempts:

```
1,000,025 //commas not permitted within constant
6 521 //white space not permitted within constant
```

Figure 5.2 contains only a partial listing of int operators. Each operation is described in terms of its syntax and mapping. A **prefix operator** is an operator that syntactically precedes the expression to which it applies. For example, any integer expression may be preceded by a minus sign (–) to cause the expression to be negated.

The proper syntax for an **infix operator** is to place it *between* its operands. For example, adding the integer 25 to 3 is denoted as follows in Java:

```
25 + 3
```

Postfix operators must be placed *after* the expression to which they apply. Java has two common postfix operators (autoincrement and autodecrement). These operators can be applied to variables to increase (autoincrement) the variable's value by 1 or decrease (autodecrement) the variable's value by 1.

Figure 5.3 summarizes the syntax of expressions of int type. This syntax diagram includes operators and constants that were described previously in Figure 5.2.

Many of the Java int expressions borrow their notation from common arithmetic expressions. Below are two examples:

```
17 + 3 / 2
(25 + 14) * (80021 - 3422)
```

The asterisk (*) symbol denotes multiplication, and the slash (/) denotes integer division. An integer division results from dividing two integer expressions, and the result of an integer division is an integer quotient. Therefore, the expression

```
17 / 3 evaluates to  5
```

and the expression

```
-5 / 4 evaluates to  -1
```

When the % operation is applied to two positive integers, the result is the remainder of an integer division. Therefore, the expression

```
17 % 3 evaluates to  2
```

Figure 5.3 IntExpression syntax

IntExpression (abridged version of *Expression*)

Syntax

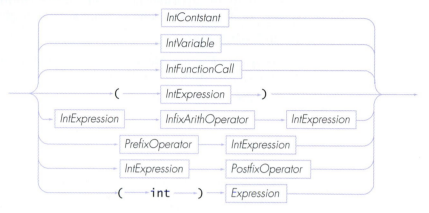

Negative operands do not change the magnitude of the result of evaluating an % expression, and the result of the expression will have the same sign as the first operand. The examples below illustrate.

```
-17 %  3    evaluates to  -2
 17 % -3    evaluates to   2
-17 % -3    evaluates to  -2
```

Assignment instructions can be used to assign values to int variables. Three example assignment instructions are listed below. (The identifiers must be declared as int variables.)

```
slicesOfBread = 24 * 10;          assigns 240 to slicesOfBread
jarsOfJelly = 100 + 1000;         assigns 1100 to jarsOfJelly
quartsOfMilk = 2000 - 2016;       assigns -16 to quartsOfMilk
```

If an int variable is used within an expression, then the variable's value is substituted for the variable when the expression evaluates. Consider the following instruction sequence:

```
dereksAge = 19;
kasandrasAge = dereksAge + 2;
```

When the second instruction executes, the value of dereksAge (19) is added to 2 in order to assign kasandrasAge the value 21.

Frequently, instructions are used to alter the existing value of an int variable. For example, executing the following instruction doubles the value of a variable.

```
cupsOfYogurt = cupsOfYogurt * 2;
```

Similarly, the following instruction decreases the value of jarsOfPeanutButter by 1.

```
jarsOfPeanutButter = jarsOfPeanutButter - 1;
```

Java supports an alternative notation for decrementing by 1. Below is another Java instruction that has the same behavior as the one above.

```
jarsOfPeanutButter--;
```

The ++ symbol also provides a more abbreviated notation for incrementing by 1. For example, executing the instruction

```
sandrasAge = sandrasAge + 1;
```

has the same result as executing

```
sandrasAge++;
```

The evaluation of Java int expressions follows rules that define the order in which operators are performed. For example, the int expression

```
7 + 9 / 2
```

evaluates to 11, because 9/2 is evaluated prior to the "+" operation. The order in which operations are performed depends upon the **precedence** of the associated operators. Operators with higher precedence are performed before operators with lower precedence. In the preceding expression the "/" operator has higher precedence than "+".

Expression evaluation also depends upon the order in which equal precedence operators appear. For example, the expression

```
6 * 2 / 3
```

evaluates to 4 (the correct answer) if "*" is performed first, and 0 (incorrect) if "/" is performed first. With just a few exceptions, Java operators of equal precedence are performed left to right. Figure 5.4 contains a table of the important int operators, their precedence, and the order in which they are performed. Appendix C contains a more complete listing.

Figure 5.4 Precedence of selected int operators

Precedence	Operator	Operation	Order within
highest	--	postfix autodecrement	left to right
	++	postfix autoincrement	
second highest	--	prefix autodecrement	
	++	prefix autoincrement	right to left
	-	unary minus	
mid	/	division	
	*	multiplication	left to right
	%	remainder	
lowest	+	addition	left to right
	-	subtraction	

Java also allows parentheses within `int` expressions. When parentheses are used, the expressions within are evaluated prior to their adjacent operators. Parentheses take priority over precedence. For example, the following expression evaluates the average (mean) of its two `int` variables, because the addition is performed before the division:

```
(dereksAge + kasandrasAge) / 2
```

There are three other Java data types for integers. They are named `byte`, `short`, and `long`. The differences between the four integer types can be found in the amount of computer storage required for each and, correspondingly, the range of integer values that can be assigned to each. Figure 5.5 summarizes these differences. For example, a variable of type `byte` requires a quarter of the memory space needed to store a variable of type `int`. However, a `byte` variable is restricted to storing values within the range from –128 through 128. The same operators are supported by all four integer data types.

Figure 5.5 Summary of Java integer data types

Type	Storage Size	Minimum Value	Maximum Value
byte	8 bits	–128	127
short	16 bits	–32,768	32,767
int	32 bits	–2,147,483,648	2,147,483,647
long	64 bits	–9,223,372,036,854,775,808	9,223,372,036,854,775,807

5.3 DIFFERENCES BETWEEN PRIMITIVES AND REFERENCES

Data of primitive type often exhibits behavior that appears to be different from the behavior of reference data. In fact, data of either type can be thought of as objects, but there are differences between primitive objects and nonprimitives (reference objects).

Examining how each type of data is stored inside a computer gives insight into the differences. Every variable of primitive type is associated with its own cell of computer memory. From the previous discussion of integer data types it should be clear that the size of the memory cell depends upon the particular type. An `int` variable occupies a memory cell that is 32 bits long, while a `long` variable requires a 64-bit cell. This association between variable and memory cell does *not* require a `new` operation. In fact the `new` operation is not permitted on primitive data. For example, consider the following local variable declaration:

```
int carCount;
```

This declaration causes `carCount` to begin its lifetime, and the variable is immediately associated with a 32-bit memory cell, as pictured by the rectangle below.

carCount   [0]

Notice that the rectangle (memory cell) in the previous picture appears to have a value of zero (0). The value in the memory cell contains what the programmer thinks to be the "value of the variable." Memory cells always store some value, and Java has rules that govern the initialization of variables in certain cases. However, it is generally advisable for the program to assign its own initial values. The following instruction illustrates such an assignment.

```
carCount = 35;
```

The outcome of executing this instruction is pictured below.

carCount | 35 |

This association of a variable name to a particular memory cell will not change throughout the lifetime of the instance variable. Furthermore, no two variables share the same memory cell.

When a primitive variable is used within an expression, the variable evaluates to its cell content (variable value). Therefore, executing the third instruction in the following instruction sequence causes vehicleCount to be assigned the value 100 (the sum of the values of carCount and truckCount):

```
carCount = 35;
truckCount = 65;
vehicleCount = carCount + truckCount;
```

Parameter passage of primitive data is also impacted by this memory cell association. Java uses a style of parameter passage that is formally known as **parameter passage by value**. In parameter passage by value, each of formal parameter behaves like a local variable that receives a copy of the *value* of its corresponding argument at the time a method is called. For example, consider the following private method.

```
/* require
        fRect is constructed AND sRect is constructed
    modifies
        fRect, sRect
    postcondition
        fRect is moved d pixels to the right
        AND sRect is moved d/2 pixels to the right */
private void slideRects(int d, ARectangle fRect, ARectangle sRect)
{
    fRect.translate( d, 0 );
    d = d / 2;
    sRect.translate( d, 0 );
}
```

Suppose that the above method is called as follows:

```
slideRects( velocity, blueRectangle, greenRectangle);
```

When this call executes, the formal parameter d receives a copy of the value of velocity. Since there is no further interaction between argument and parameter, velocity will not change value by executing slideRects, even though d changes value.

In reality, there is no difference between primitive data parameter passage and reference parameter passage in Java. In both cases, parameter passage is implemented at call time by executing the equivalent of assignment instructions, assigning each argument to its corresponding formal parameter.

Every reference variable is also associated with its own cell of memory. The cell of the reference variable stores the **address** of the object that is bound to the variable. When a reference variable is first declared, its cell stores null, which is the address of nothing. When one reference variable is assigned to another, the value (address) is copied, so both variables are bound to the same object. In reference parameter passage a copy of the argument's value (an object address) is assigned to the formal parameter. This is why the method cannot alter the binding of an argument.

5.4   REAL NUMBERS (FLOAT AND DOUBLE TYPES)

Integer data types are incapable of storing numbers that require nonwhole parts. Mathematicians use a class of numbers, known as **real numbers,** to include values that lie between consecutive integer values. The number 3.2 is an example of a real number that is not an integer.

Java includes two primitive data types for storing real number values. These types are known as double and float. Figure 5.6 describes the double data type.

The operations that Java supports on real expressions are essentially the same as those for integer expressions. Figure 5.6 points out that all of the int operators, excepting %, can also be applied to double operands. Of course, double operations produce real-numbered results, so the division operator (/) performs real number division when applied to double expressions.

Figure 5.6 Summary of the double data type (operators abridged)

Name of the type: double

Usage:

A double is a real number with fifteen significant digits of accuracy

Constants:

Any consecutive sequence of zero or more decimal digits (0–9) followed by a decimal point followed by any consecutive sequence of zero or more decimal digits. (There must be a minimum of one digit either before or after the decimal point.) The entire constant may be prefixed by a "+" or "-" symbol, and an Eformat suffix is optional.

Continued on next page.

Prefix Operator (double → double)

[++ and −− cannot be applied to constants or constant expressions.]

syntax	semantics
−	negation
++	autoincrement
−−	autodecrement

Infix Arithmetic Operators (double × double → double)

syntax	semantics
+	addition
−	subtraction
*	multiplication
/	division

Infix Relational Operators (double × double → boolean)

syntax	semantics
==	equal to
!=	not equal to
<	less than
<=	less than or equal to
>	greater than
>=	greater than or equal to

Postfix Operator (double → double)

[++ and −− cannot be applied to constants or constant expressions.]

syntax	semantics
++	autoincrement
−−	autodecrement

The syntax of a `double` constant is also distinct from Java integer constants. A syntax diagram for this syntax is given in Figure 5.7. The **Eformat** suffix permits using a scientific notation. For example, 3.92E+5 denotes $3.92 * 10^5$ or 392,000.

The `float` type in Java is nearly the same as `double`. The only differences stem from a difference in memory size.

- `float` values occupy 32 bits, whereas `double` values occupy 64 bits.
- `float` constants use the `double` syntax with an "f" character appended.

The fixed size of `float` and `double` storage imposes two limitations upon representing real numbers—limited accuracy and a restricted range of values. Figure 5.8 summarizes these restrictions.

Figure 5.7 Syntax of `DoubleConstant`

DoubleConstant

Syntax

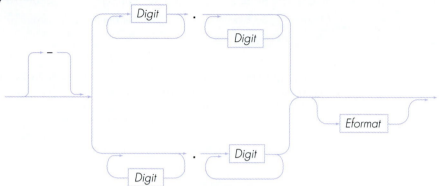

Eformat

Syntax

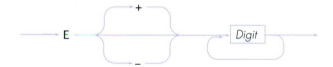

Digit

Syntax

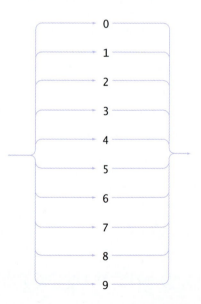

Note

All symbols in *DoubleConstant*, *Eformat*, and *Digit* must be consecutive (no intervening blanks or ends of lines).

Figure 5.8 Limitations of double and float

Type	Size	Accuracy	Minimum	Maximum
double	64 bits	15 significant digits	about 10^{-308}	about 10^{308}
float	32 bits	7 significant digits	about 10^{-38}	about 10^{38}

Computers cannot always store the exact value of a real. This limitation is a byproduct of the fixed length of the memory cells used to store double (64 bits) and float (32 bits) values. Even the mathematician cannot express all real numbers exactly in a limited number of digits. For example, the value 1/3 must be approximated to 0.3333 when using only four **significant digits** of accuracy. (Significant digits include all digits excluding any leading or trailing zeros.)

5.5 SYSTEM.OUT.PRINTLN REVISITED

Frequently, programmers find it useful to be able to display the values of variables during the program execution. This is particularly important for testing and debugging code as a way to examine intermediate states of various objects. Chapter 3 describes the System.out.println method for displaying the state of objects that belong to an *aLibrary* class.

Fortunately, this same method can be used for other objects. A System.out.println call accepts any data type for an argument, and executing System.out.println displays information regarding the state of its argument. If the argument to System.out.println is a primitive type expression, then the value of that expression is displayed. For example, when the following instruction executes

```
System.out.println( 25 + 3 * 2 );
```

the value 31 is displayed. Similarly, executing the instruction

```
System.out.println( 98.2 - 0.4 );
```

displays the value 97.8.

The println method outputs the value of its argument and then terminates the output line. Therefore, two consecutive calls to System.out.println result in two consecutive lines of output. The print method offers an alternative that performs the same task as println except that it does not terminate an output line. For example, two consecutive calls to System.out.print cause their values to be displayed consecutively on the *same* line.

5.6 MIXED-TYPE NUMERIC EXPRESSIONS

A **mixed-type numeric expression** is any expression that involves two or more different numeric data types. Java permits mixed-type numeric expressions. At the foundation of Java's handling of mixed-type expressions is a concept known as

widening. Some of Java's primitive types are said to be **wider** than other primitive types. Figure 5.9 describes this relation among the data types. The arrows in this diagram extend from narrower to the next-wider type. Any type that can be reached by a path following one or more arrows is a wider type. Therefore, `double` is wider than `float`, and both `double` and `float` are wider than `int`.

Figure 5.9 Widening relation for primitive types

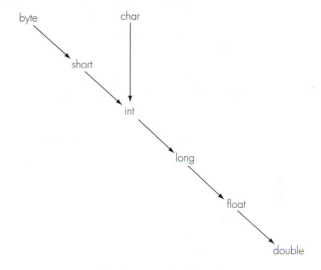

(arrows lead to immediately wider types)

Conceptually, a wider type variable can represent all of the values from a narrower type. For this reason Java considers a conversion from narrower to wider to be a **safe conversion**. Such safe conversions are often performed automatically. For instance, Java considers any primitive type to conform to any wider primitive type. This permits an `int` expression to be assigned to a `double` variable or a `long` argument to be passed to a parameter of type `float`. In fact all of the following assignment instructions result in the appropriate widening type conversion. The type of each variable below is indicated by its name.

```
doubleVar = floatVar;
doubleVar = longVar;
doubleVar = intVar;
doubleVar = shortVar;
doubleVar = byteVar;
doubleVar = charVar;
floatVar = longVar;
floatVar = intVar;
floatVar = shortVar;
floatVar = byteVar;
floatVar = charVar;
longVar = intVar;
longVar = shortVar;
```

```
longVar = byteVar;
longVar = charVar;
intVar = shortVar;
intVar = byteVar;
intVar = charVar;
shortVar = byteVar;
```

Widening also occurs during the evaluation of mixed type expressions. Whenever an operator is evaluated with two operands (subexpressions) of different types, Java uses the operation from the wider type and automatically converts the narrower value before performing the operation. This means that the expression

```
7.0 / 2
```

evaluates as 7.0/2.0 or the double value 3.5. These conversions propagate to later operations of the same expression as well. For example the expression

```
(8 + 10.3) / 3
```

evaluates to a double value of 6.1 because the parenthesized expression evaluates first to a double.

Java will *not* perform narrowing conversions automatically. In fact, attempting an automatic narrowing conversion is a syntax error. The following instruction is such an erroneous attempted assignment:

```
intVar = doubleVar; // illegal attempt to narrow
```

Similarly, passing a wider argument to a narrower parameter is not permitted.

Narrowing isn't performed automatically because it is considered unsafe. It is unsafe to convert a long value to a short because the long value may lie outside the range of possible short values. Likewise, it is unsafe to convert from double to int because an int cannot store the fractional part of the double value.

Java provides a mechanism, known as a **cast**, so programmers may force unsafe conversions to occur in selected instances. The cast syntax and semantics are described in Figure 5.10.

Figure 5.10 CastExpression

CastExpression (abridged version of *Expression*)

Syntax

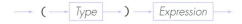

Notes

- *Type* is an identifier that names a data type.
- Some casts are not allowed because the types are incompatible.

Semantics

When a *CastExpression* executes, the *Expression* is evaluated, then converted to the data type specified by *Type*.

The evaluation of a cast is called casting. Java permits casting any primitive expression to a narrower type. Casting from a double to a float may result in a loss of accuracy, but otherwise the value is maintained.

When a real type is cast to an integer type, **truncation** occurs. Truncation means that any fractional portion of the value is lost (*not* rounded). So the expression

    (int) 24.8

evaluates to an int value of 24. Similarly, the expression

    (long) -91.6

evaluates to a long value of -91.

A cast has higher precedence than any operator, excepting the prefix operators. So the following instruction produces a compile-time error:

    intVar = (int) 25.2 + 16.9; // this contains a syntax error

This instruction should be written either as

    intVar = (int)(25.2 + 16.9);

or

    intVar = (int)25.2 + (int)16.9;

depending upon the intended result.

5.7 PRIMITIVE METHODS (INCLUDING MATH)

There are many uses for methods that return a value of primitive type. In this section there are three example applications of such methods:

1. methods to return attributes of *aLibrary* objects

2. methods to perform common mathematical operations

3. methods created by the programmer to return primitive values

Most *aLibrary* classes are defined in terms of four attributes, namely x, y, width, and height. Figure 5.11 reviews these attributes by showing an AOval object placed upon an AWindow object.

Figure 5.11 x, y, width, and height attributes

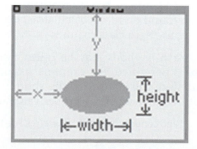

Sometimes it is useful for a program to be able to inspect these values at run time. Methods that return an attribute are often referred to as **query methods**. The Java graphical classes, including many from the *swing* and *awt* libraries as well as *aLibrary*, use a parameterless query method that returns the int value of the corresponding attribute. The name of each of these methods begins with the word get. Figure 5.12 provides specifications.

SOFTWARE ENGINEERING TIP

Names of the form "get___" are used frequently within the Java libraries to name query methods. This is an acceptable naming convention, even though it violates the preferred style of using nouns to name functions.

Figure 5.12 Query methods included in most graphical classes

Query Methods

```
public int getX( )
    postcondition
        result == x

public int getY( )
    postcondition
        result == y

public int getWidth( )
    postcondition
        result == width

public int getHeight( )
    postcondition
        result == height
```

A sample use of a query occurs when moving an ARectangle relative to its previous position. The following method call is designed to move an ARectangle, called rect, to the right by half of its width:

```
rect.translate( rect.getWidth()/2, 0);
```

This same task is accomplished by the following setLocation method call:

```
rect.setLocation( rect.getX()+rect.getWidth()/2, rect.getY());
```

Not all methods returning primitive values are query methods. The standard Java library includes a class, called Math, that supplies a number of methods that perform commonly used mathematical functions. These are the kinds of functions often found on many calculators. Figure 5.13 describes some of the Math methods. Using the Math class requires no import declaration, but a "Math." prefix is needed.

Math methods may be called from anywhere that an expression of the same type is permitted. For example, assume that side1 and side2 are double variables that store the lengths of the shorter sides of a right triangle. Then the following instruction assigns the proper value to hypotenuse (another double variable):

```
hypotenuse = Math.sqrt( side1 * side1 + side2 * side2 );
```

Since arguments are expressions, sometimes an argument contains another nonvoid method call argument. For example, the preceding instruction can be written equivalently as follows.

```
hypotenuse = Math.sqrt( Math.pow(side1,2) + Math.pow(side2,2));
```

Executing this instruction requires that Math.pow be called twice. The value of the two arguments is then passed to the Math.sqrt method.

Figure 5.13 Selected methods from the Math class

```
/* postcondition result == the absolute value of d */
double Math.abs( double d )

/* postcondition result == the absolute value of f */
float Math.abs( float f )

/* postcondition result == the absolute value of j */
int Math.abs( int j )

/* postcondition result == b raised to the power e */
double Math.pow( double b, double e )

/* postcondition result == f rounded to the nearest integer */
int Math.round( float f )

/* postcondition result == d rounded to the nearest integer */
long Math.round( double d )

/* postcondition result == the square root of d */
double Math.sqrt( double d )

/* postcondition result == the cosine of d */
double Math.cos( double d )

/* postcondition result == the sine of d */
double Math.sin( double d )

/* postcondition result == the tangent of d */
double Math.tan( double d )

/* postcondition result == the natural logarithm of d */
double Math.log( double d )

/* postcondition
       result == the mathematical constant e raised to the power d */
double Math.exp( double d )

/* postcondition
       result == a random value such that 0.0 < result < 1.0 */
double Math.random()
```

Math contains many of the common mathematical functions, such as square root (sqrt), absolute value (abs—three versions for three different types of numbers), exponentiation (pow), logarithmic functions (log and exp), and trigonometric functions (sin, cos, and tan). It is also useful for programmers to define their own methods. Below is a private method that illustrates.

```
private double average( double d1, double d2 ) {
    return (d1 + d2) / 2.0;
}
```

This average method accepts two double parameters and returns the average (arithmetic mean) of its parameter values. The average method demonstrates, once again, that the new operation isn't used to create primitive type data.

5.8 CONSTANTS (FINAL)

Mathematicians and scientists often use the concept of a constant to describe a value that is unchanging. The acceleration due to Earth's gravity is a constant and so is the Golden Ratio and Euler's constant. Java supports the concept of a constant as well.

The Math class includes two constants for the well-known mathematical constants, π and **E**. Like other Java language parts, constants are named by identifiers. Figure 5.14 contains more detail.

Figure 5.14 Constants from the Math class

```
/* E is the natural base for logarithms
        (roughly 2.7182818284590452354) */
final double Math.E

/* PI is a circle's circumference / diameter
        (roughly 3.14159265358979323846) */
final double Math.PI
```

The reserved word final provides a means of creating constants in Java. From Figure 5.15 it is evident that both Math.E and Math.PI are constants, and they are both of type double.

Constants are used almost interchangeably with variables in Java. For example, the following instruction calculates and assigns the area of a circle with a radius stored in the variable circleRadius:

```
circleArea = circleRadius * circleRadius * Math.PI;
```

The only significant difference between a final variable and other variables is that a final variable can only be assigned a value once. (For instance variables the assignment must occur before the end of the constructor method.) Any attempt to alter the value of a final variable results in an error.

Programmers can declare their own constants. Figure 5.15 shows the appropriate syntax for such declarations. The `FinalPrivateVarDecl` syntax is used to specify constants whose scope is the entire class, and `FinalLocalVariableDecl` is a notation used to declare constants that are local to a method. A `FinalPrivateVarDecl` can be placed anywhere an instance variable declaration is permitted, and a `FinalLocalVariableDecl` can be located anywhere that a local variable can be declared.

Figure 5.15 `FinalPrivateVarDecl` and `LocalVariableDecl`

FinalPrivateVarDecl (a possible *OneVarDecl*)

Syntax

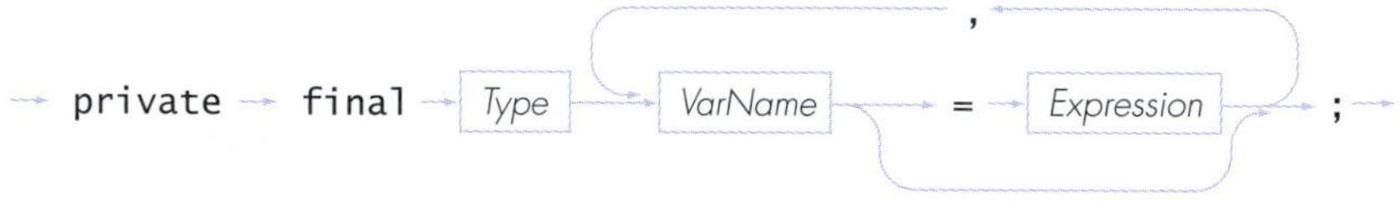

FinalLocalVariableDecl (a possible *OneStatement*)

Syntax

Semantics

A constant has the same scope and may be used in the same places as a variable with one exception—constants can only be assigned once, and for instance variables the assignment must occur before the end of the constructor method.

Notes

- The type of *Expression* must conform to *Type*.
- *Type* can be any accessible class name or primitive type.

Figure 5.15 points out that any constant can, and should, be assigned a value as part of its declaration. Below is a sample declaration that can be placed within a class to create a constant named `pintsPerGallon`:

```
private final int pintsPerGallon = 8;
```

5.9 NUMERIC EXPRESSION PATTERNS

Some numeric expressions occur with sufficient frequency that they should be highlighted as patterns. Good software developers should be familiar with these expression patterns and know how to apply them. The first pattern is designed to retain accuracy that might otherwise be lost by integer division. Such accuracy can be retained by forcing a real division, rather than integer division. The pattern to accomplish this is shown in Figure 5.16.

Figure 5.16 Expression pattern for double division with `int` expressions

(double) *integerExpression* / *integerExpression*;

A related pattern is exhibited when a real expression (say, of type `double`) must be assigned to an integer variable. A cast is needed in such a case. Applying the cast to the entire expression generally requires a set of parentheses around the expression. Figure 5.17 shows this pattern.

Figure 5.17 Assignment pattern for assigning double to `int`

intVar = (int) (*doubleExpression*);

There are many occasions in which the value of a real expression must be *rounded* to the nearest integer, rather than truncated. The `Math` class includes methods to round `float` expressions to `int` and `double` expressions to `long`. Figure 5.18 demonstrates how to use these methods to round expressions, along with a pattern for rounding without using `Math` methods.

Figure 5.18 Expression pattern for rounding

intVar = (int)Math.round(*doubleExpression*);

Yet another common instructional pattern that occurs frequently in programs is an instruction that increases the value of an integer variable by 1. There are two ways to accomplish this instruction in Java; both are shown in Figure 5.19.

Figure 5.19 Two expression patterns for incrementing a variable by 1

integerVar = *integerVar* + 1;

or

integerVar++;

The Figure 5.19 pattern is essentially a counting pattern because, if it is performed repeatedly, the effect is to cause the variable to count upwards as in 2, 3, 4,

5. . ... In some cases programs need to count within a restricted range. For example, a variable could be used to count from 0 to 4, repeatedly, as in the sequence 0, 1, 2, 3, 4, 0, 1, 2, 3, 4 . . ... This kind of counting is accomplished by the assignment instruction pattern shown in Figure 5.20.

Figure 5.20 Assignment pattern for incrementing a variable by 1 within the range 0 through *n*

$$integerVar = (integerVar + 1) \% (n + 1);$$

Yet another numeric expression pattern occurs when the program needs an integer that is randomly generated over a contiguous range. For example, a program simulating the roll of a die may need to model one roll as an integer from 1 through 6. The following Java instruction assigns to the int variable, oneDie, one of the integers from 1 through 6 with equal probability for each:

```
oneDie = (int)( Math.random() * 6.0 + 1.0 );
```

This instruction relies on the Math method, called random, and the fact that random returns random double values between (but not equal to) 0.0 and 1.0. This single instruction can be extended into a pattern expression for generating any range of integers, as shown in Figure 5.21.

Figure 5.21 Expression pattern for generating a random integer from *low* through *high*

$$(int) (Math.random() * (high - low + 1) + low)$$

5.10 DESIGN EXAMPLE—DYNAMIC HISTOGRAM

This section examines a particular program that makes use of primitive numeric data in several ways. The software requirements for this program are to display a window with three buttons and a histogram that reflects the number of times that each button has been clicked. More specifically, there is a blue filled rectangle immediately above each button. The height of each of these rectangles must be relative to the percentage of clicks of its neighboring button.

Figure 5.22 shows a snapshot of a portion of the program's execution when the buttons left to right have been clicked, respectively, 3, 2, and 5 times. For this snapshot, the height of the left bar is 30% of the maximum possible height. The middle bar is 20% of its maximum possible height, and the right bar is 50% of its maximum possible height.

A Director class for this histogram program is shown in Figure 5.23. This program uses A3ButtonWindow and the corresponding leftAction, midAction, and rightAction event handler methods.

Figure 5.22 Histogram after 3, 2, and 5 clicks

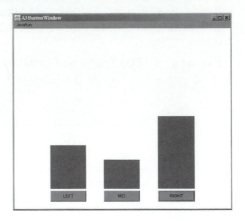

Figure 5.23 Director for button click histogram

```
// Moving Histogram Program
// Author: David Riley
// Date: January, 2000

import aLibrary.*;
import java.awt.*;

public class Director extends A3ButtonHandler{
    private A3ButtonWindow histoWin;
    private ARectangle leftBar, midBar, rightBar;
    private int leftClickCount, midClickCount, rightClickCount;
    private final int maxBarHeight = 400;

    /* postcondition
            A window is displayed that contains a histogram of the
            number of times that each window button is clicked
            as a percentage of the total number of such clicks. */
    public Director() {
        histoWin = new A3ButtonWindow(this);
        leftClickCount = 0;
        midClickCount = 0;
        rightClickCount = 0;
        leftBar = newBar(100);
        leftBar.place( histoWin );
        midBar = newBar(250);
        midBar.place( histoWin );
        rightBar = newBar(400);
        rightBar.place( histoWin );
        histoWin.show();
    }
```

```
/* precondition
        leftBar, midBar, and rightBar are instantiated
    modifies
        leftClickCount, leftBar, midBar, rightBar
    postcondition
        leftClickCount == old leftClickCount + 1
        AND all bars of the histogram are properly updated */
public void leftAction() {
    leftClickCount++;
    redrawHistogram();
}


/* precondition
        leftBar, midBar, and rightBar are instantiated
    modifies
        midClickCount, leftBar, midBar, rightBar
    postcondition
        midClickCount == old midClickCount + 1
        AND all bars of the histogram are properly updated */
public void midAction() {
    midClickCount++;
    redrawHistogram();
}


/* precondition
        leftBar, midBar, and rightBar are instantiated
    modifies
        rightClickCount, leftBar, midBar, rightBar
    postcondition
        rightClickCount == old rightClickCount + 1
        AND all bars of the histogram are properly updated */
public void rightAction() {
    rightClickCount++;
    redrawHistogram();
}


/* postcondition
        result is a filled, blue rectangle
        AND result.getWidth() == 100 AND result.getX() == j */
private ARectangle newBar(int j) {
    ARectangle tmp = new ARectangle(j, 0, 100, 0);
    tmp.setColor(Color.blue);
    tmp.setToFill();
    return tmp;
}
```

Continued on next page.

```
/* precondition
       leftBar, midBar, and rightBar are instantiated
   modifies
       leftBar, midBar, rightBar
   postcondition
       all bars of the histogram are properly updated */
private void redrawHistogram() {
    redrawOneBar(leftBar, leftClickCount);
    redrawOneBar(midBar, midClickCount);
    redrawOneBar(rightBar, rightClickCount);
}

/* precondition
       r is instantiated
   modifies
       r
   postcondition
       the y and height attributes of r are adjusted to a new
       height of maxBarHeight *
       (c/(leftClickCount+midClickCount+rightClickCount)) */
private void redrawOneBar(ARectangle r, int c) {
    int totalClicks, newHeight;
    totalClicks = leftClickCount + midClickCount +
    rightClickCount;
    newHeight = (int)((double)c / totalClicks *
    maxBarHeight);
    r.setLocation( r.getX(), 445-newHeight );
    r.setSize( r.getWidth(), newHeight );
    r.repaint();
}
}
```

The three blue histogram bars are represented by three variables, namely leftBar, midBar, and rightBar. Three int variables store the number of times the three buttons are clicked. These variables are leftClickCount, midClickCount, and rightClickCount. An int constant, named maxBarHeight, stores the maximum possible height of a blue bar as 400 pixels.

When a button click event calls the appropriate event handler, such as leftAction, the corresponding click counting variable is incremented by an instruction like the following:

```
leftClickCount++;
```

The redrawHistogram method is called after each click count variable update. In turn, redrawHistogram calls redrawOneBar once for each of the three bars. The second argument to the redrawOneBar method is the appropriate click count variable (an int).

The `redrawOneBar` method contains several examples of primitive expressions. Perhaps the most interesting is the following instruction, which is designed to calculate the height of a histogram bar:

```
newHeight = (int)((double)c / totalClicks * maxBarHeight);
```

This instruction uses two of the patterns that were presented in Section 5.9. (See Figure 5.16 and Figure 5.17.) The (double) cast is essential in the above instruction. If this cast is removed and more than one button is clicked, the division always evaluates to zero and so does the bar height. By casting to double, the bar height evaluates accurately, rather than truncating fractional values. The outer cast to int is required in order to narrow the expression's value to an int type, as required by the int variable, newHeight.

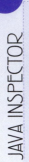

Below is a collection of hints on what to check when examining code that involves the concepts of this chapter.

✓ Reference data must be constructed before it is used, but primitive data doesn't permit construction. When you check to be certain that reference variables are nonnull, check also to be certain that there is no illegal attempt to use a new operation on primitive data.

✓ The most common errors in numeric expressions stem from a misunderstanding of operator precedence. It is wise to check each numeric expression to be certain that operations will be evaluated in the correct order. When in doubt, use parentheses.

✓ Watch out for division on integer operands. Because the fractional part is lost, an integer division often produces unwanted results. The patterns from Figures 5.17 and 5.18 are useful in avoiding such problems.

✓ Remember that a cast to an integer *truncates*; it doesn't round. The Math class provides methods for rounding.

✓ Constants (final variables) can only be assigned once, and this is best done within their declaration statement.

abs (Math function)

address (of a memory cell)

byte data type

cast

constant

cos (Math function)

double data type

E (Math constant)

Eformat

exp (Math function)

final

float data type

infix operator

int data type

literal

log (Math function)

long data type

Math (library class)

mixed-type numeric expression

parameter passage by value

PI (Math constant)

precedence

prefix operator

primitive type

postfix operator

query method

random (Math function)

real number

reference type

safe conversion

short data type

significant digit

sin (Math function)

sqrt (Math function)

System.out.println

tan (Math function)

truncation

wider (type)

widening

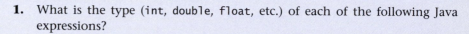

1. What is the type (int, double, float, etc.) of each of the following Java expressions?

    a. 19 / 3

    b. (int)71.7 - 2 * 3

    c. (7 + 2.3) * 3

    d. (7 % 3) + (int)18.6

    e. 2 + (int)1.9 - 2.3f

    f. ((long)7 / 2) * 1.1

2. What is the value of each expression from Exercise 1?

3. What value is assigned to the int variables j and n as a result of executing each of the following instructions. (Assume that j has an initial value of 3 and n has an initial value of 16.)

    a. j++;

    b. n = n * 2;

4. What is output by each of the following instructions?

    a. System.out.println(7 - (3 * 2.1));

    b. System.out.println(7 - 3 * 2.1);

    c. System.out.println(13 % (2+1));

    d. System.out.println((int) 4.8);

    e. System.out.println((double)1 / 8 + 2);

5. For each of the following pairs of types, identify the wider type. (Note that it is possible for neither type to be wider than the other.)

    a. int or double

    b. int or short

    c. int or float

    d. long or short

    e. byte or short

6. What is the type and the value of each of the following expressions?

    a. Math.abs(-3.4) + Math.abs(3.4)

    b. Math.abs(7 - 10 * 2)

    c. (int)(Math.PI * 2)

    d. Math.round(17 / 3.0f)

    e. Math.sqrt(Math.abs(-3) + 22)

    f. Math.pow(3, Math.pow(Math.sqrt(4.0), 2))

    g. Math.cos(Math.PI)

7. Each of the following is an incorrect attempt to write a method that returns the average (arithmetic mean) of three `int` numbers as accurately as possible, by using a `double` return type. Some of these attempts contain a syntax error and others contain logic errors. Identify specifically what is wrong with each attempt.

a.
```
private double average3( int n1, int n2, int n3 ) {
    return (double)n1 + (double)n2 + (double)n3 / 3.0;
}
```

b.
```
private double average3( int n1, int n2, int n3 ) {
    double result;
    result = new ((n1 + n2 + n3) / 3.0);
    return result;
}
```

c.
```
private double average3( int n1, int n2, int n3 ) {
    double result;
    result = (double)(n1 + n2 + n3) / 3.0);
    return result;
}
```

d.
```
private double average3( int n1, int n2, int n3 ) {
    return (double(n1) + double(n2) + double(n3)) / 3;
}
```

8. Consider the following private method:

```
public int m2(int z) {
    return z * 2;
}
```

What is output by each of the following instructions?

a. `System.out.println( m2(25) );`

b. `System.out.println( m2(7) + m2(m2(3)) );`

c. `System.out.println( m2( m2(m2(5)+1) + m2(1)) );`

9. What is the range (i.e., smallest possible number and largest possible number) that can be assigned to the `double` variable, d, as a result of executing each instruction below?

a. `d = Math.random() * 5;`

b. `d = 2 + (int)(Math.random() * 7);`

c. `d = 2 + (int)Math.random() * 7;`

d. `d = d % 25;`

10. Write a Java method for each of the following.

a. This method is a correct version of the `average3` method from Exercise 7.

b. This method returns a `double` value and has a single parameter of type `int`. When called, the method returns the area of a circle whose radius is equal to the parameter.

c. This method returns the length of a line segment given (as four parameters) the coordinates of the endpoints of the line segment. The parameters and return value should all be of type `double`.

PROGRAMMING EXERCISES

1. Write a program to simulate a sunrise. Your program must begin with a black window and a "sun" that has a diameter of 100 pixels, but is not yet visible. Using an `A3ButtonWindow`, the MID button should cause the sun to rise and the other buttons behave as described below.

   LEFT   This button is for zooming in on the sun. Clicking this button causes the sun to be enlarged by 20%. It is important to recenter the sun to the same center point whenever it enlarges.

   MID   This causes the sun to raise by 2% of its current diameter.

   RIGHT   This button is for zooming out from the sun. Clicking this button causes the sun to be reduced in size by 30%. It is important to recenter the sun to the same center point whenever it reduces its size.

2. Write a program using `A3ButtonWindow`. Initially, this program must display a green lollipop in the middle of the window. This initial lollipop consists of a green filled circle that is 100 pixels in diameter upon a "stick" constructed from an `ARectangle` that is 100 pixels long and 5 pixels wide. The bottom edge of the green circle should just touch the stick, and the stick must be centered horizontally with the green disk. The three buttons of the window have the following behavior.

   LEFT   The stick of the lollipop is resized to a length that is randomly selected from 50 through 150, and the green disk is automatically repositioned to stick precisely atop the new stick length.

   MID   The disk portion of the lollipop is resized to have a diameter that is randomly selected from 70 through 120. The upper-left corner of the disk doesn't change as a result of this resizing, but the stick must be repositioned to be horizontally centered and just touch the bottom of the disk.

   RIGHT   The entire lollipop moves to its right. The first time that the RIGHT button is clicked the lollipop moves 1 pixel to its right; the next time it moves 2 pixels to its right; the next time 3; etc.

3. Use an `A3ButtonWindow` to draw line segments using the `ALine` class. (If you don't know about `ALine`, you can teach yourself by reading the `ALine` class diagram and specifications.) The initial line segment is black and connects points (0, 0) to the opposite corner of the window. Thereafter, the buttons behave as described below.

   LEFT   Clicking this button draws a new red line segment with one endpoint that is selected randomly from the region *below* the diagonal of the original (black) line segment. The second endpoint for your new line segment must be the midpoint of the most recently drawn line segment, regardless of color.

MID   This button redraws the original black line segment.

RIGHT   Clicking this button draws a new green line segment with one endpoint that is selected randomly from the region *above* the diagonal of the original (black) line segment. The second endpoint for your new line segment must be the midpoint of the most recently drawn line segment, regardless of color.

CHAPTER 6

SUPPLIER CLASSES

"FOR NATURE DID

THAT WANT SUPPLY."

—John Dryden

OBJECTIVES

- To introduce the client-supplier (composition) relation and examine the role of supplier classes and client classes in a complete program

- To show an additional class diagram notation for composition

- To explore the differences between public and private declarations

- To revisit the Java notation for qualified expressions

- To introduce scope and lifetime rules for variables and methods

- To explore various issues of class design including selecting the best location for a feature and how to properly hide information to create thin interfaces

- To examine the notions of read-only and write-only access to data and to demonstrate a technique for implementing both kinds of restricted access

- To introduce the concept of reusing an identifier and examine Java rules for such reuse, including method overloading

- To examine the char primitive data type for implementing single characters

- To introduce the String data type for implementing a character string

- To introduce the ALabel class as a means for displaying a single line of text

T he **client-supplier relation** is common in the retail industry. Every grocery store is the client of suppliers who deliver daily stock for the grocer's shelves. Meanwhile, that same grocer is a supplier for customers (clients) who shop at the store daily. The electronic world is also no stranger to clients and suppliers. Internet Web servers act as suppliers to client computers that download Web pages, and e-mail servers supply electronic mail messages to their clients.

6.1   CLIENTS AND SUPPLIERS IN SOFTWARE

The concept of **clients** and **suppliers** also plays a central role in object-oriented software development. In software development the clients and suppliers are classes. A client class is one that borrows the facilities of another class (known as the supplier class). Sometimes the client calls a method or accesses an attribute from the supplier. Sometimes the client class uses the supplier class for one of the following:

- a variable type
- a parameter type
- the return type of one or more nonvoid methods

Figure 6.1 illustrates with a simple `Director` class that constructs a window and places a filled red `AOval` on that window. The location and size of the `AOval` are selected randomly.

The `Director` class in this example is a client of three classes: `AWindow`, `AOval`, and `Math`; this means that these three classes are all suppliers to `Director`. The `AWindow` and `AOval` classes are suppliers because `Director` includes instance variables belonging to these classes. `Math` is a supplier because `Director` uses one of its methods, namely `random`.

Since they serve as types for one or more variables, `AWindow` and `AOval` have a special relationship with `Director` known as **composition**. The term "composition" means that a client class is *composed* of instance variables and thereby of the classes that supply types for these instance variables. Another name used for composition is **aggregation**; a client class is an aggregate of its instance variables. Composition/aggregation is such an important relationship that class diagrams are often annotated with connecting lines to point out this relationship. The usual notation, as shown below, is to draw a line segment connecting the composition to its supplier with a diamond on the composite (client) end of the line.

This composition notation can be used to diagram the program from Figure 6.1. Figure 6.2 contains such a diagram for the three classes.

Prior chapters have explored how to write client code. In this chapter the focus changes to an examination of how to add supplier code.

Figure 6.1 Program to draw a random oval

```
// Random Oval Program
// Author: David Riley
import aLibrary.*;
import java.awt.*;
public class Director {
        private AWindow window;
        private AOval redOval;
        /* postcondition
                A window is displayed that contains a randomly sized
                and placed AOval. */
        public Director() {
                window = new AWindow(10, 10, 600, 500);
                redOval = new AOval( (int)(Math.random()*600),
                                     (int)(Math.random()*500),
                                     (int)(Math.random()*600),
                                     (int)(Math.random()*500) );
                redOval.setColor(Color.red);
                redOval.setToFill();
                redOval.place(window);
                window.repaint();
        }
}
```

Figure 6.2 Class diagram showing composition

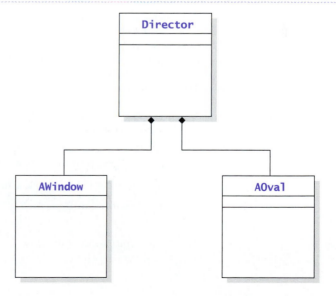

6.2   ANOTHER CLIENT

Suppliers of manufactured goods seek to provide the services most desired by their clients. Similarly, supplier classes should be designed to provide the best possible services to client classes. The "services" that a class supplies take the form of methods and instance variables. The AWindow class supplies update methods such as setColor and translate, as well as query methods like getX and getHeight. The Math class supplies constants such as PI and functions like Math.sqrt and Math.random.

The instance variables, constants, and methods of a class are said to be **encapsulated** members of that class.

Java uses the private and public prefixes to control member encapsulation. A feature that is declared to be public is available anywhere. Features that are declared to be private are the "private domain" of the class. Private features are encapsulated within the class, and not available elsewhere. These uses for public and private apply to instance variables, methods, and classes alike.

OPENING the Black Box

The Director classes encountered thus far have used fussy rules regarding the use of public and private. The Director class along with the Director constructor method, are public because these must be used elsewhere in order to create an initial Director object. Likewise, the leftAction, midAction, and rightAction methods are public because they are called from event handling objects that are external to Director.

Other Director methods and instance variables are declared to be private. This is done to keep such features localized within the class, since they aren't needed outside. These choices of how to use public and private are important software engineering decisions that will be explained later.

Consider the banking community. The primary data type for banking software is probably not an int or a double, but some form of *money*. It seems that a supplier class that provides ways to store and manipulate money would be useful for programmers developing banking software. Figure 6.3 contains the class diagram specifications for such a supplier class, called MoneyUSA. Figure 6.4 contains the class specifications for MoneyUSA.

CLOSED Black Box

The MoneyUSA class declares several public instance variables. As the warnings in Figures 6.3, 6.7, and 6.8 suggest, public instance variables are generally a poor choice. In this particular situation, public instance variables are tolerable, and they are included because they help to illustrate important concepts.

In Section 6.6, an Opening the Black Box feature explains how to write the MoneyUSA class without the use of public instance variables.

Figure 6.3 ARectangle class diagram

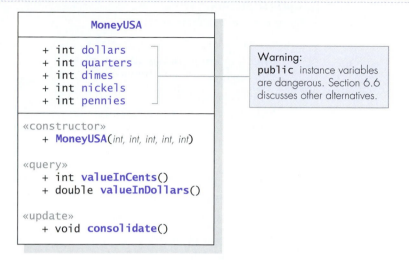

Figure 6.4 MoneyUSA class diagram and specifications

MoneyUSA Class Specifications

Invariant

A MoneyUSA object maintains a monetary amount as an integer count of dollars, quarters, dimes, nickels, and pennies so that dollars >= 0 and quarters >= 0 and dimes >= 0 and nickels >= 0 and pennies >= 0

Constructor Method

public **MoneyUSA** (int dol, int q, int di, int n, int p)

   precondition
   dol >= 0 AND q >= 0 AND di >= 0 AND n >= 0 AND p >= 0

   postcondition
   dollars == dol AND quarters == q AND dimes == di

   AND nickels == n AND pennies == p

Query Methods

public int **valueInCents**()

   postcondition
   result == dollars * 100 + quarters * 25 + dimes * 10
             + nickels * 5 + pennies

public double **valueInDollars**()

   postcondition
   result == (dollars * 100 + quarters * 25 + dimes * 10
             + nickels * 5 + pennies) / 100

Continued on next page.

> **Update Method**
> ```
> public void consolidate( )
> ```
> *modifies*
> dollars, quarters, dimes, nickels, pennies
> *postcondition*
> ```
> valueInCents() == old valueInCents()
> ```
> AND 0 <= quarters <= 3 AND 0 <= dimes <= 2
> AND 0 <= nickels <= 1 AND 0 <= pennies <= 4

A variable of type MoneyUSA will represent a single amount of money. A single program may declare as many MoneyUSA variables as needed.

The members of MoneyUSA include:

- a constructor (MoneyUSA) that has five parameters for different amounts of dollars and coins,
- a valueInCents method to return the numeric value (in cents) of the money,
- a valueInDollars method to return the dollar value of the money (as a double),
- a consolidate method to replace large numbers of small coins with larger denominations, and
- five instance variables to keep track of the exact number of each coin/dollar bill in the money

Every feature of the MoneyUSA class is declared to be public. Class diagrams use a plus sign (+) to highlight the fact that an instance variable or a method is public, while a minus sign (–) indicates a private feature.

Notice that the methods called valueInCents and valueInDollars are labeled «query». This means that they are nonvoid methods that inspect some attribute or characteristic of the object. A client program can *query* a MoneyUSA object to retrieve its monetary value either in cents (by calling valueInCents) or in dollars (by calling valueInDollars).

Figure 6.5 contains an example of a Director class that is a client of MoneyUSA. The Director class contains a constructor method and a private method, called printMoney.

The Director constructor method declares a local variable called cash that belongs to the MoneyUSA class. This variable is assigned a value by the following instruction.

```
cash = new MoneyUSA(1, 5, 1, 4, 2);
```

Executing the above instruction calls the MoneyUSA constructor, thereby initializing the monetary amount to consist of one (1) dollar, five (5) quarters, one (1) dime, four (4) nickels, and two (2) pennies. The next instruction calls the private printMoney method, passing cash as an argument. When printMoney returns, the following instruction is executed:

```
cash.consolidate();
```

Figure 6.5 Client class for MoneyUSA

```
// Money Test Program
// Author: David Riley
public class Director {
    public Director() {
        MoneyUSA cash;
        cash = new MoneyUSA(1, 5, 1, 4, 2);
        printMoney( cash );
        cash.consolidate();
        printMoney( cash );
        cash.pennies = cash.pennies * 2;
        printMoney( cash );
    }

    private void printMoney( MoneyUSA m ) {
        System.out.println( m.valueInCents() );
        System.out.println( m.valueInDollars() );
        System.out.println( m.dollars );
        System.out.println( m.quarters );
        System.out.println( m.dimes );
        System.out.println( m.nickels );
        System.out.println( m.pennies );
    }
}
```

This instruction calls the consolidate method. According to the MoneyUSA specifications, consolidate revises coin counts into the largest possible denominations without changing the total value of the money. In other words, a call to consolidate should change every five pennies into a nickel, every two nickels into a dime, every two dimes and a nickel into a quarter and every four quarters into a dollar. For example, if the total value of cash is $2.57, then a call to consolidate will ensure that this money is stored as two (2) dollars, two (2) quarters, no (0) dimes, one (1) nickel, and two (2) pennies.

The Director constructor includes the following instruction:

```
cash.pennies = cash.pennies * 2;
```

This is an assignment instruction that accesses a public instance variable. The notation

```
cash.pennies
```

denotes the pennies variable that is a part of the cash object. Therefore, this assignment instruction can be explained as doubling the number of pennies in the cash object. Figure 6.6 generalizes the notation used to reference this variable.

This description of an ObjectReference from Figure 6.6 defines the alternative ways to identify an object in Java. An object can be referred to using

1. a variable name

2. a nonvoid method call (that returns the object)

3. a local variable name

4. the name of a formal parameter

Figure 6.6 Description of `ObjectReference`

ObjectReference

Syntax

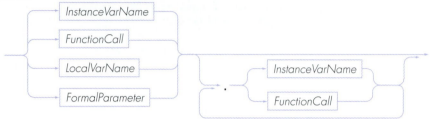

Syntax

- *InstanceVarName* is the name of an instance variable that is accessible in this context (scope)
- *FunctionCall* is the name and argument list for a nonvoid method that is accessible in this context (scope)
- *LocalVarName* is the name of a local variable (valid only if used within a method that includes a declaration for this variable)
- *FormalParameter* is the name of a formal parameter (valid only if used within a method that declares such a parameter)

Notes

- `ObjectReference` can be used anywhere that an object of the same type is permitted.
- `ObjectReference` may be used to the right of an assignment operator only if it ends with a variable or parameter name.

Of course, variable names, method calls, and formal parameters are valid only if used within the proper context. This context refers to the scope of each name. Java scope rules are examined in Section 6.4.

The `ObjectReference` description also shows that any of these four items can be used as a qualifier to be followed by a period and a different instance variable name or method call. Figure 6.5 makes use of this notation to refer to the number of quarters in a parameter (m) of type `MoneyUSA`

```
m.quarters
```

and to call `MoneyUSA` methods using expressions like the one below:

```
m.valueInDollars()
```

Expressions like those described by Figure 6.6 are often called **qualified expressions** because of the qualifiers on the left of the period. The `valueInDollars` must be *qualified* by m in order to identify the object to which the method is applied.

6.3   SUPPLIERS

When implementing a supplier class, the best place to start is the class diagram and class specifications. A class diagram shows the public features of the class, including such things as instance variable types and method names with parameter lists. The class specification goes even further by providing the software contracts (preconditions, postconditions, and class invariants) that define the desired behavior of the class.

SOFTWARE ENGINEERING TIP

To write a supplier class, start with the class diagram and class specification. These two documents dictate the features of the class and specify their behavior.

Figure 6.7 contains code for the MoneyUSA supplier class. This class consists of the same five instance variables and four methods as seen in the class diagram and specification. Even the assertions from the class specification are retained in this class to assist in code readability.

Figure 6.7 MoneyUSA class

```
public class MoneyUSA {
    /* Invariant
            A MoneyUSA object maintains a monetary amount as an
            integer count of dollars, quarters, dimes, nickels, and
            pennies AND dollars>=0 AND quarters>=0 AND dimes>=0
            AND nickels>=0 AND pennies>=0 */
    public int dollars;
    public int quarters;
    public int dimes;
    public int nickels;
    public int pennies;
    /* precondition
            dol>=0 AND q>=0 AND di>=0 AND n>=0 AND p>=0
        postcondition
            dollars == dol AND quarters == q AND dimes == di
            AND nickels == n AND pennies == p */
    public MoneyUSA(int dol, int q, int di, int n, int p) {
        dollars = dol;
        quarters = q;
        dimes = di;
        nickels = n;
        pennies = p;
    }
    /* postcondition
            result == dollars*100+quarters*25+dimes*10+nickels*5
                    +pennies */
    public int valueInCents() {
        return dollars*100+quarters*25+dimes*10+nickels*5
            +pennies;
    }
```

Warning:
public instance variables are dangerous. Section 6.6 discusses other alternatives.

Continued on next page.

```
/* postcondition
        result ==  (dollars*100+quarters*25+dimes*10+nickels*5+
                    pennies)/100 */
public double valueInDollars() {
    return valueInCents() / 100.0;
}
/* postcondition
        valueInCents() == old valueInCents() AND 0<=pennies<=4
        AND 0<=nickels<=1 AND 0<=dimes<=2 AND 0<=quarters<=3 */
public void consolidate() {
    int remainingCents = valueInCents();
    dollars = remainingCents / 100;
    remainingCents = remainingCents % 100;
    quarters = remainingCents / 25;
    remainingCents = remainingCents % 25;
    dimes = remainingCents / 10;
    remainingCents = remainingCents % 10;
    nickels = remainingCents / 5;
    pennies = remainingCents % 5;
}
}
```

The syntax used by a supplier class is no different from other classes. Like all classes, MoneyUSA must include a constructor method that has the same name as the class. Executing the MoneyUSA constructor method causes the values of its parameters to be assigned to the corresponding instance variables. Notice that while the Director class needs to use notation such as

```
cash.dimes
```

to reference an instance variable from another class, inside the MoneyUSA class the variable

```
dimes
```

is accessed using only its name.

The consolidate method is a good example of how class specifications are transformed into the necessary code. The method's postcondition asserts that executing consolidate does not alter the total monetary value of its object, but it may need to adjust the counts of individual denominations so they fall within ranges (such as 0 <= pennies <= 4). The algorithm to accomplish this is similar to the procedure a merchant uses to make change.

The first step in consolidate is to declare a local variable as follows.

```
int remainingCents = valueInCents();
```

This line not only declares a new remainingCents variable, but it also initializes its value to the total number of cents in the MoneyUSA object. The next instruction is

```
dollars = remainingCents / 100;
```

Executing this instruction assigns to `dollars` the maximum number of dollars that exist within `remainingCents`. The next instruction

```
remainingCents = remainingCents % 100;
```

subtracts the value of these dollars from `remainingCents`. At this point in the execution, the value of `remainingCents` must be less than 100. The next two instructions are designed to assign to `quarters` the maximum number of quarters in `remainingCents` and subtract their value from `remainingCents`. Similar instructions remove as many dimes and nickels as possible. Finally, `pennies` is assigned the value of `remainingCents` that is left over after the value of all larger denominations are subtracted.

Most classes are not just a supplier or a client, but serve as both a client of some classes and a supplier to others. Figure 6.8 illustrates such a class, called `PersonalBudget`. The `PersonalBudget` class is a client of `MoneyUSA` by virtue of three instance variables: `cashOnHand`, `outstandingBalance`, and `savings`. These three variables maintain the three related aspects of a person's finances. The body of the `PersonalBudget` constructor method consists of three calls to the `MoneyUSA` constructor to initialize the three instance variables to zero.

Figure 6.8 `PersonalBudget` class

```
public class PersonalBudget {
    public MoneyUSA cashOnHand;
    public MoneyUSA outstandingExpenses;
    public MoneyUSA savings;
    public PersonalBudget() {
        cashOnHand = new MoneyUSA(0, 0, 0, 0, 0);
        outstandingExpenses = new MoneyUSA(0, 0, 0, 0, 0);
        savings = new MoneyUSA(0, 0, 0, 0, 0);
    }

    /* precondition
            0<=dol AND 0<=q AND 0<=di AND 0<=n AND 0<=p
       modifies
            savings
       postcondition
            savings is old savings + dol*100+q*25+di*10+n*5+p cents
            consolidated into the largest possible denominations. */
    public void addToSavings(int dol, int q, int di, int n, int p) {
        savings.dollars = savings.dollars + dol;
        savings.quarters = savings.quarters + q;
        savings.dimes = savings.dimes + di;
        savings.nickels = savings.nickels + n;
        savings.pennies = savings.pennies + p;
        savings.consolidate();
    }
```

> Warning:
> **public** instance variables are dangerous. Section 6.6 discusses other alternatives.

Continued on next page.

```
/* precondition
        cashonHand is instantiated AND savings is instantiated
   postcondition
        result = the value of cashOnHand plus savings consolidated
                into largest possible denominations */
public MoneyUSA totalAssets() {
    MoneyUSA assets;
    assets = new MoneyUSA( cashOnHand.dollars
                         + savings.dollars,
                         cashOnHand.quarters +
                         savings.quarters,
                         cashOnHand.dimes + savings.dimes,
                         cashOnHand.nickels +
                         savings.nickels,
                         cashOnHand.pennies +
                         savings.pennies );

    assets.consolidate();
    return assets;
}
// additional methods can be included here
}
```

The `totalAssets` method illustrates how `PersonalBudget` accesses the different `MoneyUSA` variables. Executing the instruction

```
assets = new MoneyUSA( cashOnHand.dollars + savings.dollars,
                       cashOnHand.quarters + savings.quarters,
                       cashOnHand.dimes + savings.dimes,
                       cashOnHand.nickels + savings.nickels,
                       cashOnHand.pennies + savings.pennies );
```

constructs a new `MoneyUSA` object and assigns it to the local `assets` variable. Notice that the number of dollars in `assets` becomes the total of the number of dollars in the `cashOnHand` and `savings` objects.

To illustrate how `PersonalBudget` can be a supplier as well as a client, consider the following `Director` class:

```
public class Director {
    private PersonalBudget myBudget;
    // additional variables and methods can be included here
}
```

This latest `Director` class is a client of `PersonalBudget` because it declares an instance variable, called `myBudget`, that belongs the `PersonalBudget` class.

The composition relationships among the three classes (`Director`, `PersonalBudget`, and `MoneyUSA`) is pictured in Figure 6.9. The number "3" on the line connecting `PersonalBudget` to `MoneyUSA` denotes the fact that `PersonalBudget` contains three instance variables of type `MoneyUSA`.

Class diagrams, like Figure 6.9, illustrate several useful relationships. However, class diagrams cannot capture the behavior of objects at run time. A common method to draw run-time relationships is with object diagrams. Figure 6.10 is a sample object diagram for the three classes.

An object diagram includes a separate rectangle for each reference object. The variable name of an object and its class appear underlined on the first line of the rectangle. The class to which the object belongs is preceded by a colon. Lines are drawn to connect an object with variables that are contained within the object. Primitive instance variables are included in object rectangles, along with their values.

Figure 6.9 Composition of MoneyUSA, PersonalBudget, and Director

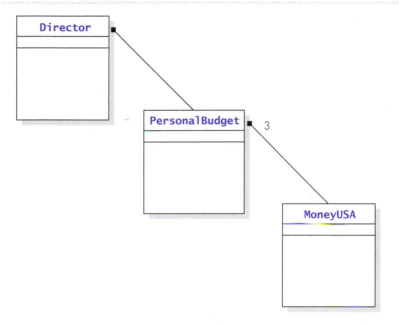

Figure 6.10 Object diagram for MoneyUSA, PersonalBudget, and Director

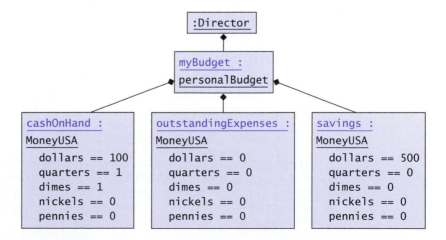

Each object diagram captures the state of objects at one instant in time. It is a kind of snapshot of a particular point during program execution. Figure 6.10 pictures an instant when the three MoneyUSA objects have been constructed and cashOnHand totals $100.35, outstandingExpenses is $0, and savings is $500.00.

At the execution time pictured by Figure 6.10, a myBudget variable has been constructed within Director. Therefore, Director can use the public features of PersonalBudget with instructions such as the following:

```
myBudget = new PersonalBudget();
myBudget.addToSavings(100, 0, 0, 0, 0);
```

It is also possible to extend the object reference notation to refer to instance variables in the suppliers of suppliers. Below is an instruction that can be placed in Director:

```
System.out.println( myBudget.savings.dollars );
```

To understand how this instruction works, it is helpful to return to a run-time picture of the objects. Notice that Director contains an object called myBudget, which contains an object called savings, which contains an int variable called dollars. This kind of dereferencing expression is permitted in Java so long as the qualifiers proceed left to right from object to contained object. Of course, the names used in such a variable reference cannot be private.

It is also possible to use a nonvoid method call as a qualifier. For example, the following expression can be used within Director to display the total dollars in the myBudget assets:

```
System.out.println( myBudget.totalAssets().dollars );
```

6.4   SCOPE AND LIFETIME

Three categories of Java variables have been explained thus far in this text.

1. private instance variables

2. public instance variables

3. local variables

Each of these categories has different **visibility** characteristics. A private instance variable is only visible within the class in which it is declared. A public instance variable is visible anywhere that an object of the supplier type can be referenced. The visibility of a local variable is the most restrictive of all, being limited to the body of the enclosing method.

Scope is the word that programmers use to refer to the region of visibility. The scope of a private instance variable is its class, and the scope of a local variable is its method. Formal parameters have scope as well. The scope of a formal parameter is the method in which it is declared, just like any of that method's local variables.

The *scope of a method* refers to the region from which the method can be called. A `private` method has scope restricted to the class in which it is declared. The scope of a `public` method extends to anywhere where an object of the supplying class is available.

In addition to scope, variables have a second property, known as **lifetime**. (Lifetime is a property of variables, *not* a property of methods.) The lifetime of a variable is the portion of run time during which the variable exists. Local variables have a lifetime that corresponds to their scope. In other words, the lifetime of a local variable begins when the enclosing scope (method body) starts to execute, and its lifetime ends when the enclosing scope completes execution.

The lifetime of instance variables is dependent upon the objects that contain them. When an object is constructed, the lifetime of all of its instance variables (both `private` and `public`) begins. An instance variable's lifetime ends only when the object is orphaned. Figure 6.11 summarizes scope and lifetime of various program entities.

Figure 6.11 Scope and lifetime of various program entities

	Scope	Lifetime
local variable	The body of the enclosing method	The period of time during which the enclosing method is running
formal parameter	The body of the enclosing method	The period of time during which the enclosing method is running
private instance variable	The class in which the variable is declared	The period of time during which the object containing the instance variable is accessible
public instance variable	Anywhere that a reference to the object containing the instance variable is available	The period of time during which the object containing the instance variable is accessible
private method	The class in which the method is declared	
public method	Anywhere that a reference to the object belonging to the method's class is available	

Good software engineers practice **defensive programming**, just as good drivers practice defensive driving. One important tenant of defensive programming is to protect supplier code from undesirable use by client code. This is analogous to a defensive driver guarding against the conduct of other drivers.

One way to program defensively is to restrict scope as much as possible. The reasoning behind this philosophy is that if clients do not have access to a variable, then they cannot assign it unwanted values.

This preference for more restrictive declaration suggests that it is better to declare a method to be `private` than `public`. Of course, some methods need to be public, but the programmer has an obligation to use caution before choosing to make a method `public`.

From a defensive programming perspective, the most preferred scope for a variable is local. However, variables sometimes need to be retained from one method call until a subsequent call of the same (or some other) method. In such cases, the variable cannot be local, so it should be declared as a `private` instance variable.

To illustrate the need for various kinds of scope and lifetime, consider the problem of implementing the class described by the interface definition from Figure 6.12.

Figure 6.12 NestedCircles class diagram and specifications

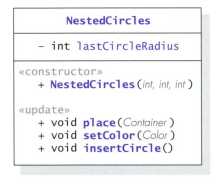

NestedCircles Class Specifications

Invariant

A NestedCircles object
    is a filled circular region, possibly with black, concentric circles upon it

Constructor Methods

public **NestedCircles** (int x, int y, int r)

    precondition

    $r > 0$

    postcondition

    A new black filled NestedCircles object is created with upper-left corner at (x, y) AND lastCircleRadius == r

Continued on next page.

Update Methods

```
public void place ( Container c )
```
   postcondition
   This NestedCircles is placed upon *c* AND removed from any prior placement.
```
public void setColor ( Color c )
```
   precondition
   c is a valid Color
   postcondition
   This filled NestedCircles is recolored using color *c*
```
public void insertCircle ( )
```
   postcondition
   lastCircleRadius == 0.8 * old lastCircleRadius AND a black outlined
   AOval with radius of lastCircleRadius is placed concentrically upon this
   object

A NestedCircles object behaves generally like an AOval that is always filled and has only four methods. The most unique feature of NestedCircles is the insertCircle method. Each call to insertCircle draws a new concentric black circle outline upon the NestedCircles object. Furthermore, each new black circle outline has a radius that is 80% of the radius of the most recent prior black circle outline on the same object. Figure 6.13 contains suitable code for the NestedCircles class.

Figure 6.13 NestedCircles class

```java
import aLibrary.*;
import java.awt.*;
/* Invariant
      A NestedCircles object...
          is a filled circular region, possibly with black,
          concentric circles upon it */
public class NestedCircles {
    private AOval background;
    private int lastCircleRadius;
    /* precondition
          r > 0
       postcondition
          A new black filled NestedCircles object is created
          with upper-left corner at (x, y)
          AND lastCircleRadius == r */
    public NestedCircles(int x, int y, int r) {
        background = new AOval(x, y, 2*r, 2*r);
        background.setToFill();
        lastCircleRadius = r;
    }
```

Continued on next page.

```
        /* postcondition
                This is placed upon c AND removed from any prior
                placement. */
        public void place(Container c) {
            background.place(c);
        }
        /* precondition
                c is a valid Color
            postcondition
                this is recolored using color c */
        public void setColor(Color c) {
            background.setColor(c);
        }
        /* postcondition
                lastCircleRadius == 0.8* old lastCircleRadius
                AND a black outlined AOval with radius of lastCircleRadius
                is placed concentrically upon this object */
        public void insertCircle() {
            AOval innerCircle;
            int newX;
            lastCircleRadius = (int)(lastCircleRadius *.8);
            newX = (background.getWidth() - 2*lastCircleRadius) / 2;
            innerCircle = new AOval(newX, newX, 2*lastCircleRadius,
                    2*lastCircleRadius);
            innerCircle.place(background);
            background.repaint();
        }
    }
```

There are four variables declared within the NestedCircles class, namely background, lastCircleRadius, innerCircle, and newX. They illustrate why a programmer might choose one category of variable over another.

The background variable is bound to the filled AOval upon which the concentric circles are placed. background is constructed by the NestedCircles method, colored by the setColor method, placed for drawing by the place method, and a call to insertCircle places an AOval upon background. Since all of these methods share a common background variable, it is impossible to declare it as a local variable.

The choice between declaring background to be public or private doesn't involve correctness because the program can be written correctly for either declaration. However, if background is public, then the client code is free to change background's dimensions, remove it from the display, or even assign it a different object. These are the kinds of unwanted variable corruption that motivate defensive programming. In this case the defensive thing to do is declare background as a private instance variable.

SOFTWARE ENGINEERING TIP

The need-to-know concept is useful in determining whether to use **public** or **private**. The supplier class needs to make things **public** only when clients "need to know." Otherwise, **private** is a better choice than **public** for variables and methods.

The `lastCircleRadius` variable is somewhat similar to background. `lastCircleRadius` needs to be maintained between consecutive calls to `insertCircle` so that each call can draw a circle outline that is 80% of the previous circle outline. Since the lifetime of local variables does not span consecutive calls, `lastCircleRadius` must be an instance variable. Furthermore, it is better defensive programming to declare `lastCircleRadius` to be private rather than public.

The `innerCircle` variable is used to construct a new circle outline. This `innerCircle` variable is never used outside the `insertCircle` method, nor is its value needed by subsequent calls to `insertCircle`. Therefore, `innerCircle` can be thought of as an implementation detail of the `insertCircle` method, and it is properly declared local to `insertCircle`. The program would still work properly if `innerCircle` were declared as an instance variable, but there is no reason to do so. Worst of all, if `innerCircle` were a `public` instance variable, it would most likely be a distraction for anyone writing client code.

The variable `newX` is even more of an implementation detail of `insertCircle`. As a matter of fact, `newX` can be eliminated altogether by passing more complicated arguments to the call to the `AOval` constructor. As with the `innerCircle` variable, sound defensive programming practice favors local declarations whenever possible.

6.5   CLASS INTERFACE DESIGN PRINCIPLES

In a large programming project it is typical to assign software development work by classes, so that each programmer has responsibility for his/her own classes. These classes *must* work cooperatively. It can be expected that one class will declare instance variables belonging to other classes and call methods written by other programmers.

This environment of separate classes, often written by different developers, places extreme importance on the quality of the **software interfaces**. A software interface is the connection between a supplier and its client classes/objects. In other words, software interfaces consist of things such as `public` instance variables and `public` methods, and the specifications of how they behave.

One of the critical steps in a software development project is designing the software interfaces. During this step of design the following decisions must be made:

- What different classes are needed to write the program?
- Which class is responsible for storing various required information?
- Which class is responsible for various required operations?
- What is the class invariant for each class?
- What are the `public` instance variables and methods of each class?
- What are the parameter lists of each method?
- What are the preconditions and postconditions for each method?

Obviously, designing software interfaces for large projects is a complex activity that requires considerable insight and skill.

The tools and techniques used in software interface design for larger projects are also quite useful for smaller programs. Class diagrams and class specifications are good examples of such tools. Even the smallest object-oriented programs use other supplier classes, and class diagrams and specifications are the best known tools for defining these suppliers. A good approach to designing software interfaces is to begin with the class diagram, then proceed to the class specification.

There are two important design principles that are key to designing a good class interface.

> ### Class Interface Design Principles
>
> 1. Locate members in the classes with strongest association.
> 2. Keep the interface thin.

The first principle is particularly important when first beginning to write suppliers. Designers must regularly choose the class that is the best location for a particular instance variable or method. When a program consists of a single `Director` class, there is no decision—everything is a feature of `Director`. As soon as you begin to write your own supplier classes, you must begin to choose where to place features.

The first design principle suggests that features should be located within the class that is most strongly associated. For example, the `valueInCents` method is more closely associated with `MoneyUSA` than with `Director`. Similarly, the `addToSavings` method is logically associated with `PersonalBudget` and not `MoneyUSA`.

One technique for measuring the association of a potential instance variable and a class is to answer the question, "Is it natural for this class to *contain* this variable?" The answer is positive for all of the following:

Yes, it is natural for `MoneyUSA` to contain a `pennies` variable.
Yes, it is natural for a `PersonalBudget` to contain `outstandingExpenses`.
Yes, it is natural for a `NestedCircles` object to contain a `lastCircleRadius`.

Sometimes the answer to the question is clearly negative.

No, it doesn't make sense for `MoneyUSA` to contain a background of type `AOval`.
No, it doesn't make sense for `NestedCircles` to contain `cashOnHand`.

At other times the issue is a matter of degrees.

It is more logical for `MoneyUSA` to contain `dimes` than for `PersonalBudget` to contain `dimes`.

Selecting the best class for a method involves a slightly different question, "Is it natural for this method to be applied to an object of this type?" Using this question as a measure of previous methods leads to the following conclusions.

It seems natural for `insertCircle` to be applied to a `NestedCircles` object.

It doesn't make sense to apply the `consolidate` method to a `NestedCircles` object.

It is more sensible to apply `valueInCents` to a `MoneyUSA` object than a `PersonalBudget`.

SOFTWARE ENGINEERING TIP

If you can think of a natural association between a feature and some other class, don't locate the feature within **Director**. It is best to keep **Director** small and reserve it for the few features that truly are central to the program.

One of the most difficult decisions is whether or not to locate methods and instance variables within the `Director` class. Prior to this chapter, all variables and methods were located within `Director`, so it is natural to want to continue to keep things in `Director`. Generally, `Director` needs to contain only a few key features—perhaps a window that is shared by many objects and a few initial objects that are widely shared.

OPENING
the Black Box

When deciding which class will contain a feature, it may be helpful to know why the name `Director` was chosen for the initial objects used in the applications of this text. A common pattern among object-oriented programs is for one object to play a central role in the program's execution. Like a motion-picture director, this object starts the action, coordinates the activities of other objects, and supervises program execution.

The second design principle, "Keep the interface thin," is related to early comments about defensive programming. Every `public` feature adds to the "thickness" of an interface. A `public` instance variable contributes more thickness than a `public` method, and update methods are thicker than queries. A **thin interface** is one that restricts the number of methods, especially those that provide opportunity for corrupting an object by unintended access.

The best technique for keeping interfaces thin is called **information hiding**. A class uses information hiding whenever it "hides" variables and methods by declaring them to be `private` or local. Information hiding leads to thin interfaces, and thin interfaces are a key aspect of defensive programming.

As an example of the use of these principles, consider a program that uses an `A3ButtonWindow` for zooming in and out on a shadowed red dot. Figure 6.14 contains a picture of the initial window.

The requirements for this program stipulate that at all times the window must display a centered red circular dot. Furthermore, this dot must have a shadow of the same size. The location of the shadow is a distance that is 10% of the dot's diameter above and 10% to the right of the dot. Initially, the dot should have a diameter of 200 pixels. The actions to be performed by the three buttons are described below.

LEFT   Each LEFT button click causes the dot (and its shadow) to increase in size by 20%, while remaining centered.

MID   Each MID button click causes the dot (and its shadow) to reset to original size and location.

RIGHT   Each RIGHT button click causes the dot (and its shadow) to decrease in size by 30%, while remaining centered.

Figure 6.14 Shadowed red dot display

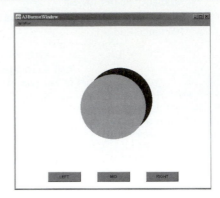

This set of requirements can be satisfied by a program with a single Director class alone. However, the shadowed red dot seems like an obvious candidate for its own supplier class. This suggests that the use of two classes, namely Director and ShadowedRedDot, is a good design decision.

The program appears to involve three main objects: a red dot, the dot's shadow, and an A3ButtonWindow (together with its buttons). The designer must locate each of these objects with one of the two classes. Using the design principle of close association, it seems best to locate the dot and shadow objects within ShadowedRedDot. However, the window object is best left in Director. The decision to locate window in Director is based on two observations: (1) windows are not really "contained" within a ShadowedRedDot, and (2) windows tend to be central to a program and are likely to be shared. (In this case the buttons and the dot share the same window.)

Designing methods begins by investigating the actions to be performed. For this set of requirements the dot must be able to *grow*, *shrink*, and be *reset* to its original size. The *grow* and *shrink* behaviors are similar to a camera lens that zooms in and zooms out. By using a parameter to capture the amount of zooming, *grow* and *shrink* can be combined into a single zoom method. Since reset and zoom methods are applied to dots, these methods are best located within ShadowedRedDot. Figure 6.15 shows class diagrams that match the design as it has been presented so far.

The class diagram for ShadowedRedDot illustrates two additional design decisions. It has been decided to keep the interface thin by declaring dot and shadow as private instance variables. Secondly, the ShadowedRedDot constructor method includes a parameter, so that the circles can be placed on their window within the same method that creates them.

Good designers typically review the class diagrams before they add more detailed software contracts. Once these diagrams appear to be complete and well organized, it is time to build class specifications. Figure 6.16 shows a set of class specifications for the ShadowedRedDot class.

Most of the specifications for a ShadowedRedDot are invariant. Both the dot and its shadow have a fixed color, remain filled, and remain placed throughout the program. The dot is always circular and always stays centered in the window. The diameter of the shadow is the same as the dot's diameter. The placement of the

Figure 6.15 Class diagrams for shadowed red dot program

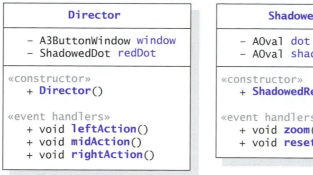
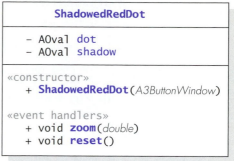

Figure 6.16 ShadowedRedDot class specifications

ShadowedRdDot Class Specifications

Invariant

A ShadowedRedDot object

- is a filled circular region colored red
- is centered in the A3ButtonWindow on which it is placed
- has a shadow that is the same size as dot and colored black
- the shadow is delta units left and above dot upon the window (delta is 10% of the diameter of dot)

Constructor Methods

public **ShadowedRedDot** (A3ButtonWindow w)

  postcondition

  dot.getWidth() == dot.getHeight() == 200

Update Methods

public void **zoom** (double d)

  postcondition

  dot.getWidth() == old dot.getWidth() * (100 + d)/100

  AND dot.getHeight()== old dot.getHeight() * (100 + d)/100

public void **reset** ()

  postcondition

  dot.getWidth() == dot.getHeight() == 200

shadow is based on a fixed percentage of the dot's diameter. About the only attribute of ShadowedRedDot that isn't invariant is the diameter of the dot.

One decision that the designer made when creating these class specifications was how to utilize the zoom method's parameter. From the specifications it is clear that the zoom parameter transmits a percentage of diameter change. For example, the following call

```
        redDot.zoom( 65.0 );
```

increases the diameter of redDot by 65%, and the call below

```
        redDot.zoom( -50.0 );
```

reduces redDot to half its prior diameter.

The class specifications provide enough information about the software interface for the Director class and the ShadowedRedDot class to be written independently. Figure 6.17 contains a suitable implementation for Director.

Figure 6.17 Director class for shadowed red dot program

```java
// Shadowed Dot Program
// Date: June, 2000
import aLibrary.*;
import java.awt.*;
public class Director extends A3ButtonHandler {
    private A3ButtonWindow window;
    private ShadowedRedDot redDot;
    /* postcondition
            A window is displayed
            AND a shadowed red dot is placed in the window's center
            AND the shadowed dot has a diameter of 200 pixels. */
    public Director() {
        window = new A3ButtonWindow(this);
        redDot = new ShadowedRedDot( window );
        window.repaint();
    }

    /* postcondition
            the shadowed dot is enlarged by 20% from its old
            diameter */
    public void leftAction() {
        redDot.zoom( 20.0 );
    }

    /* postcondition
            the shadowed dot is reset to a diameter of 200 pixels */
    public void midAction() {
        redDot.reset();
    }

    /* postcondition
            the shadowed dot is reduced by 30% from its old
            diameter */
    public void rightAction() {
        redDot.zoom( -30.0 );
    }
}
```

The implementation of Director is quite straightforward because most of the responsibility was shifted, by the various design decisions, to ShadowedRedDot. The resulting Director is short and easy to read, which is indicative of a good design.

Figure 6.18 contains an implementation for ShadowedRedDot. The assertions (class invariant, preconditions, and postconditions) from the class specifications are included in this class as documentation of code behavior.

Figure 6.18 ShadowedRedDot class

```java
import aLibrary.*;
import java.awt.*;
/* Invariant
        A ShadowedRedDot object...
        is a filled circular region colored red
        AND is centered in the A3ButtonWindow on which it is placed
        AND has a shadow that is the same size as dot and colored black
        AND the shadow is delta units left & above dot upon the window
            (delta is 10% of the diameter of dot) */
public class ShadowedRedDot {
    private AOval dot, shadow;
    /* postcondition
            dot.getWidth() == dot.getHeight == 200 */
    public ShadowedRedDot(A3ButtonWindow w ) {
        dot = new AOval(w.getWidth()/2-100,
        w.getHeight()/2-100, 200, 200);
        dot.setColor( Color.red );
        dot.setToFill();
        shadow = new AOval(dot.getX()+20, dot.getY()-20,
            200, 200);
        shadow.setColor( Color.black );
        shadow.setToFill();
        shadow.place(w);
        shadow.repaint();
        dot.place(w);
        dot.repaint();
    }
    /* postcondition
            dot.getWidth() is increased by d percent from old
            getWidth() AND dot.getHeight() is increased by d percent
            from old getHeight() */
    public void zoom(double d) {
        dot.translate( (int)(-d/200*dot.getWidth()),
                        (int)(-d/200*dot.getHeight()) );
        dot.scale( 1.0+d/100, 1.0+d/100 );
        shadow.setSize( dot.getWidth(), dot.getHeight() );
        shadow.setLocation( dot.getX()+(int)
                        (dot.getWidth()*0.1),
                         dot.getY()-(int)
                        (dot.getHeight()*0.1) );
```

Continued on next page.

```
            dot.repaint();
            shadow.repaint();
    }
    /* postcondition
            dot.getWidth() == dot.getHeight == 200 */
    public void reset() {
        int dotCenterX, dotCenterY;
        dotCenterX = dot.getX() + dot.getWidth()/2;
        dotCenterY = dot.getY() + dot.getHeight()/2;
        dot.setSize( 200, 200 );
        dot.setLocation( dotCenterX-100, dotCenterY-100 );
        shadow.setSize( 200, 200 );
        shadow.setLocation( dot.getX()+20, dot.getY()-20 );
        dot.repaint();
        shadow.repaint();
    }
}
```

Most of the work within ShadowedRedDot involves placing and recentering the dot and shadow variables. For example, the first two instructions in zoom are as follows.

```
dot.translate(  (int)(-d/200*dot.getWidth()),
                (int)(-d/200*dot.getHeight()) );
dot.scale( 1.0+d/100, 1.0+d/100 );
```

Executing the first of these two instructions recenters dot using the parameter d. This is accomplished by moving dot up and to the left by an amount that is equal to half its growth. Suppose that the ShadowedRedDot is supposed to grow by 100%; then d == 100. For this value of d the translate instruction becomes

```
dot.translate(  (int)(-100/200*dot.getWidth()),
                (int)(-100/200*dot.getHeight()) );
```

which simplifies to

```
dot.translate(  (int)(-1/2*dot.getWidth()),
                (int)(-1/2*dot.getHeight()) );
```

which signifies a move by one half of the dot's diameter.

The second instruction above calls scale to resize dot. For example, suppose again that d == 100. Substituting the value 100 for d results in the following scale method call.

```
dot.scale( 1.0+100/100, 1.0+100/100 );
```

which simplifies to

```
dot.scale( 2.0, 2.0 );
```

6.6   SEPARATING READ AND WRITE ACCESS

The concept of information hiding can be carried one step further. To understand this technique it is necessary to investigate variable usage.

Program variables are used in two different ways by code:

1. A variable may be assigned a value. (myVar = someExpression;)

2. A variable's value may be utilized in some other calculation.
(System.out.println(myVar);)

These two forms of variable access are often referred to as **write access** and **read access**, respectively. Assigning a new value to a variable is like *writing* to that variable, and using the variable's value in some expression or as a method argument is akin to *reading* the variable's content.

Instructions are permitted *both* read access and write access to all instance variables declared within the same class. However, instructions have read access only (no write access) to constants. Client classes have *neither* read access nor write access to private variables from supplier classes. On the other hand, the supplier's public instance variables are available to a client for *both* read and write access.

Sometimes it is desirable for a supplier to grant *either* read access or write access to clients without granting both. Granting read access without write access is called **read-only access**. Similarly, granting write access without read access is known as **write-only access**. The technique for providing read-only (or write-only) access requires two things:

1. declaring the instance variable to be private

2. including a method in the supplier class that provides the desired access to the private variable

For example, suppose that the programmer designing ShadowedRedDot wishes to store a read-only variable to count to the number of times zoom is called. A new zoomCounter instance variable can be included in the ShadowedRedDot class with the following private declaration:

```
private int zoomCounter = 0;
```

The zoom method must also be edited to perform the necessary counting.

The simplest way to grant read-only access to a private variable is accomplished by an **accessor method**—a nonvoid method that returns the variable. The following countOfZoomCalls illustrates use of an accessor method. This method is designed to be included within the ShadowedRedDot class.

SOFTWARE ENGINEERING TIP

Defensive programming suggests the following order of preference (from best to worst)

- no access to a variable (private variable)
- read-only access
- write-only access
- both read and write via supplier methods
- public variable (only as a last resort)

```
/* postcondition
      result == zoomCounter */
public int countOfZoomCalls() {
    return zoomCounter;
}
```

Granting write-only access is done in much the same way, except that a public void method is used to assign a value to the variable. For example, suppose that the nickels variable of MoneyUSA needs to be write-only. This can be done by declaring nickels to be private and including the following method within MoneyUSA.

```
/* precondition
      n >= 0
   modifies
      nickels
   postcondition
      nickels == n */
public void setNickels( int n ) {
    nickels = n;
}
```

Notice that the setNickels method simply assigns the value of its parameter to the nickels variable. This method gives the client a method for assigning a new value to nickels. However, the client must use a call to setNickels rather than use an assignment instruction.

OPENING
the Black Box

The following changes to the MoneyUSA class (from Figure 6.5) improve this supplier class because they make the interface thinner.

1. Change the declarations of all of the following instance variables from public to private: dollars, quarters, dimes, nickels, pennies

2. Include all of the following accessor methods: **getDollars**, **getQuarters**, **getDimes**, **getNickels**, **getPennies**

3. Include all of the following write access methods: **setDollars**, **setQuarters**, **setDimes**, **setNickels**, **setPennies**

The second design principle, "Keep the interface thin," is related to early comments about defensive programming. Library classes regularly use these techniques for granting read-only and write-only attribute access. The write access methods are often named "set..." and accessor methods are frequently named "get...". Examples of such methods from the *aLibrary* classes are getX, getWidth, setLocation, and setSize.

Color attributes are often accessed using *both* a read-only method and a write-only method. For example, AOval, ARectangle, and ARoundRectangle all include both getColor and setColor methods. This illustrates that sometimes it is possible to provide both read and write access without declaring the variable as public. Not only is it possible, but it is generally better use of information hiding. The reason for preferring separate methods is that they give the supplier more control. The setColor method can check its argument before assigning an invalid color, potentially avoiding a run-time error.

6.7 METHOD OVERLOADING

By now you have probably noticed that Java allows supplier classes to include multiple methods with the same name. Such reuse of method names is known as **overloading**. Overloading of method names is permitted within a class so long as any two methods with the same name have different parameter lists (i.e., the number of parameters and/or the type(s) of parameters differ).

The Math class, described in the previous chapter, provides two versions of the round method. One version rounds from float to int and the other from double to long. The specifications of these methods are shown below.

```
/* postcondition result == f rounded to the nearest integer */
int Math.round( float f )
/* postcondition result == d rounded to the nearest integer */
long Math.round( double d )
```

Because of the requirement for different parameter lists, overloading doesn't lead to ambiguity. If the Math.round method is called with a float type argument, then it rounds to an int. Similarly, if Math.round is called with a double argument, it rounds to a long. The compiler determines which method to call based on the type of the actual argument.

Another common usage of overloading occurs for constructor methods. Figure 6.19 contains a class diagram and Figure 6.20 a class specification for the Color class. Color is a standard Java library class from the *awt* library and used by many of the *aLibrary* classes.

The Color class diagram and specification show that this class includes two constructor methods—one with three int arguments, and one with three float arguments. These arguments determine the color intensity for red, green, and blue components, respectively, of a Color object. The values of the int arguments range from 0 (for least color intensity) to 255 (for most color intensity). The float arguments must be in the range from 0.0f (least color intensity) to 1.0f (most color intensity).

The term "overloading" is generally used to refer to using the same name for multiple methods. A closely related concept occurs when a single class uses the same name in multiple variable declarations. This is not permitted when all variables have the same scope. However, a variable name *can* be reused when the scopes differ.

The rule for such variable name reuse is: *Use the identifier declared in the innermost enclosing scope.* Suppose, as shown below, that the variable myVar is declared as both an instance variable of class MyClass and also as a local variable within the myMethod method of MyClass.

```
public class MyClass {
    public int myVar;
    public void myMethod {
        int myVar;
        . . .
    }
    . . .
}
```

An unqualified reference to myVar within the body of myMethod refers to the local variable, because this is the innermost scope. An unqualified reference to myVar within the remainder of MyClass refers to the instance variable, assuming no other myVar declarations. Figure 6.21 summarizes the rules for reusing identifiers within a class.

SOFTWARE ENGINEERING TIP

Figure 6.21 makes it evident that the rules for reusing identifiers are messy. Generally, it is safer to avoid reusing names. One notable exception is overloading, especially for constructor methods.

Figure 6.19 Color class diagram

```
                              Color
─────────────────────────────────────────────────────────────
   - int red
   - int green
   - int blue
─────────────────────────────────────────────────────────────
«constants»
   + Color Color.white     //red, green, blue values of 255,255,255
   + Color Color.black     //red, green, blue values of 0,0,0
   + Color Color.lightGray //red, green, blue values of 192,192,192
   + Color Color.gray      //red, green, blue values of 128,128,128
   + Color Color.darkGray  //red, green, blue values of 64,64,64
   + Color Color.red       //red, green, blue values of 255,0,0
   + Color Color.pink      //red, green, blue values of 255,175,175
   + Color Color.orange    //red, green, blue values of 255,200,0
   + Color Color.yellow    //red, green, blue values of 255,255,0
   + Color Color.green     //red, green, blue values of 0,255,0
   + Color Color.magenta   //red, green, blue values of 255,0,255
   + Color Color.cyan      //red, green, blue values of 0,255,255
   + Color Color.blue      //red, green, blue values of 0,0,255

«constructor»
   public color(float, float, float)
   public color(int, int, int )

«other»
   ...
```

Figure 6.20 Color class specifications

Color Class Specifications

Invariant

A Color object ...

- is a color that can be used in drawing
- 0 <= red <= 255 AND 0 <= green <= 255 AND 0 <= blue <= 255

Continued on next page.

Constructor Methods

public **Color** (float r, float g, float b)
 precondition
 $0.0 <= r <= 1.0$ AND $0.0 <= g <= 1.0$ AND $0.0 <= b <= 1.0$
 postcondition
 A new **Color** object is created with attributes as follows:
 red == r * 255 AND green== g * 255 AND blue == b * 255

public **Color** (int r, int g, int b)
 precondition
 $0 <= r <= 255$ and $0 <= g <= 255$ and $0 <= b <= 255$
 postcondition
 A new **Color** object is created with attributes as follows:
 red == r AND green == g AND blue == b

Other Methods

. . .

Figure 6.21 Rules for reusing identifiers

Within Any Class:

1. Reusing (overloading) a name for multiple methods of the same class is allowed so long as the methods have different parameter lists.

2. Reusing a name for two entities (variables, constants, or formal parameters) within the same scope is a syntax error. (For this rule, **private** and **public** entities of the same class are treated as though they have the same scope.)

3. Reusing a name within two different scopes is permitted. (**private** and **public** entities of the same class are treated as though they have the same scope.)

4. Reserved word identifiers cannot be used for any other purpose than their predefined intent.

6.8   CHAR DATA TYPE

Many computer applications process textual data. A word processor assists users in preparing documents of textual data. A compiler translates the text of a source program into object code. An e-mail program assists with reading and composing electronic messages (typically in textual form).

Not surprisingly, Java includes built-in supplier classes to support text processing. The simplest data type associated with textual data is the primitive char type. Figure 6.22 summarizes char.

A value of char data can be either a single **printable character** or a single nonprintable character. The printable characters include

- uppercase and lowercase alphabetic letters (A-Z and a-z)
- decimal digits (0-9)
- punctuation marks (period, comma, and so forth)
- and special characters (#, $, *, and so forth)

Figure 6.22 Summary of the char data type

Name of the type: char

Usage: a single (unicode) character

Constants:

Any printable character enclosed within single quotes (no intervening blanks permitted). Escape sequences can also be used to specify constants.

Postfix operator (char → char)

[cannot be applied to constants or constant expressions]

syntax	*semantics*
++	autoincrement
--	autodecrement

Widening

char automatically widens to int, long, float, or double

The printable characters can be used as char constants so long as they are enclosed within single quotation marks. For example, the following are all valid constants of type char.

```
'A'
'4'
'?'
```

Some of the char constants cannot be written using the above notation. For these characters Java supports an **escape sequence** notation. An escape sequence consists of a backslash character (\) followed by a second character. The entire escape sequence is enclosed within single quotation marks to form a char constant. Figure 6.23 includes commonly used escape sequences for char constants.

Some escape sequences are designed to denote nonprintable characters. Nonprintables include such things as tabs and linefeed characters. Other char constants requiring the use of escape sequences include the single quotation mark, the double quotation mark, and the backslash.

Since computer storage encodes everything in numeric form, char constants also have a numeric value. Java uses the **unicode** encoding scheme to encode char values. There are more than 65,000 characters included in unicode. The first 128 characters are known as the **ASCII characters**. Figure 6.24 shows the encoding for the ASCII portion of the unicode alphabet.

Figure 6.23 Escape sequence char constants

Character	Escape code constant
single quotation mark (')	'\''
double quotation mark (")	'\"'
backslash character (\)	'\\'
backspace	'\b'
tab	'\t'
linefeed (new line)	'\n'
form feed	'\f'
carriage return	'\r'

Figure 6.24 The first 128 unicode characters

Dec	Hex	char	Dec	Hex	char	Dec	Hex	char	Dec	Hex	char
0	0000	<NUL>	33	0021	!	66	0042	B	99	0063	c
1	0001	<SOH>	34	0022	"	67	0043	C	100	0064	d
2	0002	<STX>	35	0023	#	68	0044	D	101	0065	e
3	0003	<ETX>	36	0024	$	69	0045	E	102	0066	f
4	0004	<EOT>	37	0025	%	70	0046	F	103	0067	g
5	0005	<ENQ>	38	0026	&	71	0047	G	104	0068	h
6	0006	<ACK>	39	0027	'	72	0048	H	105	0069	i
7	0007	<BEL>	40	0028	(	73	0049	I	106	006A	j
8	0008	<BS>	41	0029	)	74	004A	J	107	006B	k
9	0009	<HT>	42	002A	*	75	004B	K	108	006C	l
10	000A	<LF>	43	002B	+	76	004C	L	109	006D	m
11	000B	<VT>	44	002C	'	77	004D	M	110	006E	n
12	000C	<FF>	45	002D	–	78	004E	N	111	006F	o
13	000D	<CR>	46	002E	.	79	004F	O	112	0070	p
14	000E	<SO>	47	002F	/	80	0050	P	113	0071	q
15	000F	<SI>	48	0030	0	81	0051	Q	114	0072	r
16	0010	<DLE>	49	0031	1	82	0052	R	115	0073	s
17	0011	<DC1>	50	0032	2	83	0053	S	116	0074	t
18	0012	<DC2>	51	0033	3	84	0054	T	117	0075	u
19	0013	<DC3>	52	0034	4	85	0055	U	118	0076	v
20	0014	<DC4>	53	0035	5	86	0056	V	119	0077	w
21	0015	<NAK>	54	0036	6	87	0057	W	120	0078	x
22	0016	<SYN>	55	0037	7	88	0058	X	121	0079	y
23	0017	<ETB>	56	0038	8	89	0059	Y	122	007A	z
24	0018	<CAN>	57	0039	9	90	005A	Z	123	007B	{
25	0019	<EM>	58	003A	:	91	005B	[	124	007C		
26	001A	<SUB>	59	003B	;	92	005C	\	125	007D	}
27	001B	<ESC>	60	003C	<	93	005D	]	126	007E	~
28	001C	<FS>	61	003D	=	94	005E	^	127	007F	<DEL>
29	001D	<GS>	62	003E	>	95	005F	_	128	0080	
30	001E	<RS>	63	003F	?	96	0060		...	...	
31	001F	<US>	64	0040	@	97	0061	a			
32	0020	␣	65	0041	A	98	0062	b			

<...> denotes a nonprintable character
␣ denotes a space/blank

Java recognizes one additional form of escape sequence for any char constant. This notation consists of a backslash (\) followed by a lower case "u" followed by the hexadecimal equivalent of the character. Figure 6.24 indicates the hexadecimal equivalent for the ASCII characters in the columns labeled "Hex". Using this escape code notation, the character '+' can be expressed '\u002B' and 'q' is expressed as '\u0071'.

Figure 6.24 also illustrates that each char value has a numeric equivalent. The numeric value of a character is the value resulting from widening a char to an int. The columns labeled "Dec" shows the decimal numeric equivalent for the corresponding char values. For example, the character 'Y' has a numeric value of 89 and '{' has a value of 123. Notice that the numeric value of decimal digits is different than might be expected. The character '2' has a numeric value of 50 and '9' has a numeric value of 57. Any char expression is converted to its numeric equivalent by a cast to int.

Sometimes it is useful to increment a char variable from one character to the next. Such a pattern can be used to advance the value of a char variable from one alphabetic letter to its successor or from one decimal digit character to the next. Figure 6.25 shows two patterns for accomplishing such char incrementation.

Figure 6.25 Two patterns incrementing char variables

$$charVar_{++}$$

or

$$charVar = (char) (charVar + 1);$$

The first pattern is the simpler one, but the second illustrates how char expressions can be widened automatically, as well as how to cast an int expression to a char.

6.9 STRINGS

The char data type restricts variables and expressions to representing just one character at a time. However, programs must often manipulate sequences of characters, also known as a **strings**. Java provides an appropriate library (supplier) class, called String. Figure 6.26 contains a class diagram that describes the most important String methods. Figure 6.27 gives the String class specifications.

A String is the only Java reference data type that recognizes a built-in syntax for constants. This notation consists of any sequence of characters enclosed within double quotations. Each line below contains a separate String constant.

```
"This is a string."
"1725 State Street"
"line 1\nline 2\n"
```

The last of the above three lines contains two linefeed (\n) characters, specified by escape sequences. (A linefeed character in Java separates a String into separate lines.)

Figure 6.26 String class diagram

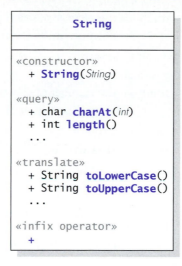

Figure 6.27 String class specifications

String Class Specifications

Invariant

A String object

- is a sequence of zero or more char values
- is immutable (cannot be altered once it is instantiated)

String Constant

A String constant consists of any sequence of char constants without enclosing single quotes. The entire string constant must be preceded and followed by double quotation marks (").

Constructor Methods

public **String** (String s)

postcondition

A new String object is created and the sequence of characters is the same as s

Other Methods

public char **charAt** (int p)

precondition

p < length()

Continued on next page.

postcondition

result == the char at position p from this string (note that zero is the
position of the leftmost character)

`public int `**`length`**` ( )`

postcondition

result == the number of characters in this string

`public String `**`toUpperCase`**` ( )`

postcondition

result == this with every lowercase letter replaced by the
corresponding uppercase letter

`public String `**`toLowerCase`**` ( )`

postcondition

result == this with every uppercase letter replaced by the
corresponding lowercase letter

Infix Operator

`+`   evaluates to a string that consists of its two operand strings concatenated (joined).

As with primitive types, the `String` constant yields an object without the use of the `new` operator. The following example instructions illustrate.

```
stateString = "Wisconsin";
System.out.println( "Your message goes here." );
```

A second unique characteristic of the `String` type is that it supports the infix "+" operator to concatenate two `String` expressions. As an example, the following instruction assigns "David D. Riley" to the `nameString` variable.

```
nameString = "David D" + "." + " Riley";
```

The "+" operator can also be used to combine a `String` expression with any other expression of primitive type. When this occurs, the primitive expression is converted to a `String` representation and concatenated with the string. For example, consider the following instruction sequence:

```
velocity = 12.5;
System.out.println( "The value of Velocity is " + velocity);
```

When the above two instructions execute, the second instruction sends the following line of text to the standard output stream:

```
The value of Velocity is 12.5
```

Objects of type `String` are **immutable** because they cannot be altered (mutated). The `String` class includes methods to query selected parts or properties of a `String` object. However, there are no "update" methods to alter an existing `String` object. Some of the methods from the `String` class include:

- length, to return the number of characters in the String object
- charAt, to return any selected char of the String object
- toLowerCase, to return the String object with uppercase letters replaced by lowercase
- toUpperCase, to return the String object with lowercase letters replaced by uppercase

CLOSED
Black Box

Any Java object can be output using System.out.println. For primitives and String expressions, System.out.println outputs the value of the expression. The default behavior of System.out.println for other objects is sometimes difficult to read. (The key to open this black box is found in Chapter 9.)

String shares some characteristics with the primitive types. However, String *is a reference type, not a primitive type.* As a result, assigning one String to another copies the binding to the same String object. Similarly, each String method returns a new String object.

Unfortunately, as a reference type, String is completely incompatible with char. This incompatibility is mentioned, because it is natural to think of a char as a String of length 1. Unfortunately, in Java the char and String types are as different as int and AOval. Some of the limitations of this incompatibility are listed below.

- You *cannot* pass a char argument to a String parameter (nor the opposite).
- You *cannot* use a char constant in place of a String constant.
- You *cannot* assign a char expression to a String variable (nor the opposite).

This last restriction is particularly troublesome, because there are many times in programs when char data and String data must be used cooperatively. Fortunately, Java provides tools to work around the incompatibility between char and String.

The charAt method is a tool for extracting a char from within a String. The charAt parameter specifies the position of the desired char (0 for leftmost character, 1 for second from the left, etc.). For example, executing the following two instructions, prints the char value 'X'.

```
String stringVar = "VWXYZ";
System.out.println( stringVar.charAt(2) );
```

Conversion from char to String requires a different approach. One such approach is to use the "+" (concatenate) operator described previously. Concatenating any char with a String of length zero (sometimes called an **empty string**) results in a String that consists of that char. The Java notation for an empty string is two consecutive double quotation marks. Therefore, the following expression

```
"" + 'B'
```

evaluates to a String of length 1, consisting of the letter B, or "B" in String constant notation. A more common use of such a conversion might be to convert the content of a char variable, as shown below:

```
// Assume that charVar is a variable of type char
// and stringVar a variable of type String
stringVar = "" + charVar;
```

The execution of this instruction assigns to stringVar a String object that consists of the single character from charVar.

This technique of constructing a String object from a char expression is easily extended to an expression pattern for converting any primitive expression into its String representation. As shown in Figure 6.28, any expression of primitive type (denoted *primitiveExpresssion*) can be converted to a String object by concatenating the primitive expression with an empty string. The result of applying this pattern is a String with the same appearance as that output by String.out.println(*primitiveExpression*);

Figure 6.28 Expression pattern for converting primitive to String

"" + *primitiveExpression*

6.10 ALABEL (OPTIONAL)

There are three classes with *aLibrary* for displaying strings. The simplest of these classes is called **ALabel**. The ALabel class is used to construct objects capable of displaying a single String on a single line. Figure 6.29 contains the class diagram for ALabel, and Figure 6.30 gives the corresponding class specification.

An ALabel object is similar to an ARectangle. Both are rectangular regions that can be placed upon other *aLibrary* objects. Both share corresponding constructor methods, as well as setLocation, setSize, setColor, repaint, getX, getY, getWidth, getHeight, and getColor methods.

The most important difference from ARectangle is that an ALabel contains a string that is displayed on top of its rectangle. The particular string to be displayed is assigned (or updated) by the setText method.

There are three options for the way that an ALabel's string to be displayed, namely **left justified**, **right justified**, and **centered**. A left-justified string is displayed as far to the left as possible within the ALabel rectangle as shown below:

```
myLabel.setText( "Eiffel" );
myLabel.setAlignmentLeft();
```

> Eiffel

The default alignment for ALabel is left justification. A right-justified string is displayed as far to the right as possible within the ALabel rectangle:

```
myLabel.setText( "Eiffel" );
myLabel.setAlignmentRight();
```

> Eiffel

A centered string is centered from left to right within the ALabel rectangle:

```
myLabel.setText( "Eiffel" );
myLabel.setAlignmentCenter();
```

> Eiffel

Figure 6.29 ALabel class diagram

```
                      ALabel
 ──────────────────────────────────────────
   - int x
   - int y
   - int width
   - int height
   - Color color
   - (one of left, right, or center) alignment
   - String text
   - int fontSize
 ──────────────────────────────────────────
 «constructor»
     public ALabel(int, int, int, int)
     ...

 «query»
     + int getX()
     + int getY()
     + int getWidth()
     + int getHeight()
     + Color getColor()
     + String getText()

 «update»
     + void repaint()
     + void setSize(int, int)
     + void setLocation(int, int)
     + void setColor(Color)
     + void setAlignmentCenter()
     + void setAlignmentLeft()
     + void setAlignmentRight()
     + void setText(String)
     + void setFontSize(int)
     + void place(Container)
     + void remove()
     ...
```

Figure 6.30 ALabel class specifications

ALabel Class Specifications

Invariant

An ALabel object

- is a rectangular region where a single line of text can be displayed on an AWindow, ARectangle, ARoundRectangle, AOval, or AView

- has an upper-left corner (when placed) that is x pixels from the left and y pixels from the top of the object upon which it is placed.

Continued on next page.

- is displayed (when placed) as a transparent rectangle with the string value from text displayed in color and aligned either to the left, right, or centered as chosen by the value of the alignment attribute. (Note that if text is too large to fit within width and/or height, then the characters are trimmed on the right and/or bottom. (*fontSize* determines the text size.)

Below is an ALabel inside an AWindow on which it is placed.

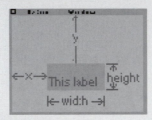

Constructor Methods

`public ALabel ( int newX, int newY, int w, int h )`

postcondition
A new ALabel object is created with attributes as follows: x == *newX* AND y == *newY* AND width == *w* AND height == *h* AND text == "" AND alignment == left AND color == Color.black AND *fontSize* == 10

. . .

Query Methods

`public int getX ( )`

postcondition
result == x

`public int getY ( )`

postcondition
result == y

`public int getWidth ( )`

postcondition
result == width

`public int getHeight ( )`

postcondition
result == height

`public int getColor ( )`

postcondition
result == color

`public String getText ( )`

postcondition
result == text

Update Methods

public void **repaint** ( )

> *postcondition*
>
> If this ALabel is placed, then its image is updated (redrawn) as soon as possible

public void **setSize** (int w, int h)

> *precondition*
> $w >= 0$ AND $h >= 0$
>
> *modifies*
> width, height
>
> *postcondition*
> width == w AND height == h

public void **setLocation** (int newX, int newY)

> *modifies*
> x, y
>
> *postcondition*
> x == *newX* AND y == *newY*

public void **setColor** (Color c)

> *precondition*
> c is a valid Color
>
> *modifies*
> color
>
> *postcondition*
> color == c

public void **setAlignmentCenter** ( )

> *postcondition*
> alignment == center

public void **setAlignmentLeft** ( )

> *postcondition*
> alignment == left

public void **setAlignmentRight** ( )

> *postcondition*
> alignment == right

public void **setText** (String s)

> *modifies*
> text
>
> *postcondition*
> text == s

Continued on next page.

```
public void setFontSize ( int f )
```

precondition

$f > 0$

modifies

fontSize

postcondition

fontSize == f

```
public void place ( Container c )
```

precondition

c != null (i.e., the c argument must be validly constructed)

postcondition

This ALabel is placed upon c and removed from any prior placement. Any portion of the ALabel that lies outside the object upon which it is placed will not be visible. (Note that a repaint() call may be necessary for the display to reflect the change.)

```
public void remove ( )
```

postcondition

This ALabel is no longer placed.

ALabel also includes a method to control the size of the ALabel text. A call to setFontSize method assigns a new height and width to all the characters within the associated ALabel object. The setFontSize method uses *points* as the unit of size. The default font size for an ALabel is 10 points, which is approximately the size used in a typical word processor. The following instructions show the effect of changing the font size.

```
myLabel.setText( "Eiffel" );
myLabel.setFontSize( 14 );
```

Eiffel

Figure 6.31 illustrates the use of ALabel and MoneyUSA objects. This program uses an A3ButtonWindow. Upon this window the program displays the count of dollars, quarters, dimes, and nickels from a monetary amount. Clicking the left button causes the number of dollars to be increased by 1. Clicking on the middle button causes the number of quarters to increase by 1 and the number of nickels to increase by 3. The right button is used to consolidate money into the largest possible denominations.

Figure 6.31 CountingMoney program

```java
// CountingMoney Driver
// Date: June, 2000
import aLibrary.*;
import java.awt.*;
public class Director extends A3ButtonHandler {
    private ALabel dollarLabel, quarterLabel;
    private ALabel dimeLabel, nickelLabel;
    private MoneyUSA money;

    /* postcondition
           A window is displayed that contains monetary denominations. */
    public Director() {
        A3ButtonWindow theWin;
        ALabel dollarLbl, quarterLbl;
        theWin = new A3ButtonWindow(this);
        dollarLabel = new ALabel(100, 10, 100, 30);
        dollarLabel.place(theWin);
        quarterLabel = new ALabel(100, 50, 100, 30);
        quarterLabel.place(theWin);
        dimeLabel = new ALabel(100, 90, 100, 30);
        dimeLabel.place(theWin);
        nickelLabel = new ALabel(100, 130, 100, 30);
        nickelLabel.place(theWin);
        money = new MoneyUSA(0, 0, 0, 0, 0);
        updateDisplay();
        theWin.repaint();
    }

    /* precondition
           money is instantiated
       postcondition
           money.dollars == old money.dollars + 1 */
    public void leftAction() {
        money.dollars++;
        updateDisplay();
    }

    /* precondition
           money is instantiated
       postcondition
           money.quarters == old money.quarters + 1
           AND money.nickels == old money.nickels + 3 */
    public void midAction() {
        money.quarters++;
        money.nickels = money.nickels + 3;
        updateDisplay();
    }
```

Continued on next page.

```
    /* precondition
            money is instantiated
        postcondition
            money.valueInCents == old money.valueInCents
            AND money consolidated into largest possible
            denominations */
    public void rightAction() {
        money.consolidate();
        updateDisplay();
    }

    /* precondition
            money is instantiated
        postcondition
            the output labels are updated to reflect the
            value of dollars, quarters, dimes, and nickels of
            the money variable */
    private void updateDisplay() {
        dollarLabel.setText( "Dollars: " + money.dollars );
        dollarLabel.repaint();
        quarterLabel.setText( "Quarters: " + money.quarters );
        quarterLabel.repaint();
        dimeLabel.setText( "Dimes: " + money.dimes );
        dimeLabel.repaint();
        nickelLabel.setText( "Nickels: " + money.nickels );
        nickelLabel.repaint();
    }
}
```

The Director class from Figure 6.31 includes a private method, called updateDisplay, to update the four labels. Each setText call assigns a string that consists of a label followed by the count of the corresponding monetary denomination. Each time that the value of the money changes, updateDisplay is called to cause the window to be properly redrawn.

JAVA INSPECTOR

Below is a collection of hints on what to check when examining code that involves the concepts of this chapter.

✓ Every feature (method or variable) should be checked for proper scope declaration. It is best to declare variables to be local. But when the lifetime of a variable must extend beyond one method execution, then it must be declared as an instance variable. It is better to declare class members to be `private` than `public`. But when a method is needed by client classes, then it is generally best for it to be declared `public`.

✓ Qualified expressions should be examined to be certain that they reference the correct object or method. The connections from one object to its `public` members read from left to right.

✓ Be careful with names that are reused. Check to ensure that the innermost enclosing declaration is the one that is desired.

✓ Method overloading requires that within one class, two methods with the same name must have different parameter lists. When overloading is used, check the parameter lists for the necessary differences.

✓ The constant notations for `char` and `String` are easily confused. Remember that `char` constants are enclosed between single quote characters, while `String` constants are enclosed between double quote characters.

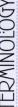

TERMINOLOGY

accessor method

aggregation (of classes)

ALabel

ASCII characters set

centered

char

client

client-supplier relation

composition (of classes)

concatenate

defensive programming

empty string

encapsulate

escape sequence

immutable

information hiding

left justified

lifetime (a property of objects)

overloading (methods)

printable character

private

public

qualified expressions

read access

read-only access

right justified

scope (a property of class features)

software interface

String

supplier

thin interface

unicode

visibility (property of identifiers)

write access

write-only access

1. Consider the following class:

```java
public class Auto {
    public int miles;
    public int gas;
    public Auto() {
        miles = 0;
        gas = 0;
    }

    public void addGas( int g ) {
        gas = gas + g ;
    }

    // additional methods belong here
}
```

a. Show the exact output that results from executing the following code (in some class other than Auto).

```java
Auto car = new Auto();
Auto compact = car;
car.miles = 2;
car.addGas( 5 );
System.out.println( car.miles );
System.out.println( car.gas);
compact.miles = car.miles + 1;
compact.addGas(7);
System.out.println( compact.miles );
System.out.println( compact.gas );
car = new Auto();
System.out.println( car.miles );
System.out.println( compact.miles );
```

b. Explain the lifetime of every miles attribute that occurs during the execution of part (a).

c. How does your answer to part (a) change if the following declaration is inserted into the addGas method?

```java
int gas;
```

d. Rewrite the Auto class so that all instance variables are private, but so that read access is provided by get... methods and write access by set... methods. Next rewrite part (a) to perform the same algorithm using these new means for reading from and writing to variables.

2. The following class makes use of the Auto class from Exercise 1.

```java
public class FamilyFleet {
    private Auto parentsCar;
    private Auto childrensCar;
    public FamilyFleet() {
        parentsCar = new Auto();
        childrensCar = new Auto();
    }
    public Auto getParentsCar() {
        return parentsCar;
    }

    public void setParentsCar( Auto a ) {
        parentsCar = a;
    }
    public Auto getChildrensCar() {
        return childrensCar;
    }

    public void setChildrensCar( Auto a ) {
        childrensCar = a;
    }
    // additional methods belong here
}
```

Using the FamilyFleet and Auto classes, assume that you are writing the code for a Director class that contains the following instance variable declaration.

```java
public class Director {
    private FamilyFleet ourCars, neighborCars;
    // additional methods belong here
}
```

For each part below, write a single Java instruction that can be placed within the Director class to perform the indicated task. (You may assume that all objects have been assigned some value by the execution of prior code.)

a. An instruction to construct a new object and assign it to ourCars

b. An instruction to output (using System.out.println) the number of miles traveled by our children's car

c. An instruction to increase the amount of gasoline in the neighbor's parent car by 15 gallons

d. An instruction to copy the amount of gasoline from our children's car into the car of the neighbor's children.

3. Draw a class diagram that includes the `Auto`, `FamilyFleet`, and `Director` classes. Be certain to include all known instance variables and methods, as well as lines to show class composition.

4. Using the environment from Exercise 2, explain what happens when the following instruction executes by drawing *before* and *after* object diagrams:

```
neighborsCars.setChildrensCar(ourCars.getParentsCar());
```

5. Consider the following two classes.

```java
public class Pizza {
    public int pepperoni;
    private int sausage;
    public int mozzarella;

    public Pizza(int p, int s, int m) {
        pepperoni = p;
        sausage = s;
        mozzarella = m;
    }
    public void enlarge() {
        pepperoni = sausage + 1;
        sausage++;
        mozzarella = sausage * 2;
    }
}
public class MyClass {
    public Pizza dinahsPie;
    private Pizza mamasPie;
    public MyClass() {
        Pizza bigJoesPie;
        dinahsPie = new Pizza(1, 2, 3);
        /* the code goes here */
    }
}
```

For each of the following parts, assume that the single instruction is substituted in place of

```
/* the code goes here */
```

What is the result? Your options are (1) an error in the parameter/argument lists, (2) a null pointer exception, (3) a compile time violation of scope rules, or (4) no compile-time or run-time errors will be detected.

a. `dinahsPie = new Pizza( pepperoni, sausage, mozzarella);`

b. `mamasPie = new Pizza(0, 0, dinahsPie.mozzarella);`

c. `dinahsPie = new Pizza(8, 9, 10);`

d. `bigJoesPie = new Pizza( p, s, m);`

e. `dinahsPie.sausage = 1000;`

f. `dinahsPie.mozzarella = 100;`

g. `dinahsPie.enlarge();`

h. `bigJoesPie.enlarge();`

6. Using the classes from Exercise 5, suppose that the following instructions replace /* the code goes here */.

```
bigJoesPie = new Pizza(10, 20, 30);
bigJoesPie.enlarge( );
bigJoesPie.enlarge( );
dinahsPie.enlarge();
```

What is the value of the following objects immediately following the execution of these instructions?

a. `bigJoesPie.pepperoni`

b. `bigJoesPie.mozzarella`

c. `dinahsPie.pepperoni`

d. `dinahsPie.mozzarella`

7. Precisely what is output by executing each of the following instructions?

a. `System.out.println( 'A' );`

b. `System.out.println( 'A' + 3 );`

c. `System.out.println( (char)98 );`

d. `System.out.println( (char)51 );`

e. `System.out.println( '\\' );`

f. `System.out.println( '\u0071' );`

g. `System.out.println( (char)('A' + 1) );`

h. `System.out.println( "A" );`

8. Precisely what is output by executing each of the following code segments?

a. ```
String s = "ABCdef";
System.out.println(s);
```

b.  ```
String s = "ABCdef";
System.out.println( s.toLowerCase() );
```

c. ```
String s = "ABCdef";
System.out.println(s + 25 + s);
```

d.  ```
String s = "ABCdef";
System.out.println( s.length() );
```

e. ```
String s = "ABCdef";
System.out.println(s.charAt(3));
```
```

PROGRAMMING EXERCISES

1. Write a separate class to maintain a counter along with an `ALabel` to display the counter, and use your class to perform the following.

   Write a program that an `A3ButtonWindow` together with two counters. The left counter is for counting the number of times that LEFT is clicked, and the right counter counts the number of times that RIGHT is clicked. Your counters should appear in the positions and sized as shown below. Initially, both counters are zero. Thereafter, the buttons behave as explained below.

   LEFT   This causes the left counter to be incremented by 1.

   MID   This causes both counters to reset to zero.

   RIGHT   This causes the right counter to be incremented by 1.

   The following picture shows a state when the "LEFT" button has been clicked twice and the "RIGHT" button five times since the last reset.

   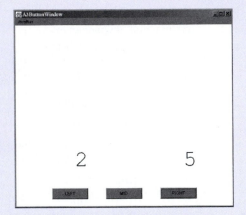

2. Write a program, using an `A3ButtonWindow`, that displays a blue triangle with filled blue `AOvals` (of diameter 10) centered on each vertex. Initially, the window should appear as follows. Thereafter, the buttons behave as explained below.

   LEFT   This causes the left vertex to move to its left by 5 pixels. The triangle and `AOval` are adjusted for this change.

   MID   This causes the top vertex to move up by 5 pixels. The triangle and `AOval` are adjusted for this change.

   RIGHT   This causes the right vertex to move to its right by 5 pixels. The triangle and `AOval` are adjusted for this change.

   Your program should include a separate class to encapsulate the triangle and its associated parts. (Note that you should look up the `ALine` specifications if you are not familiar with this class.)

3. This program allows the user to play a game that is like a mixture of ana-grams and a slot machine. When the program begins, the five four-letter words pictured below must be displayed with the same approximate size and spacing. The object of the game is to rearrange the letters to form five words that name various animals, using the three buttons, as follows.

LEFT   The second letter of each word shifts down to the same position in word below it. The second letter of the bottom word becomes the second letter of the top. (Note that this is like a slot machine wheel spinning down one notch.)

MID   The third letter of each word shifts down to the same position in word below it. The third letter of the bottom word becomes the third letter of the top.

RIGHT   The last letter of each word shifts down to the same position in word below it. The last letter of the bottom word becomes the last letter of the top.

The leftmost letter of each word never moves throughout the program execution. Your program must use a separate class to hold the words and associated features.

4. This program implements a clock face, using screen buttons to advance an hour hand and a minute hand. You must use a class called ClockHand that maintains a single one of the clock hands and associated features. Initially the clock is displayed as a 300 by 300 filled yellow circle upon an A3ButtonWindow. Button clicks produce the following results.

LEFT   The minute hand (the longer hand) is advanced by the equivalent of one minute.

MID   The value of the current hour and current minutes as displayed by the clock are output to the standard output stream. (It is okay if 12 o'clock displays as zero.)

RIGHT The hour hand (the shorter hand) is advanced by the equivalent of one hour.

[*Hints*: A ClockHand centered in an AView works well. Using cosine and sine is useful in determining the outside endpoints of the clock hands. ALine is the *aLibrary* class for drawing line segments.]

The picture below shows this clock at 3:08.

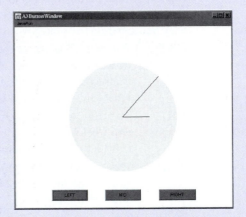

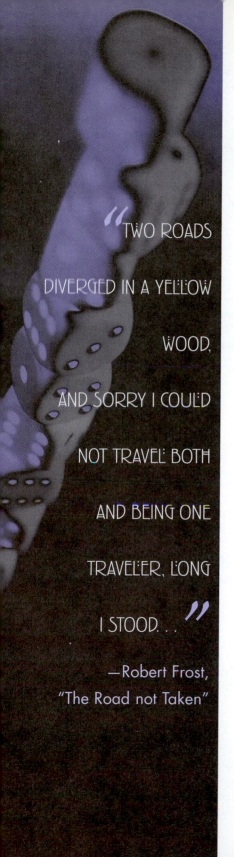

LOGIC AND SELECTION

"TWO ROADS

DIVERGED IN A YELLOW

WOOD,

AND SORRY I COULD

NOT TRAVEL BOTH

AND BEING ONE

TRAVELER, LONG

I STOOD..."

—Robert Frost,
"The Road not Taken"

OBJECTIVES

- To explore the concept of selection and the need for selection control structures

- To examine the *if* instruction in its two basic forms: *if-then* and *if-then-else*

- To emphasize the need for proper indentation styles and use of braces in control structures

- To examine Java facilities for constructing relational expressions, including == and != for all data types and <, <=, >, and >= for primitive types

- To explore the forms of Boolean expressions that are supported by Java, especially the AND (&&), OR (||), and NOT(!) operations

- To introduce the concept of conditional (short-circuit) evaluation and how it is used to avoid certain run-time errors

- To examine the `boolean` data type and illustrate how it is used in methods (predicates), variables, and parameter passage

- To introduce the discipline of logic and explore how logical reasoning and logical rules can be used to improve Boolean expressions

- To revisit the notion of assertions, examine the form of assertions that involve selections, and suggest a method for assertion testing

- To examine how *if* instructions can be nested and used as multiway selection instructions, including cascading conditions

- To introduce the *switch* instruction

- To introduce testing concepts and how logic plays a significant role in both functional testing and structural testing

Mathematics provides a foundation for science and engineering. Physics, for example, is founded to a great extent upon the concepts of calculus. Similarly, computer science is largely founded upon the mathematical field known as logic. Software requirements documents are instructions of *logic*; computer hardware is constructed from circuitry described as "digital logic"; and computer programming is a logic-based activity.

The ancient Greeks thought of logic as the basis for human reasoning. Computer scientists also use logic for reasoning—reasoning about program behavior. In addition to reasoning about programs with logic, it is possible to control program execution with a form of logic. In this chapter, logic is examined both as a means to control program execution and as a way to understand and explain software semantics.

7.1   THE IF INSTRUCTION

Humans are constantly making choices. What time shall I get out of bed? Should I write with a pencil or a pen? Which is the best route to work—the freeway or the back roads? How many hours do I need to set aside for meal preparation?

Programs must also make choices. A chess-playing program must choose its next move. A program to calculate income tax must choose which tax table is appropriate. A program to control antilock brakes must choose when to apply to the brakes.

Programming language instructions that are designed for the sole purpose of expressing choices are known as **selection instructions**. Java includes the following two selection instructions:

```
if
switch
```

The **if instruction** is the most widely used of the Java selection instructions. Figure 7.1 describes the most common version of this instruction, known as an **if-then-else instruction**. An *if-then-else* instruction has three parts:

1. a **then clause**
2. an **else clause**
3. a **condition**

When an *if-then-else* executes, either the *then* clause will execute or the *else* clause will execute, but not both. The determination of which of the two clauses to select (execute) is based upon the value of the condition. (The syntax and semantics of Java conditions are explored in Sections 7.2 through 7.4.)

Figure 7.1 ifThenElseInstruction description

ifThenElseInstruction (a possible *OneStatement*)

Syntax

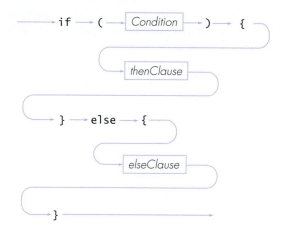

Syntax Notes

- *Condition* can be any valid *BooleanExpression*.
- *thenClause* and elseClause can be any valid *StatementSequence*.
- If *thenClause* consists of a single Java statement, then the (curly) braces immediately surrounding *thenClause* are optional.
- If *elseClause* consists of a single Java statement, then the braces immediately surrounding *elseClause* are optional.

Style Note

The reserved word if should be aligned with the "}" symbols, and all statements within *thenClause* and *elseClause* should be indented by one tab from the "if". If *Condition* cannot be completed on one line, then "{" should be placed on a separate line and aligned with its matching "}".

Semantics

Executing *ifThenElseInstruction* causes *Condition* to be evaluated. If *Condition* is found to be true, then *thenClause* is executed. If *Condition* is found to be false, then *elseClause* is executed.

SOFTWARE ENGINEERING TIP

Technically, the braces {...} can be omitted around any clause that consists of a single statement. However, it is best to include these braces, even when they are optional, for two reasons: (1) notational consistency improves code readability and (2) code maintenance frequently turns single-statement clauses into multistatement clauses.

As an initial example, suppose a program is being developed to assist an all-you-can-eat restaurant with their customer billing. This restaurant has a fixed fee of $12 per meal and a policy that children under the age of three can eat for free. The following *if-then-else* calculates the meal charge for a customer.

```java
if ( customerAge < 3 ) {
    mealCost = 0;
} else {
    mealCost = 12;
}
```

When this instruction executes, the int variable called mealCost will either be assigned 0 or 12, depending upon the value of the customerAge variable. Like every *if-then-else* instruction, there are two alternative ways for executing this instruction.

Selection instructions are called **control structures** because they control the order in which statements execute. Figure 7.2 contains an **activity diagram** to illustrate the flow of control for an *if-then-else* instruction.

Figure 7.2 Control flow of an *if-then-else* instruction

Java syntax

```
// Statement before if
if (Condition) {
        // Then Clause
} else {
        // Else Clause
}

// Statement after if
```

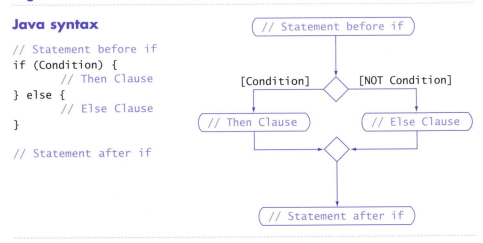

This activity diagram shows the possible ways in which this Java code may execute. Diamond-shaped polygons in an activity diagram denote locations where the path splits and/or merges. The top diamond in Figure 7.2 represents a choice of two alternative outgoing arrows. A bracketed logical expression accompanies each outgoing arrow. If Condition is true, then the path labeled [Condition] is followed; and Then Clause executes. Otherwise, if Condition is false, then the path labeled [NOT Condition] is followed; and Else Clause executes. Regardless of which clause is selected, the *if-then-else* instruction completes by executing //Statement after if. The bottom diamond in Figure 7.2 shows that both paths merge.

The program in Figure 7.3 contains another *if-then-else*. This program is designed to repeatedly move a blue dot from right to left across a window.

Figure 7.3 Program to move a dot across a window

```
import java.awt.*;
import aLibrary.*;
public class Director extends A3ButtonHandler {
    private A3ButtonWindow window;
    private AOval dot;

    /* postcondition
            window is created
            AND dot is a filled, blue circle with diameter of 100
            placed upon window at location (60, 60) */
```

```java
public Director() {
    window = new A3ButtonWindow( this );
    dot = new AOval( 60, 60, 100, 100 );
    dot.setColor( Color.blue );
    dot.setToFill();
    dot.place( window );
    window.repaint();
}

/* precondition
        dot is placed within the region of window
    postcondition
        (old dot.getX() > 19) IMPLIES
            ( dot.getX() is old dot.getX()-20 AND dot is filled )
        AND (old dot.getX() <= 19) IMPLIES
            ( dot.getX() == window.getWidth()-dot.getWidth()
        AND dot is outlined ) */
public void leftAction() {
    if ( dot.getX() > 19 ) {
        dot.translate( -20, 0 );
        dot.setToFill();
    } else {
        dot.setLocation( window.getWidth()
                            -dot.getWidth(), dot.getY() );
        dot.setToOutline();
    }
    dot.repaint();
}

public void midAction() {
}
public void rightAction() {
}
}
```

SOFTWARE ENGINEERING TIP

Indentation patterns play an important role in code readability. The clauses of every *if* instruction must be indented by three to four spaces (one tab setting) from the shell of the instruction. Examples in this section illustrate proper indentation.

The *if-then-else* instruction, located in `leftAction`, plays a key role in program behavior. Each call to this `leftAction` (i.e., each left-button click event) results in one of two options. If the blue dot is more than 19 pixels from the left edge of its background window, the dot is moved to its left by 20 pixels and set to fill. The second option for `leftAction` behavior occurs when the blue dot is within 19 pixels of the left edge. In this case, the *else* clause is executed, which causes the dot to be positioned at the right edge of the window and changed to an outline (a blue circle). Therefore, the effect of repeatedly clicking the left button is to move a solid blue dot left until it reaches the window's edge, reposition the dot (in outline form) at the right window edge, then turn it into a filled dot and repeat the entire process.

There are actually two forms of the Java *if* instruction. The *if-then-else* is one form, and the second form is known as an **if-then**. Figure 7.4 describes this form.

Figure 7.4 ifThenInstruction description

ifThenInstruction (a possible *OneStatement*)

Syntax

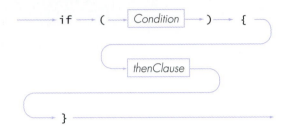

Syntax Notes
- *Condition* can be any valid *BooleanExpression*.
- *thenClause* can be any valid *StatementSequence*.
- If *thenClause* consists of a single Java statement, then the braces immediately surrounding *thenClause* are optional.

Style Note

The reserved word `if` should be aligned with the "}" symbols and all statements within *thenClause* should be indented by one tab from the "if". If *Condition* cannot be completed on one line, then "{" should be placed on a separate line and aligned with its matching "}".

Semantics

Executing *ifThenInstruction* causes *Condition* to be evaluated. If *Condition* is found to be true, then *thenClause* is executed. If *Condition* is found to be false, then execution proceeds to the statement following the *if-then*.

The *if-then* instruction provides a way to execute *optional* tasks. The *then* clause of an *if-then* instruction is executed when the instruction's condition is true, and nothing further occurs within an *if-then* with a condition that is found to be false. In other words, the execution of the *then* clause is optional. This behavior of an *if-then* instruction is pictured in the activity diagram from Figure 7.5.

The following code segment demonstrates the use of an *if-then* instruction:

```
// Assume elevationA, elevationB & maxElevation are all double
    variables.
maxElevation = elevationA;
if ( elevationB > maxElevation ) {
    maxElevation = elevationB;
}
```

Figure 7.5 Control flow of an *if-then* instruction

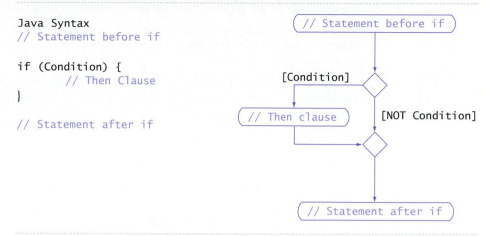

```
Java Syntax
// Statement before if

if (Condition) {
        // Then Clause
}

// Statement after if
```

There are two possible scenarios for executing this code:

Scenario 1: (elevationA < elevationB)
In this scenario, maxElevation is first assigned the value of elevationA. Next, the *if-then* instruction executes its *then* clause, causing maxElevation to be assigned elevationB.

Scenario 2: (elevationA > elevationB)
In this scenario, maxElevation is first assigned the value of elevationA. Executing the *if-then* instruction does not change the value of maxElevation.

Regardless of which scenario occurs, the execution of this code causes maxElevation to be assigned the greater value from the elevationA and elevationB variables.

SOFTWARE ENGINEERING TIP

Sometimes programmers write an *if-then* instruction when an *if-then-else* should be used. This tends to occur when the programmer is concentrating on handling one particular situation (the *then* clause) and overlooks the case in which the situation does not exist. To be safe, it is wise to begin with an *if-then-else* instruction and be certain that the *else* clause is empty, prior to choosing an *if-then*.

7.2   RELATIONAL EXPRESSIONS

A nineteenth century English mathematician, **George Boole** studied a form of a **logical expression**, which became known as a **Boolean expression**. Java makes use of Boolean expressions in many places, including as the syntax for *if* instruction conditions.

When a numeric expression is evaluated, the result is a number. When a character expression is evaluated, the result is a character. When a Boolean expression evaluates, the result is a Boolean (logical) value. The only two options for a Boolean value are **true** or **false**. Not surprisingly, these two possible values for a Boolean expression coincide with the two paths for executing an *if* instruction.

In Java the basic, and most commonly used, form of a Boolean expression is called a **relational expression**. Figure 7.6 describes the syntax and semantics of Java relational expressions.

Each relational expression is a comparison of two other expressions of compatible type, labeled "Operand1" and "Operand2." At execution time the relational expression is evaluated by performing the appropriate comparison. The result of evaluating a relational expression is either the Boolean value *true* or the value *false*. For example, the relational expression

```
3 < 4
```

evaluates to true, and the relational expression

```
'A' >= 'X'
```

evaluates to false.

Figure 7.6 RelationalExpression description

RelationalExpression (a possible *BooleanExpression*)

Syntax

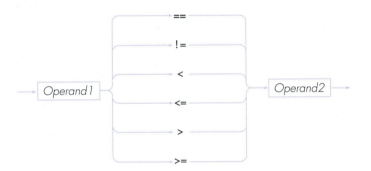

Syntax Notes

- *Operand1* and *Operand2* are expressions of conforming types.
- The <, <=, >, and >= operators require that operand types be primitive (excepting boolean).

Semantics

Executing *RelationalExpression* causes *Operand1* and *Operand2* to be compared, resulting in a true or false value. If the operands are of primitive type, then the *values* of the operands are compared. If the operands are of reference type, then the object *identities* of the operands are compared (i.e., Reference operands are equal only if they are aliases for the same object).

There are six **relational operators** in Java. They are listed below.

Operator	Meaning
==	equal
!=	not equal
<	less than
<=	less than or equal
>	greater than
>=	greater than or equal

Like any other operator, the relational operators require that their operands have compatible types. In other words, int expressions can't be compared to ARectangle expressions. For primitive types, automatic widening occurs as needed to create compatible expressions in the same way that widening occurs in the evaluation of other numeric operators. A second restriction is that four of the relational operators (<, <=, >, and >=) are supported only for non-boolean primitive expressions.

The == and != operators can be used on either primitive or reference type expressions. However, the meaning of these two operators is somewhat different for primitive data than it is for reference data. When two expressions of primitive type are compared for equality, it is their *value* that is compared. For example, the relational expression

```
myInt == yourInt
```

is true exactly when the value of the myInt integer variable is identical to the value of yourInt.

When a comparison for == or != involves two reference types, then object bindings are compared. For example, the relational expression

```
myOval == yourOval
```

is true exactly when myOval and yourOval (variables of type AOval) are both references to the same object.

These two variations on the meaning of == and != give rise to the names **value equality** and **identity equality**. Comparing primitive operands checks for value equality, whereas comparing reference operands checks for identity equality. (The differences between value equality and identity equality are consistent with the differences in the way the assignment instruction behaves for primitive and reference data.)

One particularly common comparison for a reference variable is to test for a null binding. (Recall that a variable that is equal to null has not yet been instantiated.) The following *if* instruction shows how to use the == operator to check for a dot that is instantiated. This *if* instruction will print its "ERROR" message any time that the subsequent dot.place call is about to fail on a null pointer exception:

```
if ( dot == null ) {
    System.out.println("ERROR - dot has not been assigned!");
}
    dot.place( window );
}
```

Each relational operator is paired with another operator of opposite meaning. The == operator is the opposite of !=, because A==B is true when A!=B is false, and A==B is false when A!=B is true. Similarly, < is the opposite of >=, and > is the opposite of <=. These opposite notations lead to alternative ways to express the same algorithm. For example the following *if* instruction

```
if ( someExpression < otherExpression ) {
    doThis();
} else {
    doThat();
}
```

has exactly the same run-time behavior as the following:

```
if ( someExpression >= otherExpression ) {
    doThat();
} else {
    doThis();
}
```

Neither of these alternatives is better than the other, but they do point out yet another example of how an algorithm may take different forms.

7.3 BOOLEAN EXPRESSIONS

Relational expressions are a subset of the more complete Java notation for Boolean expressions, the more complete notation for expressing an *if* condition. Figure 7.7 describes the more general syntax of Boolean expressions.

Boolean expressions are so important in Java that the language includes a separate boolean type. The boolean type is a primitive data type. Like many of the other primitive data types, boolean has a notation for constants. The two valid boolean constants are identifiers:

```
true
false
```

Java Boolean expressions also support five operators.

equal operator (==)
not equal operator (!=)
NOT operator (!)
AND operator (&&)
OR operator (||)

The first two of these operators (equal and not equal) are the same relational operators discussed in the prior section. These operators check for equality (or inequality) of values (either both true or both false).

It is often helpful to explain a Boolean expression by drawing a **truth table**. A truth table is a tabular representation of all of the possible operand value permutations and the resulting expression values. Figure 7.8 shows a truth table definition for both the equal and not equal operators, as applied to operands of boolean type.

Figure 7.7 BooleanExpression syntax

BooleanExpression

Syntax

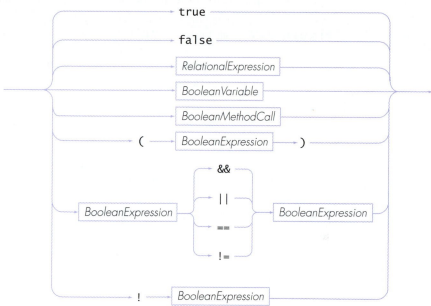

Each line of a truth table represents one of the possible value permutations for the expression. For example, the top line of each truth table in Figure 7.8 describes the situation in which both the first and the second operand have a value of false. The right column of the truth table gives the value of the expression value resulting from these particular operand values. The example shows that when both operands are false, then the == operator evaluates to true and != evaluates to false.

Figure 7.8 Truth tables for EQUAL (==) and NOT EQUAL(!=)

Operand1	*Operand2*	*Operand1 == Operand2*
false	false	true
false	true	false
true	false	false
true	true	true

Operand1	*Operand2*	*Operand1 != Operand2*
false	false	false
false	true	true
true	false	true
true	true	false

A truth table is also a good way to define the other `boolean` operators. Figure 7.9 defines the NOT operator by way of its truth table. There are only two rows in the truth table from this figure, because NOT only has one operand. Sometimes the NOT operation is called a **logical negation** operation because it evaluates to the opposite Boolean value of its operand.

Figure 7.9 Truth tables for NOT (!)

Operand	! Operand
false	true
true	false

The `boolean` AND operation has a meaning consistent with the use of "and" in English sentences. The only time that an AND operator evaluates to true is when both its operands are true. Figure 7.10 contains the truth table definition for AND.

Figure 7.10 Truth tables for AND (&&)

Operand1	Operand2	Operand1 && Operand2
false	false	false
false	true	false
true	false	false
true	true	true

The `boolean` OR operation is sometimes called an **inclusive OR**, because it evaluates to true whenever one or the other, *or both* of its operands are true. Figure 7.11 contains the truth table definition for OR.

Figure 7.11 Truth tables for OR (||)

Operand1	Operand2	Operand1 || Operand2
false	false	false
false	true	true
true	false	true
true	true	true

The NOT, AND, and OR operators can be combined to form more complicated `boolean` expressions. For example, the following *if* instruction prints a "first shift" message when the value of the integer variable hour is within the range from 7 through 16. (Note that whereas a logician might abbreviate the above condition as 7<=hour<=16, Java compilers treat this logician's abbreviation as a syntax error.)

```
if ( 7 <= hour && hour <= 16 ) {
    System.out.println( "First shift" );
}
```

A second example of Boolean operators is shown below. This *if* instruction prints a message based on the value of a char variable, called grade.

```
if ( grade=='A' || grade=='B' || grade=='C' ) {
    System.out.println( "Course grade is 'C' or better" );
} else {
    System.out.println( "Course grade is below 'C'." );
}
```

These most recent two *if* instructions are a reminder of the importance of operator precedence. The conditions in these instructions are correct, because relational operators have a higher precedence than the boolean && and || operators. Figure 7.12 adds the precedence of the boolean operators to a table of selected int operators. The two most important relationships to remember for writing boolean expressions are as follows.

1. The common numeric operations have higher precedence than the relational operators.
2. The precedence of the relational operators is higher than other Boolean operators.

Figure 7.12 Precedence of selected int and Boolean operators

Precedence	Operator	Operation	Order within
high	--	postfix autodecrement	left to right
	++	postfix autoincrement	
second highest	--	prefix autodecrement	right to left
	++	prefix autoincrement	
	-	unary minus	
	!	Boolean NOT	
mid	/	division	left to right
	*	multiplication	
	%	remainder	
low	+	addition	left to right
	-	subtraction	
second lower	<	less than	left to right
	<=	less than or equal	
	>	greater than	
	>=	greater than or equal	
third lower	==	equal	left to right
	!=	not equal	
fourth lower	&&	Boolean AND	left to right
fifth lower	||	Boolean OR	left to right

boolean expressions are similar to other primitive expressions in many ways. It is possible to parenthesize boolean expressions to force any desired order on operator evaluation. It is also possible to declare variables, constants, and methods to store boolean values, using the word "boolean" with all lowercase letters.

If an attribute of state information must either be true or false, then it is a good candidate for storing as a boolean variable. Figure 7.13 illustrates with a program that uses buttons to toggle a window label.

Figure 7.13 Program to toggle "MESSAGE"

```java
import java.awt.*;
import aLibrary.*;
public class Director extends A3ButtonHandler {
    private A3ButtonWindow window;
    private ALabel message;
    private boolean isPlaced;
    /* postcondition
            window is constructed
            AND message is constructed, placed, and set to
                "MESSAGE" */
    public Director() {
        window = new A3ButtonWindow( this );
        message = new ALabel( 200, 200, 100, 30 );
        message.setText( "MESSAGE" );
        message.place( window );
        message.repaint();
        isPlaced = true;
        window.repaint();
    }
    /* precondition
            message is constructed AND window is constructed
        postcondition
            old isPlaced IMPLIES
                (the message is removed and !isPlaced)
            AND old (not isPlaced) IMPLIES
                (the message is placed and isPlaced) */
    public void leftAction() {
        if ( isPlaced ) {
            message.remove();
        } else {
            message.place( window );
        }
        window.repaint();
        isPlaced = ! isPlaced;
    }
    public void midAction() {
    }
    public void rightAction() {
    }
}
```

The message toggling program from Figure 7.13 uses a boolean instance variable named isPlaced. The Director constructor method assigns isPlaced the value true to reflect the fact that the message label has been placed upon window. Each time that the left button is clicked, the *if* instruction uses the value of isPlaced as a condition to select between removing the message and placing the message. This causes the message to toggle off for one left button click and toggle on for the subsequent click.

Each call to leftAction must also assign isPlaced a value that is consistent with the state of the message variable. This assignment is accomplished by toggling the value of isPlaced to its opposite value (true becomes false and false becomes true) via the following instruction:

```
isPlaced = ! isPlaced;
```

7.4   CONDITIONAL EVALUATION

The Boolean AND and OR operators are evaluated in a way that is unique to these two operations. This evaluation technique is called **conditional evaluation** because the only the portion of the expression that is essential in determining its value is evaluated.

To explore the reasoning behind conditional evaluation, consider the evaluation of the following expression:

operand1 **&&** *operand2*

At run time the Java VM will first evaluate *operand1*. In the event that *operand1* has a false value, then the value of this entire expression is false, regardless of the value of *operand2*. Therefore, whenever the left operand of an AND operation is found to be false, the right operand is ignored. It is often said that the evaluation of the right operand is "short-circuited" in such cases. This gives rise to the name **short-circuit evaluation** as a synonym for "conditional evaluation." Of course, if the left operand of an AND operation is true, the operation cannot be short-circuited, and both operands must be evaluated.

Conditional evaluation is also applied to OR operations. If two operands are ORed together, then the right operand is short-circuited whenever the left operand evaluates to true because the entire expression is true regardless of the right operand's value.

It may seem that conditional evaluation is done in order to avoid wasting time evaluating unnecessary calculations. Even though efficiency is one benefit of conditional evaluation, it is not the primary reason. The better reason for conditional evaluation is to permit a left operand to guard a right operand from producing a run-time error. For example, suppose that totalWaterConsumed is an int variable representing the water consumption for a period of time given by daysPassed (another int variable). The following if instruction calculates the average water consumption per day.

```
if ( daysPassed != 0 && totalWaterConsumed/daysPassed > 100 ) {
    System.out.println( "WARNING: water consumption is high." );
    System.out.println( "This house is consuming more than 100
        units/day." );
} else {
    System.out.println( "Water consumption is acceptable." );
}
```

The *if* condition above guards against a division by zero that might occur when calculating the average by dividing by daysPassed. (Division by zero is a run-time error in Java because it an undefined arithmetic calculation.) The solution is to include a guard condition for the expression containing a potential division by zero. The guard expression in this case is daysPassed!=0. Since this guard is the left operand of an AND operation, the guard is evaluated first. If the guard is true, then daysPassed is nonzero and the remainder of the *if* condition is evaluated. However, if the guard expression is false, then the right operand is short circuited, avoiding a run-time error.

7.5   PREDICATES

Methods that return a boolean value are given a special name; they are called **predicates**. One such predicate is built into the ARectangle, AOval, and ARoundRectangle classes. It is a parameterless predicate named isFilled. A call to isFilled returns the value true if the associated object is set to fill and returns false if the object is set to outline. This method can be used in an *if* instruction, such as the one below:

```
if ( rectangle.isFilled() ) {
    rectangle.setToOutline();
}
```

Predicates, like other methods, are particularly useful for localizing code that is tedious or messy. A condition to test a character variable to see if it stores a symbol representing a English language vowel is certainly a bit messy.

```
if ( character == 'A' || character == 'E' || character == 'I'
    || character == 'O' || character == 'U' || character == 'Y'
    || character == 'W' || character == 'a' || character == 'e'
    || character == 'i' || character == 'o' || character == 'u'
    || character == 'y' || character == 'w' )
{
    System.out.println( "character is a vowel." );
}
```

The clutter of the above instruction is reduced, and its readability improved, by using an isVowel predicate as shown below.

```
if ( isVowel(character) ) {
    System.out.println( "character is a vowel." );
}
```

The code for the isVowel predicate is given in Figure 7.14. Like many predicates, isVowel has a body that consists of a single return instruction.

Figure 7.14 isVowel predicate

```
/* postcondition
    result == c is an uppercase or lowercase vowel
        (a, e, i, o , u, y, or w) */
private boolean isVowel( char c ) {
    return c=='A' || c=='E' || c=='I' || c=='O' || c=='U'
        || c=='Y' || c=='W' || c=='a' || c=='e' || c=='i'
        || c=='o' || c=='u' || c=='y' || c== 'w';
}
```

As a second example predicate, consider the task of checking whether or not two AView objects are placed on the same background in such a way that they overlap on the display. Figure 7.15 contains such a predicate called areOverlapping.

Figure 7.15 areOverlapping predicate

```
/* postcondition
    result == v1 and v2 are overlapping regions placed
        upon the same background */
private boolean areOverlapping( AView v1, AView v2 ) {
    boolean overlapHorizontally, overlapVertically;
    if ( v1 == null || v2 == null
        || v2.parentContainer() != v2.parentContainer() )
    {
        return false;
    } else {
        overlapHorizontally = v1.getX() <= v2.getX()+v2.getWidth()
            && v1.getX()+v1.getWidth() >= v2.getX();
        overlapVertically = v1.getY() <= v2.getY()+v2.getHeight()
            && v1.getY()+v1.getHeight() >= v2.getY();
        return overlapHorizontally && overlapVertically;
    }
}
```

The *if* instruction from the areOverlapping method separates the check into two cases. The first case (captured by the *then* clause) occurs when the two AView objects are *not* placed upon the same background. An AView method, named parentContainer, is called on each AView. The parentContainer method is defined to return the *aLibrary* object upon which an AView is placed. (Notice that v1 == null and v2 == null are used to short-circuit potential null pointer exception errors that could result from the calls to parentContainer when either v1 or v2 has not yet been constructed.)

The *else* clause from areOverlapping handles the case in which v1 and v2 are both placed upon the same background. In this situation the code checks separately for overlapping in the horizontal and in the vertical directions. Overlapping of the two AView parameters occurs only when *both* horizontal and vertical directions overlap, so the final expression ANDs the two boolean variables.

The test for horizontal overlapping checks to see if the left edge of v1 lies to the left of the right edge of v2 (checked by v1.getX() <= v2.getX() + v2.getWidth()). Similarly, horizontal overlapping only occurs when the right edge of v1 is to the right of the left edge of v2 (checked by v1.getX() + v1.getWidth() >= v2.getX()). Checking for overlap in the vertical direction is analogous.

7.6   NESTING IF INSTRUCTIONS

Some algorithms involve more complicated selections than possible with a single *if* instruction. Often the solution is **nesting**. An *if* instruction is said to be nested within another *if* instruction when it is contained within the *then* clause or part of the *else* clause. An example of nesting is shown in the gradePassFail method of Figure 7.16. This method returns a grade from a corresponding exam score. The particular exam has a potential range of 0 to 100 points and is scored Pass/Fail with a grade of 60 or more constituting a pass. The gradePassFail method receives the exam score as a parameter and returns a 'P' for passing or an 'F' for failing. This method also returns an 'X' and prints an error message when the parameter is out of range for a valid test score. Figure 7.16 also includes an activity diagram that pictures the control flow for gradePassFail.

The gradePassFail method contains an *if* instruction that is nested inside the *else* clause of another *if* instruction. The outer *if* checks for a valid score, while the inner *if* checks to see whether the score is passing or not. The *then* clause of the outer *if* prints an error message when the number of points is invalid (less than 0 or more than 100). The *else* clause of the outer *if* executes for any valid exam score. This outer *else* clause executes another *if* instruction to select between passing and failing.

SOFTWARE ENGINEERING TIP

Careful discipline in consistent indentation becomes more important when control structures are nested. Every clause needs to be indented from its containing statement and all indentations should use consistent distances.

Java's use of (curly) braces becomes a more significant issue as the number of braces increases due to nesting. To understand the reasoning behind braces, it is helpful to understand that the *if* instruction is designed to have a single-statement *then* clause and a single-statement *else* clause. For single-statement clauses there is no need for braces.

The braces are included in the language as a mechanism to group several statements into what is sometimes referred to as a **compound statement**. A *then* clause or *else* clause that is enclosed in braces is really just a single (compound) statement. Figure 7.17 describes the syntax and semantics of a compound statement.

Figure 7.16 gradePassFail method and its activity diagram

```
/* postcondition
        (s < 0 || s > 100) IMPLIES result == 'X'
        AND (60<=s<=100) IMPLIES result=='P'
        AND (0<=s<=59) IMPLIES result=='F' */
private char gradePassFail( int s ) {
    char result;
    if ( s < 0 || s > 100 ) {
        System.out.println("ERROR - invalid test score.");
        result = 'X';
    } else {
        if ( s >= 60 ) {
            result = 'P';
        } else {
            result = 'F';
        }
    }
    return result
}
```

Sometimes braces (compound statements) are unnecessary. The code below is a segment of the gradePassFail method (from Figure 7.16) with nonessential braces removed.

```
if ( s < 0 || s > 100 ) {
        System.out.println("ERROR - invalid test score.");
        result = 'X';
} else
```

```
if ( s >= 60 )
    result = 'P';
else
    result = 'F';
```

This second version of the gradePassFail algorithm is valid Java, and it executes the same as the original nested *if*. However, omitting the braces from control structures is discouraged because properly indented braces make the code more readable by clearly marking the beginning and ending of control structures.

Including braces also helps to avoid a problem known as the **dangling else problem**. A dangling *else* code pattern consists of an *if-then-else* instruction with an *if-then* nested as the *then* clause. Figure 7.18 contains this code pattern along with its associated activity diagram.

Figure 7.17 CompoundStatement description

CompoundStatement (a possible *OneStatement*)

Syntax

Semantics

Executing *CompoundStatement* causes the *OneStatement* statements to execute in order.

Style notes

- Statements in a sequence are best placed one per line and each line justified to the same left position (i.e., tabbed the same distance from the left margin).

- The precise location of the braces depends upon usage. The statements within a compound statement are indented to show this containment.

As shown in Figure 7.18 with braces, the dangling *else* pattern is never problematic. Executing this statement produces one of three outcomes:

1. If both *condition1* and *condition2* are true, *thenStatement* executed.
2. If *condition1* is false, *elseStatement* executes.
3. If *condition1* is true and *condition2* is false, then no further code executes within this code segment.

SOFTWARE ENGINEERING TIP

The dangling else problem is just one more reason for including braces even when they are optional.

The problem with the dangling *else* pattern only surfaces when nonessential braces are removed. The resulting code is shown in Figure 7.19.

The absence of braces in this code fails to clearly indicate the end of the *then* clause from the outer *if* instruction. In the absence of braces, the Java compiler matches *else* clauses with the most recent possibility. Therefore, the *else* clause in the code from Figure 7.19 is paired with the inner *if*, instead of the outer *if*, and the outer *if* has no *else* clause. The activity diagram in the figure illustrates the control flow of this code, and this activity diagram is inconsistent with the indentation of the code.

Figure 7.18 Dangling else pattern code and activity diagram

```
if ( condition1 ) {
        if ( condition2 ) {
                thenStatement;
        }
} else {
        elseStatement;
}
```

[condition1]   [NOT condition1]

[condition2]

[NOT condition2]

elseStatement

thenStatement

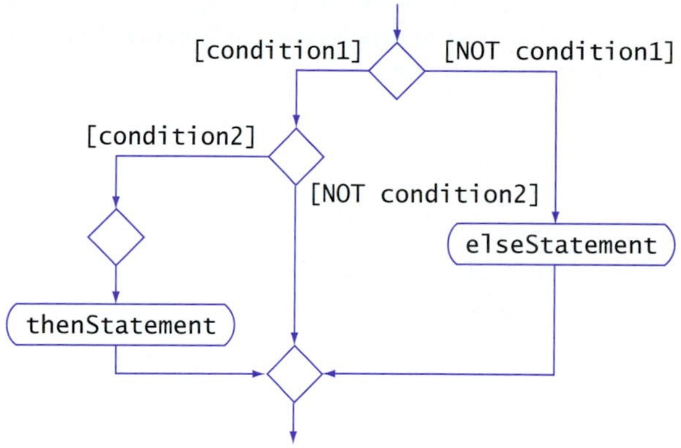

Figure 7.19 Problematic dangling else code and activity diagram

```
// WARNING: code below is improperly indented
if ( condition1 )
        if ( condition2 )
                thenStatement;
else
        elseStatement;
```

[condition1]

[condition2]   [NOT condition2]   [NOT condition1]

thenStatement   elseStatement

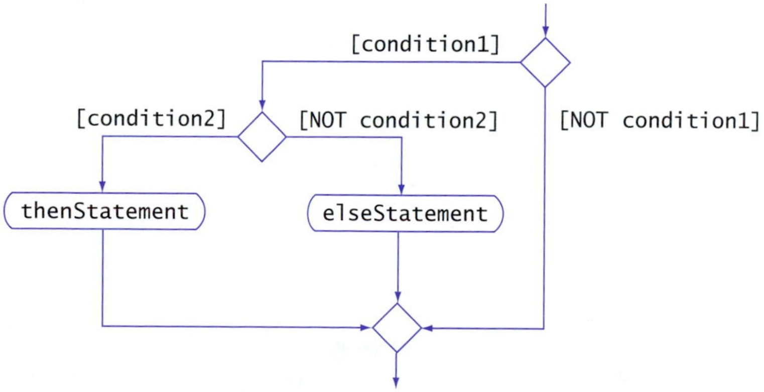

7.7 MULTIWAY SELECTION

Many selections involve more than two alternatives. An automobile has three possible directions of travel when passing through an intersection (turn left, turn right, go straight). A baseball player has nine alternatives for a fielding position. Selecting a playing card yields one of 52 possible outcomes.

The *if* instruction is designed for two-way selections. However, *if* instructions can be used as **multiway selection** instructions through nesting *if*s within *else* clauses, as below.

```
// a better notation for
// this multiway branch pattern
// is found in Figure 7.20.
if ( cond1 ) {
    alternative1;
} else {
    if ( cond2 ) {
        alternative2;
    } else {
        if ( cond3 ) {
            alternative3;
        } else {
            alternative4;
        }
    }
}
```

The preceding code represents a four-way selection using three *if-then-else* instructions, two that are nested as the *else* clause of outer *if* instructions. The notation used in this example is correct, but it is inferior because (a) the four-way selection is difficult to discern; (b) matching the braces to the closing braces is tedious and messy; and (c) if this nesting continues further, the code will run off the right side of the page.

A better notation for multiway selection via nested *if* instructions is shown in Figure 7.20. This notation indents all of the alternatives by the same distance and omits the unnecessary braces for every *else* clause.

Figure 7.20 Preferred notation for multiway selection using if instructions

```
if ( condition1 ) {
      alternative1;
} else if ( condition2 ) {
      alternative2;
} else if ( condition3 ) {
      alternative3;
      ...

} else if ( conditionN ) {
      alternativeN;
} else {
      alternativeNplus1;
}
```

As an example of multiway selection, consider a method to translate a letter from a telephone key press into the corresponding digit that is dialed. Figure 7.21 shows the standard telephone keypad. Notice that if the phone user presses the "H" key, then a "4" is dialed. Similarly, pressing the "W" key dials "9".

Figure 7.21 Telephone keypad

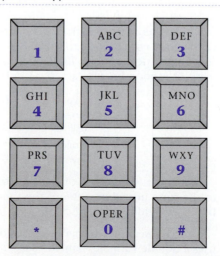

Figure 7.22 contains a `teleDigit` method to translate an alphabetic key press (the parameter c) into the corresponding digit. The `teleDigit` method displays an error and returns –1 when the char parameter represents something other than the uppercase letters contained on a telephone keypad.

Figure 7.22 `teleDigit` method

```
/* postcondition
        (c is NOT a valid uppercase letter from the telephone keypad)
                IMPLIES an error message is output AND result == -1
        (c is a valid uppercase letter from the telephone keypad)
                IMPLIES result == the keypad digit corresponding to c */
private int teleDigit( char c ) {
        if ( 'A' <= c && c <= 'C' ) {
                return 2;
        } else if ( 'D' <= c && c <= 'F' ) {
                return 3;
        } else if ( 'G' <= c && c <= 'I' ) {
                return 4;
        } else if ( 'J' <= c && c <= 'L' ) {
                return 5;
        } else if ( 'M' <= c && c <= 'O' ) {
                return 6;
        } else if ( c == 'P' || c == 'R' || c == 'S' ) {
                return 7;
        } else if ( 'T' <= c && c <= 'V' ) {
                return 8;
        } else if ( 'W' <= c && c <= 'Y' ) {
                return 9;
        } else {
                System.out.println( "ERROR - non digit key character." );
                return -1;
        }
}
```

One common pattern of multiway branching uses a concept known as **cascading conditions** to simplify the Boolean expressions used within the nested *if* instructions. For an illustration of cascading conditions, consider a code segment to randomly color an AOval in the following manner.

New AOval *Color*	*Probability*
green	0.1
yellow	0.3
orange	0.2
cyan	0.4

In other words 10% of the time the AOval should be recolored as green, 30% of the time in yellow, 20% of the time in orange, and the remaining 40% of the time it should be colored cyan.

A code segment to perform recoloring in this way is shown below. This code uses a double variable, named rand:

```
rand = Math.random();
if ( rand <= 0.1 ) {
    myOval.setColor( Color.green );
} else if ( rand <= 0.4 ) {
    myOval.setColor( Color.yellow );
} else if ( rand <= 0.6 ) {
    myOval.setColor( Color.orange );
} else {
    myOval.setColor( Color.cyan );
}
```

The code above begins execution by generating a random number through a call to the `random` method from `Math`. Since `random` returns a value randomly chosen between 0.0 to 1.0, the remainder of the code can use this value to determine recoloring probabilities. The probabilities are as follows:

- There is a probability of 0.1 that `rand` is less than 0.1.
- There is a probability of 0.3 that `rand` is between 0.1 and 0.4.
- There is a probability of 0.2 that `rand` is between 0.4 and 0.6.
- There is a probability of 0.4 that `rand` is between 0.6 and 1.0.

The cascading effect comes from the fact that the first *if* instruction checks for a rand value less than 0.1. Therefore, the second *if* instruction need not check for rand greater than 0.1, since it is impossible to reach the second *if* unless rand is greater than 0.1. Similarly, the third *if* instruction is written (rand <= 0.6) instead of (0.4 < rand && rand <= 0.6) because the conditions build upon one another in a cascade.

7.8   THE SWITCH INSTRUCTION

Java includes a second selection instruction (the **switch instruction**) that is applicable for certain algorithms. Figure 7.23 describes the syntax and semantics of the *switch* instruction.

The *switch* instruction differs from the *if* instruction in two important ways:

1. A *switch* instruction is not restricted to two-way selection, but supports multiway selection without any nesting.
2. The clause selection is based upon the value of an `int` (or `char`) expression rather than a `boolean` condition.

SOFTWARE ENGINEERING TIP

A common error when writing *switch* instructions is to omit a break instruction at the end of a clause. Such an omission does not produce a compile-time error, but it is a poor programming practice. The run-time effect of executing a case clause without a break is that execution proceeds to the subsequent case clause.

Figure 7.23 SwitchInstruction description

SwitchInstruction (a possible *OneStatement*)

Syntax

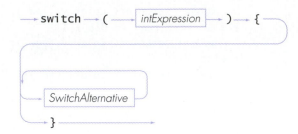

SwitchAlternative

Syntax

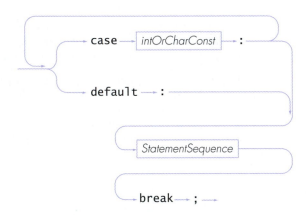

Syntax Notes

- *intExpression* is an expression of type int or char.
- *intOrCharConst* is a constant of type int or char.
- Every *intOrCharConst* must be different than all others within the same *switch* instruction.
- Only one default option is permitted within a single *switch* instruction.

Style Note

The reserved word switch should be aligned with the "}" symbol. Each case and default should be on separate lines. Each *StatementSequence* should be indented from its preceding case or default. Each break should be indented to match the *StatementSequence* that precedes it.

Semantics

Executing *SwitchStatement* causes *intExpression* to be evaluated. If the value of *intExpression* is equal to one of the *intOrCharConst* values, then the *StatementSequence* beneath the constant is executed. If none of the *intOrCharConst* is equal to *intExpression*, then the *StatementSequence* beneath default is executed. If none of the *intOrCharConst* is equal to *intExpression* and no default option is included, then no other statements from the switch instruction executes.

The syntax of a *switch* instruction consists of the reserved word `switch`, followed by the **switch expression** in parentheses, followed by zero or more **case clauses**. Case clauses begin with the reserved word `case`, followed by a **case constant**, followed by a colon and the code for the clause. (One of the case clauses for a *switch* instruction may use the reserved word `default` in place of `case`.) Each case clause should end with a break instruction. Figure 7.24 contains an example *switch* instruction in which the *switch* expression is a char variable, called `letterGrade`. The activity diagram for this *switch* instruction is also shown.

The execution of a *switch* instruction begins by evaluating the switch expression (`letterGrade`). When the value of switch expression is equal to any of the case constants, then the clause following that constant is executed. For the example *switch* instruction, two lines are output indicating that the grade is a C, which is an average grade whenever `letterGrade == 'C'`.

SOFTWARE ENGINEERING TIP

Default clauses should be included in *switch* statements unless it is absolutely certain that they aren't needed. It is best to place the *default* clause as the last of the clauses within a *switch*.

The *switch* instruction clause prefixed by `default` is known as the **default clause**. The *default* clause executes when none of the case constants match the switch expression. The example above executes its *default* clause, displaying the "`Invalid grade`" message, any time that `letterGrade` has a value other than `'A'`, `'B'`, `'C'`, `'D'` or `'F'`. Like an *else* clause, *default* clauses are optional. If a *default* clause is omitted, no clause executes when the switch expression has a value different from every case constant.

Figure 7.24 Activity diagram for the `letterGrade` switch example

```
switch ( letterGrade ) {
      case 'A' :
              System.out.println( "Your grade is an A." );
              System.out.println( "Excellent work!" );
              break;
      case 'B' :
              System.out.println( "Your grade is a B." );
              System.out.println( "Above average." );
              break;
      case 'C' :
              System.out.println( "Your grade is a C." );
              System.out.println( "Average grade." );
              break;
      case 'D' :
              System.out.println( "Your grade is a D." );
              System.out.println( "Below average." );
              break;
      case 'F' :
              System.out.println( "Your grade is an F." );
              System.out.println( "Failing." );
              break;
      default :
              System.out.println( "Invalid grade" );
              break;
}
```

Continued on next page.

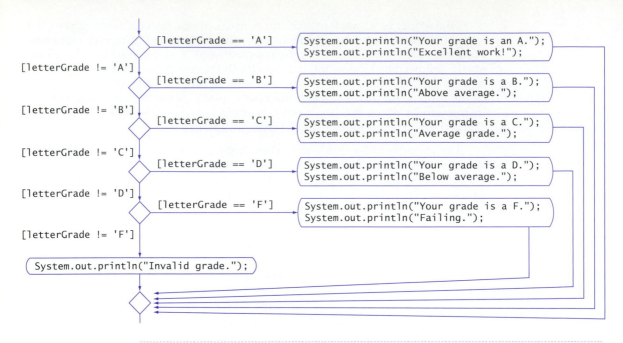

There are several restrictions imposed upon switch instructions.

- Switch expressions must be of type int or char.
- Case constants must be *constants* (not expressions involving variables, operations, or methods).
- No case constant may appear more than once within a single *switch* instruction.
- No more than one default clause may be included in a single *switch*.

There are no restrictions on the number or the ordering of case constants within a *switch* instruction. Furthermore, multiple case constants can be used for the same case clause. The following code segment illustrates:

```java
// assert 0 <= someDecimalDigit <= 9
switch ( someDecimalDigit ) {
    case 2 :
        System.out.println( "An even prime digit" );
        break;
    case 3 :
    case 5 :
    case 7 :
        System.out.println( "An odd prime digit" );
        break;
    case 0 :
    case 4 :
    case 6 :
```

```
        case 8 :
            System.out.println( "An even digit that is not prime" );
            break;
        case 9 :
            System.out.println( " An odd digit that is not prime");
            break;
        case 1 :
            System.out.println( "The number 1" );
            break;
        default :
            System.out.println( "someDecimalDigit is not a decimal
                digit." );
            break;
    }
```

Executing the preceding *switch* instruction causes one of six alternatives to occur. If the value of someDecimalDigit is 3 or 5 or 7, then the "An odd prime digit" message is output. Similarly, if someDecimalDigit is 0 or 4 or 6 or 8, then the message output is "An even digit that is not prime".

Software developers must often choose between using an *if* instruction and using a *switch* instruction. In making this choice it is best to view *switch* as a special purpose instruction and *if* as the more widely used option. A *switch* instruction is a possible choice when there is a natural integer expression to determine the selection and when the number of clauses is greater than two. The disadvantages of a *switch* instruction are the restrictions imposed upon the switch expression and case constants and the potential for neglecting to include break instructions.

7.9   SOFTWARE TESTING

Software testing is the process of exercising a program in order to uncover faults (bugs). A software tester constructs a **test suite**, consisting of different **test cases** designed to check the program under varying situations. These test suites are sometimes constructed with full knowledge of the code, and sometimes they are built without access to code details.

Testing that is done without using knowledge of specific code details is called **black-box testing**, because the program is treated like a black box. Another name for black box testing is **functional testing**, since the idea is to exercise the various functions of the code without knowledge of their implementation.

One of the advantages of functional testing is that writing test cases can begin as soon as the program requirements are known. On large programming projects it is typical to have software testers writing test suites at the same time that other software engineers are working on program design and implementation.

Logic plays an integral role in functional testing. Software requirements must be viewed as logical statements of code behavior. For example, suppose that a software tester is assigned the task of testing a single method. The best way to proceed is to examine the precondition and postcondition for the method. Since postconditions are frequently expressed as implications, one technique for selecting different test cases is to be certain to test different permutations of premises of these implications. A postcondition, such as

```
/* postcondition
        premise1 IMPLIES conclusion1
        AND premise2 IMPLIES conclusion2 */
```

can be tested once when both premises are true, once when they are both false, once when just *premise1* is true and once when just *premise2* is true. These four test cases represent four different functional situations.

Another type of functional testing examines the code for **robustness**. A robust program is one that continues to work reasonably even under unexpected conditions. Executing a method when the precondition is false is an extreme example of checking the robustness of code. A more useful form of robustness would be to consider unexpected sequences of user input events.

Unlike black-box testing, **white-box testing** is done with full knowledge of code details. White-box testing is more likely to be performed by the programmer who wrote the code, because he/she is already familiar with the code. Test cases for white-box testing cannot be written until very nearly the end of the software implementation because they depend upon the final implementation.

Another name for white-box testing is **structural testing**. As the name implies, structural testing is focused on testing the code structure. This means that the tester seeks to exercise all the different parts of the code. Test cases are often chosen to be certain to exercise certain parts of the code. The term **statement coverage** is used to measure testing. When a tester has 100% statement coverage, this means that every statement in the program has been executed by at least one test case(s). (Note that just because every statement works once, doesn't mean the code is free of bugs. Untested permutations of statements may still produce faults.)

Another form of coverage, called **path coverage**, refers to a test suite that ensures that every possible control flow path through the program has been followed by at least one test case. Selection instructions lead to alternative control flow paths. Figure 7.25 shows a segment of code consisting of two consecutive *if* instructions with a second *if* nested. The flow diagram on the right of this figure pictures the associated control flow.

There are six alternative paths that can occur when this code executes:

	Cond 1	*Cond 2*	*Cond 3*	*Resulting Execution*
1.	true	true	true	then-clause 1; then-clause 2;
2.	true	true	false	then-clause 1; else-clause 2;
3.	true	false	true	else-clause 1A; then-clause 2;
4.	true	false	false	else-clause 1A; else-clause 2;
5.	false		true	else-clause 1B; then-clause 2;
6.	false		false	else-clause 1B; else-clause 2.

This example illustrates that path coverage can be complicated even for small segments of code. While path coverage may be practical for small segments of code, it is either impractical or impossible for most programs. However, path coverage is a useful concept because it serves as the ultimate goal for structure testing.

Figure 7.25 Multiple control flow paths from three *if* instructions

```
if ( Cond1 ) {
        if ( Cond2 ) {
                then-clause1;
        } else {
                else-clause1A;
        }
}
        else-clause1B;
}

if ( Cond3 ) {
        then-clause2;
} else {
        else-clause2;
}
```

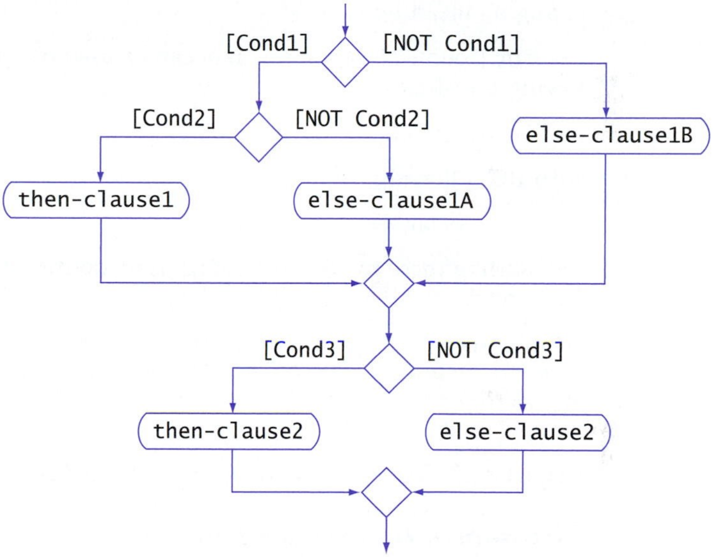

7.10   LOGIC AND PROGRAMMING (OPTIONAL)

Programming is based upon the mathematical discipline of **logic**. However, logic did not begin with computers. The ancient Greek philosopher, **Aristotle**, is generally referred to as the "Father of Logic." Aristotle examined how to use logic to reason and as a form of expression. Programmers must also reason about the correctness of their code and use logical statements to express their code.

Two obvious applications of logic in Java programs come in the form of

1. assertions
2. Boolean expressions

An understanding of the rules of logic is of great benefit to a programmer. These rules are typically expressed in the form of **logical axioms** and **logical theorems**. For example, the following theorem expresses the meaning of double negation.

> ### Double Negation Theorem
> ! (!P) ≡ P

This theorem states a **logical equivalence**. Two logical expressions are logically equivalent (symbolized by ≡) if they both mean exactly the same thing (i.e., they are both true under the same situations and both false under the same conditions). The Double Negation theorem states that NOT (NOT P) is the same as P. The symbol P in this theorem represents an arbitrary logical expression, so this theorem really means that any instance of double negation can be removed without changing meaning.

The Double Negation theorem can be used by a programmer to rewrite the following *if* instruction:

```
if ( !(myVar != 3) ) { ...
```

with the following:

```
if ( myVar == 3 ) { ...
```

Both of these two *if* instructions have identical behavior, but the second is easier to read.

Two other sets of rules that are useful to a programmer are shown in Figure 7.26. In these rules P, Q, R, P1, P2, ..., Pn all represent arbitrary logical expressions.

Figure 7.26 Distributive axioms and DeMorgan's laws

Distributive Axioms (numbered 1 and 2)

1. (P || Q) && (P || R) ≡ P || (Q && R)
2. (P && Q) || (P && R) ≡ P && (Q || R)

DeMorgan's Laws (numbered 1 and 2)

1. !(P1 && P2 && ... && Pn) ≡ !P1 || !P2 || ... || !Pn
2. !(P1 || P2 || ... || Pn) ≡ !P1 && !P2 && ... && !Pn

These axioms and theorems are useful for simplifying Boolean expressions within Java code. For example, the logical expression

```
( homeTeam==2 && visitor>3 ) || (homeTeam==2 && visitor==0)
```

can be simplified as follows by applying the second Distributive axiom:

```
homeTeam==2 && (visitor>3 || visitor==0)
```

> **SOFTWARE ENGINEERING TIP**
>
> Using logical axioms and theorems to simplify Boolean expressions is helpful for readability and debugging. One particularly useful simplification is to eliminate unnecessary NOT (!) operators.

Logic axioms and theorems can also be useful in designing code. Consider the problem of overlapping AViews presented previously. It may be simpler to identify the times that two AViews *do not* overlap than it is to identify when they *do* overlap. For example, AView v1 does not overlap AView v2 in the horizontal direction whenever v1 is completely to the right or completely to the left of v2.

v1 is right of v2 when: v1.getX() > v2.getX()+v2.getWidth()

v1 is left of v2 when: v1.getX()+v1.getWidth() < v2.getX()

Either of the above two conditions is sufficient to ensure that v1 and v2 do not overlap. Therefore, the following assignment expresses the condition for horizontal overlapping:

```
isHorizontalOverlapping =
    !( v1.getX() > v2.getX()+v2.getWidth()
    || v1.getX()+v1.getWidth() < v2.getX() );
```

The use of the second of DeMorgan's laws allows this assignment instruction to be simplified as follows:

```
isHorizontalOverlapping =
    v1.getX() <= v2.getX()+v2.getWidth()
    && v1.getX()+v1.getWidth() >= v2.getX();
```

7.11   ASSERTIONS (OPTIONAL)

Another obvious application of logic in programming is the use of program **assertions**. An assertion is a logical statement that defines the state of computation at some location within the code. Below is an assertion in the form of a Java comment:

```
makeTriangle();
/* assert
        side1 > 0 && side2 > 0 && side3 > 0
        && side1 + side2 > side3 */
```

The assertion above states that immediately after makeTriangle executes, the variables side1, side2, and side3 all have a positive value and that the sum of side1 plus side2 is greater than side3. Assertions generally include program variables, such as side1, which are expressed in logical, mathematical, and/or program notations. The above assertion borrows the Java symbol for the logical AND operator (&&), but it can just as easily be expressed as follows:

```
/* assert
        side1 > 0 AND side2 > 0 AND side3 > 0
        AND side1 + side2 > side3 */
```

Assertions don't cause the state to change. They merely document what the programmer believes (asserts) to be true regarding the state. Even though assertions perform no function at run time, they are still important tools for a programmer. An assertion provides needed insight into the how the program is intended to behave.

Because assertions are logical statements, they define what is true about the state of computation and not how this state was accomplished. This is just the opposite of program code that instructs the computer how to execute, but is less helpful with explaining what has happened at any particular code location.

Two of the most important assertions are preconditions and postconditions. Preconditions and postconditions are a pair of before and after snapshots that form a precise specification of a method's behavior.

SOFTWARE ENGINEERING TIP

Assertions must always convey *what* is true, and not *how* it became true. Such logical statements of state are more useful to someone reading the program. If there is a question about *how*, then you can read the code.

Most postconditions are expressed as a collection of several logical conditions that are *all* asserted. For example, the method in Figure 7.27 has a postcondition that defines a group of two properties that are both asserted to be true when the method completes execution, namely that the parameter ARectangle is colored green and is filled. The two conditions of the postcondition of makeFilledGreen are both expected to be true. Therefore, they are properly joined with an AND operation. As a general rule, assertions should be written as a collection of properties that must all be true and are, therefore, ANDed together.

Figure 7.27 makeFilledGreen method

```
/* precondition
        r != null
    postcondition
        r.getColor() == Color.green
        AND r.isFilled() */
private void makeFilledGreen( ARectangle r ) {
        r.setToFill();
        r.setColor( Color.green );
}
```

Assertions that describe the state resulting from selection are typically expressed in terms of separate cases using an IMPLIES operation. Figure 7.28 contains a method, called minimum, that demonstrates such a code segment. The minimum method returns the smaller of its two double parameters.

The postcondition for the minimum method defines two cases—one for the situation when the first parameter is smaller than the second and one for when the second parameter is smaller than the first. Each case is described in the form of an **implication**.

SOFTWARE ENGINEERING TIP

Software specifications often contain implications to describe what occurs under various conditions. Implications in specifications generally result in selection instructions in the associated code.

Figure 7.28 minimum method

```
/* postcondition
        (d1 <= d2) IMPLIES result == d1
        AND (d1 > d2) IMPLIES result == d2 */
private double minimum( double d1, double d2 ) {
        if ( d1 <= d2 ) {
                return d1;
        } else {
                return d2;
        }
}
```

An implication is written in the form

> *premise* IMPLIES *conclusion*

where *premise* is a logical statement that uniquely defines the computational state that produces this case and *conclusion* describes the outcome of the case. The implication

> (d1 <= d2) IMPLIES result == d1

is describing that, for the case in which d1 is smaller than or equal to d2, the method returns the value of d1.

IMPLIES is *not* a valid Java Boolean operator. However, implication is a commonly used logical operation. Figure 7.29 shows the truth table for implication.

Figure 7.29 Truth tables for the logical IMPLIES operation

Operand1	*Operand2*	*Operand1 IMPLIES Operand2*
false	false	true
false	true	true
true	false	false
true	true	true

As the truth table indicates, the implication

> (d1 <= d2) IMPLIES result == d1

is true any time that d1 > d2. Such situations in which the premise of an implication is false should be thought of as vacuously true. When the premise of an implication is false, that implication may be true, but this says nothing about the truth or falsity of the conclusion. The truth table also shows that when the premise is true, the conclusion must also be true, lest the entire implication be false.

Some programming languages include facilities for testing assertions at run time. The current version of Java does not. However, software developers can use the `boolean` expressions to create their own assertion checking tools. The `assert` method in Figure 7.30 can be included in any class as a basic tool for assertion checking.

Figure 7.30 assert method

```
/* postcondition
        (NOT b) IMPLIES msg is output */
private void assert( boolean b, String msg ) {
    if ( !b ) {
        System.out.println( "assert violated" + msg );
    }
}
```

A call to the assert method can be included wherever the programmer desires to check an assertion. When assert executes, its boolean argument is checked, and an error message is printed for a false-valued argument. Below is a version of the makeFilledGreen method that uses the assert method to test its precondition and postcondition:

```
/* precondition
        r != null
    postcondition
        r.getColor() == Color.green
        AND r.isFilled() */
private void makeFilledGreen( ARectangle r ) {
    assert( r!=null, "makeFilledGreen called with null argument" );
    r.setToFill();
    r.setColor( Color.green );
    assert( r.getColor()==Color.green && r.isFilled(),
            "makeFilledGreen violation of postcondition" );
}
```

JAVA INSPECTOR

Below is a collection of hints on what to check when examining code that involves the concepts of this chapter.

✓ Indentation patterns are crucial to the readability (and often the correctness) of control structures. If you have time to check only one thing, make it an examination that the indentation is consistent and correctly reflects the intended execution.

✓ Sometimes programs fail to handle all possible cases properly. One place to find such errors is missing *else* clauses and missing *default* clauses.

✓ Each assertion must be consistent with the code it describes. Sometimes as code is modified, the assertions are not properly updated. Don't overlook assertions in a desk check.

✓ Two-character operators (==, !=, <=, >=, &&, and ||) must be typed as two consecutive symbols with no intervening blanks.

✓ A common error is to use the assignment operator (=) when an equal operator (==) is needed. The compiler will detect errors unless both operands are `boolean`.

✓ Each equal and not equal for real numbers should be investigated. Real expressions store approximate values, and testing for equality of two approximations can produce subtle errors.

✓ Braces should be checked for proper pairing. (A good way to avoid brace pairing problems is to get in the habit of always typing a right brace immediately after its left partner, then backing up and inserting the code between.)

✓ Suspicion is indicated whenever an *if* instruction is written without braces. Situations, like the dangling else, should be investigated.

✓ Sometimes a collection of nested selection instructions is crafted in such a way that certain clauses are unreachable. The conditions inside nested instructions should be checked to make certain that they represent reasonable alternatives.

✓ Every clause of a *switch* instruction should end with a break. This requirement is easily overlooked.

✓ Humans tend to have difficulty reading NOTs. It is wise to replace Boolean expressions that are stated in terms of NOT with equivalent expressions that are stated positively. (The rules of double negation and DeMorgan's laws can help in removing NOTs.)

EXERCISES

1. What is the value of `emuCounter` following the execution of each of the following instructions, assuming it has a value of 3 just prior to this execution?

   a.
   ```
   if (emuCounter <= 3) {
       emuCounter = 5;
   } else {
       emuCounter = 17;
   }
   ```

   b.
   ```
   if (emuCounter > 3) {
       emuCounter = 83;
   } else {
       emuCounter = 94;
   }
   ```

    c. `if (emuCounter != 3) {`
           `emuCounter++;`
      `}`

2. How do your answers to Exercise 1 change if `emuCounter` has a value of 4 just before the *if* executes?

3. Assume that each of the following is used as a `boolean` expression within a Java program. Which of these expressions will evaluate to true, which will evaluate to false, and which will result in syntax errors?

    a. `7 == 7`
    b. `'b' >= 'A'`
    c. `6 < 8 && 'a' < 'b'`
    d. `true != false || 7 > 7.5`
    e. `Color.red < 3`
    f. `0 < 3 < 7`
    g. `"CAT" != null`
    h. `"Z" == 'Z'`
    i. `"A" == ""+'A'`

4. Complete the following truth tables:

a.

P	Q	!(P || Q)
false	false	
false	true	
true	false	
true	true	

b.

P	Q	R	!(P || R) && !Q
false	false	false	
false	false	true	
false	true	false	
false	true	true	
true	false	false	
true	false	true	
true	true	false	
true	true	true	

c.

P	Q	R	!((Q && R) || (P && !R))
false	false	false	
false	false	true	
false	true	false	
false	true	true	
true	false	false	
true	false	true	
true	true	false	
true	true	true	

5. Which two of the following identifiers would make the best names for `boolean` variables or methods?

```
moveThatRascal
rascalHasBeenMoved
heightOfRascal
isARascal
```

6. **a.** Executing the following *if* instruction can result in a run-time error due to a null-valued variable. Rewrite the instruction guarding the *if* condition (via conditional evaluation) so when `myRect` is `null`, the instruction behaves as if the height of `myRect` were zero.

```
if (myRect.getHeight() >= 200) {
    System.out.println("Height of myRect is 200 or more");
} else {
    System.out.println("Height of myRect is less than 200");
}
```

   b. Executing the following *if* instruction can result in a run-time error due to division by zero. Rewrite the instruction guarding the *if* condition (via conditional evaluation) so that the behavior when `divisor==0` is treated the same as `numerator==0`.

```
if (numerator/divisor > 100) {
    System.out.println("Fraction greater than 100");
} else {
    System.out.println("Fraction less than or equal to 100");
}
```

7. Consider the following predicate:

```
private boolean exclusiveOR( boolean p, boolean q ) {
        return (p || q) && !(p && q);
}
```

What value is returned by each of the following calls to this method?

   a. `exclusiveOR( false, false );`
   b. `exclusiveOR( false, true );`
   c. `exclusiveOR( true, false );`
   d. `exclusiveOR( true, true );`

8. Write a Java predicate (`boolean` method) for each of the following.

   a. This predicate is called `implies` and has two `boolean` parameters, call them *p* and *q*. The `implies` predicate returns the same `boolean` value that results *p* IMPLIES *q*.

   b. This predicate is called `inOrder` and has three `int` parameters, call them *a*, *b*, and *c*. The `inOrder` predicate returns `true` exactly when $a < b < c$.

c. This predicate is called isWider and has two ARectangle parameters. The isWider predicate returns true exactly when its first parameter has a *width* attribute greater than its second parameter.

d. This predicate is called fartherFromOrigin and has four int parameters, called *x1*, *y1*, *x2*, and *y2*. These four parameters must be thought of as the coordinates for two points: the point (*x1*,*y1*) and the point (*x2*,*y2*). The fartherFromOrigin predicate returns true exactly when point (*x1*,*y1*) is a greater distance from point (0,0) than is (*x2*,*y2*).

e. This predicate is called isUponAndWithin and has two ARectangle parameters, called *r1* and *r2*. The isUponAndWithin predicate returns true exactly when *r1* is placed upon *r2* and the boundaries of *r1* lie completely within the boundaries of *r2*.

f. This predicate is called isWithin and has two ARectangle parameters, called *r1* and *r2*. The isWithin predicate returns true exactly when *r1* and *r2* are both placed upon the same background and the boundaries of *r1* lie completely within the boundaries of *r2*.

g. This predicate is called areSidesOfRightTriangle and has three int parameters, called *s1*, *s2*, and *s3*. These three parameters must be thought of as lengths of three sides of a triangle. The areSidesOf-RightTriangle predicate returns true exactly when these three sides represent lengths for a right triangle. (*Hint*: Remember that triangles must have side lengths that are positive and that any of these sides could be the hypotenuse. The Pythagorean theorem can be used to check for proper lengths.)

9. Use the Double Negation theorem, the Distributive axioms, and DeMorgan's laws, together with your knowledge of opposite relational operators, to simplify each of the following boolean expressions. (Assume that all identifiers are int variables.)

a. !(myInt != yourInt)

b. !(someBool) && !(anotherBool)

c. (distance > 0 || time > 0) && (distance > 0 || time < 100)

d. (distance > 0 && time > 0) || (distance > 0 && time < 100)

10. Write a Java method for each of the following.

a. A method with two ARectangle parameters that returns the parameter with the larger area. (If one of the arguments is null, then the other is returned; if both arguments are null, then null is returned.)

b. A method with three double parameters that returns the value of the largest of its parameters.

c. A method to return the int value of a char parameter, if the char argument is a hexadecimal digit. Below is a table of all hexadecimal digits and their corresponding integer values. Your method should return –1 when its argument is not a valid hexadecimal digit character. (The valid hexadecimals are from '0' through '9' and from 'A' through 'F'.)

Hex	Value
'0'	0
'1'	1
'2'	2
'3'	3
'4'	4
'5'	5
'6'	6
'7'	7

Hex	Value
'8'	8
'9'	9
'A'	10
'B'	11
'C'	12
'D'	13
'E'	14
'F'	15

11. Write preconditions and postconditions for each part of Exercise 10.

12. Write a segment of Java code that takes the value from three double variables, d1, d2, and d3, and assigns them to the variables min, mid, and max so that min <= mid <= max.

13. Rewrite the teleDigit method from Figure 7.22 using a *switch* instruction instead of *if* instructions.

14. Rewrite the two *switch* instruction examples from Section 7.8 to use *if* instructions instead of a *switch*.

PROGRAMMING EXERCISES

1. Write a program to cause the LEFT button click to move an ARoundRectangle object around a window, "bouncing" off the edges. Your program must begin with a single green 300 by 300 ARoundRectangle, positioned at location (100, 100) within the window. Initially, this rectangle has a vertical velocity of 25 and a horizontal velocity of 25. The button clicks behave as follows:

LEFT   Assuming that the rectangle can do so without passing a window boundary, it moves according to its vertical and horizontal velocity. If the horizontal and vertical velocities are both 25, then the rectangle moves right 25 pixels and down 25 pixels. Positive horizontal velocities cause right movement, and negative velocities cause left movement. Similarly, a positive vertical velocity causes movement down, and negative causes movement up.

If the horizontal movement would cause the rectangle to move past the left or right edge of its window, then its horizontal velocity reverses and it moves in this new direction. The vertical movement behaves likewise with respect to the top and bottom of the window. (Note that every LEFT click causes the rectangle to move 25 pixels left or right and 25 pixels up or down.)

MID   If the rectangle has a vertical velocity moving it up, then its vertical velocity reverses to the downward value. (Note that no movement takes place, and nothing happens if the rectangle already has a positive velocity.)

RIGHT   This button causes the rectangle to change color in the following manner. A color of green becomes cyan, a color of cyan becomes yellow, and a color of yellow becomes green.

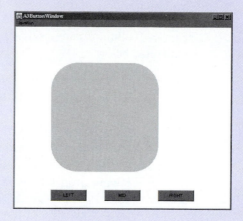

2. Wristwatch manufacturers have devised several clever techniques for setting the clock time using only two buttons on the edge of the clock. For this assignment you will use a simple one of these techniques to set the value of three-digit number. When the program begins, it displays three large 0 digits in black. The placement and size of these digits is pictured below.

LEFT   This button is used to highlight the particular digit being incremented. A highlighted digit is signified by the color red. At most one digit at a time is highlighted (colored red). Each time this button is clicked, the highlighting moves to the next digit to the left. When the leftmost digit is highlighted, clicking this button turns off all highlighting. When highlighting is turned off, clicking this button highlights the rightmost digit.

MID   The highlighted digit is advanced to the next higher digit. The digit '9' advances to '0'. If no digit is highlighted, then clicking this button has no effect.

RIGHT   This button changes the highlighting in the reverse order (i.e., left to right) of the LEFT button.

3. For this program it is best to construct a separate class to store/display a single decimal digit in the form of a seven-segment display. (A seven-segment display draws a single digit by lighting some combination of seven filled rectangles positioned as shown in the digit '8' below.) Your program should begin by displaying the digit '0' on your seven-segment display roughly centered in an A3ButtonWindow. The required button click behavior is explained below:

LEFT   Clicking this button causes the digit on the seven-segment display to advance by one. (If nine is displayed, then the digit "advances" to 0.)

MID   Clicking this button causes the digit on the seven-segment display to reduce by 1. (If zero is displayed, then the digit "reduces" to 9.)

RIGHT   Clicking this button causes the digit to be recolored with the following probabilities: 25% of the time this click causes the new color to be orange. 25% of the time this click causes the new color to be gray. 50% of the time this click causes the new color to be magenta.

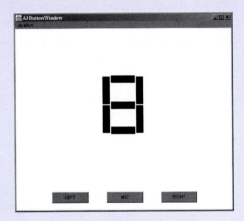

4. This program uses seven-segment digits, together with a clock built into your computer to display a digital clock. The clock display should appear as below, using four seven-segment display digits and the two dots. Clicking any button causes the clock to update to the current time. (You will need to investigate how to extract the clock time from your system. One way to accomplish this is to create a clock object from the `DateAndTime` class included within *aLibrary*.) Two possible additions to this assignment are to display the seconds (shown below), and/or to display a separate red dot to distinguish A.M. from P.M.

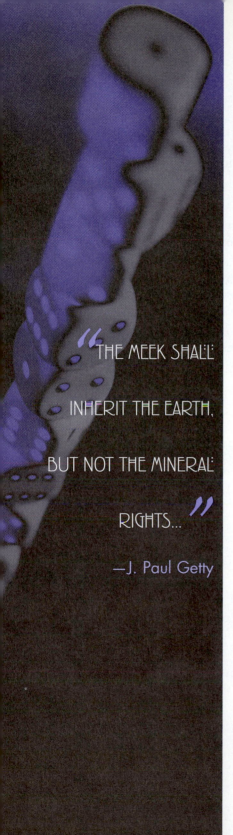

INHERITANCE

OBJECTIVES

- To examine inheritance in Java

- To explore the is_a relation as opposed to the contains_a relation, and to recognize that is_a relations lead naturally to inheritance

- To examine the semantics and limitations of overriding methods in subclasses

- To consider the concept of specialization and the particular version of specialization known as extension

- To introduce the protected declaration and its role in information hiding

- To demonstrate the utility of the callback pattern for event handling

- To examine the way that inheritance is used in event handling via the `AButton`, `EventTimer`, `AScrollbar`, and `ATextField` classes

Animals inherit characteristics from their parents. The number of legs on an insect, the shape of a bird's wings, the pattern on a snake's skin—these are all attributes that are inherited. Similarly, human children have height and hair color determined by genes inherited from their parents.

8.1   EXTENDS

Inheritance plays an important role in object-oriented software development, just as it plays an important role in biological traits. In fact, inheritance is so important that it is often identified as the primary concept separating object-oriented programming from other programming techniques.

There are two characteristics that distinguish software inheritance from biological inheritance.

1. In software, one *class* inherits from another *class*.

2. In software, inheritance is an "ideal" relationship.

Class inheritance is "ideal" in the sense that it is totally predictable, unlike biological inheritance in which inheritance is typically probabilistic. Software inheritance is also more complete than biological because all nonprivate class members are inherited.

As an initial example of inheritance, consider a software development project for a paper manufacturing company. The program uses a Parcel to keep track of the shipping information related to each outgoing paper product. Figure 8.1 is a class diagram for Parcel.

Figure 8.1 Parcel class diagram

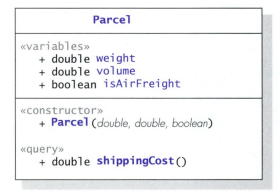

Parcel stores the weight and volume of the package, together with a method to calculate its shipping cost. The company can ship goods either by airmail or truck. The cost to ship is given below:

Air Freight: $15 + $2.75 per kilogram + ($6 per cubic meter (m³) for a parcel weighing more than 1.0 m³)

Ground Freight: $5 + $0.04 per kilogram

Figure 8.2 contains the code for Parcel.

Figure 8.2 Parcel class

```
public class Parcel {
    public double   weight;
    public double   volume;
    public boolean isAirFreight;
```

> WARNING: Declaring instance variables of a superclass as **public** is generally considered to be inferior design. In Section 8.4 a better alternative to these **public** declarations (the **protected** modifier) is introduced.

```
    /* modifies
            weight, volume, isAirFreight
        postcondition
            weight==w AND volume==v AND isAirFreight==b   */
    public Parcel( double w, double v, boolean b)   {
        weight = w;
        volume = v;
        isAirFreight = b;
    }


    /* postcondition
            isAirFreight IMPLIES result is cost to ship as air
            freight. AND !isAirFreight IMPLIES result is cost to
            ship by truck. */
    public  double   shippingCost()   {
        double   cost;
        if (isAirFreight)
            if  (weight > 1.0)
                cost = 15 + 2.75 * weight + 6 * (volume-1);
            else
                cost = 15 + weight * 2.75;
        else  // !isAirFreight
            cost = 5 + 0.04 * weight;
        return cost;
    }
}
```

The two instructions below illustrate how client code might use the Parcel class.

```
someParcel = new Parcel( 0.56, 0.3, true );
System.out.println("Cost to ship:" + someParcel.shippingCost());
```

The execution of the first instruction constructs a parcel with a weight of 0.56 kilograms and a volume of 0.3 m³ that is to be shipped as air freight. The second instruction outputs the shipping cost of this parcel by calling the shippingCost method.

This paper manufacturing company ships most of its paper goods in various-sized rectangular boxes, all weighing 677 kg/m³. A second class, called RectangularParcel (see Figure 8.3), is designed specifically for these rectangular boxes.

Figure 8.3 RectangularParcel class diagram

```
┌─────────────────────────────────────────────────────┐
│                  RectangularParcel                    │
├─────────────────────────────────────────────────────┤
│  + double weight                                      │
│  + double volume                                      │
│  + double isAirFreight                                │
│  - int parcelLength                                   │
│  - int parcelWidth                                    │
│  - int parcelHeight                                   │
│  - int weightPerCubicMeter                            │
├─────────────────────────────────────────────────────┤
│  «constructor»                                        │
│     + RectangularParcel(double, double, double, boolean) │
│                                                       │
│  «query»                                              │
│     + double shippingCost()                           │
│     + double length()                                 │
│     + double width()                                  │
│     + double height()                                 │
└─────────────────────────────────────────────────────┘
```

The commonality in the features of RectangularParcel and Parcel are a clue that inheritance can be used to write RectangularParcel. In particular, RectangularParcel uses weight, volume, isAirFreight, and shippingCost in the same way as Parcel. Therefore, it seems as if it would be simpler to use inheritance for these four members rather than duplicate them. Figure 8.4 contains a RectangularParcel class that uses inheritance in this manner.

Figure 8.4 RectangularParcel class

```java
public class RectangularParcel extends Parcel  {
    private double parcelLength, parcelWidth, parcelHeight;
    private final int weightPerCubicMeter = 677;

    /* modifies
            parcelLength, parcelWidth, parcelHeight,
            weight, volume, isAirFreight
       postcondition
            parcelLength == len  AND  parcelWidth == w
            AND  parcelHeight == h  AND  volume==len*w*h
            AND  weight == volume * weightPerCubicMeter
            AND  isAirFreight == b   */
    public RectangularParcel(double len, double w, double h,
            boolean b) {
        super(0, 0, b);
        parcelLength = len;
        parcelWidth = w;
```

```
            parcelHeight = h;
            volume = parcelLength * parcelWidth * parcelHeight;
            weight = volume * weightPerCubicMeter;
        }

    public double length()  {
        return parcelLength;
    }
    public double width()  {
        return parcelWidth;
    }
    public double height()  {
        return parcelHeight;
    }

}
```

The first thing to notice about the RectangularParcel class is the use of the reserved word extends on the class line. The word "extends" is Java notation for "inherits." RectangularParcel inherits the Parcel class. A class that is created via inheritance is called a **subclass**, and the class that is being inherited is known as a **superclass** (or **base class**). In this example RectangularParcel is a subclass of the superclass known as Parcel.

A subclass, such as RectangularParcel, automatically inherits *all* of the non-private instance variables and *all* of the nonprivate methods of its superclass. By inheriting Parcel, RectangularParcel contains all of the following members:

```
weight
volume
isAirFreight
shippingCost
```

The notation for referencing such inherited members is (with a few exceptions discussed later) the same as the notation used within the superclass. For example, the RectangularParcel constructor refers directly to volume and weight, using the same notation that is permitted inside the Parcel class.

Subclasses are not restricted solely to those features that they inherit. Just as children often develop characteristics that are not inherited, so too a subclass often includes new members. Each subclass can declare instance variables and methods like any other class. These new instance variables and methods are combined with the inherited members to define the subclass. RectangularParcel declares three new private instance variables to store the length, width, and height of a parcel, and corresponding methods to allow client code to inspect, but not alter, these values.

Constructors are handled a bit differently than other methods in Java. Since each class must have a unique name, it must also have its own constructor method(s). The RectangularParcel constructor has a different parameter list than the superclass constructor, reflecting the fact that rectangular parcels have length, width, and height. The RectangularParcel constructor also omits parameters for volume or weight since these can be calculated from its other parameters.

SOFTWARE ENGINEERING TIP

Technically, a subclass need not call a superclass
constructor method (super(...)) as its first instruction.
However, if such a call is omitted, a default call is
made anyway. It is much better to include this call
so that the intent is clear.

Java supports a notation to permit the subclass to call any constructor from its superclass. However, there are two restrictions: (1) The superclass constructor must be named with the reserved word super. (2) Such a call to a superclass constructor can be made only within constructor methods and only as their first statement. Subclass constructors should always include such calls to a superclass constructor. (Failure to include an explicit call to a superclass constructor causes the compiler to insert an automatic call to super().)

RectangularParcel includes the following explicit call to a superclass constructor:

```
super( 0, 0, b );
```

When executed, this instruction calls the Parcel constructor that in turn causes isAirFreight to be initialized to the value of parameter b. The assignment of 0 to instance variables weight and volume is unimportant, since these variables are updated to the correct values by other assignments.

Suppose the paper company also ships large rolls of paper in varying sizes. Because of their shape, paper rolls cannot be transported as airfreight. The weight of roll paper is slightly less than rectangular boxes at 600 kg/m^3. Figure 8.5 contains a CylindricalParcel class that is appropriate for such a paper roll.

Both RectangularParcel and CylindricalParcel inherit Parcel. This relationship is diagramed in the class diagram of Figure 8.6. The proper UML class diagram notation for inheritance is a closed-ended arrow drawn from the subclass to its superclass.

Figure 8.5 CylindricalParcel class

```java
public class CylindricalParcel extends Parcel  {
    private  double parcelRadius, parcelLength;

    /* modifies
            parcelLength, parcelRadius, weight, volume, isAirFreight
        postcondition
            parcelLength == len   AND   parcelRadius == r
            AND volume == len*r*r*PI
            AND weight == volume*600
            AND isAirFreight==false */
    public CylindricalParcel( double len, double r)    {
        super( 0, 0, false );
        parcelLength = len;
        parcelRadius = r;
        volume = parcelLength * Math.PI * Math.pow(parcelRadius,2);
        weight = volume * 600;
    }
```

```
public double length()  {
    return parcelLength;
}

public double radius() {
    return parcelRadius;
}
```
}

Figure 8.6 Class diagram showing inheritance relationships

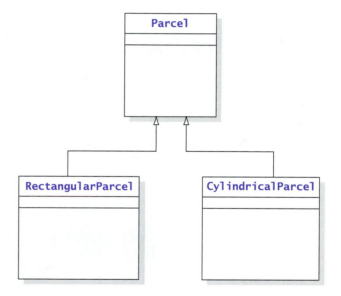

Parcel contains four members in addition to its constructor; these members are the `weight`, `volume`, and `isAirFreight` instance variables, as well as the `shippingCost` method. `RectangularParcel` and `CylindricalParcel` both inherit all four of these members. `RectangularParcel` also includes three of its own methods, namely `length`, `width`, and `height`. `CylindricalParcel` includes just two more methods than its superclass; these methods are `length` and `radius`.

As demonstrated by the `Parcel` example, it is possible to have more than one subclass of the same superclass. On the other hand, Java does not permit a subclass to have more than one superclass. This restriction is known as **single inheritance** because each class can inherit from at most one other class.

8.2 CLASS RELATIONS: CONTAINS_A AND IS_A

At first glance inheritance appears to be a convenient technique for borrowing instance variables and methods from another class (the superclass). However, proper use of inheritance deserves more investigation.

A good place to begin investigating inheritance is with the real-world concept of a **specialization**.

- *Automobile* is a special case of *transportation vehicle*.
- *Shirt* is a particular kind of *clothing*.
- *Bald eagle* is a species of *bird*.
- *Triangle* is a type of *polygon*.

This sort of relation between classes is known as an **is_a relation** because one class *is a* specialized version of the other. An is_a relation is an obvious situation for the use of inheritance.

(subclass is_a superclass)

As an example, consider the task of creating a BorderedDot class. Below is a picture of two BorderedDot objects in the same AWindow.

A BorderedDot is a filled circular region with a border around its perimeter. Furthermore, BorderedDot objects behave like other *aLibrary* objects. In other words, a BorderedDot object **is_a** AOval object with two differences:

1. BorderedDot objects are initially filled.

2. BorderedDot objects have borders around their perimeters.

Since BorderedDot and AOval exhibit an is_a relationship, inheritance seems like the obvious choice for creating a BorderedDot class. Figure 8.7 shows such a class.

Figure 8.7 BorderedDot class

```
import aLibrary.*;
import java.awt.*;
public class BorderedDot extends AOval {
   private AOval border;
   /* postcondition
           getX() == x   AND   getY() == y
           AND   getWidth() == d   AND   getHeight() == d
           AND   getColor() == borderColor() == Color.black */
   public BorderedDot( int x, int y, int d)   {
      super(x, y, d, d);
      setToFill();
      border = new AOval(0, 0, d, d);
      border.place( this );
   }


   /* postcondition
           borderColor() == c   */
   public  void  setBorderColor( Color c )   {
      border.setColor( c );
   }


   /* postcondition
           result == border.getColor()   */
   public  Color  borderColor() {
      return border.getColor();
   }


   /* postcondition
           getWidth() == d   AND   getHeight() == d   */
   public void  setSize( int d )   {
      setSize(d, d);
   }

   public void  setSize( int w, int h )   {
      super.setSize( w, h );
      border.setSize( w, h );
   }

   public void  scale( double sw, double sh )   {
      super.scale( sw, sh );
      border.scale( sw, sh );
   }
}
```

The `BorderedDot` constructor method begins by calling the inherited `AOval` object constructor, then fills the resulting `AOval`. A second `AOval` called `border` is placed on top of this inherited object. The border oval is an outline, and it has identical dimensions to the inherited `AOval`. The reserved word `this` refers to the inherited `AOval` upon which the border is placed.

The `BorderedDot` class also includes two methods to permit clients to modify and inspect the color of the border. Calling `setBorderColor` assigns a new color to the border, and the `borderColor` method returns such a color. These new methods do not disturb the inherited `setColor` method and `getColor` methods, which continue to affect the filled (`this`) `AOval`. The following code demonstrates how to create a green `BorderedDot` with a yellow border.

```
someDot = new BorderedDot( 10, 10, 100 );
someDot.setColor( Color.green );
someDot.setBorderColor( Color.yellow );
```

A subclass is permitted to **override** one or more superclass methods by including its own method(s) so long as the overriding methods have identical names, scope modifiers (`public` or `private`), and parameter lists as the superclass method(s). The last two methods of the `BorderedDot` class, `setSize` and `scale`, override methods from `AOval`. Overriding replaces the superclass method with a new version. Therefore, a call to `setSize` upon a `BorderedDot` object will execute the subclass version of `setSize`. The `setSize` and `scale` methods of `BorderedDot` alter the dimensions of *both* `this` `AOval` and its border, whereas the superclass versions of these methods do not alter `border`.

Within a subclass it is often useful to be able to call the superclass version of a method. Overriding methods can complicate this situation. For example, the code of the `scale` method must resize both the filled dot and its border. Resizing the dot can be accomplished by calling the superclass version of `scale`, but the subclass has overridden this method. Within `BorderedDot`, a call such as the following will execute the subclass version of `scale`, producing the wrong result:

```
scale( sw, sh );
```

Java includes a notation that can be used within the subclass to refer to the superclass version of any method. Figure 8.8 shows the syntax for this second use for the reserved word `super`. For example, the code within `BorderedDot` calls the superclass (`AOval`) version of `scale` with the following instruction:

```
super.scale( sw, sh );
```

The two-parameter version of `setSize` must also make use of this `super` notation.

The `BorderedDot` subclass not only *overrides* `setSize`, but also *overloads* `setSize` by including a single-parameter version of this method. The single-parameter `setSize` resizes the dot to have equal width and height.

There are two alternative ways to express the implementation of the single-parameter `setSize`. The following instruction works because it calls the subclass (`BorderedDot`) version of the double-parameter `setSize` method:

```
setSize( d, d );
```

Figure 8.8 SuperMethodCall description

SuperMethodCall (abridged version of *MethodCall*)

Syntax

Notes

- *MethodName* is the name of a nonconstructor method from the superclass.
- *argumentList* is a list of argument expressions (separated by commas) that matches in type to the corresponding parameters.
- This super notation is only permitted within a subclass.

Semantics

Executing *SuperMethodCall* causes the superclass version of the method to be executed.

The following two instructions accomplish the same thing by calling the superclass (AOval) version of setSize twice:

```
super.setSize( d, d );
border.setSize( d, d );
```

Not all relationships between two classes are is_a relations. Another common relationship is called a **contains_a relation**. (This is alternatively known as a **has_a relation**.) As the name implies, a contains_a relation occurs when an instance of one class is contained within another class.

An *automobile* contains a *steering wheel*.
A *shirt* contains a *pocket*.
A *bald eagle* has a *wing*.
A *triangle* contains a *vertex*.

A contains_a relation leads to composition—also called aggregation (see Chapter 6). Figure 8.9 demonstrates the class diagram notation for each of these two relations.

The arrow in Figure 8.9 signifies that the class called subclass inherits superclass. Such a situation is the result of an is_a relation (subclass is_a superclass). The diamond-ended line in Figure 8.9 diagrams aggregation (aggregate contains_a someclass object). Such arrows and diamond-ended lines can also be used to illustrate these relations in object diagrams.

The BorderedDot class makes use of *both* inheritance and aggregation. BorderedDot inherits AOval, and it also contains an AOval by way of the border instance variable. It is proper to diagram these relations as shown in Figure 8.10. This diagram ornaments the aggregate relation with the name of the associated instance variable.

Figure 8.9 Inheritance and aggregation in class diagrams

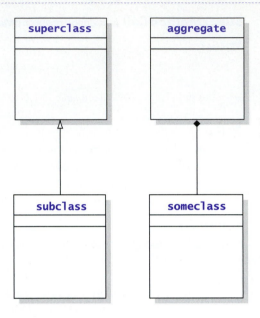

Figure 8.10 Relationship between AOval and BorderedDot

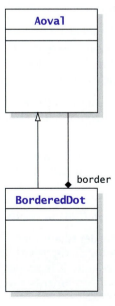

The choice between inheritance and aggregation is not always easy. For example, consider the task of implementing a class to keep track of time in military form. Military time maintains hours in the range 0 through 23 without distinction for A.M. and P.M. Figure 8.11 contains such a `MilitaryTime` class. (The `protected` qualifier in line 6 is explained in Section 8.4. For now it is sufficient to know that `protected` variables are accessible to subclasses.)

Figure 8.11 MilitaryTime class

```
public class MilitaryTime  {
    /* Invariant:
            0 <= hour <= 23
            AND   0 <= minute <= 59
            AND   0 <= second <= 59  */
    protected  int  hour, minute, second;

    /* postcondition
            hour == 1  AND  minute == 0  AND  second == 0  */
    public  MilitaryTime()    {
        hour = 1;
        minute = 0;
        second = 0;
    }


    /* postcondition
            hour == 12 AND minute == 0 AND second == 0  */
    public void setToNoon()    {
        hour = 12;
        minute = 0;
        second = 0;
    }


    /* postcondition
            old hour < 23 IMPLIES hour == old hour + 1
            AND old hour == 23 IMPLIES hour == 0  */
    public void advance1Hour()    {
        if (hour < 23)
            hour++;
        else
            hour = 0;
    }
```

```
/* postcondition
        old minute < 59 IMPLIES minute == old minute + 1
        AND old minute == 59 IMPLIES
            (minute == 0 AND hour advanced by 1)*/
public void advance1Minute()   {
    if (minute < 59)
        minute++;
    else   {
        minute = 0;
        advance1Hour();
    }
}

/* postcondition
        old second < 59 IMPLIES second == old second + 1
        AND old second == 59 IMPLIES
            (second == 0 AND minute advanced by 1)*/
public void advance1Second()   {
    if (second < 59)
        second++;
    else   {
        second = 0;
        advance1Minute();
    }
}
/* postcondition  result == hour  */
public  int  hours()   {
    return hour;
}
/* postcondition  result == minute  */
public int minutes()   {
    return minute;
}
/* postcondition result == second  */
public int seconds()   {
    return second;
}
}
```

A MilitaryTime object maintains time in the form of three variables: hour, minute, and second. Consider a second class, call it TimeWithMillisec, that is just like MilitaryTime with the addition of a millisec attribute and an advance1Millisec method for additional precision in the time keeping. A convincing argument can be made that a TimeWithMillisec timer is really a special case of MilitaryTime. Such an is_a relation suggests that TimeWithMillisec should inherit MilitaryTime. The resulting TimeWithMillisec class is shown in Figure 8.12.

Figure 8.12 TimeWithMillisec class

```
public class TimeWithMillisec extends MilitaryTime {
    protected int millisec;

    /* postcondition
            hour == 1 AND minute == 0
            AND second == 0 AND millisec == 0   */
    public TimeWithMillisec()    {
        super();
        millisec = 0;
    }


    /* postcondition
        old millisec < 999 IMPLIES millisec == old millisec + 1
        AND old millisec == 59 IMPLIES
            (millisec == 0 AND second advanced by 1)*/
    public void advance1Millisec()    {
        if (millisec < 59)
            millisec ++;
        else   {
            millisec = 0;
            advance1Second();
        }
    }
}
```

These implementations of MilitaryTime and TimeWithMillisec are a good choice, but they are not the only choice. Notice that every TimeWithMillisec contains_a MilitaryTime in the sense that it must include hours, minutes, and seconds. This observation suggests writing a class, call it TimeWithMillisec2, which does not inherit, but rather uses aggregation, as sketched in Figure 8.13

Figure 8.13 Partial class to build TimeWithMillisec2 by aggregation

```
public class TimeWithMillisec2   {
    private  MilitaryTime  hourMinuteSecond;
    private  int  millisec;
    . . .
}
```

In this case, the better choice seems to be using inheritance, because `TimeWithMillisec2` must repeat all of the query and update methods from `MilitaryTime`, whereas `TimeWithMillisec` is able to reuse these superclass methods without change. When the choice between an is_a relation and contains_a relation is not clear, software developers learn to sketch out partial solutions and draw on past experiences.

8.3   SPECIALIZATION AND EXTENSION

The is_a relationship that generally links a subclass to its superclass means that the subclass is a kind of special case (**specialization**) of the superclass. For example, a `RectangularParcel` is a specialization of `Parcel`. Inheritance is the preferred mechanism for implementing such specialization relationships.

One particular kind of specialization is known as **extension**. Extension occurs whenever a subclass adds some functionality that wasn't present in its superclass. The `RectangularParcel` class extends `Parcel` by including new instance variables to store the container's length, width, and height. The `BorderedDot` class exhibits extension by including a border and a `setBorderColor` method that aren't present in its `AOval` superclass. Similarly, the `TimeWithMillisec` class extends `MilitaryTime` to include greater time accuracy through an additional instance variable and method to increment its value.

Inheritance often involves specialization in the form of

- redefining some methods.

Inheritance also involves extension in the form of

- the addition of new instance variables.
- the addition of new methods.

One *aLibrary* class that is designed to be extended is the `AView` class. It might seem strange that a graphics class whose objects are invisible would be so useful, but the utility of `AView` lies in two of its properties.

1. An `AView` can *group* a collection of graphical objects (those that are placed upon the `AView`) into a single drawable entity.
2. The `AView` class *provides a variety of commonly used methods*, such as `place, remove, repaint, setLocation, setSize, scale, translate, getX, getY, getWidth,` and `getHeight` for subclasses to inherit.

As an example of `AView` inheritance, consider drawing a cube with a single dot on its face, like the one shown below. Figure 8.14 contains a class called `Cube` for this purpose.

Figure 8.14 Cube class

```
import java.awt.*;
import aLibrary.*;
public class Cube extends AView  {
    private ARectangle face;
    private ALine top, left, right, back, bottom;
    private AOval dot;

    /* postcondition
            this object is a cube with a single dot on its face
            AND  getX() == x  AND  getY() == y
            AND  getWidth() == s  AND  getHeight() == s  */
    public Cube( int x, int y, int s )  {
        super(x, y, s, s);
        makeAndPlaceCubeParts( s );
    }

    /* postcondition
            all parts of this object are recolored to c */
    public void setColor( Color c )   {
        face.setColor(c);
        top.setColor(c);
        left.setColor(c);
        right.setColor(c);
        back.setColor(c);
        bottom.setColor(c);
        dot.setColor(c);
    }

    /* precondition
            w > 0 AND h > 0
       postcondition
            getWidth() == w AND getHeight() == h */
    public void setSize(int w, int h)   {
        super.setSize( w, h );
        removeCubeParts();
        if ( w < h )  {
            makeAndPlaceCubeParts(w);
        } else {
            makeAndPlaceCubeParts(h);
        }
    }

    /* precondition
            sw > 0 AND sh > 0
```

```
                postcondition
                    getWidth() == old getWidth()*sw
                    AND getHeight() == old getHeight() * sh */
        public void scale(double sw, double sh)     {
            setSize( (int)(getWidth()*sw), (int)(getHeight()*sh) );
        }

        /* precondition
                getWidth() >= s AND getHeight() >= s
            postcondition
                face, dot, left, right, top, bottom, and back are all
                instantiated and placed upon this.  */
        private void makeAndPlaceCubeParts( int s )  {
            face = new ARectangle(0, s/4, s*3/4, s*3/4);
            face.place(this);
            dot = new AOval(s/4, s/2 , s/4, s/4);
            dot.setToFill();
            dot.place(this);
            left = new ALine(0, s/4, s/4, 0);
            left.place(this);
            right = new ALine(s*3/4, s/4, s, 0);
            right.place(this);
            top = new ALine(s/4, 0, s, 0);
            top.place(this);
            bottom = new ALine(s*3/4, s, s, s*3/4);
            bottom.place(this);
            back = new ALine(s, 0, s, s*3/4);
            back.place(this);
        }

        /* postcondition
                face.parentContainer()==null
                AND dot.parentContainer()==null
                AND left.parentContainer()==null
                AND right.parentContainer()==null
                AND top.parentContainer()==null
                AND bottom.parentContainer()==null
                AND back.parentContainer() == null */
        private void removeCubeParts()  {
            face.remove();
            dot.remove();
            left.remove();
            right.remove();
            top.remove();
            bottom.remove();
            back.remove();
        }
    }
```

Cube inherits AView and creates the cube image in the constructor method. A call to the Cube constructor method places an ARectangle (face), an AOval (dot), and five ALine objects upon the underlying AView. The details of creating this image are handled by a private method called makeAndPlaceCubeParts.

Since Cube inherits AView, there is an obligation to ensure that the inherited methods work properly in the context of a Cube. The AView version of methods such as place, getX, setLocation, and many others behave properly for a Cube. However, three of the AView methods do *not* work properly when applied to a Cube object. These three methods are setColor, setSize, and scale. The problem with all three methods is that in AView there are no face, dot, left, right, top, bottom, or back instance variables. As a result, AView is incapable of changing the color or size of these objects.

Since Cube methods are obligated to properly update the Cube instance variables, the Cube class must override setColor, setSize, and scale. Figure 8.14 includes the subclass versions of all three methods. The setColor method assigns colors to all seven objects placed upon the AView. setSize recreates the seven objects of the Cube for the new dimensions of the background AView. (Note that all seven objects must be removed.) The scale method uses the Cube version of setSize to accomplish most of its work.

From the client code perspective, the Cube class provides similar functionality to ARectangle and AOval; but instead of displaying a rectangle or oval, Cube displays a three-dimensional cube with a dot on its front face. The following code illustrates the client code needed to declare and construct a Cube object, color it, and display it on some other *aLibrary* object (in this case a window).

```
AWindow window;
Cube redCube;
window = new AWindow(100, 100, 300, 200);
redCube = new Cube(10, 10, 40);
redCube.place(window);
redCube.setColor( Color.red );
```

8.4 PROTECTED SCOPE

Java permits a subclass to override an inherited method, but the language imposes certain restrictions upon overriding.

- A subclass cannot override private methods, because it does not have access to superclass features that are private.
- A subclass cannot alter the scope (private, public, or protected) of an inherited method.
- The parameter list in the subclass method must contain the same number of parameters and the same types of parameters as the method from the superclass. (If the parameter lists differ, then overloading, not overriding, occurs.)
- Overriding applies only to methods, not to instance variables.

The first of two of these restrictions point out one drawback to using just pub-lic and private declarations. If a method is `public`, then *every* class has access to the method—every client class and every subclass. If a method is `private`, then *no* outside class has access—no client class and no subclass.

In order to provide a scope that differentiates subclasses from client class, Java includes the option of declaring methods and instance variables as `protected` instead of `public` or `private`. The scope of a protected feature includes any sub-class, as well as the class that declares the feature. In other words if myVar is a pro-tected instance variable of `MyClass`, then `MyClass` can access this variable as can any subclass of `MyClass`. Since subclasses inherit scope, the access to myVar extends to any direct subclass of a `MyClass` subclass, and any direct subclass of a subclass of `MyClass`. However, client classes (i.e., those that declare variables of type `MyClass`) do not have access to myVar. Figure 8.15 summarizes the scope differences of pri-vate, public, and protected class members.

Figure 8.15 Scope of `private`, `protected`, and `public` members

Member (excepting constructors)	Available within A?	Available in subclass of A?	Available elsewhere?
`private` member of class A	Yes	No	No
`protected` member of class A	Yes	Yes	No
`public` member of class A	Yes	Yes	Yes

In class diagrams, protected variables and methods are preceded with a "#" symbol, as opposed to "+" for public and "-" for private. The class diagram in Figure 8.16 illustrates. The three variables in the `MilitaryTime` class are declared to have protected scope, whereas all methods are public.

SOFTWARE ENGINEERING TIP

It is best to avoid declaring instance variables as **public**. If an instance variable is widely shared by subclasses, then **protected** is acceptable. The **Parcel** class (Figure 8.2) exhibits better informa-tion hiding if the declaration of its three instance variables is changed to **protected**.

SOFTWARE ENGINEERING TIP

Declaring methods and instance variables to be **protected** is often a good choice. As a general rule it is better to use **protected** than private any time that there is a chance the class might become a superclass.

Figure 8.16 Class diagram for `MilitaryTime`

```
                MilitaryTime

        # int hour
        # int minute
        # int second

        «constructor»
          + MilitaryTime()

        «query»
          + int hours()
          + int minutes()
          + int seconds()

        «update»
          + void setToNoon()
          + void advance1Hour()
          + void advance1Minute()
          + void advance1Second()
```

To illustrate the utility of the **protected** scope, consider the task of extending the `MilitaryTime` class to include an additional `setToMidnight` method. Figure 8.17 contains such a class.

Figure 8.17 MilitaryTimeWithSet class and class diagram

```
/* class invariant
        0 <= hour <= 23 AND  0 <= minute <= 59 AND  0 <=
        second <= 59 */
public class MilitaryTimeWithSet extends MilitaryTime {

    /* postcondition
            hour == 1  AND  minute == 0
            AND  second == 0  */
    public MilitaryTimeWithSet() {
        super();
    }
    /* postcondition
            hour == 0  AND  minute == 0
            AND  second == 0  */
    public void setToMidnight() {
        hour = 0;
        minute = 0;
        second = 0;
    }
}
```

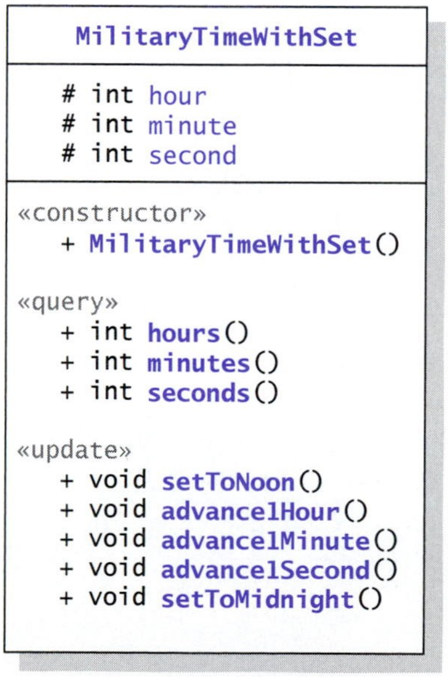

```
           MilitaryTimeWithSet
    -----------------------------------
    # int hour
    # int minute
    # int second
    -----------------------------------
    «constructor»
       + MilitaryTimeWithSet()

    «query»
       + int hours()
       + int minutes()
       + int seconds()

    «update»
       + void setToNoon()
       + void advance1Hour()
       + void advance1Minute()
       + void advance1Second()
       + void setToMidnight()
```

MilitaryTime declares hour, minute, and second to be protected instance variables. The protected scope of these variables grants subclasses full access to them, as illustrated by MilitaryTimeWithSet. Such access permits the assignment instructions that are used in the body of setToMidnight.

It would be a poor choice to declare the MilitaryTime instance variables with a scope other than protected. If these instance variables are declared private, then subclasses such as MilitaryTimeWithSet are more difficult to implement. On the other hand, if the instance variables of MilitaryTime have a public scope, then information hiding for client classes is damaged.

Java instance variables are treated differently than methods when it comes to inheritance. Whereas methods can be overridden to replace a superclass method, instance variables cannot be overridden. Unfortunately, the Java compiler does not generate errors when a subclass declares instance variables with the same name as its superclass. Instead, when a subclass declares an instance variable with the same name as a superclass instance variable, two copies of the variable will be created. The new code of the subclass has access to the subclass variable, and the inherited code from the superclass has access to the superclass variable.

SOFTWARE ENGINEERING TIP

When creating a subclass, avoid declaring instance variables that have the same names as instance variables of the superclass.

Figure 8.18 illustrates with a class called ParallelDeclarations that inherits MilitaryTime. The ParallelDeclarations class is the same as Military-TimeWithSet except for the inclusion of a declaration for hour, minute, and second in the fourth line.

Figure 8.18 ParallelDeclarations class attempt

```java
public class ParallelDeclarations extends MilitaryTime {
    /* NOTE: This class doesn't work properly.  */
    protected int hour, minute, second;

    /* postcondition
            hour == 1   AND   minute == 0   AND   second == 0   */
    public  ParallelDeclarations()   {
        super();
    }

    /* postcondition
            hour == 0   AND   minute == 0   AND   second == 0   */
    public void setToMidnight()   {
        hour = 0;
        minute = 0;
        second = 0;
    }
}
```

By including a second set of variable declarations, the `ParallelDeclarations` class has created two parallel sets of variables (hour, minute, and second), the inherited version and the newly declared version. When `super()` is called, the constructor method from `MilitaryTime` will assign values to the superclass version of the variables, and the `ParallelDeclarations` variable versions are unaltered. Similarly, the `advance1Hour`, `advance1Minute`, and `advance1Second` methods increment the superclass variables, not the newly declared variables. When `setToMidnight` is called, values are assigned to the newly declared variables and the superclass variables are unaltered. If this seems confusing, that is because it is! The moral of this example is that Java programmers should take care *not* to redeclare instance variables from a superclass.

8.5 INHERITING FOR EVENT HANDLING

Method overriding is the key to most *aLibrary* event handling. Typically, an *aLibrary* class includes event handler methods with empty bodies. An object belonging to such a type does nothing in response to an event. However, a subclass can override the event handler method, thereby providing event handling to its objects.

An example of such a library class supporting event handling is `AButton`. Figure 8.19 contains a class diagram for `AButton`.

An `AButton` object is essentially a rectangular region that can be clicked by the program user. The three characteristics of `AButton` that distinguish it from other *aLibrary* classes are as follows:

1. An `AButton` object cannot be colored, but it does have a string label on its surface.
2. Placing other *aLibrary* objects upon an `AButton` is *not* supported.
3. When the user clicks within the region of an `AButton` object, that object's `actionPerformed` method is called.

The third of these characteristics, namely the ability to respond to user clicks, is the key reason for the `AButton` class. When the user clicks an `AButton` object, the `actionPerformed` method is automatically called by the Java Virtual Machine. The Java VM also passes an `ActionEvent` parameter to the event handler, although this is of little importance for the discussion at hand.

The version of the `actionPerformed` method that is included within `AButton` has an empty body, so nothing will happen when a user clicks an `AButton` object. In order to use the `AButton` class properly, the programmer must replace the default (empty) event handling method. This is accomplished by creating a new subclass of `AButton` that overrides `actionPerformed`.

Figure 8.20 shows code for a class called `DemoButton` and an associated `Director` class. A `DemoButton` is an `AButton` with two differences: (1) Each `DemoButton` is labeled "DEMO" by virtue of the call to `setText` in the `DemoButton` constructor. (2) A `DemoButton` stores a count of the number of times it has been clicked, using the `clickCount` variable.

Figure 8.19 AButton class diagram

```
┌─────────────────────────────────────────────┐
│                    AButton                    │
├─────────────────────────────────────────────┤
│    - int x                                    │
│    - int y                                    │
│    - int width                                │
│    - int height                               │
│    - String label                             │
├─────────────────────────────────────────────┤
│  «constructor»                                │
│    + AButton()                                │
│    + AButton(int, int, int, int)              │
│    ...                                         │
│                                               │
│  «query»                                      │
│    + int getX()                               │
│    + int getY()                               │
│    + int getWidth()                           │
│    + int getHeight()                          │
│    + Container parentContainer()              │
│    + String getText()                         │
│                                               │
│  «update»                                     │
│    + void repaint()                           │
│    + void setSize(int, int)                   │
│    + void setLocation(int, int)               │
│    + void scale(double, double)               │
│    + void translate(double, double)           │
│    + void place(Container)                    │
│    + void remove()                            │
│    + void setText(String)                     │
│                                               │
│  «event handler»                              │
│    + void actionPerformed(ActionEvent)        │
│                                               │
└─────────────────────────────────────────────┘
```

Figure 8.20 DemoButton class and associated Director

```java
import aLibrary.*;
import java.awt.event.*;
public class DemoButton extends AButton  {
    private int clickCount;

    /* postcondition
            getX() == x  AND  getY() == y
        AND  getWidth() == w  AND  getHeight() == h
        AND  getText() is "DEMO"   AND  clickCount == 0  */
```

```
        public DemoButton( int x, int y, int w, int h )  {
            super(x, y, w, h);
            setText( "DEMO" );
            clickCount = 0;
        }


        /* postcondition
                a message has been sent to standard output     */
        public void actionPerformed( ActionEvent e )   {
            clickCount++;
            System.out.println("Demo click count is " + clickCount );
        }
    }


    // A client of DemoButton
    import aLibrary.*;
    public class Director  {
        private AWindow  window;
        private DemoButton button;

        public Director()  {
            window = new AWindow(10, 10, 200, 100);
            button = new DemoButton(10, 40, 180, 20);
            button.place(window);
            window.repaint();
        }
    }
```

When the program from Figure 8.20 executes, the Director constructor creates window and button. The call to the DemoButton constructor initializes the button variable to have a text label of "DEMO" and a clickCount of zero. The Director method also places button upon window, then repaints window. Figure 8.21 contains a picture that shows window as it appears with button placed.

Figure 8.21 The window resulting from the DemoButton program

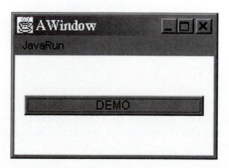

Following the execution of the Director constructor, the program awaits button clicks on the demo button. Each such click causes the overridden version of actionPerformed to be called, and each call to actionPerformed causes another line to be appended to the standard output device, creating the following output:

```
Demo click count is 1
Demo click count is 2
Demo click count is 3

. . .
```

Usually, an AButton object needs to send messages to other objects, not merely call System.out.println. For example, consider using button clicks to change the location of a Cube object. (The Cube class is given in Figure 8.14.) The MoveCubeButton from Figure 8.22 demonstrates an AButton subclass that is used for such a purpose. In particular, each time the user clicks a MoveCubeButton, the appropriate Cube object moves left five pixels and down five pixels.

Figure 8.22 MoveCubeButton class

```java
import aLibrary.*;
import java.awt.event.*;    // needed for ActionEvent class
public class MoveCubeButton extends AButton  {
    private Cube theCube;
    /* precondition
            d != null
        postcondition
            theCube == d
            AND  getX() == x   AND  getY() == y
            AND  getWidth() == 100  AND  getHeight() == 30   */
    public MoveCubeButton( int x, int y, Cube d )  {
        super(x, y, 100, 30);
        setText( "MOVE" );
        theCube = d;
    }
    /* precondition
            theCube != null
        postcondition
            theCube.getX() == old theCube.getX() + 5
            AND theCube.getY() = old theCube.getY() + 5    */
    public void actionPerformed( ActionEvent e )    {
        theCube.translate( 5, 5 );
    }
}
```

The behavior of a MoveCubeButton relies upon a new instance variable called theCube. When MoveCubeButton is instantiated, the third parameter is used to pass a Cube object. The last instruction within the MoveCubeButton constructor causes theCube to be bound to this object. This binding permits theCube to be accessed by future calls to actionPerformed. For example, consider the following client code:

```
Cube smallCube = new Cube(10, 10, 40);
MoveCubeButton exampleButton = new MoveCubeButton(20, 30,
    smallCube);
```

Following the execution of the two statements above, the theCube variable of exampleButton will be an alias for smallCube. Therefore, each time exampleButton is clicked, its actionPerformed method causes theCube (which is really smallCube) to be repositioned.

It is quite common for different classes to want to share the same object in the way that the client code above shares smallCube with exampleButton. Figure 8.23 generalizes this into a pattern for object sharing.

Figure 8.23 Shared object pattern

A Shared Object Pattern

Suppose that Object A contains an object called *sharedObject* and that Object B must also manipulate *sharedObject*. The following strategy permits such sharing.

1. Object A calls one of Object B's methods (often a constructor) and passes *sharedObject* as an argument.
2. Object B assigns *sharedObject* to one of its own instance variables. (Now both A and B have variables bound to *sharedObject*.)
3. Object A and Object B can access the shared object using their individual bindings.

(See Figure 8.22 for an example.)

Another technique often used for event handling is known as a **callback**. In a callback approach each event is "forwarded" by virtue of a method call to another object. To accomplish a callback, the actionPerformed method of an AButton subclass need execute only one instruction—a method call on some other object. The reason for the name "callback" is that the object to receive this method call is generally the object that created the button. It is as though every button event results in a "call back" to the object that created the button.

Figure 8.24 illustrates a callback with a class called recolorCallbackButton. The RecolorCallbackButton class is designed to be used in conjunction with an object of type Director. The constructor method of RecolorCallbackButton begins in much the same way as MoveCubeButton. Following the execution of the first two RecolorCallbackButton instructions, a button is created and labeled with the name RECOLOR. The third instruction in the constructor method is different, because it is assigns d to callbackDestination. This constructor method is expecting the Director object to pass its own identity. Subsequently, every actionPerformed event causes a call to the recolor method to be performed upon the callbackDestination object.

The general requirements of the callback pattern are explained in Figure 8.25.

Figure 8.24 RecolorCallbackButton class

```
import aLibrary.*;
import java.awt.event.*;   // needed for ActionEvent class
public class RecolorCallbackButton extends AButton {
    private Director callbackDestination;

    /* precondition
            m != null
        postcondition
            callbackDestination == d
            AND  getX() == x   AND   getY() == y
            AND  getWidth() == 100   AND   getHeight() == 30   */
    public RecolorCallbackButton( int x, int y, Director d )  {
        super(x, y, 100, 30);
        setText( "RECOLOR" );
        callbackDestination = d;
    }
    /* precondition
            callbackDestination != null
        postcondition
            the postcondition from callbackDestination.recolor(). */
    public void actionPerformed( ActionEvent e )   {
        callbackDestination.recolor();
    }

}
```

Figure 8.25 Callback pattern for event handling

A Callback Pattern

A callback pattern consists of an event-producing object (from class *EventProducer*) forwarding each event by calling a method on another object (from class *Target*). For a true callback, the *Target* object is the one that created the *EventProducer* object.

The following four steps are needed to accomplish this kind of callback scheme for handling events.

1. Class *EventProducer* includes an instance variable of type *Target* (call it t), and a method (usually the constructor) to assign this variable.
2. Class *Target* constructs an object of type *EventProducer* and passes its own identity so that t is bound to the *Target* object.
3. The body of the event handler method from method *EventProducer* consists of a single instruction of the following form: **t.someMethod();**
4. Class *Target* includes a method with the same name and parameter list as *someMethod*.

(See Figure 8.24 for an example in which class *EventProducer* is RecolorCallbackButton, class *Target* is Director, and the t variable is named callbackDestination.)

Figure 8.26 completes the code for this example by showing an appropriate Director class. This class creates two cubes and two buttons, one button of type MoveCubeButton and one of type RecolorCallbackButton.

Figure 8.26 Director class for the Cube buttons

```java
// Cube Director
// Author: Riley -- June, 2000
import java.awt.*;
import aLibrary.*;
public class Director  {
    private AWindow window;
    private Cube smallCube, bigCube;
    private MoveCubeButton moveButton;
    private RecolorCallbackButton recolorButton;

    public Director()  {
        window = new AWindow(10, 10, 600, 400);
        smallCube = new Cube(10, 10, 40);
        smallCube.place(window);
        smallCube.setColor( Color.red );
        moveButton = new MoveCubeButton(100, 370, smallCube);
        moveButton.place(window);
        moveButton.repaint();

        bigCube = new Cube(150, 150, 200);
        bigCube.setColor( Color.green );
        bigCube.place( window );
        recolorButton = new RecolorCallbackButton(300, 370, this);
        recolorButton.place( window );
        recolorButton.repaint();
        window.repaint();
    }

    public void recolor()    {
        float redness, greeness, blueness;
        redness = (float) Math.random();
        greenness = (float) Math.random();
        blueness = (float) Math.random();
        Color c = new Color(redness, greenness, blueness);
        bigCube.setColor( c );
        bigCube.repaint();
    }
}
```

The `Director` class from Figure 8.26 begins execution by constructing `smallCube`, coloring it red, placing it upon a window, and passing it as the third argument in the construction of `moveButton`. Next, a second and larger cube, called `bigCube`, is constructed. As the `recolorButton` is constructed, it is passed the identity of the `Director` object (namely *this*). The computer screen should contain a window that appears something like the one shown in Figure 8.27 after the `Director` constructor finishes execution.

Figure 8.27 Window produced by code from Figure 8.26

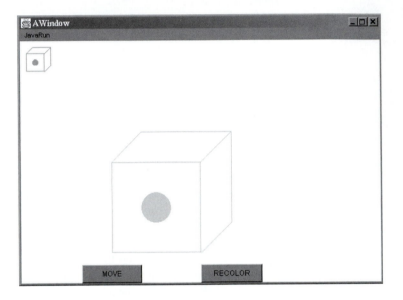

The Figure 8.27 window becomes fully event driven once the `Director` constructor completes. At such time the state of the program's execution includes five key objects: the `Director` object, `smallCube`, `bigCube`, and the two buttons. Figure 8.28 shows the key relationships among these five objects, labeling each line with the appropriate instance variable name.

Figure 8.28 Key object bindings from the Cube button example

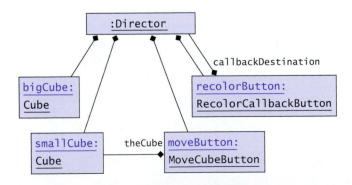

Figure 8.28 shows a two-way aggregation between the Director object and recolorButton. Such two-way aggregation is typical of a callback pattern. A user click on the RECOLOR button causes the actionPerformed method from recolorButton to be executed, and this event handler calls the recolor method upon callbackDestination (the Director object).

The MOVE button does not use a callback pattern like the RECOLOR button. Instead, moveButton contains an instance variable called theCube. A user click on the MOVE button causes the actionPerformed method from moveButton to be performed. As a result, the object named theCube (alias smallCube) moves down and to its right.

OPENING
the Black Box

The A3ButtonWindow class is just a class that declares three buttons (LEFT, MID, and RIGHT). This class is also designed to deliver all event handling by way of a callback pattern. This is why the constructor calls to A3ButtonWindow use this as their argument, as shown below:

```
public class Director extends A3ButtonHandler {
    public A3ButtonWindow window;
    public Director() {
        ...
        window = new A3ButtonWindow(this);
        ...
            }
    }
```

Chapter 9 contains another insert that explains a bit more about A3ButtonHandler.

8.6   ANIMATING BY INHERITING EVENTTIMER (OPTIONAL)

The callback object pattern can also be used to implement animations. This section demonstrates with the assistance of an *aLibrary* class called EventTimer.

A motion picture results from a sequence of individual photographs stored on film. When these photos are projected in rapid succession, they give the appearance of real-life motion. A computer animation can be produced in much the same way. The primary difference is that each image from a motion picture is created by projecting light through a single cell of the film, while each image of a computer animation is created by the execution of a program segment.

One effective way to produce animations is the use of events. The EventTimer class is designed to produce just such events. Figure 8.29 contains a class diagram for EventTimer.

An EventTimer object is like an alarm clock. Once the EventTimer is instantiated, the "alarm clock" is armed by a call to scheduleEvents. The scheduleEvents parameter specifies a delay time (in seconds). As soon as scheduleEvents has been called, the "alarm" goes off repeatedly with a time interval specified by the scheduleEvents parameter. These alarms continue to occur until the program either quits executing or the stop method is called.

Figure 8.29 EventTimer class diagram

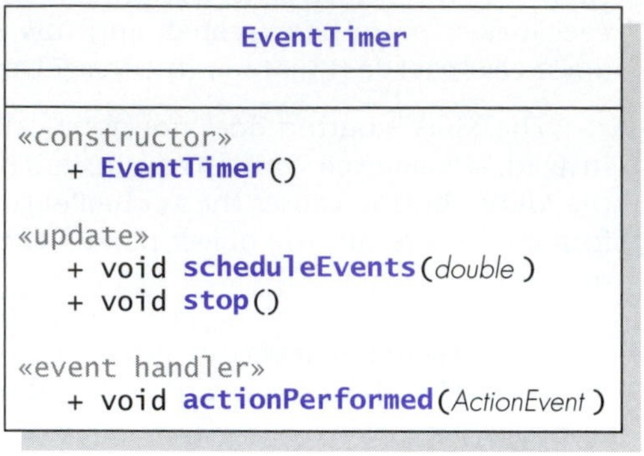

```
┌─────────────────────────────────────────────┐
│                 EventTimer                    │
├─────────────────────────────────────────────┤
│                                               │
├─────────────────────────────────────────────┤
│  «constructor»                                │
│      + EventTimer()                           │
│                                               │
│  «update»                                     │
│      + void scheduleEvents(double )           │
│      + void stop()                            │
│                                               │
│  «event handler»                              │
│      + void actionPerformed(ActionEvent )     │
└─────────────────────────────────────────────┘
```

Instead of a true alarm, the EventTimer class produces an event. For example, the following code declares and instantiates an EventTimer object, then causes the object to generate events every half second:

```
EventTimer sampleTimer = new EventTimer();
sampleTimer.scheduleEvents( 0.5 );
```

The EventTimer class uses the same actionPerformed event handler method as AButton. Therefore, the code above causes an empty actionPerformed method to be called repeatedly upon the sampleTimer object on half-second intervals.

Consider the problem of animating a dot so that it appears to move side to side within a window. For this particular animation it is assumed that the ball moves without gravity or friction, always maintaining a constant velocity. However, the ball must reverse direction when it reaches either side of the window in which it is bouncing. Figure 8.30 contains a Director class for one solution to this dot animation problem.

Figure 8.30 Director class for dot animation

```
import aLibrary.*;
public class Director  {
    private AWindow window;
    private AOval dot;
    private DotCallbackTimer clock;
    private int velocity;

    /*  postcondition
            window != null AND dot is placed at the left edge of
            window
        AND velocity = 1
        AND clock is scheduled for 1/50 sec. repeated events */
    public Director()   {
        window = new AWindow(10, 10, 400, 200);
```

```
        dot = new AOval(0, 90, 20, 20);
        dot.setToFill();
        dot.place( window );
        velocity = 1;
        clock = new DotCallbackTimer( this );
        clock.scheduleEvents( 0.02 );
        window.repaint();
    }


    /* precondition
            dot != null
        modifies
            dot.getX(), velocity
        postcondition
            dot.getX() == old dot.getX() + old velocity
            AND (old velocity == -1 && dot at left edge of window)
                IMPLIES velocity == 1
            AND (old velocity == 1  && dot at right edge of window)
                IMPLIES velocity == -1  */
    public void moveDot( )    {
        dot.translate( velocity, 0 );
        dot.repaint();
        if (velocity==1
                && dot.getX()+dot.getWidth() >= window.getWidth()) {
            velocity = -1;
        } else if (velocity == -1  &&  dot.getX() <= 0)    {
            velocity = 1;
        }
    }
}
```

The Director class in Figure 8.30 relies upon four instance variables. The dot variable represents a black AOval with a diameter of 20 pixels that will be moved back and forth within the AWindow called window. The velocity variable is used to maintain the travel direction of dot. When velocity is 1, dot is moving to the right; when velocity is –1, dot is moving to the left.

This program makes use of a callback pattern to move dot. The Director object instantiates an object called clock to initialize the callback, and clock belongs to a class called DotTimer that is designed for such a callback. DotTimer is shown in Figure 8.31.

A DotTimer object contains a single instance variable called theDirector. This theDirector variable is bound to the Director object that will serve as the true event handler. When DotTimer is instantiated, it assigns theDirector the value of its lone parameter. Thereafter, every timed event for the DotTimer object calls actionPerformed, which in turn calls theDirector.moveDot.

Figure 8.31 DotCallbackTimer class

```
import aLibrary.*;
import java.awt.event.*;
public class DotCallbackTimer extends EventTimer  {
    private Director theDirector;

    /* precondition
            d != null
       postcondition
            theDirector == d  */
    public DotCallbackTimer( Director d )  {
        super( );
        theDirector = d;
    }

    /* precondition
            theDirector != null
       postcondition
            the moveTheBall method from theDirector is performed */
    public void actionPerformed( ActionEvent e )   {
        theDirector.moveDot( );
    }
}
```

The Figure 8.30 Director class code activates a DotTimer object, called clock, with the following instructions:

```
clock = new DotTimer( this );
clock.scheduleEvents( 0.02 );
```

Executing the first of the two instructions instantiates clock and establishes the Director object (passed as this) as the callback target. The second instruction causes clock to begin generating events every .02 seconds.

The key associations among these classes are diagrammed in Figure 8.32. This diagram shows two classes (Director and DotCallbackTimer) that are each an aggregate including the other. This two-way aggregation picture is a characteristic of the callback pattern.

Figure 8.32 Class diagram of the relations for the dot timer callback

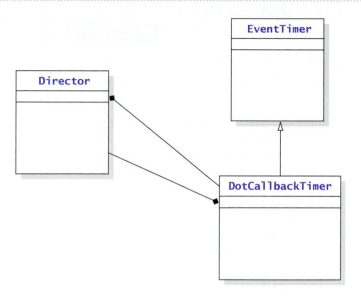

8.7 DESIGN EXAMPLE WITH SCROLLBARS AND TEXT FIELDS (OPTIONAL)

In computer programming the terms **input** and **output** are used to refer to data transfer to and from an executing program. System.out.println is considered to be an output method because programs use this method to provide information from the executing program to the user. Drawing *aLibrary* images on a computer screen is another form of computer output.

When an AButton object is clicked, this is a form of input. The name "input" indicates that the program is receiving something *from* the user. An AButton object's input is quite limited, since it cannot pass any information to the program except an actionEvent. Two other *aLibrary* classes allow the user to input more information. These two classes are AScrollbar and ATextField.

The AScrollbar class supplies a graphical event-driven technique to input integer values. AScrollbar objects appear somewhat like the image shown in Figure 8.33. (The actual image may look slightly different on different computer systems.)

Figure 8.33 An AScrollbar image

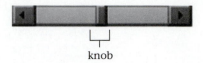

knob

On the face of every AScrollbar object is a knob. With a pointing device such as a mouse, the user can drag the knob back and forth. The AScrollbar object generates events periodically as the knob is being dragged. Sometimes scrollbars also have arrow buttons, like those on each end of the Figure 8.33 picture. Clicking these arrow buttons also moves the knob and generates events.

Each AScrollbar maintains an int value that increases as the knob is moved to the right and decreases as the knob moves left. This int value represents the position of the knob, proportional to its minimum and maximum possible values.

AScrollbar objects can be either horizontal or vertical in orientation. A horizontal scrollbar has a knob that moves left and right, whereas a vertical scrollbar's knob moves up and down. When an AScrollbar is constructed or its size changed, the horizontal/vertical orientation is determined. An AScrollbar that is wider than its height uses horizontal orientation, and an AScrollbar that is higher than its width uses vertical orientation.

Figure 8.34 contains a class diagram for AScrollbar. The place, remove, repaint, setLocation, setSize, scale, translate, and constructor methods behave as they do for other *aLibrary* classes.

There are three methods unique to AScrollbar:

- The setMinMaxVal method assigns a smallest possible value, a largest possible value, and a current value to the AScrollbar. The smallest possible value is the value of the scrollbar when the knob is positioned all the way to the left (or top), and the largest is when the knob is all the way right (or bottom).
- The getValue method returns the integer value of the knob position. This value is proportional to the distance of the knob from the left (or top) relative to the minimum and maximum possible values. For example, if the knob is three-fourths of the way from left to right for a minimum of 100 and a maximum of 200, then getValue() is 175.
- The setValue method assigns a new value to the object, and the knob is positioned appropriately.

The adjustmentValueChanged method is the event handler method for AScrollbar. User actions to change the knob position generate events that call adjustmentValueChanged. Overriding this method permits subclasses a way to capture user events associated with AScrollbar objects. Figure 8.35 illustrates the use of scrollbars with a Director class and an associated PrintingScrollbar class.

Figure 8.34 AScrollbar class diagram

```
┌──────────────────────────────────────────────────┐
│                    AScrollbar                       │
├──────────────────────────────────────────────────┤
│                                                    │
├──────────────────────────────────────────────────┤
│ «constructor»                                      │
│     + AScrollBar()                                 │
│     + AScrollBar(int, int, int, int )              │
│     ...                                            │
│                                                    │
│ «query»                                            │
│     + int getX()                                   │
│     + int getY()                                   │
│     + int getWidth()                               │
│     + int getHeight()                              │
│     + Container parentContainer()                  │
│     + int getValue()                               │
│     + int getMinimum()                             │
│     + int getMaximum()                             │
│                                                    │
│ «update»                                           │
│     + void repaint()                               │
│     + void setSize(int, int )                      │
│     + void setLocation(int, int )                  │
│     + void scale(double, double )                  │
│     + void translate(double, double )              │
│     + void place(Container )                        │
│     + void remove()                                │
│     + void setValue(int )                          │
│     + void setMinMaxVal(int, int, int )            │
│                                                    │
│ «event handler»                                    │
│     + void adjustmentValueChanged(AdjustmentEvent )│
└──────────────────────────────────────────────────┘
```

Figure 8.35 PrintingScrollbar example program

```java
import java.awt.*;
import aLibrary.*;
public class Director  {
    private AWindow  window;
    private PrintingScrollbar  upperScrollbar, lowerScrollbar;

    public Director()  {
        window = new AWindow(10, 10, 200, 120);
        upperScrollbar = new PrintingScrollbar(10, 10, 25, 80);
        upperScrollbar.setMinMaxVal(100, 200, 100);
        upperScrollbar.place( window );
```

```
                    lowerScrollbar = new PrintingScrollbar(30, 100, 120, 15);
                    lowerScrollbar.setMinMaxVal(-100, 100, 0);
                    lowerScrollbar.place( window );
                    window.repaint();
            }
    }


    import aLibrary.*;
    import java.awt.event.*;
    public class PrintingScrollbar extends AScrollbar {
        /* postcondition
                this scrollbar object is constructed
                AND getX() = x AND getY() = y
                AND getWidth() == w AND getHeight() == h */
        public PrintingScrollbar( int x, int y, int w, int h )  {
            super(x, y, w, h);
        }

        /* postcondition
                the integer value of this scrollbar is output */
        public void adjustmentValueChanged( AdjustmentEvent e )   {
            System.out.println( getValue() );
        }
    }
```

When the program in Figure 8.35 executes, two scrollbars are displayed in a window. Any event on either scrollbar causes the value of that scrollbar to be output to the standard output stream.

Another *aLibrary* class, called ATextField, supports textual (String) input. Figure 8.36 contains a class diagram for ATextField.

An ATextField object is a rectangular region in which a user can type a single line of text. (Typically, the user must select the ATextField with a mouse click prior to typing.) If the user strikes the *return* key (sometimes called an *enter* key) while typing in an ATextField, then an actionPerformed event occurs on the object. Below is a picture of an ATextField object in which a user has typed "abc".

A program can access the string within an ATextField object (with or without an event) through several methods. The getText method returns the entire String value that is within the object. If the text within the ATextField object happens to represent an integer (i.e., uses the same syntax as a Java int constant), then calling the getInt method returns the int value of this text. If the text within the object is a valid real or integer constant, then calling getDouble returns the double value of the text. If the text is true or false, then calling getBoolean returns the boolean value of the text.

Figure 8.36 ATextField class diagram

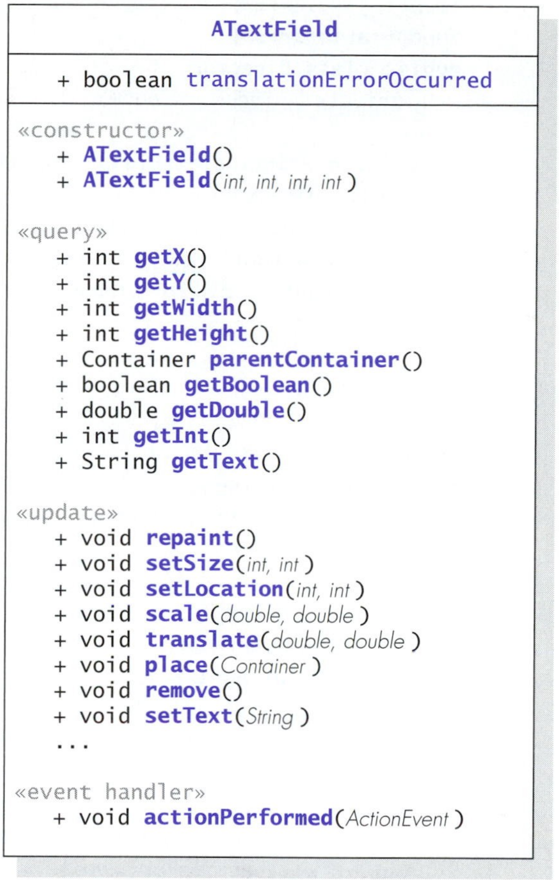

```
┌─────────────────────────────────────────────────┐
│                   ATextField                     │
├─────────────────────────────────────────────────┤
│  + boolean translationErrorOccurred              │
├─────────────────────────────────────────────────┤
│  «constructor»                                   │
│     + ATextField()                               │
│     + ATextField(int, int, int, int )            │
│                                                  │
│  «query»                                         │
│     + int getX()                                 │
│     + int getY()                                 │
│     + int getWidth()                             │
│     + int getHeight()                            │
│     + Container parentContainer()                │
│     + boolean getBoolean()                       │
│     + double getDouble()                         │
│     + int getInt()                               │
│     + String getText()                           │
│                                                  │
│  «update»                                        │
│     + void repaint()                             │
│     + void setSize(int, int )                    │
│     + void setLocation(int, int )                │
│     + void scale(double, double )                │
│     + void translate(double, double )            │
│     + void place(Container )                     │
│     + void remove()                              │
│     + void setText(String )                      │
│     . . .                                        │
│                                                  │
│  «event handler»                                 │
│     + void actionPerformed(ActionEvent )         │
└─────────────────────────────────────────────────┘
```

The ATextField class includes an instance variable, called translationErrorOccurred, to keep track of whether or not the most recent translation is valid. When the text within the ATextField object has proper syntax for the call to one of the get methods, then translationErrorOccurred is assigned false. However, if these methods are called when the text represents invalid syntax (for example the user has typed "abc" at the time of a call to getInt), then

1. translationErrorOccurred is assigned true
2. the inspector method returns a default value (0 for getInt, 0.0 for getDouble, false for getBoolean).

Figure 8.37 contains a simple program to illustrate the use of an ATextField object. This program creates such an object and the object causes its string content to be output in response to each user event.

Figure 8.37 PrintingTextField example program

```java
// PrintingTextField Program Director
import java.awt.*;
import aLibrary.*;
public class Director  {
    private AWindow  window;

    private PrintingTextField  inputBox;
    public Director()  {
        window = new AWindow(10, 10, 200, 100);
        inputBox = new PrintingTextField( 50, 50 );
        inputBox.place( window );
        window.repaint();
    }
}


import aLibrary.*;
import java.awt.event.*;
public class PrintingTextField extends ATextField {
    /* postcondition
            this text field object is constructed
            AND getX() = x AND getY() = y
            AND getWidth() == 100 AND getHeight() == 25    */
    public PrintingTextField( int x, int y )  {
        super(x, y, 100, 25);
    }

    /* postcondition
            the text and integer value from this object are output */
    public void actionPerformed( ActionEvent e )    {
        System.out.println( getText() );
        System.out.println( getInt() );
        if (translationErrorOccurred)    {
            System.out.println( "    invalid int constant");
        }
    }
}
```

The setText method allows a Java program to use ATextField object for output, as well as input. Suppose a set of requirements call for a program to translate from Fahrenheit temperature to Celsius, utilizing a user interface as shown in Figure 8.38.

This program accepts events either from the ATextField object labeled "Fahrenheit" or from the scrollbar. In response to these events the program translates the associated Fahrenheit temperature into its Celsius equivalent and displays this temperature in the ATextField labeled "Celsius."

Figure 8.38 User interface from temperature conversion program

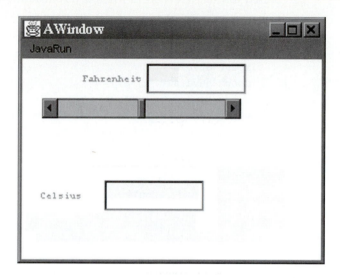

The Fahrenheit to Celsius temperature conversion program is designed around four key objects, as pictured in Figure 8.39. The Director object contains three instance variables: a scrollbar and two text fields (one for Fahrenheit and one for Celsius). If the user updates the value of the Fahrenheit text field, then the resulting event is handled by a callback to the Director object, which in turn updates the Celsius temperature. If the user drags the scrollbar, then the resulting tempScrollbar event uses the theField alias to update the Fahrenheit temperature. (Any scrollbar update will indirectly alter celsiusFld by creating a fahrenFld event.)

Figure 8.39 Object diagram for temperature conversion

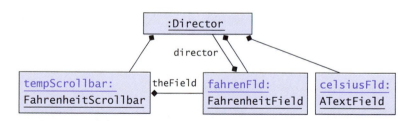

Figure 8.40 contains the code for FahrenheitField, the class of the Fahrenheit text field object. FahrenheitField inherits ATextField, and also declares an ALabel instance variable, called label. The label object is used to display a red "Fahrenheit" string next to the text field. The place method is overridden to ensure that both the ATextField object and its label are placed by the same method call.

Figure 8.40 also shows the callback code that FahrenheitField uses to handle events. Whenever the actionPerformed method is called, FahrenheitField responds by calling updateCelsius upon director. The identity of director was passed to FahrenheitField when it was instantiated.

Figure 8.40 FahrenheitField class from temperature conversion program

```
import aLibrary.*;
import java.awt.*;
import java.awt.event.*;
public class FahrenheitField extends ATextField {
    private Director director;
    private ALabel label;

    /* precondition
            d != null
        postcondition
            director == d
            AND getX() == x AND getY() == y
            AND getWidth() = 60 AND getHeight() == 30  */
    public FahrenheitField( int x, int y, Director d )  {
        super(x+65, y, 100, 30);
        label = new ALabel(x, y, 60, 30);
        label.setText( "Fahrenheit" );
        label.setForeground(Color.red);
        director = d;
    }

    /* precondition
            director != null
        postcondition
            the postconditon of director.updateCelsius() */
    public void actionPerformed( ActionEvent e )   {
        director.updateCelsius();
    }

    /* precondition
            c != null
        postcondition
            label is placed on c    AND    this is placed on c */
    public void place(Container c)   {
        label.place(c);
        super.place(c);
    }
}
```

Figure 8.41 contains the scrollbar class associated with the temperature conversion program. When the FahrenheitScrollbar is constructed, it must be passed a FahrenheitField object. The theField variable is bound to this passed object.

Whenever the user generates a FahrenheitScrollbar event, the actionPerformed method is performed upon theField, which updates the Celsius text field. This illustrates that event handling methods can be called directly, just like any other method.

Figure 8.41 FahrenheitScrollbar class from temperature conversion program

```
import aLibrary.*;
import java.awt.event.*;
public class FahrenheitScrollbar extends AScrollbar {
    private FahrenheitField theField;

    /* precondition
            f != null
        postcondition
            theField == f
            AND getX() == x AND getY() == y
            AND getWidth() = 200 AND getHeight() == 20   */
    public FahrenheitScrollbar( int x, int y, FahrenheitField f ) {
        super(x, y, 200, 20);
        theField = f;
    }

    /* precondition
            theField != null
        postcondition
            theField.getInt() == intValue
            AND the postcondition of theField.actionPerformed(null) */
    public void adjustmentValueChanged( AdjustmentEvent e )    {
        theField.setText(""+getValue());
        theField.repaint();
        theField.actionPerformed(null);   //null is a dummy argument
    }
}
```

A Director class to create the appropriate user interface is given in Figure 8.42. Executing Director creates a window, two text fields, and a scrollbar object. The text field called fahrenFld belongs to FahrenheitField, while celsiusFld belongs to the ATextField class. The reason that this second text field object does not require a separate class like FahrenheitField is that celsiusFld is used only for output, so it need not process events.

Figure 8.42 shows the code that is called in response to all user events. The updateCelsius method retrieves the value from the input text field by way of the following method call:

```
fahrenFld.getDouble()
```

A Fahrenheit temperature is translated into Celsius by subtracting 32 degrees and then multiplying by 5/9. The resulting value is assigned to `celsiusFld` by way of a `setText` method. Recall that a `"" +` expression pattern converts the expression value into a `String`.

Figure 8.42 Director class from temperature conversion

```
// Temperature Program Director
import java.awt.*;
import aLibrary.*;
public class Director {
    private  AWindow  window;
    private  FahrenheitField  fahrenFld;
    private  FahrenheitScrollbar  tempScrollbar;
    private  ATextField  celsiusFld;

    public Director() {
        ALabel celsiusLabel;
        window = new AWindow(10, 10, 300, 200);
        fahrenFld = new FahrenheitField(60, 5, this);
        fahrenFld.place(window);
        celsiusLabel = new ALabel(20, 120, 60, 30);
        celsiusLabel.setText("Celsius:");
        celsiusLabel.setForeground(Color.red);
        celsiusLabel.place(window);
        celsiusFld = new ATextField(85, 120, 100, 30);
        celsiusFld.place(window);
        tempScrollbar = new FahrenheitScrollbar(20, 40, fahrenFld);
        tempScrollbar.setMinMaxVal(-100, 300, 0);
        tempScrollbar.place(window);
        window.repaint();
    }

    public void updateCelsius() {
        celsiusFld.setText("" + (fahrenFld.getDouble() - 32.0)
            * 5.0/9.0 );
        celsiusFld.repaint();
    }
}
```

8.8 RECAP

One important characteristic of successful manufacturing is **reuse**. Automotive designers frequently design the next generation of vehicles by borrowing from pre-existing components, such as tires, door handles, and light bulbs. Computer manufacturers design new laptop computers around available processors, LCD panels, and keyboard technologies.

These forms of reuse do not reuse the objects themselves; no one expects to remove spark plugs from an older car in order to insert them into a new vehicle. Instead, this is reuse of design and of architecture. The automotive designer can avoid the cost of designing spark plugs by using existing designs. The computer manufacturer can avoid considerable expense by using existing computer processor architectures.

Object-oriented software development provides two major opportunities for software reuse:

1. reuse of a supplier class
2. reuse of a superclass

Chapter 6 focused on the concept of supplier classes. Through relations, such as aggregation, a client class is able to reuse the facilities (instance variables and methods) that are part of a supplier class. This same supplier class may play a similar role in many different programs and/or for many client classes within a single program. Client code developers have the benefits of reusing the design, implementation, prior testing, and documentation associated with any shared supplier class.

This chapter introduces another way that reuse is supported in object-oriented languages, namely *inheritance*. When one class inherits another, it borrows members of the superclass.

Inheritance is a mechanism for one class (the superclass) to be reused to create another *class* (the subclass). This is unlike aggregation, in which a supplier class is used to give form to the *objects* of the client. Most software libraries make extensive use of inheritance, not only to save development costs, but also to provide software consistency.

Ideally, inheritance represents an is_a relationship in which the subclass is_a superclass. A subclass is best viewed as a specialization of its superclass. The subclass may provide additional functionality (new methods and instance variables). The subclass may refine the behavior of inherited methods by overriding them. However, the well-conceived subclass should be more than just a way to borrow functionality from another class; it should be a specialized/extended version of its superclass.

One effective application of inheritance is to provide a mechanism for event handling. Each subclass can define its own event handling behavior by overriding the event handler method of its superclass. This chapter included a discussion of four such *aLibrary* classes. The `AButton` class is used to create clickable buttons, the `ATextField` class provides for GUI window panes where the user can type text, and the `AScrollbar` class is for graphical slider objects that maintain an integer value in the form of a sliding knob.

The fourth class supporting events is `EventTimer`. The `EventTimer` class is unlike the other three classes in the sense that its events result from the passage of time, instead of some user action.

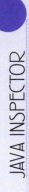

JAVA INSPECTOR

Below is a collection of hints on what to check when examining code that involves the concepts of this chapter.

✓ Whenever a class is designed, care should be taken to check the scope of each instance variable and method. Those methods that are genuinely needed by clients must be public. Most of the remaining members should be protected. The private declaration should be reserved for those situations where a class will never be inherited or where subclasses will never require the use of the private feature.

✓ The first instruction of any subclass constructor method should call one of the superclass constructors.

✓ It's a good idea to check the instance variables declared in a subclass to be certain they do not duplicate the name of some superclass instance variable. Such parallel variables can be the source of extremely subtle errors.

✓ When creating a new subclass, each method from the superclass should be checked to be certain that its behavior is proper for the subclass. Those superclass methods that don't behave properly should be overridden.

✓ If one method is intended to override another, it is always best to check for identical parameter lists. If the parameter lists are different, overloading will occur, potentially leading to unexpected behavior.

✓ The postcondition for an overriding method should always satisfy the postcondition of the method it overrides. In other words, the subclass version of the method should perform a task upon the subclass object that is analogous to the task performed by the superclass version.

✓ Check each overriding method to be certain that it does not try to call itself accidentally. Calls to the superclass method version of an overridden method must be prefixed with super.

✓ Every use of the shared object pattern must include a variable to alias the shared variable and the proper code to assign this variable the correct binding.

✓ Every use of the callback pattern must include a variable to alias the object that is the destination of the callback and the proper code to assign this variable the correct binding.

✓ Event-handling objects need to be completely initialized *before* it is possible for the user to generate events. Watch out for any event handling code that modifies other objects that handle events. This can be tricky.

✓ A call to setMinMaxVal should always be included in AScrollbar object initialization. Failure to set the minimum and maximum values can lead to strange scrollbar behavior.

TERMINOLOGY

AButton	extension	protected
AScrollbar	has_a relation	single inheritance
ATextField	inheritance	specialization
base class	input	subclass
callback	is_a relation	super
contains_a relation	output	superclass
extends	override (a method)	

EXERCISES

1. For each part below, two classes of real-world objects are given. For each pair of objects, select the best of the following five relationship possibilites.

> (1) left class **is_a** right class
>
> (2) right class **is_a** left class
>
> (3) left class **contains_a** right class
>
> (4) right class **contains_a** left class
>
> (5) None of the above relations seem appropriate.

  a. **furniture** and **desk**

  b. **desk** and **drawer**

  c. **hammer** and **handle**

  d. **hammer** and **nail**

  e. **boat** and **canoe**

  f. **bass** and **fresh water fish**

  g. **stringed instrument** and **bass**

  h. **tuba** and **brass instrument**

  i. **tuba** and **trombone**

  j. **cockpit** and **airplane**

  k. **footwear** and **shoelace**

  l. **footwear** and **boot**

  m. **footwear** and **shoe store**

  n. **retail establishment** and **shoe store**

  o. **plant** and **leaf**

  p. **rose bush** and **plant**

  q. **rose bush** and **thorn**

  r. **tea cup** and **saucer**

s. **tea cup** and **dishes**

t. **book** and **table of contents**

u. **book** and **library**

v. **beverage** and **coffee**

w. **liquid** and **beverage**

x. **liquid** and **coffee**

y. **animal** and **elephant**

z. **tail** and **elephant**

2. For each part of Exercise 1 answer the following question: "If these were software classes, should inheritance be used, and if so, which should be the subclass and which the superclass?"

Use the classes below to complete Exercises 3 through 8.

```java
public class Bird {
    private int wingLength;
    protected double brain;
    public boolean canFly;
    public Bird() {
        wingLength = 11;
        brain = 100;
        canFly = false;
    }
    public void setWingLength( int w ) {
        wingLength = w;
    }
    public void setBirdBrain( double d ) {
        brain = d;
    }
}
public class Pelican extends Bird {
    public int beakVolume;
    private int age;
    public Pelican() {
        // Pelican instruction here
    }
    public void setBirdBrain( double d ) {
        brain = d*2;
    }
}
public class TwoBirds {
    public Bird bigBird;
    public Pelican zeke;
```

```
    public TwoBirds() {
        bigBird = new Bird();
        zeke = new Pelican();
        // TwoBirds instruction here
    }
}
```

3. For each part below, suppose that the instruction were inserted in place of "// TwoBirds instruction here" in the TwoBirds class of Exercise 2. Which of the following best explains the result of this code insertion?

   (1) The instruction references an instance variable or method that is outside its scope.

   (2) The instruction compiles and executes without error.

   a. zeke.brain = 3.2;

   b. zeke.wingLength = 7;

   c. zeke.canFly = true;

   d. zeke.age = 3;

   e. zeke.beakVolume = 4;

   f. zeke.setWingLength(7);

4. For each part below suppose that the instruction were inserted in place of "// Pelican instruction here" in the Pelican class of Exercise 2. Which of the following best explains the result of this code insertion?

   (1) The instruction references an instance variable or method that is outside its scope.

   (2) The instruction compiles and executes without error.

   a. brain = 3.2;

   b. wingLength = 7;

   c. canFly = true;

   d. age = 3;

   e. beakVolume = 4;

   f. setBirdBrain(1.2);

   g. setWingLength(4);

   h. Bird();

   i. super();

5. Draw a class diagram that shows all of the aggregation and inheritance relationships from the Bird, Pelican, and TwoBirds classes of Exercise 2.

6. Suppose that the following instruction is inserted in place of "// Pelican instruction here" in the Pelican class of Exercise 2. Precisely what value is assigned to the object's brain attribute as a result executing this code?

   setBirdBrain(2.4);

7. Suppose that the following instruction is inserted in place of "`// Pelican instruction here`" in the `Pelican` class. Precisely what value is assigned to the object's brain attribute as a result executing this code?

```
super.setBirdBrain( 2.4 );
```

8. There is one instruction that should be first in the `Pelican` constructor method. What is it?

9. Below is a class designed to construct a button for repeatedly toggling the color of an `ARectangle` object from black to white.

```
import aLibrary.*;
import java.awt.event.*;
public class ToggleButton extends AButton {
   protected ARectangle theRectangle;

   public ToggleButton( ARectangle r ) {
   super(10, 10, 100, 20);
   setText( "Toggle" );
      // Instruction missing here
   }
   public void actionPerformed( ActionEvent e ) {
      if (theRectangle.getColor() == Color.white) {
         theRectangle.setColor( Color.black );
      } else {
         theRectangle.setColor( Color.white );
      }
   }
}
```

   a. Does this code appear to be using the shared object pattern or the callback pattern?
   b. What instruction needs to be substituted for "`// Instruction missing here`" in order to complete the pattern?
   c. Show all of the code that the client needs to execute in order to construct and initialize a `ToggleButton` to manipulate a `myRectangle` variable.
   d. Show the complete code for a class called `ToggleButtonWithSet` that inherits `ToggleButton` and adds the functionality necessary to change the `ARectangle` that same `ToggleButton` manipulates at run time.
   e. Draw a picture of the class diagrams, including all inheritance and aggregation connections between your client class, the `ToggleButton` class, and the `AButton` class.

10. Below is a client class designed to repeatedly toggle the color of `myRectangle` object from black to white. This program accomplishes the same basic task as examined in Exercise 9. Supply the necessary code for the `ToggleButton2` class that completes the program.

```
import aLibrary.*;
public class Director {
    private ARectangle myRectangle;
    private AWindow window;
    private ToggleButton2 button;

    public Director() {
        window = new AWindow(10, 10, 300, 200);
        myRectangle = new ARectangle(50, 50, 150, 50);
        myRectangle.setColor( Color.black );
        myRectangle.setToFill();
        myRectangle.place( window );
        button = new ToggleButton2( this );
        button.place( window );
    }
    public void toggleMyRect() {
        if (myRectangle.getColor() == Color.white) {
            myRectangle.setColor( Color.black );
        } else {
            myRectangle.setColor( Color.white );
        }
    }
}
```

11. Draw a picture of the class diagrams, including all inheritance and aggregation connections between the Director class, the ToggleButton2 class, and the AButton class from Exercise 10.

12. What specific user actions result in generating an event for each of the following objects?

   a. An ARectangle object

   b. An AScrollbar object

   c. An ATextField object

13. For each part below, draw a picture of the AScrollbar object that results from this initialization. Your picture should indicate whether the AScrollbar has horizontal or vertical orientation and the position of the AScrollbar's knob.

   a. AScrollbar scroller = new AScrollbar(30, 30, 20, 100);
      scroller.setMinMaxVal(1, 10, 1);

   b. AScrollbar scroller = new AScrollbar(30, 30, 100, 20);
      scroller.setMinMaxVal(10, 100, 30);

   c. AScrollbar scroller = new AScrollbar(30, 30, 200, 20);
      scroller.setMinMaxVal(-10, 10, 0);

   d. AScrollbar scroller = new AScrollbar(30, 30, 200, 20);
      scroller.setMinMaxVal(0, 100, 100);
      scroller.setValue(0);

14. For each part below show precisely what output results from the `System.out.println` instructions when this code executes.

a.
```
ATextField field = new ATextField(10, 10, 150, 20);
field.setText( "23.5" );
System.out.println( field.getText() );
System.out.println( field.getDouble() );
System.out.println( field.getInt() );
```

b.
```
ATextField field = new ATextField(10, 10, 150, 20);
field.setText( "abc" );
System.out.println( field.getText() );
if (field.translationErrorOccurred) {
   System.out.println( "Error occurred in getText" );
}
System.out.println( field.getInt() );
if (field.translationErrorOccurred) {
   System.out.println( "Error occurred in getInt" );
}
```

c.
```
ATextField field = new ATextField(10, 10, 150, 20);
field.setText( "true" );
System.out.println( field.getDouble() );
if (field.translationErrorOccurred) {
   System.out.println( "Error occurred in getDouble" );
}
System.out.println( field.getBoolean() );
if (field.translationErrorOccurred) {
   System.out.println( "Error occurred in getBoolean" );
}
```

d.
```
ATextField field = new ATextField(10, 10, 150, 20);
field.setText( "256" );
System.out.println( field.getDouble() );
if (field.translationErrorOccurred) {
   System.out.println( "Error occurred in getDouble" );
}
System.out.println( field.getInt() );
if (field.translationErrorOccurred) {
   System.out.println( "Error occurred in getInt" );
}
```

1. Modify the temperature program from Section 8.7 in the following way:

   a. It includes a second scrollbar for specifying Celsius temperature.
   b. Events on either the Celsius field or the Celsius scrollbar result in a translation from Celsius to Fahrenheit.
   c. Any event on one of the four interactive objects (the Fahrenheit scrollbar and text field, as well as the Celsius scrollbar and text field) update the other three to have the corresponding values.

2. Using inheritance, write a class called SpottedRect. A SpottedRect object displays an ARectangle with a filled AOval centered within. The AOval must be half as wide and half as high as its ARectangle. Your constructor must include parameters to allow the SpottedRect objects to be placed anywhere and be of any size. However, once constructed, SpottedRect objects should not change in size. Your SpottedRect class must include a setColor method with three int parameters for redness, greenness, and blueness. These parameters accept int arguments in the range from 0 through 255 with the same meaning as the Color constructor method. Calling this new setColor method must cause the ARectangle object to be colored as specified and the inner AOval to be colored in the "opposite" color. For example, for spottedRect.setColor(0, 255, 100), the ARectangle should have redness of 0, greenness of 255 and blueness of 100, while the AOval has redness of 255, greenness of 0, and blueness of 155.

   Write a Director class that constructs two AWindows. One AWindow is filled with four SpottedRect objects. The second AWindow contains three AScrollbars, labeled Red, Green, and Blue. All of the SpottedRect objects should respond to any change to the scrollbars by taking on the new color specified by the three scrollbars.

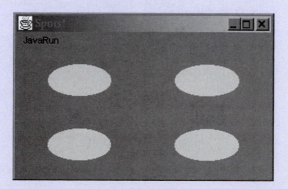

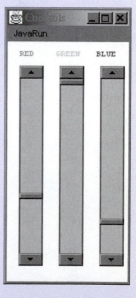

3. This program is an early prototype of an employee payroll system. For this program three windows appear on the screen. The left window is a place for the user to type information about a single fixed-salary employee. The middle window is a place to enter information about a piece rate employee. The right window is for an hourly employee. All three windows have labeled `ATextFields` for first name, last name, and job title. All three windows also include a "Display Employees" button across the bottom. Since the three types of employees are all different, the remainder of each window is different. A fixed salary is paid a certain fixed amount each week, so the left window includes a labeled `ATextField` named Weekly Salary. A piece rate employee is a production worker paid according to the number of items produced. The center window has two labeled `AtextFields`—one titled Piece Count and the other Rate per Piece. (If the piece count is 10,000 and the rate per piece is 0.03, then the payment for this work is $300.00.) The hourly employee is paid an hourly wage, plus time-and-a-half for any work over 40 hours. The right window has two labeled `ATextFields` named Wage per Hour and Hours Worked.

Your program should display all three windows throughout its execution. The user is expected to type information into the various `ATextFields`, but no `ATextField` events need be processed. Clicking the Display button in the associated window is the user's way to complete the input. This button should cause six lines of output (two for each window) to be appended to the standard output stream. The first line for a window is the name and job title of the employee, and the second line is the total wage for the week, given the values specified by the user.

Hint: Use a superclass, called `Employee`, to keep the things that are common to all employees and inherit from this class to make the three different kinds of employee. A separate `LabeledField` class is also helpful.

4. Using inheritance, construct a new class called `AScrollField`. Every `AScrollfield` object is a filled, rectangular region that is 50 pixels tall and 200 pixels wide. An `AScrollfield` contains the following three things:

1. an `ALabel` in the upper-left corner with the same background color as the `AScrollbar`, a width of 100 pixels, and a height of 20 pixels

2. an `ATextField` in the upper-right corner with a width of 80 pixels and a height of 20 pixels

3. an `AScrollbar` centered across the bottom with a width of 150 pixels and a height of 20 pixels

The behavior of an `AScrollField` should link the scrollbar and the text field, so that any user action on the scrollbar causes the text field to be updated with the new value of the scrollbar. Similarly, any event upon the text field should cause the scrollbar to take on the value from the text field. In addition to updating the opposite object, any scrollbar or text field event should call an `AScrollField` event, called `scrollFieldUpdated`. This is a parameterless method that can be overridden like an event handler. Below is a complete list of the methods that must be included in your `AScrollField` class. (Some can be inherited, and others will need to be overridden.)

`AScrollField()` constructs all the `AScrollField` parts described above.

`getX()` is the same as the `getX` for the `ARectangle` background.

`getY()` is the same as the `getY` for the `ARectangle` background.

`getWidth()` is the same as the `getWidth` for the `ARectangle` background.

`getHeight()` is the same as the `getHeight` for the `ARectangle` background.

`setLocation(int, int)` is the same as the `setLocation` for the `ARectangle` background.

`translate(double, doouble)` is the same as the `translate` for the `ARectangle` background.

`place(Container)` is the same as the `place` for the `ARectangle` background.

`remove()` is the same as the `remove` for the `ARectangle` background.

`repaint()` is the same as the `repaint` for the `ARectangle` background.

`setColor(Color)` assigns the `ARectangle` color and the background color for the `Alabel`.

`setText(String)` is the same as the `setText` for `Alabel`.

`setMinMaxVal(int, int, int)` sets the values of both the `ATextField` and the `AScrollbar`.

`setValue(int)` sets the values of both the `ATextField` and the `AScrollbar`.

`getValue()` is the same as the `getValue` method from `Ascrollbar`.

You should also disable the `setSize` and `scale` methods so that clients cannot alter the size of an `AScrollField` object. (Note that your implementation of `AScrollField` will require other classes.)

Use two `AScrollField` objects to rewrite the temperature conversion program from Section 8.6, so that any change to Fahrenheit updates Celsius and any change to Celsius updates Fahrenheit.

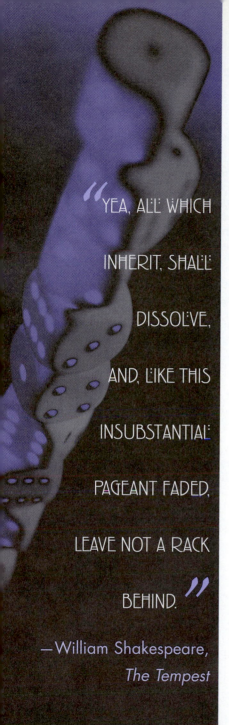

INHERITANCE HIERARCHIES AND POLYMORPHISM

OBJECTIVES

- To explore the concept of hierarchies among classes

- To define type conformance of one object/class to another and to examine the type conformance rules that Java enforces within its expressions, assignments, and parameter passage

- To introduce the `instanceOf` notation as a way to test for the actual type of an expression

- To examine how methods are associated with objects, rather than variables

- To introduce ways in which polymorphism enhances software flexibility and extensibility

- To examine the impact of dynamic binding and polymorphism on run-time execution

- To introduce abstract classes as a mechanism for implementing hierarchical classes that neither require nor permit instantiation

- To introduce the concept of a root class, called `Object`

- To examine the `toString` method as an example of a root class member that is utilized polymorphically

- To compare and contrast identity equality and content equality and to explore how content equality is implemented via the `equals` method

The working world of the modern software engineer consists of a rich collection of interrelated software libraries. There are libraries to provide graphical user interaction, such as *aLibrary*. There are libraries to provide common system utilities and methods, such as `System` and `Math`. There are libraries more specifically tailored to the needs of the software development firm. Remembering, organizing, and utilizing all of these software classes is part of the challenge of modern software development.

The key to using and creating libraries wisely lies in understanding inheritance and the many opportunities it provides. Indeed, most substantive libraries make extensive use of inheritance.

9.1   INHERITANCE HIERARCHIES

Like many object-oriented concepts, inheritance is best understood by examining its parallels in the real world. The is_a relation and associated concept of specialization provide strong clues to the nature of inheritance.

There are numerous examples of whole *systems* of is_a relationships in the real world. For example, a chair is a piece of furniture, but so is a bed. Furthermore, there are different specializations of both chairs and beds. Figure 9.1 illustrates one way to look at this system of is_a relations.

Figure 9.1 A partial hierarchy of is_a relations among furniture types

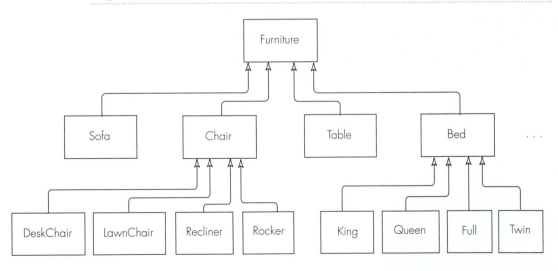

It is evident from the inheritance relationships of various types of furniture that this system forms a hierarchy. A group of sibling subclasses (i.e., those that share a common superclass) inherit behavior (methods) from their superclass. Part of the behavior of a chair is that it is designed for people to sit upon, so subclasses of chair should share this behavior. Despite the similar behavior of various chairs, there are also differences. Desk chairs are designed to work ergonomically for office usage; rockers incorporate a rocking mechanism; recliners are capable of tilting backward; lawn chairs must withstand the weather conditions of the outdoors.

Beds are also furniture, but beds are categorized a bit differently than chairs. A bed is typically categorized by its size. A twin bed accommodates a single person, while a king bed is designed for two people. The common property that beds seem to share is that they are designed as places for people to rest.

The furniture hierarchy is one example of a system of is_a relations, but there are many others. Perhaps the most complete example of a system of is_a relations is the biological classification system. Scientists classify every animal and plant using an eight-level hierarchy. Each organism belongs to a kingdom, a phylum, a class, an order, a family, a genus, a species, and a variety.

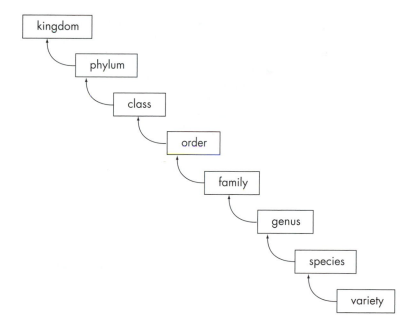

Every genus defines certain properties for the organisms that belong to that genus. Some of the properties of a *genus* are inherited from its *family* and are therefore shared by any other *genus* of the same *family*. Similarly, some of the properties of the *family* are inherited from the more general characteristics of the *order* to which the *family* belongs.

Inheritance is really a cumulative process. A particular *species* inherits its traits from the *genus* to which it belongs, while that *genus* inherits some traits from its *family*, and the *genus' family* inherits some traits from its *order*, and so on. Therefore, a particular species is an accumulation of the traits of the *kingdom*, *phylum*, *class*, *order*, *family*, and *genus* to which it belongs—together with the traits that are unique to the *species*.

This cumulative process of inherited characteristics works the same for Java classes. Each subclass inherits the instance variables and methods that are declared in the superclass, as well as all instance variables and methods that may have been inherited by the superclass. For this reason it is helpful to think of the superclass as a **parent** class. This leads to the notion of **ancestor** classes as the accumulation of parent, parent of the parent, parent of the parent of the parent, and so on. Similarly, class D is defined to be a **descendant** of class A if A is an ancestor of D. Any Java class can be thought of as the accumulation of its own instance variables and methods together with those inherited from its ancestors.

The concept of a **system of classes**, or an **inheritance hierarchy**, is extremely useful in software design. Figure 9.2 illustrates such a hierarchy from *aLibrary*. The JComponent class, shown in Figure 9.2, comes from the standard Java library known as *swing*. Informally, the JComponent class can be thought of as supplying those facilities necessary for implementing a drawable object. Among the many methods of JComponent are getX, getY, getWidth, getHeight, repaint, setLocation, and setSize.

JComponent inherits much of its functionality from another standard Java class, called Container, and Container inherits a class called Component. Both Container and Component are part of the standard *awt* Java library. The *awt* classes have provided standard graphical facilities for Java programmers since Version 1.0 of the language. The *swing* library became standard with Java Version 1.2. The *swing* library is not separate from *awt*. Instead, *swing* both complements and extends *awt*, and much of this extension is provided through inheritance, such as is illustrated in Figure 9.2.

OPENING
the Black Box

The *aLibrary* classes inherit most of their functionality from similar classes in the *swing* and *awt* classes that are included in the current standard libraries of Java. AView inherits JComponent; AButton inherits JButton; AWindow inherits JFrame; etc. This means that by learning *aLibrary* you already know a great deal about the *swing* classes. Appendix D explains the few adjustments that are needed to use *swing* without *aLibrary*.

The AView class plays a central role in the *aLibrary* inheritance hierarchy. AView inherits support for drawing and placing drawings from JComponent. AView adds a few methods of its own, including setToFill, setToOutline, place, remove, scale, and translate.

Figure 9.2 shows that ARectangle is treated as a specialization of AView. In fact, the only significant difference between AView and ARectangle is that one is transparent and the other opaque. Since the drawing is implemented within private classes, the class hierarchy shows no additional methods within the ARectangle class. Similarly, AOval and ARoundRectangle are both AView objects that look a bit different when placed. All four of these classes have differing constructor methods, but all constructors use the same four parameters in the same manner.

Figure 9.2 Hierarchy of some *aLibrary* classes

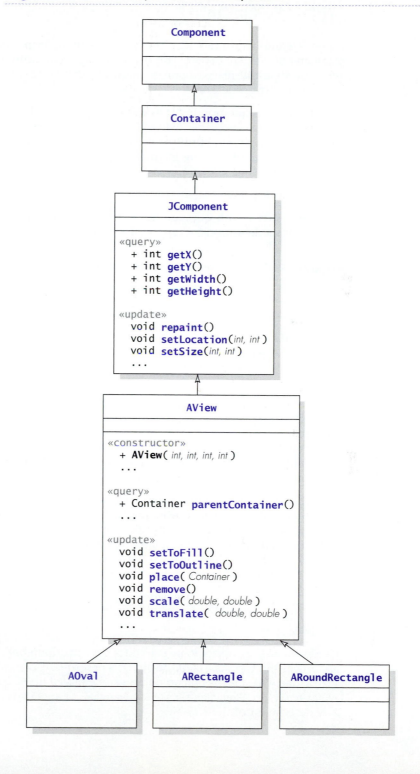

9.2 TYPE CONFORMANCE

Figure 9.2 also illustrates that the place method, from the AView class, has a parameter of type Container. This decision may seem unusual, since AView objects are more typically placed upon AWindow objects. Furthermore, the subclasses of AView do not override place.

The obvious question is, "How can *aLibrary* objects be placed upon something that is not of type Container, when the place method requires a Container parameter?" For example, suppose that donut and donutHole are both variables of type AOval. Why is the following instruction permitted, since donut belongs to AOval and not Container?

```
donutHole.place( donut );
```

The answer to this question lies in Java rules for **type conformance**. Figure 9.3 contains a definition for type conformance and the associated usage rule.

Figure 9.3 Type conformance rules for reference types

Definition
An expression type *conforms to* its own class or any ancestor class.

Usage Rule
An expression can be used anywhere that its type conforms to the required class type.

The definition of conformance states that the type of any object *conforms to* any and all ancestor classes. By this definition, the type of donut conforms to Container because the type of donut (AOval) is a descendant of Container. The usage rule from Figure 9.3 points out that it is acceptable to use an expression as long as its type conforms to the required type. Therefore, donut is an acceptable argument in the previous call to place.

Type conformance adds pliability to methods. The same place method can be used to place donut upon an ARectangle or an AWindow or an AView, because all of these classes are descendants (and thereby conform to) Container. Type conformance also allows donut to be placed upon any object from a new class that the software developer might create, so long as the developer's new class inherits from Container or one of its descendant classes.

OPENING
the Black Box

The *aLibrary* place method relies upon type conformance. Executing the call

```
myRect.place(z);
```

causes the myRect object to be placed for drawing upon object z. This call is valid so long as the type of z conforms to (is a descendant class of) an *awt* class called Container. This means that an object can be placed upon an AView, an AOval, an ARectangle, an ARoundRectangle, an AWindow, or an A3ButtonWindow, along with any descendant of these classes.

So long as inheritance taxonomies represent is_a relations, type conformance tends to behave as expected. It is reasonable to expect that if donut can be placed upon a Container, then a donut can be placed upon anything else that is_a Container.

As a second example of type conformance, consider the task of writing a boolean method to identify whether or not two ARectangle objects overlap one another when they are drawn upon the same background. Section 7.5 contains a predicate to check for such situations among AView objects. This predicate is repeated in Figure 9.4.

Figure 9.4 areOverlapping predicate

```
/* postcondition
        result == v1 and v2 are overlapping regions placed
                    upon the same background     */
private boolean areOverlapping( AView v1, AView v2 )    {
    boolean overlapHorizontally, overlapVertically;
    if ( v1 == null  ||  v2 == null
            || v2.parentContainer() != v2.parentContainer() )
    {
        return false;
    } else {
        overlapHorizontally = v1.getX() <= v2.getX()+v2.getWidth()
            && v1.getX()+v1.getWidth() >= v2.getX();
        overlapVertically = v1.getY() <= v2.getY()+v2.getHeight()
            && v1.getY()+v1.getHeight() >= v2.getY();
        return overlapHorizontally && overlapVertically;
    }
}
```

SOFTWARE ENGINEERING TIP

Type conformance of parameters adds pliability to methods. When the same method is rewritten for different parameter types, it is an indication to consider placing the method in a superclass. The areOverlapping method illustrates this idea.

This areOverlapping predicate accepts two AView arguments and checks to see if they overlap. Because of type conformance, the arguments to areOverlapping can be of any type conforming to AView. Therefore, areOverlapping can be used to check whether two ARectangles overlap, or even can be used to check whether an ARectangle overlaps the bounding box of an AOval. It would be a waste of time to write a separate predicate to test for overlapping ARectangles, since areOverlapping already performs such a check for a more general type of parameter (AView parameters).

Type conformance is directional. In other words, for any two different types, if *type1* conforms to *type2*, then *type2* does not necessarily conform to *type1*. To illustrate the directionality of type conformance, consider the proper classification of the following set of geometric figures:

circle
closed figure (any two-dimensional region with a well-defined perimeter)
hexagon
polygon
quadrilateral
square
triangle

The following statements summarize the usual definitions of these figures.

- A *circle* is a *closed figure*.
- A *hexagon* is a six-sided *polygon*.
- A *polygon* is a *closed figure*.
- A *quadrilateral* is a four-sided *polygon*.
- A *square* is a *quadrilateral* with four sides of equal length and corners forming right angles.
- A *triangle* is a three-sided *polygon*.

Figure 9.5 diagrams the appropriate inheritance hierarchy for the is_a relations from the above definitions.

Figure 9.5 Inheritance hierarchy for selected closed figures

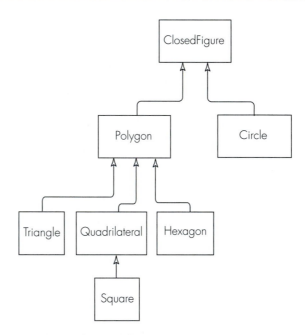

The directional nature of conformance means that it is acceptable to pass an actual argument of type `Square` when the corresponding formal parameter is of type `Polygon`. Similarly, it is acceptable to pass a variable belonging to `Hexagon` for a parameter of `ClosedFigure` type. However, a `Polygon` expression cannot be passed when a `Triangle` parameter is required. Neither can a variable of type `ClosedFigure` be passed when the formal parameter type is `Quadrilateral`.

Previous examples have considered type conformance for parameter passage. A second important use for type conformance applies to assignment instructions. For example, suppose that myPolygon, myTriangle, myQuadrilateral, myHexagon, and mySquare are all variables with the type indicated by their name. The rules of type conformance permit assignments such as the following.

```
myPolygon = myTriangle;
myQuadrilateral = mySquare;
myPolygon = mySquare;
```

However, the following instructions are all illegal.

```
// The instructions below all violate type conformance rules.
myTriangle = myPolygon;
mySquare = myTriangle;
myTriangle = myHexagon;
```

Once again, the is_a relation is the key in understanding how type conformance works in assignment instructions. Since Triangle, Quadrilateral, Hexagon, and Square all have an is_a relation with Polygon, it is sensible to allow a Polygon variable to name any of these kinds of objects. (The type of the object is_a(n) instance of the type of the variable.) On the other hand, it does not make sense to allow a Square variable to name a Polygon nor a Triangle nor a Quadrilateral nor a Hexagon object, because none of these objects are necessarily squares. More specifically, not every polygon can be expected to take the form of a hexagon, so the following assignment is illegal.

```
// The instruction below violates type conformance rules.
myHexagon = myPolygon;
```

On the other hand, every hexagon is certain to be a polygon, so the following instruction is allowed:

```
myPolygon = myHexagon;
```

Since a variable can be assigned an object of a different type, it is useful to have a programmatic means for checking the actual type of the variable's object. Java provides for such a check in the form of a relational operator called **instanceOf**. Figure 9.6 describes the syntax and semantics of instanceOf.

As an example usage of instanceOf, consider the need to check for what type of object is assigned to the myPolygon variable. The *if* instruction below performs such a test and prints out a message that is appropriate for each possible type.

```
if (myPolygon instanceOf Square) {
    System.out.println( "myPolygon references a Square." );
} else if (myPolygon instanceOf Triangle) {
    System.out.println( "myPolygon references a Triangle." );
} else if (myPolygon instanceOf Hexagon) {
    System.out.println( "myPolygon references a Hexagon." );
} else if (myPolygon instanceOf Quadrilateral) {
    System.out.println( "myPolygon references a Quadrilateral." );
} else if (myPolygon instanceOf Polygon) {
    System.out.println( "myPolygon references a Polygon." );
}
```

Figure 9.6 Instanceof description

Instanceof (a *BooleanExpression*)

Syntax

Notes

- *ObjectExpression* is any expression that evaluates to some object, such as a variable name, parameter, method, and so on.
- *TypeName* is the name of some known class or primitive type.

Semantics

Executing *InstanceofTest* returns the value `true` exactly when the value of *ObjectExpression* conforms to *TypeName*.

9.3 SUBTYPE POLYMORPHISM

The rules of type conformance allow a variable of one type to bind to an object of another type (so long as the object type conforms to the variable's class). This permits, for example, a variable belonging to the `ClosedFigure` class to bind to an object of type `Circle` or `Square`. It is even possible for the `ClosedFigure` variable to be assigned both kinds of objects at different times during a program's execution. This ability of a variable to bind to varying objects (including objects of varying type) is referred to as **dynamic binding**.

When a variable changes its binding there is always the potential that the class of the new object differs from the variable's own type (so long as the new type conforms). For example, executing the following instruction binds `myPolygon` to some object of type `Square`.

```
myPolygon = squareExpression;
```

If at some future time the following instruction executes

```
myPolygon = hexagonExpression;
```

`myPolygon` becomes dynamically bound to a different object, and this new object belongs to the `Hexagon` class.

The ability of a single variable (or parameter) to refer to objects of differing type is known as **subtype polymorphism** or just **polymorphism**. The roots of this word come from Greek words "poly," meaning *many* and "morph," meaning *structure* or *shape*.

The key to understanding polymorphism can be expressed in two statements:

1. Objects do not change the class to which they belong, but a variable may be bound dynamically to different types of objects.
2. The behavior of each object (i.e., which methods are called) is determined by the *object's class*, rather than the variable's type.

The second statement is a direct result of encapsulation. An object is very much like the class to which it belongs. The object contains all instance variables that are declared or inherited by its class. Similarly, the object utilizes the methods whose code comes from its class. This connection between object and method is particularly important when overriding occurs, making different versions of the same method available within the class hierarchy.

For example, suppose that the ClosedFigure class includes a method, called perimeter, to return the perimeter of ClosedFigure objects. Figure 9.7 contains partial classes for Circle and Square. The Circle and Square classes each contain their own version that override the perimeter method. Each version uses a calculation for perimeter that is appropriate for that particular kind of closed figure. The Circle class includes a radius variable, so the perimeter method returns (radius * 2 * Math.PI). The Square class includes a variable called sideLength, so the perimeter method returns (sideLength * 4).

Figure 9.7 Overridden perimeter method for Circle and Square class

```
public class Circle extends ClosedFigure   {
    private  double   radius;
    // Additional code omitted from here.

    /*  postcondition
            result == radius * 2 * Math.PI  */
    public  double  perimeter()  {
        return radius * 2 * Math.PI;
    }
}


public class Square extends ClosedFigure   {
    private  double   sideLength;
    // Additional code omitted from here.

    /*  postcondition
            result == sideLength * 4  */
    public  double  perimeter()  {
        return sideLength * 4;
    }
}
```

Now suppose the following instruction is executed:

```
System.out.println( closedFigureVar.perimeter() );
```

This instruction calls the version of perimeter that is consistent with the object bound to closedFigureVar. If closedFigureVar has been assigned a Circle object, then Circle's method is called, calculating perimeter based upon radius. If closedFigureVar has been assigned a Square type object, then Square's method is called and perimeter is calculated based upon sideLength.

To see a more complete program demonstrating polymorphism, consider a program to draw cake cutting geometry. Cake cutting is done in different ways for different cake shapes. To slice a rectangular cake into eight slices, most people would cut the pieces as shown below.

However, if a person is asked to slice a round cake into eight equal pieces, the more typical solution results in the wedge-shaped cake slices shown below.

These options lead to a programming solution that uses a superclass called Cake and two subclasses, namely CircularCake and SquareCake. Figure 9.8 shows the class diagram for this collection of classes.

Figure 9.8 Class diagram for Cake classes

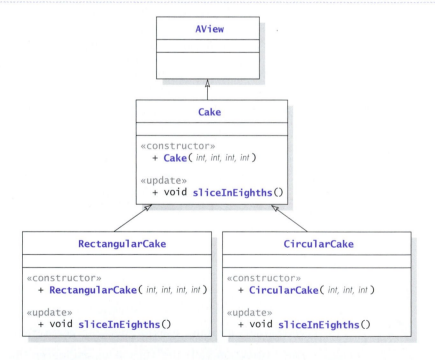

The polymorphic method of interest is called sliceInEighths. The Cake class contains an initial version of sliceInEighths and each of the other two cake classes overrides this method to define their own versions of sliceInEighths. Figure 9.9 shows code for the rectangularCake class.

Figure 9.9 The RectangularCake class

```java
import aLibrary.*;
import java.awt.*;
public class RectangularCake extends Cake   {
    private    ARectangle theCake;
    /*  postcondition
            the cake is rectangular with a yellow color
            AND getwidth() == w AND getheight() == h
            AND getX() == x AND getY() == y   */
    public RectangularCake( int x, int y, int w, int h )   {
        super(x, y, w, h);
        theCake = new ARectangle(0, 0, w, h);
        theCake.setColor( Color.yellow );
        theCake.setToFill();
        theCake.place(this);
    }


    /*  postcondition
            two black lines (one vertical and one horizontal) divide
                the cake into fourths
            AND getwidth() > getheight() IMPLIES the cake is
                separated by two additional vertical lines making
                eight pieces of equal size.
            AND getwidth() <= getheight() IMPLIES the cake is
                separated by two additional horizontal lines making
                eight pieces of equal size. */
    public void sliceInEighths( )    {
        ALine horizontalLine, verticalLine, line1, line2;
        int w = getWidth();
        int h = getHeight();
        horizontalLine = new ALine( 0, h/2, w, h/2 );
        horizontalLine.place( theCake );
        verticalLine = new ALine( w/2, 0, w/2, h );
        verticalLine.place( theCake );
        if ( w > h )    {
            line1 = new ALine( w/4, 0, w/4, h );
            line2 = new ALine( w*3/4, 0, w*3/4, h );
        } else {
            line1 = new ALine( 0, h/4, w, h/4 );
            line2 = new ALine( 0, 3*h/4, w, 3*h/4 );
        }
        line1.place( theCake );
        line2.place( theCake );
    }
}
```

The constructor method for RectangularCake constructs a yellow, filled ARectangle object, called theCake, and places it upon this (which is the AView object inherited by Cake). Executing sliceInEighths causes four ALine objects to be constructed and placed upon the cake. The horizontalLine and verticalLine objects divide the cake into quarters. The line1 and line2 objects subdivide the longer side into fourths.

Figure 9.10 shows the code for the CircularCake class. Since CircularCake has a round shape, an AOval instance variable is used for theCake. The CircularCake constructor is quite similar to the constructor method from RectangularCake, except for the color (pink) and cake's shape (AOval).

Similar to the RectangularCake method, the sliceInEighths method of CircularCake sections the cake by drawing one line (horizontalLine) to split the cake into a top and bottom halves and a second line (verticalLine) to split the cake into right and left halves.

Calculating the coordinates of the endpoints for the two diagonal lines is slightly more involved. Figure 9.11 shows how program variables are used to accomplish the diagonal line positioning.

Figure 9.10 The CircularCake class

```java
import aLibrary.*;
import java.awt.*;
public class CircularCake  extends Cake  {
    private AOval theCake;
    /*  postcondition
            the cake is circular with a diameter == d
                a color of pink
            AND  getX() == x   AND   getY() == y   */
    public CircularCake( int x, int y, int d )  {
        super(x, y, d, d);
        theCake = new AOval(0, 0, d, d);
        theCake.setColor( Color.pink );
        theCake.setToFill();
        theCake.place(this);
    }

    /*  postcondition
            four black lines are drawn through the cake center to
            form eight wedge-shaped pieces of equal size.   */
    public void sliceInEighths( )   {
        int ds, dl;
        ALine horizontalLine, verticalLine;
        ALine diagonalLine1, diagonalLine2;
        ds = (int)( (getWidth() - getWidth()/Math.sqrt(2.0)) / 2 );
        dl = (int)( getWidth() - ds );
        horizontalLine = new ALine( 0, getHeight()/2,
                                    getWidth(), getHeight()/2 );
```

```
        horizontalLine.place( theCake );
        verticalLine = new ALine( getWidth()/2, 0,
                                  getWidth()/2, getHeight() );
        verticalLine.place( theCake );
        diagonalLine1 = new ALine( ds, ds, dl, dl );
        diagonalLine1.place( theCake );
        diagonalLine2 = new ALine( ds, dl, dl, ds );
        diagonalLine2.place( theCake );
    }
}
```

Figure 9.11 The CircularCake diagonal lines

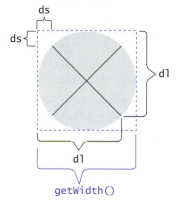

The dashed-line square in Figure 9.11 represents the border of the AView background for the cake. The gray AOval upon this square has a width that is identical to its height, and the AOval for the cake just touches the AView on all four sides. The local variables ds and dl are used to calculate the coordinates of the endpoints for the diagonals. The ALine called diagonalLine1 is drawn from coordinate (ds, ds) to (dl, dl), and diagonalLine2 is drawn from coordinate (ds, dl) to (dl, ds). Formulas for the values of ds and dl can be discovered by examining the following CircularCake with a chord (the dotted line below) connecting the endpoints of the two diagonals.

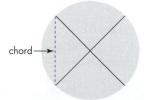

This chord is the hypotenuse of a right triangle that has halves of the diagonal lines for legs. Since the length of each leg is getWidth()/2, the Pythagorean theorem suggests that

$$\text{chord}^2 \;==\; (\text{getWidth}()/2)^2 + (\text{getWidth}()/2)^2$$

which simplifies to

chord == getWidth() / $\sqrt{2}$

Next notice that the length of one side of the AView (getWidth()) is equal to the chord plus twice ds. This leads to the conclusion that

ds == (getWidth() - getWidth() / $\sqrt{2}$) /2

The value of d1 can be calculated by adding the length of the chord to the ds, as shown below.

d1 == getWidth() - ds

These last two equations for ds and d1 are used within the CircularCake class.

To observe how polymorphism encapsulates differences *inside* the classes, it is useful to examine a client of these two cakes. Figure 9.12 illustrates such a client in the form of a Director class.

Figure 9.12 The Director class for the cake program

```java
import java.awt.*;
import aLibrary.*;
public class Director  {
    private AWindow  window;
    private Cake theCake;
    private CakeButton sliceButton;
    /* postcondition
            window is created at (10, 10) with width and height
                of 400
            AND sliceButton is placed on window
            AND theCake is constructed as a CircularCake object */
    public Director()  {
        window = new AWindow(10, 10, 400, 400);
        sliceButton = new CakeButton( 5, 5, this);
        sliceButton.setText("Slice another cake");
        sliceButton.place( window );
        theCake = new CircularCake(100, 100, 200);
        theCake.place(window);
        window.repaint();
    }
    /* precondition
            theCake != null
        postcondition
            old theCake is removed from window
            AND a new theCake was constructed & placed on window
                (The new cake has a 50-50 chance of being circular
                or rectangular. */
    public void  cutTheCake()  {
        theCake.remove();
```

```
if (Math.random() > 0.5)    {
    theCake = new CircularCake(100, 100,
        (int)(Math.random()*200 + 1));
} else {
    theCake = new RectangularCake(100, 150, 200,
        (int)(Math.random()*300 + 1));
}
theCake.place(window);
theCake.sliceInEighths();
window.repaint();
    }
}
```

Every call to the cutTheCake method in the class from Figure 9.12 constructs a new object and assigns it to theCake. This new object is randomly selected to either be of type CircularCake or RectangularCake. The following instruction from the cutTheCake method is polymorphic:

```
theCake.sliceInEighths();
```

Executing this instruction performs a task that depends upon the type of object that is bound to theCake. If theCake is a CircularCake, then the CircularCake code for sliceInEighths is executed and the cake is cut into wedges. If theCake is bound to a RectangularCake object, then the RectangularCake version of sliceInEighths executes, and the cake is cut into rectangular pieces.

This Director class is designed for use in conjunction with a button, whose event handler calls back to cutTheCake for every button click action. Figure 9.13 contains the code for such a CakeButton class.

Polymorphism frequently improves code **extensibility**. Extensibility refers to the ease with which software can be modified (extended) to solve problems other than the initial intent. To see how the cake program is extensible consider the problem of adding additional types of cakes (perhaps a heart-shaped cake, a triangular cake, and/or cake shaped like a diamond). These new cake shapes are implemented in the form of a class that inherits Cake and overrides cutTheCake. Clients can use these new cake classes with minimal modification.

Subtype polymorphism relies upon method overriding in the context of inheritance. Polymorphism means that theCake variable simultaneously assumes both the identity and the associated behavior of each object assigned to it. When theCake is bound to a CircularCake object, then sliceInEighths uses circular cake behavior. When theCake is bound to a RectangularCake, then sliceInEighths uses rectangular cake behavior.

The superclass (Cake in the example) plays a critical role in this polymorphism for two reasons:

1. Different kinds of objects conform to theCake, because they inherit from Cake.
2. Cake provides a superclass method, namely sliceInEighths, that can be overridden.

Figure 9.13 The CakeButton class

```
import aLibrary.*;
import java.awt.*;
import java.awt.event.*;
public class CakeButton extends AButton  {
    private Director director;

    /* precondition
            d != null
        postcondition
            getX() == x   AND   getY() == y
            AND   getWidth() == 120   AND   getHeight() == 30
            AND   director == d   */
    public CakeButton( int x, int y, Director d)  {
        super(x, y, 120, 30);
    director = d;
    }


    /* precondition
            director != null
        postcondition
            the cutTheCake method from director was performed.
        note
            this method is called as an event handler */
    public void actionPerformed( ActionEvent e )   {
    director.cutTheCake( );
    }
}
```

The Java compiler permits a method to be called upon a variable only if that method is appropriate for the *declared* type of the variable. In other words, since theCake is declared to of type Cake, the compiler will allow Cake only methods to be called upon theCake. Therefore, sliceInEights *must* be a method within the Cake class. Figure 9.14 contains such a Cake class. Interestingly, the body of sliceInEighths is empty in this Cake superclass. In cases where a method is intended only for override by subclasses, it is acceptable to write an empty body. (The next section examines another alternative to creating classes that contain methods with empty bodies.)

This general solution of having a superclass with methods that are ultimately implemented in different forms by subclasses is used so often that it is given a special name, the **template design pattern.** The word "template" is appropriate since the superclass is never really intended to be used for creating objects, but to be inherited only by subclasses that supply object types. Figure 9.15 explains the template design pattern further.

Figure 9.14 The Cake class

```
// This class is better implemented as shown in Figure 9.18
import aLibrary.*;
public class Cake extends AView  {
    /*  postcondition
            AND   getX() == x    AND    getY() == y
            AND   getWidth() == w   AND   getHeight() == h */
    public Cake( int x, int y, int w, int h)  {
        super(x, y, w, h);
    }


    /*  postcondition
            This method version does nothing.  It is expected to be
            overridden so as to cut this cake into eight equal-sized
            pieces.  */
    public void sliceInEighths( )   {
    }
}
```

Figure 9.15 The template design pattern

Template Design Pattern

When a variable, call it v, must take on the value of differing types of objects and perform different tasks for the same method, then the following approach should be used.

- Declare v to belong to class S.
- Class S must include all methods whose behavior will be overridden by subtypes. (Some or all of these methods may have empty bodies in S.)
- Subclasses of S should override the methods and supply the behavior that is specific to their class.
- Assigning v objects from the subclasses of S permits the overridden methods to use the behavior from the subclass.

(See Section 9.3 for an example.)

The template design pattern is the usual mechanism through which polymorphism provides extendibility. The template class includes methods, like sliceInEighths, that allow for extension. A cake class for a different-shaped cake is obligated to provide its own version of sliceInEighths.

The template design pattern also demonstrates another form of encapsulation and information hiding. The differences between each cake are largely encapsulated within different versions of the sliceInEighths method. This provides effective information hiding, because the client code does not need to know that different types of cakes require different cake-cutting code.

9.4 ABSTRACT CLASSES

There are times a class exists solely to serve as a template superclass, supplying methods that can be overridden. The Cake class from Section 9.3 illustrates this, because Cake need *never* be instantiated. Client code may declare variables of type Cake, but it is the subclasses of Cake that are instantiated and the resulting objects that are bound to Cake variables. If a Cake object is instantiated, it can serve no useful purpose. An object of type Cake has no visible form. Worse yet, an object of type Cake has a sliceInEighths method that does nothing when executed.

> **SOFTWARE ENGINEERING TIP**
>
> When a class is needed solely to serve as a template class (i.e., it will never be instantiated), then such a class should be written as an **abstract class**. Abstract classes are still able to supply code and can be inherited, making them useful within a class hierarchy.

Java provides an alternative mechanism for declaring a class that need never be instantiated, such as Cake. This mechanism is called an **abstract class**. Abstract classes are virtual entities because it is impossible to construct an object belonging to an abstract class. Abstract classes, however, are still quite useful, since they can be used as the type for variables and parameters. Abstract classes can also be inherited, and their protected and public instance variables and methods are available for use by a subclass.

Figure 9.16 contains the syntax and semantics necessary to specify an abstract class. Syntactically, the only required change for the class shell is the reserved word "abstract" that must appear immediately before the "class" identifier.

Figure 9.16 AbstractClass description

AbstractClass (abridged version of *Class*)

Syntax

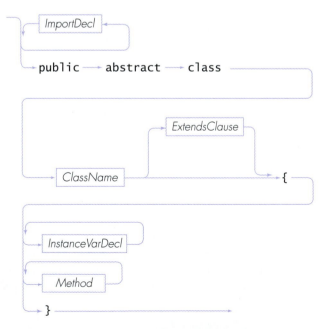

Semantics

An abstract class *can* be used as the type of a variable or parameter. It *can* be inherited. Its protected and public instance variables and methods are available to subclasses. An abstract class *cannot* be instantiated via new.

An abstract class *can* contain abstract methods (see Figure 9.17). If a class contains an abstract method, then the class *must* be an abstract class.

Notes

- *ImportDecl* is any single import declaration.
- *ClassName* is an identifier that names the abstract class.
- *ExtendsClause* is an optional inheritance clause.
- *InstanceVarDecl* is any valid instance variable declaration.
- *Method* is any valid method declaration, including an abstract method.

> **SOFTWARE ENGINEERING TIP**
> Declaring a method to be abstract forces a concrete subclass to provide an implementation. Abstract methods are a good idea when subclasses should be forced to tailor the method to their particular needs.

In Java, classes are called **concrete classes** unless they are declared to be abstract. Declaring a class to be abstract is done by simply inserting the word abstract prior to the word class.

One of the benefits of an abstract class over a concrete class is the possibility of including **abstract methods**. Figure 9.17 shows the syntax and semantics for an abstract method. An abstract method is one in which the body of the method is left unspecified. Syntactically, Java requires that a semicolon (;) be placed in an abstract method where the curly braces and body are located in non-abstract methods.

Figure 9.17 AbstractMethod description

AbstractMethod (abridged version of *Method*)

Syntax

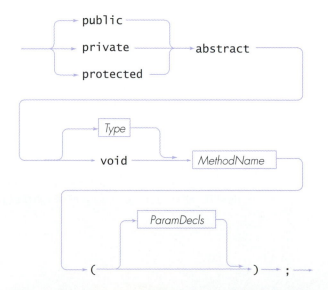

Semantics

An *AbstractMethod* has no body. Therefore, the class that contains an abstract method must be declared as an abstract class. Furthermore, any class that inherits an abstract method must either override it to be non-abstract or be declared as an abstract class.

Notes

- *MethodName* is an identifier. Each method within the same class must either have a unique name or a different number and/or type of parameters.
- *ParamDecls* is a list of formal parameters and their types.
- *Type* can be any accessible class name.

There are two key rules regarding the inclusion of abstract methods:

1. Any class that includes an abstract method is required to be an abstract class and must be so declared.
2. Any class inheriting a class with abstract methods must either override the methods or else it too is an abstract class.

The Cake class from the program discussed in Section 9.3 is an ideal candidate to be coded as an abstract class. Like many of the template design pattern situations, the Cake class is included only to provide a common superclass for the more specific kinds of cakes. Furthermore, sliceInEighths should be an abstract method, because there is no sensible implementation without knowing more about the particular kind of cake being cut. Figure 9.18 contains an appropriate abstract class for Cake.

> **SOFTWARE ENGINEERING TIP**
> Often there is a choice between using an abstract method or a method that provides a default behavior. For example, the *aLibrary* event handler classes are all written to have a default behavior of doing nothing. An abstract method is the better choice if subclasses should be forced to supply behavior.

Figure 9.18 The Cake abstract class

```
import aLibrary.*;
public abstract class Cake extends AView  {
    /* postcondition
            getX() = x  AND  getY() = y
            AND getWidth() = w  AND  getHeight() = h */
     public Cake( int x, int y, int w, int h)  {
        super(x, y, w, h);
     }

    /*  postcondition
            It is expected to be overridden so as to cut the cake
            into eight equal-szied pieces.  */
    public abstract void sliceInEighths();
}
```

It might seem curious that an abstract class, like Cake, includes a constructor method, since abstract classes cannot be instantiated. However, subclasses of Cake will need to call super within their constructor methods. Therefore, Cake's constructor method is included to provide a means to invoke the underlying AView constructor.

Class diagrams use a special notation for abstract classes and methods. An abstract class is denoted by the inclusion of the property **abstract** within curly braces following the class name. Methods are identified as abstract by italicizing their names. Figure 9.19 illustrates with the class diagram hierarchy for the cake program that uses the abstract Cake class.

Figure 9.19 Class diagram for cake classes with an abstract Cake class

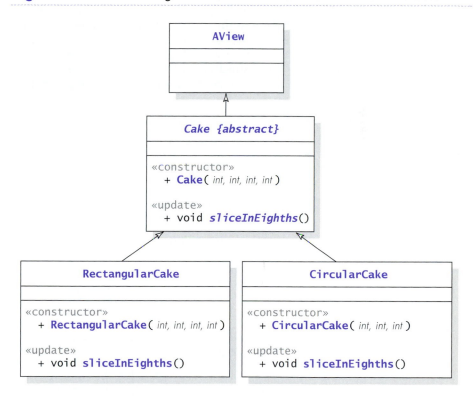

As a second example of the use of abstract classes and methods, consider the problem of storing and printing calendar date information. The Gregorian calendar is widely recognized around the world as a way to keep track of a date in terms of a year number (A.D.), a month within that year, and a day within the month.

There is far less agreement about precisely how to represent a date. In written letters many people represent a date in a form such as the one below:

```
Mar. 27, 1951
```

Around the time of the American Revolution, the English language was written in more formal notations. In those days the date above may well have been written as follows.

Day 27 during the month of March in the year of our Lord, 1951

Today, Americans tend to abbreviate dates in the form *month/day/year*, often representing the month as a number and the year with only the last two digits. Using this notation the above date is denoted as follows.

3/27/51

In Europe it is more common to use an abbreviated form like *day.month.year*, which leads to the following representation:

27.3.51

This variation in the way that dates are represented suggests that the template design pattern might be a good way to implement an abstract class called Date. Figure 9.20 contains a class diagram for Date, together with three concrete subclasses. The key abstract method within Date is called dateString. This method is expected to return the desired form of the date representation.

Figure 9.20 Class diagram for Date classes

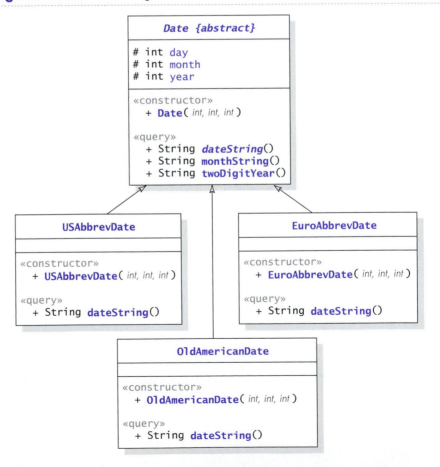

The code for the `Date` class is shown in Figure 9.21. Notice that abstract classes may contain many nonabstract parts. The `Date` class contains three instance variables, as well as a `monthString` method to return the `String` representation of month, and a `twoDigitYear` method to return the rightmost two digits of the year.

Figure 9.21 The Date class

```
public abstract class Date {
    protected int day;      // day within a month
    protected int month;    // 1 <= month <= 12
    protected int year;     // full calendar year (A.D.)

    /* precondition
            1 <= m <= 12
            AND d is a sensible day for month m
                (Note that this method doesn't check date validity)
        postcondition
            day == d   AND   month == m   AND   year == y   */
    public Date( int d, int m, int y ) {
        day = d;
        month = m;
        year = y;
    }

    /* postcondition
            result is the English name for month   */
    public String monthString()    {
        if (month == 1)
            return  "January";
        else if (month == 2)
            return  "February";
        else if (month == 3)
            return  "March";
        else if (month == 4)
            return  "April";
        else if (month == 5)
            return  "May";
        else if (month == 6)
            return  "June";
        else if (month == 7)
            return  "July";
        else if (month == 8)
            return  "August";
        else if (month == 9)
            return  "September";
        else if (month == 10)
            return  "October";
```

```
            else if (month == 11)
                return  "November";
            else if (month == 12)
                return  "December";
            else
                return  "???";
        }


        /* postcondition
                result is the last two digits of year  */
        public String twoDigitYear()    {
            return "" + year % 100;
        }


        /* postcondition
                result is some appropriate string form of the date  */
        public abstract String dateString();

    }
```

Abstract classes frequently include non-abstract methods that are expected to be useful to subclasses. The `monthString` and `twoDigitYear` classes are examples. The `Date` class stores each month as a number. The `monthString` method returns that month as a `String` that contains the English word for the month. Similarly, the `Date` class stores a year as a four-digit number. Many date abbreviations depict just the last two digits of the year, so the `twoDigitYear` method is included to return such a value.

Figure 9.22 shows the code for three possible concrete subclasses, `USAbbrevDate`, `EuroAbbrevDate`, and `OldAmericanDate`. Each of these classes is designed for a different form of date representation.

Figure 9.22 `USAbbrevDate`, `EuroAbbrevDate`, and `OldAmericanDate`

```
public class USAbbrevDate extends Date {
    /* precondition
            1 <= m <= 12
            AND d is a sensible day for month m
                (Note that this method doesn't check date validity)
        postcondition
            day == d   AND   month == m   AND   year == y   */
    public USAbbrevDate( int d, int m, int y )   {
        super(d, m, y);
    }
    /*postcondition
            result is a string in the form "<m>/<d>/<y2>"
                where <m> is the month number, <d> is the day number
                and <y2> is the last two digits of the year.    */
```

```
    public String dateString()   {
        return "" + month + "/" + day + "/" + twoDigitYear();
    }
}


public class EuroAbbrevDate extends Date {
    /* precondition
            1 <= m <= 12
            AND d is a sensible day for month m
                (Note that this method doesn't check date validity)
        postcondition
            day == d  AND  month == m  AND  year == y  */
    public EuroAbbrevDate( int d, int m, int y )  {
        super(d, m, y);
    }
    /*postcondition
            result is a string in the form "<d>.<m>.<y2>"
                where <d> is the day number, <m> is the month number
                and <y2> is the last two digits of the year.   */
    public String dateString()   {
        return "" + day + "." + month + "." + twoDigitYear();
    }
}


public class OldAmericanDate extends Date {
    /* precondition
            1 <= m <= 12
            AND d is a sensible day for month m
                (Note that this method doesn't check date validity)
        postcondition
            day == d  AND  month == m  AND  year == y  */
    public OldAmericanDate( int d, int m, int y )  {
        super(d, m, y);
    }
    /*postcondition
            result is a string in the form
                "day <d> during the month of <m> in the year of our
                Lord, <y>" where <d>, <m> and <y> are, respectively,
                day, month & year. */
    public String dateString()   {
        return "day " + day + " during the month of " +
            monthString() + " in the year of our Lord, " + year;
    }
}
```

Figure 9.26 A Date class that implements equals

```java
public abstract class Date   {
    // The innards of the Date class from Figure 9.21 have been
    // omitted for clarity reasons.  They should be placed here.

    public boolean equals( Object z )    {
        return
            z instanceOf Date
            && day == ((Date)z).day
            && month == ((Date)z).month
            && year == ((Date)z).year;
    }
}
```

SOFTWARE ENGINEERING TIP

There are many times when content equality tests are useful. The proper technique for providing tests for content equality is to overload the **equals** method.

This line causes equals to return an instruction to short circuit the Boolean expression and return false whenever it is applied to a Date object with an argument whose type does not conform to Date.

The following code illustrates a potential use for the equals method:

```java
Date jasonBirthday, jeremyBirthday;
jasonBirthday = new USAbbrevDate(20, 4, 1976);
jeremyBirthday = new USAbbrevDate(20, 4, 1976);
if ( jasonBirthday.equals(jeremyBirthday) ) {
    System.out.println( "Content Equality" );
} else {
    System.out.println( "Content Inequality" );
}
```

In the event that the Date class used for the above code was redefined to include an equals method as shown in Figure 9.26, then executing the code above outputs the following message:

```
Content Equality
```

If equals is not overloaded, then the Object version of equals is used and the resulting output is shown below:

```
Content Inequality
```

Below is a collection of hints on what to check when examining code that involves the concepts of this chapter.

✓ With any collection of several classes it is generally helpful to sketch out a class diagram that shows the inheritance relationships.

✓ Every assignment instruction of nonprimitives should be checked for type conformance. The expression on the right of the assignment must have the same type or a descendant type as the variable on the left. (Syntax errors result from nonconformance.) Sometimes the code may need to include an `instanceOf` check to ensure type conformance.

✓ Every nonprimitive argument should be checked for type conformance to its formal parameter. The argument must have the same type or a descendant type of the formal parameter. (Syntax errors result from nonconformance.)

✓ Overriding methods should be examined to ensure that their parameter lists match that of the method they override. If the parameter lists differ, then overloading occurs without causing a syntax error.

✓ A method that overrides an inherited method should accomplish at least as much as the postcondition from the superclass version.

✓ When the template design pattern is being used, it is wise to check the superclass (i.e., the template) to be certain that it contains all of the methods that require override.

✓ When polymorphism is involved, each class should be considered to ensure that the version of each polymorphic method is correct for objects of this type.

✓ Each class from which no objects are created should be considered as a candidate to become an abstract class.

✓ Overriding the `toString` method should be considered for each class.

✓ Providing a content equality test by overriding `equals` should be considered for each class.

TERMINOLOGY

abstract class

abstract method

ancestor class

Component (an awt class)

concrete class

Container (an awt class)

content equality

descendant classes

dynamic binding

equals (method from Object)

extensibility (of software)

identity equality

inheritance hierarchy

instanceOf

JComponent (a swing class)

Object (the root class)

parent class

polymorphism

root class

subtype polymorphism

system of classes

template design pattern

toString (method from Object)

type conformance

EXERCISES

Use the five classes below to complete Exercises 1 and 2.

```
public class Great {
// several methods not shown
}

public class Greater extends Great {
// several methods not shown
}

public class Greatest extends Greater {
// several methods not shown
}

public class Wonderful extends Greater {
// several methods not shown
}

public class Superlative {
    public Wonderful wonder;
    // several methods not shown
}
```

1. Draw a class diagram that shows all of the inheritance and aggregation relationships among these classes.

2. Using the five classes above, assume the following instance variable declarations.

```
public Great g;
public Greater ger;
```

```
public Greatest gest;
public Wonderful won;
public Superlative sup;
```

Which of the following parts are valid according to the rules of type conformance?

a. g = ger;

b. gest = ger;

c. gest = won;

d. won = ger;

e. sup = won;

f. won = sup;

g. g = won;

h. ger = sup.wonder;

Use the classes below to complete Exercises 3 and 4.

```java
public class Weather {
    // other methods omitted
    public void report {
        System.out.println( "No Warnings or watches." );
    }
}

public class HighWind extends Weather {
    // other methods omitted
    public void report {
        System.out.println( "Wind Advisory." );
    }
}

public class StormWatch extends Weather {
    // other methods omitted
}

public class TornadoWarning extends StormWatch {
    // other methods omitted
    public void report {
        System.out.println( "TORNADO WARNING!!" );
    }
}

public class MyWarning {
    public TornadoWarning bigWind;
    // other methods omitted
    }
}
```

3. Using the five classes above, assume the following instance variable declarations.

```
public Weather w;
public HighWind hw ;
public StormWatch sWatch ;
public TornadoWarning tWarn;
public MyWarning warn;
```

Which of the following assignment instructions are valid according to the type conformance rules of Java?

a. w = hw;

b. w = sWatch;

c. sWatch = warn;

d. warn = tWarn;

e. tWarn = hw;

f. warn.bigWind = tWarn;

g. tWarn = warn.bigWind;

h. w = warn.bigWind;

4. Assuming that all variables from Exercise 3 have been attached to objects of the same type, give the output that results from executing the following code segment.

```
w.report();
w = tWarn;
w.report();
w = sWatch;
w.report();
```

5. Figures 9.8, 9.9, and 9.17 contain the RectangularCake, CircularCake, and Cake classes, respectively.

a. Show all of the modifications needed to include a toString method within RectangularCake to properly override the toString from the Object class.

b. Show all of the modifications needed to include a toString method within CircularCake to properly override the toString from the Object class.

c. Show all of the modifications needed to include a equals method within RectangularCake to properly overload the equals from the Object class and implement content equality.

d. Show all of the modifications needed to include a equals method within CircularCake to properly overload the equals from the Object class and implement content equality.

e. Which version of equals is used when a RectangularCake object is compared to a CircularCake argument as follows?

   myRectangularCake.equals(myCircularCake)

f. Why does it seem unnecessary to override toString within Cake?

g. Why does it seem unnecessary to overload equals within Cake?

6. Consider the following three classes.

```java
public class Bumper {
    public int theNum;
    public Bumper() {
        theNum = 1;
    }
    public void bumpIt() {
        theNum = theNum + 1;
    }
    public void printTheNum() {
        System.out.println( theNum );
    }
}

public class Bumper20 extends Bumper {
    public Bumper20() {
        theNum = 100;
    }
    public void bumpIt() {
        theNum = theNum + 20;
    }
}

public class Bumper300 extends Bumper20 {
    public Bumper300() {
        super();
    }
    public void bumpIt() {
    the_num = the_num + 300;
    }
}
```

Assume the following instance variable declarations use the classes declared above.

```java
public Bumper bumped;
public Bumper20 lumped;
public Bumper300 gumped;
```

Precisely what is output when the following code segment executes?

```
lumped = new Bumper20();
gumped = new Bumper300();
gumped.printTheNum();
lumped.bumpIt();
lumped.printTheNum();
bumped = lumped;
bumped.bumpIt();
bumped.printTheNum();
bumped = new Bumper300();
bumped.bumpIt();
bumped.printTheNum();
```

7. Write the complete code for a SameBumper class. Your class must inherit the Bumper class from Exercise 6. SameBumper must also implement the equals method is such a way that two SameBumper objects are considered equal exactly when theNum of the first has the same value as theNum of the second.

PROGRAMMING EXERCISES

1. Dr. Seuss wrote a story, entitled "The Zax"[1] about two fictional characters that were so stubborn that they refused to walk in any direction but one. The North-Going Zax walks only northward and the South-Going Zax walks only to the south. You are expected to write a program to simulate this Zax problem. The window for this program begins with the following content.

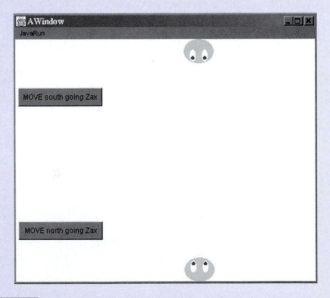

---

[1] Published in *The Sneetches and Other Stories*, Random House, 1953.

Each Zax is displayed as an oval with blue eyes pointing in the direction of movement. The South-Going Zax is at the top of the window, and the North-Going Zax is at the bottom. Each Zax moves only when its associated button is clicked. A Zax moves forward by two pixels unless it "bumps into" the other Zax; then no one moves because they are deadlocked.

Your program must include a superclass called `Zax` and two subclasses for each type of Zax. A method, called `goForward`, must be used polymorphically in all three classes.

2. Young children are often taught about real-world objects by using manipulatives. This programming assignment is to construct a "busy box" that can be used to teach about three objects: an automobile, a balloon, and a helicopter. Your program should use an `A3ButtonWindow` to display the three objects above the buttons as shown below.

Each of the three buttons *selects* the object above (thereby deselecting the previously selected object). Scrollbar events manipulate only the selected object. If the selected object is the automobile, then it moves horizontally to match the scrollbar value (i.e., as the scrollbar is moved left, the auto moves left). When the helicopter is selected, it moves up or down to respond to scrollbar changes. When the balloon is selected, it grows and shrinks with changes to the scrollbar.

You must have a superclass from which you create classes for the three screen images. Use polymorphism to implement the action of the scrollbar.

3. The basic idea of this program is to provide a programming tool for performing room layout. This program is capable of manipulating a sofa, two chairs, a desk, a table, and the room itself. The user tools include a horizontal scrollbar, vertical scrollbar, and two buttons. The Select Next Item button is used to select one of the items. It cycles through the possibilities, leaving the selected item highlighted as a red solid rectangle. (The nonselected items are outlines.) The screenshot shows the program appearance.

The two scrollbars and the Alter button operate upon the selected item. When a sofa, chair, desk, or table is selected, the scrollbars work to reposition the selected item within the room space. The scrollbars change the size of the room when it is selected.

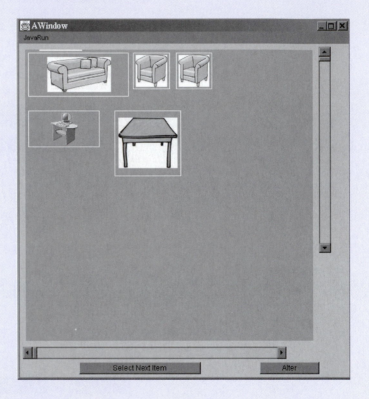

The Alter button behaves differently for different objects.

For the *sofa:* The Alter button causes the sofa to turn 90 degrees. (The image need not change.)

For the *chairs:* The Alter button causes the chair to toggle between a 30" by 30" chair using one chair image to a 22" by 22" chair using a different chair image.

For the *desk*: The Alter button causes the desk to cycle between four possible configurations: (1) a 60" wide by 30" high desk, (2) a 72" by 36" desk, (3) a 36" by 72" desk, and (4) a 30" by 60" desk. (The image doesn't change.)

For the *table*: The Alter button does nothing.

For the *room*: The Alter moves the door opening (the white opening) from one wall to another.

4. Computer-drawn sketches are useful in many ways. For example, law enforcement officials often use computer drawing to help identify suspects. For this assignment you will create a prototype drawing program to display and manipulate faces. Your solution should be designed to take advantage of inheritance and polymorphism.

The program uses two windows, one to draw the face and the other to control the drawing. Initially, the windows should appear as shown below.

The face consists of a head, two eyes, a nose, and a mouth. Each of these parts is selected by clicking the mouse within the border of the object. The eyes are selected as a pair, so clicking either eye selects them both. When one face part is selected, all previous selections are forgotten.

The control window (called "Inspector") operates upon only the selected object. A click on the Change Image button performs the following task, depending upon the selected face part.

For a selected *head*: The head changes color from green to yellow to purple and back to green.

For a selected *nose*: The nose image changes to another of three possible nose images.

For a selected *mouth*: The mouth image changes to another of three possible mouth images.

For selected *eyes*: The eye images change to another of four possible pairs of eye images.

The scrollbar behavior also depends upon the selected image.

For a selected *head*: The head gets wider or narrower with scrollbar value changes.

For a selected *nose*: The nose image moves up or down with scrollbar value changes.

For a selected *mouth*: The mouth gets wider or narrower with scrollbar value changes.

For selected *eyes*: The eyes move closer together or farther apart with scrollbar value changes.

AView objects (and their subclass objects from ARectangle, AOval, and AImage) support the following mouse events: mouseClicked, mousePressed, mouseReleased, mouseEntered, mouseDragged, mouseMoved, and mouse-Exited. All have a single MouseEvent type parameter, and all are called automatically in response to the associated event. The AView class defines these methods to perform no task, but subclasses may redefine them. For example, MyRectangle inherits from ARectangle and includes the following method.

```java
public void mouseClicked(MouseEvent e) {
    System.out.println("Hi, Mom.");
}
```

Every time the user clicks the mouse while pointing inside an object of type MyRectangle, the resulting message, "Hi, Mom.", is displayed in the standard output stream.

It is also noteworthy (although not needed for this assignment) that the MouseEvent parameter can be used to identify the precise location of the mouse. The methods getX() and getY() return the corresponding coordinates of the mouse position when applied to the MouseEvent parameter.

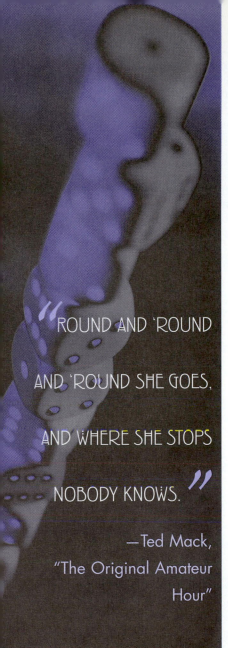

REPETITION

OBJECTIVES

- To introduce the concept of repetition in control structures

- To examine the syntax and semantics of two of Java's three repetition instructions, namely, the *while* instruction and the *do* instruction

- To emphasize the importance of loop initialization, primary work, and making progress code in the correctness of a loop

- To introduce the ATextArea object as a multiline output object

- To caution against common loop difficulties, including infinite loops and off-by-1 loops

- To examine nested loops

- To explore loop invariants and their role in loop design

- To introduce the event loop mechanism used by the Java Virtual Machine

- To revisit the EventTimer class as a mechanism and its relationship to loops

- To examine the impact of loops on software testing

"ROUND AND 'ROUND AND 'ROUND SHE GOES, AND WHERE SHE STOPS NOBODY KNOWS."

—Ted Mack, "The Original Amateur Hour"

Computers are often thought of as faithful servants because they perform large numbers of instructions with accuracy and without protest. This characteristic equips computers particularly well for performing repetitive procedures.

Java includes three instructions whose purpose is to control repetitive execution. The three instructions are

```
while
do
for
```

355

These instructions are referred to as **repetition control structures** because of their ability to control execution by causing statements to execute repeatedly. This chapter explores the first two repetition control structures: while and do. Chapter 12 examines the for instruction.

10.1   THE WHILE LOOP

The **while instruction** or **while loop** is the most commonly used of all repetition structures and is incuded in many programming languages. Figure 10.1 describes the syntax and semantics of this Java statement.

Figure 10.1 whileInstruction description

whileInstruction (a possible *OneStatement*)

Syntax

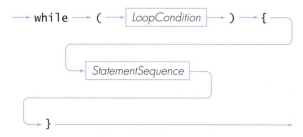

Alternate syntax (when the loop body is a single statement)

Note

LoopCondition can be any valid boolean-valued expression.

Style Notes

The reserved word while should be aligned with the "}" symbol that ends the *whileInstruction* and all statements within *StatementSequence* should be indented by at least one tab from the *while*. If *LoopCondition* requires multiple lines, then the initial loop brace "{" should be placed on a separate line and indented the same as its matching "}".

Semantics

Executing *whileInstruction* causes *LoopCondition* to be evaluated. If *LoopCondition* is found to be true, then *StatementSequence* (or *OneStatement*) executes and the process repeats. If *LoopCondition* is found to be false, then execution proceeds to the next statement following the *while* instruction.

A *while* loop has two main parts:

1. a **loop condition**
2. a **loop body**

The loop condition is a boolean-valued expression, similar to the condition used in an *if* instruction. The condition of a *while* loop determines how long the repetition will proceed. As the name of the instruction implies, a *while* loop continues to repeat as long as its loop condition remains true-valued.

The group of statements that are repeated for each loop iteration are called the "loop body." The loop body in Java is treated like a single unit in the same way that the *then* clause and the *else* clause of an *if* instruction are treated as units.

Figure 10.1 demonstrates two possible alternatives for *while* instruction syntax. The first alternative is generally preferred. This syntax can be used in all cases. The Alternative Syntax can only be used when the loop body consists of a single statement.

Figure 10.2 contains a description of the run-time behavior of a *while* instruction in the form of an activity diagram.

Figure 10.2 The control flow of a *while* instruction

Java Syntax

A *while* instruction begins execution by evaluating the loop condition. If the value of the loop condition is true, then execution proceeds to execute the loop body. Each time that the loop body is executed, the loop condition is reevaluated, and the body executes again so long as the condition is true. At any time that the loop condition is evaluated and found to be false, execution proceeds to the statement after the loop.

The control flow depicted in Figure 10.2 illustrates this repetition by following the downward arrow out of the diamond when the loop condition is true, and the right arrow when the condition is false. The downward arrow begins a control flow path that passes through the loop body and back to the loop condition. This circular control path is common for all repetition control structures, and the circular nature of the path is the reason for the name "loop" for this kind of control.

Following is a sample *while* loop that uses an `int` variable called `powerOfTwo`. (Comments are included to number certain of the statements.)

```
int powerOfTwo;
powerOfTwo = 2;     //(1)
while (powerOfTwo < 10 ) { //(2)
    System.out.println( "Next power: " + powerOfTwo ); //(3)
    powerOfTwo = powerOfTwo * 2; //(4)
}
System.out.println( "the end." ); //(5)
```

A trace of the execution of the above code is shown in Figure 10.3. Execution proceeds from the top of this trace to the bottom. The number of each statement executed is indicated in the leftmost column, labeled Line No. The action taken during the execution of each statement is explained briefly in the Execution Action column. The value assigned to the powerOfTwo variable is shown in the third column, and the rightmost column shows the output, if any, generated by the statement.

Figure 10.3 Trace of the execution of the powerOfTwo loop

Line No.	Execution Action	powerOfTwo	Output
//(1)	powerOfTwo assigned	2	
//(2)	(powerOfTwo < 10) evaluates to true		
//(3)	Output		Next power: 2
//(4)	powerOfTwo updated	4	
//(2)	(powerOfTwo < 10) evaluates to true		
//(3)	Output		Next power: 4
//(4)	powerOfTwo updated	8	
//(2)	(powerOfTwo < 10) evaluates to true		
//(3)	Output		Next power: 8
//(4)	powerOfTwo updated	16	
//(2)	(powerOfTwo < 10) evaluates to false		
//(5)	Output		The end.

Another way to display program output is to make use of an ATextArea object. ATextArea is an *aLibrary* class designed for displaying lines of text. Figure 10.4 contains a class diagram for ATextArea.

ATextArea is different from ATextField, because ATextArea does not support input, nor does it supply any event handling. ATextArea is different from ALabel because an ATextArea object may contain several lines of text, whereas ALabel objects can display only one line. The text content of an ATextArea object (returned by the getText method) is a String made up of all its lines of text concatenated together with "\n" characters between lines.

ATextArea includes most of the same methods as other *aLibrary* classes. The three new methods that distinguish this class are as follows:

setText(*s*)   Replaces the entire content (all lines) of the text area with *s*
append(*s*)   Appends *s* onto the end of the text area

appendln(*s*)   Appends *s* onto to the end of the text area and begins a new line

Figure 10.5 illustrates how to use the ATextArea class to create an output region. This Director class contains the same basic loop that was presented earlier for calculating powers of 2. However, this new version of the loop sends output to the outPane object, rather than using System.out.println.

Figure 10.4 ATextArea class diagram

```
┌─────────────────────────────────────────────┐
│              ATextArea                       │
├─────────────────────────────────────────────┤
│                                              │
├─────────────────────────────────────────────┤
│  «constructor»                               │
│      + ATextArea()                           │
│      + ATextArea(int, int, int, int )        │
│                                              │
│  «query»                                     │
│      + int getX()                            │
│      + int getY()                            │
│      + int getWidth()                        │
│      + int getHeight()                       │
│      + Container parentContainer()           │
│      + String getText()                      │
│                                              │
│  «update»                                    │
│      + void repaint()                        │
│      + void setSize(int, int )               │
│      + void setLocation(int, int )           │
│      + void scale(double, double )           │
│      + void translate(double, double )       │
│      + void place(Container )                │
│      + void remove()                         │
│      + void setText(String )                 │
│      + void append(String )                  │
│      + void appendln(String )                │
└─────────────────────────────────────────────┘
```

Figure 10.5 A Director for the powerOfTwo loop

```
import aLibrary.*;
import java.awt.*;
public class Director  {
    private AWindow window;
    private ATextArea outPane;

    /*  postcondition
            A window is created containing a text area
            AND the text area contains the powers of 2 less than
            100 */
```

```
public Director()   {
    int  powerOfTwo;
    window = new AWindow(10, 10, 200, 110);
    outPane = new ATextArea(20, 20, 150, 80);
    outPane.place(window);
    powerOfTwo = 2;
    while ( powerOfTwo < 100 )   {
        outPane.appendln("Next power: " + powerOfTwo);
        powerOfTwo = powerOfTwo * 2;
    }
    window.repaint();
}
}
```

Executing the Director code from Figure 10.5 displays the following window. Notice how the ATextArea automatically provides scrollbars to allow the user to scroll to any text that lies outside the displayed region. In the case below, the first three lines have scrolled off the top of the text area but can be viewed by pulling up on the right scrollbar knob.

An algorithm to display the Fibonacci number sequence is also a good use for a *while* loop. Fibonacci numbers were discovered by a thirteenth-century mathematician, Leonardo Fibonacci. Originally, this sequence of numbers was discovered as a way to model the population growth for rabbits, but has since been observed in numerous other natural situations.

The complete collection of Fibonacci numbers form an infinite sequence of positive integers. The first two integers in the sequence are both 1. Thereafter, each number in the sequence is calculated by adding the two numbers that immediately precede it. The first 10 numbers of the sequence are 1, 1, 2, 3, 5, 8, 13, 21, 34, and 55. Figure 10.6 contains a Director class to output the first 30 Fibonacci numbers to an ATextArea object.

Figure 10.6 A Director to display Fibonacci numbers

```
import aLibrary.*;
import java.awt.*;
public class Director   {
    private AWindow window;
```

```
        private ATextArea outPane;
        /* postcondition
                the first 100 Fibonacci numbers are displayed,
                one per line, on an ATextArea object       */
        public Director()    {
            int   aFibo, nextFibo, newFibo, linesOutput;
            window = new AWindow(10, 10, 500, 400);
            outPane = new ATextArea(20, 20, 80, 300);
            outPane.place(window);
            aFibo = 1;
            nextFibo = 1;
            linesOutput = 0;
            while ( linesOutput != 30 )    {
                outPane.appendln("" + aFibo);
                newFibo = aFibo + nextFibo;
                aFibo = nextFibo;
                nextFibo = newFibo;
                linesOutput++;
            }
            window.repaint();
        }
    }
```

Loops contain at least three critical parts:

1. the **initialization** code
2. code to accomplish the **primary work** to be performed
3. code for **making progress** to loop termination

The initialization code is responsible for initializing the state properly to begin the loop. This code must execute prior to the while and is best placed immediately before while. The initialization code for the powers-of-2 loop is the following single statement.

```
powerOfTwo = 2;
```

This instruction assigns powerOfTwo the proper value to begin the loop. If this instruction is removed, the resulting program prints nothing but zeros.

The second part of a loop performs the primary work of the loop body. This portion of the loop is generally the reason that the loop was written. The primary work of the powers-of-2 loop is performed by the following instruction.

```
outPane.appendln("Next power: " + powerOfTwo);
```

Loop termination (completion) for a *while* loop is defined as the time when the loop condition is false. The loop body generally includes instructions to *make progress* toward this eventual termination. The powers-of-two program makes progress with the following instruction.

```
powerOfTwo = powerOfTwo * 2;
```

To further illustrate the three loop parts, Figure 10.7 labels the Fibonacci program loop appropriately.

Figure 10.7 Fibonacci program loop parts identified

```
                    ┌  aFibo = 1;
   initialization ──┤  nextFibo = 1;
                    └  linesOutput = 0;
                       while ( linesOutput != 30 )    {
                    ┌    outPane.appendln("" + aFibo);
                    │    newFibo = aFibo + nextFibo;
   primary work ────┤    aFibo = nextFibo;
                    └    nextFibo = newFibo;

   make-progress ──────── linesOutput++;
                       }
```

The linesOutput variable from the Fibonacci program is used in the loop condition, so it seems an obvious candidate to be initialized. The assignment of the value zero to linesOutput properly establishes the count of the number of lines that have been appended to the outPane object.

The need for the assignments to aFibo and nextFibo within initialization may be less obvious. aFibo maintains the Fibonacci number about to be output, and nextFibo maintains the successor to aFibo. Both of these variables must store consecutive Fibonacci numbers for the loop body to be able to calculate subsequent Fibonacci numbers.

10.2   COUNTING LOOPS

There is one looping pattern that occurs so frequently that it is given a special name. The **counting loop pattern** is, as its name implies, characterized by counting. This counting is accomplished by a variable, called a "counter variable." The typical counting loop uses its counter variable to determine when to stop repeating. The types of tasks that are well suited to counting loop solutions include the following:

- Display the first 15 prime numbers.
- Print the first 50 Unicode characters.
- Display twelve 10-by-10 blue rectangles across an AWindow.
- Show the value of PI approximated to 30 digits.

All of these tasks involve a count of times (15, 50, 12, and 30) that a task must be performed. The counting pattern, and associated *while* loop, are shown in Figure 10.8.

The Fibonacci number loop from Figure 10.6 is an example of a counting loop. The counter variable is linesOutput for the Fibonacci program.

Figure 10.8 Counting loop pattern

Counting Loop Pattern

A counting loop is a good choice for any algorithm (a task) that needs to be repeated some fixed number of times. Below is a skeleton of this code.

```
someCounter = 0;
while  ( someCounter != numberOfRepetitions )    {
    //perform primary work
    someCounter++;
}
```

An application of this pattern requires the following:

* *numberOfRepetitions* is to be replaced by the count repetitions required.
* *//perform primary work* is replaced by the code for a single task.
* someCounter is some variable declared as one of the integer data types.

Not all counting loops match the pattern perfectly. Sometimes it makes sense to start the counting with a value other than zero, so the initialization might become

```
someCounter = n;
```

where n is 1 or some other integer. Sometimes it is more convenient to decrease the counter, rather than increase it, so the loop body instruction for making progress might be

```
someCounter--;
```

Sometimes it is better to count by some integer other than by 1. There are many variations in this counting loop pattern, but they all follow the basic theme of using a counter variable and the following steps:

* Initialize the counter before the loop
* Increment (or decrement) the counter in the body of the loop
* Use the counter in the condition to determine when to terminate repetition

A second example of a counting pattern is the displayPrimes method shown from Figure 10.9. This method has a single int parameter called n. When displayPrimes is called, it displays the first n prime numbers. displayPrimes uses primeCount as its counter variable.

The displayPrimes method represents a variation on the basic counting loop pattern because it does not increment primeCount for each time the loop body is executed. Instead, the loop body tests the value of potentialPrime using a boolean method called isPrime, which returns true if and only if its parameter is a prime number. (The code for isPrime will be given shortly.) As a result, primeCount is incremented only when potentialPrime is found to be a prime number.

Figure 10.10 contains the code for the isPrime method referred to by displayPrimes. This method is designed to identify whether or not parameter p is a prime number. This is accomplished by yet another variation on a counting loop pattern. The isPrime algorithm tests each potential divisor from 2 through the square root of p. A boolean variable, looksPrime, is initially assigned true and is changed to false only if a factor of p is found.

Figure 10.9 displayPrimes method

```
/* precondition
        n >= 0
   postcondition
        the first n prime numbers are output in outPane */
public void displayPrimes( int n )    {
    int potentialPrime, primeCount;
    outPane.setText(" ");   // clear the pane
    outPane.appendln("Primes");
    potentialPrime = 2;
    primeCount = 0;
    while  (primeCount != n)   {
        if ( isPrime(potentialPrime) ) {
            outPane.appendln("       " + potentialPrime);
            primeCount++;
        }
        potentialPrime++;
    }
}
```

Figure 10.10 isPrime method

```
/* precondition
        n >= 2
   postcondition
        result == p is a prime number */
public boolean isPrime( int p )    {
    int divisor;
    boolean looksPrime;
    looksPrime = true;
    divisor = 2;
    while (divisor <= Math.sqrt(p))    {
        if (p/divisor == (double)p/divisor)    {
            looksPrime = false;
        }
        divisor++;
    }
    return looksPrime;
}
```

The loop counter for the `isPrime` method is `divisor`. This variable is initialized to 2 before the loop begins. Each time through the loop body the next `divisor` value is tested, and if `divisor` turns out to be a factor of p, then `looksPrime` is assigned false. If the loop completes and `looksPrime` is still true, then there can be no factors of p from 2 through $\sqrt{p}$, so p must be prime. The following condition is used to test whether or not `divisor` is a factor of p.

```
(p/divisor == (double)p/divisor)
```

This condition compares the integer value of p divided by `divisor` to the same division done on `double` numbers. If these two divisions are equal, then a factor has been found.

10.3 SENTINEL LOOPS

Not all loops follow the counting loop pattern. Many loops simply repeat the body until some threshold condition exists. Such noncounting loops are often called **sentinel loops**. The tasks below suggest the use of sentinel loops.

- Display the all prime numbers up to and including 37.
- Print all of the Unicode characters that precede the letter 'Z'.
- Display as many 10-by-10 blue rectangles across an `AWindow` as possible.

Another example that shows the repetition of a noncounting threshold is the action of dropping an object from height *h* until it reaches Earth's surface. Earth's gravity causes falling objects to accelerate at a rate of 9.81 meters per second². This means that the velocity (meters per second) of the frictionless object falling from a resting position can be calculated as *V* in the following equation:

```
V = 9.81 * T
```

T in this equation denotes the number of seconds of free fall from rest. The distance, D (meters), that the object falls is explained by the following equation.

```
D = 4.9 * T2
```

If the object begins falling from a height, *H*, then its height after falling for T seconds can be described as shown below.

```
ActualHeight = H - D = H - 4.9*T2
```

For example, suppose that a bowling ball is dropped from a helicopter hovering over the ocean at a height of 177 meters. The picture in Figure 10.11 demonstrates the results. This picture displays three values for each second of bowling ball travel:

1. The number of seconds that have passed since the ball was dropped.
2. The bowling ball's height (in meters) above Earth's surface.
3. The downward velocity of the ball at that particular instant in time.

A typical `AWindow` image for a program to demonstrate this drop is shown in Figure 10.12. This program uses an `ATextArea` to display the heights and velocities for a drop.

Figure 10.13 contains the code for the bowling ball program.

Figure 10.11 Bowling ball dropping into ocean

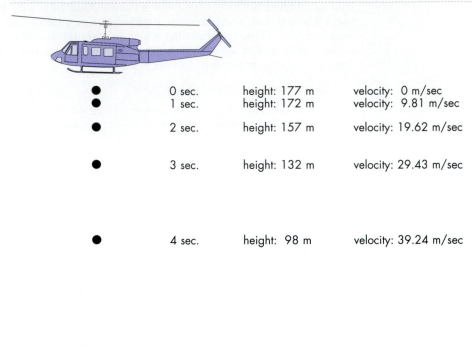

•	0 sec.	height: 177 m	velocity: 0 m/sec
•	1 sec.	height: 172 m	velocity: 9.81 m/sec
•	2 sec.	height: 157 m	velocity: 19.62 m/sec
•	3 sec.	height: 132 m	velocity: 29.43 m/sec
•	4 sec.	height: 98 m	velocity: 39.24 m/sec
•	5 sec.	height: 54 m	velocity: 49.05 m/sec

6 sec.   height: 0 m   velocity: 58.86 m/sec

Figure 10.12 Output from the bowling ball program

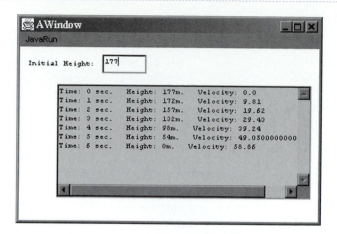

Figure 10.13 Falling object program

```
import aLibrary.*;
import java.awt.*;
public class Director   {
    private AWindow window;
    private ATextArea outPane;
    private HeightField inField;
    private ALabel label;

    /* postcondition
            window != null   AND   outPane != null
            AND inField!=null
            AND outPane, inField are both displayed in window   */
    public Director()     {
        window = new AWindow(10, 10, 400, 230);
        outPane = new ATextArea(50, 50, 340, 150);
        outPane.place(window);
        label = new ALabel(10, 10, 100, 25);
        label.setText("Initial Height:");
        label.place(window);
        inField = new HeightField(110, 10, this);
        inField.place(window);
        window.repaint();
    }
```

```java
        /* precondition
                h > 0   AND   outPane != null
           postcondition
                outPane is reset to contain one line for each second of
                drop from a height of h through last height
                before zero. Each line gives the height of the dropped
                object and its velocity at that second.    */
    public void displayFall( int h )    {
        int   seconds;
        outPane.setText("");    // clear the text area of prior
                                // content

        seconds = 0;
        while ( h-seconds*seconds*4.9 > 0 )    {
            outPane.append("Time: " + seconds +" sec.    ");
            outPane.append("Height: "+(int)
                        (h-seconds*seconds*4.9)+"m");
            outPane.appendln("   Velocity: " + seconds*9.81);
            seconds++;
        }
        outPane.repaint();
    }
}
import aLibrary.*;
import java.awt.*;
import java.awt.event.*;
public class HeightField extends ATextField {
    private Director director;

    /* precondition
            d != null
       postcondition
            director == d
            AND getX() == x AND getY() == y
            AND  getWidth() == 60 AND getHeight() == 25 */
    public HeightField( int x, int y, Director d )    {
        super(x, y, 60, 25);
        director = d;
    }

    /* precondition
            director != null
       postcondition
            the displayFall method from director is performed
            upon the getInt() value of this. */
    public void actionPerformed( ActionEvent e )    {
        director.displayFall( getInt() );
    }
}
```

The key loop of the falling-object program occurs in the `displayFall` method. This method simulates the fall by advancing one second for each loop repetition. This loop has many similarities to counting loops because the `seconds` variable is assigned an initial value of zero and is incremented by 1 for each loop repetition. The difference between this loop and most counting loops is that the loop condition is the following:

```
( h - seconds*seconds*4.9 > 0 )
```

This condition tests to see if the height of the falling object is greater than zero, which is a sentinel condition.

10.4 LOOP DESIGN CAUTIONS

The process of designing loops can be tricky. Consider the following program loop that is designed to print the integers from 1 through `num`.

```
counter = 1;
while ( counter != num+1 ) {
    System.out.println( counter );
    counter++;
}
```

This loop works properly if `num` has a value greater than or equal to 1. However, if `num` has a negative value, then this loop will continue to increment `counter` forever. A loop like this that never stops repeating is known as an **infinite loop** or a **dead loop**. A common way to accidentally create an infinite loop is by forgetting to include a portion of the loop body to make progress toward loop completion. For example, the loop above is guaranteed to be an infinite loop if the following line is omitted from the loop body.

```
counter++;
```

The first time you observe the execution of an infinite loop, you may believe that the program has stopped running. Actually, just the opposite has occurred; the program can't stop running!

A second difficulty in loop design is the subtle relationships between the three portions of the loop code:

- the initialization part
- the primary work part
- the making-progress part

For the loop counting from 1 to *n*, these three parts are identified as follows:

```
initialization ———— counter = 1;
                    while (counter != num+1)    {
primary work ———————— System.out.println( counter );
make-progress ————— counter++;
                    }
```

The examples shown so far are largely organized so that the primary work part precedes the making-progress part. This is one typical way to write many algorithms. However, it is almost always possible to write equivalent loops with the primary work and making-progress parts reversed. For example, the following loop performs the same task of printing the integers from 1 through num, but increments counter *before* the println call.

```
counter = 1;
while (counter != num + 1) {
    counter++;
    System.out.println( counter - 1 );
}
```

In order to make this code produce the proper output, the argument to println is changed to counter - 1. Yet a third equivalent loop is shown below:

```
counter = 0;
while (counter != num) {
    counter++;
    System.out.println( counter );
}
```

This last example uses a println argument of counter, but alters the initialization and loop condition code to compensate. These equivalent loops point out the close relationships among loop initialization, loop conditions, the primary work part, and the making-progress part. Any change to one of these parts may induce needed changes to the others.

One common programming error is the **off-by-1 loop**. An off-by-1 loop results when a loop body is repeated one time too many or one time too few. The following code results in such an error, because it will print only the values from 1 through num - 1 (not 1 through num):

```
counter = 1;
while (counter != num) {
    System.out.println( counter );
    counter++;
}
```

10.5 NESTED LOOPS

Nested loops occur when one loop is placed within the body of another. The inner loop is said to be "nested" within the outer loop. As an illustration of how to use nested loops, Figure 10.14 contains the code for a "polka dot" program.

Figure 10.14 Polka dot program

```
// PolkaDot Program
import aLibrary.*;
import java.awt.*;
public class Director {
    private AWindow window;
```

```
public Director()   {
    int  yCount, xCount;
    AOval dot;
    Color rowColor;
    window = new AWindow(10, 10, 200, 200);

    yCount = 0;
    while ( yCount != 12 )   {
        rowColor = new Color(yCount/13.0f,
                        yCount/13.0f, yCount/13.0f);
            // rowColor is gray, an intensity of yCount/13.
            // (0.0f is black and 1.0f is white)
        xCount = 0;
        while ( xCount != 8 )   {
            dot = new AOval(xCount*25, yCount*15, 10, 10);
            dot.setColor(rowColor);
            dot.setToFill();
            dot.place(window);
            xCount++;
        }
        yCount++;
    }
    window.repaint();
}
}
```

To observe the run-time behavior of the polka dot program, consider the following shell of its two loops, along with the corresponding activity diagram.

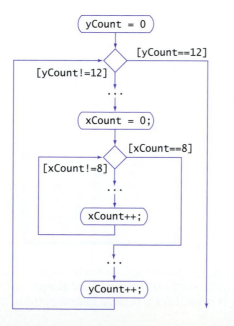

```
yCount = 0;
while ( yCount != 12 ) {
    ...
    xCount = 0;
    while ( xCount != 8 ) {
        ...
        xCount++;
    }
    yCount++;
}
```

This shell reveals that the outer loop is a counting loop that counts from 0 through 12, and the inner loop is also a counting loop, counting from 0 through 8. Tracing this skeleton code shows that, for yCount==0, the inner loop body executes eight times. When yCount==1, the inner loop executes another eight times, and so forth. Shown to the right is a trace table of the order in which yCount and xCount are assigned values.

Every time that the outer loop body executes, the inner loop body executes eight times. Therefore, the total number of AOval dots constructed in the body of the inner loop is 12 * 8 or 96.

Examining the execution of the outer loop reveals more about how the dots are arranged. Each time that the body of the outer loop executes, the value of yCount increases by 1. This yCount value is used to determine the intensity of the rowColor object. The 12 executions of the outer loop body result in 12 different rowColor values that range from black for the first outer loop body repetition to a very light gray for the last repetition.

yCount	xCount
0	0
0	1
0	2
0	3
0	4
0	5
0	6
0	7
0	8
1	0
1	1
1	2
...	...
1	8
2	0
2	1
...	...
2	8
.	.
.	.
.	.
12	8

The inner loop body constructs a new AOval for each repetition. Since xCount is initialized to zero before the inner loop, the first AOval constructed will be located at x==0*25==0 and y==0*15==0. The second AOval will be located at x==25 and y==0, the third at x==50 and y==0 and so forth. In other words, the xCount variable is changing value more frequently than yCount, resulting in AOvals that are drawn across rows. Figure 10.15 shows the complete AWindow displayed by executing the polka dot program.

Figure 10.15 Window displayed by the polka dot program

The pattern of nesting one loop within a single outer loop, such as the polka dot loops, is sometimes called **doubly nested loops**. The two-dimensional nature of the polka dots is typical for a doubly nested pattern. The outer loop proceeds from row to row, and the inner loop proceeds across columns within a row. The result is the construction of AOvals that proceeds from the top of the window to the bottom, and left to right within each row.

There is no reason that the creation of AOvals must always be done row by row. Suppose that a programmer wishes to construct AOvals, column by column, with the left column as black dots and proceeding to lighter gray dots on the right. Figure 10.16 shows such a window.

Figure 10.16 Window displayed by looping across columns

The shell of the looping structure that proceeds across the columns is shown below:

```
xCount = 0;
while ( xCount != 8 ) {
    colColor = new Color(xCount/9.0f, xCount/9.0f, xCount/9.0f);
    yCount = 0;
    while ( yCount != 12 ) {
        . . .
        yCount++;
    }
    xCount++;
}
```

The primary difference between this code and that of the original polka dot program is that the role of the two loops is interchanged. The outer loop of the new algorithm changes xCount, thereby proceeding from left to right across the columns. For each outer loop repetition, the inner loop varies yCount so as to advance from the top to bottom row.

SOFTWARE ENGINEERING TIP

The bodies of the inner nested loops have the greatest potential for repetition. Programmers looking to improve the execution speed of their programs often look first at speeding up the innermost loops.

A **triply nested** loop pattern consists of a doubly nested loop that is nested within a third loop. Triply nested loops are well suited to processing three-dimensional structures in the same way that doubly nested loops work well for two-dimensional structures.

Nested loop repetition can be deceptively repetitious. For example, consider triply nested loops in which each loop is repeated 100 times. The skeleton of such a structure is given as follows.

```
x = 0;
while (x != 100) {
    y = 0;
    while (y != 100) {
        z = 0;
        while (z != 100) {
            // work of innermost loop goes here
            z++;
        }
        y++;
    }
    x++;
}
```

When the above code executes, the "`// work of innermost loop goes here`" line is executed 100*100*100 or one million (1,000,000) times!

10.6 THE DO LOOP

while loops are said to perform their test for loop exit at the **top of the loop**. The phrase "top of the loop" refers to the fact that the *while* loop's condition is checked *before* the loop body is executed. Java supports a second kind of loop that checks for loop exit at the **bottom of the loop**. This instruction is referred to as a **do instruction**. Figure 10.17 describes the syntax and semantics of the Java *do* instruction. The run-time behavior of a *do* instruction is shown as a control flow diagram in Figure 10.18.

Figure 10.17 doInstruction description

doInstruction (a possible *OneStatement*)

Syntax

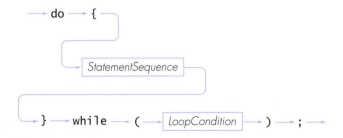

Alternate syntax (when the loop body is a single statement)

Note

LoopCondition can be any valid boolean-valued expression.

Style Notes

The reserved word do should be aligned with the "}" symbol that ends the *doInstruction* body and all statements within *StatementSequence* should be indented by at least one tab from the while.

Semantics

Executing *doInstruction* causes *StatementSequence* to execute once. Following each execution of *StatementSequence*, *LoopCondition* is to be evaluated. If *LoopCondition* is found to be true, then *StatementSequence* is executed again and the process repeats. If *LoopCondition* is found to be false, then execution proceeds to the next statement following the *do* instruction.

Figure 10.18 The control flow of a *do* instruction

Java Syntax

```
// Statement before do
do {
    // Loop Body
} while ( LoopCondition );
// Statement after do
```

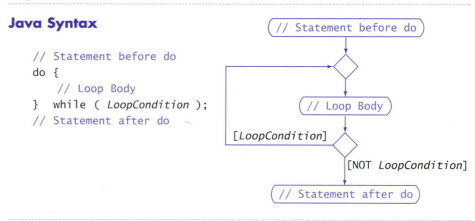

The fact that *do* loops test their condition at the bottom of the loop means that the loop body executes a minimum of one time for each execution of the entire *do* loop. This is different than a *while* loop, whose body is not executed when the loop condition is initially false. Except for this difference, however, a *do* loop behaves like a *while* loop.

Figure 10.19 contains an example program, using a *do* loop. This program displays a table of sine and cosine values for degree measurements from 0 degrees through 90 degrees (in 10-degree increments). The table is placed in three ATextArea objects: degreePane displays the degrees, sinePane displays the corresponding sine values, and cosinePane displays the cosine values.

Each time the body of the *do* instruction from displayTable repeats, another line is appended to each of the three ATextArea objects. When the program completes execution, the window that is displayed appears as shown in Figure 10.20.

Figure 10.19 A program to display a table of sine and cosine values

```java
import aLibrary.*;
import java.awt.*;
public class Director  {
    private AWindow window;
    private ATextArea degreePane, sinePane, cosinePane;

    public Director()    {
        window = new AWindow(10, 10, 250, 250);
        degreePane = new ATextArea(10, 20, 50, 220);
        degreePane.place(window);
        sinePane = new ATextArea(70, 20, 80, 220);
        sinePane.place(window);
        cosinePane = new ATextArea(160, 20, 80, 220);
        cosinePane.place(window);
        displayTable();
        window.repaint();
    }

    /* postcondition
            degreePane, sinePane, and cosinePane contain s table of
            sine and cosine values beginning with 0 degrees through
            90 degrees in 10 degree increments.   */
    private void displayTable( )    {
        int degrees = 0;
        degreePane.appendln("Deg.");
        degreePane.appendln("----");
        sinePane.appendln("Sine");
        sinePane.appendln("-------");
        cosinePane.appendln("Cosine");
        cosinePane.appendln("-------");
        do {
            degreePane.appendln("" + degrees );
            sinePane.appendln("" + Math.sin(degrees/180.*Math.PI));
                // Math trig functions use radian measures for
                // angles
            cosinePane.appendln("" + Math.cos(degrees/180.*Math.PI));
            degrees = degrees + 10;
        } while (degrees != 100);
    }
}
```

The choice to use a *do* loop in the program to display a table of sine and cosine values is reasonable because this program must display more than one row of the table. The same algorithm could also have been written with a *while* loop instead of a *do* loop.

Figure 10.20 Output from the sine/cosine table program

SOFTWARE ENGINEERING TIP

How does a software developer choose between a *while* loop and a *do* loop? Most of the time, either loop will work well. In such cases *while* loops are generally used. The preference for *while* is simply that a *do* instruction always executes its loop body at least once, and the *while* works even if the loop body should not execute.

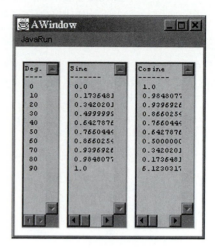

10.7   LOOP INVARIANTS

Assertions have been shown to be useful as class invariants, as well as method preconditions and postconditions. Assertions can also be useful in loop design. The particular kind of assertion that is used within loops is known as a **loop invariant** (not to be confused with a *class* invariant).

A loop invariant captures the state of computation within a loop. This assertion should be placed just prior to the loop condition. Figure 10.21 shows how a loop invariant is located within a *while* loop.

Figure 10.21 Placement of a loop invariant within a *while* loop

Java Syntax

```
// Statement before while


while (LoopCondition)   {

    // Loop Body

}

// Statement after while
```

// Statement before while

loop invariant

[NOT *LoopCondition*]

[*LoopCondition*]

// Loop Body

// Statement after while

Informally, a loop invariant captures the work of the loop by showing relationships that hold each time this location is encountered during code execution. For example, the following counting loop sums the numbers from 1 through num.

```
sum = 0;
counter = 1;
while /*invariant location*/ (counter != num + 1) {
    sum = sum + counter;
    counter++;
}
```

The loop invariant for this code can be discovered by tracing the code while writing down the values of both variables. Such a trace results in the following table.

sum	counter	
0	1	before the loop body executes the first time
1	2	before the loop body executes the second time
3	3	before the loop body executes the third time
6	4	before the loop body executes the fourth time
10	5	before the loop body executes the fifth time
15	6	before the loop body executes the sixth time
etc.	etc.	

A careful examination of this table shows that the following relation between sum and counter exists for each line of the table.

```
sum == 1 + 2 + ... + (counter - 1)
```

This is a loop invariant for this loop.

As another example loop invariant, reconsider the Fibonacci loop:

```
aFibo = 1;
nextFibo = 1;
linesOutput = 0;
while ( linesOutput != 30 ) {
    outPane.appendln("" + aFibo);
    newFibo = aFibo + nextFibo;
    aFibo = nextFibo;
    nextFibo = newFibo;
    linesOutput++;
}
```

An appropriate loop invariant for this code is given below.

> The first linesOutput Fibonacci numbers have been output
> AND aFibo == the (linesOutput + 1)th Fibonacci number
> AND nextFibo == the (linesOutput + 2)th Fibonacci number

Once the loop invariant is known, it can be used in many ways. A loop invariant can be used to test to see if initialization is done properly. This is accomplished by substituting the result of loop initialization into the loop invariant and checking to see if the resulting expression must be true. For example, the initialization code for the Fibonacci loop assigns linesOutput==0,

---

SOFTWARE ENGINEERING TIP

Writing loop invariants can be challenging at first. However, the unique perspective provided by a loop invariant is valuable.

SOFTWARE ENGINEERING TIP

Loop invariants are a useful way to reason about loops. A good loop invariant captures the purpose of the loop by expressing what must be true every time the loop condition is tested, and includes sufficient information to guarantee the desired result at loop completion.

`aFibo==1`, and `nextFibo==1`. Substituting these three values for their variables in the loop invariant results in the following:

> The first 0 Fibonacci numbers have been output
> AND 1 == the (0 + 1)th Fibonacci number
> AND 1 == the (0 + 2)th Fibonacci number

The above statement is clearly true since nothing is output before the loop begins and since 1 is both the first and second Fibonacci number. The fact that this statement is true reveals that the initialization code is correct.

The loop invariant can also be used to verify that the loop condition is correct. For example, consider the summing loop. An appropriate loop invariant is

> `sum == 1 + 2 + ... + (counter - 1)`

Since this loop's condition is (`counter != num + 1`), it must be that `counter == num + 1` when the loop terminates. Substituting `num + 1` for `counter` into the loop invariant results in the following assertion, which verifies that the loop completes properly:

> `sum == 1 + 2 + ... + (num + 1-1) == 1 + 2 + ... + num`

Similarly, the loop invariant for the Fibonacci loop states, among other things, that "The first `linesOutput` Fibonacci numbers have been output." Therefore, a loop that is supposed to output the first 30 Fibonacci numbers should properly begin with

> `while ( linesOutput != 30 )`

The position of a loop invariant for a *do* loop should also be just prior to the loop condition. Below is an example, using a loop borrowed from the sine/cosine table program:

```
degrees = 0;
do {
    degreePane.appendln( " " + degrees );
    sinePane.appendln( " " + Math.sin(degrees/180.*Math.PI) );
    cosinePane.appendln( " " + Math.cos(degrees/180.*Math.PI) );
    degrees = degrees + 10;
    // Loop Invariant:
    // the sine/cosine table is completed from 0 through degrees
} while (degrees != 100);
```

Loop invariants are also useful for designing code. The general procedure for designing a loop from a loop invariant consists of the following four steps:

Step	*Action*
1	Select a loop invariant.
2	Choose loop initialization statements to make the loop invariant true initially.
3	Select a loop condition that, when false, ensures that the loop invariant implies the intended loop postassertion (i.e., the assertion that is required just following the loop).
4	Complete a loop body that preserves the invariant, while making progress.

As an example of using this four-step procedure to create a loop, consider the task of writing a loop to calculate the factorial of *n*, an integer variable. The factorial of *n* is defined to be 1*2*···*n*. The notation "*n*!" is used to denote *n* factorial.

Figure 10.22 contains the shell of a loop to calculate *n*!. The italicized portions of this figure show code that remains to be designed. The Assert comments (assertions) express desired run-time for their respective code locations. The assertion following the loop captures the intended purpose of the loop.

Figure 10.22 Shell of a loop to calculate *n*! (*n* factorial)

```
// Assume the declaration of three int variables: n, j, factorial
// Assert:   0 <= n <= 12
// initialization code
while     // Loop invariant
( SomeCondition )    {
    // Loop Body
}
// Assert: factorial = n!
```

The first step in designing the *n* factorial loop is to select a loop invariant. An appropriate choice for this loop is

```
// Loop invariant: factorial == j!
```

This choice is based on the knowledge that a loop invariant generally has a form similar to the assertion following the loop, but needs to represent an intermediate condition. Figure 10.23 shows the shell of the loop following Step 1.

Figure 10.23 Shell of *n*! loop with loop invariant (after Loop Design Step 1)

```
// Assume the declaration of three int variables: n, j, factorial
// Assert:   0 <= n <= 12
// initialization code
while   // Loop Inv:  factorial == j!
( SomeCondition )    {
    // Loop Body
}
// Assert: factorial = n!
```

Step 2 of the loop design is to use the loop invariant to derive the initialization code. Initialization code must guarantee that the loop invariant is true the first time it is encountered. The simplest initialization code in this situation sets both factorial to 1 and j to 0. (Note that 0! = 1 by the definition of factorial.) Figure 10.24 shows the loop shell with this initialization code included.

Figure 10.24 Shell of *n*! loop with initialization (after Loop Design Step 2)

```
// Assume the declaration of three int variables: n, j, factorial
// Assert:  0 <= n <= 12
factorial = 1;
j = 0;
while   // Loop Inv:  factorial == j!
( SomeCondition )   {
    // Loop Body
}
// Assert: factorial = n!
```

Step 3 of loop design is to use the loop invariant to determine the proper loop condition. This step is achieved by noting that the assertion following the loop must be true when the loop terminates. If `factorial==n!` (from the assertion after the loop) and `factorial==j!` (from the loop invariant), then it must be that `n==j`. A loop condition of

$$(j != n)$$

ensures that `n==j` when the loop terminates, which in turn assures the desired assertion following the loop. Figure 10.25 shows the loop shell with this loop condition inserted.

Figure 10.25 Shell of *n*! loop with condition (after Loop Design Step 3)

```
// Assume the declaration of three int variables: n, j, factorial
// Assert:  0 <= n <= 12
factorial = 1;
j = 0;
while   // Loop Inv:  factorial == j!
( j != n )   {
    // Loop Body
}
// Assert: factorial = n!
```

The final step of loop design, Step 4, is to complete the code for the body of the loop. This step involves recognizing two things:

- A loop must make progress toward completion.
- A loop must preserve its loop invariant.

The initialization code causes the variable, j, to have an initial value of 1. The loop condition makes it clear that j will have a value of n when the loop terminates. Therefore, the value of j must increase if the loop body is to make progress. The following loop body makes progress and ensures that the loop invariant is still true.

```
        j++;
        factorial = factorial * j;
```

Inserting this loop body completes the factorial program as shown in Figure 10.26.

Figure 10.26 Shell of *n!* loop with body (after Loop Design Step 4)

```
// Assume the declaration of three int variables: n, j, factorial
// Assert:  0 <= n <= 12
factorial = 1;
j = 0;
while  // Loop Inv:  factorial == j!
( j != n )    {
        j++;
        factorial = factorial * j;
}
// Assert: factorial = n!
```

SOFTWARE ENGINEERING TIP

The four-step procedure for using a loop invariant to design a loop should be remembered even when it isn't used explicitly. The four-step procedure assists in writing loops that are correct *the first time*.

Most programmers don't repeat the entire four-step procedure to design every loop. However, they do borrow from the reasoning that is used. Furthermore, several remarkably efficient algorithms have been discovered using this procedure to design loops from their invariants.

10.8 LOOPING AND EVENT HANDLING

Loops appear to provide a convenient way to animate graphics. For example, the following code may seem like a tempting way to cause an AOval to move across a window.

```
// Warning: The following code may be deceptive.
AWindow window;
AOval oval;
window = new AWindow(10, 10, 200, 100);
oval = new AOval(0, 30, 20, 20);
oval.place(window);
while ( oval.x() < 200 ) {
    oval.translate( 20, 0 );
}
```

Clearly, the initialization code places oval on the left edge of window. Just as clearly, the loop body causes oval to move to the right for each repetition. However, when this code executes oval does *not* move. The behavior of this code relies upon an understanding of the workings of the Java Virtual Machine. The following insert explains how the Java VM works in this case.

OPENING
the Black Box

Java programs can be thought of as largely *reactive*. A program may begin by executing the Director constructor, but then it becomes idle. Whenever an event occurs, the program reacts by executing an event handler, then once again, the program is idle. The next event results in another event handler "reaction." This pattern of reacting to events then becoming idle is precisely what the Java VM expects from a program.

In order to support this react-then-become-idle pattern, the Java VM essentially leaves the graphical display unaltered until an "idle" time. In other words, a call to repaint() doesn't result in an immediate change to a display. Instead, the display is updated only when the program becomes idle. Therefore, using a loop to animate is futile.

The correct way to animate an AOval so that it moves across a window is accomplished with events, using a class such as EventTimer shown in Chapter 8.

10.9   TESTING AND LOOPS

In Chapter 7 the idea of structure testing was examined. Loops pose unique problems for software testers who are concerned with testing paths through the control flow. It is essentially impossible to achieve path coverage when testing most code that contains one or more loops. The problem is that the control path for executing the loop body just once is different from the path for executing it twice and from the path for executing the body three times, and so forth. This leads to the conclusion that there are an enormous number (often an infinite number) of possible execution paths for even a single loop.

A reasonable alternative to path coverage, sometimes called **loop coverage**, is to ensure that each loop body is executed multiple times. It is a good practice to include at least three possibilities in the loop coverage:

- Ensure that at least one test case checks a *while* loop body that is skipped (i.e., the loop condition causes immediate loop exit).
- Ensure that at least one test case checks for a loop body that executes exactly once.
- Ensure that at least one test case checks for multiple consecutive loop body executions.

Of these three kinds of structure tests, it is generally conceded that the last one is the most important.

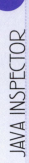

Below is a collection of hints on what to check when examining code that involves the concepts of this chapter.

✓ It is always a good idea to simulate the execution of a loop on your desktop by tracing a few repetitions. Ideally, the loop should be traced for its first two or three repetitions and its last two or three.

✓ Most programmers concentrate on the portion of the loop body that performs the primary work of the loop. It is always wise to check that the portion of the loop body that makes progress is correct.

✓ Every loop needs some initialization. A loop should be examined to ensure proper initialization before its first repetition.

✓ One extremely effective means of verifying a loop is to express a loop invariant, and then use it to check the loop in the following ways:
   1. Is the initialization code sufficient to assure that the loop invariant is true the first time it is encountered?
   2. Do the loop invariant and the negation of the loop condition imply the desired result of the loop?
   3. Does the loop body preserve the invariant after each repetition?

✓ When loops are nested, it is the inner loop that does most of the work. The inner loop should always be examined for statements that can be moved outside of its body without changing the final result of the code. Such statements should be moved outside of the inner loop for more efficient code.

✓ If a *do* loop is used, it is best to check that its loop body must always execute at least once. If the loop might need to skip the body under certain circumstances, then a *while* loop is better.

✓ The Java VM event loop can get swamped by inefficient event handlers. Each event handler should be examined for unnecessary code or inefficiencies. Can some of the event handler code be performed when the object is initialized? Are there any `repaint` calls that are unnecessary?

TERMINOLOGY

bottom of the loop

counting loop pattern

dead loop

do instruction

do loop

doubly nested loops

infinite loop

initialization (of a loop)

loop body

loop condition

loop coverage

loop invariant

making progress (in a loop body)

nested loops

off-by-1 loop

primary work

repetition control structures

sentinel loop

top of the loop

triply nested loops

while instruction

while loop

EXERCISES

1. Show the exact output that is produced by executing each of the following loops.

a.
```
int k;
k = 0;
while (k < 9) {
    System.out.println( k*5 );
    k++;
}
```

b.
```
int k;
k = 11;
while (k != 19) {
    System.out.println( k );
    k = k + 2;
}
```

c.
```
int k;
k = 10;
while (k != 13) {
    System.out.println( k );
    k = k + 2;
}
```

d.
```
int k;
k = 0;
while (k != -9) {
    k = k - 1;
    System.out.println( k );
    k = k - 2;
}
```

```
e. int k;
   k = 1;
   while (k != 9) {
      System.out.println( k );
   }
f. int k;
   k = 1;
   while (k != 9) {
      k = k + 2;
      System.out.println( k );
      k = k - 1;
   }
g. int k, j;
   k = 33;
   j = 1;
   while (k < j) {
      k = k + 10;
      System.out.println( k );
      j = j * 2;
   }
h. int k;
   k = 1;
   do {
      k++;
      System.out.println( k );
   } while (k != 9);
i. int k;
   k = 1;
   while (k != 33) {
      k++;
      System.out.println( k );
      k++;
   }
```

2. Which of the Exercise 1 loops are infinite loops?

3. Show the content of outPane following the execution of each of the following code segments:

```
a. AWindow window = new AWindow(10, 10, 200, 200);
   ATextArea outPane = new ATextArea(50, 50, 100, 100);
   outPane.place( window );
   outPane.appendln( "This is a test" );
   outPane.append( "of an ATextArea object." );
   outPane.appendln( "This is only a test." );
```

b.
```
AWindow window = new AWindow(10, 10, 200, 200);
ATextArea outPane = new ATextArea(50, 50, 100, 100);
char oneChar;
outPane.place( window );
oneChar = 'a';
while ( oneChar < 'y' ) {
    outPane.append( oneChar );
    oneChar++;
}
outPane.appendln("/");
```

4. Show the exact output that is produced by executing each of the following loops.

a.
```
int j, k;
k = 0;
while (k < 3) {
    j = 5;
    while (j > 0) {
        System.out.println( "j == " + j );
        j = j - 2;
    }
    System.out.println( "k == " + k );
    k++;
}
```

b.
```
int j, k;
k = 1;
while (k < 7) {
    j = 5;
    while (j > 0) {
        System.out.println( "j == " + j );
        System.out.println( "k == " + k );
        j--;
    }
    k = k * 2;
}
```

c.
```
int j, k;
k = 1;
j = 10;
while (k < 8) {
    while (j > 0) {
        System.out.println( "j == " + j );
        System.out.println( "k == " + k );
        j--;
    }
    k = k * 2;
}
```

```
d. int j, k;
   k = 1;
   while (k < 8) {
       j = 5;
       while (j > k) {
           System.out.println( "j == " + j );
           System.out.println( "k == " + k );
           j--;
       }
       k = k * 2;
   }
```

5. What is the value of the sum variable following the execution of the following code segment?

```
int j, k, m, n, sum;
sum = 0;
j = 0;
while (j != 20) {
    k = 0;
    while (k != 100) {
        m = 0;
        while (m != 50) {
            n = 0;
            while (n != 10) {
                sum++;
                n++;
            }
            m++;
        }
        k++;
    }
    j++;
}
```

6. Consider the code below:

```
int k, prod;
// initialization code here
while (k != lastInt) {
    prod = prod + 7;
    k = k + 1;
}
/* Assert: prod == 7 * lastInt */
```

Below is a proper loop invariant for this loop.

```
prod = 7 * k
```

a. What initialization code needs to be inserted to make this loop work properly?

b. Which part of this code is the primary work and which is the make-progress part of the loop?

c. For what values of `lastInt` does this code result in an infinite loop?

d. How does the assertion following the loop change if the two instructions of the loop body are reversed to become

```
k = k + 1;
prod = prod + 7;
```

e. What is the proper loop invariant resulting from the changes described in part (d)?

f. Rewrite this code to perform the original task (i.e., the assertion after the loop is the same) but the value of k *decreases* by one for each loop body execution.

g. Rewrite this code to perform the original task using a *do* loop instead of a *while* loop.

7. Each part below shows a "final assertion" and a loop invariant for a while loop. Your task is to write a loop that, when executed, makes the final assertion true and also has the given loop invariant. Be certain to include the declaration of all needed variables and proper initialization code. You may assume that all variables are of type `int`.

a. final assertion
```
    sum = 1 + 2 + ... + 100
```
loop invariant
```
    sum = 1 + 2 + ... + intVar
```

b. final assertion
```
    sum = 1 + 3 + 5 + ... + 999
```
loop invariant
```
    sum = 1 + 3 + ... + intVar AND intVar % 2 = 1
```

c. final assertion
```
    sum = 3 + 4 + 5 + ... + 999
```
loop invariant
```
    sum = intVar + (intVar + 1) + (intVar + 2) + ... + 999
```

1. Write a program to factor any positive integer. Below is an example of such a program that accepts the value to be factored in an `ATextField` and displays all of the prime factors in an `ATextArea`.

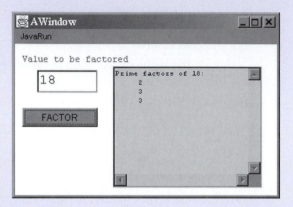

2. Write a program that calculates both the greatest common divisor (GCD) and least common multiple (LCM) of two positive integers. If either input value is nonpositive or not an integer, a proper error message should be displayed. Below is an example of such a program, using `ATextField` objects and a button for user input.

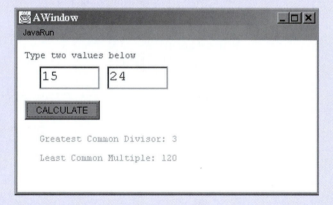

The greatest common divisor is the largest integer that divides evenly (with a remainder of zero) both input numbers. The least common multiple is the smallest integer than can be evenly divided by both input numbers.

3. This program is designed to draw a ruler of up to 10 inches in length. The interface to this program is a Control Window with two text fields and a button. The top text field is for the user to specify the length of the ruler (in whole inches). The bottom text field allows the user to specify graduations

(1 for inches only; 2 for inches and half inches; 4 for inches, half inches, and quarter inches; 8 for inches, halves, quarters, and eighths; 10 for inches and tenths of an inch; and everything else for inches, halves, quarters, eighths, and sixteenths of an inch).

The ruler is drawn in a separate window in response to a button click. Be certain that every button click draws a new ruler using the text field values at that time. Below is a picture of the way a ruler should be drawn. Note that each button click causes the ruler to redraw to the user's specifications.

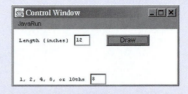

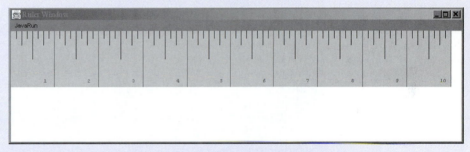

4. Pythagorean triples are any three positive integers for which the square of the largest equals the sum of the squares of the other two. For example, 3, 4, and 5 are a Pythagorean triple because $3^2 + 4^2 == 5^2$. Write a program to display all Pythagorean triples whose individual values are less than a user-specified value. Below is an example in which the maximum value is 17.

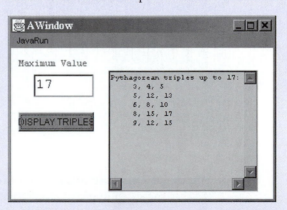

5. For this assignment you must design and implement the code necessary to display a calendar for any specified month and year. When the program begins, it must display a single window that appears like the one following. The user is expected to type a year and a month (as integers) into two text

fields and then to click the Show Calendar button. In response to the Show Calendar click, your program must display a calendar for that particular month (i.e., dates must be arranged in columns for the correct week days). Every month must be displayed with the leftmost column of numbers corresponding to Sunday.

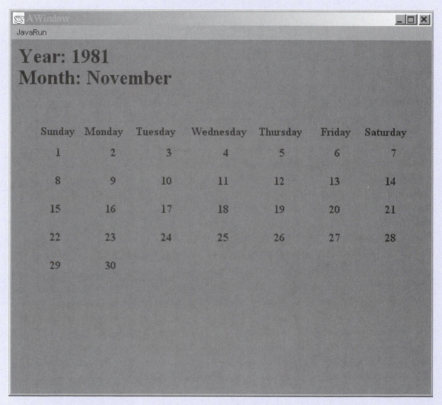

Where did our calendar come from?

It takes the earth approximately 365.24219878 days to orbit the sun. The ancient Egyptians invented a calendar with a 365-day year. Although this may have kept the seasons consistent with the calendar during the length of the Egyptian empire, this calendar clearly drifts after time. In fact, the calendar loses an entire year of time after 1508 years. The Romans detected the error in the Egyptian calendar and created the so-called Julian Calendar, which added a day to every fourth year. It takes the Julian Calendar about 47 centuries to gain a year of time, but it still has considerable drift. In 1582 Pope Gregory XIII approved the calendar which was named for him, the Gregorian Calendar. We continue to use the Gregorian calendar today.

Using the Gregorian calendar there are still 365 days in most years, and every year that has 366 days (i.e., leap year) does so by virtue of Feb. 29. The rule for determining leap year is as follows. Leap year occurs for any year that is evenly divisible by four (i.e., year % 4 == 0) that is not evenly divisible by 100, unless it is evenly divisible by 400.

Why the long description of leap year? Because you need to calculate the number of days that have passed in order to decide which day of the week is day 1 for a particular month. In other words, if you calculate the total number of days that occurred since the first day A.D. modulo (%) seven through October, 1999, then you will find the day of the week for Nov. 1, 1999. (By the way, January 1 in year 1 is a Monday, based on this method.)

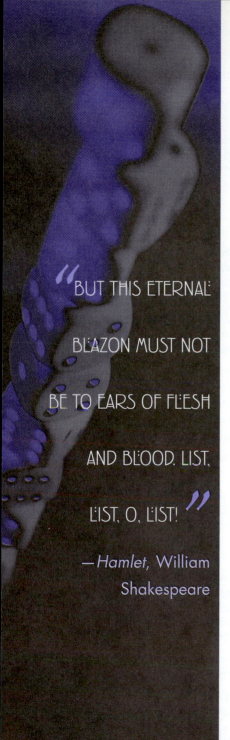

CONTAINERS

"BUT THIS ETERNAL

BLAZON MUST NOT

BE TO EARS OF FLESH

AND BLOOD. LIST,

LIST, O, LIST!"

—*Hamlet*, William
Shakespeare

OBJECTIVES

- To examine the utility of containers as both a receptacle for items and a way to organize items

- To explore Bag as a simple container that provides a measure of genericity in the form of items that belong to the Object class

- To emphasize the importance of type safety and three ways to provide for it

- To introduce wrapper classes and show how they are used to allow containers of Object to store primitive information

- To examine a class, called SimpleList, that implements a list container with an internal iterator

- To examine how an iterator is used in conjunction with other list operations

- To introduce the concept of a list traversal algorithm pattern and examine several such algorithms

- To explore linear searching algorithms as a method of looking for list data satisfying certain properties

- To introduce the concept of a sorted container and show how to maintain a sorted list by means of the insertion method

- To demonstrate how the Java *awt* library uses a class called Container in order to implement the placement of graphical objects upon one another

Vending machines, video rental stores, and banks all have something in common. They all store items that are dispensed to their clients. A vending machine stores snack foods, video rental stores offer VCR tapes and DVDs, and banks are repositories for money.

In programming terminology an entity that exhibits this ability to store and dispense items as needed is referred to as a **container**. Vending machines, video rental stores, and banks are all real-world examples of containers.

11.1   CONTAINERS OF OBJECTS

People sometimes think of computers as machines for implementing containers. The employee payroll program utilizes a *container of employees*. The airline reservation system relies upon *containers of airplane seat assignments*. A university transcript is a *container of collegiate courses*.

In an object-oriented environment, containers are themselves objects, but a container is unique in the sense that its primary purpose is to serve as a storehouse for other objects. Typical container methods include the following:

- Constructor methods for initializing the container
- Methods to insert objects into the container
- Methods to remove objects from the container
- Methods to inspect the content of the container
- Methods to return the size and other container properties

In addition, container classes sometimes include other methods to organize their content or to assist client software in locating content with special properties.

The standard Java *awt* library includes a class called Container that is a particular kind of container. Objects belonging to Container are used to keep track of items that are being displayed. *aLibrary* makes use of such containers. Figure 11.1 shows the inheritance structure of several library classes that are descendants of Container.

The method that is called by the *aLibrary* classes in order to insert a new object into a Container is called place. Whenever a program places one *aLibrary* object upon another, it is really placing the object into a Container. Figure 11.1 shows the five *aLibrary* classes that are Container descendants: AWindow, AView, AOval, ARectangle, and ARoundRectangle. These are the five *aLibrary* objects upon which other objects can be placed.

The *aLibrary* classes support two typical container methods.

- The place method inserts an object into a Container.
- The remove method extracts an object from its Container.

Below is a list of all of the *aLibrary* classes that support being placed and removed.

```
AButton, AImage, ALabel, ALine, AOval,
ARectangle, ARoundRectangle, AScrollbar,
ATextArea, ATextField, AView
```

The *aLibrary* place method serves a dual purpose. Executing the call

```
a.place(b);
```

1. causes object a to be displayed upon object b.

2. causes object a to be retained as an item within the b container.

It is this second property that permits an *aLibrary* object to continue to be displayed even though it is assigned to a variable whose lifetime has ended or has been reassigned. For example, executing the following code results in the construction of two AOval objects placed on window:

```
AOval oval1, oval2;
oval = new AOval(10, 10, 10, 10);
oval.place( window );
oval = new AOval(30, 30, 30, 30);
oval.place( window );
```

When the second AOval object is constructed it is bound to the oval variable in place of the first object. However, the first object remains visible in the window because it continues to be stored within the window container.

Figure 11.1 Descendants of the Container class

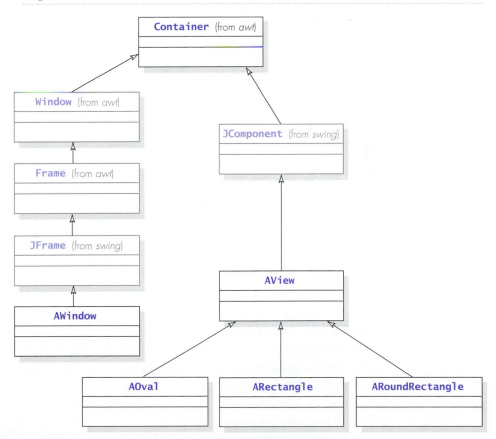

In addition to their ability to be placed and removed, objects from these 11 classes share another method related to Container. A parentContainer() method is included in all of these classes to return the Container upon which the object is placed. (The value of parentContainer() == null for an object that isn't placed.)

11.2 GENERIC CONTAINERS

The Container class from the *awt* library is a useful technique for storing graphical objects, but there are many other container needs that this particular class cannot satisfy. One way to meet these other needs is to use a general-purpose container. Among the most general-purpose containers are those that accept items of varying type. Such containers are known as **generic containers** because the type of the objects they contain is not restricted.

Figure 11.2 contains a class diagram for a simple generic container, called **Bag**. The methods of the Bag class are typical for a container class. These methods include

- insert—to put an item into a Bag
- remove—to remove an item from a Bag
- item—a method to return (inspect) one value entity from within a Bag without removing it
- count—a method to return the integer count of the number of items in a Bag

Figure 11.2 Bag class diagram

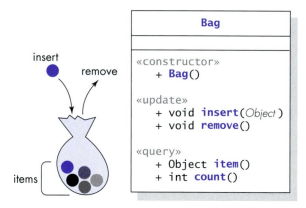

Figure 11.3 explains more details about the Bag class and its methods in the form of a class specification. Notice that the lack of a precondition on insert means that there is no limit on the number of items that can be inserted.

Below is a segment of code that creates a Bag object and inserts String objects into this Bag:

```
Bag nameCollection;
nameCollection = new Bag();
nameCollection.insert( "Richard" );
```

```
nameCollection.insert( "Eddie" );
nameCollection.insert( "Marion" );
nameCollection.insert( "Richard" );
nameCollection.remove();
System.out.println( "Number of names stored:
    " + nameCollection.count() );
```

Figure 11.3 Bag class specifications

Bag Class Specifications

Invariant

A Bag object

- is a container of zero or more other objects
- is capable of storing anything that conforms to `Object`

Constructor Method

public **Bag** ( )

> *postcondition*
> `this` is an empty bag (i.e. `count()` == 0)

Query Methods

public int **count** ()

> *postcondition*
> result == the number of items in `this`

public Object **item** ( )

> *precondition*
> `count() > 0`
>
> *postcondition*
> result == one of the items from `this` Bag

Update Methods

public void **insert** (Object z)

> *postcondition*
> `this` == old `this` with z inserted
> AND `count() = old count() + 1`

public void **remove** ()

> *precondition*
> count() > 0
>
> *postcondition*
> `this` == old `this` with one item removed
> AND `count() == old count() - 1`

When the above code executes, it constructs an empty bag, called nameCollection. The code continues by inserting four String objects, "Richard", "Eddie", "Marion", and "Richard" again. Next, one of the names is removed from the bag. The final instruction outputs the message

```
Number of names stored: 3
```

The type of the items that can be inserted into a Bag is Object. This use of Object means that Bag is a generic container in the sense that objects within a Bag can be of any reference (i.e., nonprimitive) type. In the example, the type of the objects inserted into nameCollection is String. However, there is nothing to prohibit the program from inserting ARectangle objects or AButton objects into this same Bag, because all reference types conform to Object.

11.3 TYPE SAFETY, CASTING, AND INSTANCEOF

One of the difficulties with building generic containers with Object for the item type is that methods for returning the items of the container return things of type Object, instead of the actual item type. For example, consider the following four Java instructions:

```
Bag nameCollection;
String nameString;
nameCollection = new Bag();
nameCollection.insert( "Tim" );
nameString = nameCollection.item(); // This is a syntax error.
```

This code creates a Bag called nameCollection and inserts into this Bag the single String object, "Tim". The intent of the fourth instruction is to assign the item "Tim" to nameString. The state of program execution following the insert is that nameCollection stores the single item, "Tim". Unfortunately, this code will never execute, because of a syntax error in the last instruction. The problem is a type conformance issue. The item method returns an Object, and Object does not conform to String (even though this particular item happens to be a String).

The erroneous instruction can be modified to work as expected by incorporating the cast shown below:

```
nameString = (String)nameCollection.item();
```

When executed, this last instruction properly assigns the string "Tim" to nameString. However, the following instruction is also acceptable to the compiler and yet it makes no sense within this program:

```
AOval circle = (AOval)nameCollection.item(); // This is wrong.
```

The Java compiler is extremely permissive regarding type casts, sometimes allowing them when they aren't sensible. This last instruction isn't sensible, because the value returned by the item method is of type String, and yet the instruction casts it to AOval. The result of executing such an instruction is a run-time error.

Software developers speak of **type safety** in situations such as this. It is *unsafe* to cast an object to any type to which it fails to conform. A lack of type safety is particularly troublesome, because an improper type casts lead to run-time errors.

There are three viable alternatives to adding type safety to the use of the Bag class. The first alternative is to avoid the use of genericity. Using this approach, the generic Bag class is abandoned in favor of the BagOfString class, described in Figure 11.4.

Figure 11.4 BagOfString class diagram

```
┌─────────────────────────────────┐
│         BagOfString             │
├─────────────────────────────────┤
│                                 │
├─────────────────────────────────┤
│ «constructor»                   │
│    + Bag()                      │
│                                 │
│ «update»                        │
│    + void insert(String )       │
│    + void remove()              │
│                                 │
│ «query»                         │
│    + String item()              │
│    + int count()                │
└─────────────────────────────────┘
```

BagOfString provides type safety by permitting nothing but String objects to be inserted in the container. The code to insert the "Tim" string into a BagOfString and then inspect it via the item method is shown below.

```
BagOfString nameCollection;
String nameString;
nameCollection = new BagOfString();
nameCollection.insert( "Tim" );
nameString = nameCollection.item();
```

This technique of using a different class for each type of content has the advantage of providing a container that is type safe. The consequence of this approach is that the generic property (and the reusability it fosters) is sacrificed.

A second approach for ensuring type safety is to always write client code that tests for type safety *before* casting. The instanceof test, introduced in Chapter 9, can be used for this purpose.

The code to insert and inspect the "Tim" string, using instanceof to check for type conformance, is shown below. The key feature of this code is that the call to the item method has been made type safe by attempting such a call only when it is guaranteed to be successful.

```
Bag nameCollection;
String nameString;
nameCollection = new Bag();
nameCollection.insert( "Tim" );
```

```
if (nameCollection.item() instanceof String) {
    nameString = (String) nameCollection.item();
} else {
    System.out.println( "Attempt to call item() for a non-String." );
}
```

The advantage of using instanceof is that Bag can be used generically, supporting content items of all class types. The disadvantage is that the container class (Bag) does not guarantee type safety. Instead, programmers must provide their own protection in the form of an instanceof test before each call to item.

A third approach to providing type safety can be thought of as a combination of the first two techniques. This approach relies upon the creation of a nongeneric class, like BagOfString. However, this class is designed to inherit the generic class and only redefine those methods that would otherwise require casting. Figure 11.5 shows how to code BagOfString using this third approach.

Figure 11.5 BagOfString class inheriting Bag

```
public class BagOfString extends Bag {
    /*  postcondition
            this is an empty bag. */
    public BagOfString()  {
        super();
    }
    /*  precondition
            the type of z conforms to String
        postcondition
            this == old this with z inserted
            AND count() == old count + 1  */
    public void insert(Object z)    {
        if (z instanceof String)    {
            super.insert(z);
        } else {
            System.out.println( "Inserting non-string violates type
                safety." );
        }
    }
    /*  precondition
            count() > 0
        postcondition
            result == one of the items from this */
    public String itemString()    {
        return (String)super.item();
    }
}
```

SOFTWARE ENGINEERING TIP

It is best to make generic classes type safe, either by creating parallel classes that are nongeneric or by checking every type conversion with **instanceof**. One method for reusing generic classes safely is to inherit them to build a non-generic class by adding only those methods that would otherwise be unsafe.

The BagOfString class overrides insert to ensure that only String objects can be inserted into bags of this type. Changing only the one method guarantees that any use of the BagOfString class will be type safe.

The BagOfString class from Figure 11.5 has one additional difference from the prior class specification. A method called itemString has been added to this class. This new method is used to return a String item so that client code need not perform type casts.

The BagOfString class is not a generic class, having sacrificed the generic property for type safety. Nonetheless, it is still important to write a generic Bag class, because it forms the proper foundation for creating classes such as BagOfString. The same techniques used to create the BagOfString class can be used to create type-safe classes such as BagOfAOval and BagOfAView that are subclasses of Bag.

11.4 WRAPPER CLASSES

In addition to the type safety limitations, containers of Object items have a second limitation—they are not truly generic. Primitive types do not conform to Object. As an example of this restriction, the second instruction below results in a compile-time error.

```
Bag nameCollection = new Bag();
nameCollection.insert( 33 ); // This is a syntax error.
```

The value 33 is of type int and int does *not* conform to Object.

The Java library includes a set of classes to compensate for this inconsistency between the primitive and reference types. These classes are called **wrapper classes**, because their purpose is to provide a way to "wrap up" a single primitive value within a reference object. As shown in Figure 11.6, there is one wrapper class to correspond to every primitive type.

Wrapper classes often share the name of their corresponding primitive type, except for capitalizing the first letter of the name. The two exceptions to this rule are for primitive types int and char. The wrapper class for int is Integer, and the wrapper class for char is Character.

Each wrapper class includes two key methods:

1. A constructor method that accepts a single parameter of its corresponding primitive type. This constructor creates an object that stores the value of its argument.
2. A method to return the primitive value stored within the wrapper. These methods are always named with the primitive type followed by the suffix "Value", and they are parameterless.

Figure 11.7 illustrates these two methods by supplying the class specifications for the Integer wrapper class.

Figure 11.6 Wrapper classes corresponding to primitive types

Primitive Class	*Corresponding Wrapper Class*
boolean	Boolean
byte	Byte
char	Character
double	Double
float	Float
int	Integer
long	Long
short	Short

Figure 11.7 Integer class specifications

Integer Class Specifications

Invariant

An Integer object

- is a wrapper around an embedded value of type int.
- implicitly inherits Object like other classes.
- does not support int operators such as +, −, <, etc.

Constructor Method

public **Integer** (int j)

   postcondition
   the embedded value of this == j

Query Method

public int **intValue** ()

   postcondition
   result == the embedded value of this

...

The wrapper classes provide the tools necessary for converting primitive type data to and from a type that belongs to a full-fledged class. This means that wrapper class objects can be placed within a Bag just like other objects whose type conforms to Object.

For example, the following instruction generates a syntax error for an int variable, called someInt, because int expressions do not conform to Object (the type of the insert method parameter).

```
bag.insert( someInt ); // this results in a syntax error
```

However, the intent of the previous instruction can be accomplished by the following:

```
bag.insert( new Integer(someInt) );
```

Executing this instruction causes the value of `someInt` to be wrapped (embedded) within an `Integer` object that is inserted into bag. The following code will output such a wrapper value from within the container:

```
if ( bag.item() instanceof Integer) then {
    System.out.println( ((Integer)bag.item()).intValue() );
}
```

The expression `((Integer)bag.item()).intValue()` inspects the wrapped item as a three-step expression:

1. The `item` method returns the value within a wrapper.

2. An `Integer` cast permits the wrapped item to be treated in its proper `Integer` type.

3. The `intValue` method is applied to the `Integer` object to extract the embedded `int` value.

The two key patterns for using wrapper classes are summarized in Figure 11.8. The first pattern is an expression to return a wrapper object with an embedded primitive value. The second pattern is an expression to return a copy of the primitive value from within the wrapper class object. The variable `intVar` is assumed to be of type `int`; the variable `integerVar` is of type `Integer`; and the variable `charVar` is of type `char`.

Figure 11.8 Two patterns for converting to/from wrapper objects

---

To convert from primitiveExpression to WrapperType:
```
new WrapperType( primitiveExpression )
```

Examples:
```
integerVar = new Integer(33);
myBag.insert( new Character(charVar) );
```

To convert from wrapperExpression to primitiveType:
```
wrapperExpression.primitiveTypeValue()
```

Examples:
```
intVar = integerVar.intValue();
System.out.println( characterExpression.charValue() );
```

These two patterns are used in `BagOfInt`, a type safe version of `Bag` for `int` values. The code for `BagOfInt` is shown in Figure 11.9.

Figure 11.9 BagOfInt class

```
public class BagOfInt extends Bag {
    /* postcondition
            this is an empty bag (i.e. count() == 0) */
    public BagOfInt()  {
        super();
    }


    /* precondition
            count() > 0
       postcondition
            result == one of the items from this */
    public int itemInt()   {
        return ( (Integer)super.item() ).intValue();
    }


    /* postcondition
            z is of type Integer
                IMPLIES (result == old this with j inserted
                AND count() == old count() + 1
            z is NOT of type Integer   IMPLIES  error message */
    public void insert(Object z)   {
        if (z instanceof Integer)   {
            super.insert( z );
        } else {
            System.out.println( "Attempt to insert a non-Integer." );
        }
    }


    /* postcondition
            result == old this with j inserted
            AND count() == old count() + 1 */
    public void insert(int j)   {
        super.insert( new Integer(j) );
    }
}
```

BagOfInt inherits Bag and both overrides and overloads the insert method.
The overriding version of insert (i.e., the one with the Object parameter) ensures
type safety by prohibiting non-Integer type data from being inserted into the bag.
The overloaded version of insert (i.e., the one with the int parameter) is included to relieve client code from the need to translate an int to an Integer. This new
insert method wraps its parameter's int value within an Integer object, then
inserts this value within the bag. BagOfInt also includes a new itemInt method
that unwraps an Integer item from the bag and returns the embedded int value.

The BagOfInt class stores all objects within Integer wrappers, but this fact is largely transparent to client code. The client code below illustrates this idea. This sequence of instructions inserts three int values into a BagOfInt, removes one, and outputs one of the items from the bag.

```
BagOfInt intBag;
intBag = new BagOfInt();
intBag.insert( 11 );
intBag.insert( 22 );
intBag.insert( 33 );
intBag.remove();
System.out.println( intBag.itemInt() );
```

One caution is in order regarding wrapper classes. Although wrapper classes provide a technique for storing primitive values within full-fledged objects, they have many limitations. The arithmetic operations like + and – that are supported for many of the numeric primitive data types are *not* permitted on wrapper objects. Neither are relational operators, such as < and >=, or logical operators (!, &&, and ||) supported. Furthermore, the wrapper classes have no built-in syntax for constants, and Java does not permit primitive constants to be assigned directly to variables belonging to wrapper classes. All of these restrictions mean that wrapper classes are really only useful for situations in which primitives need to be treated like reference objects.

11.5 LISTS

The Bag class and all of its variants provide useful illustrations of the basics of generic Java container classes, but programmers rarely use a Bag class. Bag's shortcoming is that it provides no mechanisms for maintaining the order of items within the container. The remove method from Bag is permitted to remove *any* item. Similarly, a call to item inspects (returns) one of the items from a Bag, but which one? Most algorithms require containers that provide better control over the order in which items are removed and inspected.

One of the best known ordered containers is called **list**. Lists treat their content as a single file line of items. Every item in the list, except the front item, has another item preceding it, and every item, except the back item, has an item behind it. Like links on a chain, every list item is located in a specific position within the list. Also like a chain, inserting or removing links doesn't alter the relative position of the other links in the chain.

front ←————————————————————————————————→ back

Actually, a list is not a single kind of container because there are many different kinds of lists. For the purposes of this text a particular kind of list, known as SimpleList, is examined. Figure 11.10 contains the class diagram for SimpleList. In addition to its constructor, SimpleList has only three methods that are different from Bag, namely start, forth, and isOff. Figure 11.11 shows the class specifications for these three methods, as well as the rest of the class.

Figure 11.10 SimpleList class diagram

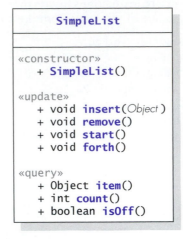

Figure 11.11 SimpleList class specifications

SimpleList Class Specifications

Invariant

A SimpleList object

- is a container of zero or more objects arranged in a linear order.

- can store any type of item that conforms to Object.

- maintains an *iterator* that is positioned either in front of the first item, beyond the last item, or between two consecutive list items. (The iterator can be thought of as an integer that counts the number of items preceding its position.)

Constructor Method

public **SimpleList** ( )

   postcondition
   this is empty (i.e., count() == 0)

   AND iterator == 0 (i.e. the iterator has zero items before it)

Update Methods

public void **insert** (Object z)

   postcondition
   this == the old this list with z inserted at the old iterator position

   AND count() == old count() + 1

   AND iterator == old iterator + 1

```
public void remove ()
```
   postcondition
   NOT isOff() IMPLIES

       (this == old this with the item following old iterator removed

       AND count() == old count() – 1)

   AND isOff() IMPLIES nothing changed

```
public void start ()
```
   modifies
   iterator

   postcondition
   iterator == 0 (i.e., positioned before all items in the list)

```
public void forth ()
```
   modifies
   iterator

   postcondition
   not isOff() IMPLIES iterator == old iterator + 1;

   AND isOff() IMPLIES nothing changes;

Query Methods
```
public int count ()
```
   postcondition
   result == the number of items in this list

```
public Object item ( )
```
   postcondition
   NOT isOff() IMPLIES

       result == the item immediately following the iterator;

   AND isOff() IMPLIES result == null

```
public boolean isOff ( )
```
   postcondition
   result == (iterator == count()) (i.e.. result is true exactly when
   iterator is positioned at the rear of this list)

SOFTWARE ENGINEERING TIP
There are many kinds of lists. Some lists separate the notion of the list from that of an iterator. `SimpleList` combines the two concepts by including an iterator as an integral part of the list.

Nearly every `SimpleList` method involves the notion of an **iterator**. An iterator is a device to keep track of list positions. Like a counter on a tape recorder, an iterator measures how much of the list precedes its current position. For example, following is a picture of a list containing three string items. The front item in the list is the string "Moe", the middle item is "Larry", and the back item is "Curly".

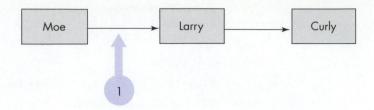

Each `SimpleList` container has a single iterator built into the container. It is best to think of this iterator as always positioned *between* items, unless it precedes or follows the entire list. The arrow attached to the oval in the above diagram denotes the iterator for the list. At this time the iterator is positioned between the "Moe" item and the "Larry" item. The value shown within the iterator is "1" and reflects the fact that the number of items preceding the iterator is 1. (The `SimpleList` class specifications explain the iterator in terms of this integer value.)

The `SimpleList` class includes two methods specifically to manipulate the position of the iterator. Whenever the `start` method is called upon a list, the iterator is positioned at the very front of the list, as shown below.

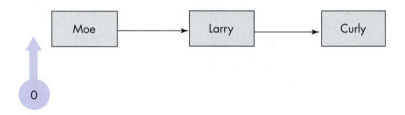

The purpose of the `forth` method is to advance the iterator by one position within the list. For example, the two pictures below show "before" and "after" states when `forth` is called:

BEFORE calling `forth()`

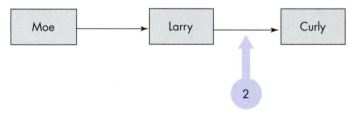

AFTER calling `forth()`

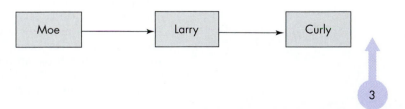

When the iterator is positioned at the back of the list (as shown immediately previous), it is said that the iterator is **off the list**. Calling forth when the iterator is off the list does not advance the iterator because it is impossible to advance any farther.

SimpleList includes a method to check whether or not the iterator is off the list. The isOff method returns true when the iterator is positioned off the list and false otherwise. This method is particularly important in light of the insert and item methods.

A call to insert inserts the new item at precisely the location of the iterator. To illustrate, the following two pictures show the list before and after inserting the string "Frank".

BEFORE calling insert

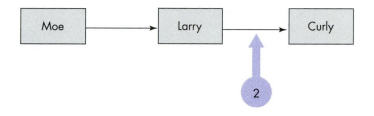

AFTER calling insert("Frank");

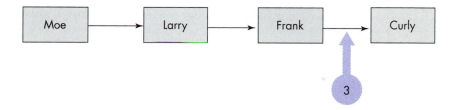

Notice that a call to insert leaves the previous list items intact. In addition, the iterator is always positioned just after the item that was inserted. If the iterator is positioned at the front of the list (has a value of zero) prior to an insert, then the inserted item becomes the new front of the list. If the iterator is off the list at the time of an insertion, then the inserted item is the new back of the list.

The item method is designed to return the item that *follows* the iterator. For the picture below, a call to item will return the String "Curly".

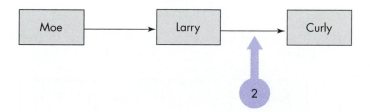

In the event that the iterator is positioned off the list at the time of a call to item, then null is returned. The remove method also operates upon the item that *follows* the iterator. This is the item that is removed from the container. The pictures below illustrate.

BEFORE calling remove

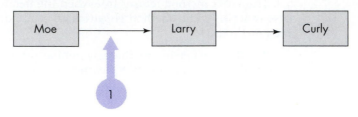

AFTER calling remove();

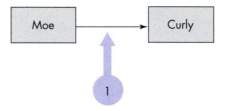

Calling remove does not alter the sequencing of any list items except the item removed, nor does it change the iterator's position. An attempt to remove an item when the iterator is off the list changes nothing.

The following code combines several SimpleList method calls.

```
SimpleList egList;
egList = new SimpleList();
egList.start();
egList.insert("Elinor");
egList.start();
egList.insert("Susan");
egList.start();
egList.forth();
egList.insert("Gina");
egList.forth();
egList.insert("Patty");
egList.insert("Diane");
egList.insert("Gillian");
```

A careful trace of this code reveals that the resulting list can be pictured as follows:

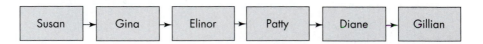

Type safety is just as important for a list as it is for a Bag. Fortunately, the inclusion of an iterator does not complicate the issue of type safety. The techniques that provided type safety for the Bag class can be used on SimpleList as well. Figure 11.12 illustrates with a ListOfAOval class to provide a SimpleList to store AOval objects in a manner that is type safe.

Figure 11.12 ListOfOval a type safe subclass of SimpleList

```
import aLibrary.*;
public class ListOfAOval extends SimpleList  {
    /*  postcondition
            this is empty
            AND iterator == 0      */
    public ListOfAOval()  {
        super();
    }


    /*  postcondition
            not isOff  IMPLIES                              \
                result == the item immediately following the
                iterator ;
            isOff IMPLIES result == null  */
    public AOval itemAOval()  {
        return  (AOval)super.item();
    }


    /*  postcondition
            z is of type AOval
                IMPLIES
                    (this == old this list with z inserted at
                    iterator position
                    AND  count() = old count() + 1
                    AND  iterator == old iterator + 1 )
                AND z is NOT of type AOval
                    IMPLIES  error message */
    public void insert( Object z )    {
        if (z instanceof AOval) {
            super.insert(z);
        } else {
            System.out.println("ERROR: Attempt to insert
                non-AOval");
        }
    }
}
```

11.6 LIST TRAVERSAL

The SimpleList class provides three methods (start, forth, and isOff) specifically to assist client code in manipulating iterators. The previous section illustrates
how these methods can be used to control the order in which items are inserted,
removed, and/or inspected.

These three methods also provide the tools needed to perform **list traversal
algorithms**. A list traversal algorithm consists of processing each list item, one at
a time. Figure 11.13 contains an example method, called printList, to output all
of the String items of its list parameter.

Figure 11.13 printList method

```
private void printList( SimpleList list )   {
        list.start();
        while(!list.isOff())   {
            if (list.item()  instanceof  String)   {
                System.out.println( (String) (list.item()) );
            } else {
                System.out.println("item is not of type String");
            }
            list.forth();
        }
    }
```

When printList executes, it begins by positioning the list's iterator at the
front of the list using the following instruction.

```
list.start();
```

The value of the each item of the list is output by the instruction

```
System.out.println( (String)(list.item()) );
```

The final instruction in the loop body advances the iterator to the next item.
Each succeeding loop body repetition causes the subsequent list item to be output
and the iterator to advance to the next item. When the last item is output, the iterator advances off the list and the loop terminates.

The printList method is but one illustration of a list traversal algorithm. In
particular this is a traversal that outputs each item. However, there are many other
algorithms, such as the following:

- A list traversal of a list of AOval objects to change the color of each AOval
  to green
- A list traversal of a list of double values to calculate the square root of each
  item
- A list traversal of a list of ATextField objects to input the value from each
  item

These, and countless other list traversal algorithms, can all be accomplished using the same algorithmic pattern shown in Figure 11.14.

Figure 11.14 List traversal algorithm pattern for `SimpleList`

The following pattern assumes `list` is of type `SimpleList`:

```
list.start();
while ( !list.isOff() )   {
    // Process list.item()
    list.forth();
}
```

As a further illustration of list traversal algorithms, consider the program in Figure 11.15. The `Director` constructor method constructs a horizontal row of `AOval` objects, placing them upon an `A3ButtonWindow`. Each `AOval` is also inserted into a list called `circleList`. (The class to which `circleList` belongs is shown in Figure 11.12.)

Figure 11.15 List traversal algorithm for a list of `AOval`s

```
import java.awt.*;
import aLibrary.*;
public class Director extends A3ButtonHandler {
    private A3ButtonWindow window;
    private ListOfAOval circleList;

    /* postcondition
            window is created
            AND a row of black circles is stored in the circleList
                container
                (These circles span the window horizontally.) */
    public Director()   {
        AOval tempCircle;
        int horizontalPos;
        window = new A3ButtonWindow(this);
        circleList = new ListOfAOval();
        horizontalPos = 5;
        circleList.start();
        while   ( horizontalPos < window.getWidth() )   {
            tempCircle = new AOval(horizontalPos, 100, 10, 10);
            tempCircle.place( window );
            circleList.insert( tempCircle );
            horizontalPos = horizontalPos + 15;
        }
        window.repaint();
    }
```

```
    /* postcondition
           all AOvals within circleList are colored green */
    public void leftAction()    {
        circleList.start();
        while(!circleList.isOff())    {
            circleList.itemAOval().setColor( Color.green );
            circleList.itemAOval().repaint();
            circleList.forth();
        }
    }


    /* postcondition
           all AOvals within circleList are colored blue and
           filled */
    public void midAction()    {
        circleList.start();
        while(!circleList.isOff())    {
            circleList.itemAOval().setToFill();
            circleList.itemAOval().setColor( Color.blue );
            circleList.itemAOval().repaint();
            circleList.forth();
        }
    }


    /* postcondition
           the x coordinate of all AOvals within circleList are
           output */
    public void rightAction()    {
        circleList.start();
        while(!circleList.isOff())    {
            System.out.println( "X coordinate of circle: "
                            + circleList.itemAOval().getX() );
            circleList.forth();
        }
    }
}
```

The leftAction, midAction, and rightAction methods from Figure 11.15 each contain a list traversal algorithm. The leftAction algorithm uses the traversal to assign the color green to every item of circleList. The midAction algorithm assigns each item the color blue and also sets each item to be filled. The rightAction algorithm outputs the horizontal (getX) coordinate of each of the AOval items.

11.7   LINEAR SEARCHING

SimpleList containers can be used for countless purposes. A program used by a Web-based retailer might use a SimpleList to store all customers. A university's student registration information program could incorporate a SimpleList of student records. A program used by a dairy farmer to maintain information about milk production might utilize a SimpleList to store milk production information for many cows.

One algorithm that is commonly used by list programs is called a **search algorithm**. The Web-based retailer may need to *search* for a customer who has just requested the status of a purchase. The Registrar's Office responds to student requests for college transcripts by *searching* for each student's record. In response to a recently illness for some cow, the dairy farmer might *search* for that cow's milk production.

All search algorithms share the need to locate some object or set of objects from within a container. The most common kind of search is to locate a particular object given an identifying characteristic, such as a customer name or a student ID number.

Searches within SimpleList are referred to as **linear searches** because of the linear nature of the container and the way that list traversal algorithms proceed from the front of the list toward the back. In fact an algorithm to search a SimpleList is just a special kind of list traversal algorithm.

Figure 11.16 contains a subclass of SimpleList that adds a new method called contains that has a single parameter of type Object. It performs a linear search of the SimpleList and returns true exactly when the parameter's value is found to be one of the items in the container.

A call to contains initiates a linear search of the list until one of two things occurs:

1. The iterator has been advanced off the list.
2. The item identified by the iterator is the same item as the search object (z).

The loop terminates the first time that either of these conditions is true. Following the loop, the result variable is assigned the proper value (true if and only if the z value has been found). This particular contains method alters the location of the iterator. Both the *postcondition* and the second call to start highlight this fact.

The contains search checks for the presence of an object, but does not attempt to return the item's position or value. The forthTo method from Figure 11.17 is a different search that illustrates how searching can sometimes make use of the iterator. In this case the forthTo method is searching for an AOval with getX and getY coordinates matching its xPos and yPos parameters. When such an item is found within the list, the method returns, leaving the iterator positioned at the item that was found. The client code can now access the item or even remove it.

Figure 11.16 SimpleList extended to include a contains method

```
import aLibrary.*;
public class SearchList extends SimpleList {
    /* postcondition
             this is empty
             AND iterator == 0      */
    public SearchList()  {
        super();
    }

    /* modifies
             iterator
         postcondition
             result == (this list contains z)
             AND  iterator == 0 */
    public boolean contains(Object z)   {
        boolean  result;
        start();
        while ( !isOff()  &&  z != item() )   {
            forth();
        }
        result = (!isOff()  &&  z == item());
        start();
        return result;
    }
}
```

Figure 11.17 AOvalList extended to include a forthTo method

```
import aLibrary.*;
public class SearchListOfAOval extends ListOfAOval  {
    /* postcondition
             this is empty
             AND iterator == 0     */
    public SearchListOfAOval()  {
        super();
    }

    /* modifies
             iterator
         postcondition
             There exists an item with getX & getY coordinates of
                 xPos & yPos
```

```
            IMPLIES itemAOval().getX()==xPos &&
                itemAOval().getY()==yPos;
            No such item exists IMPLIES isOff()==true */
    public void forthTo(int xPos, int yPos)    {
        start();
        while ( !isOff()
                && !(itemAOval().getX()==xPos
                    && itemAOval().getY()==yPos) )    {
            forth();
        }
    }
}
```

The loops from Figures 11.16 and 11.17 make use of conditional evaluation of boolean expressions in a way that is common for list search algorithms. It is important to guard any call to inspector method calls like item or itemOval for times when the iterator might be positioned off the end of the list. This is accomplished by locating the !isOff() test at beginning of the boolean expressions.

11.8 SORTING BY INSERTION

Sometimes it is helpful to maintain lists in a **sorted** fashion. Residential portions of telephone books are sorted by peoples' last names. The index for this textbook is sorted in alphabetic order. Teachers often sort exam scores from highest to lowest.

There are two important ways in which to sort items. An **ascending sort** arranges items from least to greatest, and **descending sorts** arrange items from greatest to least. A list that is sorted via an ascending sort is said to be in **ascending order**, whereas a descending sort produces a list in **descending order**.

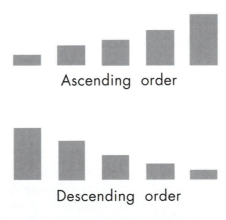

Ascending order

Descending order

One convenient technique for producing a sorted list is accomplished by a different insertion method that ensures every new item is located so as to preserve the desired sort property (either ascending or descending). Figure 11.18 contains a class called AscendingListOfInt that implements sorting in this way.

The key code that keeps the AscendingListOfInt sorted is the loop within the insert method, which is repeated below:

```
start();
while (!isOff() && j > itemInt()) {
    forth();
}
super.insert(new Integer(j));
```

This loop results in a search for the first list item that is greater than or equal to the value to be inserted (j). When such a larger value is found, the loop terminates and inserts j at the resulting iterator position (i.e., j is inserted immediately in front of the larger value). In the case that the loop terminates only when the iterator is off the list, then j is appropriately inserted at the back of the list.

The AscendingListOfInt class also overrides the insert method for parameters of type Object. This is done for two reasons:

1. Overriding insert prohibits this method from inserting non-int data.
2. Overriding insert prohibits this method from violating the sorted property of the list.

An object of type AscendingListOfInt remains sorted because the only method for putting items into the container ensures that this property holds. Other methods that move the position of the iterator or methods to return list information do not alter the order of the items. Even the remove method cannot alter the ascending order of this list.

Figure 11.18 AscendingListOfInt class

```
import aLibrary.*;
/* Invariant
        An AscendingListOfInt contains Integer objects in ascending
        order. */
public class AscendingListOfInt extends SimpleList  {
    /* postcondition
            this is empty
            AND iterator == 0      */
    public AscendingListOfInt()   {
        super();
    }
    /* postcondition
            not isOff   IMPLIES
                result == item immediately following the iterator ;
            AND isOff IMPLIES result == 0   */
    public int itemInt()   {
        return  ((Integer)super.item()).intValue();
    }
```

```
          /*  modifies
                  iterator
              postcondition
                  this list == old this list with j inserted (note that
                      the sorted property from the class invariant is
                      maintained)
                  AND iterator is positioned immediately after newly
                      inserted j */
          public void insert(int j)  {
              start();
              while (!isOff()  &&  j > itemInt())   {
                  forth();
              }
              super.insert(new Integer(j));
          }
          /* modifies
                  iterator
              postcondition
                  z is of type Integer
                      IMPLIES
                          this list == old this list with j.intValue()
                              inserted (note that the class invariant is
                              maintained)
                          AND iterator positioned immediately before
                              newly inserted j
                  AND z is NOT of type Integer  IMPLIES  error message */
          public void insert(Object z)   {
              if (z instanceof Integer)   {
                  insert( ((Integer)z).intValue() );
              } else {
                  System.out.println("ERROR: Attempt to insert
                      non-Integer.");
              }
          }
      }
```

To investigate the behavior of sorting a sequence of numbers, consider the following code:

```
AscendingListOfInt sortList = new AscendingListOfInt();
sortList.insert( 3 );
sortList.insert( 1 );
sortList.insert( 5 );
sortList.insert( 2 );
sortList.insert( 1 );
```

When this code executes, the first call to the insert method occurs on an empty list. Therefore, isOff is immediately true, and the insertion value (3) is inserted as the only item in the list.

j == 3

The second call to insert, namely sortList.insert(1), passes the value 1 as an argument corresponding to parameter j. This call to insert causes the list iterator to be reset to the start of the list and compares the item following the iterator (itemInt()) to parameter j. Since the value of j is 1 and the value of itemInt() is 3, the loop from the insert method never executes its body. The super.insert call inserts j at the iterator position, which is immediately before 3.

j == 1

The third call to insert is sortList.insert(5). This call to insert passes the value 5 for parameter j and causes the list iterator to be reset to the start of the list, as shown below:

j == 5

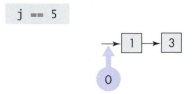

Since itemInt() has a value of 1 at this time, the insert method's *while* loop condition is true. This results in the first execution of the loop body, as pictured below:

j == 5

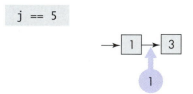

Now itemInt() has a value of 3, and the insert method's *while* loop condition is true again. The resulting second loop body execution produces the following state:

j == 5

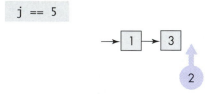

At this time isOff is true, so the loop terminates execution and the value of j is inserted at the iterator position (i.e., at the end of the list).

The fourth call to insert is sortList.insert(2). This call to insert passes the value 2 for parameter j and causes the list iterator to be reset to the start of the list, as shown below:

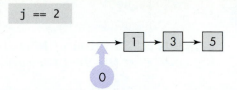

The first loop condition test for this call of insert finds that the value of j (2) is greater than the value of itemInt(), which is 1. Therefore, the loop body is executed once to advance the iterator as shown below:

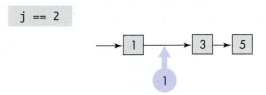

Now the value of j (2) is less than the value of itemInt(), so the loop terminates and j is inserted at this iterator position. The fifth, and final, call to insert resets the iterator to the loop beginning as shown below:

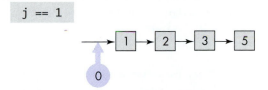

Since the value of j (1) is equal to the value of itemInt(), the loop terminates immediately and j is inserted at this iterator position, as shown below:

This example illustrates how each call to insert performs a traversal of the list to find the proper location for the new value and then inserts the value in its place. The property of sortedness is thereby maintained.

Below is a collection of hints on what to check when examining code that involves the concepts of this chapter.

✓ Type safety is a significant concern for generic containers. To enhance reusability many container classes store `Object` data, or have superclasses that store `Object` data. This leaves it up to the software developer to ensure that container items have the correct type. It is best to use classes that ensure type safety. Otherwise, every instruction that accesses a container item should be examined to be certain that it is type safe.

✓ Wrapper classes are best avoided within client code. When they must be used, care must be taken to avoid attempting to treat a wrapper object interchangeably with its primitive counterpart.

✓ The `item` and `remove` methods for lists should always be examined for the possibility of a call when the iterator is off the list.

✓ When inheriting a list, be careful to scrutinize *all* of the methods of the superclass. Sometimes these methods should be overridden to avoid situations where, if used, they could violate some intended property of the subclass.

✓ Every list traversal algorithm should be checked to ensure that the `forth` method has been called within the loop body. Forgotten `forth`s are a common cause for infinite loops.

✓ Don't forget to test code that manipulates a container to be certain that it works when the container is empty.

✓ Be careful about assuming too much regarding an iterator. Many methods, such as search methods, can disturb the position of an iterator.

ascending order

ascending sort

Bag

Boolean (the wrapper class)

Byte (the wrapper class)

Character (the wrapper class)

container

Container (the awt class)

count (a container method)

descending order

descending sort

Double (the wrapper class)

Float (the wrapper class)

forth (a list method)

generic container

insert (a container method)

Integer (the wrapper class)

isOff (a list method)

item (a container method)

iterator

linear search

list container

list traversal algorithm

Long (the wrapper class)

off the list

remove (a container method)

search algorithm

Short (the wrapper class)

sort

start (a list method)

type safety

wrapper classes

1. Following the execution of each code segment below, indicate how many String items are stored in myBag and the strings these items represent.

a.
```
Bag myBag;
myBag = new Bag();
myBag.insert( "abc" );
myBag.insert( "xyz" );
myBag.insert( "abc" );
```

b.
```
Bag myBag;
myBag = new Bag();
myBag.insert( "abc" );
System.out.println( (String)myBag.item() );
myBag.insert( "xyz" );
myBag.insert( "abc" );
```

c.
```
Bag myBag;
myBag = new Bag();
myBag.insert( "abc" );
myBag.remove();
myBag.insert( "xyz" );
myBag.insert( "abc" );
```

d.
```
Bag myBag;
myBag = new Bag();
myBag.insert( "abc" );
myBag.insert( "xyz" );
myBag.insert( "abc" );
myBag.remove();
```

2. Suppose you are writing a section of code that includes a variable, called viewBag, belonging to the Bag class. Further suppose that that your code has inserted into viewBag a number of AView objects, and nothing else. The next instruction you wish to write is an assignment of one of the viewBag items to a variable, called view. The following attempt is the correct basic idea, but it generates a compiler error.

```
AView view = viewBag.item();
```

a. What is wrong with this instruction?

b. Correct the problem so that the instruction performs the intended task without a compiler error.

c. Show how to enclose this instruction within an *if* instruction that ensures type safety for this assignment.

3. Suppose that `letterBag` is created as follows.

   `Bag letterBag = new Bag();`

   a. Show the code that is needed to insert the character "W" into `letterBag`. (*Hint*: You will need to use a wrapper class.)
   b. Write a single `System.out.println` instruction to output the value of an item from `letterBag`, assuming that all `letterBag` contents are inserted in the same way as you did for part (a).

4. Each of the following examples gives a "BEFORE" picture of the state of a `SimpleList`, named `myList`, just prior to executing the code. You should assume that all list items contain `String` values. Draw the new picture that results after the code executes.

   a. BEFORE

   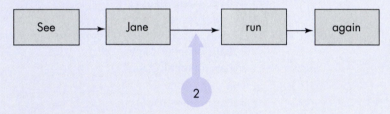

   CODE
   ```
   myList.insert( "and Jim" );
   myList.start();
   ```

   b. BEFORE

   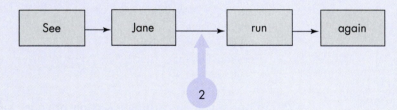

   CODE
   ```
   myList.remove();
   myList.forth();
   myList.insert( "?" );
   myList.start();
   myList.insert( "May I" );
   ```

c. BEFORE

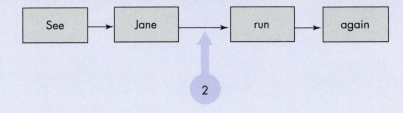

CODE
```
myList.start();
while( !myList.isOff() ) {
    myList.forth();
}
myList.insert( "and again" );
```

5. Complete the code for the body of the following methods that use a parameter(s) of type `SimpleList`.

a.
```
/* precondition
      list.count() > = 2
   postcondition
      list == old list with the first and last items removed */
private void trimEnds( SimpleList list ) {
   // your code goes here.
}
```

b.
```
/* modifies
      destList
   postcondition
      destList is a copy of the content of sourceList */
private void copyList( SimpleList sourceList, SimpleList
   ( destList ) {
   // your code goes here.
}
```

c.
```
/* modifies
      destList
   postcondition
      destList is old destList with every item that is
      somewhere in sourceList removed */
private void removeDups( SimpleList sourceList, SimpleList
   ( destList )
{
   // your code goes here.
}
```

6. Complete the code for the body of the following methods that use a parameter(s) of type ListOfOval (Figure 11.12).

a. ```
/* precondition
      oList.count() > = 3
   postcondition
      result == the color of the third item of oList */
private Color thirdColor(ListOfOval oList) {
   // your code goes here.
}
```

b. ```
/* modifies
      oList
   postcondition
      all items in oList are the same as old oList excepting
      all are colored white. */
private void whiteWash( ListOfOval oList ) {
   // your code goes here.
}
```

c. ```
/* precondition
      oList.count() > = 1
   postcondition
      result == getX() value of oList item that is farthest
      left */
private int leftmostX(ListOfOval oList) {
   // your code goes here.
}
```

d. ```
/* modifies
      oList
   postcondition
      oList contains the same items as old oList, but these
      items are reordered so that the getY values are arranged
      in descending order */
private void sortDescendingOnY( ListOfOval oList ) {
   // your code goes here.
}
```

1. This program permits the user to create and manipulate a night sky as a container. Initially, the program displays a black A3ButtonWindow. Each click on the black window creates a new gray "star" at the position of the user's mouse click. (Note that ARectangles can handle mouseClick events, and getX(), getY() methods applied to a MouseEvent parameter retrieve its position.) Stars are AOvals with a diameter of 2. The three buttons of the window behave as follows.

   LEFT   A click on this button causes the first, third, fifth, seventh, etc. stars to be recolored in white.

   MID   A click on this button causes the second, fourth, sixth, eighth, etc. stars created to be recolored in yellow.

   RIGHT   A click on this button causes the most recently created star to be recolored in red.

2. This program is designed to use an A3ButtonWindow to control the behavior of space ships (gif images). When the program begins the window appears as follows. Thereafter, the buttons behave as explained below:

   LEFT   A click on this button causes the top row of spaceships to all move downward by 2 pixels. In addition, these ships should all be recolored—blue ships become red, red ships become green, green ships become black, and black ships become blue.

   MID   A click on this button affects the ships in the bottom row. It causes the rightmost ship, the ship third from the right, the ship fifth from the right, ... to all move up by 2 pixels.

   RIGHT   A click on this button removes the rightmost space ship from the bottom row

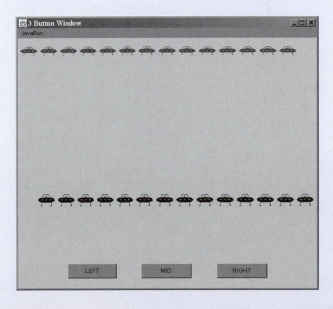

3. Write a program to maintain a list of names with associated telephone numbers. Your user interface should appear like the one below:

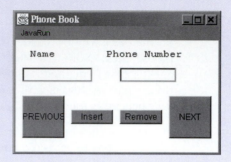

The two ATextFields below "Name" and "Phone Number" display one name and the corresponding phone number from the list. Initially, they are blank, because the list is empty. The four buttons behave as described below.

PREVIOUS   A click on this button causes the "Name" and "Phone Number" fields to be updated to display the previous phone number in the list. If the first number is displayed, then clicking this button has no effect.

NEXT   A click on this button causes the "Name" and "Phone Number" fields to be updated to display the subsequent phone number in the list. If the last number is displayed, then clicking this button causes the fields to turn blank. If the fields are already blank, then clicking this button has no effect.

INSERT   A click on this button causes the value in the "Name" and "Phone Number" field to be inserted into the list immediately *before* the fields that were displayed. Furthermore, fields should again display the item that follows immediately after the newly inserted item. (The expectation is that the user will use PREVIOUS and NEXT to position the display, then type new values into the fields, then click INSERT.)

REMOVE   A click on this button removes the displayed item, and updates the "Name" and "Previous Number" fields to the subsequent item. The fields are updated to blank when the last list item is removed.

4. This program gives the user certain controls over a festive light display. Initially, the program consists of a large dark gray window with small AOvals just inside the window's perimeter. (There should be 40 to 50 AOvals on each side of the window. The AOvals are to be treated as a continuous, circular string of light bulbs so that all the way around the window there are consecutive pairs of yellow AOvals with a blue AOval separating them from adjacent pairs. These lights should be operating as a marquee light moving in the counterclockwise direction. At a rate of five times per second the color of each AOval should be assigned to its counterclockwise neighbor. In addition a large "LIGHT SHOW!" message should blink on and off in the center of the window at a rate of once per second.

In a separate small window are three buttons that behave as described below.

MARQUEE Causes the behavior to revert to the initial program behavior.

REVERSE Causes the AOvals to become pairs of blue AOvals separated by yellow, and the marquee action should be clockwise.

FLASH Causes the entire string to take on a single color and flash from one color to another at a rate of five times per second. All AOvals first become green, then all become red, then all become white, then all become green and the sequence repeats.

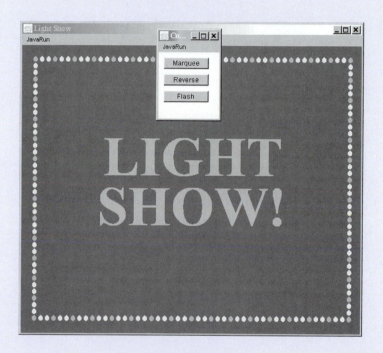

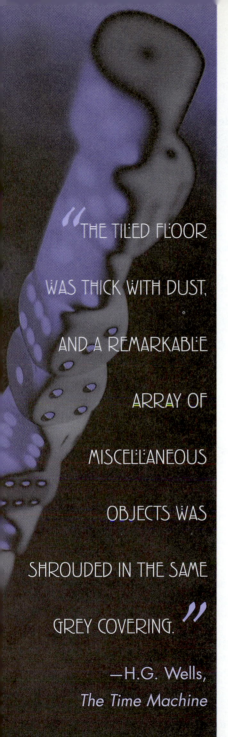

INTRODUCTION TO ARRAYS

OBJECTIVES

- To explore the concept of arrays as direct access containers

- To examine the syntax and semantics of array declaration and instantiation

- To explore the use of index expressions for referencing array items

- To introduce the possibility of index boundary violations

- To examine uses for the length feature for arrays

- To explore the *for* loop as a tool for sequentially processing arrays

- To examine aggregate treatment of arrays in parameter passage, method value return, and assignment instructions, as well as to introduce the Java syntax for an aggregate array expression

- To examine the use of arrays to store tabular information

- To illustrate inherent limitations of arrays

- To examine the selection sort algorithm

- To introduce two-dimensional arrays

Tape recorders are **sequential access** storage devices. As the tape rolls forward, the music (or video) that is stored on the tape is played in the same order it was recorded. The only way to play a song from the middle of a tape is to advance (fast-forward) past the front portion. List containers, like those presented in Chapter 11, also exhibit mandatory sequential access. The only way to reach the middle of a list is to call `forth` multiple times.

Compact disks and DVDs are **direct access devices**. The term "direct access" stems from their ability to skip directly to a particular track without scanning all preceding information. This chapter is all about direct access containers.

12.1 ONE-DIMENSIONAL ARRAYS

Containers, as described in Chapter 11, are receptacles used to store other objects. The most commonly used direct access container is the **array**. Like a compact disk (CD) of music, an array stores a collection of data that is conceptually linear. The music CD is considered linear because musical songs (cuts) are ordered one after another from the first cut to the last. Arrays store objects in the same linear sequence. Figure 12.1 pictures an example array in which all items are `String` objects.

Figure 12.1 An example array of `Strings`

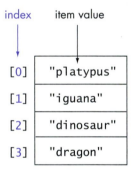

Another similarity between musical CDs and arrays is that they both number their items. The songs of a CD are numbered 1, 2, 3, ..., and the items of an array are numbered 0, 1, 2, ... An array identification number is called an **index** (**indices** when plural) or **subscript**. An index is needed when referencing a particular array item in the same way that a song number is needed to advance directly to a cut on a CD. The Figure 12.1 example depicts an array in which the item with an index of zero (0) is "platypus", and the item with index of two (2) is "dinosaur".

In Java, arrays must be declared just like other variables. Such a declaration of an array may occur as an instance variable or as a local variable. Figure 12.2 shows the syntax needed to specify an array declaration.

An array declaration defines both the name of the array and the type of items that it will contain. For example, the declaration below specifies a private instance variable, called `animals`, that names an array in which every item is a `String`.

```
private String[] animals;
```

Figure 12.2 ArrayDecl description

ArrayDecl (a possible *OneVarDecl*)

Syntax

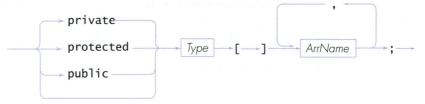

Alternative syntax

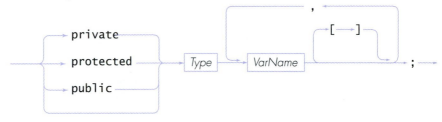

Note

Type and *ArrName* must be *Identifiers*. *Type* must either be a primitive type or it must name a class name that is known within this scope.

Usage

Each *ArrName* from "Syntax," as well as each *ArrName* that is followed by [ ] from "Alternative syntax," refers to an array in which each item must conform to *Type*.

The following line declares a local variable, called ageTable, that is an array of double items.

        double[] ageTable;

Below is a declaration that declares a protected instance variable, rowOfSquares, that will serve as an array of ARectangle items.

        protected ARectangle[] rowOfSquares;

Figure 12.2 also points out an alternative syntax for declaring arrays by placing the square brackets [ ] immediately after the variable name, instead of after the type name. Either notation produces the same result. (However, square brackets must not be located in *both* places.)

Before an array can be used it must be constructed (instantiated) just like any other object. Figure 12.3 describes the Java notation for instantiating an array.

The specific size (number of items) of an array is determined at the time that the array is instantiated. The following instruction instantiates the animals array to contain a total of four items, similar to the picture shown in Figure 12.1.

```
animals = new String[4];
```

Similarly, the instruction below will construct an array of ten items:

```
ageTable = new double[10];
```

Figure 12.3 ArrayConstruction description

ArrayConstruction (a possible *Expression*)

Syntax

Note

integerExpression is an expression of type int.

Semantics

integerExpression is first evaluated. Assuming that the *integerExpression* has a nonnegative value, an array is instantiated to contain this number of items. The items will be indexed from 0 through *integerExpression* − 1. If *integerExpression* is negative, then a run-time exception occurs when this construction executes.

Java always numbers array indices beginning at zero. Therefore, the index range for the ageTable array is 0 through 9. The following instruction constructs an array of one hundred ARectangle items with indices ranging from 0 through 99.

```
rowOfSquares = ARectangle[100];
```

SOFTWARE ENGINEERING TIP

The use of an array always involves three tasks.

- Declare the array (to provide the array name and the type of its items).

- Instantiate the array (to provide the size – number of items).

- Use the array items as though they were variables (using array item reference notation).

Once an array has been declared and instantiated, array items can be treated as though they were variables. The notation that is used to refer to such items is described in Figure 12.4. This array item syntax consists of the name of the array, followed by an integer expression for an index enclosed in square brackets. Therefore, animals[2] references the item from the animals array that has an index of 2. Likewise, ageTable[0] refers to the item of the ageTable array with an index of 0.

To illustrate the complete process of declaring, constructing, and using an array, consider the execution of the following segment of Java code:

```
char[] initials;
int someInt;
initials = new char[6];
initials[2] = 'B';
```

```
initials[0] = 'E';
initials[3] = 'S';
initials[1] = 'M';
initials[4] = 'R';
System.out.println( initials[3] );
someInt = 2;
System.out.println( initials[someInt*2] );
initials[someInt+1] = initials[0];
```

Figure 12.4 ArrayItemReference description

ArrayItemReference (a possible *Variable*)

Syntax

Note

integerExpression is an expression of type `int`.

Semantics

integerExpression is first evaluated. Assuming that the *integerExpression* is a valid index, then *ArrayItemReference* refers to the item within the array named *ArrName* that has an index of *integerExpression*. If *integerExpression* is not valid, then a run-time exception (`ArrayIndexOutOfBoundsException`) occurs.

The first statement in the code segment above declares an array object. This statement specifies that the name of the array is `initials` and that each of its individual items will store a `char` value. Therefore, after the following two statements are executed:

```
char[] initials;
int someInt;
```

the state of execution includes the two variables pictured below. (Notice that `initials` array is `null` at this point in the execution.)

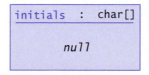 

Executing the instruction below causes the `initials` array to be instantiated with six items (indexed from 0 through 5).

```
initials = new char[6];
```

Following the execution of this instruction, the state of execution changes as shown below:

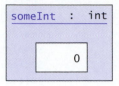

Execution proceeds to a number of assignment instructions that use indices to refer to specific items of the `initials` array. For example, the first assignment instruction is

```
initials[2] = 'B';
```

Following the execution of this instruction, the item with index of 2 is assigned the character `'B'`. The resulting state is shown below:

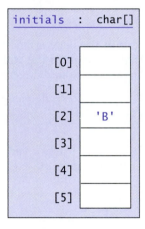
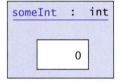

The remainder of the consecutive assignment instructions from this example are as follows.

```
initials[0] = 'E';
initials[3] = 'S';
initials[1] = 'M';
initials[4] = 'R';
```

Following the execution of these instructions, the state of execution has been updated in the following picture:

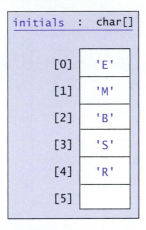
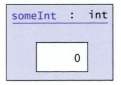

The next instruction executed,

```
System.out.println( initials[3] );
```

causes the value of the array item with an index of 3 to be output. In this case, the character 'S' is output.

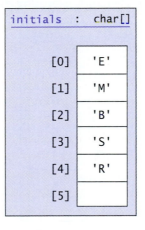
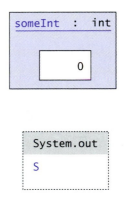

The instruction that follows is

```
someInt = 2;
```

Executing the previous instruction assigns someInt the value 2, as shown below:

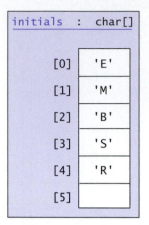

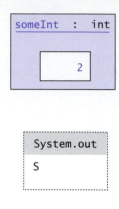

The next instruction to execute is repeated below:

```
System.out.println( initials[someInt*2] );
```

This instruction has a more complicated integer expression for an index. Every array index expression must be evaluated before the item can be identified. In this case, the expression someInt*2 must first be evaluated in order to discover that the necessary index is 4. Therefore, executing this instruction causes 'R' to be output:

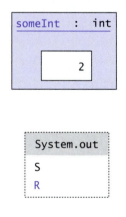

The final instruction in this code segment is as follows.

```
initials[someInt + 1] = initials[0];
```

When this instruction executes, the index expression someInt + 1 is evaluated to the value 3. Therefore, this instruction results in the state pictured below:

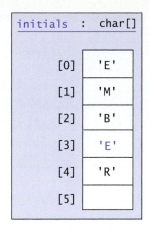
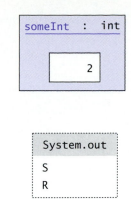

Array items behave like variables of the same type. Since the `initials` array contains items of primitive (`char`) type, these items can be used just like any other `char` variable.

Items that belong to classes (i.e., reference type items) also behave like variables of the same type. For example, the following code declares and instantiates an array of three `AWindow` items:

```
AWindow[] windowPanes;
windowPanes = new AWindow[3];
```

Following the execution of these two instructions, the array contains three items, but none of the items are bound:

```
windowPanes  :  AWindow[]

    [0]    null

    [1]    null

    [2]    null
```

Instructions such as the following are needed in order to construct the content of the individual array items:

```
windowPanes[1] = new AWindow(5, 5, 100, 100);
```

Executing this last instruction alters the state as shown below:

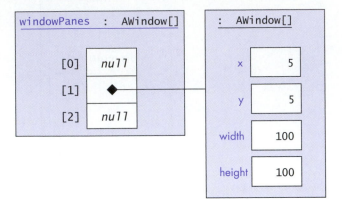

Once the second item of windowPanes has been assigned an AWindow in this manner, that item can be used just like any other AWindow variable. Therefore, the following instructions produce the usual AWindow behavior.

```
windowPanes[1].setLocation(100, 200);
windowPanes[1].repaint();
windowPanes[1].show();
```

12.2   KEEPING INDICES IN BOUNDS

The most common programming error involving arrays is an index that is **out of bounds**. An out-of-bounds index is any index expression that evaluates to an integer that is one of the following:

- less than zero
- greater than the array's maximum possible index

For an array of 25 items, all index expressions must be within the range from 0 through 24. Any other value for an index is invalid (out of bounds) for the array.

When an index is found to be out of bounds, a **boundary violation** has occurred. Boundary violations are detected as run-time exceptions by the Java VM. The resulting error messages from such errors contain information like the following:

```
ArrayIndexOutOfBoundsException
```

Since all arrays begin with a smallest index of zero, a Java program can easily test to ensure that an index isn't too small using code similar to that shown below.

```
if ( indexExpression >= 0 ) {
    CodeUsingIndexExpression
}
```

Java also includes an additional feature to assist in testing array indices from becoming too large. This feature is called `length`. An array reference (array name) can be followed by

```
.length
```

to form an `int` expression returning the number of items in the array. The following instruction uses `length` to ensure that the integer variable `index` is valid for the `initials` array:

```
if ( 0 <= index && index < initials.length ) {
    System.out.println( initials[index] );
}
```

SOFTWARE ENGINEERING TIP

Index boundary violations are quite common in programs involving arrays. Java programmers sometimes find it necessary to use the **length** facility to ensure that an index is within bounds before it is used.

Notationally, `length` behaves like a public read-only (`final`) variable of every array. `length` cannot be directly assigned a value, and it does require a variable declaration.

12.3 SEQUENTIAL PROCESSING WITH FOR LOOPS

Index expressions permit a program to directly access any array item. Sometimes it is convenient to process arrays sequentially from the first item to the last (or last to first).

SOFTWARE ENGINEERING TIP

Arrays are often processed sequentially. However, if *all* array processing is sequential, then a list may be a better container. The inherently sequential nature of lists tends to make some algorithms easier to code.

Java includes another looping instruction that is particularly well suited to the kind of sequential processing required by arrays. The **for instruction** is described in Figure 12.5.

Below is a sample of the use of a *for* loop:

```
for (int k=1; k!=100; k++) {
    System.out.println( k );
}
```

The "Semantics" section of Figure 12.5 describes the behavior of a *for* loop in terms of an equivalent *while* loop. According to this description, the following code should behave like the sample *for* loop:

```
int k=1;
while (k!=100 ) {
    System.out.println( k );
    k++;
}
```

Therefore, this example *for* loop is a counting loop with k as its counter variable. When the loop executes the values from 1 through 99 are output.

Another way to explain the execution of *for* loops is in terms of the key parts of the loops (using names borrowed from Figure 12.5).

SOFTWARE ENGINEERING TIP

The alternative syntax for the *for* instruction omits braces. This should generally be avoided; code modifications tend to be easier if multi-instruction loop bodies are assumed.

- `initInstr` is a single initialization instruction that is executed before the rest of the loop begins.
- `LoopCond` is tested at the top of the loop. If `LoopCond` is true, then the body of the loop is executed, and the process repeats. When `LoopCond` is tested and found to be false, then the loop terminates.
- `statementSequence` is the loop body.
- `progressInstr` is a single instruction that is executed immediately after every loop body repetition.

Figure 12.5 `forInstruction` description

forInstruction (a possible *OneStatement*)

Syntax

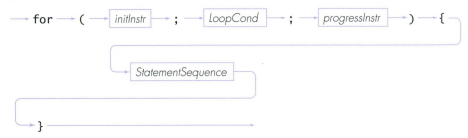

Alternate syntax (when the loop body is a single instruction)

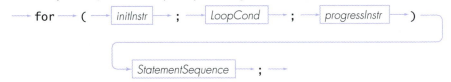

Notes

- *initInstr* is some valid instruction. If this includes a variable declaration, then the variable is local with scope and lifetime restricted to this execution of the *for* instruction.
- *LoopCond* can be any valid boolean-valued expression.
- *progressInstr* is some valid instruction.

Style Notes

The reserved word *for* should be aligned with the "}" symbol that ends the *forInstruction* and all instructions within *InstructionSequence* (i.e., the loop body) should be indented by at least one tab from the *for*. If the parenthesized code cannot be completed on one line, then "{" should be placed on a separate line and aligned with "}".

Semantics

Executing *forInstruction* behaves like the following code.

```
initInstr;
while  ( LoopCond )   {
    StatementSequence;
    progressInstr;
}
```

SOFTWARE ENGINEERING TIP

The default choice for a loop should be the *while* loop, since it works reasonably well for all situations. However, the *for* loop works well for simple counting loops or when the number of loop repetitions is known in advance. When using a *for* instruction, programmers typically use `initInstr` to declare and initialize a counting variable, `progressInstr` to increment the counter, and `LoopCond` to test the counter.

The *for* loop is a good choice for counting loops, because `initInstr` can be used to both declare and initialize a counter variable. Declaring the counter within `initInstr` is a good idea because it localizes the scope and the lifetime of the variable to the execution of the *for* loop. The `progressInstr` is also useful for counting loops as a way to assist the programmer to remember to include the "make-progress" part of the loop body. Often `progressInstr` is used to increment (or decrement) the counter variable.

When a *for* loop is used to process an array sequentially, the loop can either proceed from the first index (0) to the last index (`length - 1`) or from the last to the first. The counter variable is correspondingly incremented or decremented.

Figure 12.6 contains a `Director` that constructs a table of square root values. This program constructs an array of 11 `double` items.

Figure 12.6 Construct and output a table of square roots

```
public class Director  {
    /* postcondition
           (for all j, 0<=j<=10) [ sqrtTable[j] == Math.sqrt(j) ]
           AND all square roots from 0 through 10 have been
               output. */
    public Director()   {
        double[] sqrtTable;
        sqrtTable = new double[11];

        for (int k = 0; k!=sqrtTable.length; k++)   {
            sqrtTable[k] = Math.sqrt(k);
        }
        for (int k = 0; k!=sqrtTable.length; k++)   {
            System.out.println("The square root of " + k + " is "
                + sqrtTable[k]);
        }
    }
    ...
}
```

The first *for* loop assigns the square root of the counter variable (k) to the array item indexed by k. The second *for* loop processes the array from first to last item and outputs the following 11 lines.

```
The square root of 0 is 0.0
The square root of 1 is 1.0
The square root of 2 is 1.4142135623730951
The square root of 3 is 1.7320508075688772
The square root of 4 is 2.0
The square root of 5 is 2.23606797749979
The square root of 6 is 2.449489742783178
The square root of 7 is 2.6457513110645907
The square root of 8 is 2.8284271247461903
The square root of 9 is 3.0
The square root of 10 is 3.1622776601683795
```

The two *for* loops from Figure 12.6 follow a common pattern for sequential array processing. Figure 12.7 explains this pattern.

Figure 12.7 Pattern for sequential loop array processing

The following *for* instruction can be used to sequentially process the array called *arr* from the first item to the last:

```
for (int ndx = 0; ndx!=arr.length; ndx++)   {
    // process arr item indexed by ndx
}
```

This sequential loop array processing is also present in the example shown in Figure 12.8. This program simulates the action of marquee lights.

Figure 12.8 Marquee lights program

```
// Marquee lights program
import java.awt.*;
import aLibrary.*;
public class Director extends A3ButtonHandler {
    private A3ButtonWindow window;
    private AOval[] dots;
    /* postcondition
            window is created
            AND a row of filled circles is assigned to the dots
                array. (These circles span the window horizontally.)
            AND any dot with a multiple of 3 for an index is dark
                gray while all other dots are white.  */
```

```
    public Director()  {
        int xPos = 5;
        dots = new AOval[32];
        window = new A3ButtonWindow( this );
        window.setColor( Color.black );
        for  ( int j=0; j!=32; j++ )    {
            dots[j] = new AOval(xPos, 100, 10, 10);
            if ( j % 3 == 0 )   {
                dots[j].setColor( Color.darkGray );
            } else {
                dots[j].setColor( Color.white );
            }
            dots[j].setToFill();
            dots[j].place( window );
            xPos = xPos + 15;
        }
        window.repaint();
    }

    /*  postcondition
            all dot's old colors are moved to the left by one dot
            AND the rightmost dot gets the old color of the
            leftmost */
    public void leftAction()    {
        Color leftmostDotColor;
        leftmostDotColor = dots[0].getColor();
        for  ( int j=0; j!=31; j++ )    {
            dots[j].setColor( dots[j+1].getColor() );
        }
        dots[31].setColor( leftmostDotColor );
        window.repaint();
    }

    // The methods below do nothing.
    public void midAction()    {
    }

    public void rightAction()    {
    }
}
```

An array of AOval objects called dots plays the role of the light string. The Director constructor method instantiates this array. Next, Director includes a *for* loop to instantiate 32 AOval circles. Each AOval is constructed and assigned to a unique array item by the following instruction.

```
dots[j] = new AOval(xPos, 100, 10, 10);
```

One third of the dots items (i.e., those with an index that is a multiple of 3) are colored dark gray and the others are colored white. All of the dots items are filled by the following instruction.

```
dots[j].setToFill();
```

This instruction calls a method upon a dots item using the same notation that would be used to call the method upon any AOval variable.

The leftAction method from Figure 12.8 contains an algorithm for simulating marquee lighting. Executing this method causes each of the dots items (except the last) to take on the color of its neighbor with next greater index. The following *for* loop accomplishes such recoloring.

```
for ( int j=0; j!=31; j++ ) {
    dots[j].setColor( dots[j+1].color() );
}
```

The repetitions of this loop perform the following work.

dots[0] is assigned the color of dots[1]
dots[1] is assigned the color of dots[2]
dots[2] is assigned the color of dots[3]
. . .
dots[30] is assigned the color of dots[31]

The loop condition for this leftAction *for* loop terminates the loop when j==31, instead of j==32. This is essential to the loop correctness, because the index expression of j+1 (used within the loop body) would result in a bounds violation if j==31.

This process of reassigning colors causes the old color of the first item in the dots array to be replaced in the very first loop repetition. Since the last item needs to be assigned the old color of the first, it must be saved prior to the loop. A variable, called leftmostDotColor, stores this color until it can be assigned to the last dots item.

12.4 TREATING ARRAYS IN AGGREGATE

Previous sections have demonstrated that array items behave like variables. The dots array, declared in Figure 12.8, consists of items of type AOval. Therefore, any item of dots can be assigned a new AOval with an instruction such as

```
dots[3] = new AOval(10, 10, 50, 50);
```

This instruction instantiates an AOval object and assigns it to the dots[3] array item.

Methods can also be applied to array items, such as the following two method calls, which apply the setColor and setToFill methods to the object assigned to the dots[3] array item.

```
dots[3].setColor( Color.orange );
dots[3].setToFill();
```

Furthermore, any array item can be passed as an argument, so long as its type conforms to the corresponding formal parameter type. The following call to the place method illustrates by passing the object assigned to the dots[3] item as an argument:

```
Oval innerOval = new AOval(10, 10, 30, 30);
innerOval.place( dots[3] );
```

As a result of executing these two instructions, innerOval is placed upon the dots[3] object.

For some algorithms this ability to process an array by way of its individual items isn't enough. There needs to be a way to treat an array as a whole. A so-called **aggregate array operation** is one in which the *entire* array behaves as a single entity. One type of aggregate array manipulation in Java is **aggregate array parameter** passage. When an array is passed in aggregate, the whole array is passed via a single parameter. In order to pass an aggregate array, the formal parameter must be declared using the syntax shown in Figure 12.9.

Figure 12.9 aggregateArrayParameter description

----

aggregateArrayParmeter (a possible *Type* for declaring formal parameters)

Syntax

$$\longrightarrow \boxed{Type} \longrightarrow [\longrightarrow] \longrightarrow$$

Notes

Type is a primitive type or a class name known within this scope

Semantics

Any aggregate array of items in which the item type conforms to *Type* is permitted for a parameter of this type.

As an example of aggregate array parameter passage, consider a method, called countOfZeros, which returns the number of zero-valued items from an array of int. Figure 12.10 contains such a method. This method utilizes an aggregate array parameter, named arr, to pass the particular array to be examined.

Within the countOfZeros method, arr is treated like any other array of int. The countOfZeros algorithm consists of a search loop. This search uses length in order to determine the maximum index for its parameter. When countOfZeros is called, arr is an alias for the actual array argument. Therefore, the value of arr.length is the same as the length of the argument array. Such use of length is common in methods with aggregate array parameters, because it permits the same method to be applied to arrays of differing sizes.

Suppose that the countOfZeros method is being used to count the number of students who didn't take an examination, thereby receiving an exam score of zero. The program stores exam scores in an array declared and instantiated as follows:

```
int[] examScores;
examScores = new int[15];
```

Figure 12.10 countOfZeros method

```
/*  postcondition
            result == the count of arr items that == 0 */
    public int countOfZeros( int[] arr )   {
        int result;
        result = 0;
        for ( int k=0; k!=arr.length; k++ )   {
            if (arr[k] == 0)  {
                result++;
            }
        }
        return result;
    }
```

The countOfZeros method has a single parameter, called arr. This parameter will accept an aggregate array of int items. An appropriate call to countOfZeros is shown below:

```
int studentsAbsent = countOfZeros(examScores);
```

This call passes examScores in aggregate, and within the code of the countOfZeros method this array is given the arr alias. This permits countOfZeros access to every part of the examScores array.

As a second example of passing an aggregate array as a parameter, consider the initializeTo method from Figure 12.11. This method illustrates that the content of an array can be altered when it is passed in aggregate.

Figure 12.11 initializeTo method

```
/*  postcondition
            for all j from 0 through arr.length, arr[j] == d */
    public void initializeTo( double[] arr, double d )   {
        for ( int k=0; k!=arr.length; k++ )   {
            arr[k] = d;
        }
    }
```

When initializeTo is called, it is passed an array of double values. The second parameter for initializeTo is named d and is of type double. Executing intializeTo causes every cell of its array parameter to be assigned the value of d. To illustrate, suppose the following three statements are executed:

```
double[] measureTable;
measureTable = new double[ 1000 ];
initializeTo( measureTable, Math.PI );
```

The result of these three instructions is to instantiate an array of one thousand cells, called measureTable, and to assign the value of the mathematical constant PI to every cell of this array.

A second kind of aggregate array operation supported by Java is an aggregate assignment. This allows one array to be assigned to another in a single assignment instruction. For example, if someDoubleArray is declared

```
double[] someDoubleArray;
```

then the following assignment instruction is permissible:

```
someDoubleArray = measureTable;
```

This is called an **aggregate assignment** because it assigns an entire array, as opposed to a single item of the array. Aggregate assignments behave like any other assignment of one reference object to another. The variable name on the left of the assignment is bound to the same array as the expression on the right. For the example above, someDoubleArray becomes an alias for the measureTable array. The array expression being bound must have an item type that conforms to the item type of the array name being assigned.

A third way that arrays can behave in aggregate is when they are returned as the value of a method. Figure 12.12 illustrates with a method called arrayCopy.

Figure 12.12 arrayCopy method for double arrays

```
/* postcondition
        result.length == source.length
        AND (for 0 <= j < source.length)
            [result[j] == source[j]]  */
private int[] arrayCopy( int[] source )  {
    int[] result;
    result = new int[ source.length ];
    for (int ndx = 0;  ndx != source.length;  ndx++)    {
        result[ndx] = source[ndx];
    }
    return result;
}
```

When called, the arrayCopy method returns a complete copy of its source parameter. For example, the following statement causes someIntArray to be assigned an array that has the same length and item content as examScores, but is a separate array:

```
int[] someIntArray = arrayCopy( examScores );
```

Executing the body of arrayCopy begins by declaring a local array called result. The result array is instantiated to have the same length of the source parameter. A *for* loop copies the value of every item from source into result. The return instruction at the end of arrayCopy returns the aggregate result array.

Java supports an **aggregate array expression** notation as yet another way to treat arrays in aggregate. This notation is particularly useful for initializing arrays. Figure 12.13 describes the syntax and semantics of aggregate array expressions.

Figure 12.13 aggregateArrayExpression description

---

aggregateArrayExpression (a possible *Expression*)

Syntax

Note

- *itemExpression* is a valid expression of the same type as the array item

Semantics

An aggregate array is instantiated with length equal to the number of *itemExpressions*. Each item of this array has the value of the corresponding *itemExpression*.

Each aggregate array expression instantiates a new array. For example, the following array picture is repeated from the beginning of the chapter:

[0]	"platypus"
[1]	"iguana"
[2]	"dinosaur"
[3]	"dragon"

This array can be declared as follows:

```
private String[] animals;
```

The assignment instruction below makes use of an aggregate array expression to construct the content of the array as pictured above.

```
animals = { "platypus", "iguana", "dinosaur", "dragon" };
```

An aggregate array expression determines both the length of the array and the value of every array item. The assignment above instantiates an array of length four with particular `String` constants for item values.

Below is a second use of an aggregate array expression that creates an array of two items, each bound to separate `AOval` objects:

```
AOval[] circles = { new AOval(0,0,5,5), new AOval(10,10,8,8) };
```

12.5 TABLES

A **table**, sometimes called a **look-up table**, is a convenient way to store and retrieve information. Chemists use the Periodic Table to record facts regarding the elements, such as their atomic weight. Tax tables are often used to determine personal income tax. An international banker performs monetary conversions using tables of exchange rates.

Arrays provide an efficient tool for implementing many tables. Figure 12.14 contains a table of the number of days in a month during a non–leap year.

Figure 12.14 Table of the length of each month in a non–leap year

Month	Num	Length
January	1	31
February	2	28
March	3	31
April	4	30
May	5	31
June	6	30
July	7	31
August	8	31
September	9	30
October	10	31
November	11	30
December	12	31

Figure 12.15 shows a Java method that returns the number of days in a month, without the use of an array. This daysPerMonth method assumes that its parameter is the month number and uses a collection of *if* instructions to select the correct number of days.

A more efficient implementation of daysPerMonth is possible by using an array. Figure 12.16 contains a monthLength array constant and the associated daysPerMonth method. A call to this new method returns the appropriate monthLength item. Note that the array index is m - 1, because humans number months from 1, whereas arrays have a lowest index of zero.

Using an array look-up to replace a system of *if* instructions is referred to as **table-driven code**. Figure 12.17 contains a second example of table-driven code. This table shows the gravitational force of the planets relative to earth.

Figure 12.15 daysPerMonth method using *if* instructions

```
/* precondition
       1 <= m    and    m <= 12
   postcondition
       result == number of days in month m (for a non-leap year)
   note
       the version in Figure 12.16 is more efficient. */
private int daysPerMonth( int m )    {
    if(m==1 || m==3 || m==5 || m==7 || m==8 || m==10 || m==12) {
        return 31;
    } else if (m==4 || m==6 || m==9 || m==11)    {
        return 30;
    } else {
        return 28;
    }
}
```

Figure 12.16 daysPerMonth method using an array

Array (table) Declaration
```
private final int[] monthLength
        = {31, 28, 31, 30, 31, 30, 31, 31, 30, 31, 30, 31};
```

Method Using the Table
```
/* precondition
       1 <= m   <= 12
   postcondition
       result == number of days in month m (for a non-leap year) */
private int daysPerMonth( int m )    {
    return monthLength[m-1];
}
```

Figure 12.17 Table of relative gravity for planets

Planet	Gravity
Mercury	0.37
Venus	0.78
Earth	1.00
Mars	0.38
Jupiter	2.64
Saturn	1.16
Uranus	1.07
Neptune	1.21
Pluto	0.05

The information from this gravity table can be stored in the `relativeGravity` array declared and initialized below:

```
private final double[] relativeGravity
    = {0.37, 0.78, 1.00, 0.38, 2.64, 1.16, 1.07, 1.21, 0.05};
```

To make this array easier to use and the program easier to read, the following constant declarations are included:

```
private final int mercury = 0;
private final int venus = 1;
private final int earth = 2;
private final int mars = 3;
private final int jupiter = 4;
private final int saturn = 5;
private final int uranus = 6;
private final int neptune = 7;
private final int pluto = 8;
```

Given these constants, looking up the relative gravity of Saturn is expressed as

```
relativeGravity[ saturn ];
```

SOFTWARE ENGINEERING TIP

Sometimes table keys don't map naturally onto integer indices. At such times **int** constants with meaningful names can greatly improve code readability.

12.6 ARRAYS OF OBJECTS

Arrays are containers of items. Sometimes the array items have a primitive type, in which case the array is really a container of primitive values. At other times the array items belong to a class, and in these cases the array consists of an array of objects. Like any variable that belongs to a class, the items from an array of objects really store bindings.

For example, suppose a class called `Name` is used to declare arrays. The `Name` class is shown in Figure 12.18.

Figure 12.18 Name class

```
public class Name    {
    public String first;
    public String last;

    public Name( String fs, String ls )    {
        first = fs;
        last = ls;
    }
}
```

```
public Name deepClone()    {
    Name result;
    result = new Name( new String(first), new String(last) );
    return result;
}
}
```

Below is a declaration of two arrays with items that belong to the `Name` class.

```
private Name[] politicians, presidents;
```

These arrays can be instantiated as follows.

```
politicians = new Name[3];
presidents = new Name[3];
```

Following the execution of the two instructions above, all array items are null. The pictures below illustrate:

politicians

[0]	null
[1]	null
[2]	null

presidents

null	[0]
null	[1]
null	[2]

Next, assume that these instructions assign values to items of the `politicians` array:

```
politicians[0] = new Name( "George", "Washington" );
politicians[1] = new Name( "Abraham", "Lincoln" );
```

Following the execution of these assignments, the first two items from politicians are updated as shown below.

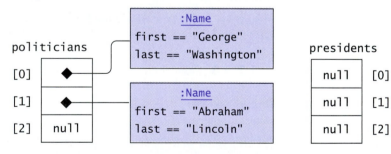

Executing the following three instructions assigns the first two items from politicians to the corresponding items of presidents.

```
presidents[0] = politicians[0];
presidents[1] = politicians[1];
```

Since the items of these arrays are objects, these assignments copy the bindings, resulting in the following:

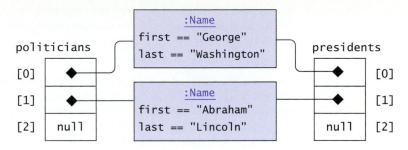

The result of these last assignments leaves both arrays bound to the same two objects. For many applications such multiple bindings are acceptable. However, there are other times when the program needs to ensure that each array contains separate objects.

To make such a complete copy it is necessary to construct a second set of item objects. The deepClone method from the Name class provides a facility for returning a complete copy of any Name object. This method can be used as follows to create and assign item copies.

```
presidents[0] = politicians[0].deepClone();
presidents[1] = politicians[1].deepClone();
```

The picture below shows the structure following the execution of these last two instructions.

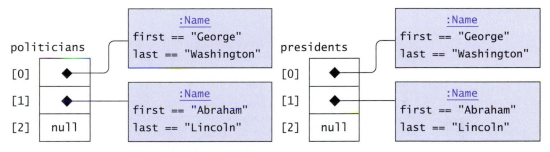

The result of executing the two assignment instructions is that both the items of the presidents array are bound to their own copies of objects with the same content as those objects bound to the politicians array.

12.7 ARRAYS AND OBJECTS

In many ways arrays act as though they are like other objects. These similarities between arrays and other objects are summarized by the following.

1. Every array name must be declared before it is used.
2. Arrays have a value of null until they are bound to an array of conforming type.
3. Arrays must be instantiated using the new operator.
4. An aggregate assignment performs a binding copy.
5. A method may return an aggregate array.

6. An equality test (==) between one aggregate array and another checks for identity equality (i.e. for == to be true, both operands must bind to the same array).

7. Aggregate arrays implicitly conform to `Object`.

This last similarity deserves special comment. Since an array conforms to `Object`, every aggregate array can be stored in a generic container that is implemented as a container of `Object`. For example, `SimpleList` (presented in the previous chapter) is a container in which each item must be of type `Object`. This container of `Object` design permits the objects belonging to any class or aggregate array objects to be inserted.

All the similarities between arrays and objects tend to suggest that arrays are really objects with a special notation for indexing. However, there are two ways in which Java treats arrays unlike full-fledged objects:

1. It is impossible to inherit an array.

2. `Object` methods cannot be overridden by any array.

There are many places where the Java syntax requires a *type* be specified:

Variable declarations require a type.

        private *type* varName;

Formal parameters must specify their type.

        public void methodName(*type* parameterName) { ... }

The type must precede the name of each method.

        public *type* methodName() { ... }

In all of these example cases an aggregate array may be used as a valid type. However, it is *not* possible to use an aggregate array in an inheritance specification.

        public class className extends *type* { ... } //aggregate array invalid

The second way in which arrays are unlike other objects deserves comment. All Java classes implicitly inherit `Object`. Among other things, inheriting `Object` gives each class the ability to override `Object` methods such as `toString` and `equals`. Aggregate arrays share this property in the sense of conforming to `Object`. However, an array is incapable of overriding inherited methods such as `toString` and `equals`.

12.8   SORTING—THE SELECTION SORT

In Chapter 11, **sorting algorithms** were introduced. A sorting algorithm rearranges the items within a container to place them in some particular order. The most common kinds of sorting algorithms perform either an ascending sort (ordering items from smallest to largest) or a descending sort (ordering items from largest to smallest).

There are many different algorithms for sorting arrays. One of the most common is the **straight selection sort**, informally called a **selection sort**. The name "selection" comes from the fact that this algorithm repeatedly *selects* items in sorted order.

People commonly utilize selection sorts in their everyday activities. For example, a selection sort to order the batting averages of nine professional baseball players in ascending order would proceed as follows:

1. Select the smallest batting average and place it first in the new order, removing it from further consideration in the sorting process.
2. Select the next smallest batting average and place it second, removing it from further consideration in the sorting process.
3. Select the next smallest batting average and place it third, removing it from further consideration in the sorting process.

   ...

8. Select the next smallest batting average and place it eighth, removing it from further consideration in the sorting process.
9. Place the remaining batting average ninth.

The shell of this algorithm can be expressed shown in Figure 12.19. (Note that all comments in this algorithm are informal statements requiring further implementation.)

Figure 12.19 Step 1 of the design of the selection sort algorithm

```
/* Loop initialization code goes here */
while  ( /* the array is not yet sorted */ )    {
        /* Select the smallest value from those remaining */
        /* Move the smallest value into "next" position */
}
```

Suppose that the name of the array to be sorted in ascending order is arr. Then the first time the body of this loop executes, it selects a value for arr[0]. The second loop body execution selects the value for arr[1]. Each subsequent loop body repetition selects another item and assigns it to the arr item with next greater index.

As the sorting algorithm proceeds, the array remains partitioned into two parts: the front part of the array (with lower indices) contains the sorted values that have already been selected, and the rear part of the array contains the unsorted values that have not yet been selected. Figure12.20 pictures this situation.

Figure 12.21 shows how an int variable, called lastSorted, can be used to maintain the index of the last item that was selected and assigned.

One effective way to identify a selected array item is to store the index of the selected item in an int variable. Using a variable called selectedIndex, the selection sort algorithm can be refined as shown in Figure 12.22.

Figure 12.20 The state of the arr array in the midst of selection sort

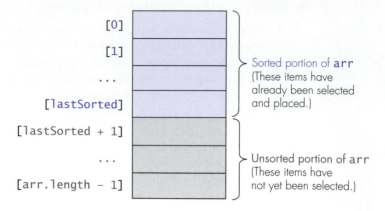

Figure 12.21 Step 2 of the design of the selection sort algorithm

```
int lastSorted = -1;
while ( lastSorted != arr.length - 1 )   {
    /* Select the smallest value from those remaining */
    lastSorted++;
    /* Move the smallest value into the lastSorted position */
}
```

Figure 12.22 Step 3 of the design of the selection sort algorithm

```
int selectedIndex;
int lastSorted = -1;
while ( lastSorted != arr.length-1 )   {
    /* Assign the index of the smallest value from those remaining to
       selectedIndex */
    lastSorted++;
    /* Swap arr[selectedIndex] and arr[lastSorted] */
}
```

The portion of the selection sort algorithm that selects the smallest valued item begins by assuming that arr[lastSorted + 1] is smallest, then checks all subsequent arr items to find the smallest. This search for the smallest value is accomplished by the following code:

```
selectedIndex = lastSorted + 1;
for (int k = lastSorted + 2; k<arr.length; k++) {
    if (arr[k] < arr[selectedIndex]) {
        selectedIndex = k;
    }
}
```

Plugging this code and the swap code into the algorithm shell results in the completed selection sort code shown in Figure 12.23. This method assumes that the array items are of type double.

Figure 12.23 The complete selection sort method

```
/*  postcondition
        arr is the same as old arr with item values permuted
        AND  for all j [0<=j<arr.length-1] [ arr[j] <= arr[j+1]] */
public void selectionSort( double[] arr )   {
    int selectedIndex;
    double selectedValue;
    int lastSorted = -1;
    while  ( lastSorted != arr.length-1 )   {
        selectedIndex = lastSorted+1;
        for (int k = lastSorted+2; k<arr.length; k++)   {
            if (arr[k] < arr[selectedIndex])   {
                selectedIndex = k;
            }
        }
        lastSorted++;
        /* swap arr[selectedIndex] with arr[lastSorted] */
        selectedValue = arr[selectedIndex];
        arr[selectedIndex] = arr[lastSorted];
        arr[lastSorted] = selectedValue;
    }
}
```

The behavior of the selection sort algorithm can be observed by tracing the execution of selectionSort for specific array content. Figure 12.24 contains such a trace. This picture progresses left to right. The leftmost column depicts the array and lastSorted value just before executing the body of the selectionSort *while* loop for the first time. The state of execution just prior to each subsequent repetition of the *while* loop body is shown in the next column. Arrows indicate swapped array items.

Figure 12.24 Execution trace of selectionSort

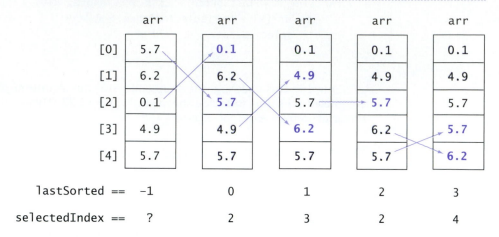

12.9 TWO-DIMENSIONAL ARRAYS

The arrays examined thus far are called **one-dimensional arrays**. As demonstrated, a one-dimensional array is a linear sequence of items. Java also supports arrays of greater dimension, because each array item can be any object, including another array. For example, a **two-dimensional array** is an array in which each array item is a separate one-dimensional array. Figure 12.25 shows a picture of the one-dimensional arrays in comparison to two-dimensional arrays.

Figure 12.25 One-dimensional and two-dimensional arrays

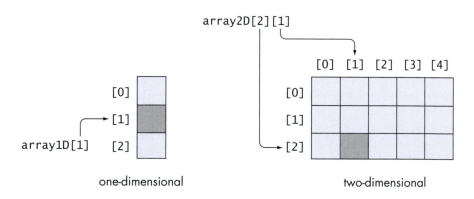

Two-dimensional arrays can be thought of as having rows and columns. Each item is in one row and one column of the array. Therefore, two indices are required. Figure 12.26 shows that the syntax for declaring a two-dimensional array uses two sets of square brackets, signifying the two indices for each item.

Figure 12.26 ArrayDec2D description

ArrayDec2D (a possible *OneVarDecl*)
Syntax

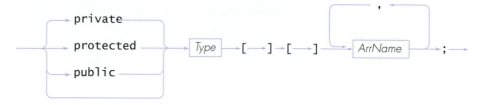

Alternative syntax

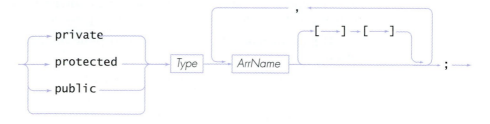

Note

Type and *ArrName* must be *Identifiers*. *Type* must either be a primitive type or it must name a class name that is known within this scope.

Usage

Each *ArrName* from "Syntax," as well as each *VarName* that is followed by [ ] from "Alternative syntax," refers to a two-dimensional array in which each item must conform to *Type*.

As an example, consider a two-dimensional array for storing a table of mileage for highway travel between cities. Figure 12.27 diagrams such a table.

Figure 12.27 Table of mileage between four cities

	Chicago	Los Angeles	Miami	New York
Chicago	0	2095	1360	840
Los Angeles	2095	0	2713	2915
Miami	1360	2713	0	1330
New York	840	2915	1330	0

The information from this mileage table can be stored in a two-dimensional `mileage` array using the following code.

```
private final int chicago = 0;
private final int los_angeles = 1;
private final int miami = 2;
private final int new_york = 3;
private int mileage[][] = {        {0, 2095, 1360, 840},
                                   {2095, 0, 2713, 2915},
                                   {1360, 2713, 0, 1330},
                                   {840, 2915, 1330, 0}        };
```

The declaration of `mileage` demonstrates that Java extends the aggregate array notation to allow an aggregate to contain aggregates. Each row of the two-dimensional array corresponds to one of the inner aggregate array expressions (shown on separate lines). The inner array expressions are separated by commas and enclosed in braces to form the two-dimensional array expression.

The instruction below can be used to print the mileage from Chicago to Miami:

```
System.out.println( mileage[chicago][miami] );
```

As shown above, the notation used for identifying individual items of a two-dimensional array requires an index for the row of the item and an index for the column. The row index for `chicago` is 0 and the column index for `miami` is 2.

As a second example of two-dimensional arrays, consider the picture of a checkerboard below. A checkerboard consists of eight rows and eight columns of squares that alternate from red to black. This particular checkerboard contains a white checker in the second row and seventh column. Figure 12.28 is a `Director` class to construct this image.

The checkerboard program from Figure 12.28 illustrates several characteristics that are common to programs that utilize two-dimensional arrays. The two-dimensional array to store the checkerboard is declared with the following line:

```
private ARectangle[][] checkerboard;
```

Figure 12.28 Program to draw a checkerboard

```
import aLibrary.*;
import java.awt.*;
public class Director {
    private ARectangle[][] checkerboard;
    private AWindow window;
    private AOval whitePiece;

    public Director()  {
        window = new AWindow(100, 100, 160, 160);
        checkerboard = new ARectangle[8][8];
        for (int row=0; row!=checkerboard.length; row++)  {
            for (int col=0; col!=checkerboard[0].length; col++)  {
                checkerboard[row][col] = new ARectangle(col*20,
                    row*20, 20, 20);
                checkerboard[row][col].setToFill();
                if ((row+col) % 2 == 0)  {
                    checkerboard[row][col].setColor( Color.black );
                } else {
                    checkerboard[row][col].setColor( Color.red );
                }
                checkerboard[row][col].place(window);
            }
        }
        whitePiece = new AOval(2, 2, 16, 16);
        whitePiece.setColor( Color.white );
        whitePiece.setToFill();
        whitePiece.place( checkerboard[1][6] );
        window.repaint();
    }
}
```

To instantiate a two-dimensional array as a full grid requires specifying both the number of rows and the number of columns. The following instruction instantiates checkerboard to have eight rows and eight columns (each indexed from 0 through 7):

```
checkerboard = new ARectangle[8][8];
```

The items of two-dimensional arrays require two consecutive index expressions—a row index and a column index. Two-dimensional array items, like one-dimensional array items, can be used like variables of the same type. The following instruction assigns an ARectangle object to an array item:

```
checkerboard[row][col] = new ARectangle(col*20, row*20, 20, 20);
```

Similarly, the instruction below places an item from checkerboard on the window:

```
checkerboard[row][col].place(window);
```

Placing the white checker piece onto the square in the second row and seventh column is performed by the following instruction:

```
whitePiece.place( checkerboard[1][6] );
```

The checkerboard program also includes an instance of a common pattern for processing all of the items of an array. This pattern is explained in Figure 12.29.

Figure 12.29 Two-dimensional array processing pattern

Two-dimensional Array Processing Pattern

Processing every item in a two-dimensional array (arr), proceeding row by row and column by column within each row, is accomplished by the following pattern:

```
for   (int r=0; r!=arr.length; r++)    {
    for (int c=0; c!=arr.length[0].length; c++)   {
        // process item arr[r][c]
    }
}
```

An application of this pattern requires that the arr array must be instantiated with all rows of equal length.

In Java two-dimensional arrays are actually a one-dimensional array of items that are one-dimensional arrays. Therefore, the notation checkerboard.length refers to the number of rows in the checkerboard. The number of columns can be found by accessing the length attribute of any of the rows, such as checkerboard[0].length.

While two-dimensional arrays often have rows of equal length, this is not required in Java. Each row can be instantiated separately and assigned to the row item, thereby creating different lengths for different rows.

Java also permits more than two dimensions in an array. A **multidimensional array** is any array of dimension two or greater. The same notations that are used in two-dimensional arrays are extended to dimensions of three and more.

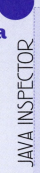

Below is a collection of hints on what to check when examining code that involves the concepts of this chapter.

✓ Array index out of bounds exceptions are arguably the most common difficulty in array processing. Each index expression should be considered as a potential run-time error.

✓ Java arrays always begin with an index of zero. When an array is instantiated with a length of *n*, the largest valid index is *n* – 1. Index expressions need special attention to ensure that the 0*th* item isn't forgotten.

✓ When the type of array items belong to classes, the items are bound to objects. These bindings are like variables. Instantiating such arrays does not instantiate the individual items. You should check to ensure that the items are instantiated separately.

✓ Arrays have many of the properties of classes. However, arrays lack many polymorphic properties because they cannot be inherited, nor can they override Object methods. In a few cases a different type of container may be required to circumvent these restrictions.

✓ If an array is accessed only via sequential algorithms, then perhaps a list would be a better container choice.

TERMINOLOGY

aggregate array expression

aggregate array operation

aggregate array parameters

aggregate assignment

array

boundary violation

direct access device

for instruction

index (indices)

length (of an array)

look-up table

multidimensional array

one-dimensional arrays

out of bounds

selection sort (straight selection)

sequential access

sorting algorithm

subscript

table

table-driven code

two-dimensional arrays

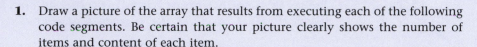

1. Draw a picture of the array that results from executing each of the following code segments. Be certain that your picture clearly shows the number of items and content of each item.

   a. ```
String[] message;
message = new String[6];
message[1] = "Write home.";
message[3] = "Send money.";
message[5] = "I cannot tell a lie.";
message[3] = "Please retransmit";
```

   b. ```
double[] number;
number = new double[4];
number[0] = 1.2;
number[1] = 3.4;
number[2] = 5.6;
number[3] = 7.8;
number[0] = number[3];
number[2] = number[1] + number[3];
```

   c. ```
int[] distance;
distance = new int[6];
distance[0] = 4;
distance[1] = 3;
distance[2] = 2;
distance[3] = 1;
distance[4] = distance[distance[1]];
distance[5] = 2 + distance[distance[3]-1] + distance[1+1]
```

   d. ```
AOval[] elipse;
elipse = new AOval[4];
elipse[0] = new AOval(0, 0, 10, 10);
elipse[1] = new AOval(1, 1, 21, 21);
elipse[2] = new AOval(2, 2, 32, 32);
elipse[3] = elipse[2];
elipse[1].setColor( Color,green );
elipse[3].setSize(43, 43);
elipse[1].setLocation( elipse[0].getX(), elipse[3].getX() );
```

2. Draw a picture of the array that results from executing each of the following code segments. Be certain that your picture clearly shows the number of items and content of each item.

   a. ```
double[] number;
number = new double[5];
for (int j = 0; j != 5; j++) {
   number[j] = (j+1) * 3;
}
```
```

b.
```
int[] money;
money = new int[8];
for (int k = 1; k != 7; k++) {
   money[k-1] = k * k;
}
```

c.
```
int[] pizza;
pizza = new int[8];
for (int k = 0; k != 8; k++) {
   pizza[k] = k;
}
for (int j = 1; j != 8; j++) {
   pizza[j-1] = pizza[j];
}
```

d.
```
int[] inventory;
inventory = new int[8];
for (int k = 0; k != 8; k++) {
   inventory[k] = k;
}
for (int j = 6; j != 0; j--) {
   inventory[j-1] = inventory[j];
}
```

e.
```
int[] box;
box = new int[8];
for (int k = 0; k != box.length; k++) {
   box[k] = k;
}
for (int j = box.length-2; j != 0; j--) {
   box[j] = box[j]*box[j];
}
```

f.
```
int[] canoe, kayak;
canoe = new int[5];
kayak = new int[5];
for (int k = 0; k != canoe.length; k++) {
   canoe[k] = k*2;
   kayak[k] = canoe[k] + 1;
}
for (int j = 0; j != 3; j++) {
   canoe[j] = kayak[j]+ canoe[j+1];
}
```

3. Show the output that results from executing each of the following segments of code.

a.
```
double[] dog, cat;
dog = new double[8];
cat = new double[8];
for (int j = 0; j != 8; j++) {
```

```
        dog[j] = j;
    }
    for (int j = 0; j != 8; j++) {
        cat[j] = dog[j];
    }
    for (int j = 0; j != 8; j++) {
        cat[j] = j*10;
    }
    for (int j = 0; j != 8; j++) {
        System.out.println( dog[j] );
        System.out.println( cat[j] );
    }
```

b.
```
double[] tree, shrub;
tree = new double[5];
for (int j = 0; j != 5; j++) {
    tree[j] = j;
}
shrub = tree;
for (int j = 0; j != 5; j++) {
    shrub[j] = j*10;
}
for (int j = 0; j != 5; j++) {
    System.out.println( tree[j] );
    System.out.println( shrub[j] );
}
```

c.
```
ARectangle[] frontFace, backFace;
frontFace = new ARectangle[3];
for (int k = 0; k != 3; k++) {
    frontFace[k] = new ARectangle(0, 0, k*20, k*10);
}
backFace = new ARectangle[3];
for (int k = 0; k != 3; k++) {
    backFace[k] = frontFace[k];
}
for (int k = 0; k != 3; k++) {
    backFace[k].scale(1, 2);
}
for (int k = 0; k != 3; k++) {
    System.out.println( frontFace[k].getHeight() );
    System.out.println( backFace[k].getHeight() );
}
```

4. Draw a picture of the array that results from executing each of the following code segments. Be certain that your picture clearly shows the number of items and content of each item.

   a. `double[] number = { 1.05, 2.05, 3.05, 4.05, 5.05 };`
   b. `char[] initial = { 'w', 'x', 'y', 'z' };`

c. `String[] color = { "red", "green", "blue" };`

d.
```
AWindow[] pane = { new AWindow(0, 0, 50, 50),
                   new AWindow(100, 100, 60, 60),
                   new AWindow(200, 200, 70, 70)   };
```

5. Show all of the code needed for a table lookup to perform the same task as the following *if* instructions.

a.
```
/* precondition
      0 <= c and c <= 4 */
private int monetaryValue( int c ) {
   if (c==0) {
      return 1;
   } else if (c==1) {
      return 5;
   } else if (c==2) {
      return 10;
   } else if (c==3) {
      return 25;
   } else {
      return 100;
   }
}
```

b.
```
/* precondition
      2 <= m and m <= 10 */
private int mysteryValue( int m ) {
   if (m==2 || m==3 || m==5 || m==7) {
      return 100;
   } else if (m==4 || m==6 || m==8) {
      return 200;
   } else {
      result = 500;
   }
}
```

6. Complete each of the following method bodies so that each method follows the specifications from the precondition, postcondition, and modifies clauses.

a.
```
/* modifies
      names
   postcondition
      all items in names are assigned the letter 'R' */
private void makeAllRs( char[] names ) {
   // your code goes here.
}
```

b.
```
/* precondition
      arr.length > = 2
   modifies
      arr[0], arr[1]
   postcondition
      the values in arr[0] and arr[1] are swapped from their old
      values */
private Color swapFirstTwo( double[] arr ) {
   // your code goes here.
}
```

c.
```
/* precondition
      dArray.length > = 1
   postcondition
      result is the largest double value of any item in dArray
*/
private double biggestValue( double[] dArray ) {
   // your code goes here.
}
```

d.
```
/* precondition
      dArray.length > = 1
   postcondition
      result is the index of the largest-valued item in dArray
*/
private int biggestIndex( double[] dArray ) {
   // your code goes here.
}
```

e.
```
/* precondition
      target.length == dest.length
   modifies
      target
   postcondition
      the item values in target are reversed in order from dest
*/
private void copyReversed( char[] dest, char[] target ) {
   // your code goes here.
}
```

PROGRAMMING EXERCISES

1. Write a program to analyze user messages. Your program should display an ATextField in which the user types a message. When the user strikes the return key on the ATextField, a set of 26 histogram bars are displayed across the bottom of the window. Each bar represents the number of times the corresponding alphabetic letter occurs in the user's message. The most frequently occurring letter should be 150 pixels high and all others proportional to their occurrence count relative to the maximum. Below is a picture of a typical analysis.

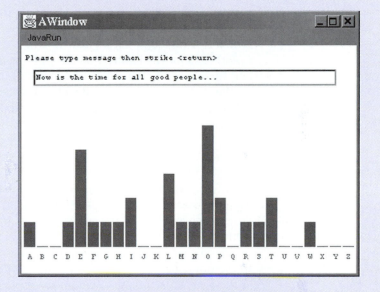

2. Write a program to score a bowling game. The initial GUI of the program should appear as shown below. The user enters the appropriate scores in the ATextField cells and then click the "Score the game" button. The program responds by completing the scores and filling in a frame-by-frame running total.

BEFORE SCORING:

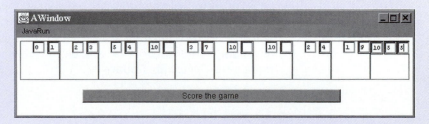

AFTER SCORING:

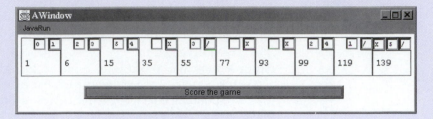

Here is a brief summary of bowling scoring. Ten frames make up a single bowling game. (Each frame in this program is represented by the larger square.) The first nine frames are alike. At the beginning of each frame ten bowling pins are reset on the alley and the bowler throws a first ball. The number of pins downed on this first ball is always placed in the leftmost ATextField for the frame. If all ten pins are downed, this is called a "strike" and the bowler is finished for the frame. If fewer than ten pins are downed on the first ball, then a second ball is thrown at the remaining pins and the number of pins downed by the second ball is recorded in the right ATextField for the frame. If all the pins are downed after the second ball, this is called a "spare." The tenth frame begins the same with all ten pins reset and the number of pins downed by the first ball recorded in the left ATextField. If the bowler gets a strike on the first ball of the tenth frame, then the pins are reset and a second ball is thrown. If there was no strike, then the user throws a normal second ball at the remaining pins. The number of pins downed by the second ball in the tenth frame is placed in the center ATextField. If the bowler gets either a strike on the first ball or a spare on the second ball, he/she is given a third roll. If all pins were downed after the second ball, then they are again reset; otherwise, the third ball is thrown at the pins left standing. The number of pins rolled on the third ball of the tenth frame is recorded in the rightmost ATextField.

Scoring a bowling game is accumulated left to right. If there are no strikes or spares, then a frame's score is the total of the number of pins downed by both balls thrown in the frame added to the score from the previous frame. If the frame is a spare, then the score for the frame is 10 plus the next ball thrown after the spare added to the score from the previous frame. If a strike is thrown, then the score is 10 plus the total pins downed on the next *two* balls added to the score from the previous frame.

For some extra effort you might want to substitute a "/" in place of any score that constitutes a spare and "X" in the roll for a strike. (In all but the tenth frame, the strike "X" should be placed in the right ATextField of the frame.) See the example above.

3. Write a program that uses the GUI pictured below. It consists of a red dot upon a two-dimensional (3 by 4) grid of squares, along with four buttons. Clicking any of the buttons causes the dot to move to the next grid cell in the direction indicated. The dot cannot move off the grid, so some button clicks must be ignored. Be certain to use a two-dimensional array of ARectangle in your solution.

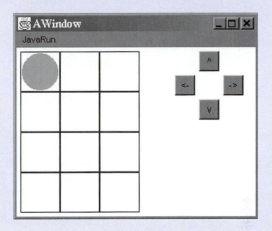

4. Write a program that draws a grid of ATextField objects in five rows and three columns, like the picture below. This grid is to be treated like a ledger in which each ATextField stores a single real number. When the Total Rows button is clicked, the program responds by subtotaling across every row, leaving the sum subtotals in ALabels to the right of the grid. Similarly, a button click to Total Columns causes the five columns to be subtotaled. You must use a two-dimensional array of ATextField for the grid and loops to perform the algorithms.

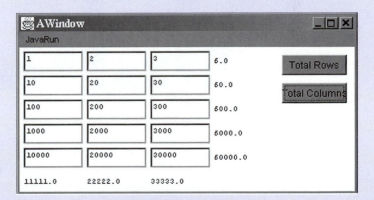

5. This program should construct an array of ten bars. (Each bar is 40 units wide and 1 unit tall. Ten units separate consecutive bars.) Store the bars in an array and display them on a window

Clicking the "Update one bar" button causes one bar to change height. The particular bar to resize is supplied by the user in the Bar Number field. (The bars are numbered from the left, beginning with the numeral 1.) The new height for the selected bar comes from the New Height field.

A click of the New Bars button causes all of the previous bars to be destroyed and replaced by an evenly spaced row of bars. The height of these new bars is 1 pixel, and the Bar Count field gives the number of new bars. The width of each bar should be 400 divided by the number of bars, and the space between bars is 25% of a bar's width. You will want to create a new array, using the same array name, after first removing all of the items from the old array.

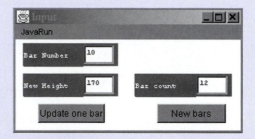

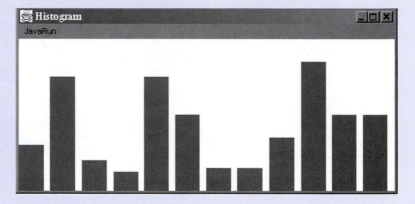

6. Cryptography (i.e., the science of how to send secret messages) has long been an important area of study within computer science. For this program you will use a simple translation table to encode a message. The user interface for this program is shown as follows.

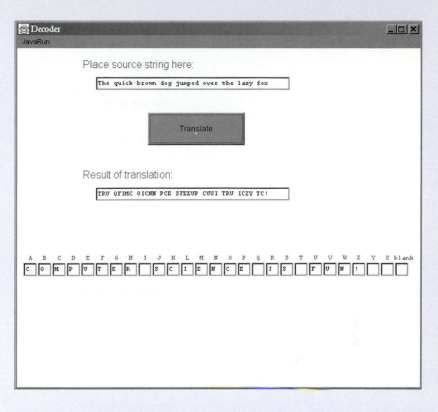

The user is expected to type a message string into the top text field and to define the translation mappings via the bottom row of text fields. When the "Translate" button is clicked, your program must display the correct decoded form of the message in the text field just below the button. This translation must proceed as follows:

- The decoded message will contain the same number of characters as the source.
- Every alphabetic character will be replaced by the leftmost character from the corresponding translation field box, assuming that that the field is not the empty string. (that is, if the user has placed a "+" in the box below "H", then every occurrence of "H" or of "h" in the source string will be replaced by "+" in the translated string.)
- Every alphabetic letter in the source string that has a corresponding text field containing an empty string remains unaltered in the translated string.
- Every blank character in the source string is replaced by the first character from the string in the text field beneath "blank". (Just as in the alphabetic translation, if the blank text field contains an empty string, blanks should remain unaltered.)
- All other characters (i.e., nonalphabetic and nonblank) remain unchanged in the decoding process.

CHAPTER 13

FILE INPUT AND OUTPUT

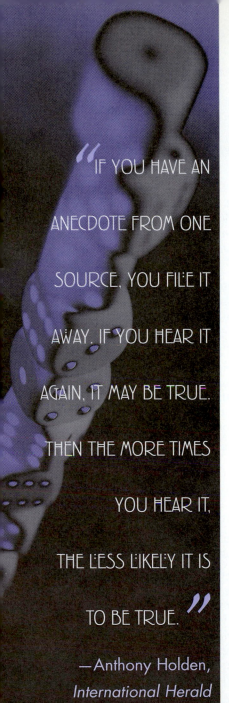

"IF YOU HAVE AN ANECDOTE FROM ONE SOURCE, YOU FILE IT AWAY. IF YOU HEAR IT AGAIN, IT MAY BE TRUE. THEN THE MORE TIMES YOU HEAR IT, THE LESS LIKELY IT IS TO BE TRUE."

—Anthony Holden, *International Herald Tribune*, June 9, 1979

OBJECTIVES

- To introduce the concept of a file system and the associated use of files and directories

- To examine the way that files are named with both relative and absolute file names

- To examine the `File` class as a way to manage files and file systems programmatically

- To introduce the exception handling mechanisms needed to perform I/O in Java

- To explore the Java concepts of streams, readers, and writers, and the way such objects are used to read from and write to files

- To suggest a general-purpose algorithm for file input and another for file output

- To explore binary file I/O using `DataInputStream` and `DataOutputStream`

- To examine the concept of an end of file condition and the many different ways in which it is detected

- To explore text file I/O using `PrintWriter` and `BufferedStream`

- To introduce terminal-style file I/O using `System.in` and `System.out`

- To explore persistent object implementation using `ObjectInputStream` and `ObjectOutputStream`

- To introduce the use of `JFileChooser` as a means to allow the user to specify file names

Programs store and manipulate data. Sometimes the program's data is of primitive type, and sometimes it consists of objects belonging to one or more classes. Sometimes data is referenced by a variable, and sometimes it is part of a container of data. Sometimes the data is publicly accessible, and sometimes its scope is more restricted.

There is one important property of all of the program data examined thus far—such data is transient in the sense that, when the program completes execution, all of this program data is lost. The lifetime of some data, such as local variables and formal parameters, can even end long before the program terminates.

This transient nature of program data leads to questions regarding the potential need for more permanent forms of data storage. For example, an insurance company is likely to have many programs to manipulate its client data. There might be one program to enter a new client, another to generate notices for premium invoices, and a third to process an insurance claim. Certainly, client data must be retained from the time that any of these programs execute until the next executes.

13.1 FILES

The need to retain data between program executions is supported by something called a **file**. Files are categorized as **persistent**, rather than transient, because the data of the file *persists* even when programs are not executing.

If you've ever written and executed a Java application, then you have used at least two files. A Java program typically consists of many source code files. A `Director` class is generally stored as a file called *Director.java*. Some type of text editor program is used to create the *Director.java* file. When the *Director.java* program is compiled, a second bytecode file, called *Director.class*, is produced. This *Director.class* file is used by the Java VM during program execution. In other words, the *Director.java* file is shared by the text editor and the Java compiler, while the *Director.class* file is shared by the Java compiler and the Java VM.

Another difference between program variables and files is in the physical devices where they are stored. The data referenced by program variables and parameters are stored within computer memory (sometimes called the "main memory" or "RAM") of the computer. The transient nature of this kind of data is underscored by the fact that turning off the power to most computers causes main memory to be erased.

Files are retained by different devices than main memory. Hard disks, floppy disks, compact disks, various forms of computer tapes, and DVDs are all capable of storing files. The name **secondary storage** is commonly used to refer to the type of storage used for files, and the devices that manipulate secondary storage are called **secondary storage devices**. Since data stored in secondary storage must be persistent, secondary storage devices *do not* automatically erase their content when power to the computer is lost.

Computer systems use **file systems** to organize all of secondary storage. Modern file systems organize their storage using (1) files and (2) directories. The file is the basic unit of secondary storage. Data must first be collected into a file before it can be stored within secondary storage. A **directory** is a mechanism for cataloging. A collection of files can be grouped together into a single directory. Sometimes directories, and possibly other files, are grouped together into larger directories.

Many computer systems refer to directories as **folders** because of the similarity between a computer directory and a file folder. Just as printed documents can be grouped together in file folders, computer files can be grouped together in computer folders.

Figure 13.1 pictures a small segment of a typical file system. Each rectangle in this picture depicts a separate file or directory. The rectangles with folder icons are directories, and those without the icon are files.

Figure 13.1 Example file system

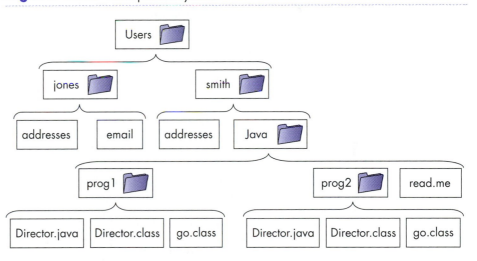

The root of the file system shown in Figure 13.1 is a directory named *Users*. The *Users* directory contains two other directories, namely *jones* and *smith*. The *jones* directory consists of two files: one called *addresses* and one called *email*. The *smith* directory contains one file, called *addresses*, and one directory called *Java*.

Figure 13.1 also illustrates that each file and each directory has its own name. These **file names** and **directory names** follow a syntax that is defined by the particular file system. In general, these names can include alphabetic letters and periods. It is also possible for two files and or directories to share the same name so long as they are not within the same immediate directory.

The file system provides two different ways to identify a particular file. The first technique uses a **path name**. The complete path name for a file is formed by joining all of the containing directories (from most distant to immediate) followed by the file name. Each directory or file name is separated from adjacent names using a separator symbol ("/" for Unix and Apple file systems and "\" for Windows file system). The path name for the *read.me* file would be as follows for a Unix or Apple file system:

```
/Users/smith/Java/read.me
```

The path name for this same file in a Windows file system is as follows:

```
\Users\smith\Java\read.me
```

The first symbol in each of these names is a file separator to signify that the path name begins with the master directory for the entire device.

The second way to identify a file uses a **current directory** (also called a **working directory**). Many programs keep track of such a working directory, and it is generally possible to change the working directory from one folder to another. For example, Unix shells and DOS both use the **cd command** to allow the user to specify a new current directory.

The purpose of a current directory is to simplify the identification of files. When a current directory is established, a file can be identified by a **relative path name** that consists of the substring of the complete path name that omits the names up to and including the current directory. For example, the complete path name for the *go.class* file that is within prog2 is given below:

```
/Users/smith/Java/prog2/go.class   (in Unix/Apple notation)
```

or

```
\Users\smith\Java\prog2\go.class   (in Windows notation)
```

However, if the current directory is set to the *prog2* folder, then the following relative path name will uniquely identify the same file:

```
go.class
```

Notice that complete path names begin with a file separator symbol and relative path names omit this character.

It is common for a Java Virtual Machine and the Java compiler to treat the directory of the class that initiates program execution (such as directory containing *go.class*) as its current directory. This explains why import declarations are unnecessary in situations where all class files are grouped together in a common directory, and the CLASSPATH variable is properly set. (See Chapter 15 for a discussion of the CLASSPATH system variable.)

13.2 THE JAVA FILE CLASS

Java includes many file-related classes within a library package called *java.io*. Some of these classes are used to build objects to extract data from files and some are used to place data within files. Still another of the classes from the *java.io* package is designed to provide Java programs with a mechanism for interacting with the file system. This class is called `File`. Figure 13.2 contains a class diagram for some of the most commonly used methods of the `File` class.

Figure 13.2 File class diagram

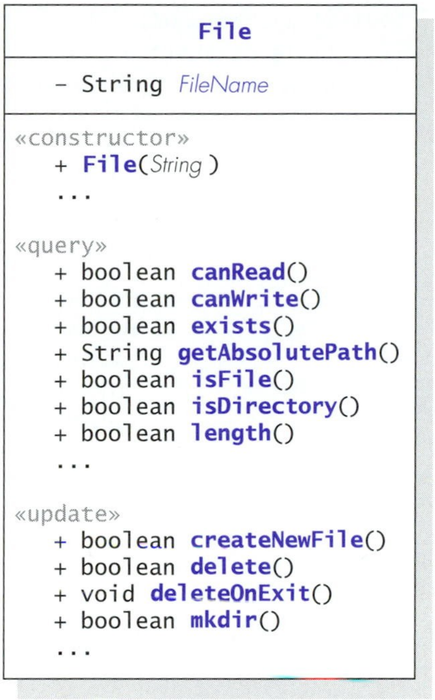

```
┌─────────────────────────────────────────┐
│                  File                   │
├─────────────────────────────────────────┤
│   - String FileName                     │
├─────────────────────────────────────────┤
│  «constructor»                          │
│      + File(String )                    │
│      . . .                              │
│                                         │
│  «query»                                │
│      + boolean canRead()                │
│      + boolean canWrite()               │
│      + boolean exists()                 │
│      + String getAbsolutePath()         │
│      + boolean isFile()                 │
│      + boolean isDirectory()            │
│      + boolean length()                 │
│      . . .                              │
│                                         │
│  «update»                               │
│      + boolean createNewFile()          │
│      + boolean delete()                 │
│      + void deleteOnExit()              │
│      + boolean mkdir()                  │
│      . . .                              │
└─────────────────────────────────────────┘
```

Using the standard `File` class it is possible to check for the existence of a file and print an appropriate message with the following segment of code:

```
// Note that the code below requires exception handling (see
// Section 13.3)

File file = new File( "EXAMPLE" );
if ( !file.exists() ) {
    System.out.println( "No file or directory with a relative path"
    + "name of EXAMPLE exists." );
} else if (file.isFile()) {
    System.out.println( "A file with name EXAMPLE exists." );
} else if (file.isDirectory()) {
    System.out.println( "A directory with name EXAMPLE exists." );
}
```

The code above demonstrates how an object of type `File` can be used to examine a file system by checking for the existence of a file (`exists`) and by checking to see whether the relative path name represents a file (`isFile`) or a directory (`isDirectory`). It is also possible to use `File` to ascertain the complete path name (by calling `getAbsolutePath`) or to check a file's size (by calling `length`).

To illustrate how a `File` object can be utilized to create a new file, consider the following code:

```
// Note that the code below requires exception handling
// (see Section 13.3)
File file = new File( "myFile.fil" );
boolean operationOK;
if ( !file.exists() ) {
    operationOK = file.createNewFile();
} else {
    System.out.println( "A file/directory with name myFile.fil
exists." );
}
```

SOFTWARE ENGINEERING TIP

When manipulating the file system from a program, it is best to take care regarding the unexpected cases. For example, don't attempt to create a new file without first checking to see if one already exits. Don't attempt to delete a file unless it is known to be a file and not a directory. Don't attempt to make a new directory without first checking for a previous file or directory of the same name. Fortunately, the Java File class provides many methods to test for these unexpected conditions.

When the file variable is instantiated, it is associated with the relative name of *myFile.fil*. If a file with this name already exists, then the *else* clause executes, displaying a suitable message. If no file named *myFile.fil* already exists, then the *then* clause will execute. The resulting call to `createNewFile` in the above example performs two functions. This method attempts to create a new file with the given name. Secondly, the `createNewFile` method returns a true or false, indicating whether or not such a creation was properly performed.

Figure 13.3 summarizes a class specification for the most widely used of the `File` class members.

Figure 13.3 File class specifications

File Class Specifications

Invariant
A `File` object
- represents the file with the name given by *FileName*. (This name can either be a complete path name or a name relative to the current directory used by the Java VM.)

Constructor Method
public **File** (String s)

> *postcondition*
> A new `File` object is created and, if possible, associated with a file named s.
> AND *FileName* == s (either a complete path name or a relative name)

Query Methods
public boolean **canRead**( )

> *postcondition*
> result == true if and only if the file exists and it is permissible for the program to read from this file

```
public boolean canWrite( )
```

postcondition
result == true if and only if the file exists and it is permissible for the program to write to this file

```
public boolean exists( )
```

postcondition
result == true if and only if the file or directory identified by *FileName* already exists

```
public boolean getAbsolutePath( )
```

postcondition
result == the complete path name associated with *FileName* (even if the file doesn't exist)

```
public boolean isFile( )
```

postcondition
result == true if and only if a file identified by *FileName* already exists

```
public boolean isDirectory( )
```

postcondition
result == true if and only if a directory identified by *FileName* already exists

```
public int length( )
```

postcondition
(exists() IMPLIES result == the number of bytes occupied by the file/ directory)
AND (NOT exists() IMPLIES result == 0)

Update Methods

```
public boolean createNewFile( )
```

postcondition
A new, empty file called *FileName* was created. (Note that any existing file with the same name was lost.)
AND result == the file creation was properly performed

```
public boolean delete( )
```

precondition
exists()

postcondition
The file identified by *FileName* has been deleted from the file system.
AND result == the deletion was properly performed

```
public void deleteOnExit( )
```

precondition
isFile()

postcondition
At the time that the currently executing program terminates, the file identified by *FileName* will be deleted from the file system

```
public boolean mkdir( )
```
precondition
NOT exists()

postcondition
An empty directory identified by *FileName* has been constructed.
AND result == the directory creation was properly performed

```
public void setToReadOnly( )
```
precondition
isFile()

postcondition
The file identified by *FileName* has permissions that prohibit writing new values into the file.

13.3 I/O EXCEPTIONS

There are many things that can go wrong when a program accesses files or the file system. For example, file systems generally enforce security restrictions that protect files and directories from unwanted access. These security systems may prohibit file access to certain programs.

Java incorporates a mechanism, known as **exception handling**, to manage run-time errors that are detected by the Java VM, including those that result from illegal file usage. The term exception refers to a run-time failure. It said that the program **throws** an exception when it encounters a run-time error that is too severe to continue normally. For example, a file security violation within a program results in an exception. Similarly, when a program attempts to create a new file on a hard disk that is already full, an exception is thrown.

The creators of Java felt that most of the exceptions associated with files are so severe that they are categorized as **checked exceptions**. Any checked exception forces programs to include special code to account for such possibilities. The preferred way to deal with checked exceptions is to include exception handling code and, in Java, this requires the use of a **try instruction**. Figure 13.4 contains a description of the *try* instruction.

A *try* instruction is a Java statement that has a body, much the way a method has a body. When the *try* statement executes, its body executes. If no exceptions are thrown during the execution of the *try*'s body, then the *catch* clauses are ignored, and execution proceeds as though there were no *try* instruction.

Every Java exception has some type, and if an exception is thrown within a *try* body and if that exception has a type matching one of the *catch* clauses, then the remainder of the *try* body is skipped and the matching *catch* clause is executed.

The type of exceptions that can occur while using methods from the file-related classes all belong to the IOException type. Therefore, the particular form of *try* instruction that is often used for file manipulation is shown in Figure 13.5.

Figure 13.4 tryStatement description

tryStatement (a possible *OneStatement*)

Syntax

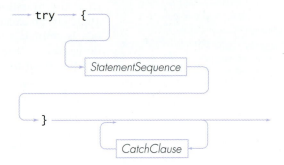

CatchClause

Syntax

Semantics

When a *try* is executed, its *StatementSequence* is executed. If an exception matching the *ExceptionType* of one of the *catch* clauses is thrown while executing the *try*, then the matching *catch* clause is executed and the remainder of the *try* instruction is aborted.

Note

ExceptionType is an identifier that names a valid Java exception.

Style notes

1. The body of the *try* instruction should be indented.
2. The *catch* clauses should be left aligned with their corresponding *try* and their bodies should be indented

Figure 13.5 Form of the *try* instruction needed for file-related methods

```
try  {
    // Code with potential to throw exceptions goes here.
}
catch ( IOException e)  {
    // Code to handle the exception goes here.
}
```

SOFTWARE ENGINEERING TIP

The entire collection of related code that would be impacted by an exception should be collected together within a **try** instruction body. For file-related code this usually means that all of the code for a single algorithm performed upon the same file should be kept together.

SOFTWARE ENGINEERING TIP

Catch clauses should display an error message to notify the user that something has gone wrong.

When writing programs to manipulate files, it is best to put the entire collection of instructions associated with one file within a single *try* instruction. This kind of grouping ensures that when an exception is thrown that the remainder of the file access is aborted. Typically, an exception thrown by the file-related methods is nonrecoverable. Therefore, the exception handling code of the *catch* clause can do little more than print an error message.

Figure 13.6 contains a complete `Director` class designed to attempt a new file creation and report on the outcome. This class includes an import declaration of *java.io* in order to import both the `File` class and the `IOException` class.

Figure 13.6 Director class to attempt to create a new file

```
import java.io.*;
public class Director  {
    public Director()   {
        try{
            File  file;
            boolean createOK;
            file = new File( "example.txt" );
            if ( file.exists() )   {
                if ( file.isDirectory() )   {
                    System.out.println( file.getAbsolutePath()
                            + " is a directory.  No file created.");
                } else {
                    boolean deleteOK = file.delete();
                    if ( deleteOK )   {
                       System.out.println("Existing file deleted.");
                       createOK = file.createNewFile();
                       if ( createOK )   {
                          System.out.println("File created. ");
                       } else {
                          System.out.println( "Unable to create
                             file " + file.getAbsolutePath() );
                       }
                    } else {
                       System.out.println( "Unable to delete file "
                                          + file.getAbsolutePath() );
                    }
                }
```

```
        } else {  // file doesn't exist
            createOK = file.createNewFile();
            if ( createOK )    {
                System.out.println("File created. ");
            } else {
                System.out.println( "Unable to create file "
                                      + file.getAbsolutePath() );
            }
        }
    }
    catch (IOException e)    {
        System.out.println( "I/O error occured");
    }
  }
}
```

The code to create a new file from Figure 13.6 is nested within a *try* instruction. If an IOException is thrown at any time during the execution of the Director method, then the remainder of the method is aborted and the *catch* clause prints an error message

If this program executes without an exception being thrown, then it first instantiates a File object for a file with the relative path name of *example.txt*. The outer *if* instruction tests to see if this file/directory already exists or not. In the event that exits() returns true, the program proceeds to check whether the existing entity is a file or a directory. If it is a directory, a message is output without attempting to replace this with a file. If, however, it is a file that already exists, then that file is first deleted and a new file created. The boolean value returned by these delete and create operations are assigned, respectively, to the deleteOK and createOK variables. These variables are used to print an appropriate message. If the file doesn't exist in the first place, then a new file is created and an appropriate message displayed.

13.4 INPUT AND OUTPUT

Computer scientists use the term **I/O** (short for **Input/Output**) to refer to the transfer of data between a program and some external device, such as a secondary storage device. The operation of sending data *to* a device is called **writing**, and the data are the program **output**. The operation of retrieving data *from* a device is called **reading**, and the data are the program **input**.

The File class includes methods for creating new files and deleting existing files. However, a File object alone is incapable of reading from or writing to a file. Fortunately, the *java.io* package includes a rich collection of different classes to support I/O. Different classes provide for different ways for programs to organize and retrieve data. Various classes accommodate the differences between the various I/O devices.

The notion of a **stream** is fundamental to Java I/O. Java programs do not communicate directly with external devices. Instead, a program creates a stream object to connect a program to some device. Each stream functions like a conduit that establishes a path for the data to flow between the program and the I/O device. Figure 13.7 illustrates this connection by showing an executing program with an input stream to serve as a conduit for reading data from a file and an output stream to serve as a conduit for writing data to a file

Figure 13.7 Using streams with readers and writers

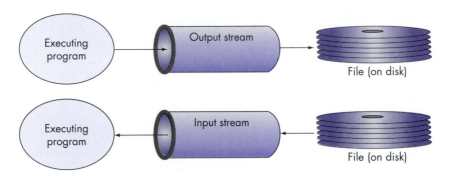

In this book **sequential files** are examined. An essential characteristic of every sequential file is that data be processed from the beginning. An input stream will supply the data from the file in precisely the order in which that data is stored, starting with the first data item. An output stream causes data to be written from the file's beginning and in the order that write methods are executed.

Java supports several different kinds of streams for different purposes. Figure 13.8 diagrams some of the most commonly used Java stream classes. This figure also includes arrows to depict the inheritance relations among these classes.

The stream classes shown in Figure 13.8 are subdivided into two categories, those that are used for input and those that are used for output. The FileInputStream and FileOutputStream classes are not particularly useful by themselves, since these kinds of streams provide for data flow only in the form of bytes. The DataInputStream and DataOutputStream are more useful, since they provide methods for reading and writing data of any primitive data type, as well as String data. The ObjectInputStream and ObjectOutputStream classes include methods for reading and writing whole objects. Section 13.5 discusses DataInputStream and DataOutputStream, while Section 13.7 examines ObjectInputStream and ObjectOutputStream.

Before exploring the particulars of each of these streams, it is instructive to explore the basic algorithms employed by programs that perform I/O. Figure 13.9a contains a basic algorithm for reading from a file.

This algorithm shows that files must be **opened** before it is possible to read from them. Opening a file for input consists of associating a file from the file system with the appropriate input stream object(s). Opening a file generally positions the file data so that it is read from the beginning of the file. The Java stream objects include constructor methods that are used to open files.

Figure 13.8 Inheritance relations for selected stream classes

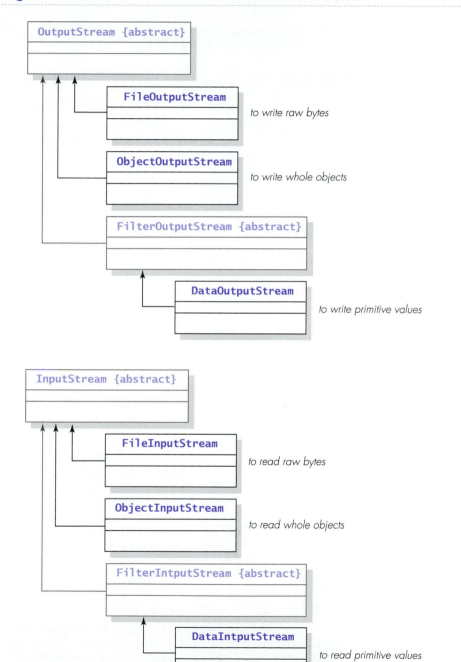

Figure 13.9a General algorithm for reading from a file

1. Open the file for input, instantiating associated stream objects.
2. Call read methods to retrieve the stream's content.
3. Close the file/stream.

SOFTWARE ENGINEERING TIP

Streams are closed automatically when the program completes with or without a call to a **close** method. However, it is still best to explicitly call **close** for two reasons:

1. An explicit **close** makes it clear when the programmer expects to be finished performing I/O.
2. Once a file is closed it is possible to reopen the file .

After a program is finished reading from a file it is wise to close the file. Most streams include a parameterless **close** method for this purpose.

The basic algorithm for writing to a file is similar to the reading algorithm. Figure 13.9b contains the writing algorithm.

Figure 13.9b General algorithm for writing to a file

1. Open the file for output, instantiating associated stream objects.
2. Call read methods to write data into the stream.
3. Flush the stream.
4. Close the file/stream.

The additional requirement of the writing algorithm is shown in Step 3, Flush the stream. This step is usually accomplished by calling a parameterless **flush** method upon the appropriate output stream. Flushing is done to ensure that all data has reached the output file and none is left in the stream conduit.

SOFTWARE ENGINEERING TIP

Before opening a file for output, it is best to check whether or not a file with the same name already exists. For most Java streams, opening a new output stream deletes any earlier file with the same name.

Another difference between input and output algorithms is the behavior of their open operations. When a file is opened for input, it is expected that the file already exists. The stream for the newly opened input file begins to supply the first data that is stored within the file. When a file is opened for output, it is because the program intends to place data into a file. For all but some specialized streams, the program will place *all* of the data into the file. Therefore, the process of opening a file for output typically creates a new file. Even if the file already exists, opening an output stream on a file should be expected to create a new file.

The stream class constructors in Java are designed in a curious way. Two of the *java.io* streams, namely FileInputStream and FileOutputStream, can be connected directly to a file. Few other *java.io* stream classes include the proper constructor methods to allow the program to specify a file name or to use a File object. This unique property of FileInputStream and FileOutputStream gives these two classes special importance. Figure 13.10 contains a class diagram and class specifications for the FileInputStream class.

Figure 13.10 FileInputStream class diagram and specifications

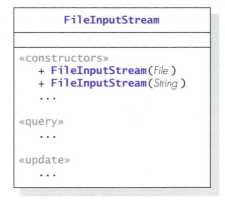

FileInputStream Class Specifications

Invariant

An FileInputStream object

serves as a conduit for input from a file specified at the time this object is instantiated.

Constructor Methods

public **FileInputStream** (File f)

precondition
f.isFile()

postcondition
A new FileInputStream object is created and, if possible, associated with a file named *f*.
AND the file is positioned to begin reading from the beginning.

throws
If file *f* does not exist, is a directory, or cannot be opened, then a FileNotFoundException (subclass of IOException) is thrown.

public **FileInputStream** (String s)

precondition
s is a pathname for an existing file

postcondition
A new FileInputStream object is created and, if possible, associated with a file named *s*. (*s* may be either a complete path name or a relative name.)

AND the file is positioned to begin reading from the beginning.

throws
If file *s* does not exist, is a directory, or cannot be opened, then a FileNotFoundException (subclass of IOException) is thrown.

There are only two `FileInputStream` methods of interest to this discussion—the two constructor methods. These are the methods that make `FileInputStream` unique from other streams. The first constructor instantiates a `FileInputStream` object and connects it to the file from a `File` object. The code segment below illustrates how to open a file using this constructor.

```
try{
    File file;
    FileInputStream inStream;
    file = new File( "sampleFile" );
    inStream = new FileInputStream( file );
    // The code to read the file and close it belongs here.
}
catch (IOException e) {
    System.out.println( "I/O error occured" );
}
```

When this code executes, a `file` object is instantiated and connected to a file with the relative path name *sampleFile*. Next, a `FileInputStream` object, named `inStream`, is instantiated and connected to the same file by passing `file` as an argument to the constructor method. The *try* instruction captures any I/O exceptions that might occur.

This first example of opening a stream via a `File` object is useful whenever the program needs to check other file properties, through `File` queries like `isDirectory()`, `exists()`, or `length()`. However, if the program doesn't require such tests, then using the second constructor method leads to abbreviated code for opening the same file. This code is shown below:

```
try{
    FileInputStream inStream;
    inStream = new FileInputStream( "sampleFile" );
    // The code to read the file and close it belongs here.
}
catch (IOException e) {
    System.out.println( "I/O error occured" );
}
```

The `FileOutputStream` class includes two constructor methods that parallel those from `FileInputStream`. Figure 13.11 contains their specifications.

13.5   DATAINPUTSTREAM AND DATAOUTPUTSTREAM

As mentioned previously, the `DataInputStream` and `DataOutputStream` classes are well suited for reading and writing data of primitive type. Figure 13.12 illustrates this by showing that `DataOutputStream` includes a separate method to output each primitive type.

Figure 13.11 FileOutputStream constructor specifications

FileOutputStream Constructor Specifications

public **FileOutputStream** (File f)

precondition
NOT *f*.isDirectory()

postcondition
A new **FileInputStream** object is created and, if possible, associated with an empty file named *f*.

AND the file is positioned to begin writing from the beginning.

throws
If file *f* is a directory, cannot be created, or cannot be opened for any reason, then a **FileNotFoundException** (subclass of **IOException**) is thrown.

public **FileOutputStream** (String s)

precondition
s is not the path name for an existing directory

postcondition
A new **FileInputStream** object is created and, if possible, associated with an empty file named *s*. (*s* may be either a complete path name or a relative name)

AND the file is positioned to begin writing from the beginning.

throws
If the file named *s* is a directory, cannot be created, or cannot be opened for any reason, then a **FileNotFoundException** (subclass of **IOException**) is thrown.

Opening a DataOutputStream is complicated by the fact that the constructor method has a parameter of type OutputStream, rather than File or String (for the file's name). However, FileOutputStream inherits from OutputStream. This permits a DataOutputStream to be opened by first instantiating a FileOutputStream object, then passing this object as an argument to instantiate a DataOutputStream. The resulting situation is pictured in Figure 13.13.

Figure 13.14 shows the code needed to open a file in this way. Figure 13.14 also illustrates how to write, flush, and close such a file.

The first four statements in the body of the *try* instruction constitute the code needed to open the stream for a file named *example.bin*. The third statement instantiates a FileOutputStream object, called outStream, and the fourth statement uses outStream as an argument to instantiate dataStream. All subsequent method calls are appropriately directed to dataStream, not outStream.

Figure 13.12 DataOutputStream class diagram

```
┌─────────────────────────────────────────────┐
│            DataOutputStream                   │
├─────────────────────────────────────────────┤
│                                               │
├─────────────────────────────────────────────┤
│ «constructor»                                 │
│   + DataOutputStream(OutputStream )           │
│   ...                                         │
│                                               │
│ «update»                                      │
│   + void close()                              │
│   + void flush()                              │
│   + void writeBoolean(boolean )               │
│   + void writeByte(byte )                     │
│   + void writeChar(char )                     │
│   + void writeDouble(double )                 │
│   + void writeFloat(float )                   │
│   + void writeInt(int )                       │
│   + void writeLong(long )                     │
│   + void writeShort(short )                   │
│   + void writeUTF(String )                    │
│   ...                                         │
└─────────────────────────────────────────────┘
```

Figure 13.13 Connecting a DataOutputStream to a file

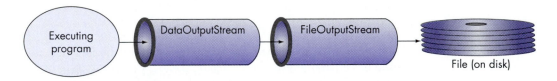

Figure 13.14 Director to write to a binary file

```java
import java.io.*;
public class Director  {

    public Director()    {
        try{
            FileOutputStream outStream;
            DataOutputStream dataStream;
            outStream = new FileOutputStream( "example.bin" );
            dataStream = new DataOutputStream( outStream );
            dataStream.writeInt( 12 );
            dataStream.writeBoolean( true );
            dataStream.writeDouble( 98.7 );
```

```
            dataStream.writeUTF( "hello world" );
            dataStream.writeChar('Z');
            dataStream.flush();
            dataStream.close();
        }
        catch (IOException e)  {
            System.out.println("ERROR writing." );
        }
    }
}
```

The `DataOutputStream` and `DataInputStream` classes are designed to perform I/O using a storage format that essentially matches the format used to store data in memory. So, the content of the *example.bin* file following the execution of the code from Figure 13.14 can be pictured as follows:

Content of the *example.bin* file:

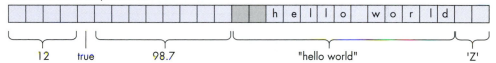

Each of the small squares in this picture represents one byte of the file. The first four bytes store the `int` value 12; this is what was output by the `writeInt` instruction of the program. The fifth byte stores `boolean` value. When the `writeDouble` method is called, eight bytes are written to store the value 98.7.

You might be wondering why `DataOutputStream` has no `writeString` method. As is evident in the above example, the `writeUTF` method plays this role. The "UTF" in the name of this method refers to a particular technique for storing `String` data efficiently. A single unicode character occupies two bytes of storage. However, a UTF encoding reduces this to one byte for most commonly used symbols. The above example shows each character in the `"hello world"` string stored within a single byte. The two gray bytes preceding this string are also part of the overhead required for UTF encoding.

The methods of `DataInputStream` parallel those of `DataOutputStream`. Figure 13.15 shows a class diagram for `DataInputStream`.

The most significant differences between `DataOutputStream` and `DataInputStream` are (1) `DataInputStream` has no `flush` method and (2) the void `write` methods from `DataOutputStream` are replaced by nonvoid parameterless `read` methods in `DataInputStream`.

Figure 13.16 illustrates how to use `DataInputStream` to read the file that was created by the code from Figure 13.14.

Figure 13.15 DataInputStream class diagram

```
┌─────────────────────────────────────────────┐
│            DataInputStream                   │
├─────────────────────────────────────────────┤
│                                              │
├─────────────────────────────────────────────┤
│ «constructor»                                │
│     + DataInputStream(InputStream )          │
│     ...                                       │
│                                              │
│ «query»                                       │
│     + boolean readBoolean()                   │
│     + byte readByte()                         │
│     + char readChar()                         │
│     + double readDouble()                     │
│     + float readFloat()                       │
│     + int readInt()                           │
│     + long readLong()                         │
│     + short readShort()                       │
│     + String readUTF()                        │
│     ...                                       │
│                                              │
│ «update»                                      │
│     + void close()                            │
└─────────────────────────────────────────────┘
```

Figure 13.16 Director to read and print the binary file created by Figure 13.14

```java
import java.io.*;
public class Director  {

    public Director()    {
       try {
             int inInt;
             boolean inBool;
             double inDouble;
             String inStr;
             char inCh;
             FileInputStream inStream;
             DataInputStream dataStream;
             inStream = new FileInputStream( "example.bin" );
             dataStream = new DataInputStream( inStream );

             inInt = dataStream.readInt();
             inBool = dataStream.readBoolean();
             inDouble = dataStream.readDouble();
             inStr = dataStream.readUTF();
             inCh = dataStream.readChar();
             dataStream.close();
```

```
                    System.out.println( inInt );
                    System.out.println( inBool );
                    System.out.println( inDouble );
                    System.out.println( inStr );
                    System.out.println( inCh );
                }
              catch (IOException e)  {
                    System.out.println("ERROR reading." );
                }
            }
          }
```

The `Director` method from Figure 13.16 opens the file for input using a `FileInputStream` object in the same way that `FileOutputStream` was used for opening an output stream. Each of the values is read from the input file and assigned to a separate variable. The method uses `System.out.println` to display each of these variables.

The most important thing to remember when using `DataInputStream` is that *data must be read (by type) in the same order it was written*. The order used to write the *example.bin* file is as follows:

an int ➔ a boolean ➔ a double ➔ a String ➔ a char

Therefore, it must be read with the following order of calls:

`readInt, readBoolean, readDouble, readUTF, readChar.`

Reading data in the wrong order from a `DataInputStream` can produce extremely unusual behavior. Consider the following code segment (a variation from the Figure 13.16 code).

```
inStream = new FileInputStream( "example.bin" );
dataStream = new DataInputStream( inStream );
inBool = dataStream.readBoolean();
inInt = dataStream.readInt();
```

When `readBoolean` is called, it will consume the first byte from the file. Unfortunately, the file's first byte was one fourth of an `int` value. When the `readInt` method is called, it consumes the next four bytes from the file. The result is that `inInt` is assigned a value formed from three fourths of an `int` value appended to a `boolean` value. The values assigned to `inBool` and `inInt` resulting from the execution of this code are simply not sensible, but no error will be reported.

Sometimes the author of the input program does not know the exact amount of data in a file. In such cases the program must test for a condition known as end of file. An **end of file condition** becomes true when all data from an input file has been read completely.

`DataInputStream` handles an end of file condition by throwing an `EOFException` when any `read` method is called that would retrieve more bytes of data than remain unread in the stream. This condition can be caught by a separate *catch* clause. For example, suppose that *fileOfInts* is a file that is known to contain exclusively int values. The following code will read every value from this file and print it with System.out.println.

```
try {
    FileInputStream inStream;
    DataInputStream dataStream;
    inStream = new FileInputStream( "fileOfInts" );
    dataStream = new DataInputStream( inStream );

    while (true) {
        System.out.println( dataStream.readInt() );
    }
}
catch (EOFException e) {
    // This occurs normally when reading past the last int.
}
catch (IOException e) {
    System.out.println("ERROR reading." );
}
```

The loop in the above program may appear to be infinite, but remember that each execution of the loop body causes another int value to be read from the stream. When readInt is called after all values from the stream have been read, then an EOFException is thrown. The exception is handled by its own *catch* clause, which does nothing.

13.6 TEXT FILES

A file that contains exclusively char data is said to be a **text file**. Memos, letters, and manuals are often stored in the computer in the form of text files. Your source code (*.java*) files are also stored as text files. Text editors are programs that create and modify text files.

Not all files are in text file format. For example, any file created using DataOutputStream is unlikely to be a text file, unless only writeChar methods are used. Nontext files are referred to collectively as **binary files**. When a binary file is opened by a text editor, it tends to appear as a random collection of symbols.

Since humans like text separated into separate lines, text files make use of a special character (written '\n' in Java) to separate consecutive lines. Figure 13.17 shows three lines of text the way they would be read by humans, and the corresponding characters as they would be stored in a text file.

The *java.io* package includes several classes to manipulate text files. Many of these classes use the concepts of **reader** and **writer** objects to massage stream data.

In a sense, the data that comes from a stream is like crude oil. It is possible to use crude oil in its natural form. However, crude oil is useful in a wider variety of applications after it has been refined and repackaged. Readers and writers provide tools to refine and repackage data.

Figure 13.17 Text file storage format for lines

Three lines of text:

This
is a
test

Content of a text file storing three lines:

T	h	i	s	\n	i	s		a	\n	t	e	s	t

Figure 13.18 pictures a typical way to utilize readers and writers for performing I/O. In order to write to a file a program creates two objects—a writer object and an output stream. The actual output methods will be performed upon the writer. Similarly, a program can input from a file by way of a reader object that is connected to an input stream object.

Figure 13.18 Using streams with readers and writers

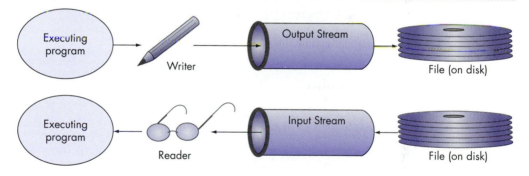

Figure 13.19 contains a class diagram for one writer class, called `PrintWriter`. The `PrintWriter` class is an output class that produces only text files.

On the surface the `PrintWriter` class looks somewhat similar to `DataOutputStream`. Both classes use the same `close` and `flush` methods. Both classes include separate methods for most of the primitive data types, although `PrintWriter` does so by overloading its `print` and `println` methods. Even the constructor method of the two classes uses the same type of stream parameter.

The primary difference between `DataOutputStream` and `PrinterWriter` is that `DataOutputStream` writes data in binary form, whereas `PrintWriter` transforms all data into a textual form before writing. For example, the following `DataOutputStream` method call writes its data in the form of an eight-byte double:

```
dataStream.writeDouble( 1234567890.1 );
```

Figure 13.19 PrintWriter class diagram

```
┌─────────────────────────────────────┐
│              PrintWriter             │
├─────────────────────────────────────┤
│                                      │
├─────────────────────────────────────┤
│ «constructor»                        │
│    + PrintWriter(OutputStream)       │
│    ...                               │
│                                      │
│ «update»                             │
│    + void close()                    │
│    + void flush()                    │
│    + void print(boolean)             │
│    + void print(char)                │
│    + void print(double)              │
│    + void print(float)               │
│    + void print(int)                 │
│    + void print(long)                │
│    + void print(Object)              │
│    + void print(String)              │
│    + void println()                  │
│    + void println(boolean)           │
│    + void println(char)              │
│    + void println(double)            │
│    + void println(float)             │
│    + void println(int)               │
│    + void println(long)              │
│    + void println(Object)            │
│    + void println(String)            │
│    ...                               │
└─────────────────────────────────────┘
```

However the corresponding PrintWriter method call below writes a sequence of 12 characters, including the decimal point, to represent the same output data in textual form:

```
printWriterObject.print( 1234567890.1 );
```

The PrintWriter class includes println methods to make the insertion of end of line separations more convenient. Each call to the parameterless version of println writes a single end of line character into the output stream. In other words, a call to the method

```
println();
```

performs the same function as the following instruction:

```
print('\n');
```

When an argument is passed to println, an end-of-line character is appended to the stream *following* the textual representation of the argument.

Figure 13.20 contains a complete Director method that uses PrintWriter to create a text file. The file that is created by executing the Director method writes the same data as the class from Figure 13.14. Figure 13.20 also shows the content of the text file that is produced by executing the Director method.

Figure 13.20 Director using PrintWriter

```java
import java.io.*;
public class Director  {

    public Director()    {
        try {
            FileOutputStream outStream;
            PrintWriter printWriter;

            outStream = new FileOutputStream( "example.txt" );
            printWriter = new PrintWriter( outStream );
            printWriter.print( 12 );
            printWriter.print( true );
            printWriter.println( 98.7 );
            printWriter.print( "hello world" );
            printWriter.print('Z');
            printWriter.flush();
            printWriter.close();
        }
        catch (IOException e)  {
            System.out.println("ERROR writing." );
        }
    }
}
```

Content of the resulting *example.txt* file:

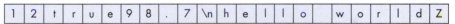

| 1 | 2 | t | r | u | e | 9 | 8 | . | 7 | \n | h | e | l | l | o | | w | o | r | l | d | Z |

OPENING the Black Box

The notation System.out refers to a variable of type PrinterWriter. So method calls like

    System.out.println()

are calling the methods described in this section.

Reading from a text file can be accomplished in many ways. One way to read from a text file is one character at a time. Another way to read from a text file is to read an entire line in a single method call. The BufferedReader class provides for both of these options. Figure 13.21 contains a class diagram for BufferedReader.

The constructor method of BufferedReader differs from previously presented input classes because it cannot accept an argument of type FileInputStream. However, there is another *java.io* class, called FileReader, which is a subclass of Reader and can be used in the same way as FileInputStream.

Figure 13.21 BufferedReader class diagram

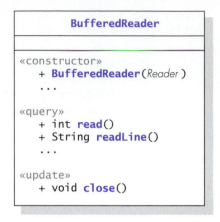

Each call to the BufferedReader readLine method returns the next unread line as a String value. There are two important things to remember when calling readLine.

1. The String returned by readLine does *not* include the end of line character ('/n'), but the end of line is consumed by the method call.
2. When readLine is called after reaching the end of file, then null is returned.

Below is a segment of code to open the *example.txt* file and read its contents line by line:

```
try {
    String inStr;
    FileReader inReader;
    BufferedReader bReader;
    inReader = new FileReader( "example.txt" );
    bReader = new BufferedReader( inReader );
    inStr = bReader.readLine();
    while ( inStr != null ) {
        System.out.print(inStr + "//");
        inStr = bReader.readLine();
    }
    bReader.close();
}
catch (IOException e) {
    System.out.println( "ERROR reading." );
}
```

In order to read a file character by character, BufferedReader provides a method called read. The read method is a bit unusual because it returns an int value rather than a char. A cast is required before the read method's value can be used as a char. Another characteristic of the read method is that it returns the value –1 to indicate any attempt to read past the end of file. Below is an example of reading an entire text file character by character, while checking for end of file.

```java
try {
    int inInt;
    char inChar;
    FileReader inReader;
    BufferedReader bReader;
    inReader = new FileReader( "example.txt" );
    bReader = new BufferedReader( inReader );

    inInt = bReader.read();
    while ( inInt != -1 ) {
        inChar = (char) inInt;
        System.out.println(inChar);
        inInt = bReader.read();
    }
    bReader.close();
}
catch (IOException e) {
    System.out.println( "ERROR reading." );
}
```

13.7 TERMINAL-STYLE I/O (OPTIONAL)

Prior to the use of graphical user interfaces, the most common form of I/O between an executing program and the user was **terminal-style I/O**. This type of I/O is so named because it behaves like an old-fashioned computer terminal. A computer terminal consists of a keyboard and an output device (either a video screen or a printer). An executing program typically communicates with the terminal in a kind of dialog. The program might display several lines of output and then request input from the user. Typically, an input request causes the program to suspend execution until the user supplies input in the form of keystrokes. Even though textual computer terminals are largely devices from the past, terminal-style I/O is still utilized in many places. For example, both the DOS prompt from the Windows operating system and Unix shells operate on terminal-style I/O.

The creators of Java felt that terminal-style I/O was sufficiently important that they included two objects to provide programs convenient access to a standard way of emulating computer terminal like I/O.

1. The System.out object is an output stream, analogous to a computer terminal display.
2. The System.in object is an input stream for the computer keyboard.

The System.out object is of type PrintStream. System.out can be used directly without initialization by calling the print and println methods. Executing either of these methods causes the argument to be displayed in the standard output stream (usually a window of textual display).

The System.in object is of type InputStream, so using System.in requires a bit of initialization in order to accomplish terminal-style I/O. In particular, since computer terminals typically read data one line at a time, it is best to use a BufferedReader to process the input from System.out. Figure 13.22 illustrates.

Figure 13.22 Example of terminal-style I/O

```java
import java.io.*;
public class Director {

    public Director()    {
        try {
            String userInput;
            InputStreamReader inReader;
            BufferedReader bReader;

            inReader = new InputStreamReader( System.in );
            bReader = new BufferedReader( inReader );

            System.out.print("Type your message: ");
            userInput = bReader.readLine();
            System.out.println("Your message is as follows. "
                                        + userInput);
        }
        catch (IOException e)   {
            System.out.println("ERROR reading." );
        }
    }
}
```

The Director method from Figure 13.22 connects System.in with two other objects, namely inBuffer (of type InputStream) and bReader (of type BufferedReader). The inReader object is instantiated and attached to System.in via the following instruction.

```java
inReader = new InputStreamReader( System.in );
```

The bReader object is instantiated and attached to inReader via the following instruction:

```java
bReader = new BufferedReader( inReader );
```

These two instructions properly initialize System.in so that all subsequent input can be processed through bReader.

Terminal-style I/O usually begins when the program displays a prompt for the user. The following instruction is an example of how to produce such a user prompt.

```java
System.out.print("Type your message: ");
```

Next the program executes the following instruction.

```
userInput = bReader.readLine();
```

Since this particular bReader is reading from System.in, the execution of this instruction will cause the program to delay until the user has typed an input line terminated by striking the "return" key. The string that represents this line of keystrokes is returned by the readLine method and assigned to userInput.

The delay that is a part of any readLine from System.in is unlike event-driven code. Such a readLine suspends execution until such time that the user has supplied the proper input.

13.8   PERSISTENT OBJECTS (OPTIONAL)

Sometimes whole objects must be retained from one program execution to the next. Such persistent objects require that a program store the complete state of the object in some file. This object and its state can be restored at a later time by reading the data back from the file.

One situation that calls for persistent objects is a program that keeps track of its final state to use as the initial state the next time the program is executed. For example, consider a computer program that plays the game of chess against the human that executes the program. It might be desirable to write the chess-playing program so that the user could suspend a game and turn off the computer to resume the game at a later date. Such a program is written by making the game board persistent, along with its associated chess piece objects.

It is possible to use *java.io* streams, like DataOutputStream and DataInputStream, as a crude mechanism for implementing persistent objects. Using DataOutputStream and DataIntputStream to implement persistence requires that all of its key individual attributes of the persistent object be written and read. For complicated objects this is a tedious approach.

A better technique for implementing persistent objects is provided by way of the ObjectOutputStream and ObjectInputStream classes. These classes include methods to read or write an entire object at once.

Figure 13.23 contains an example use of ObjectOutputStream. Executing this Director method writes two objects (from window and dot) to a binary file.

Figure 13.23   Writing objects with ObjectOutputStream

```
import java.io.*;
import aLibrary.*;
public class Director   {
    public Director()    {
        AWindow window;
        AOval dot;
        window = new AWindow(10, 10, 300, 200);
        dot = new AOval(125, 75, 50, 50);
```

```
        dot.setToFill();
        dot.place(window);
        window.repaint();

        try{
            FileOutputStream outStream;
            ObjectOutputStream objStream;
            outStream = new FileOutputStream( "example.obj" );
            objStream = new ObjectOutputStream( outStream );
            objStream.writeObject( window );
            objStream.writeObject( dot );
            objStream.flush();
            objStream.close();
        }
        catch (IOException e)  {
            System.out.println("ERROR writing." );
        }
    }
}
```

The method used to write persistent objects to an ObjectOutputStream is writeObject. Executing the writeObject method outputs the complete state of its argument object. If the object is an aggregate, then the state of its instance variables is also written. This inclusion of referenced objects is applied transitively so that the complete state of the object can be retained.

One requirement of the use of ObjectOutputStream is that any argument to the writeObject method must be **serializable**. A class is made serializable by simply adding the expression

```
implements Serializable
```

just prior to the opening brace for the class. For example, the AOval class begins as follows:

```
public class AOval extends AView implements Serializable {
```

If a persistent object is stored using ObjectOutputStream, then it should be restored using ObjectInputStream and its readObject method. Figure 13.24 demonstrates with a Director class to restore the objects written by the Figure 13.23 code.

There are three requirements that must be observed to input objects using ObjectInputStream.

1. Objects must be read in the same order they were written.
2. The value returned by readObject is of type Object and must be cast to the proper type.
3. A call to readObject may throw various exceptions, requiring a different *catch* clauses.

Figure 13.24 Reading objects with `ObjectInputStream`

```java
import java.io.*;
import aLibrary.*;
public class Director  {

    public Director()    {
        AWindow window;
        AOval dot;
        try{
            FileInputStream inStream;
            ObjectInputStream objStream;
            inStream = new FileInputStream( "example.obj" );
            objStream = new ObjectInputStream( inStream );
            window = (AWindow) objStream.readObject();
            dot = (AOval) objStream.readObject();
            objStream.close();
            window.repaint();
            dot.repaint();
        }
        catch (Exception e)   {
            System.out.println("ERROR reloading object." );
        }
    }
}
```

The code in Figure 13.24 observes all of these three requirements. The first object read is assumed to be an `AWindow`, and the second is an `AOval`. Both of the calls to `readObject` are immediately cast to the proper type. The *catch* clause uses a parameter of type `Exception`, which is a superclass of `IOException` and includes all of the required types of exceptions that must be handled by this code.

13.9 JFILECHOOSER (OPTIONAL)

Most modern operating systems include graphical file browser windows to make it easier for the user to select a file from within the file directory. It is also common for computer applications to permit the user to select an input file or an output file using a similar file browser.

The *swing* package includes a graphical file browser class for just this purpose. Figure 13.25 contains a class diagram for this `JFileChooser` class, along with a picture of a typical `JFileChooser` window as it would be appear to a user.

Figure 13.25 JFileChooser class diagram and sample image

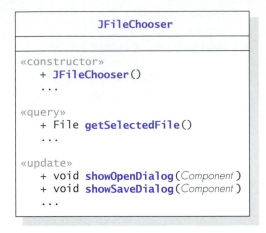

A JFileChooser object can be instantiated from a parameterless constructor. Such an object becomes visible by executing either of two methods:

1. showOpenDialog is called to display a JFileChooser that is appropriate for selecting an input file.
2. showSaveDialog is called to display a JFileChooser that is appropriate for selecting a new output file.

Note that null can be used as an argument for both showOpenDialog and showSaveDialog.

After having called showOpenDialog or showSaveDialog to display the file finder, the program should call getSelectedFile. This method performs three tasks:

1. Execution is suspended until the user selects a file or cancels the action in the JFileChooser window.
2. A File object is returned for the user-selected file. (null is returned if the user canceled this action or selected an invalid file.)
3. If a valid file is selected, then that file is opened for input or output from the beginning of the file.

Figure 13.26 illustrates how to use a JFileChooser object to open a file for input. The code in this example reads all characters from a user-specified text file, writing them to System.out.

Figure 13.26 Using JFileChooser to read from a file

```
import java.io.*;
import javax.swing.*;
public class Director   {

    public Director()    {
        try {
            JFileChooser chooser = new JFileChooser();
            int tmp = chooser.showOpenDialog( null );
            File file = chooser.getSelectedFile();
            if (file != null)    {
                FileInputStream inStream;
                InputStreamReader reader;
                int inInt;
                inStream = new FileInputStream(file);

                reader = new InputStreamReader( inStream );
                inInt = reader.read();
                while (inInt != -1)    {
                    System.out.print( (char)inInt );
                    inInt = reader.read();
                }
                reader.close();
            } else {
                System.out.println("No file name selected.");
            }
        }
        catch (FileNotFoundException e)   {
            System.out.println("ERROR opening input stream." );
        }
        catch (IOException e)   {
            System.out.println("ERROR reading." );
        }
    }
}
```

The three lines from this example that are needed to display a JFileChooser and open the specified file are as follows.

```
JFileChooser chooser = new JFileChooser();
int tmp = chooser.showOpenDialog( null );
File file = chooser.getSelectedFile();
```

Executing the first of these three lines instantiates a JFileChooser object called chooser. The second instruction displays chooser in a form that is proper for opening an existing file. The call to getSelectedFile causes the program to suspend execution until the user has selected some file or canceled the selection via the chooser window. If the user selects a valid file name, then the associated file is opened and assigned to the file variable. If the user makes an invalid selection or cancels the selection, then file is assigned null.

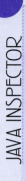

Below is a collection of hints on what to check when examining code that involves the concepts of this chapter.

✓ The standard Java I/O packages are located together in the `java.io` folder. It is best to include a declaration like the following when using these libraries: `import java.io.*;`

✓ When a program opens a file with its path name, care must be taken to be certain that the file's name and directory match the file system upon which the program executes.

✓ Always check to be certain that the file is properly opened before attempting to read from it or write to it.

✓ Opening a file for output generally deletes any existing file with the same path name. If this deletion is unwanted, then a `File` object should be used to check for its existence prior to executing the opening code.

✓ Always ensure that a file is closed after the I/O is complete on it. Output files usually require the additional step of calling `flush` before closing.

✓ Most I/O operations throw checked exceptions. You must remember to handle these exceptions by enclosing your I/O code within a *try* instruction and catching the appropriate type of exceptions (`IOException` is the superclass for most exceptions that occur during I/O.)

✓ Java contains many classes for I/O. The proper selection of classes is needed to perform I/O properly. Below is a list of the classes associated with certain types of I/O:

— To read *bytes* from a binary file, connect a `FileInputStream` object to the file.

— To write *bytes* to a binary file, connect a `FileOutputStream` object to the file.

— To read *primitive values* and/or *Strings* from a binary file, connect a `DataInputStream` object to a `FileInputStream` object connected to the file.

— To write *primitive values* and/or *Strings* to a binary file, connect a `DataOutputStream` object to a `FileOutputStream` object connected to the file.

— To read *chars* and/or *Strings* from a text file, connect a `BufferedReader` object to a `FileReader` object connected to the file.

— To write *primitive values* and/or *Strings* to a text file, connect a `PrintWriter` object to a `FileOutputStream` object connected to the file.

— To read persistent *Objects* from a binary file, connect an `ObjectInputStream` object to a `FileInputStream` object connected to the file.

— To write persistent *Objects* to a binary file, connect an `ObjectOutputStream` object to a `FileOutputStream` object connected to the file.

— To read *lines* in terminal-style from the standard input stream, connect a `BufferedReader` object to a `InputStreamReader` object connected to `System.in`.

— To write *primitive values* and/or *Strings* to the standard output stream, use `PrintWriter` methods upon `System.out`. (No additional objects are required).

✓ When reading from a file, there must be some familiarity with the type of data stored within the file. If the file is a binary file it must be read as a binary file. If there are different types of data in the file, then the data must be read in the order (by type) that they were written. Failure to read in the proper order results in meaningless input and/or thrown exceptions.

✓ Always check input code to ensure proper handling of the end of file condition. Java provides different ways to check for end of file. When reading past end of file on a `DataInputStream` object, an `EOFException` is thrown. When reading reference data (such as a `readLine` applied to a `BufferedReader` object), an attempt to read past end of file returns `null`. A call to `read` that normally returns the next character from a `BufferedReader` object will return –1 when reading beyond the end of file.

✓ Objects that are made persistent via `ObjectInputStream` and `ObjectOutputStream` must belong to classes that implement `Serializable`.

TERMINOLOGY

binary file	File	persistent
cd command	file name	read (from an input
checked exception	file system	device)
current directory	folder	reader (file input object)
directory	input	relative path name
directory name	I/O (Input/Output)	secondary storage
end of file condition	open	secondary storage device
exception	output	sequential file
exception handling	path name	serializable

stream	throw (an exception)	write (to an output
terminal-style I/O	try instruction	device)
text file	working directory	writer (file output
		object)

1. Figure 13.1 contains a sample file directory. Using this particular directory specify the names for each of the following files:

   a. The complete path name for the `email` file

   b. The complete path name for the `Director.java` file from `prog1`

   c. The complete path name for the `Director.class` file from `prog2`

   d. The relative path name for the `email` file if the current directory is `/Users`

   e. The relative path name for the `Director.class` file from the `prog2` file if the current directory is `/Users/smith`

   f. The relative path name for the `Director.class` file from the `prog2` file if the current directory is `/Users/smith/prog2`

2. Figure 13.13 depicts the connections that are used to write to a binary file. For each part below, draw a picture in this same style that describes the indicated example. Your figures must label the classes involved in this output and show the proper connection sequence.

   a. The objects used to read from *example.bin* within the code in Figure 13.16

   b. The objects used to write to *example.txt* within the code in Figure 13.20

   c. The objects used to write to *example.obj* within the code in Figure 13.23

   d. The objects used to read from *example.obj* within the code in Figure 13.24

3. Label each of the following standard Java I/O classes with the best choice from the following descriptions:

   (1) Writes data in binary form

   (2) Reads data in binary form

   (3) Writes data in textual form

   (4) Reads data in textual form

   a. `BufferedReader`

   b. `DataInputStream`

   c. `DataOutputStream`

   d. `PrintWriter`

   e. `ObjectInputStream`

   f. `ObjectOutputStream`

4. Suppose that the following code segment is executed:

```
try{
    FileOutputStream outStream;
    DataOutputStream dataStream;
    outStream = new FileOutputStream( "Ex3File" );
    dataStream = new DataOutputStream( outStream );
    dataStream.writeInt( 34 );
    dataStream.writeLong( 644 );
    dataStream.writeFloat( 7.3f );
    dataStream.writeDouble( 12.345 );
    dataStream.writeFloat( 9.87f );
    dataStream.flush();
    dataStream.close();
}
catch (IOException e) {
    System.out.println("ERROR writing." );
}
```

a. Assuming that no file named *Ex3File* exists prior to executing this code, how many bytes in total are written to *Ex3File* after the code finishes execution?

b. How does your answer to part (a) change if a file with the name *Ex3File* already exists before this code executes?

c. Picture the content of the *Ex3File* created by this code, depicting the number of bytes devoted to each output value.

5. Suppose that following code segment is executed:

```
try{
    FileOutputStream outStream;
    PrintWriter printWriter;
    outStream = new FileOutputStream( "Ex4File" );
    printWriter = new PrintWriter( outStream );
    printWriter.print( 34 );
    printWriter.println( 644 );
    printWriter.print( 7.3f );
    printWriter.print( 12.345 );
    printWriter.print( 9.87f );
    printWriter.flush();
    printWriter.close();
}
catch (IOException e) {
    System.out.println( "ERROR writing." );
}
```

a. Assuming that no file named *Ex4File* exists prior to executing this code, how many bytes in total are written to *Ex4File* after the code finishes execution?

b. Picture the content of the *Ex4File* created by this code, depicting the actual characters devoted to each output value.

6. Assume that the following code has just executed:

```
try {
    FileOutputStream outStream;
    DataOutputStream dataStream;
    outStream = new FileOutputStream( "sample" );
    dataStream = new DataOutputStream( outStream );
    dataStream.writeInt( 101 );
    dataStream.writeDouble( 102.0 );
    dataStream.writeInt( 103 );
    dataStream.writeInt( 104 );
    dataStream.writeInt( 105 );
    dataStream.flush();
    dataStream.close();
    outStream = new FileOutputStream( "sample" );
    dataStream = new DataOutputStream( outStream );
    dataStream.writeInt( 201 );
    dataStream.writeDouble( 202.0 );
    dataStream.writeInt( 203 );
    dataStream.writeInt( 204 );
    dataStream.writeInt( 205 );
    dataStream.flush();
    dataStream.close();
    outStream = new FileOutputStream( "sample2" );
    dataStream = new DataOutputStream( outStream );
    dataStream.writeUTF( "Cows R not us" );
    dataStream.writeUTF( "Cows R them" );
    dataStream.flush();
    dataStream.close();

    int j1, j2, j3, j4;
    String str;
    FileInputStream inStream;
    DataInputStream dataInStream;
    inStream = new FileInputStream( "sample" );
    dataInStream = new DataInputStream( inStream );
    j1 = dataInStream.readInt();
    j2 = dataInStream.readInt();
    j2 = dataInStream.readInt();
    j2 = dataInStream.readInt();
    dataInStream.close();
    inStream = new FileInputStream( "sample" );
    dataInStream = new DataInputStream( inStream );
    j3 = dataInStream.readInt();
    dataInStream.close();
```

```
    inStream = new FileInputStream( "sample2" );
    dataInStream = new DataInputStream( inStream );
    str = dataInStream.readUTF();
    dataStream.close();
    // variable values from HERE.
}
catch (IOException e) {
    System.out.println( "ERROR in I/O." );
}
```

a. Is the first output file created above a binary file or a text file?

b. What values are assigned to the variables below by the end of this second code segment?

j1 _____

j2 _____

j3 _____

str _____

PROGRAMMING EXERCISES

1. For this assignment you must write a program that copies text files in a peculiar manner. When your program executes it accepts input from a file called *source.txt*. The program creates a new text file called *copyOfSource.txt* that contains the same lines as *source.txt* except that the order of the lines has been reversed. Note that keeping both files within the same folder as your code is easiest. Also note that you can use a text editor program to create text files for *source.txt*.

2. Using your favorite program that utilizes *aLibrary* to construct a graphical display, modify the program so that the objects of the display are made persistent. In particular, the program must remember the state of the display each time that it quits, and it must reload this state each time it starts. (You may use a separate SAVE button to cause the state to be saved and assume that the user clicks this button prior to terminating the program's execution.)

3. Programming Exercise 1 from Chapter 12 analyzes the characters that are typed into an ATextField object. Write this same program, except that your version must analyze all of the characters from a text file file named *letters.txt*.

4. Programming Exercise 2 from Chapter 12 displays bowling scores that are typed into several ATextField objects. Write this same program, except your version must input all scores as consecutive int values from a binary file called *pins.bin*. (Note that you will need to create a separate program to create the initial content of a *pins.bin* file to use for test data.)

5. Modify Programming Exercise 1 above to allow the user to select the name for the output file by using a JFileChooser object.

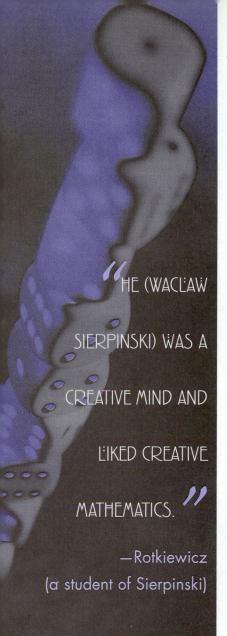

CHAPTER 14

RECURSION

*"*HE (WACLAW

SIERPINSKI) WAS A

CREATIVE MIND AND

LIKED CREATIVE

MATHEMATICS.*"*

—Rotkiewicz
(a student of Sierpinski)

OBJECTIVES

- To introduce recursion as a form of control

- To explore the concept of recursive definition and how it leads naturally to recursive methods

- To examine the run-time behavior of recursion in the form of activation records

- To compare and contrast loops and recursion

- To examine more complicated forms of recursion, including multiple recursive calls from a single method and indirect recursion

Programming languages often include instructions, called **control structures**, that are tools for manipulating control flow. An *if* instruction is a control structure that supports selection. The *while*, *do*, and *for* loops are control structures, providing repetition. The call and return mechanism of a method is still another control structure, often called "control abstraction."

This chapter explores a way to utilize control abstraction to produce a repetition-like form of control. The result is a sufficiently different form of control to deserve its own name—**recursion**.

14.1 RECURSIVE DEFINITION

Long before computer programs made use of recursion as a form of control flow, people were using recursion as a definitional tool. In fact, mathematicians have long accepted recursion as a sound method for defining properties.

Informally, a **recursive definition** can be described as a definition of some property that is self-referential. In other words, a property is defined in terms of itself. For example, consider the task of defining **odd positive integer**. Mathematicians might offer two relevant observations about the *odd positive integers*.

1. The smallest odd positive integer is 1.

2. Every odd positive integer, except 1, is two greater than some other odd positive integer.

These two observations are transformed into a recursive definition, presented in Figure 14.1. This definition is expressed in two parts, namely a **basis clause** and a **recursive clause**. All recursive definitions include these two parts.

Figure 14.1 Recursive definition of *odd positive integer*

Basis Clause

The number 1 is an *odd positive integer*.

Recursive Clause

If $K == N + 2$ and N is an odd positive integer, then K is an *odd positive integer*.

The basis clause defines the property for one or more situations that can be defined nonrecursively. The basis clause can be thought of as defining the property for the simplest case(s). In the definition of an odd positive integer, the basis clause defines that 1 is an odd positive integer. The number 1 is the "simplest" case because it is the smallest of all odd positive integers.

The recursive clause defines the property for all cases not examined in the basis. This makes the recursive clause the more general case. For the definition of *odd positive integer*, the recursive clause defines that any value, K, is an odd positive integer so long as it is $K == N + 2$ where N is also an odd positive integer. A recursive clause is characterized by the fact that it defines a property by using the same property. The recursive clause from Figure 14.1 defines an *odd positive integer K* by using another *odd positive integer* called N.

To see how this definition is applied, consider the question of whether or not the integer 3 is an *odd positive integer*. Substituting "3" for "K" in the recursive clause leads to the following statement:

If $3 == N + 2$ and N is an *odd positive integer*, then 3 is an *odd positive integer*.

According to the above statement, it is possible to conclude that 3 is an odd positive integer by satisfying two requirements: (1) to find some value N for which

3 == N + 2, and (2) to verify that this same value N is itself an odd positive integer. If the value 1 is selected for N, then 3 == N + 2 is satisfied. Furthermore, 1 is known to be an odd positive integer according to the basis clause.

It is more complicated to reason why a larger number, such as 9, is an odd positive integer. The five steps below offer an appropriate analysis.

Step 1: According to the recursive clause,

If 9 == N + 2 and N is an odd positive integer, then 9 is an odd positive integer.
Since 9 == 7 + 2, the above statement means
If 7 is an odd positive integer, then 9 is an odd positive integer.

Step 2: To decide about 7: According to the recursive clause,

If 7 == N + 2 and N is an odd positive integer, then 7 is an odd positive integer.
Since 7 == 5 + 2, the above statement means
If 5 is an odd positive integer, then 7 is an odd positive integer.

Step 3: To decide about 5: According to the recursive clause,

If 5 == N + 2 and N is an odd positive integer, then 5 is an odd positive integer.
Since 5 == 3 + 2, the above statement means
If 3 is an odd positive integer, then 5 is an odd positive integer.

Step 4: To decide about 3: According to the recursive clause,

If 3 == N + 2 and N is an odd positive integer, then 3 is an odd positive integer.
Since 3 == 1 + 2, the above statement means
If 1 is an odd positive integer, then 3 is an odd positive integer.

Step 5: To decide about 1: According to the basis clause,

The number 1 is an odd positive integer.

Therefore, by the reasoning in Step 4, 3 is an odd positive integer; and by Step 3, 5 is an odd positive integer; and by Step 2, 7 is an odd positive integer; and by Step 1, 9 is an odd positive integer.

The five steps above follow a typical pattern of repeatedly applying the recursive clause until the issue is reduced to something that is satisfied by the basis clause. It is this repeated application of the recursive clause that permits recursive definitions to define properties that extend to an infinite number of elements.

SOFTWARE ENGINEERING TIP

Using recursion in programming begins with recursive thinking. Studying recursive definitions is a good way to learn recursive thinking.

Every recursive definition (and every recursive Java method) has both a basis and a recursive part. The basis must work for the "first" or "simplest" situation(s). The recursive part is self-referential in such a way that it makes progress toward the basis.

A recursive definition is useful only if the basis and recursive clauses of a recursive definition work in concert with one another. The recursive clause must be written so that repeated applications of this clause will eventually lead to the basis clause, and the basis clause must define the property for some small number of elements.

The key characteristic of the basis clause is that it must provide the "first" occurrence(s) of the definition. Suppose that the basis clause for *odd positive integer* was changed as follows.

INCORRECT ATTEMPT TO DEFINE: *odd positive integer*

Basis Clause

Seven (7) is an **odd positive integer**.

Recursive Clause

If $K == N + 2$ and N is an odd positive integer, then K is an **odd positive integer**.

This basis step may be a correct statement regarding the number 7. However, this new basis makes it impossible to conclude that 1, 3, and 5 are odd positive integers; this conclusion is contrary to the usual notion of odd positives.

The key characteristic of a proper recursive clause is that it provides a way to "make progress" toward use of the basis clause. Suppose that the recursive clause of the odd positive integer definition were altered as shown below:

ANOTHER INCORRECT ATTEMPT TO DEFINE: *odd positive integer*

Basis Clause

1 is an **odd positive integer**.

Recursive Clause

If $K == N - 2$ and N is an odd positive integer, then K is an **odd positive integer**.

This new recursive clause may be a correct statement mathematically, but it isn't useful in a recursive definition. For example, consider applying this recursive clause to consider whether or not the value 11 is an odd positive integer. The recursive clause can be translated into the following by substituting 11 for K.

If $11 == N - 2$ and N is an odd positive integer, then 11 is an **odd positive integer**.

Since $11 == N - 2$, N must have a value of 13. However, this is progressing *away* from the basis clause in the sense that the basis clause defines the property for 1 and 13 is a further away from 1 than 11.

Technically, every recursive definition should also include a third clause, known as an **extremal clause**. The extremal clause defines the situations where the property is *not* true. Figure 14.2 adds an extremal clause for the definition of odd positive integer. Frequently, extremal clauses are not included in definitions, because they are taken for granted. In the case of odd positive integer it is reasonable to assume that any number that satisfies neither the basis nor the recursive clause must *not* be an odd positive integer.

Figure 14.2 Recursive definition of *odd positive integer* with extremal clause

Basis Clause

The number 1 is an *odd positive integer*.

Recursive Clause

If $K == N + 2$ and N is an *odd positive integer*, then K is an *odd positive integer*.

Extremal Clause

Anything that cannot satisfy the basis clause and cannot satisfy the recursive clause is *not* an *odd positive integer*.

Some recursive definitions are more complicated. For example, Figure 14.3 contains a definition of *even integer*. This definition requires a two-part recursive clause, because there are even integers that are greater than the basis value of zero, and there are even integers that are smaller than zero.

Figure 14.3 Recursive definition of *even integer*

Basis Clause

Zero (0) is an *even integer*.

Recursive Clause

(Option 1)

 If $K == N - 2$ and N is an even integer, then K is an *even integer*.

(Option 2)

 If $K == N + 2$ and N is an even integer, then K is an *even integer*.

This definition contains two possible alternatives, labeled Option 1 and Option 2, within the recursive clause. Both of these options are true, and both can be used when applying the definition. Option 1 must be applied repeatedly in order to reason that a value less than zero is an *even integer*. Option 2 must be applied repeatedly for reasoning about positive numbers.

The basis clause of the definition of *even integer* is also interesting. The value zero really isn't the "first" even integer. The *even integer* property is a somewhat unusual situation in which any particular even number can be substituted for zero and the basis will still lead to an equivalent workable definition.

Recursive definitions can also be applied to nonmathematical properties. For example, consider the task of defining what it means to be an *ancestor of Person X*.

Both of X's parents are ancestors of X.
A parent of a parent of X (i.e., a grandparent of X) is an ancestor of X.
A parent of a parent of a parent of X (i.e., a great grandparent of X) is an ancestor of X.

 . . .

Figure 14.4 supplies a recursive definition for *ancestor of X*.

Figure 14.4 Recursive definition of *ancestor of X*

Basis Clause

Every parent (mother or father) of X is an ancestor of X.

Recursive Clause

Every ancestor of a parent of X is an ancestor of X.

Arguably, the simplest form of an ancestor is a parent. Therefore, Figure 14.4 supplies a basis clause that defines *ancestor of X* in terms of *parent of X*. To see how the recursive clause can be applied to make progress toward the basis, consider the following partial family tree for Tim.

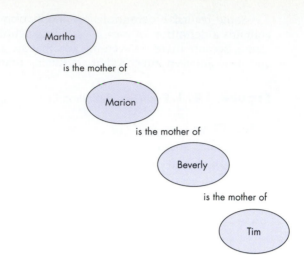

The definition of ancestor from Figure 14.4 can be used to see that Martha is an ancestor of Tim by the following reasoning steps.

Step 1: According to the recursive clause,

Every ancestor of a parent of Tim is an ancestor of Tim.

Since Beverly is Tim's mother (parent), it is concluded that Martha is Tim's ancestor so long as Martha is an ancestor of Beverly.

Step 2: Using the recursive clause a second time, it is concluded that Martha is Beverly's ancestor so long as Martha is Marion's ancestor.

Step 3: According to the basis clause,

Every parent of Marion is an ancestor of Marion.

Since Martha is Marion's mother (parent), it is concluded that Martha is an ancestor of Marion.

Therefore, using Step 2, Martha is Beverly's ancestor.

Therefore, using Step 1, Martha is Tim's ancestor.

Recursive definitions can also be an effective tool for defining programming language syntax. For example, Figure 14.5, contains the definition of a Boolean expression that partially defines the syntax supported in Java. This definition of Boolean expression syntax includes two options in the basis clause, one for each Boolean constant. The recursive clause options define the syntax of various Boolean operators and parentheses.

Using the definition from Figure 14.5, it is possible to conclude that each of the lines below represent valid syntax for a *Boolean expression*.

```
true
! true
( false )
false && ( true )
!( false || (true && !false))
```

Figure 14.5 Recursive definition of *Boolean expression* syntax

Basis Clause

The strings below are each syntactically valid *Boolean expressions*:

    true
    false

Recursive Clause

(Option 1)

If *expr* is any syntactically valid *Boolean expression*, then so is each of the following lines:

    !   *expr*
    (*expr*)

(Option 2)

If *expr1* and *expr2* are both syntactically valid *Boolean expressions*, then so is each of the following lines:

    expr1   **&&**   *expr2*
    expr1   **||**   *expr2*

Some properties, like the Java Boolean expression, are inherently recursive. Syntax diagrams regularly utilize recursion in the form of a box that refers to the expression being defined. For example, the following syntax diagram for `booleanExpression` refers to itself in order to define the proper use of parentheses to surround a Boolean expression.

ParenthesizedBooleanExpression

Syntax

The concept of ancestor, discussed earlier, is another example of a definition that is inherently recursive. It is impossible to define properties such as ancestor or a parenthesized Boolean expression without resorting to recursion, formally or informally.

14.2 FROM RECURSIVE DEFINITION TO METHOD

The Fibonacci sequence is another example of something that is an inherently recursive concept. Figure 14.6 supplies a definition for the *j*th value in the Fibonacci number sequence.

The recursive clause of the Fibonacci definition indicates that the fourth Fibonacci number is the sum of the third Fibonacci number plus the second. The recursive clause also indicates that the third Fibonacci number is the sum of the second plus the first Fibonacci numbers. Since the basis clause states that the first and second Fibonacci numbers are both 1, the entire definition indicates that the third Fibonacci is 2 and the fourth Fibonacci is 3.

Figure 14.6 Recursive definition of the jth Fibonacci number

Basis Clause

(Option 1)

> 1   is the first Fibonacci number.

(Option 2)

> 1   is the second Fibonacci number.

Recursive Clause

If $J1$ is the $(j-1)$st Fibonacci number and $J2$ is the $(j-2)$nd Fibonacci number, then $J1 + J2$ is the jth Fibonacci number.

This definition for the jth Fibonacci number can be transformed into a recursive Java method. Figure 14.7 contains this code.

Figure 14.7 jth_Fibonacci method

```
/*  precondition
        j >= 1
    postcondition
        result == the jth number in the Fibonacci sequence  */
// CAUTION: There are more efficient ways to write this code.
private int jth_Fibonacci( int j )   {
    if (j == 1  ||  j == 2)   {
        return 1;
    } else   {
        return jth_Fibonacci(j-1) + jth_Fibonacci(j-2);
    }
}
```

The jth_Fibonacci method uses its parameter to indicate the position of the value within the Fibonacci sequence (1 for the first Fibonacci, 2 for the second, etc.). Whenever the j parameter is 1 or 2, the method returns 1. This corresponds to the two options of the basis clause in the definition of a Fibonacci number. Whenever the j parameter value is greater than 2, the jth_Fibonacci returns the sum of the $(j-1)$st and $(j-2)$nd Fibonacci numbers. This is consistent with the recursive clause of the Fibonacci number definition.

The thought of a method calling itself may seem unusual, but it is perfectly acceptable Java code. A method that calls itself is known as a **recursive method**. Figure 14.8 explains the values returned by this method for arguments 1 through 6. The source of the values of the later calls can be found in the earlier ones.

Figure 14.8 Values returned by jth_Fibonacci method for arguments 1 to 6

jth_Fibonacci(1)

    return 1

jth_Fibonacci(2)

    return 1

jth_Fibonacci(3)

    return jth_Fibonacci(2) + jth_Fibonacci(1) == 1 + 1 = 2

jth_Fibonacci(4)

    return jth_Fibonacci(3) + jth_Fibonacci(2) == 2 + 1 = 3

jth_Fibonacci(5)

    return jth_Fibonacci(4) + jth_Fibonacci(3) == 3 + 2 = 5

jth_Fibonacci(6)

    return jth_Fibonacci(5) + jth_Fibonacci(4) == 5 + 3 = 8

As a second example of a recursive method, consider the problem of testing whether or not one *swing/awt* object is an ancestor container for another. Figure 14.9 gives a recursive definition for the meaning of *ancestor container*. This method is based upon the notion that Component objects (such as buttons and ARectangles) can be placed upon Container objects (such as windows and AViews). The *swing/awt* getParent returns the Container upon which its object is placed, unless there is no placement, in which case getParent returns null.

Figure 14.9 Recursive definition of *ancestor container*

Basis Clause

If c.getParent() == a, then a is an ancestor container of c.

Recursive Clause

If a is an ancestor container of c.getParent(),

then a is an ancestor container of c.

The definition of the concept of an ancestor container is turned into a boolean in Figure 14.10. The isAncestorContainer is designed to return true exactly when its first argument is an ancestor container of its second argument.

Figure 14.10 isAncestorContainer

```
/*  postcondition
        result == a is an ancestor container of c  */
private boolean isAncestorContainer (Container a, Component c)    {
    if (c == null)    {
        return false;
    } else if (c.getParent() == a)    {
        return true;
    } else    {
        return isAncestorContainer( a, c.getParent() );
    }
}
```

The isAncestorContainer closely resembles the definition from Figure 14.9 except for the first check for c == null. This check corresponds to an extremal clause test; it handles the situation where all possibilities have been exhausted and false must be returned.

14.3   RECURSIVE METHODS

Recursive method calls can be made to void methods as well as nonvoid methods. For example, consider the problem of displaying all ancestor containers of a Component. In particular, a method called displayAncestorWidths is designed to print the width of each ancestor container from the most distant ancestor to the closest ancestor. To illustrate this, Figure 14.11 diagrams a collection of Component objects. In this picture, each rectangle is placed upon the next larger rectangle with the largest rectangle placed upon the window.

Figure 14.11 A group of ancestor containers

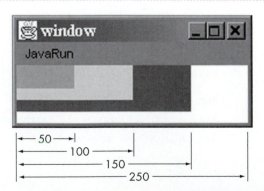

If the `displayAncestorWidths` method is called upon the smallest rectangle from Figure 14.11, the widths of each `Component` should be output in the following order.

250

150

100

50

Figure 14.12 shows the code for this method. Like many recursive methods, `displayAncestorWidths` is deceptively short for the algorithm performed.

Figure 14.12 `displayAncestorWidths` method

```
/*  postcondition
        all ancestor widths are displayed - most distant ancestors
        first  */
private void displayAncestorWidths( Component c )    {
    if (c != null)    {
        displayAncestorWidths( c.getParent() );
        System.out.println( "Width: " + c.getBounds().width );
    }
}
```

When this method is called, it is passed a `Component`, c. If this component is `null`, then the work of the method is complete, and it does nothing. If `displayAncestorWidths` is called with a non-`null` parameter, then it first proceeds to call itself recursively with c's parent container as an argument. This recursive call should cause the widths of all ancestor containers to be displayed, and when the recursive call returns, the `System.out.println` instruction displays the width of c.

It is wise to remember two points when designing recursive methods.

1. There must be a nonrecursive way to execute the method.

2. Every recursive call must make progress toward the nonrecursive alternative.

The first point is analogous to the basis clause of a recursive definition. There must be a way to exit the recursion in the same way that there must be at least one basis situation. The second point is also reminiscent of recursive definitions. Each time a method is called recursively, it is important that the call is moving the algorithm closer to the nonrecursive (basis) alternative.

SOFTWARE ENGINEERING TIP

When writing a recursive method, think first about the "simplest" or "first" case(s). These can often be found by answering the question, "Under what circumstances can this method complete its work nonrecursively?"

In the case of `displayAncestorWidths`, a nonrecursive call occurs when the parameter c is `null`. This is appropriate since a `null` `Component` has no width, nor ancestor containers. The recursive call in `displayAncestorWidths` is guaranteed to make progress because it passes a parent container as the argument for the next call. If recursion to the parent container is repeated enough times, the window frame at the background of the placement will be encountered. This parent of the background window is always `null`.

14.4 RECURSIVE EXECUTION

Tracing the execution of a recursive method reveals the run-time behavior of recursion. In order to trace recursion it is important to keep track of all **activations**. A method activation is defined to be a separate, single call to that method. Each activation has its own copy of all parameters and local variables, collectively called an **activation record**. This activation record also includes the location of the currently executing instruction. Consider a trace of the `displayAncestorWidths` method upon the smallest rectangle from Figure 14.11. When `display-AncestorWidths` is called with the smallest rectangle as an argument, its activation record can be pictured as shown in Figure 14.13

Figure 14.13 Initial activation of `displayAncestorWidths`

```
Initial activation record of displayAncestorWidths

Parameter
            smallest rectangle
     c

Method code (arrow indicates point of execution)

 →   if (c != null)    {
         displayAncestorWidths( c.getParent() );
         System.out.println( "Width: " + c.getBounds().width );
     }
```

This activation record shows that the c parameter is bound to the smallest rectangle. The activation also records the point of execution within the method's code (pictured as an arrow). This arrow points just before the *if* instruction to indicate that execution is about to begin to execute the *if* instruction.

As this first activation proceeds to execute, it is discovered that c is not `null`. Therefore, the `displayAncestorWidths` method is called recursively, and the parent container of c (the middle rectangle) is passed as the argument. This second call produces a second activation record, as shown in Figure 14.14.

This second activation is drawn on top of the first activation to illustrate that both activations are in progress at the time of this execution snapshot. The first activation is on hold in the sense that it has performed a recursive call. The location of the instruction that caused this call is pictured by the light blue arrow. The second activation is beginning to execute at the darker arrow.

Notice that both activations have their own c parameter. The c parameter of the first activation continues to bind to the smallest rectangle, whereas the c parameter of the second activation is bound to the middle rectangle.

As the execution of this second activation proceeds, it will call `displayAncestorWidths` a third time, passing the parent container (i.e., the larger rectangle). The recursive third activation results in yet a fourth activation of the method that passes the background window. Figure 14.15 illustrates the state of the four activation records as this fourth call begins.

Figure 14.14 Two activations of `displayAncestorWidths`

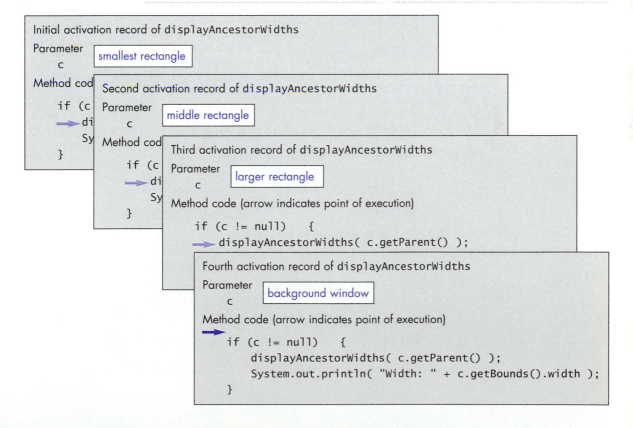

Figure 14.15 Four activations of `displayAncestorWidths`

The execution snapshot from Figure 14.15 shows the different values for each c parameter. The first three activations are executing in the midst of their call instruction. The fourth activation is about to begin executing. Executing the fourth activation causes getParent to be applied to the background window. Since the background window has no parent container, getParent returns null. Therefore, the argument passed to the fifth activation is null. Figure 14.16 illustrates the start of the fifth activation.

Figure 14.16 Five activations of displayAncestorWidths

Initial activation record of displayAncestorWidths

Parameter
c   smallest rectangle

Method code (arrow indicates point of execution)

```
    if (c !=
 ──▶disp
        Syst
    }
```

Second activation record of displayAncestorWidths

Parameter
c   middle rectangle

Method code (arrow indicates point of execution)

```
    if (c !=
  ──▶disp
        Syst
    }
```

Third activation record of displayAncestorWidths

Parameter
c   larger rectangle

Method code (arrow indicates point of execution)

```
    if (c != null)    {
 ──▶displayAncestorWidths( c.getParent() );
        System.out.println( "Width: " + c.getBounds().width );
```

Fourth activation record of displayAncestorWidths

Parameter
c   background window

Method code (arrow indicates point of execution)

```
    if (c != null)    {
 ──▶displayAncestorWidths( c.getParent() );
        System.out.println( "Width: " + c.getBounds().width );
```

Fifth activation record of displayAncestorWidths

Parameter
c   null

Method code (arrow indicates point of execution)

```
──▶
    if (c != null)    {
        displayAncestorWidths( c.getParent() );
        System.out.println( "Width: " + c.getBounds().width );
    }
```

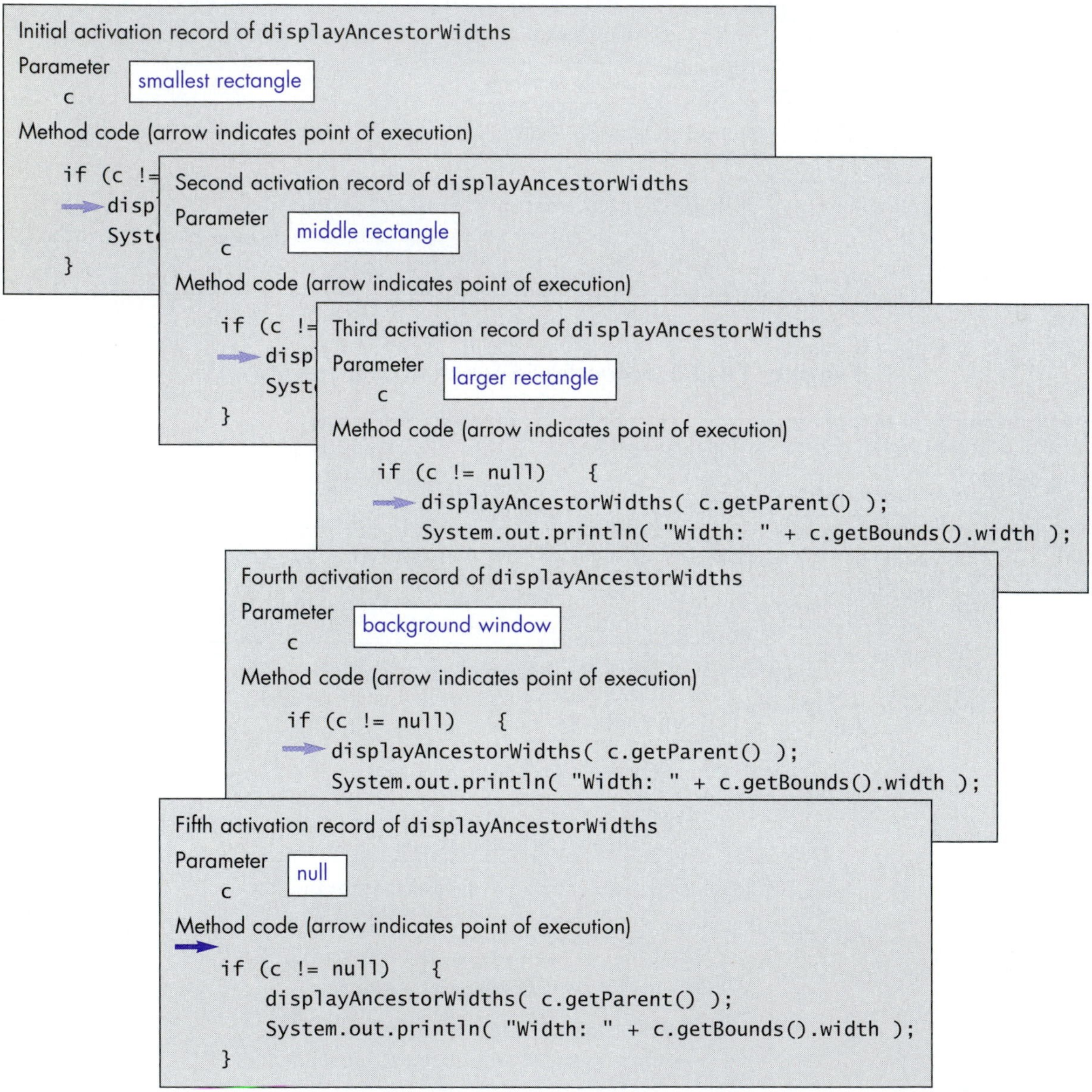

The fifth activation of `displayAncestorWidths` returns without another call, because its parameter c is `null`. This returns to the fourth activation in the state pictured in Figure 14.17.

Figure 14.17 After return from the fifth activation of `displayAncestorWidths`

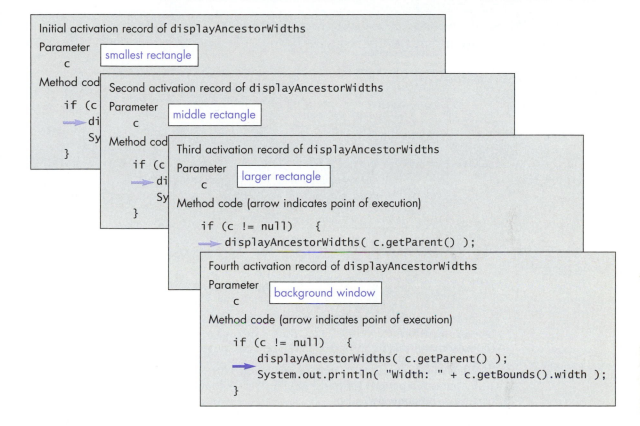

Again, in the fourth activation, the output instruction executes and displays the width of its c parameter. The width of the window (250) is displayed. Next, this fourth activation returns to the third, as shown in Figure 14.18.

The third activation proceeds to display the width of the larger rectangle (150). Then the third activation returns to the second. Similarly, the second activation displays the width of the middle rectangle (100) and returns to the first activation. Finally, the first activation displays the width of its smallest rectangle parameter (50), then returns.

Figure 14.18 Four activations of displayAncestorWidths

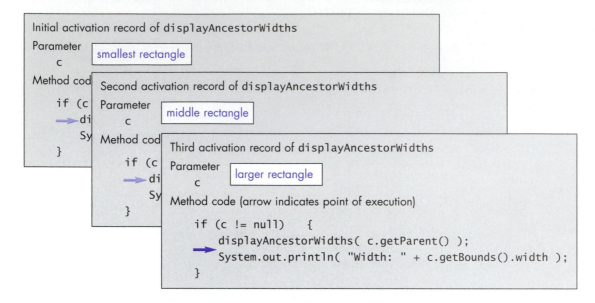

14.5 RECURSION AND REPETITION

Recursion resembles looping (repetition) in many ways. Just like looping, recursion is used to perform repetitive tasks. Both forms of control require attention to initialization and making progress. Both have the potential for unending execution.

It is always possible to replace repetition with recursion. To illustrate, Figure 14.9 contains a pattern for translating any *while* loop into a recursive method that performs the same algorithm.

Figure 14.19 A *while* loop and the corresponding recursive method

A *while* algorithm

```
while ( theCondition )   {
    loopBody;
}
```

The corresponding recursive method

```
private void recWhile()   {
    if ( theCondition )   {
        loopBody;
        recWhile;
    }
}
```

Calling the recWhile method results in the same operation as the *while* algorithm of Figure 4.19. The execution of recWhile begins by checking the value of theCondition. If this boolean condition is false, then recWhile returns in the same way that the *while* loop algorithm completes execution whenever theCondition is found to be false. Whenever the test finds theCondition to be true, recWhile executes loopBody and calls itself recursively. This is the same behavior as the *while* algorithm that executes loopBody whenever theCondition is true.

Translating in the opposite direction, namely from recursion into loops, is not so simple, nor is it always feasible. Part of the difficulty stems from the fact that recursive methods often incorporate parameter passage, which is not easily mimicked by a loop.

Despite the difficulties in translating from recursion to loops, there is one category of recursion, called **tail recursion**, that can be routinely translated into repetition. Tail recursion is a category of recursive methods in which the recursive call is the last instruction to be executed by an activation. For example, the isAncestorContainer, repeated below, uses tail recursion:

```
private boolean isAncestorContainer (Container a, Component c) {
    if (c == null) {
        return false;
    } else if (c.getParent() == a) {
        return true;
    } else {
        return isAncestorContainer( a, c.getParent() );
    }
}
```

Whenever isAncestorContainer makes a recursive call, it does so from within the *else* clause. Such a recursive call is the last task isAncestorContainer performs prior to its return.

Tail recursion can be eliminated by using a loop that does the following:

- Captures the recursive work within the loop body
- Utilizes a loop condition(s) corresponding to the basis step of the recursion

For example, a nonrecursive version of isAncestorContainer is shown in Figure 14.20. This new version of isAncestorContainer utilizes a local variable, called newC, to play the same role as the c parameter within the recursive version. The loop causes the value of newC to change from Component to its parent container, just as occurred in the recursive calls. The loop terminates when either of the two basis conditions, (newC==null) or (c.getParent==a), is true.

Figure 14.20 Nonrecursive version of isAncestorContainer

```
private boolean isAncestorContainer (Container a, Component c)    {
        Component newC = c;
        while ( newC!=null && c.getParent != a )    {
            newC = newC.getParent(); }
        return newC != null; }
```

In contrast to isAncestorContainer, the displayAncestorWidths method, repeated below, is not tail recursive. This is because the System.out.println is called *after* the recursive call. It is typically more difficult to translate nontail recursive code into loops. A loop to do the work of displayAncestorWidths would need to progress through all parent Containers while somehow "remembering" all of the Components along the way.

```
private void displayAncestorWidths( Component c ) {
    if (c != null) {
        displayAncestorWidths( c.getParent() );
        System.out.println( "Width: " + c.getBounds().width );
    }
}
```

A final similarity between recursion and loops is that both have the potential for infinite execution. A method that calls itself without making progress toward the basis clause is similar to an infinite loop. The only difference is that such "infinite recursion" halts with a **stack overflow** exception.

The name "stack overflow" comes from the fact that the Java VM stores each activation record within a so-called "run-time stack." When a method is called recursively without end, the Java VM will eventually exhaust all of the available space for method activations, and the exception message results.

14.6　MORE COMPLICATED FORMS OF RECURSION

Nontail recursion is more complicated than tail recursion in the sense that nontail recursion is not easily translated into an equivalent loop. Another way in which one algorithm can be more complicated than another is to perform multiple recursive calls per activation. The jth_Fibonacci method from Section 14.2 is an example of a method that calls itself twice for each recursive activation.

Many **fractal** algorithms also require such multiple recursive calls. Fractals are visualized as drawing patterns that repeat in varying scales. For example, the Sierpinski gasket is a particular kind of fractal created by Waclaw Sierpinski, a famous Polish mathematician (1882–1969). The Sierpinski gasket appears within an equilateral triangle with the apex pointing directly up. (Call this outer gray triangle the *bounding triangle*.) The recursive pattern used to draw a Sierpinski gasket is to draw a second equilateral triangle inside the bounding triangle, as shown in Figure 14.21. In this picture, the bounding triangle is a solid gray and the second triangle is the white-center triangle. The white triangle is formed by connecting the midpoints of the sides of the bounding triangle. A Sierpinski gasket is formed by applying this drawing pattern recursively using the remaining gray triangles as bounding triangles.

Figure 14.21 The Sierpinski gasket pattern

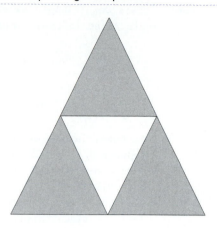

Drawing fractals, like the Sierpinski gasket, is performed recursively by levels. A level $N + 1$ fractal consists of a level N fractal with the next smaller copy of the pattern included. For the Sierpinski gasket, a level $N + 1$ fractal is formed by drawing half-sized triangles in the center of every solid gray (bounding) triangle of a level N gasket. Figure 14.22 illustrates.

Figure 14.22 Level 1 through level 4 Sierpinski gasket fractals

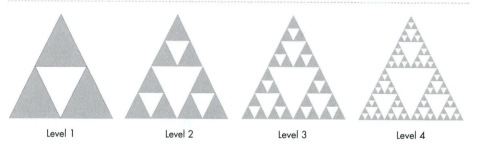

| Level 1 | Level 2 | Level 3 | Level 4 |

Figure 14.23 shows a class, called DownTriangle, that creates an appropriate triangle for use in a Sierpinski gasket fractal. The DownTriangle constructor is a non-recursive method that is passed the apex (x,y) and height (h) of a bounding triangle. DownTriangle draws a downward pointing triangle within the specified bounding triangle.

Figure 14.24 diagrams the bounding triangle as a dashed gray line and the triangle to be drawn in solid black. After the black triangle is drawn, its three surrounding triangles are potential bounding triangles for other DownTriangle objects. As shown in Figure 14.24, the height of each of these three new bounding triangles is h/2, and the apex of each is (x, y), (x – h/4, y + h/2) and (x + h/4, y + h/2).

Figure 14.23 DownTriangle class

```java
import aLibrary.*;
import java.awt.*;
public class DownTriangle extends AView  {
    private ALine leftSide, rightSide, base;

    /*  postcondition
              getX() == x-h/4 AND getY() == y+h/2
              AND getWidth() == h/2 AND getHeight() == h/2
              AND an equilateral triangle fills this AView
                  (The apex of the triangle is at the bottom.)   */
    public DownTriangle(int x, int y, int h )    {
        super(x-h/4, y+h/2, h/2, h/2);
        base = new ALine(0, 0, h/2, 0);
        base.place(this);
        leftSide = new ALine(0, 0, h/4, h/2);
        leftSide.place(this);
        rightSide = new ALine(h/2, 0, h/4, h/2);
        rightSide.place(this);
    }
}
```

Figure 14.24 DownTriangle drawing

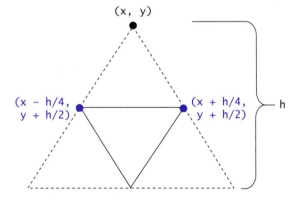

Figure 14.25 contains the code for a displayGaskets method that recursively draws Sierpinski gaskets. Each activation of displayGaskets draws a single triangle. The first three parameters to displayGaskets are the *x* and *y* coordinates of the bounding triangle's apex along with the height of the bounding triangle. The fourth parameter is the level of the drawing. Each activation of displayGaskets begins by constructing a DownTriangle. Assuming that an activation has a level

parameter greater than 1, it will result in three more activations—one for each of the surrounding triangles. Notice that the height argument for the recursive calls is half the height of the method's own height parameter. Progress is made toward completion, because each recursive call uses a level argument that is one less than its calling activation.

The displayGaskets method requires three recursive calls to accomplish its task. This leads to a more complicated form of recursion that is extremely difficult to implement without the use of recursion.

Figure 14.25 Sierpinski gasket program

```
import aLibrary.*;
import java.awt.*;
public class Director  {
    private AWindow win;

    public Director()    {
        win = new AWindow(10, 10, 600, 600);
        displayGaskets(300, 0, 600, 5);
        win.repaint();
        win.show();
    }


    /*   precondition
             lev > 0
         postcondition
             Sierpinski gaskets of level lev are drawn on win
             within a triangle with upper apex at (x, y)
             and height of h    */
    private void displayGaskets( int x, int y, int h,   int lev ) {
        DownTriangle gasket;
        gasket = new DownTriangle(x, y, h);
        gasket.place(win);
        if (lev > 1)    {
            displayGaskets(x, y, h/2, lev-1);
            displayGaskets(x-h/4, y+h/2, h/2, lev-1);
            displayGaskets(x+h/4, y+h/2, h/2, lev-1);
        }
    }
}
```

Another form of recursion is known as **indirect recursion**. Indirect recursion occurs when a method can produce simultaneous activations of itself without calling itself directly. Such a situation occurs only when a method calls some sequence of other methods that eventually result in another call to the original method. Figure 14.26 shows a variation on the Sierpinski gasket program that is accomplished by indirect recursion.

Figure 14.26 displayDownTriangle and displayUpTriangle

```
private void displayDownTriangle( int x, int y, int h,  int lev )
{
    DownTriangle triangle;
    triangle = new DownTriangle(x, y, h);
    triangle.place(win);
    if (lev > 1)    {
        displayUpTriangle(x, y+h, h/2, lev-1);
    }
}

private void displayUpTriangle( int x, int y, int h,  int lev )
{
    UpTriangle triangle;
    triangle = new UpTriangle(x, y, h);
    triangle.place(win);
    if (lev > 1)    {
        displayDownTriangle(x, y-h, h/2, lev-1);
    }
}
```

The displayDownTriangle method is similar to the method by the same name from the Sierpinski gasket program. This method draws a DownTriangle in the same way as before. However, this new method does not call itself, but calls displayUpTriangle instead. The displayUpTriangle method mirrors the behavior of displayDownTriangle. The displayUpTriangle method uses a bounding triangle with its apex at the bottom. A call to one of these methods draws a triangle and passes the newly drawn triangle to the other method, where it will be used as a bounding triangle. displayUpTriangle calls displayDownTriangle, and displayDownTriangle calls displayUpTriangle. The indirect recursion terminates when the lev parameter is no longer greater than 1. The picture drawn by calling these methods is a collection of triangles nested inside each other as shown in Figure 14.27.

Both multiple recursive calls and indirect recursion contribute to algorithm complexity. Both can be difficult to replace with loops.

Figure 14.27 Image from displayDownTriangle and displayUpTriangle

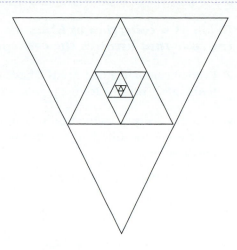

Below is a collection of hints on what to check when examining code that involves the concepts of this chapter.

✓ Every recursive method needs a basis clause that causes the recursion to terminate. Checking for the presence of such a clause is always helpful.

✓ When a recursive method calls itself, it must be making progress toward the basis clause. Checking for such progress can often eliminate the stack overflow errors.

TERMINOLOGY

activation	fractals	recursive definition
activation record	indirect recursion	recursive method
basis clause	recursion	stack overflow
control structure	recursive clause	tail recursion
extremal clause		

EXERCISES

1. Write a recursive definition for each of the following:

   a. Define what it means for one positive expression to be greater than (>) another positive expression. This should be defined in terms of + and ==.

   b. Define what it means for an airline to have to fly from A to B. Note that flying from A to B may require several individual connecting flights.

2. Consider the following method:

```java
private void munge( int x ) {
   System.out.println( x );
   if ( x != 10 ) {
      munge( x+3 );
   }
   System.out.println( x );
}
```

What output results from each of the following calls?

a. `munge(10);`

b. `munge(1);`

c. `munge(11);`

d. `munge(0);`

3. Consider the following method:

```java
private int times( int k, int m ) {
   if ( k != 0 ) {
      return m + times( k-1, m );
   } else {
      return 0;
   }
}
```

What output results from the instructions in parts (a)–(d)?

a. `System.out.println( times(3, 2) );`

b. `System.out.println( times(2, 3) );`

c. `System.out.println( times(100, 75) );`

d. `System.out.println( times(-1, 2) );`

e. Write a precondition and a postcondition to describe the behavior of this `times` method.

4. Show how to replace each of the following methods with a recursive method that produces the same output without a loop.

a.
```java
private void printProducts( int j, int k ) {
    while (j < k) {
       System.out.println( j*k );
       j++;
       k = k - 2;
    }
}
```

b.
```java
private void print0toN( int n ) {
    for (int k=0; k!=n + 1; k++) {
       System.out.println( k );
    }
}
```

5. Rewrite the code for the `jth_Fibonacci` function so that it performs the same task as the method from Figure 14.7 without using recursion in your method.

6. Show how to replace the following method with a recursive method that returns the same values when executed.

```
private int sum1ThruN( int n ) {
    int sum = 1;
    int k = 1;
    while (sum <= n) {
        sum = sum + k;
        k++;
    }
    return sum;
}
```

7. Figure 14.19 shows a recursive method that mimics the execution of a *while* loop.

   a. Supply a similar recursive method to mimic the behavior of the following *do* loop pattern.

   ```
   do {
       loopBody;
   } while ( theCondition );
   ```

   b. Supply a similar recursive method to mimic the behavior of the following *for* loop pattern.

   ```
   for ( ; theCondition; progressStatement) {
       loopBody;
   }
   ```

1. Write a program to draw a Sierpinski carpet fractal pattern. This Sierpinski carpet begins with a black background square. The drawing pattern is a black square with a filled white square centered within the black square. The side length of the white square is one-third the side length of the black square on which it is placed.

The fractal pattern is repeated upon the eight black squares that surround the white center square. Dashed lines following show the location of these eight squares.

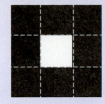

Your program must be capable of drawing Sierpinski carpets to different levels. Below is an illustration of the repeated pattern:

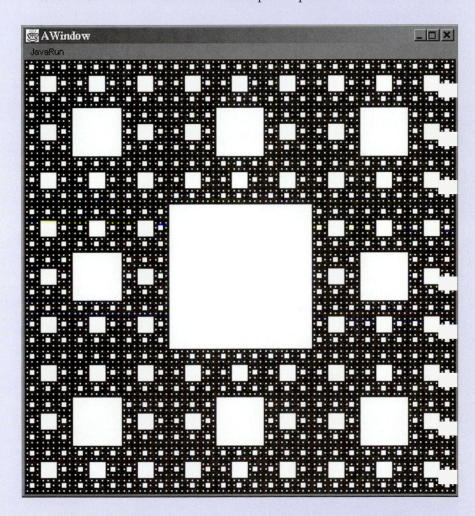

2. Write a program to produce fractal images based upon a regular hexagon. A level 0 image consists of a hexagon with the following form.

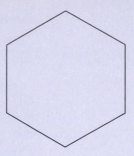

The repeated pattern is to draw six more hexagons at the corners of the larger hexagon. These six new hexagons have side length that is half of their predecessor. The level 1 picture below illustrates.

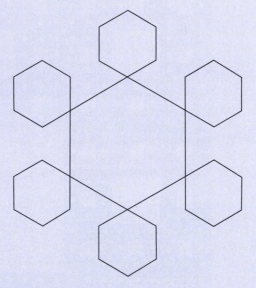

The picture that follows shows a level 4 version of this fractal pattern.

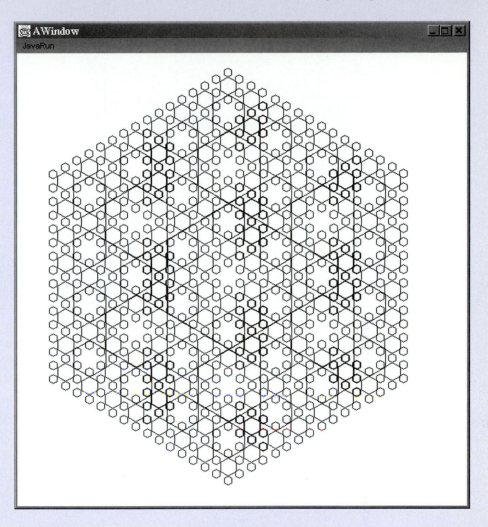

CHAPTER 15

LIBRARY ISSUES: PACKAGES, STATICS, APPLETS, AND DELEGATION

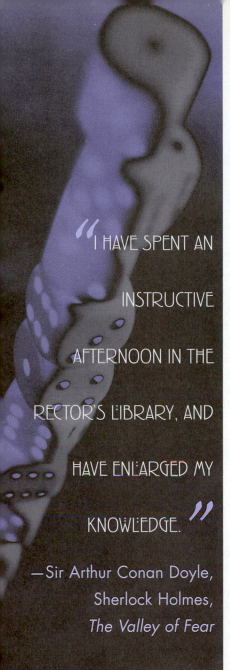

OBJECTIVES

- To explore how Java packages are grouped into package libraries

- To examine how Java uses import declarations and the CLASSPATH variable to support package access

- To introduce the concept of `static` methods and their utility in designing libraries of pure functions, such as the `Math` package

- To examine applications, the `main` method, and the *go.java* file used to implement the applications in this text

- To explore the use of `static` variables for sharing constants and for sharing data storage among objects

- To introduce applets and how they are invoked by browsers via HTML files

- To introduce event handling by delegation

549

Extensibility is a major advantage of object-oriented programming languages like Java. Java doesn't include all of the specific classes needed to support all software development, but the language includes the facilities necessary to create your own class libraries. Java doesn't include square root as a built-in language construct, but the standard Java libraries include a Math class that implements a square root function. Java doesn't have a predefined type for declaring rectangular images, but an *aLibrary* was created to include an ARectangle class for this purpose.

This extendibility of a programming language leads to perhaps the most important benefit of object-oriented programming: software **reuse**. Every time an AWindow variable is declared or an AWindow method is called, the AWindow class is reused. Every code segment that includes a String constant reuses the String class. Every class that inherits AView is reusing the superclass. Software reuse saves time, money, and can ultimately improve software quality.

In real life people often organize their surroundings based upon reusability. A young student's school backpack is filled with pencils, pens, paper, books, and any other items that might be useful for the school day. This backpack serves as a convenient package that supplies those items most likely to be used and reused.

Good software development environments should also be organized for reuse. Code that is reused once or twice can be kept in classes that are shared among the client and/or subclasses. Software that is more widely shared is elevated in importance, and those classes that are expected to see the most frequent reuse are included in **class libraries**. As the name "library" implies, a class library is a collection of classes designed for reuse through sharing.

In this chapter several different features of Java are explored. The common thread among them is that they all play a role in building good software libraries.

15.1   CREATING PACKAGES

A collection of related library classes that are available in a programming environment is called an **Application Programming Interface** or **API**. The complete API of a Java system includes all of the library classes that are available.

The Java API is further subdivided into **packages**, where each package is a group of related classes. Some packages, like *awt* and *swing*, are standard to all current Java systems. Other packages, such as *aLibrary*, are available in some, but not all, Java systems. Figure 15.1 shows a few of the packages that are part of the standard Java API. Selected classes from several of these packages have been used in earlier examples of this text.

SOFTWARE ENGINEERING TIP

The Java compiler allows any combination of classes to be included in a package. It is up to the programmer to group classes that are logically related to one another.

Java provides the tools to permit programmers to build their own packages. Creating a new package begins by placing the source code for all of the package's classes (i.e., the *.java* files) into a single folder. Each of these classes must be edited to insert a **package declaration** containing the name for the package. Figure 15.2 shows the syntax for a package declaration.

Figure 15.1 A partial list of packages from the standard Java API

Package	Purpose
java.lang	Includes wrapper classes and `System`, `String`, `Object`
java.util	Includes classes for building containers, dates, etc.
java.applet	Includes `Applet`
java.io	Includes classes for file manipulation
java.net	Includes classes to support Internet communication
java.awt	Includes graphical user interface classes
java.awt.event	Includes various event handling classes
javax.swing	Includes graphical user interface classes

Figure 15.2 `PackageDeclaration` description

PackageDeclaration

Syntax

Notes

- If included, a *PackageDeclaration* is the first noncomment, nonblank line in the class file. (This declaration precedes the "class" line.)
- There may be no more than one *PackageDeclaration* per file.

Semantics

- Following their compilation, the class(es) within the file containing a *PackageDeclaration* become part of the package.
- The name of the package is formed by the *Identifiers* used in the declaration. For example, package `A.B`; specifies that the class(es) of the file should be compiled into a package called "A.B".
- The .*class* files of the package that result from compilation will be placed into a folder with the same name as the package. For example, compiling a file with the declaration package `A.B`; places the resulting .*class* file(s) into a folder called "B" that is within a folder called "A".

Suppose that the Java library of an international bank includes software classes for currency for individual nations: `Dollar` for United States currency, `Euro` for European currency, `Yen` for Japanese currency, etc. These different monetary classes can be grouped together into a single package called `money` by performing the following three steps.

Step 1. Include the following package declaration in every class to be included in the package.

```
package money;
```

Figure 15.3 sketches the skeleton of the three classes for the different money types.

Figure 15.3 Three source files of the money package

Dollar.java file:

```
package money;
public class Dollar {
    /* innards ommitted
}
```

Euro.java file:

```
package money;
public class Euro {
    /* innards ommitted
}
```

Yen.java file:

```
package money;
public class Yen {
    /* innards ommitted
}
```

Step 2. Place all of the source files within a single folder. For this example, suppose that the folder is called *MoneyPackage*. Figure 15.4 pictures the file directory hierarchy at this stage for the three money files.

Figure 15.4 Money package folder prior to compilation

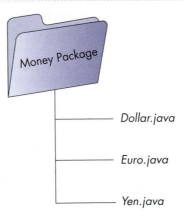

Dollar.java

Euro.java

Yen.java

Step 3. Compile all of the files in the *MoneyPackage* folder using the following command:

```
javac -d. *.java
```

This will create a new folder within *MoneyPackage* that stores the compiled code (i.e., the *.class* files.) Figure 15.5 illustrates.

Figure 15.5 Money package folder following compilation

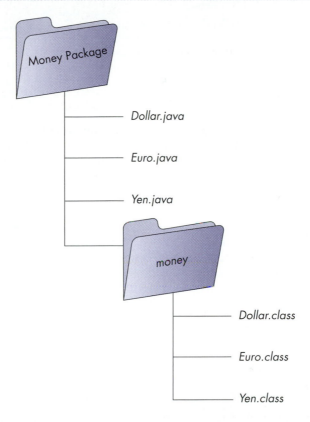

The classes examined throughout this text have been *public classes*. The word "`public`" before "`class`" marks a class as `public`. Public classes, like `public` methods and `public` variables, have a scope that makes them available to any other class.

OPENING
the Black Box

The *aLibrary* package is constructed from a collection of different source code classes (*AWindow.java, AButton.java,* etc.) These classes all contain the same first line:

```
package aLibrary;
```

These classes were compiled and are distributed in the form of a folder called *aLibrary*.

Java also allows the creation of classes that have **package scope**. A class with package scope can be used by any other class from the same package, but nowhere else. The syntax for a class with package scope is identical to the syntax of a `public` class, except for the omission of the word "`public`" from the class line.

(Package scope may also be applied to instance variables and methods, using the same notation of omitting the scope qualifier.)

Suppose, for example, that the *money* package requires the facilities of a MoneyExchanger class in order to calculate exchange rates among the various currencies. If it is best to encapsulate this class within the package, then the following file appropriately defines MoneyExchanger to have package scope.

MoneyExchanger.java file:

```
package money;
class MoneyExchanger{
    /* innards ommitted
}
```

Package scope is useful in this situation because MoneyExchanger is needed by several other classes within the class and nowhere else. However, the need for package scope is fairly limited and should not be overused.

15.2 USING PACKAGES

Once a package is created and compiled, its public classes become available. However, client classes and subclasses generally include **import declarations** in order to provide reasonable access to the public classes of the packages. An import declaration specifies classes that can be used by the client or subclass. Figure 15.6 explains.

Import declarations denote classes using a syntax that is essentially a file system path name. The names of classes being imported begin with a package name and proceed using periods as separators between folder/file names. For example, to import the *Dollar.class* file, the following import declaration is used.

```
import money.Dollar;
```

Figure 15.6 ImportDeclaration description

ImportDeclaration

Syntax

Notes

- If included, an *ImportDeclaration* must follow after any *PackageDeclaration* and precede the "class" line.
- There may be several *ImportDeclarations* per file.
- The *java.lang* package is automatically available without import.

Semantics

- The notation of *Identifiers* with period separators refers to file folders. For example,

  ```
  import A.B;
  ```

  specifies that the class called "B.class" is to be imported from a folder called "A".
- The naming of a class to be imported begins with the name of the folder that contains the package.
- An asterisk (*) signifies that all possible identifiers should be included.

Frequently, a class is the client of many other classes from the same package. When this occurs, it is convenient to include an asterisk (*) to denote all matching names. For example, the following declaration imports *every* public class within the *money* package:

```
import money.*;
```

The standard Java API package, called *java.lang*, is imported by default. It is the one package that can be used without an import declaration. The *java.lang* package includes, among other classes, the following:

```
System
String
Object
```

This explains why these classes are always accessible, but never imported.

Import declarations work properly only if the computer performing the compile and/or executing the program use a proper value for **CLASSPATH**. CLASS-PATH is an operating system variable (*not* a Java variable) that Java compilers and Java VMs use to help locate the file folders containing packages. In order to import the *money* package, the folder containing *money* must be included in CLASSPATH. Figure 15.7 shows how to accomplish this for three different operating systems.

Figure 15.7 Setting CLASSPATH to include the *money* package

Assume

The *MoneyPackage* folder (diagramed in Figure 15.5) is placed at the root of the directory system for the hard disk. (This folder could be placed elsewhere as long as the CLASSPATH address reflects its location.)

To set CLASSPATH to access money

For Windows (assuming the use of hard disk c:)

If the c:\autoexec.bat file does *not* already contain a "set CLASSPATH" line, then include the following line in this file:

```
set CLASSPATH=.;c:\MoneyPackage
```

If autoexec.bat already contains a "set CLASSPATH" line, then append the text below to the end of the set CLASSPATH line:

```
;c:\MoneyPackage
```

(*The computer must be rebooted to activate these changes.*)

For UNIX systems using a C shell, including OS X (Apple Computer)

Edit the .login file as follows:

If the .login file does *not* already contain a "setenv CLASSPATH" line, then include the following line in this file:

```
setenv CLASSPATH .:/MoneyPackage
```

If .login already contains a "setenv CLASSPATH" line, then append the text below to the end of the setenv CLASSPATH line:

```
:/MoneyPackage
```

(These changes become active upon next login.)

For UNIX systems using either a Bourne shell or a Korn shell

If .profile file does *not* already contain a "CLASSPATH=" line, then include the following two lines in this file:

```
CLASSPATH=.:/MoneyPackage
export CLASSPATH
```

If .profile already contains a "CLASSPATH=" line, then append the text below to the end of the CLASSPATH= line":

```
:/MoneyPackage
```

(These changes become active upon next login.)

15.3 STATIC METHODS

Most methods make use of the "this object" in some way. Nonvoid methods frequently return some attribute of this, and update methods alter the state of this. There are a few nonvoid methods that do not require a this object. Such methods are sometimes called **pure functions** because, like a mathematical function, they return the result of some calculation that is based solely upon their parameters. The square root function (Math.sqrt) is a pure function. A double argument is passed to the square root method and it returns the square root of this value without the need for any object except the argument.

Pure functions are good candidates to be written as **static methods**. The syntax for declaring a static method is the same as any other method with the exception of the inclusion of the static reserved word between the scope identifier (either private, protected, or public) and the method's return type.

```
private static TypeName methodName(...)
```

The advantage of a static method is that it can be called without instantiating an object. The notation that Java supports for calling static methods consists of the class name followed by the name of the static method and its argument list.

```
ClassName.methodName(...);
```

Usually, static methods are called using just the name of their class. For this reason static methods are also known as **class methods**. static methods can also be called in the same manner as other methods. In other words, (1) a static method can be called by qualifying the method name with the class name; (2) a static method can be called using an object from its class as a qualifier; and (3) within the static method's class no qualifier is needed to call the method.

OPENING
the Black Box

The Math class contains many static methods. A sample of these methods is listed below:

```
public static double abs( double num )
public static int abs( int num )
public static double cos( double num )
public static double pow( double b, double exp )
public static double random()
public static int round( float b)
public static long round( double b)
public static double sin( double num )
public static double sqrt( double num )
public static double tan( double num )
```

Since these methods are all static methods, there is no need to instantiate an object of type Math. To invoke a method, all that is needed is to use the name of the class. This is why the following instruction is valid.

```
double rand = Math.random();
```

SOFTWARE ENGINEERING TIP

static methods are best avoided except for rare cases. One good use for **static** methods is for methods that return values based solely upon primitive-type parameters.

static methods have one major disadvantage—the body of a static method is prohibited from referencing any non-static instance method or non-static instance variable. This restriction is imposed because, unlike non-static methods, static members are never associated with the lifetime of the this object. (Note that the inability of a static method to utilize non-static instance variables does not prohibit a static method from constructing and manipulating *local* non-static objects.)

Java follows the tradition of programming languages like C and C++ that use one particular static method as the predefined starting point for program execution. Every Java application begins its execution with a void method called main. Furthermore, the main method *must* be static. This fact has been hidden in this text by using go.class.

The go class serves to create a local Director object and call its constructor method. This technique has the advantage of avoiding the restrictions of a static method (main). The following box shows the entire go.java file.

The Java applications in this book use a class named go to initiate their execution. The code for this class is shown below.

go.java:

```java
public class go {
    public static void main(String args[])  {
        Director director = new Director;
    }
}
```

Java requires that every application begin executing from a main method that is static, void, and has the parameter list shown above. The go class follows these rules with a main method that does just one thing—it instantiates a Director object by calling the Director constructor.

15.4   STATIC VARIABLES

Not everything in a program is object-oriented, and not all libraries are associated with objects. The Math library is a good example of a library that isn't object-oriented and doesn't require any objects, except parameters. The static methods of the Math class are widely used by Java programs to manipulate primitive data.

A second Java language feature that is not really object-oriented, but useful for library classes, is a **static variable**. Any instance variable (not a local variable) can be declared to be static by inserting the static label immediately before the type name in the variable's declaration.

private static *TypeName variableName*;

The Math library class includes two static variables. The E and PI constants are declared within the Math class as shown below:

```java
public final static double E = 2.7182818284590452354;
public final static double PI = 3.14159265358979323846;
```

static variables are referenced using class names (or object names), just like static methods. This means that any external class can refer to the PI constant as

Math.PI

The most significant difference between static variables and non-static variables is that throughout a program's execution, only one instance exists of each static variable. static variables belong to classes, rather than objects. Therefore, creating multiple objects of the same class does not create new static instance variables. If, for example, a program declares several Math objects, there is just one PI constant that must be shared by all of the Math objects.

Figures 15.8 and 15.9 illustrate the difference between static and non-static variables. Figure 15.8 contains a supplier class called NonStat and a segment of client code using NonStat. The object diagram in this figure illustrates the usual behavior of non-static instance variables. Each of the three objects (non1, non2, and non3) contain their own copy of the instance variable called nonStatVar. Each of these copies can be assigned independently.

Figure 15.8 Creating objects containing non-static variables

Supplier class:

```
public class NonStat   {
    private int nonStatVar;
    public NonStat()  {  //The constructor method.
    }
}
```

Client code:

```
NonStat non1, non2, non3;
non1 = new NonStat();
non2 = new NonStat();
non2 = new NonStat();
```

Object diagram after executing client code:

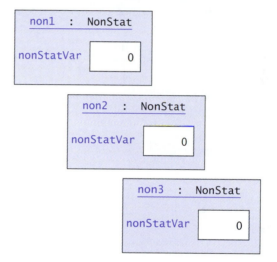

Figure 15.9 contains an example that is almost the same as Figure 15.8, except that the supplier's non-static instance variable has been replaced by a static instance variable. The binding lines in the object diagram demonstrate that none of the objects (stat1, stat2, and stat3) contain their own copy of the static variable (statVar). Instead, all three objects share the same variable. Therefore, if the value of statVar is changed in one of the objects, then it is changed for all.

static variables are useful for situations where data needs to be shared among different objects. For example, suppose that a particular application needs to ensure efficient display update by restricting the total number of AImage objects to 10 or less. Figure 15.10 shows a class, named AImageWithCheck, that extends AImage. This new class causes a warning message to be displayed any time that an AImageWithCheck object is placed along with 10 or more other such objects.

Figure 15.9 Creating objects containing `static` variables

Supplier class:
```
public class Stat    {
    private static int statVar;
    public Stat()   { //The constructor method.
    }
}
```

Client code:
```
Stat stat1, stat2, stat3;
stat1 = new Stat();
stat2 = new Stat();
stat2 = new Stat();
```

Object diagram after executing client code:

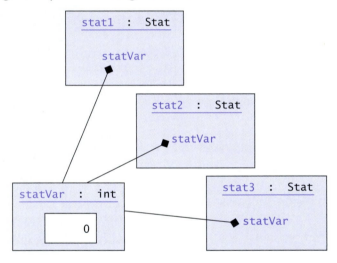

Figure 15.10 AImageWithCheck class

```
/* This class is a version of AImage that prints
   warning messages whenever a place is called that
   results in more than ten simultaneously placed
   AImage objects.    */
import aLibrary.*;
import java.awt.*;
public class AImageWithCheck extends AImage   {
    private static int placedCount = 0;

    public AImageWithCheck( int x, int y, int w, int h )   {
        super(x, y, w, h);
    }
```

```
        public void place( Container c )    {
        if (parentContainer() == null)    {
            // parentContainer()==null means this not currently
            // placed
            placedCount++;
            if (placedCount > 10)    {
                System.out.println("Warning - too many AImages");
            }
        }
        super.place(c);
    }


    public void remove( )    {
        if (parentContainer() != null)    {
            super.remove();
            placedCount--;
        }
    }
}
```

The AImageWithCheck class contains a static variable called placeCount to maintain the number of AImageWithCheck objects that are simultaneously placed. This variable is initialized to zero in its declaration. (Such an initialization is performed only once for static variables.) The place and remove methods, inherited from AImage, are overridden. The AImageWithCheck version of remove decrements placedCount so long as the object was placed prior to call remove. The place method defined in AImageWithCheck will increment placedCount whenever it is called upon an image not already placed. If the new value for placedCount exceeds 10, then a warning message is displayed.

The AImageWithCheck class is only possible because placedCount is static. If placedCount were non-static, then each AImageWithCheck object would have its own instance variable and none would store a total count. Furthermore, without static variables there is no convenient way for the library classes to provide any service that relies upon such counting of library objects.

The characteristics of a static variable can be combined with the characteristics of a final variable (constant) to form a **static constant**. A static variable declaration guarantees that there is just a single instance of the *variable*, but it fails to ensure that the binding to this variable cannot change. As a program executes, a static variable can be bound to different objects at different times. A final variable cannot be rebound. A static final variable has both properties—it has only one instance and is bound just once.

One advantage of static final variables is that they can be shared like primitive constants. For example, the Color class declares Color constants using declarations like the following.

```
public final static blue = new Color(0,0,255);
```

The *aLibrary* classes assign each separate object an identification number. Identification numbers are assigned so that each object has an ID that is different from the IDs of all other objects of the same type. When an *aLibrary* object is passed to System.out.println, this ID number is output.

Assigning each object a unique ID is accomplished by including an instance variable, called idNum, to maintain the ID of each object. In addition, a second (class) variable called idShared is used.

For example, the AView class contains the following declarations:

```
private static int idShared = 0;
private int idNum;
```

In addition, each AView constructor must include the following two instructions:

```
AView.idShared++;
idNum = AView.idShared;
```

The first of these instructions increments a static counter variable (idShared) that is shared by every AView object. The second assignment copies the value of the shared variable into a private variable that is encapsulated by the object (idNum). Therefore, the first AView object constructed by the program has idNum==1; the second has idNum==2; and so forth.

Such a declaration specifies blue as a static constant and assigns blue to the object returned by the Color constructor method. This initialization of blue will occur only once during a program's execution, so the Color.blue constant is shared throughout the program with the same object binding.

Suppose that a Java program assigns a blue color to an AOval with the following code.

```
AOval circle;
circle = new AOval(0, 0, 10, 10);
circle.setColor( Color.blue );
```

A later test, such as the one below, tests for the same blue color:

```
if ( circle.color() == Color.blue ) {...
```

Normally, checking for identity equality like this is dangerous for objects. In this case there is no danger, because a static color constant is only instantiated once (any reference to Color.blue refers to the same variable) and because color constants cannot change their binding.

The Color class from the *awt* library uses static constants for 13 predefined colors:

```
public final static Color black = new Color(0,0,0);
public final static Color blue = new Color(0,0,255);
public final static Color cyan = new Color(0,255,255);
public final static Color darkGray = new Color(64,64,64);
public final static Color gray = new Color(128,128,128);
```

```
public final static Color green = new Color(0,255,0);
public final static Color lightGray = new Color(192,192,192);
public final static Color magenta = new Color(255,0,255);
public final static Color orange = new Color(255,200,0);
public final static Color pink = new Color(255,175,175);
public final static Color red = new Color(255,0,0);
public final static Color white = new Color(255,255,255);
public final static Color yellow = new Color(255,255,0);
```

The Color constructor method specifies, respectively, the amount of redness, greenness, and blueness (255 is the maximum intensity of each color).

Because they are static, each of these constants can be referenced using the Color class name, as illustrated below.

```
Color.black
```

SOFTWARE ENGINEERING TIP

static variables should be avoided unless absolutely necessary. They are not object-oriented so they tend to present unwanted surprises to those expecting object-oriented code.

static final variables are safer than non-final static variables. Private static variables are safer than public.

The facility of static variables to provide shared data can be enticing for a number of different tasks. It is tempting, for example, to construct a window object that every other object can share without the need for passing parameters and storing aliases. Such temptations are best avoided.

The great danger with static variables is that they represent a form of shared data that is easily overlooked and not encapsulated. A static variable is not part of the state of any particular object, so class invariants don't describe its behavior. Furthermore, since static variables are shared, a single assignment to a static variable has the potential to alter the behavior of all objects that are relying upon that variable.

Generally, it is possible to determine which code segments have access to which variables by looking only at scope and parameter passage. static variables can also circumvent these normal access constraints. As a result, debugging can become more complicated when static variables are involved.

15.5 APPLICATIONS AND APPLETS

The standard Java libraries support two ways in which to run a Java program, namely **applications** and **applets**. This book has focused on applications. An application is the closest thing that Java offers to a traditional program.

Every application

1. can be executed by a Java Virtual Machine.

2. begins executing with a static main method.

Executing the go class, repeated below, upon a Java VM causes the main method to execute, which in turn constructs a Director object by calling the Director constructor.

go.java:

```
public class go {
    public static void main(String args[])  {
        Director director = new Director;
    }
}
```

Applets offer a different way to execute a program. One of the design principles of Java is to support programs that are delivered through the Internet. Applets are intended for such use. Applets can be executed via Web browsers, such as Netscape Navigator or Microsoft's Internet Explorer. Applets can also be executed using a Sun Microsystems tool called **appletviewer**.

There are two files required to run an applet, regardless of whether the applet is run from a browser or from *appletviewer:*

1. The first is a *.class* file containing the compiled form of the applet.
2. The second is an HTML (Web page) file to invoke the applet's execution.

The *.class* file must be a class that inherits Applet (java.applet.Applet). Figure 15.11 contains the code for such an applet, called AppletStarter. When an AppletStarter object is instantiated by a Web browser or appletviewer, such an instantiation invokes the AppletStarter constructor method. In turn the AppletStarter method instantiates a Director object. (*Note*: If the program uses *aLibrary*, then care must be taken with browsers that ignore CLASSPATH. A simple fix for some browsers is to include a copy of the *aLibrary*, generally compressed into a jarfile, folder into the same folder as the applet's class.)

Figure 15.11 AppletStarter class

```
import java.applet.Applet;
public class AppletStarter extends Applet{
    public AppletStarter()  {
        Director director = new Director();
    }
}
```

The AppletStarter method from Figure 15.11 contains similar code to the main method from the go class. Each of these techniques of initiating program execution begins by instantiating a Director object; and each can be used to begin the execution of programs in this book—go is used to execute a program as an application, and AppletStarter is used to execute a program as an applet.

Applets are not executed directly by Web browsers or appletviewers. Instead, an intermediate file, known as an HTML file, is required. The Web browser or appletviewer loads the HTML file, which, in turn, initiates the execution of the applet. A brief description of Web browsers is necessary to understand the reason for HTML files.

Internet Web browsers display information in units known as **Web pages**. Web pages are generally stored in text files using a notation known as **hypertext markup language** or **HTML**. Web pages are also referred to as **HTML files**, because of this notation. HTML files are named with a suffix of ".html" (or sometimes ".htm").

HTML uses special symbols, known as **tags**, to control the page layout. (A complete discussion of HTML tags is not included in this text.) The **applet tag** that is required to begin the execution of an applet is written as shown below:

```
<APPLET CODE = "XYZ.class" WIDTH=someInteger HEIGHT=someInteger>
</APPLET>
```

These lines cause the browser to execute the applet called **XYZ**. Typically, this applet file is in the same folder as the HTML file with the associated applet tag. If the applet file is elsewhere, then **XYZ** must be the complete file directory path name for the applet file. Figure 15.12 contains the text for an HTML file that will initiate the execution of the AppletStarter applet, assuming both files are in the same folder.

Figure 15.12 go.html class

go.html:

```
<HTML>
<HEAD>
<TITLE>Example of how to use a Java Applet</TITLE>
</HEAD>
<BODY>
<APPLET CODE = "AppletStarter.class" WIDTH=200 HEIGHT=100>
</APPLET>
</BODY>
</HTML>
```

If the go.html file is opened by a browser, then the AppletStarter.class code will execute. Alternatively, the following command will initiate the execution of the AppletStarter applet, assuming that both the AppletStarter,class file, and the go.html file are stored within the current directory when the command is issued:

```
appletviewer go.html
```

One difference between an applet and an application is that every applet is implicitly associated with a graphical window. When the applet executes, this window is displayed within a region of the browser or appletviewer. The WIDTH and HEIGHT options in the APPLET tag establish the initial dimensions for this applet window.

The applet window is part of the Applet class because Applet inherits an *awt* class called Frame, and Frame is a general-purpose GUI window. In fact Frame is the same class that is inherited by AWindow, so applets support many of the same methods as AWindow. Since an applet *is* a Frame, these methods are applied directly to the applet in order to apply them to the applet's window.

Figure 15.13 contains an HTML file, named `sunrise.html`, which is designed to execute a second applet. The applet tag within this file specifies three things:

1. The applet to be invoked is called "GrowingDot".
2. The initial width of the applet's window is 200 pixels.
3. The initial height of the applet's window is 100 pixels.

Figure 15.13 `sunrise.html` file

```
<HTML>
<HEAD>
<TITLE>An applet to repeatedly animate a sunrise</TITLE>
</HEAD>
<BODY>
<APPLET CODE = "GrowingDot.class" WIDTH=200 HEIGHT=100 >
</APPLET>
</BODY>
</HTML>
```

The growing dot applet can be executed via the following command:

```
appletviewer sunrise.html
```

For this command to work properly, the current directory must include the `sunrise.html` file, the `GrowingDot.class` file, a `DotTimer.class` file, and the *aLibrary* directory of files.

Figure 15.14 shows an appropriate `GrowingDot` class, as well as the associated `DotTimer` class. The `GrowingDot` class combines many elements from applets and *aLibrary*. Such utilization of many library packages is evident in the collection of import declarations. Since `GrowingDot` is an applet, it must use the `java.applet.Applet` class. Importing *aLibrary* permits `GrowingDot` to utilize `AOval` as a type for its image. The import of `java.awt.*` allows for access to `Color.red`. The animation of the `GrowingDot` applet is accomplished via the `EventTimer` class, which is supported by importing `aLibrary.*`.

All *aLibrary* windows use a so-called "null layout manager" to control window layout. Any applet window that wishes to use *aLibrary* objects must also use a null layout manager. The use of a null layout manager is ensured upon the `GrowingDot` applet window by executing the first instruction of the constructor method, as repeated below:

```
setLayout( null );
```

SOFTWARE ENGINEERING TIP

An applet is compatible with *aLibrary* objects, so long as it uses a null layout manager.

Figure 15.14 GrowingDot applet and DotTimer class

```java
import java.applet.Applet;
import aLibrary.*;
import java.awt.*;


/* invariant
    redDot.getWidth() == redDot.getHeight()
    AND   redDot.getX() == 100 - redDot.getWidth()/2
    AND   redDot.getY() == 100 - redDot.getHeight()/2 */
public class GrowingDot extends Applet {
    private AOval redDot;
    private DotTimer clock;

    /*  postcondition
            redDot is placed on this window
            and clock is scheduled for 30 millisec. repeated
            events */
    public GrowingDot()    {
        setLayout(null);
        resize(200, 100);
        redDot = new AOval(90, 95, 10, 10);
        redDot.setColor( Color.red );
        redDot.setToFill();
        redDot.place( this );
        repaint();
        clock = new DotTimer( this );
        clock.scheduleEvents( 0.1 );
    }


    /* precondition
            redDot != null
        modifies
            redDot
        postcondition
            (old redDot.getWidth() == 200)
                IMPLIES (redDot.getWidth() == 20
                    AND redDot.getHeight() == 20)
            AND (old redDot.getWidth() != 200)
                IMPLIES (redDot.getWidth()
                    == old redDot.getWidth() + 2
                AND redDot.getHeight()
                    == old redDot.getHeight() + 2) */
    public void grow()    {
        if (redDot.getWidth() == 200)   {
            redDot.setSize(10, 10);
            redDot.setLocation(90, 95);
        } else {
```

```
                    redDot.setSize(redDot.getWidth()+2,
                        redDot.getHeight()+2);
                    redDot.setLocation(100-redDot.getWidth()/2, 100-
                        redDot.getHeight()/2);
            }
            redDot.repaint();
        }
    }

import aLibrary.*;
import java.awt.event.*;
public class DotTimer extends EventTimer{
    private GrowingDot theDot;

    /* postcondition
            theDot = d */
    public DotTimer( GrowingDot d )    {
        super();
        theDot = d;
    }

    public void actionPerformed( ActionEvent e )    {
        theDot.grow();
        }
}
```

The second instruction of the GrowingDot method is included to make the size of the applet window clear to anyone reading this program. The resize method performs the same operation upon an Applet that setSize performs upon an AWindow.

Once the GrowingDot applet window has been resized, the code instantiates redDot and places it upon the applet. The GrowingDot method also instantiates a DotTimer object (clock), and causes clock to start generating events in intervals of one-tenth of a second.

Each clock event is handled by a callback to the grow method. Calling grow usually causes the dot's diameter to increase by two pixels, and the dot is recentered within the applet frame. When the dot fills the frame (has a diameter of 200), a call to grow resizes the dot to its initial diameter of 10 pixels.

When an applet is designed to be executed by a Web browser, rather than by appletviewer, three additional precautions should be observed:

1. The init, start, stop, and destroy methods should be used to control applet execution.
2. Supplier classes should be compressed into jar files.
3. Not all Web browsers provide proper support for Java.

The `Applet` class includes the following four parameterless methods to permit an applet to respond to the control buttons of a typical Web browser:

`init()` is called when the browser first loads the HTML page with the applet tag.

`start()` is called each time the applet's HTML page is displayed.

`stop()` is called each time the Web browser stops displaying the applet's HTML page.

`destroy()` is called each time the Web browser is no longer maintaining the applet's HTML page.

For example, the user selects an HTML page by entering its URL or clicking a link to the page. If a newly selected HTML page contains an applet tag, then the applet's constructor method is called, followed by its `init` method, followed by its `start` method. If the user selects a different Web page, then the running applet's `stop` method is automatically called to notify the applet that it is no longer displayed within the Web browser.

Web browsers often maintain recently displayed pages in **cache** (a kind of backup storage). So long as an applet's HTML page is maintained in cache, the `start` method will be called each time the user reselects the page. At some time the browser will be finished maintaining the applet's HTML page—perhaps because the page isn't recent enough to qualify for caching or perhaps because the browser is about to quit executing. The browser calls any executing applet's `destroy` method to notify the applet that it should complete its execution.

These `init`, `start`, `stop`, and `destroy` methods are used by programmers to synchronize an applet's behavior with the Web browser. The `init` method should provide the code necessary to initiate applet execution. The `stop` method should perform tasks such as closing external windows created by the applet. A `start` method might need to reopen external windows that were closed by a prior call to `stop`. The `destroy` method must perform any necessary final cleanup.

Figure 15.15 illustrates with a different version of the `GrowingDot` applet that is designed for execution by a Web browser. This `GrowingDot` applet replaces the need for a constructor method by `init`. This new version of `GrowingDot` also includes a `stop` method to turn off timed event generation and a `start` method to reinitiate timed events. There is no particular need for a `destroy` method in this example, because the applet doesn't create external windows or initiate other execution threads except for the timed events. (Note that `stop` is always called prior to any call to `destroy`.)

Figure 15.15 GrowingDot revised for use by Web browsers

```
import java.applet.Applet;
import aLibrary.*;
import java.awt.*;

/* invariant
    redDot.getWidth() == redDot.getHeight()
    AND  redDot.getX() == 100 - redDot.getWidth()/2
    AND  redDot.getY() == 100 - redDot.getHeight()/2 */
```

```
public class GrowingDot extends Applet implements ActionListener{
    private AOval redDot;
    private DotTimer clock;

    /* postcondition
           redDot is placed on this window
           AND clock != null */
    public init()    {
        setLayout(null);
        resize(200, 100);
        redDot = new AOval(90, 95, 10, 10);
        redDot.setColor( Color.red );
        redDot.setToFill();
        redDot.place( this );
        repaint();
        clock.scheduleEvents( 0.1 );
    }

    /* precondition
           clock != null
       modifies
           clock
       postcondition
           clock event generation has been terminated */
    public void stop()    {
        clock.stop();
    }

    /* precondition
           clock != null
       modifies
           clock
       postcondition
           clock is scheduled for 30 millisec. repeated events */
    public void start()    {
        clock.scheduleEvents( 0.1 );
    }

    /* precondition
           redDot != null
       modifies
           redDot
       postcondition
           (old redDot.getWidth() == 200)
               IMPLIES redDot.getWidth() == 20
                   AND redDot.getHeight() == 20
```

```
                   AND (old redDot.getWidth() != 200)
                       IMPLIES (redDot.getWidth()
                               == old redDot.getWidth() + 2
                           AND redDot.getHeight()
                               == old redDot.getHeight() + 2) */
       public void grow()    {
           if (redDot.getWidth() == 200)   {
               redDot.setSize(10, 10);
                   redDot.setLocation(90, 95);
           } else {
               redDot.setSize(redDot.getWidth()+2,
                   redDot.getHeight()+2);
               redDot.setLocation(100-redDot.getWidth()/2, 100-
                   redDot.getHeight()/2);
           }
           redDot.repaint();
       }
   }
```

When a Web browser retrieves files over the Internet, it executes an applet more efficiently when supplier class files are delivered quickly. File delivery speeds are improved when groups of supplier class files are compressed into a **jar file**. The Sun Java system provides a jar software tool for creating such jar files. The *aLibrary* files have been compressed into a single jar file, called *aLibrary.jar*, which is included with the supplementary materials for this book. Figure 15.16 shows a sunrise.html file that is appropriate for using this jar file.

Figure 15.16 sunrise.html file that uses a jar file

```
<HTML>
<HEAD>
<TITLE>An applet to repeatedly animate a sunrise</TITLE>
</HEAD>
<BODY>
<APPLET CODE = "GrowingDot.class" ARCHIVE="aLibrary.jar"
                WIDTH=200 HEIGHT=100 >
</APPLET>
</BODY>
</HTML>
```

The HTML file from Figure 15.16 includes an *ARCHIVE* option that is used to specify the name of the jar file containing the *ALibrary* code. This particular *ARCHIVE* indicates that a jar file called *aLibrary.jar* should be retrieved from the folder containing the GrowingDot.class file. The *ARCHIVE* option also permits the use of absolute file addressing.

15.6 EVENT DELEGATION (OPTIONAL)

Historically, library classes have used one of two general techniques for handling events.

1. An event is handled by the object associated with the event.
2. An event is delegated to some other object and handled there.

The first technique has been used in prior event handling examples. You have seen classes like AButton that include an actionPerformed method to serve as its event handler. Subclasses of AButton override the actionPerformed method to supply the actual event handling code for the objects of the subclass.

The EventTimer class, used in conjunction with the GrowingDot applet from Figure 15.14, provides another example of an event that is handled by the object that generates the event. In this example, a DotTimer object, called clock, generates events. This same clock object must handle each event through the execution of its own event handler method. For objects inheriting from EventTimer, the actionPerformed method serves as the designated event handler.

A second style of event handling supported in Java is known as **delegation**. In the delegation model of event handling, the task of handling events can be assigned to an object that is different from the object where the event occurs. Figure 15.17 shows a slightly different form of the GrowingDot applet, called GrowingDotDelegate, that handles timed events by way of delegation.

Figure 15.17 GrowingDotDelegate applet

```
import java.applet.Applet;
import aLibrary.*;
import java.awt.*;
import javax.swing.Timer;
import java.awt.event.*;
/* invariant
      redDot.getWidth() == redDot.getHeight()
      AND  redDot.getX() == 100 - redDot.getWidth()/2
      AND  redDot.getY() == 100 - redDot.getHeight()/2 */
public class GrowingDotDelgate extends Applet
        implements ActionListener {
    private AOval redDot;
    private EventTimer clock;
    /*  postcondition
            redeDot is placed on this window
            and clock is scheduled for 30 millisec. repeated
                events */
    public GrowingDotDelegate()    {
        setLayout(null);
        resize(200, 100);
        redDot = new AOval(90, 95, 10, 10);
```

```
                    redDot.setColor( Color.red );
                    redDot.setToFill();
                    redDot.place( this );
                    repaint();
                    clock = new EventTimer( );
                    clock.addActionListener( this );
                    clock.scheduleEvents( 0.1 );
                }
        /*  precondition
                    redDot != null
                modifies
                    redDot
                postcondition
                    (old redDot.getWidth() == 200)
                        IMPLIES redDot.getWidth() == 20
                                AND redDot.getHeight() == 20
                    AND (old redDot.getWidth() != 200)
                        IMPLIES (redDot.getWidth()
                                    == old redDot.getWidth() + 2
                              AND redDot.getHeight()
                                    == old redDot.getHeight() + 2) */
            public void actionPerformed( ActionEvent e )    {
                if (redDot.getWidth() == 200)   {
                    redDot.setSize(10, 10);
                    redDot.setLocation(90, 95);
                } else {
                    redDot.setSize(redDot.getWidth()+2,
                        redDot.getHeight()+2);
                    redDot.setLocation(100-redDot.getWidth()/2,
                        100-redDot.getHeight()/2);
                }
                redDot.repaint();
            }
        }
```

Assigning `GrowingDotDelegate` to become the event handler for `clock` requires three things.

1. `GrowingDot` must include an `implements ActionListener` clause.
2. `GrowingDot` must include an `actionPerformed` method with the indicated parameters.
3. Prior to the first event, `GrowingDot` must execute an `addActionListener` method.

The generalized form of these three items are required for every event that is to be delegated.

1. The class of the delegate object must include an `implements_____Listener` clause.

2. The class of the delegate object must override the appropriate event handler method.

3. Prior to the first event, an add_____Listener method must be called.

The standard Java *awt* and *swing* libraries contain several events that may be delegated. The types of events that can be handled in *awt* include the following:

ActionEvent	Invoked when a button is clicked or timer event occurs (Button and Timer classes)
AdjustmentEvent	Invoked when an adjustable object changes (Scrollbar class)
ComponentEvent	The root class for all Component subclass events (Component class)
FocusEvent	Invoked when the component gains or loses keyboard focus (Component class)
ItemEvent	Invoked when items are selected (Checkbox class)
KeyEvent	Invoked in response to keyboard events (Component class)
MouseEvent	Invoked when mouse is altered upon some object (Component class)
TextEvent	Invoked when text changes (TextComponent class)
WindowEvent	Invoked when a window is opened, closed, iconified, etc. (Window class)

Each type of *awt* event has a corresponding **event listener** with a corresponding name. Event listeners are grouped together in a package known as *java.awt.event*. This list of *awt* listeners includes ActionListener, AdjustmentListener, ComponentListener, ContainerListener, FocusListener, ItemListener, KeyListener, MouseListener, MouseMotionListener, TextListener, and WindowListener.

Each event listener class is a Java **interface**. An interface is like an abstract class in which every method must be empty. Each of the event listener classes contains the signature(s) for one or more event handler methods. For example, the ActionListener class contains the actionPerformed method. Similarly, the AjustmentListener class contains adjustmentValueChanged.

The first requirement for delegation is that the class of the delegate object must include an implements clause for the proper event listener interface. Figure 15.18 describes the syntax of the **implements clause**.

Any class that implements an interface is obligated to implement the methods of the interface. Therefore, the delegate class that implements a listener interface is required to include the event handler method that is included in the particular listener.

When a class includes an *implements* clause for an event listener and implements the appropriate event handler method, it has the capability of serving as a class for delegates. However, event delegation can only begin at run time by executing an *add____Listener* method, such as addActionListener, addMouseListener, or addAdjustmentListener. (The notation "____" in *add____Listener* denotes the fact that there are several different such methods that share the name prefix of "*add*" and suffix of "*Listener*" with the event type between.) These *add____Listener* classes all have a single method that is used to pass the identity of the object to serve as an event delegate.

Figure 15.18 ImplementsClause description

ImplementsClause

Syntax

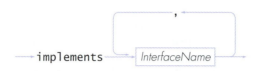

Note

- *interfaceName* is the name of an interface known within this scope.
- An *ImplementsClause* is placed immediately before the "{" for the class.

Usage

The class containing an *ImplementsClause* is obligated to implement (override) every method from that interface and can be used like a subclass of the interface type.

Figure 15.19 contains a second illustration of delegation. This example consists of a Director class that delegates button events. The class of the delegate object is called ButtonHandler.

Figure 15.19 Classes for an AButton delegation example

```
import aLibrary.*;
public class Director  {
    private AWindow window;
    private AButton button;
    private ButtonHandler delegate;

    public Director(){
        window = new AWindow(10, 10, 200, 200);
        button = new AButton(50, 50, 100, 100);
        button.place(window);
        delegate = new ButtonHandler();
        button.addActionListener( delegate );
        window.repaint();
    }
}

import java.awt.event.*;
public class ButtonHandler implements ActionListener  {
    public ButtonHandler()  {
    }
```

```
        /* postcondition
               A message is output. */
        public void actionPerformed( ActionEvent e )    {
            System.out.println( "Some button was clicked." );
        }
    }
```

Executing the Director constructor creates an AButton object, known as button, and places this object upon an AWindow. A third object, called delegate, is also constructed by Director. The following instruction establishes delegate as the event handling delegate for the button object:

```
    button.addActionListener( delegate );
```

Following the execution of this instruction, every user click to the button results in an event that is handled by the delegate object, rather than the button object. Therefore, the actionPerformed method invoked by button events is found in the class to which delegate belongs. This class is called ButtonHandler.

The ButtonHandler class includes both elements that are necessary to serve as a delegate class. Firstly, ButtonHandler includes an *implements* clause. By implementing ActionListener, the ButtonHandler class has the capability of handling ActionPerformed events. The second requirement for a delegate class is to implement the event handling method. This requirement is accomplished by including actionPerformed in the ButtonHandler class.

OPENING
the Black Box

The *aLibrary* classes accomplish event handling by delegating events to themselves. The following shell of the AScrollbar class demonstrates how this is done.

```
import java.awt.*;
import java.awt.event.*;
public class AScrollbar extends Scrollbar
    implements AdjustmentListener {
        public AScrollbar(int x, int y, int w, int h) {
            ...
            addAdjustmentListener(this);
        }
        ...
    public void adjustmentValueChanged(AdjustmentEvent e) { }
}
```

Event handler methods utilize a single event parameter. This event handler parameter becomes increasingly important when events are delegated. Suppose that two different buttons delegate their event handling to the same delegate object. Without using the ActionEvent parameter, the delegate object cannot distinguish which of the two buttons generated the event.

Java passes key information to the event handler method through the event parameter. Perhaps the most useful of all such information is the identity of the object that generated the event. A parameterless method called getSource can be applied to any of the GUI event parameters, and getSource returns the object that generated the event. Using getSource permits a delegate object to distinguish which button was clicked.

Figure 15.20 contains an example use of getSource. The ScrollHandler class in this figure is designed to construct a suitable object that can be delegated event handling for AScrollbar(s).

Figure 15.20 Using getSource in delegating AScrollbar events

```java
import java.awt.event.*;
import aLibrary.*;
public class ScrollHandler implements AdjustmentListener
{
    public ScrollHandler()  {
    }

    /*   postcondition
            The current value of the AScrollbar generating the
            event is output. */
    public void adjustmentValueChanged( AdjustmentEvent e )   {
        AScrollbar scroller = (AScrollbar)(e.getSource());
        System.out.println( "Scrollbar value: " +
            scroller.getValue() );
    }
}
```

In order for an AScrollbar delegate to be able to display the value of the scroll bar, it must first ascertain the identity of the AScrollbar object. The following instruction is used by this example to retrieve the AScrollbar from the event parameter and assign it to the scroller variable.

```java
AScrollbar scroller = (AScrollbar)(e.getSource());
```

Note that the cast to AScrollbar is required, since getSource returns an Object.

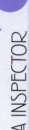

Below is a collection of hints on what to check when examining code that involves the concepts of this chapter.

✓ When you are creating packages, all classes of the package must include the package declaration and it must be the first noncomment line of the file.

✓ The *.class* files stored within a package are available only when the client class includes a proper import declaration and the CLASSPATH variable includes the file folder of the package.

✓ `static` methods and `static` variables should be eliminated whenever possible. Public, non-`final` `static` variables are especially risky. If an alternative exists to `static`, it should be given serious consideration.

✓ Event delegation requires three elements: (1) an `implements` clause within the event handling class, (2) an overridden event handler, and (3) a call to perform the delegation. It is best to check the details of the name of the event handler and its parameters with the appropriate event listener class from the *java.awt.event* package.

applet

applet tag

appletviewer

application

Application
    Programming
    Interface (API)

class library

class method

CLASSPATH

delegation

event listener

files

hypertext markup
    language (HTML)

implements (clause)

import declaration

interface

main (method)

package

package declaration

package scope

pure function

reuse (of software)

static constant

static method

static variable

tag

Web page

EXERCISES

1. Suppose that the first line of some class is as follows:

   ```
   package MyPackage;
   ```

   Further suppose that the CLASSPATH variable includes the following reference that is intended to include the package for the class mentioned above:

   ```
   /Java/Library
   ```

   a. In what folder should the *.class* file for this class be placed?

   b. Where in the directory system should this folder be located?

2. Suppose that you are creating a new class, call Blob. A Blob object is a three-dimensional thing that can be placed on an AWindow. Each of the methods below is being considered for inclusion within the Blob class. Which of the following are suitable candidates for static methods and which must be non-static?

   a. A parameterless method that returns the volume of the this Blob

   ```
   private static? double volume() { ... }
   ```

   b. A method that is passed a Blob parameter and returns its volume

   ```
   private static? double volume( Blob b ) { ... }
   ```

   c. A method that is passed two Blob parameters and returns the one with greater volume

   ```
   private static? double biggerBlob( Blob b1, Blob b2 ) { ... }
   ```

   d. A method to recolor a Blob

   ```
   private static? void recolor( Color c ) { ... }
   ```

   e. An equals method to compare the this Blob to another Blob passed as a parameter

   ```
   private static? boolean equals( Blob b ) { ... }
   ```

3. Suppose that a Java application is written without the use of the go class. Instead, the application will begin executing from a class called TestApplication, shown in part below:

   ```
   import aLibrary.*;
     public class TestApplication {
        private static AOval squirrel;
        private AOval moose;
        public static void main(String args[]) {
           //code goes here
        }
     }
   ```

Which of the following code segments can validly be located in place of "`//code goes here`", and which will cause compile-time errors?

a. `squirrel = new AOval(10, 10, 50, 50);`

b. `moose = new AOval(10, 10, 50, 50);`

c. `AOval localSquirrel = new AOval(10, 10, 50, 50);`

d. `static Oval localSquirrel = new AOval(10, 10, 50, 50);`

4. Consider the following class:

```
import aLibrary.*;
public class ThreeSquares {
   public ARectangle square1 = new ARectangle( 0, 0, 10, 10 );
   public static ARectangle square2 = new ARectangle(0,0,10,10);
   public static final ARectangle square3 =
      new ARectangle(0,0,1,1);
   public static void ThreeSquares() {
      square2 = new ARectangle( 0, 0, 100, 100 );
   }
}
```

For each part that follows, identify whether or not the code is syntactically correct. If it is incorrect, then why? If is it correct, show what values are output when this code executes.

a. `System.out.println( ThreeSquares.square1.getWidth() );`

b. `System.out.println( ThreeSquares.square2.getWidth() );`
   `System.out.println( ThreeSquares.square3.getWidth() );`

c. `ThreeSquares squarePair;`
   `squarePair = new ThreeSquares();`
   `System.out.println( squarePair.square1.getWidth() );`
   `System.out.println( squarePair.square2.getWidth() );`
   `System.out.println( squarePair.square3.getWidth() );`

d. `ThreeSquares squarePair;`
   `squarePair = new ThreeSquares();`
   `squarePair.square3 = new ARectangle(0, 0, 200, 200);`
   `System.out.println( squarePair.square1.getWidth() );`

e. `ThreeSquares squarePairA, squarePairB;`
   `squarePairA = new ThreeSquares();`
   `squarePairB = new ThreeSquares();`
   `squarePairB.square1 = new ARectangle(0, 0, 200, 200);`
   `squarePairB.square2 = new ARectangle(0, 0, 2000, 2000);`
   `System.out.println( squarePairA.square1.getWidth() );`
   `System.out.println( squarePairA.square2.getWidth() );`
   `System.out.println( squarePairB.square1.getWidth() );`
   `System.out.println( squarePairB.square3.getWidth() );`

5. Which of the following parts output the message "Same color" when executed?

a.
```java
Color lightColor, whiteColor;
lightColor = Color.white;
whiteColor = Color.white;
if (lightColor == whiteColor) {
    System.out.println( "Same color" );
}
```

b.
```java
Color lightColor, whiteColor;
lightColor = new Color(0, 0, 0);
whiteColor = new Color(0, 0, 0);
if (lightColor == whiteColor) {
    System.out.println( "Same color" );
}
```

c.
```java
Color lightColor, whiteColor;
lightColor = Color.white;
whiteColor = new Color(0, 0, 0);
if (lightColor == whiteColor) {
    System.out.println( "Same color" );
}
```

d.
```java
Color lightColor, whiteColor;
lightColor = new Color(0, 0, 0);
whiteColor = lightColor;
if (lightColor == whiteColor) {
    System.out.println( "Same color" );
}
```

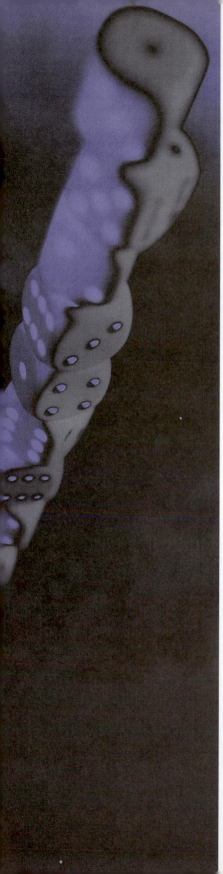

INTRODUCTION TO COMPUTING SYSTEMS

OBJECTIVES

- To introduce the basic hardware components of a computer

- To examine the difference between digital and analog devices as an explanation for some of the behavior of digital computers

- To explore the fundamentals of bit strings and binary numbers, as used by computers to represent information

- To relate common terminology used to measure computer memory size and computer speed

- To introduce basic networking techniques and terminologies

Today's computers are sophisticated devices. Even an ordinary home computer is capable of executing millions of instructions per second, storing billions of individual pieces of data, and transferring messages throughout the world in a fraction of a second. This appendix provides a glimpse of some of the fundamental issues of computing systems that make all this possible.

A.1   WHAT IS A COMPUTER?

Technically, any device that performs automated calculations can be called a **computer**. Computers are embedded in everything from cameras to automobiles and are frequently hidden from sight. However, when most people use the word "computer," they refer to a separate, visible, machine. The most common such computer is called a **personal computer**, because it is serves a single person.

Computers have four basic hardware components.

- **I/O devices**
- A **main memory**
- A **central processing unit**
- **secondary storage**

The first things that most people notice about a computer are the I/O devices. I/O is an abbreviation for input/output, and an I/O device is anything that is intended to get information into or out of a computer. Most I/O devices are designed to interact with humans. The most obvious I/O devices on most personal computers are **keyboards**, **mice, printers,** and computer **monitors** (also called computer **displays**). See Figure A.1.

Figure A.1 Parts of a typical personal computer

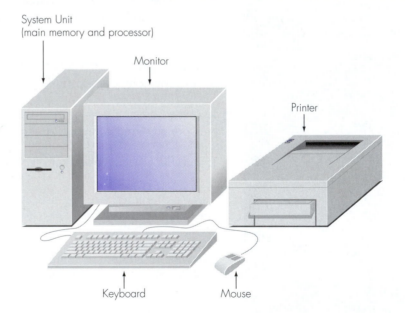

Less obvious than the I/O devices is the box that contains the innards of the computer, often referred to as the **system unit**. Inside the system unit are the main memory and the central processing unit of the computer. Main memory is the part of the computer that stores data while it is being processed. Section A.3 examines the basics of computer storage.

The central processing unit (**CPU** or **processor**) is the computational part of the computer. Some of the common brand names for current processors include the Athalon, Celeron, Pentium III, Pentium IV, and PowerPC G4. Processors are measured primarily in terms of their **clock speed**. The processor's clock is an internal device that regulates the speed at which the processor functions. Generally, a computer with a higher clock speed is faster than one with a lower clock speed. Clock speeds for computers in the year 2000 were typically in the range from 500 MHz to 1+ GHz.

The unit "MHz" stands for a measure of frequency known as **megahertz**. One megahertz is equal to one million cycles per second, so a 500 MHz clock "ticks" a half billion times per second. In 2000, many personal computer processors passed into the **gigahertz** (GHz) range. One gigahertz is one billion cycles per second. Computer processor speeds continue to double approximately every 18 months.

When the computer is turned on, its processor begins to execute instruction after instruction in what is known as the **fetch-execute cycle** (see Figure A.2). Conceptually, the CPU fetches an instruction from main memory, then executes that instruction. Next, the CPU fetches another instruction and the process repeats.

Figure A.2 The fetch-execute cycle

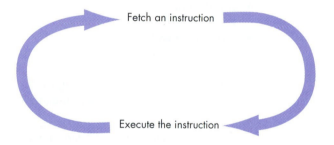

Fetch an instruction

Execute the instruction

The instructions that are fetched from main memory constitute the **program** that is being executed. The form of these instructions is called **machine language** because they are in a form that is conveniently decoded by the machine (i.e., the CPU). CPUs usually cannot execute one machine instruction per clock cycle. However, the exact number of instructions that are executed per second is difficult to measure, because this rate depends upon the speed of main memory, the processor's ability to overlap the execution of multiple instructions, and the task performed by each particular instruction.

Each machine instruction performs a simple function. For example, a single machine instruction might add two pieces of data. The data that is used by a program is also stored in main memory. Therefore, the execution of an instruction often retrieves data from main memory and stores results back in main memory.

This dual usage of main memory to store both program instructions and data is called the **von Neumann architecture**. This is named after John von Neumann who developed the concept in the 1940s.

Other machine instructions carry out tasks to transfer information to and from the I/O devices. One instruction might transfer the data that represents a keystroke, and another instruction transfers a character to be displayed on the monitor.

Data stored in main memory is transient. Before a program begins to execute, both the instructions and the data for the program must be placed (loaded) into memory. Since there is only a limited amount of main memory, it must be reused. A newly executing program is frequently loaded into memory space made available from an earlier program that has completed. This means that a program should consider everything it stores in main memory to be lost once its execution is finished. A second way in which main memory is transient is that it is usually built using technologies that erase when the current is shut off. This transient nature of data stored in main memory is the reason why computers generally include more permanent storage, called **secondary storage**.

Data stored on secondary storage can be maintained indefinitely. Many secondary storage devices have removable media that can be transported from one computer to another.

A secondary storage device is often named after its media. For example, a floppy disk drive uses floppy disks for a storage media. Other common forms of secondary storage media include the following:

- **hard disks** The primary storage for large files and programs integral to computer operation
- **floppy disks** Removable magnetic disks approximately 3.5 inches square
- **compact disks (CD)** Plastic disks storing information as reflective/non-reflective dots
- **DVD** A CD-like medium with greater capacity
- **magnetic tapes** Ribbons of magnetically coated plastic

Sometimes the same basic technology has variations. A **CD-ROM** device is capable of playing data that has been previously stored on a CD. However, a CD-ROM cannot write new data to CDs. The acronym "ROM" represents "read only memory," which means that the CPU is restricted to reading from the CD. A different form of secondary storage, known as **CD-RW**, can both retrieve data from a CD and store (burn) new data onto the CD. The "RW" symbols stand for "read" (retrieve data) and "write" (store new data).

A.2   ANALOG OR DIGITAL?

Most of today's computers are **digital computers**, although certain special-purpose nondigital (**analog**) computers exist. Many aspects of computer behavior are defined by its digital nature.

Analog devices are based on continuously varying systems, while digital devices support only a fixed (discrete) number of alternatives. An elevator is an analog device because it rises gradually and continuously from one floor to the next. A stairway is discrete, not analog, because it divides its rise into a certain number of steps. A motion picture exhibits this same discrete property. Every motion picture is made from a film of individual photos (frames) that, when played at the rate of 30 frames per second, give the illusion of continuous motion. Figure A.3 lists several real-life systems that have both discrete and continuous (analog) counterparts.

Discrete systems are conveniently represented as digits. A light switch is either off or on. The "off" position can be represented by the digit 0 and the "on" position by the digit 1. Similarly, the clicking volume buttons can be used to raise and lower the value of an integer ranging from 0 (no sound) to 100 (maximum volume).

Figure A.3 Discrete systems as opposed to continuous systems

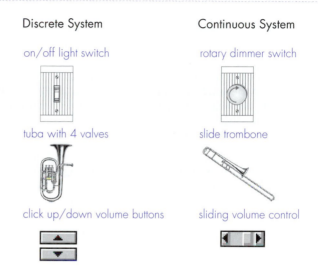

Two of the more common devices that are available in either digital or analog are automobile speedometers and wristwatches. An analog speedometer has a needle that moves continuously from 0 miles per hour up. Digital speedometers display the auto's speed in the form of numeric digits. A digital speedometer displays "25" or "26", but nothing between. An analog wristwatch has hands that sweep around the dial in an infinite number of positions, while its digital counterpart displays time in the form of a fixed collection of numbers.

The concept of digitization is key to understanding the modern computer. Images displayed on a computer monitor are not drawn as a collection of continuous lines, but are rather displayed upon a grid of small rectangular figures called **pixels** (short for picture elements). Figure A.4 illustrates. The letter "A" on the right is displayed in a grid of pixels that is 7 wide and 9 high. Most modern computer displays have sufficiently many pixels that the quality of images is better than the pixelized "A" from Figure A.4. (A common computer monitor today measures 17 inches diagonally and has a visible region of 1280 pixels horizontally by 1024 pixels vertically or roughly 100 pixels per inch.) However, even the best computer displays have limitations.

Figure A.4 Displaying a letter in a continuous and pixelized form

Continuous Letter   Pixelized Letter

The color and intensity of graphical images are also digitized. Color resolution can differ. One commonly used digitization technique is like mixing three colors of paint. Every color is made from mixing a certain amount of redness with an amount of greenness and an amount of blueness. The colors are digitized by storing the intensity of each color as an integer in the range from 0 through 255. This means that 256 different intensities of red that can be mixed with 256 different intensities of green and 256 different intensities of blue. The result is 256 × 256 × 256 = 1,677,216 potential colors.

Sound on a computer is also stored digitally. Phonograph records and analog tape recorders store sound in analog form as an infinite number of different frequencies and amplitudes. Compact disks and MP3s encode sound as a sequence of numbers that are sampled thousands of times per second. Playing this digitized sound is like playing a motion picture, stringing the sound associated with the numbers so close together that the human ear hears continuity.

A.3 HOW IS DATA STORED?

By now it should be clear that a digital computer stores data in digitized (i.e., numeric) form. Images are stored as numbers, sounds are stored as numbers, machine instructions are stored as numbers. Everything that is stored within a digital computer is encoded as a number.

The numbers stored in a computer are represented in an elementary form, known as a **bit string**. A bit string is a sequence of several **bits**, where "bit" is an abbreviation for **binary digit**. A bit is limited to just two possible values, either 0 or 1.

To understand why bits are important, it is necessary to examine a little more about computer technology. Computers store things in one of three forms: electrically, magnetically, or optically. The main memory and CPU use largely electrical storage. CDs and DVDs store data optically. Most secondary storage, including hard disks, floppy disks, and tapes, utilize magnetic storage technologies.

Figure A.5 shows that each of these three storage techniques has a natural method for encoding a bit. An electrical circuit can be designed to store either a positive voltage (V+) or an electrical ground (gnd). A positive voltage can represent a bit value 1, and a ground can represent 0. An optical circuit is either light or dark, representing 0 and 1. A magnetic field can be polarized in one of two directions, commonly referred to as "north" and "south." One of these two magnetic polarities can be used to represent a 0 and the other a 1.

Figure A.5 Storing a bit electrically, optically, or magnetically

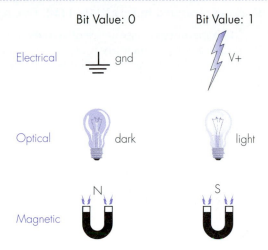

A single bit of data can only store one of two configurations: 0 or 1. Therefore, in order to store more complex forms of data, bits must be strung together in a sequence. Conceptually, a string of eight bits is like eight parallel wires, each with their own value (V+ or gnd) or eight spots on a CD each capable of reflecting light or dark. Any such string that is exactly eight bits long is called a **byte**.

One byte of storage is sufficient to store a simple character or an integer in the range from 0 through 255. A byte is also the base measurement used to describe the volume of data. Figure A.6 shows several common measurements that are based in quantities of bytes.

Figure A.6 Commonly used computer storage measures

Measure	Abbrev	Quantity (in bytes)
byte	B	$2^0 = 1$
kilobyte	KB	$2^{10} = 1,024$
megabyte	MB	$2^{20} = 1,048,576$
gigabyte	GB	$2^{30} = 1,073,741,824$
terabyte	TB	$2^{40} = 1,099,511,627,776$

One **kilobyte (KB)** of data is roughly one thousand bytes. The transfer of data over telephone lines is in the range of 20 to 30 kilobytes per second. One **megabyte (MB)** is slightly more than a million bytes. Main memory sizes are generally measured in megabytes. A personal computer may be advertised with 128 MB of main memory. Secondary storage is typically much larger and much slower than main memory. Therefore, secondary storage devices are generally measured in **gigabytes (GB)**. One gigabyte exceeds a billion bytes. While a typical hard disk size is 30 GB, it is possible for a large computer installation to have computing databases measured in **terabytes (TB)**. One terabyte is over a trillion bytes.

Main memory is a sequence of **words** of data, where each word is a bit string. The size of a word of memory is dependant upon the particular computer with one to eight bytes being common word length. Figure A.7 diagrams this view by showing a portion of main memory.

Figure A.7 Segment of main memory

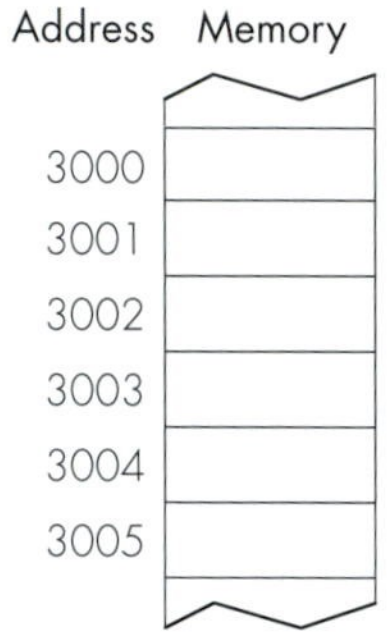

Figure A.7 also illustrates that each separate word of memory has its own numeric address. Like the street address of a townhouse, the memory address uniquely identifies the location of a particular word of data. The CPU fetches an instruction by specifying the address of the memory word(s) where the instruction is stored. Similarly, an address is required any time that the CPU retrieves data from or stores data into memory.

A.4 WHAT ARE BINARY NUMBERS?

When bit strings must represent numeric values, the obvious encoding choice is that of **binary numbers**. A binary number, also known as a **base-2 number**, uses 0 and 1 as its only two digits

To understand binary numbers it is helpful to review the more familiar **decimal numbers**. A decimal integer is written as a sequence of decimal digits (0 through 9) in which each digit position has a different weight, and this weight indicates how much a position contributes to the integer's value. The rightmost digit position is called the "1's position," because the rightmost digit represents a number of 1s in the integer value. The second position from the right is the 10s position, because the digit in this position contributes ten times its value to the integer. The third position from the right is the 100s position; the fourth position is the 1000s position; and so on.

Figure A.8 illustrates with a particular decimal number, namely "3704". The integer value of this number is calculated as $3 \times 1000 + 7 \times 100 + 0 \times 10 + 4 \times 1$.

Figure A.8 The value of a decimal integer

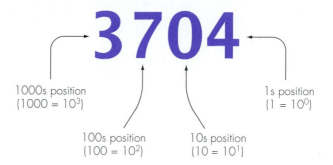

From Figure A.8 it is evident that the weight of each position in a decimal number is a power of 10 and that these powers increase from right to left. The weight of the rightmost position in a decimal integer is $1 = 10^0$. The second position from the right has a weight of $10 = 10^1$. The third position has a weight of $100 = 10^2$, and the fourth position has a weight of $1000 = 10^3$.

The binary number system is like the decimal system if you substitute 2 for 10. The decimal system has 10 digits (0 through 9); and the binary system has two digits (0 and 1). The weights of the digit positions of a decimal number are powers of 10. The weights of the digit positions in a binary number are powers of 2. Therefore, the rightmost digit in a binary number is still the 1s position (2^0). The second position from the right in a binary number is the 2s position (2^1). The third position is the 4s position (2^2). The fourth position is the 8s position (2^3).

Figure A.9 The value of a binary integer

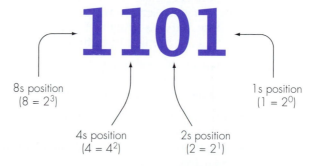

The decimal value of any binary number can be calculated by summing the product of each digit times its weight. The value of the binary number 1101 (shown in Figure A.9) is $1 \times 8 + 1 \times 4 + 0 \times 2 + 1 \times 1 = 13$. Figure A.10 illustrates how to count from 0 through 16 (decimal) with binary numbers.

Figure A.10 Binary numbers from 0 through 16 (decimal)

Binary		Decimal
0	=	0
1	=	1
10	=	2
11	=	3
100	=	4
101	=	5
110	=	6
111	=	7
1000	=	8
1001	=	9
1010	=	10
1011	=	11
1100	=	12
1101	=	13
1110	=	14
1111	=	15
10000	=	16

Just as with decimal numbers, leading zeros (zeros on the left of an integer) contribute nothing to the value of a binary number. This means that 00010 = 10.

Since the positional weights of binary digits grow by powers of 2, it is helpful to be familiar with powers of two when using this system. Figure A.11 diagrams a table of the powers of 2 from 2^0 through 2^{10}. This powers of 2 table verifies that one kilobyte is 1024 bytes, rather than 1000 bytes. Similarly, this table provides insight about why the main memory of a computer is generally 64 KB or 256 KB, rather than more even decimal quantities.

The powers of 2 can also be used to count the number of unique values for a bit string of a given length. For example, there are 32 (2^5) different bit strings that can be formed from a string of five bits. Similarly, there are 256 (2^8) different bit strings that have a length of eight bits.

The powers of 2 table can also be used to assist in the conversion of a decimal number into its binary representation. For example, the value of 625 can be converted to a decimal number as follows:

- The largest power of 2 contained within 625 is 512 (2^9). Subtracting 625 – 512 leaves 113.
- The largest power of 2 contained within 113 is 64 (2^6). Subtracting 113 – 64 leaves 49.
- The largest power of 2 contained within 49 is 32 (2^5). Subtracting 49 – 32 leaves 17.
- The largest power of 2 contained within 17 is 16 (2^4). Subtracting 17 – 16 leaves 1.

Figure A.11 Value of the powers of 2 (2^0 through 2^{10})

2^0	1
2^1	2
2^2	4
2^3	8
2^4	16
2^5	32
2^6	64
2^7	128
2^8	256
2^9	512
2^{10}	1024

Using the above reasoning, the binary equivalent of 625 can be constructed as follows:

$$
\begin{aligned}
625 \text{ (decimal)} \ &= \ 1 \times 2^9 + 1 \times 2^6 + 1 \times 2^5 + 1 \times 2^4 + 1 \times 2^0 \\
&= \ 1 \times 2^9 + 0 \times 2^8 + 0 \times 2^7 + 1 \times 2^6 + 1 \times 2^5 + 1 \times 2^4 + 0 \times 2^3 \\
&\quad + 0 \times 2^2 + 0 \times 2^1 + 1 \times 2^0 \\
&= \ 1001110001 \text{ (binary)}
\end{aligned}
$$

This technique converting a decimal number to binary by repeatedly subtracting the largest possible power of 2 is somewhat difficult for larger numbers. Another technique for translating from decimal to binary representation is to perform repeated integer divisions by 2. This method starts with a decimal number and divides the number by 2, recording both the quotient and the remainder of this division. The quotient of the first division is divided by 2 again, noting the quotient and remainder of this second division. The quotient of the second division is divided by 2 again, and so on. These repeated divisions by 2 continue until the resulting quotient is zero. The binary number is formed from the bit string of all remainder bits joined together with the earliest remainders on the right end of the bit string.

To illustrate the technique of converting to binary by repeated division a notation is used for division that is useful for pen and paper calculations. The calculation "97 divided by 2 results in a quotient of 48 and a remainder of 1" is diagrammed as follows.

$$
2 \ \overline{\left)\ 97 \right.}
$$

$$
48 \qquad \text{R: 1}
$$

Figure A.12 demonstrates the conversion of 625 (decimal) into its binary equivalent through repeated division by 2. It is important to notice that the remainders form the binary value from *bottom to top*.

Figure A.12 Convert 625 (decimal) into binary via repeated division by 2

To convert 625 to binary:

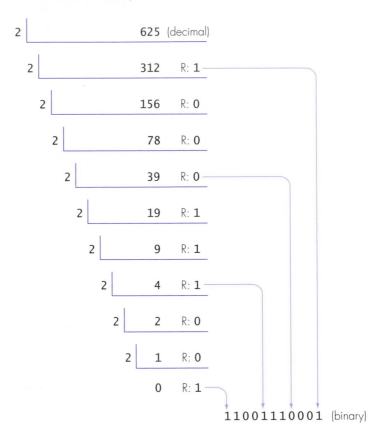

Just like decimal numbers, binary numbers can represent fractional values. Decimal numbers use a decimal point to separate the integer part of the number from the fractional part. The weight of the digits to the right of the decimal point continue the sequence of powers of two by using negative powers of 10. (Recall that $10^{-x} = 1/10^x$.) Binary numbers also use a period to separate the integer portion from the fractional part, and the weight of the positions right of the period are negative powers of 2. Figure A.13 illustrates.

Converting a binary value into decimal is done the same with or without fractional parts. That is, you sum the weights of each binary 1 bit position. Below are two examples.

11.01 (binary) = 2 + 1 + 1/4 = 3.25
0.101 (binary) = 1/2 + 1/8 = 0.625

Figure A.13 The value of a binary integer with fractional part

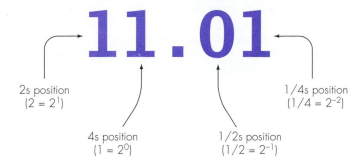

Converting a decimal number into its binary representation is slightly different when the number contains a fractional part. The technique of repeatedly subtracting powers of 2 still works as previously described; however, the technique of repeated division by 2 does not. To convert the fractional part to binary, a repeated multiplication by 2 is used.

The complete technique for converting decimal values into binary representations is to separate the portion of the binary number to the left of the period (the integer part) from the portion right of the period (the fractional part). The integer part is converted as previously described. The fractional part is converted by repeatedly *multiplying* the fractional part by 2 and retaining all of the resulting integer bits. (The integer bits are ordered from greatest weight to least.) This process is pictured in Figure A.14.

Figure A.14 Convert decimal into binary via repeated multiplication by 2

To convert 0.6875 to binary:

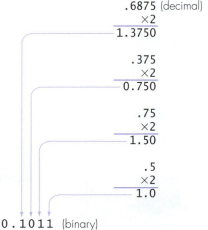

Representing fractional parts in binary form sometimes makes it impossible to store exact values. Even decimal numbers cannot represent all real numbers exactly with a finite number of digits. For example, the value 1/3 = 0.33333... where the "..." denote the fact that 3s repeat forever. The binary numbers are able to represent even fewer real numbers exactly. For example, the decimal number 0.2 is a repeating number in binary, as demonstrated by the following steps of converting 0.2 into binary:

$$
\begin{array}{ccc}
\begin{array}{r} .2 \\ \times\, 2 \\ \hline 0.4 \end{array}
&
\begin{array}{r} .8 \\ \times\, 2 \\ \hline 1.6 \end{array}
&
\begin{array}{r} .2 \\ \times\, 2 \\ \hline 0.4 \end{array}
\\[2em]
\begin{array}{r} .4 \\ \times\, 2 \\ \hline 0.8 \end{array}
&
\begin{array}{r} .6 \\ \times\, 2 \\ \hline 1.2 \end{array}
&
\end{array}
$$

This inability to store fractional values exactly with a fixed number of digits leads to the fact that computers often store numbers as approximations.

A.5 HOW DO COMPUTERS COMMUNICATE?

One of the most important facilities of the modern computer is its ability to communicate with other computers, and thereby with other people. Such communication is made possible by connecting computers to one another in a computer **network**, as shown in Figure A.15. The computers within a particular office suite or small building often form a **local area network** (**LAN**). The technologies that are used to manage LAN communications are often restricted by distance to a few hundred meters. Networks that cover larger distances are referred to as **wide area networks (WANs)**.

Figure A.15 Networked computers

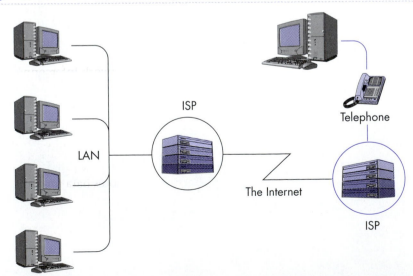

Most of today's LANs and WANs are ultimately connected to each other by the **Internet**. The Internet is really not a single entity, but is actually a collection of separate networks that are interconnected with few regulations and almost no centralized management. However, computers on the Internet do share a few **protocols** (communication conventions).

Internet service providers (ISPs) are companies who sell physical connections to the Internet. Each ISP has its own connection to the Internet that is made available to customers who connect to ISP computers.

A computer used at home typically makes use of existing telephone lines to communicate with their ISP. Telephone lines, commonly referred to as **voice lines**, are not specifically designed to handle computer communication, so a device called a **modem** is required within any computer communicating in this way. Modems are typically capable of a communications **bandwidth** (i.e., capacity) of 56 Kb per second. (Note that communication speeds are given in *kilobits* per second, not kilobytes per second. The small "b" in Kb denotes this difference.) A second technology that is gaining popularity among home computer users borrows the use of cable television wires. **Cable modems** transfer data at a rate of 1.5 **Mbps** (**megabits per second**).

A LAN is more likely to use so-called **data lines,** instead of telephone wires, to carry computer transmissions. Data lines are preferred because of their additional bandwidth. LAN bandwidth typically ranges from 10 Mbps for the commonly used **Ethernet** technology to 12.8 gigabits per second (Gbps) for **asynchronous transfer mode (ATM)**. Wireless technologies are beginning to reach levels of bandwidth and cost that make them practical for LAN usage.

Data lines used to transmit over longer distances, such as those connecting LANs to an ISP, often use Tx lines to communicate. The most common such communication uses either T1 lines (1.5 Mbps) or T3 lines (45 Mbps).

There is more to a network than just wires. Networks actually consist of at least three different kinds of devices:

- **client computers**
- **network interconnection devices**
- **servers**

A client computer refers to any computer that is making use of the services provided by a network. Home computers and office computers are generally thought of as client computers. A network interconnection device is any piece of equipment needed to connect the wires of the network and make certain that transmissions are directed along the proper paths. Switches, routers, and hubs are among the devices that provide such network infrastructure.

One of the greatest advantages of a computer network is for sharing of resources. Servers are the primary resource providers. A server is just another computer, but unlike client computers, servers are designed to respond to requests from other computers. A database server stores data for access by selected individuals. A compute server provides the ability to perform calculations at high speeds. A Web server provides World Wide Web pages to be displayed on client computers using a Web browser such as Internet Explorer or Netscape Navigator.

Suppose that you wish to send e-mail to a friend. You compose your e-mail on your personal computer (a client computer) and then request that the message be sent. Your message is directed through the Internet from router to router using the address you specify in the "to field" to guide it to its destination. Eventually, this message will be stored in the e-mail server that is used by your friend. Still later, your friend, using another client computer, requests mail from the e-mail server and your message is delivered. This example illustrates that even a simple e-mail message requires the cooperation of many different devices, including client computers, servers, and the network interconnection devices that lie between.

So if a computer is connected to a LAN operating at 10 Mbps, then why do Web pages sometimes arrive at speeds less than 10 Kbps? The answer to this question is as complicated as the Internet itself. It is possible that the Web server is simply receiving requests for its Web pages faster than it is able to retrieve them from disk, so it selectively puts client computers "on hold." Another possible explanation is that the local computer is busy performing other tasks that restrict the CPU time that is available for network communication. While these end computers may be the source of some bottlenecks, a more likely reason for slow communication is the network itself.

LANs and WANs make use of shared interconnections. For example, a LAN may operate at 10 Mbps, but if there are 100 computers on the LAN, the average bandwidth available to each is less than 0.1 Mbps. Similarly, data transmission lines that connect two ISPs act like trunk lines that can be shared by thousands of individual computers. This explains why the Internet is often called the "data superhighway." A frequent concern is that there are more "on-ramps" onto the Internet than the "number of driving lanes" can handle.

A.6 WHY ARE COMPUTERS CALLED "SYSTEMS"?

We have seen that modern computer hardware can perform some pretty remarkable feats: Execute millions of machine instructions per second, store trillions of bytes on a hard disk, communicate with other computers at a rate of thousands of bytes per second. However, computer hardware can do none of these things without computer **software**. Computer hardware without software is like a DVD player without a DVD disk, a baseball glove without a ball, a movie projector without film.

The term "software" refers to any collection of computer instructions. These instructions serve as commands for the CPU. Software instructions might command the CPU to add two values, to store something into main memory, to display the character "R" on the computer monitor, or to transmit a byte of information to some other Internet address.

Instructions are grouped together to form computer programs. A single program is designed to perform one application. Word processors are programs to help people write and edit textual documents. Database applications are programs to assist computer users in information storage and retrieval. Web browsers are programs designed to make it convenient to "surf" the Internet.

At the center of all computer activity is a very special program, known as the **operating system (OS)**. Common operating systems for personal computers include UNIX, LINUX (a version of UNIX), OS X, Solaris (another version of UNIX), Windows 98, Windows NT, and Windows 2000. The operating system is responsible for coordination of all computer functions, including how various parts of the hardware interact with each other and with the executing software. The following items are some of the key functions performed by operating systems.

- The OS maintains a file system to keep track of all data stored on secondary storage. Such a file system identifies each file by a name and allows files to be organized into folders (also called "directories").
- The OS manages the main memory loading new programs into memory so they can execute and reserving separate memory space to store the program's data.
- The OS ensures the integrity of several programs that are simultaneously active. If you run a word processor at the same time as a Web browser, it is the operating system that does the "behind the scenes" work needed to guarantee that both of these programs can operate independently at the same time.
- The OS provides a **graphical user interface** (**GUI**). The elements of a typical GUI include menus for selecting tasks, windows for displaying text and graphics on a computer monitor, buttons for clicking, and scrollbars for dragging. The GUI elements work closely with the computer keyboard and mouse to give the user control over the computer.

Computers are called "computer systems" to refer to the collaborative nature of the computer hardware and its operating system.

JAVA SYNTAX DIAGRAMS

This appendix defines the syntax of the Java programming language in syntax diagram format. Each rectangle contains the name of a separate syntax diagram. Semantic qualifiers are denoted using a <...> suffix. For example, **ID <class>** denotes the syntax diagram called "ID" that names a class. Below is an alphabetized list of diagram names and their corresponding page number within this appendix.

CompilationUnit

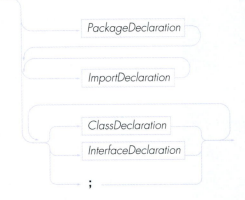

PackageDeclaration

ImportDeclaration

ClassBody

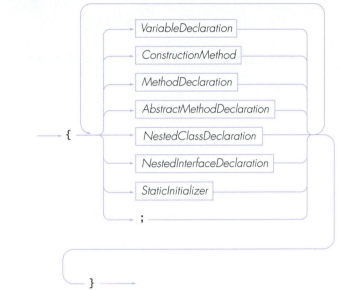

ClassDeclaration

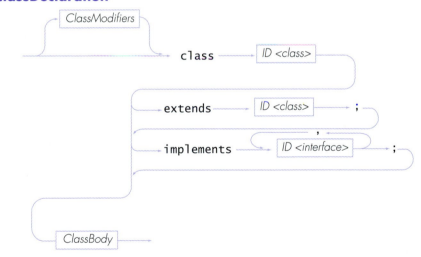

ClassModifiers

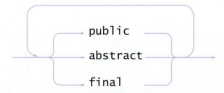

Note: Each modifier can occur at most once for the same modified unit.

InterfaceDeclaration

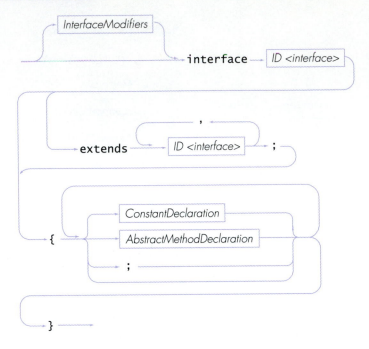

InterfaceModifiers

public

NestedClassDeclaration

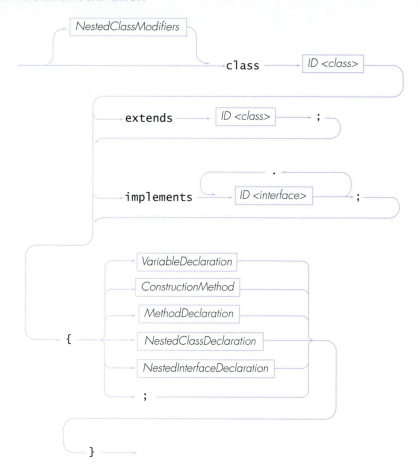

NestedClassModifiers

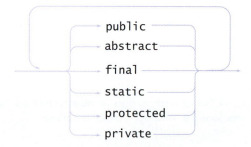

Notes:

- Each modifier can occur at most once for the same modified unit.
- The following modifiers are mutually exclusive: public, protected, private.

NestedInterfaceDeclaration

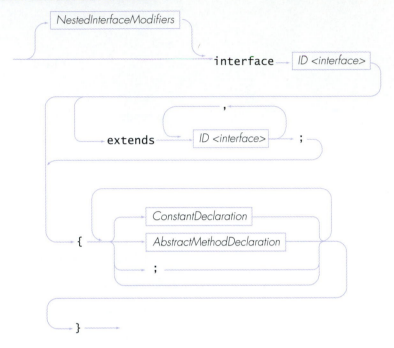

ConstantDeclaration

Note: A constant declaration must include the "final" modifier.

AbstractMethodDeclaration
ConstructorMethod

Note: Within an abstract class an abstract method must include an "abstract" modifier. Within an interface the "abstract" modier is not used.

ConstructorMethod

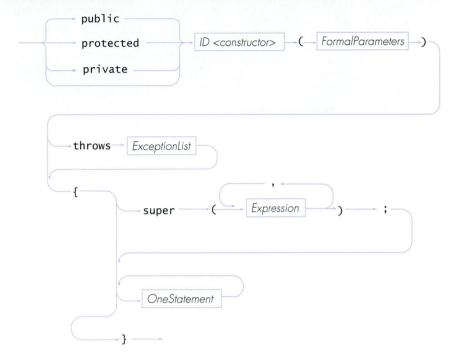

FormalParameters

FormalParameter

ExceptionList

Type

MethodDeclaration

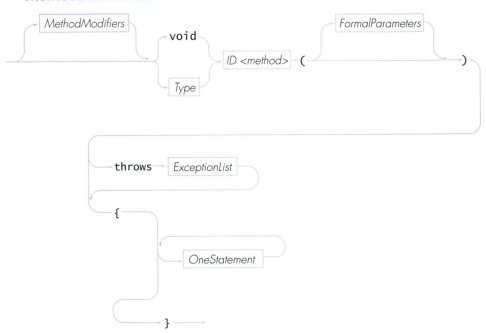

MethodModifiers

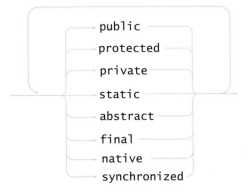

Note: Each modifier can occur at most once for the same modified unit. The following modifiers are mutually exclusive: `public`, `protected`, `private`.

VariableDeclaration

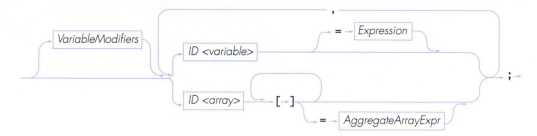

VariableModifiers

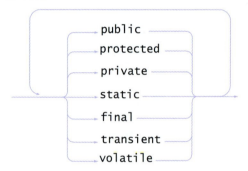

Note: Each modifier can occur at most once for the same modified unit. The following modifiers are mutually exclusive: public, protected, private.

StaticInitializer

OneStatement

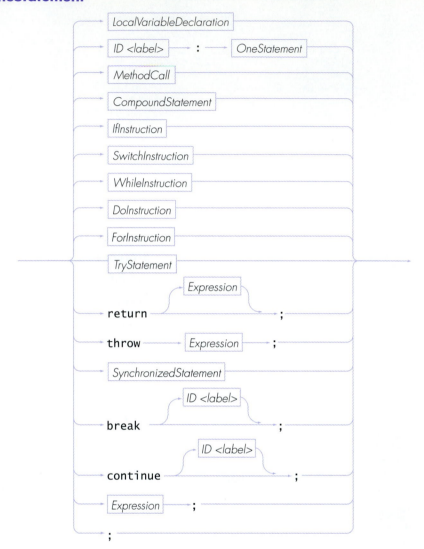

LocalVariableDeclaration

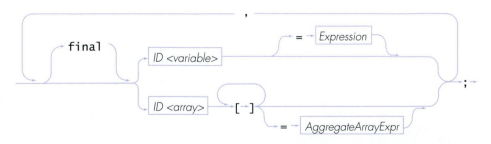

AggregateArrayExpr

MethodCall

Arguments

CompoundStatement

IfInstruction

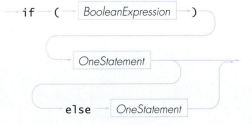

SwitchInstruction

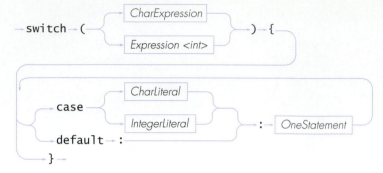

Note: No more than one *default* clause is permitted per switch instruction.

WhileInstruction

DoInstruction

ForInstruction

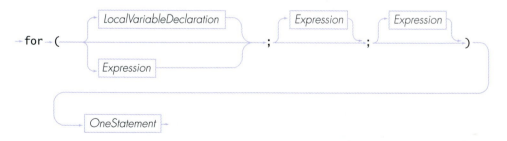

TryStatement

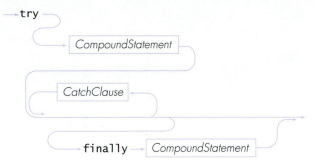

CatchClause

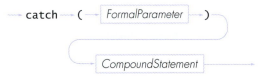

SynchronizedStatement

Expression

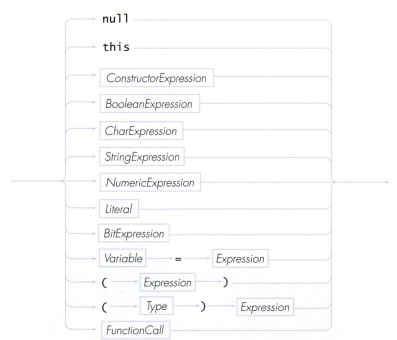

ConstructorExpression

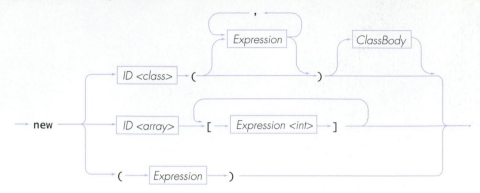

PrimitiveExpression

Note: A PrimitiveExpression must be of type boolean, byte, char, float, int, long, or short.

BooleanExpression

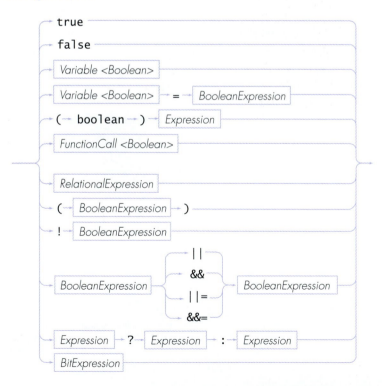

RelationalExpression

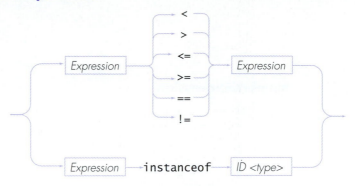

CharExpression

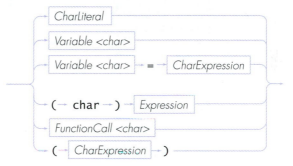

CharLiteral

Note: Extra blanks, tabs, and line breaks are not permitted within CharLiteral.

StringExpression

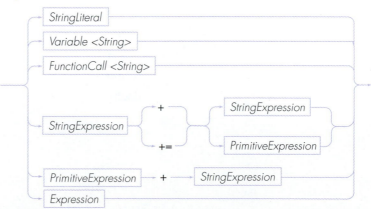

StringLiteral

NumericExpression

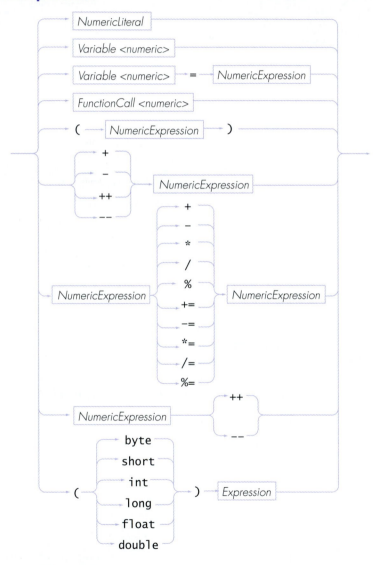

NumericLiteral

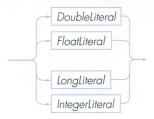

DoubleLiteral

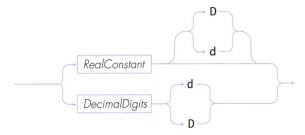

Note: Blanks, tabs, and line breaks are not permitted within `DoubleLiteral`.

FloatLiteral

Note : Blanks, tabs, and line breaks are not permitted within `FloatLiteral`.

LongLiteral

Note : Blanks, tabs, and line breaks are not permitted within `LongLiteral`.

RealConstant

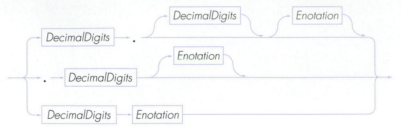

Note : Blanks, tabs, and line breaks are not permitted within RealConstant.

Enotation

Note : Blanks, tabs, and line breaks are not permitted within Enotation.

IntegerLiteral

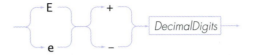

Note : Blanks, tabs, and line breaks are not permitted within IntegerLiteral.

Literal

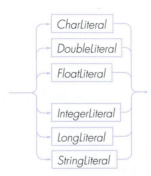

BitExpression

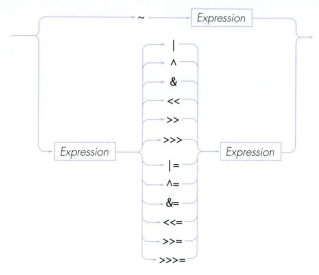

DecimalDigits

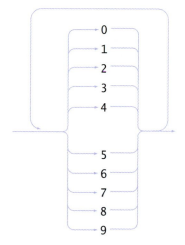

Note : Blanks, tabs, and line breaks are not permitted within `DecimalDigits`.

HexadecimalDigits

Note : Blanks, tabs, and line breaks are not permitted within `HexadecimalDigits`.

HexadecimalDigit

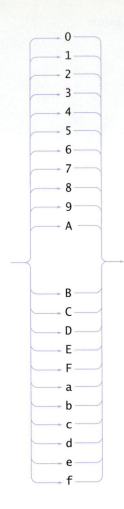

FunctionCall

Object Reference

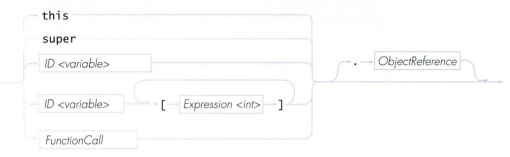

Variable

NumericVariable

Note : NumericVariable is a variable of type byte, double, float, int, long, or short.

ID

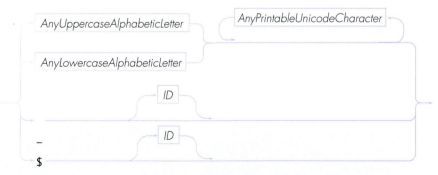

Note : Blanks, tabs, and line breaks are not permitted within ID.

OneCharacter

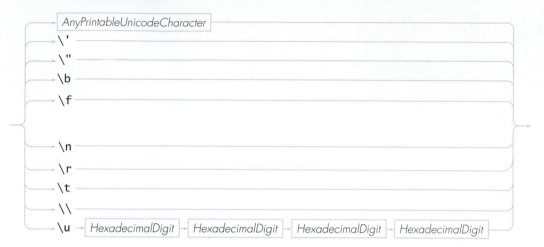

Note : Blanks (except for a single blank character), tabs, and line breaks are not permitted within OneCharacter.

Comment

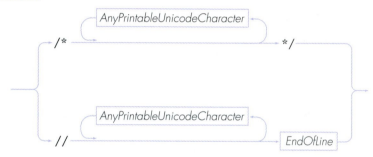

PRECEDENCE OF JAVA OPERATIONS

This table indicates the 15 Java precedence levels and associated operators. The textbook sections that describe the various operations are included. ("N.C." means not covered.)

Precedence	Operator	Operation	Text coverage	Order within
high (Postfix)	--	postfix autodecrement	Sect. 5.2	Left to right
	++	postfix autoincrement	Sect. 5.2	
	.	qualified expression	Sect. 2.2 & 6.2	
	[ ]	array indexing	Sect. 12.1	
2nd (Unary)	+	unary plus	N.C.	Right to left
	-	unary minus	Sect. 5.2	
	!	boolean NOT	Sect. 7.3	
	--	prefix autodecrement	N.C.	
	++	prefix autoincrement	N.C.	
	~	bitwise NOT	N.C.	
3rd (Cast)	new	object construction	Sect. 2.4	Right to left
	(*type*)	cast	Sect. 5.6	
4th (Multiplicative)	/	division	Sect. 5.2	Left to right
	*	multiplication	Sect. 5.2	
	%	remainder (modulus)	Sect. 5.2	
5th (Additive)	+	addition	Sect. 5.2	Left to right
	-	subtraction	Sect. 5.2	
	+	String concatenation	Sect. 6.9	
6th (Shift)	<<	shift left	N.C.	Left to right
	>>	shift right	N.C.	
	>>>	shift right with 0	N.C.	
7th (Relational)	<	less	Sect. 7.2	Left to right
	<=	less or equal	Sect. 7.2	
	>	greater	Sect. 7.2	
	>=	greater or equal	Sect. 7.2	
	instanceof	type comparison	Sect. 9.2	
8th (Equality)	==	equality (identity)	Sect. 7.2 & 9.6	Left to right
	!=	inequality	Sect. 7.2	
9th	&	bitwise AND	N.C.	Left to right
10th	^	bitwise XOR	N.C.	Left to right
11th	|	bitwise OR	N.C.	Left to right
12th	&&	boolean AND	Sect. 7.3	Left to right

Precedence	Operator	Operation	Text coverage	Order within
13th	||	boolean OR	Sect. 7.3	Left to right
14th	?:	conditional	N.C.	Right to left
15th	=	assignment	Sect. 2.4	Right to left
(Assignment)	+=	add, then assign	N.C.	
	+=	concatenate, then assign	N.C.	
	/=	divide, then assign	N.C.	
	*=	multiply, then assign	N.C.	
	%	modulus, then assign	N.C.	
	-=	subtract, then assign	N.C.	
	<<=	shift left, then assign	N.C.	
	>>=	shift right, then assign	N.C.	
	>>>=	shift right with zero, then assign	N.C.	
	&=	bitwise AND, then assign	N.C.	
	|=	bitwise OR, then assign	N.C.	
	^=	bitwise XOR, then assign	N.C.	

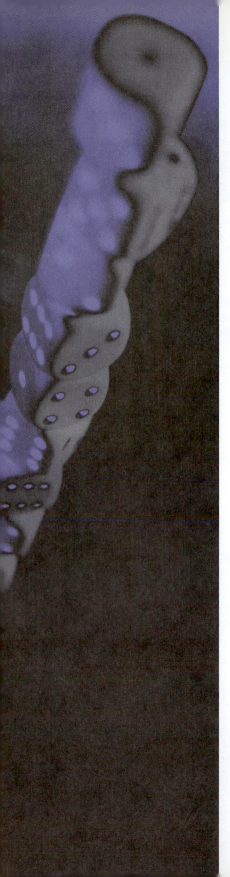

SWING, AWT, AND aLIBRARY

The graphical classes of *aLibrary* constitute an extension of the standard Java graphical environment that is defined in the standard *swing* and *awt* libraries. Most *aLibrary* functionality is inherited directly from classes of these two libraries. This appendix is included to explain how to use *swing* and *awt* directly without *aLibrary*. This is a substantial introduction to *swing* and *awt*, but a complete presentation of these extensive libraries is beyond this book.

D.1 BACKGROUND ON AWT AND SWING

Since the earliest versions, Java has included a library, known as *awt* (short for Abstract Windowing Toolkit). The *awt* library includes numerous classes that are useful for building graphical user interfaces. As the Java language matured, it was felt that *awt* lacked some of the features needed for certain graphical applications, so the *swing* library was developed as an extension of *awt*. By Version 1.2 of Java both *awt* and *swing* were standard parts of the Java API.

It is virtually impossible to separate *awt* and *swing* because most of the key *swing* classes inherit much of their functionality from *awt* classes. Furthermore, many of the *swing* classes are clients of other *awt* classes. Therefore, the notation "*swing/awt*" is often used to refer to the collective programming environment formed by these combined libraries.

Figure D.1 diagrams the inheritance relationships of the *aLibrary* classes, along with related *swing* and *awt* classes. The *aLibrary* classes are shaded. The *swing* classes in this particular figure include those that begin with the letter "J", as well as `AbstractButton`.

Every concrete graphical *aLibrary* class (i.e., any nonabstract class whose names begins with the letter "A") inherits either a *swing* or an *awt* class, and *aLibrary* classes generally adopt names that are similar to their *swing/awt* superclass. The primary goals of *aLibrary* are (1) to reduce some of the complexity associated with production APIs like *swing/awt*, (2) to provide a programming environment specifically designed for learning about object-oriented software development. One of the byproducts of learning *aLibrary* is a useful first step toward learning *swing/awt*.

D.2 TRANSITIONING COMMON FEATURES

There is one class that is shared without inheritance by *aLibrary*, *swing* and *awt*, namely the `Color` class. `Color` is part of the `java.awt` package. Therefore, `Color` is used in exactly the same way by both *aLibrary* and *swing/awt*.

Many of the *aLibrary* methods are common to several classes. These methods are explained individually below. Following each method is an explanation of how to perform the same task in *swing/awt*.

```
getBackground()
```

This method is inherited, so its behavior is identical in either *aLibrary* or *swing/awt*.

```
getForeground()
```

This method is inherited, so its behavior is identical in either *aLibrary* or *swing/awt*.

Figure D.1 Class hierarchy for selected *swing*, *awt*, and *aLibrary* classes

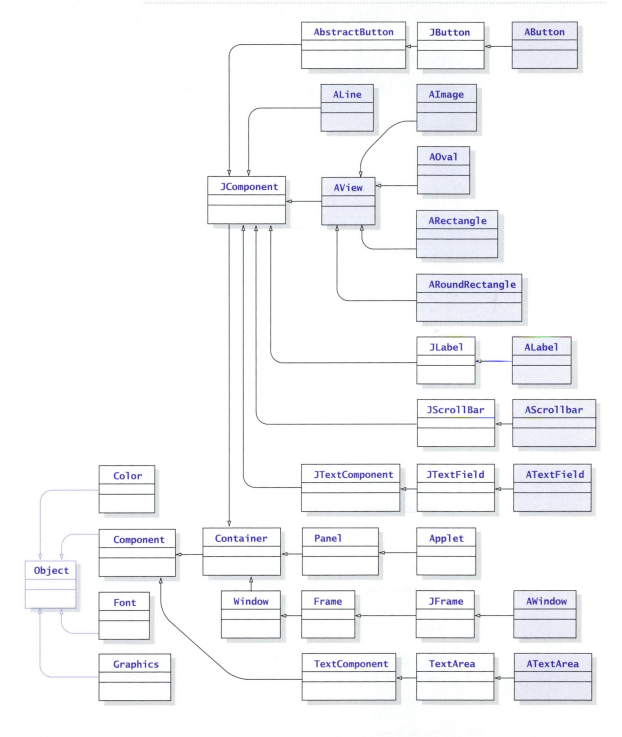

`getHeight()`

This method is inherited, so its behavior is identical in either *aLibrary* or *swing/awt*.

`getText()`

This method is inherited, so its behavior is identical in either *aLibrary* or *swing/awt*.

`getWidth()`

This method is inherited, so its behavior is identical in either *aLibrary* or *swing/awt*.

`getX()`

This method is inherited, so its behavior is identical in either *aLibrary* or *swing/awt*.

`getY()`

This method is inherited, so its behavior is identical in either *aLibrary* or *swing/awt*.

`parentContainer()`

This method is an *aLibrary* extension. Below is a roughly equivalent way to replace this method. The `aj` object is assumed to be the *swing/awt* version of the a object.

> *aLibrary* expression
> ```
>     a.parentContainer()
> ```
> *swing/awt* equivalent
> ```
>     aj.getParent()
> ```

A difference between `parentContainer` and `getParent` occurs when `parentContainer` returns an object of type `AWindow`. In such cases `getParent` will return the content pane of the corresponding `JFrame`. (A more complete explanation of this issue is given in Section D.3.)

`place( Container )`

This method is an *aLibrary* extension. Below is a functionally equivalent way to replace this method. The `aj` object is assumed to be the *swing/awt* version of the a object. Similarly, the `bj` object is the *swing/awt* version of b.

> *aLibrary* statement
> ```
>     a.place( b );
> ```
> *swing/awt* equivalent[1]
> ```
>     bj.add( aj, 0 );
> ```

---

[1] This replacement does not work for a `JFrame` replacement for an `AWindow`. See Section D.3 for details.

Notice that the role of object and argument (a and b) are reversed from *aLibrary* to *swing/awt*. The second argument should always be zero (0) to guarantee that a later placement is displayed "on top."

`remove()`

This method is an *aLibrary* extension. Below is a functionally equivalent way to replace this method. The aj object is assumed to be the *swing/awt* version of the a object.

aLibrary statement
```
a.remove();
```

swing/awt equivalent
```
if ( aj.getParent() != null) {
    aj.getParent().remove(aj);
}
```

`scale( double, double )`

This method is an *aLibrary* extension. Below is a functionally equivalent way to replace this method. The aj object is assumed to be the *swing/awt* version of the a object.

aLibrary statement
```
a.scale( d1, d2 );
```

swing/awt equivalent
```
aj.setSize( (int)(aj.getWidth()*d1),
    (int)(aj.getHeight()*d2) );
```

`setBackground( Color )`

This method is inherited, so its behavior is identical in either *aLibrary* or *swing/awt*.

`setForeground( Color )`

This method is inherited, so its behavior is identical in either *aLibrary* or *swing/awt*.

`setLocation ( int, int )`

This method is inherited, so its behavior is identical in either *aLibrary* or *swing/awt*.

`setSize( int, int )`

This method is inherited, so its behavior is identical in either *aLibrary* or *swing/awt*.

`setText( String )`

This method is inherited, so its behavior is identical in either *aLibrary* or *swing/awt*.

```
translate( double, double )
```

This method is an *aLibrary* extension. Below is a functionally equivalent way to replace this method. The aj object is assumed to be the *swing/awt* version of the a object.

   aLibrary statement
```
        a.translate( d1, d2 );
```

   swing/awt equivalent
```
        aj.setLocation( (int)(aj.getX()+d1), (int)(aj.getY()+d2) );
```

One key difference between *aLibrary* classes and their *swing/awt* counterparts is that the constructor methods perform important initialization. In particular it is *always* necessary to call setBounds to establish the dimensions for a graphical *swing/awt* object. This and other details of constructor methods are explained in later sections of this appendix.

D.3 JFRAME INSTEAD OF AWINDOW

The AWindow class inherits JFrame. There are four major differences between AWindow and JFrame.

1. The drawing region of a JFrame object is called a "content pane." Many of the methods that can be called directly upon an AWindow must be called upon the content pane of the corresponding JFrame. A method called getContentPane() is provided to return the necessary component.

2. AWindow adds a menu with a quit button and activates the close button. This menu and button are not included in a simple JFrame. (When Java applications are activated from a UNIX shell or a DOS window, they can generally be terminated by holding down the CTRL key and simultaneously striking the C key.)

3. AWindow supports mouse event handling. This can be accomplished in JFrame via event delegation. Section D.8 explains more about mouse event handling.

4. AWindow supports key event handling. Section D.8 explains more about key event handling.

Below is a list of the most commonly used AWindow methods and how to perform the same tasks in *swing/awt*. Common methods that were fully explained in Section D.2 are not repeated.

```
AWindow( int, int, int, int )
```

This constructor method performs numerous initializations. Below are the essential parts for constructing a corresponding JFrame. The wj object is assumed to be the *swing/awt* version of the w object.

   aLibrary statement
```
        w = new AWindow ( x, y, wid, h );
```

corresponding *swing/awt*

```
wj = new JFrame();
wj.setBounds( x, y, wid, h );
wj.getContentPane().setLayout( null );
wj.show();
```

The call to `setBounds` is necessary to establish the dimensions of the window. The call to `setLayout` establishes that the content pane will use the so-called "null layout manager." This method is needed in order to be able to precisely specify the locations of objects placed upon the `JFrame`. The `show` command is required to make the `JFrame` visible.

dispose()

This method is inherited, so its behavior is identical in either *aLibrary* or *swing/awt*.

getColor()

This method is an *aLibrary* extension. Below is a functionally equivalent way to replace this method. The `wj` object is assumed to be the *swing/awt* version of the `AWindow`, called `w`.

aLibrary statement
```
w.getColor()
```

swing/awt equivalent
```
wj.getContentPane().getBackground()
```

getTitle()

This method is inherited, so its behavior is identical in either *aLibrary* or *swing/awt*.

place(Container)

This method is an *aLibrary* extension. When placing upon an `AWindow`, this method is a bit different than explained in Section D.2. Below is a functionally equivalent way to replace this method. The `aj` object is assumed to be the *swing/awt* version of the a object. Similarly, the `wj` object is the *swing/awt* version of the `AWindow` object, called `w`.

aLibrary statement
```
a.place( w );
```

swing/awt equivalent
```
wj.getContentPane().add( aj, 0 );
```

setColor(Color)

This method is an *aLibrary* extension. Below is a functionally equivalent way to replace this method. The `wj` object is assumed to be the *swing/awt* version of the `AWindow` object, called `w`.

aLibrary statement

```
    w.setColor( c );
```

swing/awt equivalent

```
    wj.getContentPane().setBackground( c );
```

setTitle(String)

This method is inherited, so its behavior is identical in either *aLibrary* or *swing/awt*.

Figure D.2 contains an example program that uses *swing/awt* classes directly to produce a "Hello world" message upon a window. An equivalent program using *aLibrary* is included following the *swing/awt* program.

Figure D.2 Program to create a window in *swing*

```java
import javax.swing.*;   //provides access to JFrame and JLabel
import java.awt.*;   //provides access to Color
public class Director  {
    private JFrame window;
    private JLabel message;
    /* postcondition
            a window is displayed containing a "Hello world!"
            message. */
    public Director()   {
        window = new JFrame();
        window.setBounds(10, 10, 200, 150);
        window.getContentPane().setLayout( null );
        window.show();

        message = new JLabel();
        message.setBounds(10, 20, 170, 30);
        message.setText( "Hello world!" );
        message.setForeground( Color.blue );
        window.getContentPane().add( message );
        message.repaint();
    }
}
```

Corresponding *aLibrary* version:

```java
import java.awt.*;
import .*;
public class Director  {
    private AWindow window;
    private ALabel message;
```

```
/* postcondition
        a window is displayed containing a "Hello world!"
        message. */
public Director()    {
    window = new AWindow(10, 10, 200, 150);

    message = new ALabel(10, 20, 170, 30);
    message.setText("Hello world!");
    message.setForeground( Color.blue );
    message.place( window );
    message.repaint();
}
}
```

D.4 JLABEL INSTEAD OF ALABEL

The ALabel class inherits JLabel. The differences between these classes are fairly minor, and are explained in the list of ALabel methods below.

ALabel(int, int, int, int)

Below are the necessary parts for constructing a functionally equivalent JLabel. The aj object is assumed to be the *swing/awt* version of the a object. (If the last two lines are omitted, a standard font will be used.)

aLibrary statement
```
a = new ALabel ( x, y, w, h );
```

corresponding *swing/awt*
```
aj = new JLabel();
aj.setBounds( x, y, w, h );
aj.setForeground( Color.black );
aj.setBackground( Color.white );
Font newFont = new Font( "Courier", Font.PLAIN, 10 );
aj.setFont( newFont );
```

The call to setBounds is necessary to establish the dimensions of the JLabel. The last two instructions assign the use of a font, known as Courier, with a size of 10. Notice that the Font class is part of the *awt* library.

getFontSize(int)

This method is an *aLibrary* extension. Below is a functionally equivalent way to replace this method. The aj object is assumed to be the *swing/awt* version of the ALabel object, called a.

aLibrary statement
```
a.getFontSize()
```

swing/awt equivalent
```
aj.getFont().getSize()
```

setAlignmentCenter(), setAlignmentLeft(), setAlignmentRight()

These methods are *aLibrary* extensions that can be duplicated using a JLabel method called setHorizontalAlignment, along with a static constant from an *awt* class called Label. Below is a functionally equivalent way to replace the setAlignmentCenter method. The aj object is assumed to be the *swing/awt* version of the ALabel object, called a.

aLibrary statement
```
a.setAlignmentCenter();
```

swing/awt equivalent
```
aj.setHorizontalAlignment( Label.CENTER );
```

The replacements for setAlignmentLeft and setAlignmentRight are analogous. Note that the name of the constant must be all capital letters, such as "CENTER".

setFontSize(int)

This method is an *aLibrary* extension. Below is a functionally equivalent way to replace this method. The aj object is assumed to be the *swing/awt* version of the ALabel, called a.

aLibrary statement
```
a.setFontSize( k );
```

swing/awt equivalent
```
Font newFont = new Font(getFont().getName(), Font.PLAIN, k);
aj.setFont( newFont );
```

D.5 JCOMPONENT INSTEAD OF AVIEW, AOVAL, ARECTANGLE, AND AROUNDRECTANGLE

The AView class inherits JComponent. AOval, ARectangle, and ARoundRectangle inherit AView, which means that they indirectly inherit from JComponent. There are three major differences between the AView class and subclasses and the JComponent class.

1. The *aLibrary* classes are graphical objects, while using JComponent requires that the proper method calls for drawing. The impact of this difference is explained in more detail below.
2. JComponent does not support the notion of filled/outlined as an attribute.
3. AView and its subclasses support mouse event handling. This can be accomplished in JComponent via event delegation. Section D.8 explains mouse event handling.

A major difference between *swing* and *aLibrary* is the way in which graphical objects are drawn. Graphical images in *aLibrary* always result from placing graphical objects from classes such as AOval and ARectangle. The *swing/awt* approach to graphical objects is to provide *methods* rather than *classes* for drawing. Methods, such as drawOval, drawRect, fillOval, and fillRect are included in the *swing* library

A JComponent object must be declared, instantiated, and added to some visible Container, such as a JFrame, before it becomes visible. Once added, the drawing of an JComponent object is generally initiated by a call to the repaint method. Calling repaint signals the Java VM to redraw the image for the JComponent as soon as possible.

When the Java VM is able to redraw the JComponent object, it does so by calling the object's update method. The update method performs three tasks in the following order.

1. Clear the background rectangle for the JComponent by filling it with the appropriate background color.
2. Set the drawing color for the current graphical context to the appropriate foreground color.
3. Call the paint method for the current graphical context.

The third task performed by a call to update consists of a call to paint. JComponent is designed with the intention that software developers override the paint method in order to perform drawing. Figure D.3 illustrates.

Figure D.3 Triangle class (subclass of JComponent)

```
import javax.swing.*;
    import java.awt.*;   //provides access to Graphics
    public class Triangle extends JComponent  {
        public Triangle( int x, int y, int w, int h )  {
            super( );
            setBounds(x, y, w, h);
        }
        /* postcondition
               A triangle is drawn with base as the bottom of the
               getBounds() rectangle and apex at the midpoint of
               the top of the region of this JComponent. */
        public void paint( Graphics g )    {
            int width = getWidth();
            int height = getHeight();
            g.setColor( getForeground() );
            g.drawLine( 0, height - 1, width, height - 1 );
            g.drawLine( 0, height - 1, width/2, 0 );
            g.drawLine( width/2, 0, width, height - 1 );
        }
    }
```

The `Triangle` class demonstrates several things about extending `JComponent` classes. Each `JComponent` has a bounding rectangle, much like `AView`, that defines the drawing region for the `JComponent` object. The location and size of these bounding rectangles must be established by calling `setBounds`. Every `JComponent` object also has both a foreground color and a background color to be used in drawing. These colors are assigned values by the `setForeground` and `setBackground` methods.

The key to writing code for a `paint` method is to realize that *swing/awt* draws using a graphical context. Every call to `paint` supplies the appropriate graphical context in the form of a parameter belonging to `Graphics` (an *awt* class). The *swing/awt* methods for drawing are contained within this `Graphics` class. One such method, used by the `Triangle` class, is `drawLine`. The following call

```
g.drawLine(x1, y1, x2, y2)
```

causes a line segment to be drawn within the graphical context of object g. This line segment connects points (x1, y1) and (x2, y2) using the coordinate system of the `JComponent` whose `paint` method is executing.

Figure D.4 completes this example with a `Director` class that draws two triangles using the `Triangle` class from the previous figure.

Figure D.4 `Director` example using `Triangle`

```
import javax.swing.*;
import java.awt.*;
public class Director   {
    private JFrame window;
    private Triangle blueTri, greenTri;

    public Director()   {
        window = new JFrame();
        window.setBounds(10, 10, 200, 200);
        window.getContentPane().setLayout( null );

        blueTri = new Triangle( 10, 10, 20, 20 );
        blueTri.setForeground( Color.blue );
        window.getContentPane().add( blueTri );

        greenTri = new Triangle( 110, 110, 60, 30 );
        greenTri.setForeground( Color.green );
        window.getContentPane().add( greenTri );

        window.show();
    }
}
```

Changing the body of its paint method causes a JComponent to draw a different picture. Figure D.5 shows paint methods for the six options for the AOval, ARectangle, and ARoundRectangle images.

Figure D.5 Six possible images for AOval, ARectangle, and ARoundRectangle

AOval that is outlined

```java
public void paint( Graphics g )    {
    g.setColor( getForeground() );
    g.drawOval( 0, 0, getWidth(), getHeight() );
}
```

AOval that is filled

```java
public void paint( Graphics g )    {
    g.setColor( getForeground() );
    g.fillOval( 0, 0, getWidth(), getHeight() );
}
```

ARectangle that is outlined

```java
public void paint( Graphics g )    {
    g.setColor( getForeground() );
    g.drawRect( 0, 0, getWidth(), getHeight() );
}
```

ARectangle that is filled

```java
public void paint( Graphics g )    {
    g.setColor( getForeground() );
    g.fillRect( 0, 0, getWidth(), getHeight() );
}
```

ARoundRectangle that is outlined

```java
public void paint( Graphics g )    {
    g.setColor( getForeground() );
    g.drawRoundRect( 0, 0, getWidth(), getHeight(),
        min(getWidth(),getHeight())/2,
        min(getWidth(),getHeight())/2 );
}
```

ARoundRectangle that is filled

```java
public void paint( Graphics g )    {
    g.setColor( getForeground() );
    g.fillRoundRect( 0, 0, getWidth(), getHeight(),
        min(getWidth(),getHeight())/2,
        min(getWidth(),getHeight())/2 );
}
```

Figure D.5 demonstrates that many of the drawing methods from the `Graphics` class occur in pairs—a `drawX` method and a corresponding `fillX` method. The only difference between the methods is that `drawX` produces an outlined image, while `fillX` produces a filled image.

Below is a list of the most commonly used `AView` methods and how to perform the same tasks in *swing/awt*. Common methods that were fully explained in Section D.2 are not repeated.

```
AView ( int, int, int, int )

AOval ( int, int, int, int )

ARectangle ( int, int, int, int )

ARoundRectangle ( int, int, int, int )
```

These constructor methods are explained in the following example. The `aj` object is assumed to be the *swing/awt* version of the `a` object.

> *aLibrary* statement
> ```
> a = new AView ( x, y, w, h );
> ```

> corresponding *swing/awt*
> ```
> aj = new JComponent();
> aj.setBounds( x, y, w, h );
> aj.setOpaque( false );
> ```

The call to `setBounds` is necessary to establish the dimensions of the `JComponent`. The call to `setOpaque` is essential so that other objects placed (added) on top of this `JComponent` will be visible.

```
getColor()
```

This method is an *aLibrary* extension. Below is a functionally equivalent way to replace this method. The `aj` object is assumed to be the *swing/awt* version of the `AView`, called `a`.

> *aLibrary* statement
> ```
> a.getColor()
> ```

> *swing/awt* equivalent
> ```
> aj.getForeground()
> ```

```
setColor( Color )
```

This method is an *aLibrary* extension. Below is a functionally equivalent way to replace this method. The `aj` object is assumed to be the *swing/awt* version of the `AView`, called `a`.

> *aLibrary* statement
> ```
> a.setColor( c );
> ```

> *swing/awt* equivalent
> ```
> aj.setForeground( c );
> ```

D.6   JCOMPONENT INSTEAD OF ALINE

The ALine class inherits JComponent. Drawing a line segment in *swing/awt* is best accomplished by placing the appropriate call to drawLine with the JComponent's paint method. See Section D.5 for an explanation of paint and drawLine.

D.7   JCOMPONENT INSTEAD OF AIMAGE

The AImage class inherits AView, which in turn inherits JComponent. Drawing a graphical image, like those drawn via AImage, is accomplished upon a JComponent by creating another object of type Image (an *awt* class). The following instruction can be located within a JComponent class to assign an Image object derived from the GIF or JPEG file named *imageFile* (a String).

```
imageObject = getToolkit().getImage( imageFile );
```

Drawing such an image requires that the paint method call drawImage. Below is a sample paint method:

```
public void paint( Graphics g ) {
    g.drawImage( imageObject, 0, 0, getWidth(), getHeight(), this );
}
```

A call to drawImage causes the Image object specified by the first argument to be drawn according to the x, y, width, and height dimensions specified, respectively, by the second through fifth arguments. All drawing is relative to the JComponent's bounding rectangle, and the image is reshaped to fill the region indicated by the four arguments. Note that the last argument can be ignored by passing the JComponent object that is performing the paint (i.e., the this object).

Figure D.6 contains a class, called SimpleImage, that uses a JComponent to draw such an Image object. The SimpleImage class captures the essential drawing facilities that are used by AImage.

Figure D.6 SimpleImage class (subclass of JComponent)

```
import javax.swing.*;
import java.awt.*;    //provides access to Graphics and Image
    public class SimpleImage extends JComponent  {
        private Image imageObject;

        public SimpleImage( int x, int y, int w, int h )  {
            super( );
            setBounds(x, y, w, h);
        }
```

```
              /* postcondition
                       imageObject == an image derived from the file
                       named s. */
              public void setImage( String s )   {
                  imageObject = getToolkit().getImage(s);
              }


              /* postcondition
                       The image assigned to imageObject is drawn filling
                       the bounding rectangle of this component. */
              public void paint( Graphics g )   {
                  g.drawImage( imageObject, 0, 0, getWidth(), getHeight(),
                      this );
              }
      }
```

The code below illustrates how to create an image, using `SimpleImage`, and display it upon a `JFrame` (window).

```
JFrame window = new JFrame();
window.setBounds(10, 10, 200, 200);
window.setLayout( null );
window.show();
SimpleImage im = new SimpleImage( 10, 10, 20, 20 );
im.setImage( "ufoBlue.GIF" );
window.add( im );
im.repaint();
```

D.8   HANDLING MOUSE AND KEY EVENTS

A mouse event occurs as the result of some user action that involves the computer's pointing device (a mouse, trackball, etc.) There are seven possible kinds of events, named below by their corresponding event handler methods.

`mouseClicked`

occurs when the mouse button is pressed, then released, while pointing to a `JComponent`.

`mousePressed`

occurs when the mouse button is pressed down, while pointing to a `JComponent`.

`mouseReleased`

occurs when the mouse button is released from being pressed, while pointing to a `JComponent`.

`mouseEntered`

occurs when the mouse button is moved from the outside into the region of a `JComponent`.

mouseExited

occurs when the mouse button is moved from the inside to outside the region of a JComponent.

mouseDragged

occurs when the mouse button is held down at the same time that the mouse is moved within the region of a JComponent.

mouseMoved

occurs when the mouse is moved within the region of a JComponent, but the mouse button is *not* held down.

Mouse events can be handled by a subclass of a JComponent using the steps below:

1. The JComponent object must receive a call to addMouseListener (which delegates mouseClicked, mousePressed, mouseReleased, mouseEntered, and mouseExited events) and/or a call to addMouseMotionListener (to delegate mouseDragged and mouseMoved events).

2. The object delegated to handle mouse events must include an implements clause for either java.awt.event.MouseListener (for the first five MouseListener events) or java.awt.event.MouseMotionListener (for the last two MouseMotionListener events) or javax.swing.MouseInputListener (for all seven events).

3. The delegate's class must include event handler methods for all events that are delegated to its objects. Each mouse event handler has a single parameter of type MouseEvent.

Figure D.7 illustrates how to delegate mouse events in this manner. The Director class in this example creates a Triangle object. (The Triangle class was shown previously in Figure D.3.) Executing the following instruction

mouser.addMouseMotionListener(this);

establishes the Director object as the delegate for handling mouse motion events. Correspondingly, the Director class implements MouseMotionListener and overrides the mouseDragged and mouseMoved methods.

When the application executes, a blue triangle is displayed within a JFrame. Anytime that the user drags the mouse or moves the mouse across this blue triangle the application will generate events, thereby outputting messages. It is worth noting that events depend upon the bounding rectangle of the JComponent and not the image that it draws. In this case, mouse events are generated anywhere within the rectangular region that bounds the blue triangle, not just within the triangle.

Figure D.7 also illustrates how to ascertain the exact position of the cursor at the time that a mouse event occurs. The MouseEvent parameter that is sent to all mouse event handlers supports getX() and getY() calls to return the position of the cursor relative to the JComponent's coordinates.

Figure D.7 Director handling mouse events for a Triangle

```java
import javax.swing.*;
import java.awt.event.*;
import java.awt.*;
public class Director implements MouseMotionListener {
    private JFrame window;
    private Triangle mouser;

    public Director(){
        window = new JFrame();
        window.setBounds(10, 10, 200, 200);
        window.getContentPane().setLayout( null );
        mouser = new Triangle( 10, 10, 100, 100 );
        mouser.setForeground( Color.blue );
        mouser.addMouseMotionListener( this );
        window.getContentPane().add( mouser );
        window.show();
    }

    public void mouseDragged( MouseEvent e ) {
        System.out.println( "Mouse dragged event" );
    }

    public void mouseMoved( MouseEvent e ) {
        System.out.println( "Mouse moved event" );
        System.out.println( "   x: " + e.getX() );
        System.out.println( "   y: " + e.getY() );
    }
}
```

A key event occurs as the result of striking one of the keys on the keyboard. Such an event is delivered to the frame that has focus (i.e., the frame that is highlighted in the foreground of the screen). There are three possible kinds of key events, named below by their corresponding event handler methods.

keyPressed

occurs when the key is pressed down.

keyReleased

occurs when the key is released from being pressed.

keyTyped

occurs when the key has been both pressed and released.

Key events can be handled by a subclass of a JComponent using the steps below.

1. The JComponent object must receive a call to addKeyListener (which delegates keyPressed, keyReleased, and keyTyped events).

2. The object delegated to handle key events must include an implements clause for java.awt.event.KeyListener.
3. The delegate's class must include event handler methods for all events that are delegated to its objects. Each key event handler has a single parameter of type KeyEvent.

Figure D.8 illustrates how to delegate mouse events in this manner. The Director class in this example creates a JFrame object. Executing the following instruction

```
win.addKeyListener( this );
```

establishes the Director object as the delegate for handling key events. Correspondingly, the Director class implements KeyListener and overrides the three event handlers.

When the application executes, a window is displayed. When this window is in the screen's foreground, it will add a message to the standard output stream for every time a key is struck. The message will indicate the integer value of the key that was struck. This example illustrates how to use getKeyCode() (a method from KeyEvent) in order to determine which key was struck.

Figure D.8 Director handling key events

```java
import javax.swing.*;
import java.awt.event.*;
import java.awt.*;
public class Director implements KeyListener {
    private JFrame window;

    public Director(){
        window = new JFrame();
        window.setBounds(10, 10, 200, 200);
        window.getContentPane().setLayout( null );
        window.addKeyListener( this );
        window.show();
    }

    public void keyTyped( KeyEvent e ) {
        System.out.println( "The key which was struck is "
            + e.getKeyCode() );
    }

    public void keyPressed( KeyEvent e ) {
    }

    public void keyreleased( KeyEvent e ) {
    }
}
```

D.9   JBUTTON INSTEAD OF ABUTTON

The AButton class inherits JButton. Except for those things unique to all *aLibrary* classes, AButton is similar to JButton. The primary difference between the two classes is the way in which events are handled. The AButton class delegates events to itself. Using JButton requires that events be explicitly delegated.

The only event supported by JButton is ActionPerformed. An ActionPerformed event occurs every time that the user clicks on the button. The appropriate listener interface for such event is called ActionListener, and the form of the event handler method is shown below:

```
public void actionPerformed(ActionEvent e) { ... }
```

Figure D.9 contains a Director class that creates two JButtons. The Director object serves as the event handler for both buttons. The getSource method is used to distinguish between the buttons.

Figure D.9 Director serves as a delegate for JButton events

```
import javax.swing.*;
import java.awt.event.*;
public class Director implements ActionListener {
    private JFrame window;
    private JButton onButton, offButton;

    public Director()    {
        window = new JFrame();
        window.setBounds(10, 10, 200, 240);
        window.getContentPane().setLayout( null );
        onButton = new JButton( );
        onButton.setBounds( 5, 200, 90, 30 );
        onButton.setText( "ON" );
        onButton.addActionListener( this );
        window.getContentPane().add( onButton );
        offButton = new JButton( );
        offButton.setBounds( 105, 200, 90, 30 );
        offButton.setText( "OFF" );
        offButton.addActionListener( this );
        window.getContentPane().add( offButton );
        window.show();   }

    public void actionPerformed( ActionEvent e )    {
        if (e.getSource() == onButton)    {
            System.out.println( "ON button clicked" );
        } else if (e.getSource() == offButton)    {
            System.out.println( "OFF button clicked" );   }   }

}
```

D.10 JSCROLLBAR INSTEAD OF ASCROLLBAR

The AScrollbar class inherits JScrollBar. There are two signifcant differences between these classes.

1. AScrollbar objects are automatically oriented toward the longer dimension. (When width is greater than height, then an AScrollbar is horizontal. Otherwise, it has a vertical orientation.) JScrollBar includes a method to assign such orientation. Within any subclass of JScrollBar the following method call is used to assign the object a horizontal orientation:

```
setOrientation(HORIZONTAL);
```

Similarly, a vertical orientation is assigned as follows:

```
setOrientation(VERTICAL);
```

2. JScrollBar uses delegation for handling the events resulting from movement of the scrollbar's knob. The appropriate interface for such events is adjustmentListener and the form of the associated event handler is shown below:

```
public void adjustmentValueChanged(AdjustmentEvent e) { ... }
```

The methods that are unique to AScrollbar are explained below:

AScrollbar (int, int, int, int)

Below are the necessary parts for constructing a roughly equivalent JScrollBar. The aj object is assumed to be the *swing/awt* version of the a object.

> *aLibrary* statement
> ```
> a = new AScrollbar ( x, y, w, h );
> ```

> corresponding *swing/awt*
> ```
> aj = new AScrollBar();
> aj.setBounds( x, y, w, h );
> aj.setOrientation( HORIZONTAL );
> ```

The call to setBounds is necessary to establish the dimensions of the JScrollBar. The last instruction can use VERTICAL in place of HORIZONTAL.

getMinimum()

getMaximum()

getValue()

These methods are inherited, so their behavior is identical in either *aLibrary* or *swing/awt*.

setMinMaxVal(int, int, int)

This method is an *aLibrary* extension. Below is a functionally equivalent way to replace this method. The aj object is assumed to be the *swing/awt* version of the AScrollbar, called a.

> *aLibrary* statement
> ```
> a.setMinMaxVal( mn, mx, v );
> ```
>
> *swing/awt* equivalent
> ```
> aj.setValues( v, 0, mn, mx );
> ```

setValue(int)

This method is inherited, so its behavior is identical in either *aLibrary* or *swing/awt*.

D.11 TEXTAREA INSTEAD OF ATEXTAREA

The ATextArea class inherits TextArea. This inheritance is somewhat unique because TextArea is in the *awt* library, while most other *aLibrary* classes inherit from *swing* classes. There is also a JTextArea class in the *swing* library, but it does not directly support automatic scrollbars. The differences between TextArea and ATextArea are fairly minor, and are explained in the list of ATextArea methods below.

ATextArea(int, int, int, int)

Below are the necessary parts for constructing a functionally equivalent TextArea. The aj object is assumed to be the *swing/awt* version of the a object. (If the last two lines are omitted, a standard font will be used in place of the specific font used by *aLibrary*.)

> *aLibrary* statement
> ```
> a = new ATextArea ( x, y, w, h );
> ```
>
> corresponding *swing/awt*
> ```
> aj = new TextArea();
> aj.setBounds( x, y, w, h );
> aj.setForeground( Color.black );
> aj.setBackground( Color.white );
> Font newFont = new Font( "Courier", Font.PLAIN, 10 );
> aj.setFont( newFont );
> aj.setEditable( false );
> ```

The call to setBounds is necessary to establish the dimensions of the TextArea. The last instruction turns off the user's ability to edit the text displayed with such objects.

append(String)

This method is inherited, so its behavior is identical in either *aLibrary* or *awt*.

```
appendln( String )
```

This method is an *aLibrary* extension. Below is a functionally equivalent way to replace this method. The aj object is assumed to be the *swing/awt* version of the ATextArea, called a.

> *aLibrary* statement
> ```
> a.appendln( s );
> ```

> *swing/awt* equivalent
> ```
> aj.append( s + "\n" );
> ```

D.12 JTEXTFIELD INSTEAD OF ATEXTFIELD

The ATextField class inherits JTextField. There are two significant differences between these classes.

1. ATextField includes the following inspector methods to retrieve the text within the text field in various representations: getBoolean, getDouble, getFloat, getInt. None of these methods are part of JTextField, nor is the translationErrorOccurred instance variable.

2. JTextField uses delegation for handling the events resulting from the user *striking* the return key while the text field is selected. The appropriate interface for such events is ActionListener (like JButton) and the form of the associated event handler is shown below:

   ```
   public void actionPerformed(ActionEvent e) { ... }
   ```

The methods that are unique to ATextField are explained below:

```
getBoolean()
```

This method is an *aLibrary* extension. Below is a functionally equivalent way to replace this method. The aj object is assumed to be the *swing/awt* version of the ATextField, called a.

> *aLibrary* statement
> ```
> booleanVariable = a.getBoolean();
> ```

> *swing/awt* equivalent
> ```
> translationErrorOccurred = false;
> if ("FALSE".equalsIgnoreCase(aj.getText().trim()) ) {
>     booleanVariable = false;
> } else if ("TRUE".equalsIgnoreCase(aj.getText().trim()) ) {
>     booleanVariable = true;
> } else { //This results from a translation error
>     booleanVariable = false;
>     translationErrorOccurred = true;
> }
> ```

getDouble()

This method is an *aLibrary* extension. Below is a functionally equivalent way to replace this method. The aj object is assumed to be the *swing/awt* version of the ATextField, called a.

aLibrary statement

```
doubleVariable = a.getDouble();
```

swing/awt equivalent

```
translationErrorOccurred = false;
try{
    doubleVariable =
        (Double.valueOf(aj.getText())).doubleValue();
}
catch (NumberFormatException e) {
    doubleVariable = 0.0; //This results from a translation
                          //error.
    translationErrorOccurred = true;
}
```

getFloat()

This method is an *aLibrary* extension. Below is a functionally equivalent way to replace this method. The aj object is assumed to be the *swing/awt* version of the ATextField, called a.

aLibrary statement

```
floatVariable = a.getFloat();
```

swing/awt equivalent

```
translationErrorOccurred = false;
try{
    floatVariable = (Float.valueOf(aj.getText()))
                    .floatValue();
}
catch (NumberFormatException e) {
    floatVariable = 0.0f; //This results from a translation
                          //error.
    translationErrorOccurred = true;
}
```

getInt()

This method is an *aLibrary* extension. Below is a functionally equivalent way to replace this method. The aj object is assumed to be the *swing/awt* version of the ATextField, called a.

aLibrary statement

```
intVariable = a.getInt();
```

swing/awt equivalent

```
translationErrorOccurred = false;
try{
    intVariable = (Integer.valueOf(aj.getText()))
                    .intValue();
}
catch (NumberFormatException e) {
    intVariable = 0; //This results from a translation
                    //error.
    translationErrorOccurred = true;
}
```

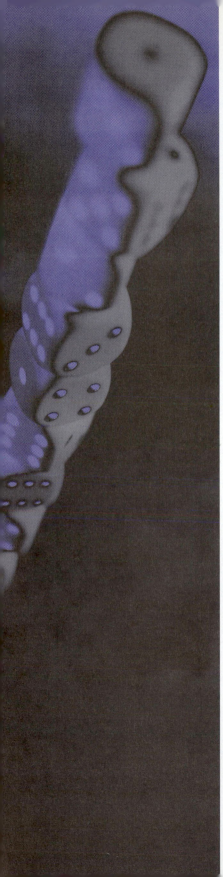

UML
NOTATIONS

The unified modeling language (UML) is a collection of many graphical notations used to diagram various aspects of software artifacts. The standards for these notations were published by the Object Management Group (OMG) in September of 1997. UML has seen widespread adoption, and is commonly used throughout the software engineering community. This appendix explains the subset of UML that is used within this textbook. For a more complete explanation of UML see *The Unified Modeling Language Reference Manual* by Rumbaugh, Jacobson, and Booch (Addison Wesley).

E.1 CLASS DIAGRAMS

Class diagrams capture classes, their key properties, and relationships with other classes. These pictures represent a view of classes as they appear at compile time (i.e., a *static* view).

Using this notation, each class is diagrammed as a separate rectangle with three compartments, separated by horizontal lines. The top compartment contains the name of the class, the middle compartment contains the class's attributes and the bottom compartment contains the class's methods. Some or all of the attributes and methods may be omitted, in order to highlight the remaining members and/or class relationships. Three consecutive dots are sometimes included to indicate that some attributes or methods have been omitted.

Each attribute is specified on a separate line with its type followed by its name. (Note that this is a common notation for variables in C-based languages, such as Java. An alternative UML notation is to specify the variable as the name, followed by a colon, followed by the variable's type.)

Each method is specified on a separate line with its return type, followed by its name, followed by a parameter list. Constructor methods have no return type. Parameters are specified by their type, but are not necessarily named. (UML allows an alternative notation for methods that is similar to that for attributes. The alternative notation has the return type at the end, preceded by a colon.)

Every attribute and method is optionally preceded by a symbol to indicate its scope. The appropriate symbols for Java are public (+), private (–) and protected (#). Methods can be grouped into categories that are preceded by notations like constructor, query, or update.

Figure E.1 contains an example class diagram that shows a typical class, called StreetAddress. The corresponding Java code is shown prior to the class diagram.

Figure E.1 Example class diagram with matching Java code

```java
public class StreetAddress {
    private String city;
    private String state;
    private int zipcode;

    public StreetAddress
        ( String h, String st, int z)
    {
        //code omitted
    }

    public String getCity() {
        //code omitted
    }
```

```java
public String getState() {
    //code omitted
}
public int getZipcode() {
    //code omitted
}
public String getAddress() {
    //code omitted
}

public void setCityState( String c, String s )
{
    //code omitted
}

protected void setZipcode( int z )
{
    //code omitted
}
}
```

StreetAddress
- String city - String state - int zipcode

«constructor»
   + **StreetAddress**(*String, String, int*)
 	
«query»
   + String **getCity**()
   + String **getState**()
   + int **getZipcode**()
   ...
 	
«update»
   + void **setCityState**(*String, String*)
   # void **setZipcode**(*int*)

Three dots indicate omitted method(s), such as getAddress.

Interfaces and abstract classes are diagrammed in a similar fashion to classes. An interface is distinguished from a class by including the stereotype "interface" above the class name in the top compartment of the interface rectangle. An abstract class is distinguished by italicizing the class name (and abstract methods). For clarity, the name abstract should also be included in braces following the class name. Figure E.2 shows an example interface, and Figure E.3 diagrams an abstract class.

Figure E.2 Example interface

```
public interface ActionListener {

    // All variables and methods omitted
}
```

```
          «interface»
         ActionListener
```

Figure E.3 Example abstract class

```
public abstract class Date {
    protected int day;
    protected int month;
    protected int year;

    public Date( int, int, int )    {
        // code omitted
    }

    public abstract String dateString();

    public String monthString()    {
        // code omitted
    }
}
```

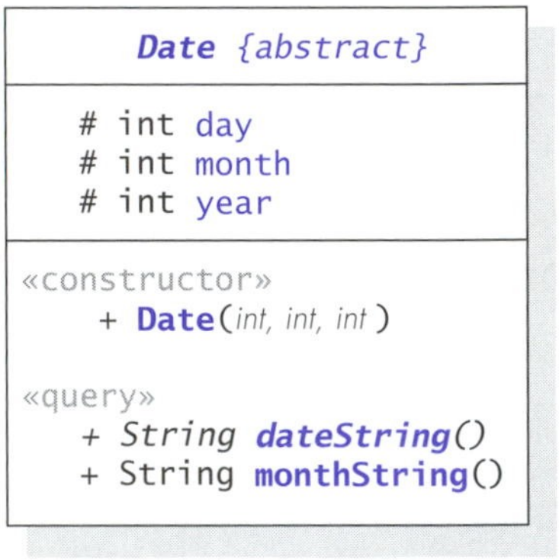

```
          Date {abstract}

    # int day
    # int month
    # int year

    «constructor»
        + Date(int, int, int )

    «query»
        + String dateString()
        + String monthString()
```

There are two kinds of relationships among classes that are diagrammed in this text. Association is a relationship that occurs any time that one class is used within another. If the association results from the declaration of a parameter or local variable, then it is diagrammed as a line segment connecting the two classes.

Aggregation is a special kind of association that results when a client class contains of one or more instance variables belonging to another type. Aggregation is diagrammed as a line segment connecting the aggregate (client) to any constituent (supplier) class with a diamond drawn on the aggregate end of the line. Figure E.4 illustrates aggregation between Person and String and Person and Date. Figure E.4 also shows two associations that are not aggregation. These associations are between Person and AWindow and Person and ATextArea.

Figure E.4 Example of association and aggregation

```
public class Person {
    public String name;
    public Date birthday;

    public void display(AWindow w)
    {
        ATextArea area;
        // remaining code omitted
    }
    // Additional methods omitted
}
```

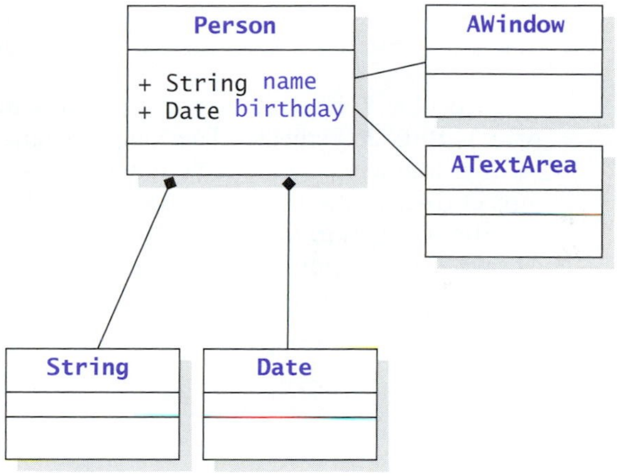

The inheritance relationship is diagrammed as an arrow connecting a subclass to its superclass. The head of the arrow points toward the superclass. Implementing an interface is diagrammed similar to inheritance, except that a dashed arrow points from the implementation to the interface. Figure E.5 illustrates both inheritance and interface implementation.

Figure E.5 Example of inheritance

```
public class MyOval extends AOval
    implements MouseListener {

    // All methods omitted
}
```

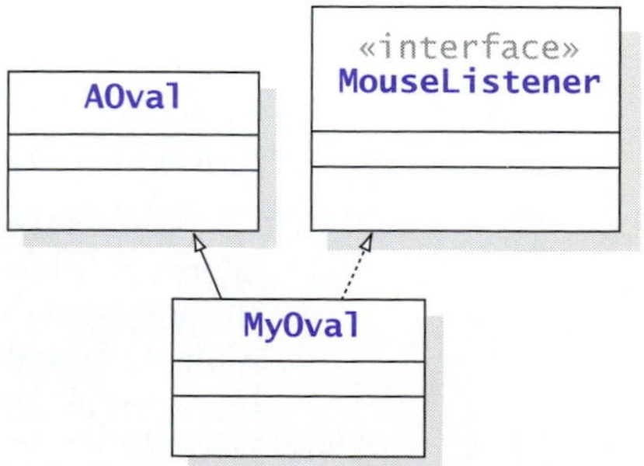

E.2 OBJECT DIAGRAMS

Object diagrams picture the run-time (dynamic) behavior of a program. Each object diagram is a snapshot of one particular computational state. An object diagram shows a collection of objects and their assigned values from a specific instant in time.

The UML notation for a single object consists of a rectangle with the name of the object at the top of the rectangle, followed by a colon, followed by the object's type. The name and type are underlined to distinguish object rectangles from class rectangles. This text uses the additional notation of a light blue fill to denote object diagrams.

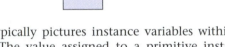

An object diagram typically pictures instance variables within the object in which they are created. The value assigned to a primitive instance variable is shown following the variable name and a "==" separator. Figure E.6 contains an object diagram that depicts a local variable, called `clock`, after it has been created via the instruction in the gray box. The `StopWatch` class to which `clock` belongs is shown on the right side of Figure E.6.

Figure E.6 Example object diagram and associated `StopWatch` class

```
StopWatch   watch;
watch = new StopWatch(4, 9.3);
```

```
public class StopWatch {
    private int minute;
    private double second;

    public StopWatch( int
           m, double s)  {
        minute = m;
        second = s;
    }
}
```

The object diagram below shows the state of `clock` upon executing the two statements above.

```
watch   :   StopWatch

   minute == 4
   second == 9.3
```

When an object is the aggregate of other objects, the instance variables of the aggregate can be diagrammed by using the same symbol (a line segment with a diamond on the aggregate end) as a class diagram. Figure E.7 illustrates.

Variable names, like `startTime` and `endTime`, are repeated both inside the aggregate object and inside the object. Including instance variable names within the aggregate object is useful in situations where an object is assigned multiple names (aliases). Figure E.8 demonstrates with an object diagram for an object that has been assigned to `clock1` and `clock2`.

Figure E.7 Example object diagram and associated `SplitTimer` class

```
SplitTimer clock = new SplitTimer();
clock.setStart(10, 5.3);
clock.setEnd(12, 7.1);
```

The object diagram below shows the state that results from executing the above statements.

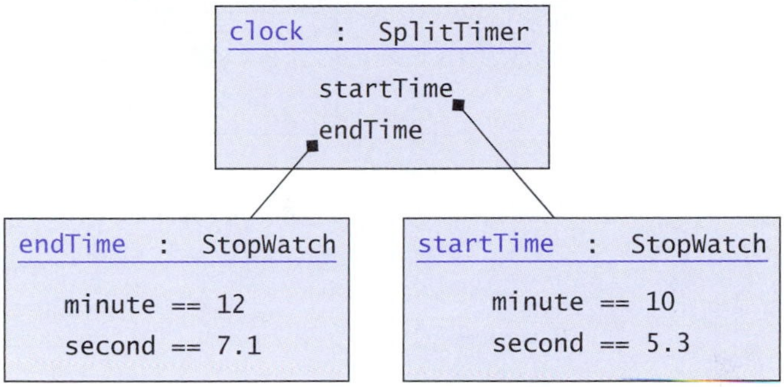

```java
public class SplitTimer {
    public StopWatch startTime;
    public StopWatch endTime;

    public SplitTimer() {}

    public void setStart(int m, double s)
    {
        startTime = new StopWatch(m, s);
    }

    public void setEnd(int m, double s)
    {
        endTime = new StopWatch(m, s);
    }
}
```

Figure E.8 also demonstrates that it is acceptable to omit the name within an object rectangle, such as the StopWatch object. This omission is commonly used for anonymous objects, and when an object has multiple names.

Figure E.8 Example object diagram

```
SplitTimer clock = new SplitTimer();
clock.setStart(10, 5.3);
clock.endTime = clock.startTime;
```

The object diagram below shows the state that results from executing the above statements.

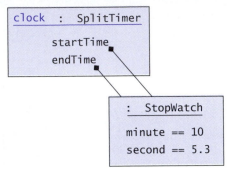

E.3 ACTIVITY DIAGRAMS

An activity diagram pictures actions and their dependencies. Each activity diagram in this textbook is used to show the alternative control flows for possible program executions. In this context an action consists of the execution of one or more Java statements.

The right side of Figure E.9 contains an activity diagram for the Java code segment on the right. Each action is diagrammed as an oval that contains the Java statement. Run-time control flow is indicated by arrows directed from each action state to its subsequent action.

Figure E.9 Activity diagram for sequential actions

```
int length = 12;
int width = 7;
int perimeter = length*2
        + width*2;
int area = length * width;
```

int **length** = 12;

int **width** = 7;

int **perimeter** = length*2 + width*2;

int **area** = length * width;

Alternatives in control flow require branch and merge symbols. A branch symbol is a small diamond with multiple outgoing arrows. The outgoing arrows symbolize alternative execution paths, and each is labeled with the condition (in square brackets). An outgoing arrow is followed only when its guard condition is true. If alternative execution flows eventually merge to perform the same actions, then a diamond may be used with multiple incoming arrows and a single outgoing arrow. It is also possible to combine branching and merging in a single diamond.

Figure E.10 illustrates a single branch (the top diamond). This branch represents a choice in program execution. If the condition a > b is true, then execution follows the left arrow; otherwise, the right arrow is followed. Regardless of the chosen branch, both paths merge prior to executing the System.out.println call.

Figure E.10 Activity diagram including branching

```
public void printMax( int a, int b) {
    int max;
        if (a > b)  {
            max = a;
        } else {
            max = b;
        }
        System.out.println(max);
}
```

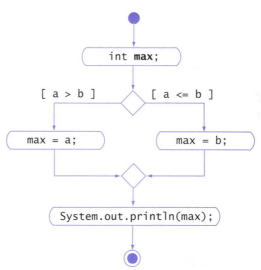

INDEX

that: (a) you distribute the Redistributables complete and unmodified (unless otherwise specified in the applicable README file), and only bundled as part of the Java™ applets and applications that you develop (the "Programs:); (b) you do not distribute additional software intended to supersede any component(s) of the Redistributables; (c) you do not remove or alter any proprietary legends or notices contained in or on the Redistributables; (d) you only distribute the Redistributables pursuant to a license agreement that protects Sun's interests consistent with the terms contained in the Agreement, and (e) you agree to defend and indemnify Sun and its licensors from and against any damages, costs, liabilities, settlement amounts and/or expenses (including attorneys' fees) incurred in connection with any claim, lawsuit or action by any third party that arises or results from the use or distribution of any and all Programs and/or Software. 3. Separate Distribution License Required. You understand and agree that you must first obtain a separate license from Sun prior to reproducing or modifying any portion of the Software other than as provided with respect to Redistributables in Paragraph 2 above. 4. Java Technology Restrictions. You may not modify the Java Platform Interface ("JPI", identified as classes contained within the "java" package or any subpackages of the "java" package), by creating additional classes within the JPI or otherwise causing the addition to or modification of the classes in the JPI. In the event that you create an additional class and associated API(s) which (i) extends the functionality of a Java environment, and (ii) is exposed to third party software developers for the purpose of developing additional software which invokes such additional API, you must promptly publish broadly an accurate specification for such API for free use by all developers. You may not create, or authorize your licensees to create additional classes, interfaces, or subpackages that are in any way identified as "java", "javax", "sun" or similar convention as specified by Sun in any class file naming convention. Refer to the appropriate version of the Java Runtime Environment binary code license (currently located at http://www.java.sun .com/jdk/index.html) for the availability of runtime code which may be distributed with Java applets and applications. 5. Trademarks and Logos. You acknowledge and agree as between you and Sun that Sun owns the Java trademark and all Java-related trademarks, service marks, logos and other brand designations including the Coffee Cup logo and Duke logo ("Java Marks"), and you agree to comply with the Sun Trademark and Logo Usage Requirements currently located at http://www.sun.com/policies/trademarks. Any use you make of the Java Marks inures to Sun's benefit. 6. Source Code. Software may contain source code that is provided solely for reference purposes pursuant to the terms of this Agreement. 7. Termination. Sun may terminate this Agreement immediately should any Software become, or in Sun's opinion be likely to become, the subject of a claim of infringement of a patent, trade secret, copyright or other intellectual property right. License Agreement: Forte for Java, release 2.0, Community Edition for All Platforms To Obtain Forte for Java, release 2.0, Community Edition for All Platforms, you must agree to the software license below. Sun Microsystems Inc., Binary Code License Agreement READ THE TERMS OF THIS AGREEMENT AND ANY PROVIDED SUPPLEMENTAL LICENSE TERMS (COLLECTIVELY "AGREEMENT") CAREFULLY BEFORE OPENING THE SOFTWARE MEDIA PACKAGE. BY OPENING THE SOFTWARE MEDIA PACKAGE, YOU AGREE TO THE TERMS OF THIS AGREEMENT. IF YOU ARE ACCESSING THE SOFTWARE ELECTRONICALLY, INDICATE YOUR ACCEPTANCE OF THESE TERMS BY SELECTING THE "ACCEPT" BUTTON AT THE END OF THIS AGREEMENT. IF YOU DO NOT AGREE TO ALL THESE TERMS, PROMPTLY RETURN THE UNUSED SOFTWARE TO YOUR PLACE OF PURCHASE FOR A REFUND OR, IF THE SOFTWARE IS ACCESSED ELECTRONICALLY, SELECT THE "DECLINE" BUTTON AT THE END OF THIS AGREEMENT. 1. LICENSE TO USE. Sun grants you a non-exclusive and non-transferable license for the internal use only of the accompanying software and documentation and any error corrections provided by Sun (collectively "Software"), by the number of users and the class of computer hardware for which the corresponding fee has been paid. 2. RESTRICTIONS. Software is confidential and copyrighted. Title to Software and all associated intellectual property rights is retained by Sun and/or its licensors. Except as specifically authorized in any Supplemental License Terms, you may not make copies of Software, other than a single copy of Software for archival purposes. Unless enforcement is prohibited by applicable law, you may not modify, decompile, or reverse engineer Software. You acknowledge that Software is not designed, licensed or intended for use in the design, construction, operation or maintenance of any nuclear facility. Sun disclaims any express or implied warranty of fitness for such uses. No right, title or interest in or to any trademark, service mark, logo or trade name of Sun or its licensors is granted under this Agreement. 3. LIMITED WARRANTY. Sun warrants to you that for a period of ninety (90) days from the date of purchase, as evidenced by a copy of the receipt, the media on which Software is furnished (if any) will be free of defects in materials and workmanship under normal use. Except for the foregoing, Software is provided "AS IS". Your exclusive remedy and Sun's entire liability under this limited warranty will be at Sun's option to replace Software media or refund the fee paid for Software. 4. DISCLAIMER OF WARRANTY. UNLESS SPECIFIED IN THIS AGREEMENT, ALL EXPRESS OR IMPLIED CONDITIONS, REPRESENTATIONS AND WARRANTIES, INCLUDING ANY IMPLIED WARRANTY OF MERCHANTABILITY, FITNESS FOR A PARTICULAR PURPOSE OR NON-INFRINGEMENT ARE DISCLAIMED, EXCEPT TO THE EXTENT THAT THESE DISCLAIMERS ARE HELD TO BE LEGALLY INVALID. 5. LIMITATION OF LIABILITY. TO THE EXTENT NOT PROHIBITED BY LAW, IN NO EVENT WILL SUN OR ITS LICENSORS BE LIABLE FOR ANY LOST REVENUE, PROFIT OR DATA, OR FOR SPECIAL, INDIRECT, CONSEQUENTIAL, INCIDENTAL OR PUNITIVE DAMAGES, HOWEVER CAUSED REGARDLESS OF THE THEORY OF LIABILITY, ARISING OUT OF OR RELATED TO THE USE OF OR INABILITY TO USE SOFTWARE, EVEN IF SUN HAS BEEN ADVISED OF THE POSSIBILITY OF SUCH DAMAGES. In no event will Sun's liability to you, whether in contract, tort (including negligence), or otherwise, exceed the amount paid by you for Software under this Agreement. The foregoing limitations will apply even if the above stated warranty fails of its essential purpose. 6. Termination. This Agreement is effective until terminated. You may terminate this Agreement at any time by destroying all copies of Software. This Agreement will terminate immediately without notice from Sun if you fail to comply with any provision of this Agreement. Upon Termination, you must destroy all copies of Software. 7. Export Regulations. All Software and technical data delivered under this Agreement are subject to U.S. export control laws and may be subject to export or import regulations in other countries. You agree to comply strictly with all such laws and regulations and acknowledge that you have the responsibility to obtain such licenses to export, re-export, or import as may be required after delivery to you. 8. U.S. Government Restricted Rights. If Software is being acquired by or on behalf of the U.S. Government or by a U.S. Government prime contractor or subcontractor (at any tier), then the Government's rights in Software and accompanying documentation will be only as set forth in this Agreement; this is in accordance with 48 CFR 227.7201 through 227.7202-4 (for Department of Defense (DOD) acquisitions) and with 48 CFR 2.101 and 12.212 (for non-DOD acquisitions). 9. Governing Law. Any action related to this Agreement will be governed by California law and controlling U.S. federal law. No choice of law rules of any jurisdiction will apply. 10. Severability. If any provision of this Agreement is held to be unenforceable, this Agreement will remain in effect with the provision omitted, unless omission would frustrate the intent of the parties, in which case this Agreement will immediately terminate. 11. Integration. This Agreement is the entire agreement between you and Sun relating to its subject matter. It supersedes all prior or contemporaneous oral or written communications, proposals, representations and warranties and prevails over any conflicting or additional terms of any quote, order, acknowledgment, or other communication between the parties relating to its subject matter during the term of this Agreement. No modification of this Agreement will be binding, unless in writing and signed by an authorized representative of each party. JAVA(TM) DEVELOPMENT TOOLS FORTE(TM) FOR JAVA(TM), RELEASE 2.0, COMMUNITY EDITION SUPPLEMENTAL LICENSE TERMS These supplemental license terms ("Supplemental Terms") add to or modify the terms of the Binary Code License Agreement (collectively, the "Agreement"). Capitalized terms not defined in these Supplemental Terms shall have the same meanings ascribed to them in the Agreement. These Supplemental Terms shall supersede any inconsistent or conflicting terms in the Agreement, or in any license contained within the Software. 1. Software Internal Use and Development License Grant. Subject to the terms and conditions of this Agreement, including, but not limited to Section 3 (Java(TM) Technology Restrictions) of these Supplemental Terms, Sun grants you a non-exclusive, non-transferable, limited license to reproduce internally and use internally the binary form of the Software complete and unmodified for the sole purpose of designing, developing and testing your [Java applets and] applications intended to run on the Java platform ("Programs"). 2. License to Distribute Redistributables. In addition to the license granted in Section 1 (Redistributables Internal Use and Development License Grant) of these Supplemental Terms, subject to the terms and conditions of this Agreement, including but not limited to Section 3 (Java Technology Restrictions) of these Supplemental Terms, Sun grants you a non-exclusive, non-transferable, limited license to reproduce and distribute those files specifically identified as redistributable in the Software "README" file ("Redistributables") provided that: (i) you distribute the Redistributables complete and unmodified (unless otherwise specified in the applicable README file), and only bundled as part of your Programs, (ii) you do not distribute additional software intended to supersede any component(s) of the Redistributables, (iii) you do not remove or alter any proprietary legends or notices contained in or on the Redistributables, (iv) for a particular version of the Java platform, any executable output generated by a compiler that is contained in the Software must (a) only be compiled from source code that conforms to the corresponding version of the OEM Java Language Specification; (b) be in the class file format defined by the corresponding version of the OEM Java Virtual Machine Specification; and (c) execute properly on a reference runtime, as specified by Sun, associated with such version of the Java platform, (v) you only distribute the Redistributables pursuant to a license agreement that protects Sun's interests consistent with the terms contained in the Agreement, and (vi) you agree to defend and indemnify Sun and its licensors from and against any damages, costs, liabilities, settlement amounts and/or expenses (including attorneys' fees) incurred in connection with any claim, lawsuit or action by any third party that arises or results from the use or distribution of any and all Programs and/or Software. 3. Java Technology Restrictions. You may not modify the Java Platform Interface ("JPI", identified as classes contained within the "java" package or any subpackages of the "java" package), by creating additional classes within the JPI or otherwise causing the addition to or modification of the classes in the JPI. In the event that you create an additional class and associated API(s) which (i) extends the functionality of the Java platform, and (ii) is exposed to third party software developers for the purpose of developing additional software which invokes such additional API, you must promptly publish broadly an accurate specification for such API for free use by all developers. You may not create, or authorize your licensees to create, additional classes, interfaces, or subpackages that are in any way identified as "java", "javax", "sun" or similar convention as specified by Sun in any naming convention designation. 4. Java Runtime Availability. Refer to the appropriate version of the Java Runtime Environment binary code license (currently located at http://www.java.sun.com/jdk/index.html) for the availability of runtime code which may be distributed with Java applets and applications. 5. Trademarks and Logos. You acknowledge and agree as between you and Sun that Sun owns the SUN, SOLARIS, JAVA, JINI, FORTE, STAROFFICE, STARPORTAL and iPLANET trademarks and all SUN, SOLARIS, JAVA, JINI, FORTE, STAROFFICE, STARPORTAL and iPLANET-related trademarks, service marks, logos and other brand designations ("Sun Marks"), and you agree to comply with the Sun Trademark and Logo Usage Requirements currently located at http://www.sun.com/policies/trademarks. Any use you make of the Sun Marks inures to Sun's benefit. 6. Source Code. Software may contain source code that is provided solely for reference purposes pursuant to the terms of this Agreement. Source code may not be redistributed unless expressly provided for in this Agreement. 7. Termination for Infringement. Either party may terminate this Agreement immediately should any Software become, or in either party's opinion be likely to become, the subject of a claim of infringement of any intellectual property right. For inquiries please contact: Sun Microsystems, Inc., 901 San Antonio Road, Palo Alto, California 94303.